r Trade Northwest to 1870

Churchill Factory

Lac-du-Brochet

York Factory

Indian Lake

Split Lake

Deer's Lake · Nelson House
Nelson River
Rat River

Oxford House · Gods Lake
Jackson Bay
Cross Lake · Merry's House

Pelican Lake

ac la Ronge

Island Lake
Norway House II · Rossville
Cumberland House · Moose Lake · Norway House I
The Pas

Nipawin · Grand Rapids · Poplar River
Fort-à-la-Corne · Cedar Lake
se · Red Deer River · Shoal River · Berens River
Pigeon
Little Grand Rapids

Egg Lake · Swan Lake · Duck Bay
Waterhen River
Fort Pelly · Partridge Crop
d Hills · Little · Beaver Hills · Salt Point · Fairford
Touchwood Hills

Riding
Mountain · Manitobah · Fort Alexander
House · Lac du Bonnet
Oak Point · Eagle Nest
Qu'Appelle · Fort Ellice · Big Point · Netley Creek
White · Lower Fort Garry
Horse Plain · Upper Fort Garry
Portage · Shoal Lake
Tattooed Tent · la Prairie · Saint Boniface
Oak Lake · Brandon House · Lake of
Moose Mountain · the Woods
Souris River · Rivière Long · Pembina
Old Wives' Creek · Turtle Mountain · Roseau Lake
Saint-Joseph

1:9,500,000

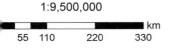

55   110   220   330   km

By: Anne Krahnen, CPRC, Nov. 2007.
Sources: Department of Natural Resources Canada. All rights reserved.
         Historical Atlas of Canada: Vol II, The Land Transformed,
         1800-1891 (Toronto: University of Toronto Press, 1990), Plate 17.

The Early Northwest

The Early Northwest

edited by Gregory P. Marchildon

2008

Canadian Plains Research Center
University of Regina
Regina, Saskatchewan S4S 0A2
Canada
Tel: (306) 585-4758/Fax: (306) 585-4699
e-mail: canadian.plains@uregina.ca
http://www.cprc.uregina.ca

Library and Archives Canada Cataloguing in Publication
    The early Northwest / edited by Gregory P. Marchildon.

(History of the Prairie West series 1914-864X 1)
Includes bibliographical references and index.
ISBN 978-0-88977-207-6

        1. Northwest, Canadian--History. I. Marchildon, Gregory P., 1956-
II. University of Regina. Canadian Plains Research Center III. Series.

FC3206.E37 2008   971.2'01   C2008-905698-1

Cover design: The Noblet Design Group, Regina
Cover illustration, Frances Anne Hopkins, "Voyageurs at Dawn/Voyageurs à l'aube," 1871, courtesy Library and Archives Canada C-2773.
Index prepared by Patricia Furdek (pafurdek@yahoo.com)
Printed and bound in Altona, Manitoba, Canada by Friesens.

Publisher's Note:
We acknowledge the financial support of the Government of Canada through the Book Publishing Industry Development Program (BPDIP) for our publishing activities. We also acknowledge the support of the Canada Council for the Arts for our publishing program.

Contents

Preface

Since its inception in 1975, *Prairie Forum* has been a major repository of articles on the history of the northern Great Plains, in particular the region encompassed within the current political boundaries of the three Prairie Provinces of Manitoba, Saskatchewan and Alberta. The purpose of the *History of the Prairie West* series is to make available the very best of *Prairie Forum* to as broad an audience as possible. Each volume in this series is devoted to a single, focused theme. Accompanied by dozens of new illustrations and maps as well as a searchable index, these volumes are intended to be of interest to the general reader as well as the professional historian.

The editor of the *History of the Prairie West* series is Gregory P. Marchildon, Canada Research Chair in Public Policy and Economic History at the Johnson-Shoyama Graduate School of Public Policy at the University of Regina campus. In addition to selecting and organizing the articles based upon their quality and thematic connections to the volumes, he has chosen a cover painting for each volume which reflects the essence of each period and theme.

Introduction to *The Early Northwest*

Gregory P. Marchildon

The "Early Northwest" is both a geographical and an historical reference. Geographically, it means the region north of the prairie and parkland encompassed by the fur trade. Over time, it took on a more local meaning as many of those retiring from the fur trade took up residence in the Red River Settlement, the core of what would eventually become the province of Manitoba. Although the geographical definition captures some of the content in this volume, I use the Early Northwest in its broader, historical sense. For me, it means the first phase of the history of the Prairie West before the region was settled on a large scale by Euro-Canadianfarmers, ranchers and townspeople.

The chapters in *The Early Northwest* have been divided up into four parts: 1) Aboriginal history in the pre-European and early contact eras; 2) Aboriginal-newcomer relations as they evolved during the course of the fur trade in western Canada; 3) the beginning of colonization and settlement in the Red River colony and the transfer of Rupert's Land from the Hudson's Bay Company to newly created Dominion of Canada; and 4) the ensuing conflict between the Aboriginal occupants of the Northwest and the Canadian government just before settlers from central Canada, Europe and the United States streamed into the region.

Early Aboriginal History

The events and lives presented in Part I have been reconstructed on the basis of archeological, anthropological, linguistic and environmental evidence supplemented where possible by written sources. Here, we meet the original inhabitants of the Northwest. We witness their struggle with the extreme climate. We experience their cycles of feast and famine, and their efforts to adapt to, and take advantage of, the first wave of Europeans who were, at least initially, highly dependent on them.

Olive Patricia Dickason's chapter offers us a sweeping overview of pre-European contact and early post-contact Aboriginal history in the Prairie West.[1] When it appeared in *Prairie Forum* in 1980, Dickason's essay was a clear indication of what would come 12 years later in her magisterial *Canada's First Nations: A History of Founding Peoples from Earliest Times*.[2] Of Métis descent herself, Dickason led the way for a fundamental re-interpretation of the role of Indigenous peoples in Canadian history. In her original abstract, she put the issue bluntly: "We would do well to re-evaluate our perception of Canada as a 'new world' without traditions of civilization before the arrival of Europeans."[3] Her work marked the beginning of an outpouring of Aboriginal history involving a generation of Canadians actively questioning past Euro-centric assumptions and biases.

This new generation of path-breaking scholars included Ted Binnema. In 2001, he caused a major stir with the appearance of *Common and Contested Ground: A Human and Environmental History of the Northwestern Plains*.[4] Combining ethnohistory with physical history, Binnema emphasized long-neglected physical influences, especially climatic variability, to explain the movement and development of Aboriginal societies in the prairie region. In the guise of a review article, James Daschuk presents a sweeping account of the environmental and human history of the Prairie West based in part on his own scholarly investigation. Daschuk agrees with Binnema that climatic forces, including a prolonged drought in the 1790s that was likely the most severe of the last 500 years, were at least as important a factor as the arrival of Europeans in unleashing intertribal wars and shifting political boundaries in the northern Great Plains.

In the absence of a written record, our understanding of pre-European contact history is highly dependent on the painstaking reconstructions of Aboriginal life by archaeologists. An excavation at an Aboriginal gathering place in the Saskatchewan River valley known as Pasquatinow provides a much-needed window on this earlier history. David Meyer, Terry Gibson and Dale Russell provide us with an historical interpretation of this site, shedding light on other centres at which hunters and gatherers would gather in the Saskatchewan River valley.[5] These were not permanent communities but places where local bands—usually dispersed in an effort to get enough food to stay alive—would rendezvous in the late winter or early spring. At such sheltered meeting places, while waiting for the fish-spawning runs to begin and the waterfowl to return, marriages and religious ceremonies would be celebrated and disputes would be resolved.

An anthropologist, Charles Bishop recounts the seasonal life and movements of the Western James Bay Cree, also known as the Swampy Cree, at a time when Europeans had established themselves on a few locations on Hudson Bay but had not yet penetrated into the interior of the Northwest. Members of these Swampy Cree bands eventually moved went in the lower Saskatchewan River Region in north-central Manitoba and north-eastern Saskatchewan.[6] Using the records of the Hudson's Bay Company as well as fur trade narratives, Bishop reconstructs the nature of this Aboriginal-new-comer relationship, and the extent to which fur traders were dependent on the members of this First Nation. The Swampy Cree became skilled traders in their own right, controlling the sale of European goods to other First Nations thousands of kilometers inland from the Bay and controlling the sale of food and other provisions needed for survival to the traders concen-trated at the Bay.[7] As for those "homeguard" Cree who remained in the direct vicinity of the Bay, their lives became more intertwined with these Europeans, foreshadowing the long-term shift in the dynamics of the Aboriginal-newcomer relationship.

The Fur Trade

Arthur J. Ray's research and writing has had an immense impact in shaping our understanding of the Canadian fur trade. His books, covering the peri-ods from pre-European contact through to the 20th century, have become essential reading for all scholars of the fur trade.[8] His subsequent work as an expert witness in Aboriginal land claims cases and his concern about the majority population's lack of historical understanding of Aboriginal history, then led Ray to write a more popular history of Canada's Indigenous peoples.[9] In the chapter here, Ray uses the archival record of the Hudson's Bay Company to reconstruct how the fur trade was provisioned from the buffalo herds of the Great Plains.

The two main food sources fueling the fur trade were pemmican and dried (jerked) buffalo meat. Of the two, pemmican was by far the more important. Originating from the Cree word *pimiy* meaning "grease," pemmi-can was a mixture of powdered buffalo meat mixed with fat. To be made extremely transportable, this high protein and high energy food was stored in 40 kilogram buffalo hide bags that were sealed with melted fat. Pemmican permitted huge distances to be traversed by voyageurs without having to stop to hunt or fish, to barter for food, or even to cook.[10]

Time was money to the fur traders who employed the voyageurs, and effective transportation over long distances in a single season was the key to success. The logistics were staggering. The traders relied on a spider's web of rivers of lakes, to get trade goods into, and fur pelts out, of the Northwest.[11] The choke points on this east-west route stretching from the St.

Lawrence River and Hudson Bay to the rich fur lands of the Athabasca-Mackenzie were the heights of land separating watersheds. Long and arduous portages across land were required at these points. In the east, it was the Grand Portage separating the waters flowing east to the Atlantic Ocean via the Great Lakes and the St. Lawrence River from the rivers and lakes leading to the Northwest.[12] In the Northwest, it was the almost 20-kilometre Portage La Loche (also known as Methy Portage) separating the waters flowing to Hudson Bay from those flowing northwest to the Arctic Ocean and west to the Pacific Ocean.[13] C.S. Mackinnon recounts the historic importance of Portage La Loche and explains why this isolated place in North America was once one of the busiest hubs in the Northwest.

Fur trade posts were built at strategic points along the length of the voyageur highway. Cumberland House, for example, was located at the point on the Saskatchewan River where fur traders could access a chain of lakes and rivers eventually taking them to the fur-rich Athabasca region. First established by explorer and fur trader Samuel Hearne in 1775, Cumberland House was one of the earliest and most important inland posts established by the Hudson's Bay Company in response to the competitive pressure of hundreds of traders and voyageurs from Montreal. These "pedlars" from Montreal, many of whom were Scottish or expatriate Americans, made it at point to intercept Aboriginal traders who were only to glad not to paddle all the way to Hudson Bay in order to sell their furs.

The question of how "home" is perceived goes to the heart of Aboriginal-newcomer relations in the history of the Prairie West. In Tolly Bradford's chapter, we see the different ways in which participants in the fur trade perceived their respective lives in the Northwest.[14] Old Swan was a Siksika (Blackfoot) Indian leader who had long participated in the fur trade. His "home" ranged from the prairie-parkland to the foothills. Foreseeing his own death, Old Swan said his spirit would go to a forested high ground somewhere between Red Deer and Saskatchewan rivers within sight of the Rocky Mountains. James Bird, on the other hand, was a chief trader for the Hudson's Bay Company stationed at Fort Edmonton on the North Saskatchewan River. His home was less a geographical location than the Honourable Company itself, and eventually Bird would retire to Red River where he would live out his last days in the company of other old Hudson's Bay Company warhorses.

Rupert's Land and Red River

Based on its monopoly charter of 1670, the Hudson's Bay Company laid legal claim to almost all of the Northwest for 200 years. Although contested on its interpretation by Aboriginal peoples as well as rival fur traders, Rupert's Land was still viewed as the property of the Honourable Company by the British government and the new Dominion of Canada established in 1867. As a consequence, the Red River Settlement founded in 1812 had to be carved out of the Company's existing territory. Subsequently, the new self-governing colony of Canada had to negotiate a transfer of Rupert's Land from the owners of the Hudson's Bay Company in order to create its own transcontinental nation. The land purchased would end up constituting 75% of the territory today encompassed by Canada.

A.A. den Otter is an established historian of the Prairie West.[15] He uses the 1857 British Parliamentary Inquiry into the Hudson's Bay Company to examine the long-standing but conflicting views concerning the future of Rupert's Land and, with it, the Aboriginal peoples living within the vast territory. At one extreme, they were those who argued that, at a minimum, the forested portion of Rupert's Land should remain the preserve of fur traders, hunters and trappers, a position supported both by defenders of the Hudson's Bay Company as well as its trade rivals who felt it was high time the British government removed the Honourable Company's monopoly charter and encouraged a competitive fur trade. At the other extreme, were the expansionists who argued that civilization, including the assimilation of native peoples, could only come after the agricultural settlement in the south and the introduction of forestry and other industries in the north of Rupert's Land. Not surprisingly, proponents of both extremes held similar assumptions about the mental and spiritual state of Aboriginal peoples relative to Europeans. George Simpson, the Canadian governor of the Hudson's Bay Company, spoke for the majority when he said this meant that Europeans had "the duty to instruct and civilize them."[16]

Barry Kaye's narrative focuses on the machinations surrounding the founding of the colony at Red River. The first major agricultural initiative in the northern Great Plains, the Red River Settlement was located at the junction of the Red and Assiniboine rivers. Kaye tells us why and how the colony was founded introducing us to a fascinating cast of characters in the process. From the beginning, the colony was riven with conflict. Shortly after its founding, the colony's governor issued a proclamation prohibiting the sale of pemmican. This action spurred the partners of the Montreal-based North West Company and their Métis allies to attack the colony in what became known as the Pemmican War.

History from the bottom up—as social history is popularly known—has provided us with a deep and rich understanding of the history of the Prairie West. Jonathan Anuik's chapter on the education of Aboriginal children at

Red River is a superb example of what the new social history can offer. Shortly after the establishment of the Settlement, Roman Catholic and Protestant—mainly Anglican (Church of England)—missionaries arrived. Their intention was to "civilize" the mixed blood and First Nation families who made up the majority of the population. While many Aboriginal parents wanted to see their children educated, they often resisted the so-called civilizing objectives of the missionaries. In many ways, the tension between the missionaries and Aboriginal families in Red River presaged the Indian residential school experience in the 20th century.[17]

The interests and rights of the indigenous inhabitants of the Prairie West were rarely considered by the colonial governing class as the new Dominion pushed west and north. As Frank Tough shows in his exploration of the acquisition of Rupert's Land by the Canadian government, few considered the impact of the final agreement on Aboriginal rights. Instead, it was left to the Canadian government to figure out how to deal with Indigenous land claims after it took over all of Rupert's Land. Immediately following the purchase, the Canadian governed negotiated treaties throughout the region in the 1870s. In return for transferring vast tracts of land, First Nations received small areas for their own settlements known as reservations, as well as modest annuities, some supplies including medicines, and the promise of relief during famines or similar disasters.

Resistance and "Rebellion"

The racial, religious and political strife at Red River would eventually lead to armed struggle in 1869–70. On one side were the settlement's (mainly) Roman Catholic, French-speaking and Métis inhabitants, and on the other side were Protestant and English-speaking inhabitants from Ontario and Great Britain. The immediate outcome of the resistance was the establishment of the province of Manitoba; originally seen by Prime Minister John A. Macdonald as a compromise between the provisional government set up under Louis Riel and his Protestant opponents. But with the influx of new settlers from Ontario, almost all white and Protestant, the new provincial government would soon push Riel and his supporters to the margins of the very territory they fought to have recognized.

The first two chapters in this section deal with different aspects of the Red River Resistance of 1869–70. Doug Owram's work on Anglo-Canadian imperialism and the expansionist movement into Western Canada has greatly influenced our understanding of the Prairie West.[18] Here, Owram examines the events at Red River from the perspective of the English-Canadian Protestant settlers in Manitoba who were members of what became known as the "Canada Party." For years, this group had argued that the time had come to, in their words, throw off the yoke of the Hudson's Bay Company, and put the entire territory under the control of the Canadian government and open the southern fertile belt to agricultural settlement. Of course, the members of Canada Party wanted to see the Prairie West settled in their own image; that is, Protestant, British and English-speaking. They feared that French-speaking Catholics from Quebec would attempt to perpetuate language, education and religion through the Red River Métis. As a result, they were unwilling to consider a compromise along racial, religious and linguistic lines thereby inflaming a real opposition in Quebec to the Canada Party.

The polarization which erupted in central Canada over events in Manitoba would eventually focus on two men. One was already well-known in Red River—Louis Riel. The other was largely unknown in his lifetime—Thomas Scott. An immigrant Protestant from Northern Ireland, Scott became famous only after he was tried and executed by Riel's provisional government. In death, Scott was mythologized by the Ontario supporters of the Canada Party and demonized by the Quebec supporters of Riel's movement. A prolific historian of the period, Jack Bumsted searched for the historical truth behind these polarized views of Scott.[19]

With the ascendancy of the Canada Party in Manitoba, the new settlements of Red River Métis along the banks of the Saskatchewan River further west and the desire of the Canadian government to fill up the West with non-Aboriginal farmers, the stage was set for further conflict. Immediately after the Red River Resistance, the Canadian government concluded treaties with First Nations and scrip with the Métis, and then opened the region to settlement. But some First Nations and many Métis decided to fight against what they considered highly unfair settlements which displaced their peoples and left them without a significant land base.[20]

The end result was series of clashes between the Canadian militia and the North-West Mounted Police. Of the five military encounters in 1885, only one—the battle of Batoche—was a clear victory for the Canadian government. Walter Hildebrandt presents a detailed, military history of Batoche including the Métis view of the battle. For the British-Canadians, this was a battle in the tradition of the colonial wars of the second half of the 19th century where European armies faced indigenous insurrections throughout the globe. For the Métis, this was the last chance to protect their way of life, language and culture and to defend their independence against an aggressive, encroaching enemy.

Batoche is now a national historic site, the interpretation of which has shifted significantly since the 1920s when it first opened its doors to visitors.

Collective memory means to "remember in common" and historic sites likely play at least as important role than published history in establishing, or at least reinforcing, a dominant view of events. Not surprisingly, the dominant interpretation associated with a historic site shifts over time, occasionally propelled by a professional reassessment of events as well as broader societal changes. The historic site of Batoche offers a rich case study of the extent to which this collective memory, and the assumptions which underpin it, changes over time. Because it continues to raise unresolved questions, the Rebellion of 1885 and its aftermath continues to bite hard into the collective Canadian psyche.

Notes

1. Dickason worked as a journalist long before she became a scholar. She was 57 years of age when she received her doctorate in history from the University of Otttawa in 1977. Her earlier stints with the *Regina Leader-Post* and *Winnipeg Free Press* and her subsequent residence in Edmonton when she was a history professor at the University of Alberta (1985–92) informed her historical work.

2. Olive Patricia Dickason, *Canada's First Nations: A History of Founding Peoples from Earliest Times* (Toronto: McClelland and Stewart, 1992).

3. See abstract in Olive Patricia Dickason, "A Historical Reconstruction for the Northwestern Plains," *Prairie Forum* 5, no. 1 (1980): 19.

4. Ted Binnema, *Common and Contested Ground: A Human and Environmental History of the Northwestern Plains* (Norman, OK: University of Oklahoma Press, 2001; Toronto: University of Toronto Press, 2001).

5. Dale Russell was also trained as an historian. Russell's *Eighteenth Century Western Cree and their Neighbours* (Ottawa: Canadian Museum of Civilization, Mercury Series Paper 43, 1991).

6. See Paul C. Thistle, *Indian–European Trade Relations in the Lower Saskatchewan River Region to 1840* (Winnipeg: University of Manitoba Press, 1986).

7. Also see Arthur J. Ray and Donald Freeman, *"Give Us Good Measure": An Economic Analysis of Relations between the Indians and the Hudson's Bay Company before 1763* (Toronto: University of Toronto Press, 1978).

8. See *Indians in the Fur Trade: Their Roles as Trappers, Hunters and Middlemen in the lands Southwest of Hudson Bay, 1660–1870* (Toronto: University of Toronto Press, 1974); *The Canadian Fur Trade in the Industrial Age* (Toronto: University of Toronto Press, 1990); and *"Give Us Good Measure"* which he co-authored with Donald Freeman.

9. Arthur J. Ray, *I Have Lived Here Since the World Began: An Illustrated History of Canada's Native Peoples* (1996; Toronto: Les Publishing and Key Porter, 2005).

10. Greg Marchildon and Sid Robinson, *Canoeing the Churchill: A Practical Guide to the Historic Voyageur Highway* (Regina: Canadian Plains Research Center, 2002), 48.

11. Eric Morse, *Fur Trade Canoe Routes of Canada* (1969; Toronto: University of Toronto Press, 1979). Morse was a modern day voyageur who personally paddled most of these historic routes.

12. Barbara Huck, *Exploring the Fur Trade Routes of North America* (Winnipeg: Heartland, 2000), 137.

13. On the Methy Portage (or Portage La Loche, the name Mackinnon prefers to use), see Marchildon and Robinson, *Canoeing the Churchill*, 85–97.

14. In a similar manner, Gerald Friesen surveys the history of the "Natives'" fur trade in one chapter and the history of the "Europeans' fur trade in a subsequent chapter: see *The Canadian Prairies: A History* (Toronto: University of Toronto Press, 1987), 22–65.

15. See den Otter's *Civilizing the West: The Galts and the Development of Western Canada* (Edmonton: University of Alberta Press, 1981), and *The Philosophy of Railways: The Transcontinental Railway Idea in British North America* (Toronto: University of Toronto Press, 1997). He also co-authored *Lethbridge: A Centennial History* (Lethbridge: Historical Society of Alberta, 1985) with Alex Johnston.

16. George Simpson quoted in A.A. den Otter, "The 1857 Parliamentary Inquiry, the Hudson's Bay Company, and Rupert's Land's Aboriginal People," *Prairie Forum* 24, no. 2 (1999), 167.

17. See J.R. Miller, *Shingwauk's Vision: A History of Native Residential Schools* (Toronto: University of Toronto Press, 1996).

18. Doug Owram, *Promise of Eden: The Canadian Expansionist Movement and the Idea of the West, 1900–1945* (Toronto: University of Toronto Press, 1980). Also see R.G. Moyles and Doug Owram, *Imperial Dreams and Colonial Realities: British Views of Canada, 1880–1914* (Toronto: University of Toronto Press, 1988).

19. See the following authored by Jack Bumsted: *Trials and Tribulations: The Red River Settlement and the Emergence of Manitoba, 1811–1870* (Winnipeg: Great Plains Publications, 2003); *The Red River Rebellion* (Winnipeg: Watson and Dwyer, 1996); *Louis Riel v. Canada: The Making of a Rebel* (Winnipeg: Great Plains Publications, 2001); and *Fur Trade Wars: The Founding of Western Canada* (Winnipeg: Great Plains Publications, 1999).

20. On the First Nations involvement and (perhaps more significantly) non-involvement in the 1885 Rebellion, see Blair Stonechild and Bill Waiser, *Loyal till Death: Indians and the North-West Rebellion* (Calgary: Fifth House, 1997).

Early Aboriginal History

1. A Historical Reconstruction for the Northwestern Plains[1]

Olive Patricia Dickason

Reconstructing the early history of the people of the northwestern plains of North America has been so difficult for the historian that the task is still far from completed. Because the written record began very recently, historians have had to place a heavy, and professionally uncharacteristic, reliance on unwritten resources. In effect, this has meant a dependence upon archaeology, which has been very useful up to a point. But the plains have not been kind to archaeologists either, especially in Alberta and southwestern Saskatchewan where the record has been particularly difficult to decipher.[2]

It is perhaps not surprising, under these circumstances, that it came to be believed that the plains had not been inhabited to any extent before the appearance of the European-introduced horse. Such an eminent authority as Clark Wissler wrote in 1907, "the peopling of the plains proper was a recent phenomenon due in part to the introduction of the horse and the displacement of tribes by white settlement."[3] Even as late as 1939, A.L. Kroeber concurred, adding that in his view, the plains had developed culturally "only since the taking over of the horse from Europeans."[4] These two authorities were writing principally of the plains south of the 49th parallel. If their interpretation was correct for the south, so the reasoning went, how much truer must it have been for the north?

Today, we know that such views were heavily conditioned by the inability of most 19th-century scholars, as well as some in the 20th century, to envision man as having been capable of wresting a living from the plains before the advent of the horse and gun.[5] Here archaeology has helped to set the record straight. It is on the plains, including those of the northwest, that some of our earliest evidence of human presence in North America has been found. The great advances in archaeology during recent years have dramatically lengthened our historical perspective of man in the Americas. The

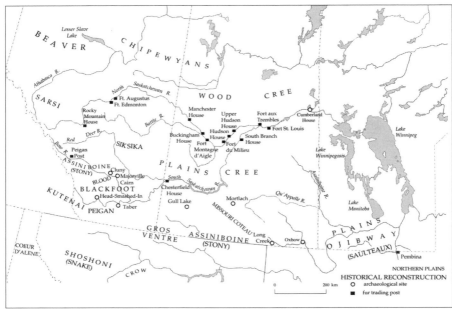

The Northwestern Plains (courtesy Canadian Plains Research Center, University of Regina).

world that Europeans labelled "New" when they became aware of it in the 15th century has turned out to be anything but new; and the people who inhabited it, considered by Europeans to be such a young race as to be still in their cultural ABCs,[6] have a history that can claim the dignified label of "ancient."

It is also a complex history. The development of stone and bone tools represented one of man's great strides forward into technological sophistication; and while such a technology can in a way be regarded as "simple," it was viable only because of acute and careful observation of nature-still a basic requirement today. As a general rule, a "simple" technology is effective in proportion as it is based upon sharp and accurate observation on the one hand, and supported by a workable social organization on the other. In other words, the intelligent manipulation of nature backed by supportive social structures makes possible man's survival under extremely difficult conditions. The process is a dynamic one; although the rates of change can and do vary, at no time can a living culture be regarded as static. As far back as we have traced the presence of man in America, his story has been one of adaptation and alteration—so slow as to be all but imperceptible in the beginning, but ever so gradually gaining momentum. This process was not characterized by a consistent rate of change, but rather by spurts or leaps

Clovis-type spear point made of yellow jasper found near Lake Diefenbaker, Saskatchewan (courtesy of Tim Jones, Saskatoon, Saskatchewan).

alternating with "idling" periods. In this context, the arrival of Europeans, horses and all, is to be viewed as part of an ongoing process; the intrusion may have accelerated or altered patterns of change, but it did not initiate change in itself.

The story of this change on the northwestern plains is the concern of this paper. Because the time span is so long, from early prehistoric to European-Amerindian contact, it will be possible to trace events only in their broad outlines, but with the hope that this will be sufficient to reveal something of underlying patterns. The term "northwestern plains" includes the southern halves of Alberta and Saskatchewan, the eastern two-thirds of Montana and the northern third of Wyoming; however, the focus will be on Alberta and Saskatchewan.

Early Big-Game Hunters (17,000–5,000 BC)[7]

The earliest consistent evidence of man on the Great Plains clusters in the period of 17,000 to 7,000 years ago. We do have some evidence from earlier dates, perhaps even as far back as 30,000 BC,[8] and there is that tantalizing skeleton of an infant found under glacial till at Taber, Alberta, which suggests considerable antiquity—more than 22,000 years, and perhaps as much as 60,000.[9] But such evidence is at present too scattered and fragmentary to be anything more than suggestive. With the big-game hunters of 12,000 or so years ago we are on firm ground. Our knowledge of their activities is derived from sites associated with kills of mammoth, contemporaries of giant beaver and giant wolves, of camels and horses, species which disappeared during the late Pleistocene megafaunal extinctions of about 11,000 years ago. We know that long before the invention of the bow and arrow, paleo-Amerindians hunted with spears tipped with bone or with fluted stone points. Very early—at least by the time of the extinctions—the "atlatl," or thrower, appeared, enabling hunters to hurl their spears with great force.[10] Used in this manner, spears have been aptly described as "guided missiles"; their effectiveness has been dramatically illustrated by the discovery of points embedded in bone, such as the rib of a mastodon or the scapula of a giant bison.

Sites associated with bison hunting date from more than 10,000 years ago; the earliest buffalo drive of which we have a record was a jump at Bonfire Shelter in southwestern Texas from about that time.[11] The greatest number of jump sites have been found in the foothills of the Rocky Mountains, where they outnumber pounds. The latter were apparently more commonly used on the plains,[12] particularly in such areas as the Missouri Coteau. Drive sites are most frequent in Saskatchewan, Alberta, Montana and Wyoming. By whatever means the herds were harvested, the archaeological record indicates that buffalo hunting has provided the basis for life on the plains for at least as long as jumps have been used. It also tells us that our previously held and much cherished picture of early hunters perpetually facing starvation does not equate with what we now know to have been the case. Although lean times certainly alternated with periods of plenty, such cycles were prepared for from a very early period by drying or otherwise preserving meat. Oddly enough, the dog does not seem to have accompanied man in the Americas during distant prehistoric days[13]; the earliest indications of its presence—and these are not undisputed—date from about 5,000 BC.

Plains Archaic (5000BC to BC/AD)

After 5,000 BC, seasonal nomadism continued, largely based on bison as a food resource. However, there was a long period called the Altithermal (5000–2500 BC), in which bison appear to have been scarce or even absent, and during which human presence also seems to have been much reduced, particularly in short-grass areas.[14] The Altithermal is believed to have been marked by higher temperatures and increased aridity which decimated the herds of giant buffalo by cutting down on their food supply. Before the Altithermal, hunters pursued giant bison; afterward, the bison available was of the smaller variety with which we are familiar.[15]

The end of the Altithermal period saw the growing elaboration of the buffalo drive, such as the jump at Head-Smashed-In, Alberta, and as indicated by campsites at Oxbow and Long Creek in Saskatchewan. In fact, sites in general increased throughout the two provinces; about 12,000 have been recorded in Alberta alone, believed to be a small proportion of those that existed[16]; their numbers reflect substantial increases in population. From this period too we can date the appearance of elaborate surface assemblages which probably indicate eastern influence.[17] Some sites include several hundred tipi rings which extend for miles; it has been estimated that there are more than a million such rings scattered throughout Alberta.[18] They may be mute testimony to the annual cycle of buffalo hunters, who in historic times gathered seasonally in large camps, for they are usually excellent observation posts for watching the movement of game, a characteristic which they share with medicine wheels.[19] Wheels found on the Canadian plains, largely in Alberta, seldom exceed 30 feet in diameter; those dating from the proto-historic period characteristically have four spokes; earlier ones may have five or even more.[20] Those found south of the 49th parallel are usually more complicated in form but are far fewer in number.

All these features were associated, particularly in the later phase, with the appearance of the small-point weapons system to which the bow and arrow belongs. This new weaponry may have been introduced by peoples filtering down from the north, such as the Athapaskans, who reached the southern limits of the plains sometime before the 16th century.[21] These were probably the people described by Spaniards during the first half of that century as "dog nomads," appearing at pueblos with as many as 500 dogs loaded with the products of the buffalo hunt to trade for farm produce as well as for manufactured items.

Plains Woodlands (250 BC–950 AD)

This was the period when plains cultures, as we know them, began to develop patterns resembling their proto-historical forms. This seems to have resulted from an accelerated infusion of eastern influences.[22] The northern plains continued as the centre for bison hunting. Pottery was now seen for the first time; its evidence indicates that ancestral Kutenai occupied southern Alberta as much as 2,000 years ago, supporting oral traditions reported by David Thompson.[23]

It was also the period in which agricultural communities appeared in those areas of the plains where rainfall and the growing season allowed— factors which still have to be contended with. The Adena and the later Hopewell cultural complexes, each named from Ohio sites where their

Reconstructed pottery vessel from the area of Cutbank, Saskatchewan (courtesy of Tim Jones, Saskatoon, Saskatchewan).

distinctive characteristics were first identified, spread in from the south. Hopewell extended further north than Adena: mounds and burials after the pattern of Hopewell have been found in Ontario, Manitoba and Saskatchewan. Such traces are also seen in ceramics, some of which have been found in southern Alberta. In the northwestern grasslands generally, hunting and gathering persisted in cultural manifestations such as the intrusive Besant and the indigenous Avonlea. At those sites especially, the developing complexities of ritualized, planned buffalo drives have been traced.[24]

Plains Village (900 AD–1750 AD)

These social units were characterized by multi-family lodges at fixed locations; permanent settlements fortified with dry moats and stockades; underground storage pits, pottery, and a wide range of artifacts in stone, bone, horn, shell and other materials. The Cluny Earth Lodge village at Blackfoot Crossing, about 70 miles east of Calgary, may have been the northernmost manifestation of this phase; according to Blackfoot legend, it was built by the Crow, in which case it would be proto-historic.[25] In any event, village life on the high plains was discouraged by recurrent droughts, to the point of disappearing entirely during the 15th century; surviving villages in peripheral areas, such as the aspen parklands, provide mute testimony to what once had been.[26] It is interesting that all historic farming peoples of the plains speak a Hokan-Siouan tongue; this language group may well be the oldest in North America.

Bison populations recovered more rapidly than human populations from these droughts. At about this time the herds reached the immense sizes reported by Francisco Vasquez Coronado in the south (1541), by Father Simon Le Moyne in the Great Lakes region (1654) and Henry Kelsey on the Saskatchewan (1690). Their spread east of the Mississippi appears to have been comparatively recent, if one is to judge from the tenuous evidence of Spanish accounts; and it was not until the late 18th century that they were seen on the Peace River west of Lesser Slave Lake.[27] These herds could well have prevented the return of village farmers to the high plains.[28] For instance, Hernando De Soto reported in 1541 that the Amerindians of Caluca in north-central Arkansas

> stated that thence toward the north, the country, being very cold, was very thinly populated; that cattle were in such plenty, no maize-field could be protected from them, and the inhabitants lived upon the meat.[29]

Colonists who tried to farm the plains before the extermination of the herds discovered to their sorrow that they were as vulnerable to depredations by bison as their Amerindian predecessors had been. Not only did the animals eat and trample crops, they were even reported to have demolished a settler's cabin in Pennsylvania about 1770.[30] The movements of such great herds rendered permanent settlements extremely precarious, both from the physical as well as the economic point of view, and they were also dangerous to hunters on foot. Canadian-born explorer Louis Jolliet, with Jesuit Jacques Marquette in 1673, reported bison as being "very fierce … not a year passes without their killing some savages." Amerindian appreciation of these dangers is graphically presented in a Caddo legend which tells how buffalo ceased to eat humans.[31]

Proto-Historic Buffalo Hunters

The buffalo-hunting way of life on the plains which today is considered "traditional" crystallized between 1600 and 1750, depending on locality; in southern Alberta and Saskatchewan, it seems to have appeared during the first half of the 18th century. It was, of course, based upon horses, which not only altered the hunt, transportation and warfare, but also, and perhaps most importantly of all, trade routes. Interestingly, horses did not generally become a source of subsistence in themselves, as they had in Asia.[32]

However, to view the changes that did occur with the introduction of the horse as simply superficial, as some have done, is to misunderstand the process of cultural evolution. Technologies change faster than institutions, and institutions change faster than ideologies. In less than two centuries on the northwestern plains, the horse in conjunction with the fur trade had heavily altered the principal institutions of plains Amerindian society; given more time, more profound ideological modifications would probably have been effected as well.[33]

While there is no doubt that horses were first reintroduced into the Americas by the Spaniards, there is considerable question as to when Amerindians began to ride and own them. In 1541 Viceroy Antonio de Mendoza provided mounts for Mexican allies during a campaign in central Mexico; about 1567, the Amerindians of Sonora rode horses and used them for food.[34] Spanish stock-raising settlements in the southwest, particularly in the neighborhood of Santa Fe, were apparently points of diffusion[35]; as for the Atlantic seaboard, where horses had been present since early in the 17th century, they do not seem to have crossed the Alleghenies until later. On the southern plains, Amerindians owned horses by 1630, and may well have had some as early as 1600. Athapaskan-speaking Apache were raiding on horseback by mid-17th century[36]; indeed, they evolved Amerindian techniques for mounted warfare, and also had become the prototype of the mounted buffalo hunter.

Although horses had such a radical effect on buffalo hunting, they were not universally suited to their new role. Some could not overcome their fear of buffalo and so could not be trained as hunters; among the Cree during the last days of bison hunting, only one tipi in ten had a good buffalo horse, although nearly all had riding and transport animals. While running buffalo became universally favoured as a hunting technique, horses were also used for surrounds, which became more efficient as a result.[37] Jumps began to fall into disuse between 1840 and 1850; the last known use was by the Blackfoot in 1873.[38] Pounds, on the other hand, continued to be used until the end of the herds. Another effect of the horse was to eliminate women from direct participation in buffalo drives, turning their attention exclusively to the preparation of meat and hides.

Apart from its usefulness for hunting and transport, the horse both extended and altered trade routes. As a consequence of all this, it became a symbol of wealth in its own right and, as always with the growth of affluence, polarized economic status both between individuals as well as between tribes. For example, in 1833 a Peigan chief, Sackomaph, was reported to own between 4,000 and 5,000 horses, 150 of which were killed upon his

Augustus Kenderdine, "The Buffalo Hunt," 1915, oil on canvas, 59.7 x 90.2 cm, MacKenzie Art Gallery, University of Regina Collection, gift of Estate of Dr. John B. Ritchie (Courtesy of the MacKenzie Art Gallery/1974-016).

death. Among tribes, the Assiniboine and Plains Cree had fewer horses than the Blackfoot. However, they were highly skilled as horse raiders; David Thompson described a spectacular raid in which a band of Assiniboines disguised as antelope made off with fifty horses from Rocky Mountain House.[39]

The Shoshoni (Snake, Gens du Serpent), seasonal residents of grasslands and plateau, are generally believed to have been the first to acquire horses on the northwestern plains.[40] Their sources were their relatives to the south, the Comanche, as well as neighbours, such as the Coeur d'Alene and Flathead from the western plateau and Columbia River, who were early large-scale herders.[41] The Shoshoni may have employed their horses at first principally for the hunt, presaging, as the Apache had done earlier, the emergence of the buffalo-based "horse cultures." By the 1730s the Shoshoni were using horses for raiding, and during the following decades they were feared mounted warriors of the plains.[42] Under the circumstances, word quickly spread of the strange animal, "swift as a deer." A Cree, Saukamapee, described to David Thompson his first encounter with the new arrival, which occurred while he and some fellow tribesmen were hunting in the territory of the Peigan, westernmost and most southerly of the four tribes of the

Blackfoot Confederacy. Attacking a lone Shoshoni, the Cree succeeded in killing his mount, and crowded in wonder around the fallen animal which, like the dog, was a slave to man and carried his burdens. So they called it "Misstutim," "big dog"[43]; later, the Blackfoot were to name it "Ponokamita," "elk dog," in recognition of its size and usefulness.[44]

Historic Residents

At this time, all of the year-round residents of the northwestern plains were Algonkian or Siouan speakers except the Sarsi, who spoke an Athapaskan language and who had broken away from the Beaver, apparently not long before the arrival of Europeans. Eventually, they became part of the Blackfoot Confederacy, along with the Siksika (Blackfoot proper), Blood and Peigan.[45] Linguistic evidence indicates a great time span of occupation for the Algonkian-speaking Blackfoot and Gros Ventre, much of it in isolation from their own language group. Speech similarities between the Blackfoot and the Kutenai may hark back to the time when the latter also lived in the area. In any event, the Blackfoot were probably the first to arrive of all the historic peoples still in the region; cultural indications are that they came from the eastern woodlands,[46] the source of much immigration to the northwestern plains. Directly to the east of the Confederacy were the allied Gros Ventre (Atsina, originally a division of the Arapaho) who may have been second to arrive in the region.[47] They share with the Blackfoot the probability of being the "Archithinue" or "Archithine" reported by Anthony Henday in 1754.[48] If we except the Plains Ojibway (Saulteaux, Bungi), who reached Saskatchewan by the late 18th century, but who did not establish a major presence on the high plains,[49] the newest arrivals on the northwestern plains are the Plains Cree. Their presence dates from some time during the 17th century; their arrival may have been in association with their close allies, the Siouan Assiniboine, who probably preceded them. To the south were the Siouan Crow, who were described in their territory of the middle Yellowstone by the Nor'Wester François Larocque in 1805. It has been estimated that at the beginning of the historic period the population of the northwestern plains averaged less than one person per 10 square miles.[50] However, there were considerable fluctuations. Tribes from surrounding areas made forays onto the plains for hunting and warfare, such forays increasing in frequency as the buffalo herds declined and then disappeared from their eastern ranges after 1850, until their final extermination in Alberta in the 1880s.[51] All of these peoples, with the exception of the Gros Ventre and Crow,[52] had been hunters and gatherers from time immemorial, so that their shift to plains life was from one form of hunting to another.

The opening of the historic period saw the southwestern parts of the region being dominated by the raiding Shoshoni. They appear to have been an aggressive people even when they were on foot; horses enabled them to extend their field of operations. According to Saukamapee's description of some of their raids during the first half of the 18th century,[53] the Shoshoni wore six-ply quilted leather armour and carried shields, but did not at that time have firearms, as they had "no Traders among them."[54] What trading connections they had were with the south, and Spaniards were reluctant to include arms in such transactions. However, the Shoshoni sinew-back bow was an efficient weapon, particularly when used with metal-tipped arrows, and was both more accurate and more reliable than guns until about the middle of the 19th century. With the principal exception of the Cree, but also of the Assiniboine and Saulteaux, it was usually preferred by Amerindians for buffalo hunting. In 1811, Alexander Henry the Younger reported that Peigans would trade a horse or a gun for such a bow.[55] The principal economic purpose of the Shoshoni raids seems to have been the acquisition of captives, who as slaves were useful to both Amerindians and Spaniards as well as to the French, and so had high trading value.

Shifting Power Balances

The acquisition of the gun by the Comanche, from the French pushing west of the Mississippi early in the 18th century, inaugurated the final phase of shifting Amerindian power balances on the plains. The gun, for all its inadequacies at that time, had been quickly adopted for warfare for its psychological effect as well as for the damage it could do; for one thing, it rendered Amerindian armour ineffective. Within twenty years the Comanche had driven the still gunless Apache south of the River Platte.[56] In the north, the Shoshoni had no such luck; they first encountered guns in the hands of their enemy the Cree, about the same time as their southern kinsmen, the Comanche, were acquiring them in trade. The Cree were blessed with two sources of the new weaponry: the English, who by that time were established on Hudson Bay, and the French, whose St. Lawrence and Great Lakes network of posts had by 1753 reached into the northwest with the establishment of Fort St. Louis on the Saskatchewan River. The Shoshoni quickly discovered that this new weaponry seriously diminished the advantage they had gained from the horse.[57] But before they could gain regular access to firearms, the French and Indian War had broken out, seriously interrupting such trade in the West. By 1770, British traders were back on the Upper Mississippi and the Saskatchewan, and were beginning to penetrate into the far northwest; but France as a power had all but disappeared from North

America, and her jurisdiction over Louisiana had been transferred to Spain. This dealt a severe blow to whatever hopes the Shoshoni might have had of obtaining enough guns to face their enemies. As the Blackfoot, now mounted, already had access to British firearms, the Shoshoni were pushed off the plains by the end of the 18th century.[58] In achieving this, the Blackfoot were powerfully aided by epidemics, especially that of 1781–82, which took a particularly heavy toll of the Shoshoni.[59] By the turn of the century, the victorious Peigans, who had been the tribe of the Blackfoot confederates mainly involved in the struggle, were referring to the once-dreaded Shoshoni as miserable old women whom they could defeat with sticks and stones.[60] With the removal of the Shoshoni threat, the fragile alliance of the Confederacy with Assiniboine and Cree lost its principal motivation, and the two expanding power groups came into collision.

Before this happened, and while they were still allies, the Blackfoot had obtained their first trade items from the Assiniboine and Cree, rather than directly from Europeans. Linguistic evidence hints that the first white men they met were French, as they designated them as "Real (or Original) Old Man People"; their term for whites in general was "Napikawan," "Old Man Person."[61] While the furthest west of the French establishments, Fort St. Louis, was located east of the forks of the Saskatchewan and thus outside Blackfoot territory, it would have been easily accessible to them. However, the first recorded meeting is the well-known encounter with Anthony Henday in 1754–55. It has been estimated that by that time the Blackfoot were all mounted; but Henday's report that they had horses was greeted with disbelief by the English on the Bay.[62] By then, the Blackfoot were well into their period of expansion; as the Peigan pushed the Shoshoni south and west, the Sarsi moved into the North Saskatchewan basin and the Gros Ventre occupied territories vacated by the Blackfoot around the Eagle Hills. By 1770, the territory along the eastern Rockies north of Yellowstone was controlled by the Blackfoot Confederacy and its allies. It was about this time that the Crow (Hidatsa) first appeared in the southern part of this region; they also took up the fight against the Shoshoni.[63]

The Blackfoot never took to trading with Europeans as had the Cree and the Assiniboine; neither Henday nor, later, Matthew Cocking had been able to persuade them, or the Gros Ventre, to make the arduous journey to the Bay. This resistance was due partly to the fact that they were already receiving trade goods through the Cree and the Assiniboine, and partly to a conflict of the demands of the fur trade with those of buffalo hunting, which provided so bountifully for them. Late fall and early winter was the best season for trapping, as pelts were then in their prime; it was also the best time for killing bison and preparing winter provisions. From the social aspect, trapping was a family affair, whereas buffalo hunting involved the whole community. Of the Blackfoot confederates, the Peigan had the most beaver in their territory, and consequently became the most active as trappers; the others, as well as their allies, were to become provisioners for the trade rather than trappers for furs. This independence of the Blackfoot and Gros Ventre helped convince the Hudson's Bay Company to build Cumberland House (near The Pas) in 1774 and Hudson House (west of Prince Albert) in 1779. These posts were, however, outside Blackfoot territory. By the time the Nor'Westers built Fort Augustus on the North Saskatchewan in 1795, and the Hudson's Bay Company had countered with Fort Edmonton that same year, Blackfoot territory was ringed with trading posts.[64] It was not until 1799, when the Nor'Westers built the first Rocky Mountain House, that a post was established within the Blackfoot sphere of control.

Trading Situation

The trading situation on the plains was complex, compounded by rivalries between tribes, between traders, between traders and Amerindians, as well as between Canada and the USA. Despite their unwillingness to meet the fur trade on its own terms, the Blackfoot and Gros Ventre felt that they were not as well treated in trade as their enemies, the Cree, particularly in the case of firearms.[65] The traders, especially the independents, did not help when they treated Amerindians badly, as happened all too frequently. The resultant tensions sometimes erupted into violence, as in 1781 when Amerindians burned the prairie around the posts, which the traders believed was done to scare game away.[66] When the Nor'Westers sought to cross the mountains and make contact with the Kutenai and other plateau peoples, the Blackfoot became seriously alarmed. David Thompson finally succeeded in building a post in Kutenai territory in 1807, which moved the Peigans, already disturbed by the killing of two of their tribesmen by members of the Lewis and Clark expedition shortly before, to raise a war party. Although Thompson was able to negotiate a peaceful settlement, the unfortunate result for him was that famous delay which cost the Nor'Westers the right to claim the mouth of the Columbia for Britain.[67] That same year (1807), a band of Bloods and Atsina pillaged the first Fort Augustus, and when the Hudson's Bay Company built Peigan Post (Old Bow Fort) in 1832 in territory controlled by the Bloods, the latter refused to allow their allies to trade there, forcing the closing of the post two years later.[68] Nor did it take long for the Blackfoot to take advantage of the new international boundary; they became adept at raiding posts built in that part of their territory claimed by the United States and then selling the proceeds to posts north of the border.[69] The situation was aggravated by the American custom of sending out white trappers instead of relying on Amerindian sources—an act which the Blackfoot considered trespassing.

It was a change in the character of the fur trade which brought about better relations between the Blackfoot and traders. In Canada, this developed because of the opening of the Athabaska region, which resulted in a greatly increased demand for pemmican to provision lengthening supply lines. Pemmican, a highly concentrated food, was particularly suitable for the transportation facilities of the northern routes which depended upon the canoe. In the US, the growing importance of buffalo robes, encouraged by the development of transportation facilities, made it practicable to traffic in the bulky, heavy hides. In either case, developing affluence was manifested in the size of tipis, which by the 1830s could be large enough to accommodate as many as 100 persons.[70] The new commerce placed a premium upon the services of women, who prepared both pemmican and hides. This encouraged polygamy, as well as a younger age for brides. Where plains Amerindian women had usually married in their late teens, girls as young as twelve now did so. Rarely could a man afford to buy a wife before he was 35, however. As polygamy developed, so did a hierarchy among wives, with the senior wife usually directing the others.[71] Women taken in raids now tended to be retained by their captors rather than to be sold, a trend that became particularly evident after the first third of the 19th century.

Commercialism and its concomitant emphasis on wealth affected other social institutions as well. A great many societies appeared, the best known of which were connected with war and the maintenance of camp and hunt disciplines. War as a way of life was a comparatively late development; for the Blackfoot, it became a means of accumulating wealth, which in turn was a route to prestige. Still, something of the old ways persisted, for although the Blackfoot were a major military power on the northwestern plains for more than a century, it remained possible in their society to become a chief without going on the warpath.[72] Bravery and generosity were the requisites, as they were among the Plains Cree and others.

Allies and Enemies

The Gros Ventre, who were established between the forks of the Saskatchewan River when Matthew Cocking visited them in 1772—he referred to them as one of the tribes of "equestrian natives"—were the easternmost of the Blackfoot allies. The expression "Gros Ventre" was first recorded by Edward Umfreville, who was in their territory from 1784 to

1788.[73] The Blackfoot term for these Algonkian-speaking agriculturalists-turned-hunters was "Atsina," "gut people"; they called themselves "Haaninin," "chalk-men" or "men of soft white stone." They impressed Cocking not only with their skill as buffalo hunters, but also in their customs and manners, which he found more like those of Europeans.[74] A later fur trader, however, described them as "lazy" and "treacherous," good only at stealing horses,[75] an opinion probably based on nothing more substantial than on poor trading relations. Weakened by the ravages of the great epidemic of 1781–82, the Gros Ventre began to be pushed south and east by the Assiniboine and Cree. In 1793, a key battle was fought near South Branch House, when Cree wiped out a Gros Ventre band which had numbered sixteen lodges. Apparently their alliance with the Blackfoot was not on a very secure basis,[76] as they received little, if any, help from them.

Such incidents greatly exacerbated the resentment shared by the Gros Ventre and the Blackfoot toward the trading success of the Cree and Assiniboine, which made possible the latter's superiority in firearms. In the eyes of the Gros Ventre, the traders were in effect allies of their enemies, so they responded to the Cree raid by attacking fur-trade posts such as Manchester House (on Pine Island, Saskatchewan River), which they looted in 1793, and in the destruction of the Hudson's Bay Company's South Branch House the following year. In both cases, nearby Nor'Wester forts had been able to defend themselves. Such raids, of course, only compounded the trading difficulties of the Gros Ventre, who apparently were responsible for pillaging Chesterfield House at the mouth of the Red Deer River in 1826; in any event, groups of them subsequently fled south to the headwaters of the Missouri, where they joined their Arapaho kinsmen.[77] The disappearance of the Gros Ventre from the Saskatchewan basin meant that there was no longer a buffer between the Blackfoot and the Assiniboine-Cree, who were thus in direct conflict.

The first European mention of Cree and their allies, the Assiniboines (Stoneys), is in the Jesuit Relations for 1640, when the latter are referred to first as the "Assinipour" and later (1657) as "Assinipoualak," "Warriors of Rock." The Assiniboines came to the attention of the French because of their connection with the Ottawa River trading system.[78] A Siouan-speaking people, they apparently broke off from the Yanktonai Dakota sometime around 1600, moving north and west, with some moving northeastward into the boreal forest. According to David Thompson, the rupture had not been peaceful, with the breakaways establishing themselves on the Red River and along the right bank of the Saskatchewan River to the foothills.[79] As the Assiniboines became more firmly associated with the fur trade, their alliance with the Cree and other Algonkian speakers strengthened, as did their hostility to their kinsmen, the Sioux.

The Cree, the most widespread of northern Amerindians, were first identified by the French as "Kristinaux" or "Killistinaux"; like the Assiniboine, they were connected with the Ottawa and Huron trading systems. Soon, however, they were in direct trading contact with the French in what is now northern Quebec, to the east of Hudson Bay, as well as north of Lake Superior. By 1684, the French had built a post on Lake Nipigon to trade with the Cree and their Assiniboine allies in the area[80]; by that time, other bands of Cree were actively trading with the English on the Bay.[81] Kelsey noted in 1690 that both Cree and Assiniboine were well armed, a situation which encouraged an already evident trend toward expansion. By 1730, Pierre Gaultier de Varennes et de La Verendrye reported a detachment of Cree south of the Saskatchewan, which the stories of Saukamapee support.[82] The Cree probably entered the northwestern plains by two routes, the Saskatchewan to the north and the Assiniboine and its tributaries to the south. That they flourished in the plains environment despite the decimations of the smallpox epidemic of 1776–77 and later is witnessed by the number of bands which developed between the Qu'Appelle Valley and Edmonton— eight, all told.[83] In the forests of the north, the Cree were finally stopped and pushed back by the Chipewyans, although bands raided as far as the Mackenzie basin in 1820, the farthest point of their expansion.[84] In the southwest, they were stopped by the Blackfoot, with whom they had once been in sporadic alliance when the Shoshoni were a common enemy. By the early 19th century, Cree and Blackfoot considered each other their worst foe.

Whether or not the Cree were introduced to plains life by the Assiniboine, as some have maintained, underlying similarities between customs of northeastern woodlands and northwestern plains meant that adaptation was not difficult. By 1772, Cree were impounding bison, but preferred the gun to the bow for the hunt, in contrast to peoples longer established on the grasslands. However, buffalo hunting lessened dependence upon the fur trade; bands of Cree acting as hunters for particular posts, known as the "home guard," were more a phenomenon of the northern forests,[85] although they were not unknown at the posts of the parklands or prairies, as for example at Fort Pembina.

Reduced dependence on the fur trade affected relationships with traders, and it was the Plains Cree who were involved in one of the most widely remembered confrontations. It occurred in 1779 in reaction to the callous behaviour of a group of independent traders at Fort Montagne d'Aigle (Eagle Hills Fort), on the Saskatchewan between Eagle Hill Creek and Battle

River. Two traders were killed and the rest forced to flee; the post was abandoned, and was apparently never permanently reoccupied. The incident also caused the abandonment that same year of the Nor'Wester Fort du Milieu and Upper Hudson House of the Hudson's Bay Company. Nor was this an isolated occurrence. For just one more example, it was the Cree who were participants in a *mêlée* in 1781 at Fort des Trembles on the Assiniboine that resulted in the death of three traders and between 15 and 30 Amerindians. Only the outbreak of the 1781–82 smallpox epidemic prevented large-scale retaliations against the traders.[86] The much-vaunted peaceful cooperation considered to be characteristic of the fur trade in the northern forests was not so evident on the plains.

In spite of this, the converging influences of the horse and the fur trade fostered an efflorescence of plains cultures, whose golden years in the northwest are usually dated from 1750 to 1880. The horse facilitated the exploitation of the buffalo herds and the extension of overland routes; the fur trade made available a new range of goods, but even more importantly, provided new markets for products of the hunt. This meant that as long as the herds lasted, plains Amerindians were able to hold their own and indeed to reach new heights of cultural expression as their socieites became increasingly complex. They were even able to overcome to a large extent the demographic disasters of introduced diseases. But they did not have time to make their own accommodations to the disappearance of the herds upon which all this was based; it was the dramatic suddenness of that event which catapulted matters beyond their control.

This flourishing of a culture soon to die was not unique to the plains: it had previously occurred in the eastern woodlands, for example, among the Ojibway, Woods Cree and Iroquois; and it occurred simultaneously and continued somewhat later on the west coast, where one of its more spectacular manifestations was the burgeoning of totem poles, not to mention the appearance of button blankets and argillite carving. But in sheer artistry of dress, the mounted plainsman achieved an elegance which has never been surpassed; as an expression of the nomadic buffalo-hunting way of life, he was his own *pièce de résistance*.

Summary

To conclude, there is now no doubt as to the considerable time span of human habitation on the northwestern plains. Indeed, some of our most ancient archaeological records have been discovered here. In Alberta, for instance, there is Head-Smashed-In Buffalo Jump and the Majorville Cairn and Medicine Wheel site, both of which have yielded evidence of continuous human use for 5,000 years or more. In Saskatchewan, Oxbow and Long Creek campsites show a similar length of habitation. However, archaeological evidence has not been found to support the hypothesis that early migrating Siberians found a corridor in the open lands east of the mountains[87]; those historic plains tribes which did originate in the northwest, all Athapaskan-speakers, arrived comparatively recently. Ancient Amerindians of the plains appear to have had more connections, however remote, indirect and sporadic, with the eastern and northeastern woodlands, as well as with the civilizations of the Mississippi, the pueblos of the southwest, and even tenuously with Mexico. Similarly, when the horse and European trade goods appeared on the northwestern plains, they filtered in from the south as well as from the east and northeast. When Europeans first began to colonize mainland America during the 16th century, they often compared Amerindians with what they imagined their own Stone Age ancestors to have been like, and even sometimes with the peoples of classical antiquity. In the hurly-burly of conquering the land, that more generous perspective was often overlooked. As archaeology reveals the richness and antiquity of our prehistoric heritage, and as its links with the historic present are slowly traced out, we would do well to re-evaluate our perception of Canada as a "new world" without traditions of civilization before the arrival of Europeans.

Notes

This article first appeared in *Prairie Forum* 5, no. 1 (1980): 19–38.

1. This paper was presented in a slightly different form to the Edmonton Branch of the Alberta Historical Society, December 6, 1979. I would like to thank Dr. Paul F. Donahue, acting director of the Archaeological Survey, Historical Resources Division, Alberta Culture, for his generous assistance, as well as Dr. L.H. Thomas and Dr. John Honsaker, both of the University of Alberta, for their thoughtful and informed comments. The conception and line of thought is entirely my responsibility.

2. H.M. Wormington and Richard G. Forbis, "An Introduction to the Archaeology of Alberta," *Proceedings of the Denver Museum of Natural History* 11 (1965): 198–99.

3. Clark Wissler, "Diffusion of Culture in the Plains of North America," *International Congress of Americanists*, 15th session (Quebec, 1906), 39–52; also cited by William Mulloy, "A Preliminary Historical Outline for the Northwestern Plains," *University of Wyoming Publications* 22, no. 1 (July 1958), 6. However, Wissler later modified this view. See Edward Adamson Hoebel, *The Plains Indians: A Critical Bibliography* (Bloomington, IN: Indiana University Press, 1977), 8–10.

4. A.L. Kroeber, *Cultural and Natural Areas of Native North America* (Berkeley, CA: University of California, 1939), 76; also cited in Mulloy, *Preliminary Historical Outline*, 6.

5. Waldo R. Wedel, *Prehistoric Man on the Great Plains* (Norman, OK: University of Oklahoma Press, 1961), 243–44, 256. Also, by the same author, "The High Plains and Their Utilization by the Indian," *American Antiquity* 29, no. 1 (1963): 1–16.

6. Michel de Montaigne, *The Complete Works of Montaigne*, translated by Donald M. Frame (Stanford, CA: Stanford University Press, 1957), 693.

7. The classification I am using was suggested by that of Waldo R. Wedel, "The Prehistoric Plains," in Jesse D. Jennings (ed.), *Ancient Native Americans* (San Francisco: W.H. Freeman, 1978), 183–219.

8. Hoebel, *Plains Indians*, 12; Zenon S. Pohorecky, "Archaeology and Prehistory: The Saskatchewan Case," in Richard Allen (ed.), *Region of the Mind* (Regina: Canadian Plains Research Center, 1973), 47–72.

9. Brian O.K. Reeves, "The Southern Alberta Paleo-Cultural Paleo-Environmental Sequence," in *Post-Pleistocene Man and His Environment on the Northern Plains* (Calgary: University of Calgary Archaeological Association, 1969), 21.

10. H.M. Wormington, *Ancient Man in North America* (Denver: The Denver Museum of Natural History, 1964), 149.

11. George W. Arthur, *An Introduction to the Ecology of Early Historic Communal Bison Hunting Among the Northern Plains Indians* (Ottawa: National Museums of Canada, 1975), 71.

12. Ibid., 72; Reeves, *Post-Pleistocene*, 22; Thomas F. and Alice B. Kehoe, "Saskatchewan," in Warren W. Caldwell (ed.), *The Northwestern Plains: A Symposium* (Billings, MT: Centre for Indian Studies, Rocky Mountain College, 1968), 21. See also Thomas F. Kehoe, *The Gull Lake Site* (Milwaukee, Milwaukee Public Museum, 1973).

13. Wedel, *Prehistoric Man*, 249.

14. There is always the possibility—even probability—that this reduction is more apparent than real. As archaeological techniques develop, traces of man's presence become more evident. For other aspects of the problem, see Brian Reeves, "The Concept of an Altithermal Cultural Hiatus in Northern Plains Prehistory," *American Anthropologist* 75 (1973): 1221–53; and W.R. Hurt, "The Altithermal and the Prehistory of the Northern Plains," *Quaternia* 8 (1966): 101–13.

15. Jennings, *Ancient Native Americans*, 202.

16. So far the Archaeological Survey of Alberta has examined about 5% of the province's surface.

17. James M. Calder, *The Majorville Cairn and Medicine Wheel Site, Alberta*, Mercury Series #62 (Ottawa: National Museum of Man, 1977), 202. See also two reports by Boyd Wettlaufer, *The Long Creek Site* (Regina: Saskatchewan Museum of Natural History, 1960), and *The Mortlach Site in The Besant Valley of Central Saskatchewan* (Regina: Department of Natural Resources, 1955); and one by Robert W. Nero and Bruce A. McCorquodale, "Report of and Excavation at the Oxbow Dam Site," *The Blue Jay* 16, no. 2 (1958): 82–90.

18. Richard G. Forbis, *A Review of Alberta Archaeology to 1964* (Ottawa: National Museum of Canada, 1970), 27.

19. Arthur, *Introduction to the Ecology*, 110ff; Forbis, *Review*, 29. See also Thomas F. Kehoe, *Indian Boulder Effigies* (Regina, Saskatchewan Museum of Natural History, 1965).

20. Forbis, *Review*, 27. On the significance of the circle, Calder cited Hyemeyohsts Storm: "It is the mirror in which everything is reflected, it is the universe and the cycle of all things that exist," and added that it represented understanding, knowledge and perception. The four great powers of the circle found at the four cardinal points are wisdom, innocence, illumination and introspection. (Calder, *Majorville Cairn*, 207.)

21. Kehoe, "Saskatchewan," 30.

22. Jennings, *Ancient Native Americans*, 203. Ceramic evidence also supports this hypothesis. See William J. Byrne, *The Archaeology and Prehistory of Southern Alberta as Reflected by Ceramics*, 3 vols., Mercury Series #14 (Ottawa: National Museum of Man, 1973), 2: 561.

23. Ibid., 2: 554; Richard Glover (ed.), *David Thompson's Narrative* (Toronto: Champlain Society, 1962), 240.

24. Reeves, *Post-Pleistocene Man*, 34–36.

25. Richard G. Forbis, "Alberta," in *Northwest Plains Symposium*, 44. An earth village described by Peter Fidler, who was in Saskatchewan late in the 18th century, has not been located. (Kehoe, "Saskatchewan," 32.)

26. Population on the high plains during the post-glacial period has been estimated at 0.2 to 0.3 persons per square mile. (Reeves, *Post-Pleistocene Man*, 37.)

27. Dolores A. Gunnerson, "Man and Bison on the Plains in the Protohistoric Period," *Plains Anthropologist* 17, no. 55 (1972): 3–4, 5–6. See also F.G. Roe, *The North American Buffalo* (Toronto: University of Toronto Press, 1972), 228–56 and 283–333.

28. Ibid., 2. It has been estimated that the buffalo may have numbered as many as 60,000,000 at their peak. (Arthur, *Introduction to the Ecology*, 11–12; F.G. Roe, *North American Buffalo*, 518–19.)

29. T.H. Lewis (ed.), "The Narrative of the Expedition of Hernando de Soto by the Gentleman of Elvas," in Frederick W. Hodge (ed.), *Spanish Explorers in the Southern United States 1528–1543* (New York: Scribner's, 1907), 213.

30. Roe, *North American Buffalo*, 235, 843–44; Gunnerson, "Man and Bison," 2. Buffalo also destroyed small trees and pushed over telephone poles. Arthur, *Introduction*, 15–16. R.G. Thwaites (ed.), *The Jesuit Relations and Allied Documents*, 73 vols. (Cleveland: Burrows Bros., 1896–1901), 59: 113; Gunnerson, "Man and Bison," 2-3, citing G.A. Dorsey, *Traditions of the Caddo* (Washington: Carnegie Institution of Washington, 1905), 50–55, 109–11.

32. Joseph Jablow, *The Cheyenne in Plains Indian Trade Relations 1795–1840*, Monograph of the American Ethnological Society 19 (Seattle and London: University of Washington Press, 1950), 14; Robert H. Lowrie, *Indians of the Plains* (New York: American Museum of Natural History, 1963), 45.

33. William Duncan Strong, "The Plains Culture Area in the Light of Archaeology," *American Anthropologist* 35 (1933), held that horse nomadism represented no more than a "thin and strikingly uniform veneer" on earlier cultural manifestations. For the lack of specific rites among the Plains Cree for the increase of horses even though they were the symbol of wealth, see David G. Mandelbaum, *The Plains Cree*, Anthropological Papers #37, Pt. 2 (New York: American Museum of Natural History, 1940, 195–96. Mandelbaum's work was reprinted by the Canadian Plains Research Center, University of Regina.

34. F.G. Roe, *The Indian and the Horse* (Norman: University of Oklahoma Press, 1951), 54.

35. John C. Ewers, *The Horse in Blackfoot Indian Culture* (Washington: Smithsonian Institution Press, 1955), 2–3.

36. Roe, *Indian and the Horse*, 74–75.

37. Arthur, *Introduction*, 66; Elliott Coues (ed.), *History of the Expedition Under the Command of Lewis and Clark*, 4 vols. (New York: Harper, 1893), 3: 1,148.

38. Arthur, *Introduction*, 72.

39. Oscar Lewis, *The Effects of White Contact Upon Blackfoot Culture With Special References to the Fur Trade*, Monographs of the American Ethnological Society 6 (New York, Augustin, 1942), 39–40; Bernard Mishkin, *Rank and Warfare Among Plains Indians*, Monographs of the American Ethnological Society 3 (Seattle and London, University of Washington Press, 1940), 10; Glover, *David Thompson*, 267–68. For other such raids, see

A.S. Morton (ed.), *The Journal of Duncan M'Gillivray of the Northwest Company at Fort George on the Saskatchewan, 1794–1795* (Toronto: Macmillan, 1979), 27.

40. Glover, *David Thompson*, 241–42; Frank Raymond Secoy, *Changing Military Patterns on the Great Plains*, Monographs of the American Ethnological Society 21 (Seattle and London: University of Washington Press, 1953), 33; Lewis, *Effects of White Contact*, 11; George E. Hyde, *Indians of the High Plains* (Norman: University of Oklahoma Press, 1959), 121, 133–34.

41. James Teit, "The Salishan Tribes of the Western Plateaus," *45th Annual Report, U.S. Bureau of American Ethnology (1927–1928)* (Washington: U.S. Bureau of American Ethnology, 1930), 109–10; Mishkin, *Rank and Warfare*, 9.

42. Secoy, *Military Patterns*, 36–38.

43. Glover, *David Thompson*, 244.

44. John C. Ewers, *The Blackfeet* (Norman: University of Oklahoma Press, 1958), 22.

45. John C. Ewers, "Was There a Northwestern Plains Sub-Culture? An Ethnographic Appraisal," *Northwest Plains Symposium*, 71. See also Hugh A. Dempsey, *Indian Tribes of Alberta* (Calgary: Glenbow-Alberta Institute, 1978).

46. Ewers, *Blackfeet*, 6–7; Hoebel, *Plains Indians*, 37; Lewis, *Effects of White Contact*, 7–9.

47. Ewers, "Ethnographic Appraisal," 73.

48. Ewers, *Blackfeet*, 24–25.

49. Cf. James Henri Howard, *The Plains-Ojibwa or Bungi, Hunters and Warriors of the Northern Prairie* (Vermillion: South Dakota Museum, University of South Dakota, 1965). Also, Edwin Thompson Denig, *Five Indian Tribes of the Upper Missouri*, edited by John C. Ewers (Norman: University of Oklahoma Press, 1961), 100. Denig says that the Ojibwa and Cree were so intermingled as to be difficult to consider separately.

50. Ewers, "Ethnographic Appraisal," 71.

51. Ibid., 72.

52. Symmes C. Oliver, *Ecology and Cultural Continuity as Contributing Factors in the Social Organization of the Plains Indians* (Berkeley and Los Angeles: University of California Press, 1962), 46.

53. Glover, *David Thompson*, 241–42; Hyde, *High Plains*, 133–34; and Secoy, *Military Patterns*, 36–37.

54. Glover, *David Thompson*, 245.

55. Elliott Coues (ed.), *New Light on the Early History of the Great Northwest, 1799–1814*, 3 vols. (New York: Harper, 1897), 2: 713–14. For a Spanish governor's ingenious argument in favour of providing guns to *indios barbaros* in order to make them less formidable, see Max L. Moorhead, *The Apache Frontier* (Norman: University of Oklahoma Press, 1968), 127–28

56. Hyde, *High Plains*, 146.

57. Secoy, *Military Patterns*, 52.

58. Glover, *David Thompson*, 107, 240.

59. Hyde, *High Plains*, 164–65.

60. Coues, *New Light*, 2: 726.

61. Ewers, *Blackfeet*, 19, 24.

62. Glyndwr Williams, "The Puzzle of Anthony Henday's Journal, 1754–55," *The Beaver*, Outfit 309, no. 3 (Winter 1978): 53.

63. Lewis, *Effects of White Contact*, 14.

64. Ibid., 17–18.

65. Morton, *Duncan M'Gillivray*, 31.

66. E.E. Rich, *The Fur Trade and the Northwest to 1857* (Toronto: McClelland and Stewart, 1967), 158.

67. Lewis, *Effects of White Contact*, 23.

68. J.B. Tyrrell (ed.), *David Thompson's Narrative of his Explorations in Western America* (Toronto: Champlain Society, 1916), xc; for a different version, see J.E.A. Macleod, "Peigan Post and the Blackfoot Trade," *Canadian Historical Review* 24, no. 3 (1943): 273–79.

69. Lewis, *Effects of White Contact*, 24.

70. Ibid., 35–36.

71. Mandelbaum, *Plains Cree*, 246; Lewis says that among the Blackfoot, the third or fourth wife had such an inferior status that she was referred to as a "slave." (Lewis, *Effects of White Contact*, 39–40.)

72. Ibid., 57.

73. Regina Flannery, *The Gros Ventres of Montana, Part 1: Social Life*, Anthropological Series 15 (Washington: The Catholic University of America Press, 1953), 4–5.

74. Ibid., 5; Alfred L. Kroeber, *Ethnology of the Gros Ventre* (New York, Anthropological Papers of the American Museum of Natural History, I, 1908), 145.

75. Morton, *Duncan M'Gillivray*, 26–27, 73–74.

76. Ibid., 62–63; Arthur J. Ray, *Indians in the Fur Trade* (Toronto: University of Toronto Press, 1974), 98; Kroeber, *Ethnology*, 146.

77. Flannery, *Gros Ventres*, 9.

78. Thwaites, *Jesuit Relations*, 18: 231; 44: 249; Ray, *Fur Trade*, 11.

79. Glover, *David Thompson*, 164.

80. Thwaites, *Jesuit Relations*, 18: 229; Ray, *Fur Trade*, 11.

81. Apparently the English on the Bay, on the advice of Medard Chouart de Groseilliers and Pierre Radisson, had entered into ceremonial alliances with the local Cree, which were ritually renewed annually with feasting and gift exchanges. One observer saw this as paying "rent." (Denig, *Five Tribes*, 112.)

82. Glover, *David Thompson*, 240ff; L.J. Burpee (ed.), *Journals and Letters by Pierre Gaultier de Varennes de La Vérendrye* (Toronto: Champlain Society, 1927), 25.

83. David G. Mandelbaum, *Anthropology and People: The World of the Plains Cree*, University Lectures 12 (Saskatoon: University of Saskatchewan, 1967), 7.

84. Mandelbaum, *Plains Cree*, 183.

85. Mandelbaum, *Anthropology and People*, 6.

86. Coues, *New Light*, 1: 292–93; 2: 498–99; Alexander Mackenzie, *Voyages from Montreal on the River St. Lawrence Through the Continent of America* (London: n.p., 1801), xiii-xiv.

87. Wormington and Forbis, *Introduction*, 183.

2. An Examination of *Common and Contested Ground: A Human and Environmental History of the Northwestern Plains*

James Daschuk

Ted Binnema's *Common and Contested Ground: A Human and Environmental History of the Northwestern Plains* (Norman, OK: University of Oklahoma Press, 2001) may be the most important book on the Aboriginal history of western Canada since the publication of Dale Russell's *Eighteenth Century Western Cree and Their Neighbours*[1] fifteen years ago. Binnema's synthesis of human and environmental change spanning more than a thousand years of northwestern plains history, though perhaps inspired by Howard Meredith's *Dancing on Common Ground: Tribal Cultures and Alliances on the Southern Plains,*[2] is truly innovative in Canadian scholarship. In addition, he has provided a detailed account of the shifting political and military situation in the 18th century, a period when horses, the fur trade, and smallpox reached the region. What makes *Common and Contested Ground* significant is its approach. It is the first work of history on the Canadian plains to truly ground its subjects on the changing landscape. Instead of an ethnohistory dealing solely with cultural phenomena, Binnema has accorded the physical environment the weight it deserves when examining the human history of the northwestern plains. By taking a balanced regional approach, he has demonstrated why some groups prevailed as others declined. *Common and Contested Ground* is the first historical work to seriously consider the role of long-term environmental change in the development of societies on the Canadian plains. Binnema rightly draws the connection between historical change among the hunting and gathering societies on the northwestern plains and the impact of climatic variability. Climatic forces have become increasingly recognized as an agent of societal change. The recent publication of Jared Diamond's *Collapse: How Societies Choose to Fail or Succeed* has introduced climate change as an historical force to a mass audience.[3] Before the arrival of the Europeans, germs, goods, and market economy, climatic variability was the predominant factor in precipitating cultural or techno- logical change in prehistoric communities.[4] With the recognition of climate change as a central force in northwestern plains history, Binnema has broken new ground in Canadian scholarship.

By considering historical processes at a macro level, Binnema has been able to avoid a common pitfall of many ethnohistories which tend to focus on small-scale changes within bands or ethnic groups. With their intimate connection to a single entity, many ethnohistorians tend to advocate for a particular group, and present the stories of their subjects from a single side of the equation. We need micro studies to understand the motivations of individual communities; they are the foundation of our understanding of past events. However, Binnema reveals how our knowledge of the impact of introduced forces, such as horses, commerce and disease, on the region as a whole, can be greatly enhanced by putting the ethnohistorical pieces together to create a large-scale interpretation of historical change.

Over the past thirty years, ethnohistoric method has been remarkably successful in showing how Aboriginal societies were active agents in their relations with European traders. Binnema's chapters on the 18th century clearly show that the inhabitants of the northwestern plains dealt with change on their own terms. Although Binnema's focus on the diplomatic and military interactions differs from most ethnohistorical studies, he is in general agreement with the prevalent interpretation in ethnohistory, that "[t]he arrival of Euroamerican traders and their wares did not bring rapid economic dependence or cultural and social disintegration but did bring profound change" (114). Among the Blackfoot, he argues that the arrival of the horse, European goods, and Euroamericans themselves actually strengthened belief systems (114).

Binnema's focus on the short-term military and diplomatic aspects of 18th-century plains life comes at a price. Binnema may have overlooked the increasing environmental risk that plains people assumed as they adopted equestrianism and integrated themselves into the fur trade. With these changes, the susceptibility of Aboriginal communities to the negative effects of climatic conditions was greatly increased. To be fair, Binnema makes sev- eral references to severe weather conditions during the winters of the last quarter of the 18th century as a factor contributing to an increase in intertrib- al tension, but he does not explicitly identify bad weather, horse depletion and conflict as a pattern driving diplomatic and military relations. The late 18th and early 19th centuries brought some of the most severe and unpre- dictable weather episodes in the region in the last thousand years. The universal adoption of a species imported from southern Europe, at a time when the Little Ice Age was at its worst, had dire ramifications for the newly equestrian-dependent peoples on the Canadian plains. Aboriginal groups may have been free agents making autonomous decisions but their choices were shaped, indeed limited, by environmental factors. When it came to intertribal violence in western Canada, climatic forces were as important as the arrival of Europeans as causative factors.

Our current preoccupation with climate change has had the unintended consequence of providing historians with an increasingly detailed picture of climatic variability in the past. Tree-ring reconstructions, for example, have detailed drought cycles in the region for the past 500 years.[5] Streamflow reconstructions of the Saskatchewan River covering an 1,100-year period, a valuable indicator of regional temperatures, have been developed.[6] The integration of proxy data from scientific sources into historical narratives can provide a new level of understanding of the interaction of human communities and their environment. Much of this new data has become available since the completion of Binnema's dissertation in the late 1990s. In light of these recent developments, the historical trends identified by Binnema regarding past occupation of the region can be supported with a greater level of precision.

During the Scandic and Neo-Atlantic climatic episodes (A.D. 250–1250), societies on the northwestern plains were relatively stable. As Binnema pointed out, the principal innovation during this period was the spread of bow and arrow technology (61–63). A recent archaeological discussion of the period notes the gradual nature of technological and human change in the region, and stresses that they were "in situ" developments rather than the intrusion of a culture from another region.[7] In regions east of Binnema's *Common and Contested Ground*, societies underwent a period of florescence during the benign weather conditions of the Neo-Atlantic climatic episode (A.D. 850–1250). Rather than Binnema's interpretation that villages on the middle Missouri were founded by "refugees" from Cahokia (66), they were probably "settlers." According to W.R. Wood, the establishment of corn agriculture in the Missouri basin was directly related to the favourable climate of the Neo-Atlantic period: "it is certainly not accident that the initial variant makes its appearance on the Prairie-plains border and High plains at the time it does… This was a warm period when more moisture was available than previously on the High Plains."[8]

The climatic deterioration that accompanied the shift to the Pacific climate episode in the mid-13th century marked the end of stable occupation on the northwestern plains. Binnema's general statement, "(t)hroughout the pedestrian era diverse human communities migrated onto the northwestern plains" (71), could have been more precise. From the beginning of the Pacific climatic episode on, the region was subjected to an unprecedented level of in-migration. The vast majority of those migrants arrived as a consequence of deteriorating conditions in their home territories. Binnema discusses the impact of the climatic decline on the horticultural communities of the Missouri and their brief foray north of the 49th parallel during this period (66–67). Diminished harvests forced the Hidatsa to the northern plains to supply meat to their increasingly strained agricultural partners (68). The period, characterized by severe drought south of the 49th parallel, forced widespread abandonment of agrarian villages and led to the adoption of the bison hunt by the Hidatsa to supplement the crops of the Missouri villages.

The climatic downturn beginning in the mid-13th century was a global phenomenon and affected all who eventually made their way to the north-western plains. Long-term climatic decline drove many groups from unsustainable woodlands to the relative stability of the bison herds on the western grasslands. Binnema describes the westward migration of numerous groups to the northern plains, yet he does not posit their reasons for doing so. He quotes ecological anthropologist Douglas Bamforth that "humans rarely engage in extremely expensive behaviour without very good reason" (58). Many new arrivals to the northern plains travelled great distances in their quest for a reliable subsistence base. Clearly, their home territories could not sustain them. By 1300, the Mortlach, the ancestors of the historic Assiniboine, moved onto the grasslands from the east, pushing the ancestors of the historic Blackfoot westward out of the South Saskatchewan River region (68). During the mid-13th century, the Atsina and their kin, the Arapaho, probably began their migration west from the Interlakes of Manitoba to the parklands and eventually to the region of the forks of the Saskatchewan River by 1550 (75). The ancestors of the Cree also moved south and west in response to the worsening conditions in the boreal forest and occupied the Lower Saskatchewan River Valley (77). Later, during the 16th century, the Shoshoni battled their way onto the northwestern plains. Binnema explains how the Shoshoni were able to invade the region but does not advance a reason for why they did so. Their invasion was probably a consequence of what has been called a "megadrought" across the western United States during the 16th century.[9] The protracted and severe desiccation would have certainly undermined food supplies in their home territory, forcing them northward to survive. Although the destination of the Shoshoni and the other migrants was arid and prone to sustained drought, their universal adoption of the pedestrian bison hunting underscores the viability of that strategy despite scarce precipitation. Although the Dirty Thirties and the droughts of the late 1980s remain in our popular consciousness, the 20th century was anomalous for its absence of sustained drought.[10]

A critical factor in understanding the allure of the northwestern plains during the prehistoric period is the issue of how communities survived under conditions of minimal precipitation. Grace Morgan asserts that the ability of pedestrian bison hunters to withstand prolonged drought was predicated on a widespread aversion to beaver hunting as a means to conserve limited water supplies.[11] According to Morgan, beavers provided prehistoric hunters with a reliable supply of water along valleys of the tributaries of major waterways through the grasslands. Ponds established in valley complexes slowed the flow of the water, a scarce but essential resource. These were the principal sites of human occupation for most of the year.[12] Morgan stressed that, without beaver, "human occupancy of the plains may not have been possible during periods of intense drought."[13] Binnema makes only passing reference to Morgan's "intriguing" discussion about the place of beaver in Blackfoot life (216–17, fn. 12), and dismisses the notion of Aboriginal beaver conservation with the statement that HBC journals "show that many Peigan did kill many beavers, but that their relatively sedentary lifestyle in winter precluded large-scale beaver hunting." With this, Binnema underestimates what was the critical factor in the survival of groups on the northwestern plains. David Smyth stresses that only a small number of Peigan ever commercially harvested beaver until well into the 19th century.[14] Binnema states that the devaluation of wolf pelts, the predominant fur brought in by the Blackfoot and the Atsina, was an important factor in the increasing tension between them and traders in the late 18th century because "they could supply few of the furs that Europeans valued most highly" (142). Smyth stated emphatically that they would not trap beaver. The central point of Smyth's thesis is that the Blackfoot allies refused to exploit beaver commercially as a matter of choice rather than simply the scarcity of the species in their territory. According to Smyth, only the Sarcee and a single band of Peigan, amounting to 30–40 tents, commercially trapped beaver during the period of Binnema's study.[15] The literature is replete with references to the Blackfoot and their allies not harvesting beaver to their commercial potential.[16] On his journey to southern Alberta in 1792–93, Peter Fidler travelled with a Peigan group who, though disgruntled at the low prices paid for their wolves, passed by ponds seemingly teeming with beaver only days from Buckingham House.[17] Fidler admonished the Peigan for their refusal to hunt beaver for trade in his journal although they were forced to adjust their travelling "entirely owing to the places where water is to be had, both for ourselves and for the horses."[18] Clearly, the availability of water placed significant constraints on the inhabitants of the northwestern plains.

Groups that did not hunt beaver and traded primarily wolves and provisions were increasingly seen as second-class customers at the posts, where beaver was prized above all else. In the case of the Blackfoot, they were also the community with the longest collective experience in the northwestern plains. New arrivals to the region such as the woodland Cree, the Saulteaux and the Iroquois were the primary beaver producers on the plains in the late 18th century. They came in association with the trade and were unencumbered by an aversion to beaver hunting, the key to long-term survival in the region. The role of the beaver in the plains ecosystem, and the aversion of those groups with a long history on the northwestern plains to commercially harvest beaver, are not fully considered by Binnema.

Another ecological issue that is not fully developed is the role of climate variability during the period identified as the "horse and gun revolution." Early in the book, he challenges the reader to consider how the "Indian of imagination" differs "from the native American of actual existence" (xiii). Binnema asserts that the adoption of equestrianism did not significantly change the cultures of those who adopted horses and that the acquisition of the species increased the power of those who took it up. While equestrianism may not have changed the cultures of those who adopted the new strategy on the northwestern plains, it must certainly have changed their relationship to the land. In addition to the ever-present need for water, groups that acquired horses had to feed their stock.[19] The timing of the diffusion of horses to the northern plains, coinciding with a long period of mild weather between the severe cold marking the first and last decades of the 18th century, was a significant factor in the spread of equestrianism across the west.[20]

Three decades ago, Dennis Rinn recognized that horses could not be naturally maintained by all groups on the Canadian prairies and that an almost constant supply of equestrian stock flowed from the mountain tribes southwest of the plains.[21] In a footnote, Binnema cites Rinn on the susceptibility of Cree and Assiniboine horses to severe weather (218, fn. 43). Rinn stated that while the Peigan lost fewer horses to cold and starvation, all groups suffered from acute depletions of their herds at least once a decade from adverse conditions.[22] Rinn also stated that none of the people north of the 49th parallel were able to maintain their herds through natural growth. Binnema provides ample evidence of the difficulty in maintaining horses during the final cold decades of the 18th century and the connection between bad weather conditions and horse raiding. Binnema does not consider the increasing

On the March.

Blackfoot camp on the march with horse and dog travois, c. 1875. Original sketch by Richard Barrington Nevitt of the North-West Mounted Police (courtesy of the Glenbow Archives/LAC-1434-30).

violence over horses in the context of long-term climatic variability and that the relationship between severe weather conditions and intertribal violence was a pattern. The years between the late 18th and early 19th centuries were among the most severe of the neo-Boreal climatic episode (A.D. 1550–1850). During the 1790s, as inter-tribal conflict grew, the northwestern plains were subjected to the worst drought of the past 500 years.[23] Horses became a military necessity, but this equestrian dependency exposed these cultures to a new level of assumed risk from the negative impact of climatic stimuli. Because intertribal conflict was inextricable from horse acquisition during the final decades of Binnema's study, the weather was as important as any other factor and heightened the level of conflicts on the western plains. In the final decades of his study, tribal populations were certainly more vulnerable to climatic variability than they were prior to their ill-fated equestrian dependency.

Climate science has advanced significantly since Binnema's research on his subject. He could not take full advantage of this unintended consequence of our new concern over global warming. Future studies that integrate the burgeoning scientific literature with existing historic sources will lead to a richer understanding of the broad strokes identified in Binnema's *Common and Contested Ground*. The recognition of climatic factors is essential to truly understand the relationship between human communities and their environment.

Some aspects of *Common and Contested Ground* may incite debate from within the ethnohistorical community. Binnema includes a discussion of Blackfoot groups travelling to York Factory during the first half of the 18th century, citing Ray's pioneering study, *Indians in the Fur Trade* (105). David Smyth categorically denies that there was direct trade between any members of the Blackfoot alliance and Europeans at Hudson Bay "ever," and that only four people from the alliance ever travelled to York Factory of their own volition.[24] Smyth raises another, perhaps more significant, issue surrounding the nature of Cree-Assiniboine relationship with the Blackfoot before the onset of open warfare in 1806. He forcefully disputed the notion of a Cree-Blackfoot alliance in this publication more than a decade ago.[25] Binnema does not repeat what, according to Smyth, was John Milloy's error.[26] Rather he uses the looser term "coalition" for the relationship that Milloy described as an alliance. Both Milloy and Binnema cite the same account by Daniel Harmon from the summer of 1806 on the outbreak of hostilities between the Cree-Assiniboine and the Blackfoot.[27] There is no question that relations between the Cree-Assiniboine and the Blackfoot alliance were hostile after 1806. It is the characterization of their relations in the decades before that remains not fully resolved. Binnema noted that occasional hostilities over horses occurred between the Cree and Archithinue bands as early as the 1750s and 1760s (99). The number of incidents between the members of Binnema's northern coalition grew toward the end of the 18th century. According to Smyth, "If such a coalition ever indeed existed, there is little evidence of it in the 1780s and 1790s."[28] Intertribal violence was predicated on the acquisition of horses or retaliation for predations on herds; climatic forces were largely responsible for the ongoing warfare in the period after Binnema's terminal date of 1806. Binnema asserts that the tenuous connection between the Blackfoot and the Cree-Assiniboine remained a coalition until the first decade of the 19th century. Smyth's view was that it was not. When Smyth's thesis gains a wider readership, the debate over the fundamental nature of indigenous relations will be given a new impetus. Regardless of which interpretation prevails, by the late 18th century, violence increased as tribal groups tried to maintain their herds in the face of conditions that were often too severe to sustain them.

Although Binnema stresses the independence and agency of Aboriginal groups inhabiting the common and contested ground, it is clear that from a climatic standpoint, communities of the northern plains were in a more precarious position at the end of the 18th century than at the beginning. As the century progressed, tribal groups took on new roles and new locations in relation to the expanding trade. Their almost universal adoption of horses created vulnerabilities that did not exist during the pedestrian era. As trade took hold as the dominant force among tribal groups on the plains, their situation became increasingly precarious. During the difficult years of the 1790s, the Blackfoot trade at Edmonton and other posts on the North Saskatchewan River slowed to a trickle because harsh weather made horse travel impossible. Over the winter of 1797, the Ojibwa, who had come west as commercial trappers, were the only group who traded at Buckingham House.[29] As Aboriginal societies turned their backs on climate as the dominant force in their decision-making in favour of the introduced factors, they assumed a level of climatic vulnerability much greater than had existed before.

In going beyond the "culturalist preoccupations" of ethnohistory, Binnema has provided a truly innovative study of historical change in western Canada. In taking a regional approach to intertribal relations to the beginning of the 19th century, he has provided us with a new level of understanding in the history of the west. For this Binnema should be applauded for his vision and its realization. With the increasing volume of scientific data of past climate, historians can no longer rely exclusively upon traditional methodologies which focus solely on the written record. The integration of historical records with scientific data cannot but render a more accurate narrative of the past. The marriage of historical method and the science of climate change is still in its infancy in the Canadian context.[30]

Binnema has opened the door to a new approach to Aboriginal scholarship. Advances from climate science have provided previously unavailable data that can be applied to historical analysis. Our growing insight into climatic variability may force scholars to reconsider longstanding beliefs developed from studies that consider human agency exclusively. The interrelationship between climatic variability and human communities identified by Binnema remain with us to the present. Recent droughts, floods and trade disputes have shaken the agricultural economy of western Canada. In this sense, the northwestern plains remains a *Common and Contested Ground*.

Notes

This article first appeared in *Prairie Forum* 31, no. 1 (2006): 141–48.

1. Dale Russell, *Eighteenth Century Western Cree and their Neighbours* (Ottawa: Canadian Museum of Civilization, 1991).

2. Howard Meredith, *Dancing on Common Ground: Tribal Cultures and Alliances on the Southern Plains* (Lawrence: University of Kansas Press, 1995).

3. Jared Diamond, *Collapse: How Societies Choose to Fail or Succeed* (New York: Viking, 2005).

4. Donald J. Lehmer, "Climate and Culture History in the Middle Missouri Valley," in W.R. Wood (ed.), *Reprints in Anthropology, Volume 8. Selected Writings of Donald J. Lehme* (Lincoln, NE: J & L Reprint Company), 59–72.

5. David Sauchyn and Walter Skinner, "A Proxy Record of Drought Severity for the Southwestern Canadian Plains," *Canadian Water Resources Journal* 26 (2001): 253–72.

6. Roslyn A. Case and Glen M. MacDonald, "Tree Ring Reconstructions of Streamflow for the Three Canadian Prairie Rivers," *Journal of the American Water Resources Association* 39 (2003): 707–16.

7. Trevor R. Peck and Caroline Hudecek-Cuffe, "Archaeology on the Alberta Plains: The Last Two Thousand Years," in Jack Brink and John Dormaar (eds.), *Archaeology in Alberta: A View from the New Millennium* (Medicine Hat: Archaeological Society of Alberta, 2003), 90.

8. W. Raymond Wood, "Plains Village Tradition: Middle Missouri," in Raymond J. DeMallie (ed.), *Handbook of North American Indians. Volume 13. Plains* (Part 1) (Washington: Smithsonian Institution Press, 2001), 190.

9. David W. Stahle, et al., "Tree-Ring Data Document 16th Century Megadrought over North America," *EOS: Transactions, American Geophysical Union* 81 (2000): 121–25.

10. David Sauchyn, E.M. Barrow, R.F. Hopkinson and P.R. Leavitt, "Aridity on the Plains," *Géographie Physique et Quaternitaire* 56 (2002): 247.

11. Grace Morgan, "Beaver Ecology/Beaver Mythology" (PhD dissertation, University of Alberta, 1991), 5.

12. Ibid., 153.

13. Ibid., 49.

14. David Smyth, "The Niitsitapi Trade: Euroamericans and the Blackfoot-Speaking Peoples to the Mid-1830s" (PhD dissertation, Carleton University, 1992), 207. Smyth quoted Alexander Henry's narrative from 1810–11 that noted only 30–40 tents of Piikani (Peigan) hunted beaver; by the mid-1820s, "beaver trapping had become widespread among the Piikani," 306.

15. Ibid., 205.

16. Although a full inventory of references to the failure of plains groups to commercially harvest beaver is beyond the scope of this review, references to the phenomenon are present from the 1730s on. G.H. Smith and W.R. Wood, *The Explorations of the La Vérendryes in the Northern Plains, 1738–43* (Lincoln: University of Nebraska Press, 1980), 44; Barbara Belyea (ed.), *A Year Inland: The Journal of a Hudson's Bay Company Winterer* (Waterloo: Wilfrid Laurier University Press, 2000), 121, For a discussion of the practice during the 18th and early 19th centuries, see Smyth, "The Niitsitapi Trade," 203–08.

17. Bruce Haig (ed.), *Journal of a Journey over Land from Buckingham House to the Rocky Mountains in 1792 & 93* (Lethbridge, AB: Historical Research Centre, 1992), 10–12.

18. Ibid., 23.

19. J.R. Vickers and T.R. Peck, "Islands in a Sea of Grass: The Significance of Wood in

Winter Campsite Selection on the Northwestern Plains," in Brian Kooyman and Jane H. Kelley (eds.), *Archaeology on the Edge: New Perspectives from the Northern Plains* (Calgary: University of Calgary Press, 2003), 98.

20. The period between 1685 and 1704 was the coldest of the past 1,000 years in western Canada. See B.H. Luckman and R.J.S. Wilson, "Summer Temperatures in the Canadian Rockies During the Last Millennium: A Revised Record," *Climate Dynamics* 24 (2005): 137. Alwynne Beaudoin, "What They Saw: The Climatic and Environmental Context for Euro-Canadian Settlement in Western Canada," *Prairie Forum* 24, no. 1 (1999): 32.

21. Dennis Rinn, "The Acquisition, Diffusion and Distribution of the European Horse among Blackfoot Tribes in Western Canada" (MA thesis, University of Manitoba, 1975,) 93.

22. Severe weather conditions included not only cold temperatures and deep snow but also unseasonable rain during winter. See Rinn, "The Acquisition, Diffusion, and Distribution of the European Horse among Blackfoot Tribes in Western Canada," 87–88.

23. Sauchyn and Skinner, "A Proxy Record of Drought Severity for the Southwestern Canadian Plains," 266.

24. Smyth, "The Niitsitapi Trade," 67–68.

25. David Smyth, "Missed Opportunity: John Milloy's *The Plains Cree*," *Prairie Forum* 17, no. 2 (1992): 337–54.

26. Ibid., 341–48.

27. John Milloy, *The Plains Cree: Trade, Diplomacy and War, 1790 to 1870* (Winnipeg: University of Manitoba Press, 1988), 35. Binnema, *Common and Contested Ground: A Human and Environmental History of the Northwestern Plains*, 196.

28. Smyth, "The Niitsitapi Trade," 214.

29. Alice M. Johnson, *Saskatchewan Journals and Correspondence: Edmonton House 1795–1800. Chesterfield House 1800–1802* (London: Hudson's Bay Record Society, 1967), 87.

30. A recent study that deals specifically with the relationship between climate change and history is Renée Fossett, *In Order to Live Untroubled: Inuit of the Central Arctic 1550 to 1940* (Winnipeg: University of Manitoba Press, 2002).

3. The Quest for Pasquatinow: An Aboriginal Gathering Centre in the Saskatchewan River Valley (1992)

David Meyer, Terry Gibson and Dale Russell

In the late 1600s, those Europeans who began to trade with the residents of northern Saskatchewan and Manitoba found that thousands of locations and landforms throughout the boreal-forest region had been named by the first peoples. Since the Cree language was the *lingua franca* of the fur trade in interior western Canada, most of the European traders gained some grasp of this tongue and learned from the Crees the local place names. In particular, they used and recorded a series of Cree toponyms along the Saskatchewan River[1] (Figure 1). Most of these referred to the locations at which the largest annual aggregations of peoples occurred.

"Pasquatinow" was one of these named places. It appears on 19th-century maps as "Pasquatinow"[2] or "Pasquatinow Hill,"[3] positioned on the north side of the Saskatchewan River, a few kilometres downstream from Tobin Rapids (Figure 1). One of the authors, David Meyer, has long been intrigued by these references to Pasquatinow. Therefore, during the summer of 1989 he, with another of the authors, Terry Gibson, travelled to the central part of the Saskatchewan River valley to try to locate the site. They were encouraged by the results of their 1989 visit and returned in the summer of 1990 to make a more formal investigation of the region. The following is a presentation and analysis of historical, geographical, archaeological and ethnographic information relating to this location. In particular, Pasquatinow will be discussed as an example of a seasonal aggregating centre, in relationship to the larger settlement pattern of the aboriginal hunters and gatherers of the Saskatchewan River valley.

Topography of the Pasquatinow Area

Pasquatinow is located on the Saskatchewan River, precisely at the point of transition between the Carrot River lowlands on the west and the

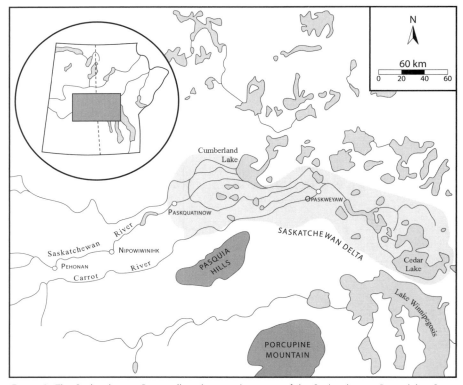

Figure 1. The Saskatchewan River valley, showing the extent of the Saskatchewan River delta. Some Cree place names are also shown.

Saskatchewan River delta (or, Cumberland Lake lowlands) on the east.[4] This part of the Carrot River lowlands lies on the flat (former) bed of glacial Lake Agassiz. It is an area of very low relief, characterized by the sandy strandlines of the latter glacial lake and by the remnants of distributary channels through which the waters of the Saskatchewan River flowed into this glacial lake.

Travelling downstream in 1910, William McInnes of the Geological Survey of Canada described the descent into the Saskatchewan River delta in this way:

> For a short distance, where the river contracts at Tobin and Squaw Rapids, the banks are again steep and high, but below the rapids fall away to a height of 10 feet or less and continue low to the mouth. This long stretch of river-valley extending to Grand rapids near the mouth, has the character of an estuary, in which the low, flat land is broken only by a

few ridges of boulder clay... The elevation of the land above the general river level is not more than 10 feet, and in many places is much less, so that in periods of flood the river overflows its banks and spreads over nearly all this low-lying land.

The low, flat country forms a broad belt along this part of the river, extending northerly from the river for 15 miles, and southerly for 25 miles to the base of the Pasquia Hills.[5]

More generally, the Saskatchewan River delta has been described as "a gently sloping plain about 30 miles wide and 120 miles long,[6] extending from just below Tobin Rapids east to Cedar Lake. Almost all of the elevated land within the delta consists of levees which border either the Saskatchewan River or channels in which it has flowed in the distant past.[7] Levees also border a number of smaller streams which flow into the delta. One of the former channels of the Saskatchewan River is the Sipanok, which trends southeast and eventually joins the Carrot River (Figure 1). The latter river empties into the Saskatchewan River at The Pas. Also within the delta are numerous lakes and marshes.

Historical Accounts

In order to understand the historical references to Pasquatinow and environs, it is necessary to consider some of the changes in the course of the Saskatchewan River which have occurred over the past two centuries (Figure 2). Just downstream of Pasquatinow, the Saskatchewan River once executed a sharp 5 km-long turn to the north. This produced a tongue of land which was known in the eighteenth and nineteenth centuries as Mosquito Point.[8] In the first half of the 1870s there was a dramatic natural event (an "avulsion"), the exact details of which do not seem to have been recorded; however, due to some combination of ice jams the spring floodwaters of the Saskatchewan River were diverted north from Mosquito Point, following Zig Zag Creek for 4 km. At this point the river waters left Zig Zag Creek and surged northward, eroding a new, 1.5 km-long channel through to the Torch River.[9] Either at the same time, or within two or three years, the river also gouged a "trench" across the base (south end) of Mosquito Point, forming the "Cut-off."[10] As a result, Mosquito Point became surrounded by river channels and now appears on topographic maps as Anderson Island. At present, the new channel (post-1873) carries most of the water of the Saskatchewan River, emptying it into the west end of Cumberland Lake. The old channel (pre-1873) only flows during periods of high water.

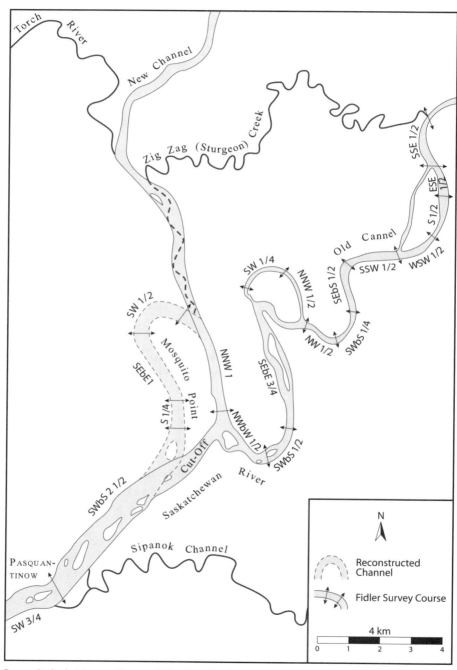

Figure 2. Saskatchewan River and Zig Zag Creek reconstructed to their approximate, pre-1870s channels, showing Peter Fidler's survey courses.

Pasquatinow regularly appeared on 19th-century maps, the earliest of which accompanied Sir John Franklin's account of his travels published in 1823.[11] On that map it is shown as a prominent hill on the north side of the Saskatchewan River, opposite the mouth of the Sipanok Channel. Other nineteenth-century maps, such as the Palliser end map,[12] also show "Pasquatinow Hill"; however, it is evident that the information on this latter map, and others, was recopied from the information on the Franklin map. Pasquatinow Hill also appears on Dominion of Canada maps produced in the 1880s under the direction of Edouard Deville, chief inspector of surveys of Canada.

We have not attempted an exhaustive search for historical accounts of Pasquatinow but have reviewed several references to this location. The earliest of these is by a Hudson's Bay Company employee, Matthew Cocking. According to the unpublished version of Cocking's journal, in the course of journeying up the Saskatchewan River in 1772, his party portaged across the base of Mosquito Point on August 6.[13] Just before camping for the night, they passed the head of the Sipanok Channel. It is possible that they camped at Pasquatinow, because in his log entry for the next day Cocking noted: "the Natives call this part Pusquatinow from its being the termination of the woody Country."[14] The next reference to Pasquatinow occurs five years later, again by Cocking. By this time he was in charge of Cumberland House and on May 13, 1777 he made this journal entry:

> Two Indians arrived having left their Canoe in Saskachiwan River, brought little or nothing with them: They tell me that they came from the Place called Puskwatinow (i.e.) high bare ground—about One Third of the way between this Place and the Pedlers nearest Settlement.[15]

Cocking's obervations, therefore, place Pasquatinow just upstream from Mosquito Point and provide a translation of the Cree name. We also learn that Crees were camping here in the spring.

More precise locational information is provided some years later by another Hudson's Bay Company trader and surveyor, Peter Fidler. His account of a survey trip up the Saskatchewan River in the autumn of 1792 is held in the Hudson's Bay Company Archives.[16] Traversing the western portion of the Saskatchewan River delta, his observations of compass directions and distance estimates for each stretch of the Saskatchewan River make it reasonably straightforward to follow his course (Figure 2). His notations of landmarks such as islands and creek mouths are also very helpful. On September 12, 1792, Fidler's party reached "the head of Sturgeon river on

North side—sometimes pass thro it in canoes, but it is farther about than to keep the Saskatchewan—it is partly supplied by this river—& 2 small rivulets that fall into it from the North."[17] In other words, they had passed the head of Zig Zag Creek, at the northern extremity of Mosquito Point.

Fidler's party canoed on for another one-half mile on a southwesterly course and then put up for the night. As indicated by the following quote, Fidler's first courses for the morning of September 13 were SEbE1 and S1/4, at which point they reached a small island (judging by contemporary aerial photographs and maps, this island no longer exists):

> At 41/2 AM, got underway, went SEbE1-S 1/4 a small Isld. SWbS 2 1/2, a pretty high bank on the North side, called Pes coo tin naw—a stony shore—T_?_etc—this is the first appearance of a good dry place since we left Oo pas qui aw [The Pas]—it only extends about 1/4 mile along the river & is the termination of a small hill from within—put out the Tracking Line & Tracked the Canoes—all below, paddling & _?etting with poles. low _?_ steep banks, etc.—& several small willow Islands—went along the North side SW 3/4 the head of Sepannuck or the Carrot river on South side that falls into this river a little above Oo pas qui aw…[18]

Fidler's account, therefore, indicates that Pasquatinow ("Pes coo tin naw") is on the north side of the riverbank, and in the vicinity of the head of the Sipanok Channel.

Additional information about Pasquatinow is provided by the travel diary of Alexander Henry the Younger. In August 1808, his party travelled up the Saskatchewan River. Having passed Mosquito Point, Henry wrote:

> At this place, which is called Barren hill, commences the first range of high land on this river; on the N., where the land is elevated near 100 feet, the soil is yellow sand covered only with short grass. The hill is a delightful spot, compared with the low marshy country we have passed, but the surrounding country looks wretched; it is overgrown with the same wood as below, which in many places appears to have been ravaged by fire, the trees lying across each other in every direction.[19]

While Henry does not refer to this location as Pasquatinow, the editor (Coues) does propose this identification. This is almost certainly correct since Pasquatinow is the Cree word *paskwatinow*, "bare/bald hill" and it is apparent that Henry has simply provided an alternate English translation ("Barren hill").

A more recent reference to Pasquatinow occurs in the official report of Otto J. Klotz, a surveyor employed by the Canadian government. He travelled the Nelson and Saskatchewan rivers in 1884 and made this observation:

> About opposite the head of the Sepenock Channel there is
> an elevation called Pasquatinas, meaning, in Cree "the little
> bare hill"; Sepenock meaning "a narrow channel making an
> island."[20]

It is puzzling that Klotz employed this variant form, "Pasquatinas," with the diminutive suffix—evidently *paskwatinis*, which Klotz correctly translated as "the little bare hill." However, the fact that Klotz recorded this place name in the diminutive is evidence that he obtained his information locally, and did not simply refer to existing maps.

Therefore, these accounts and maps indicate that the rise of land named Pasquatinow is on the north side of the Saskatchewan River, approximately across from the entrance to the Sipanok Channel. It is composed of a deposit of yellow sand that forms a valley side which rises nearly 30.5 m (100 ft.) above the river and on its summit is/was a meadow. As well, the riverbank at the base of this elevation is rocky—the first appearance of a stony river's edge on the western edge of the Saskatchewan River delta.

The Search

During our initial visit to this region on July 15–16, 1989, we walked about 1.5 km of valley side and found one location which we thought could be Pasquatinow (Figure 3). This was on the north side of the Saskatchewan River valley, roughly opposite the head of the Sipanok Channel. In the winter of 1989–90, we decided to organize a more formal project and subsequently obtained the requisite archaeological research permit. We intended to expand our walking reconnaissance, to dig some trowel holes, and to collect artifacts as warranted. In particular, we had noted a topographic high mapped just west of the south end of Anderson Island (Figure 3). It seemed that this could be the location of a hill (and, therefore, Pasquatinow) and so we determined to examine it in the summer of 1990.

Upon our return, on August 25, 1990 we first searched the forest on the west side of the entrance to the abandoned channel on the west side of Anderson Island. We found that there was no elevated area and that the topographic high shown on the map was not evident on the ground. We walked a substantial portion of the forest bordering the north side of the

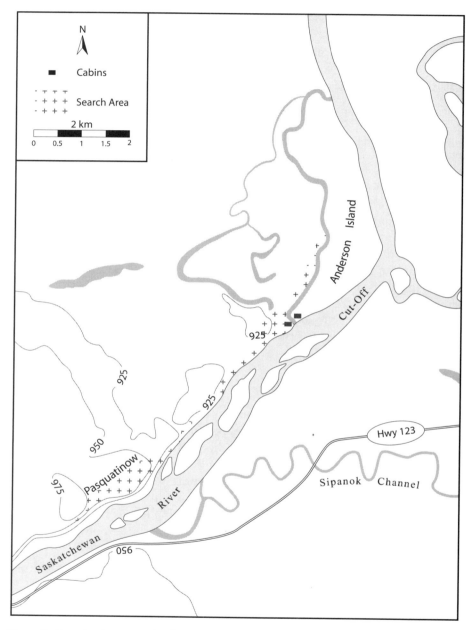

Figure 3. Map showing twenty-five-foot contour lines and section of riverbank searched between Anderson Island and the area across from the head of the Sipanok Channel.

riverbank between Anderson Island and the area across from the entrance to the Sipanok Channel (Figure 3).

In this entire area, the only terrain feature which corresponds to the historical descriptions of Pasquatinow is the valley top on the north side of the Saskatchewan River, across from the entrance to the Sipanok Channel. Therefore, we have accepted this as the location of Pasquatinow: first, this is where Peter Fidler and O.J. Klotz located it; second, the valley side here is composed of fine yellow sand, just as described by Alexander Henry; third, there are two meadows on the valley top, corresponding to Alexander Henry's observation of the grassy summit of Pasquatinow; fourth, stones and rocks which are absent immediately downstream are abundant on the riverbank here, and Peter Fidler noted that it is at Pasquatinow that the first stony shore appears; fifth, this locale is the first high land on the western edge of the delta, just as described by Alexander Henry; sixth, there is a major archaeological site at this location, which would be expected of an important camping place. The official archaeological designation of this site is FkMs-2.

A Description of Pasquatinow

When we first visited this area, our attention was immediately drawn to the treeless openings (Figure 4) along the valley summit across from the head of the Sipanok Channel. These meadows on the valley rim were obvious even from a distance of a kilometre away, out on the river. The valley summit is about 15m (50 ft.) above the river, with one small area rising above 23m (75 ft.) (Figure 3). The valley side here is a huge deposit of yellow sand, the edge of a large area of stabilized sand dunes which stretches away to the north. While this dune area becomes quite hummocky a few hundred metres north of the valley rim, at the rim itself the terrain is fairly flat.

The valley rim here supports a fringe of poplars which gives way on the north to an open jack pine forest. There is very little shrubbery within the latter forest, although blueberries and bearberries form a mat over the forest floor. In two locations, both hugging the valley rim, there are small meadows (Figure 5). In both cases, young poplars appear to be invading the margins of these grassy areas.

One of the meadows extends east-west along the valley edge for 30m and is 18m wide north-south. The second meadow is positioned some 60 m to the west and is larger, stretching along the valley rim for 45 m. We collected two samples of grasses from the former meadow. Dr. Vernon Harmes of the Fraser Herbarium, University of Saskatchewan, has identified one of the samples as Kentucky bluegrass, an introduced European species, and the

Figure 4. View of Pasquatinow from the Saskatchewan River, looking northeast. The arrows in the centre of the photograph indicate the locations of two grassy openings on the valley edge. The arrow on the right indicates the eastern end of Pasquatinow, beyond which is the Saskatchewan River delta.

Figure 5. Meadow on the valley top at Pasquatinow, looking west.

Figure 6. The sandy valley side at Pasquatinow, looking north. Note the rocky shore and the figure standing at the water's edge.

other as sand reed grass, *Calamovilfa longifolia*, a species characteristic of the Prairies to the south. Dr. Harmes pointed out that this location is an extension of the known range of the latter species, as the nearest known occurrence is some 80 km to the southwest, south of the town of Nipawin. Sand reed grass is the dominant grass of both of the small meadows.

The valley side at Pasquatinow is steep and, except for the upper quarter, supports a forest of young aspens, with willows just above the river-bank (Figure 6). The upper part of the valley side is sparsely vegetated, and sand is exposed in many areas; however, judging by the many rocks exposed on the river's edge here (Figure 6), this deposit of sand must rest on glacial till.

Archaeological Observations

A 375 m-long stretch of the outer edge of the valley rim is exposed in a narrow "cutbank," up to .5 m high, below which is a steep slope of slumped sand (Figure 7). Some portions of the upper valley side have been trampled by the resident elk and are free of vegetation. Apparently, these elk search out areas near the valley top where they can stand in the breeze in an attempt to escape their insect tormentors. There are, therefore, some sizeable areas of open sand here, which we examined for visible archaeological remains.

Figure 7. The eroding upper edge of the valley side at Pasquatinow, looking west.

Along the cutbank we observed an intermittent scatter of archaeological materials (Table 1), all originating from the thin, exposed "A" horizon (topsoil) within a few centimetres of the surface. These included bone fragments, bits of fire-cracked rock and some lithic debitage. A well-incised elk trail follows the valley summit, while another, roughly parallel trail is situated deeper in the forest (up to 40 m north of the valley rim). We walked these trails and regularly observed fire-cracked rock. Indeed, some pieces of fire-cracked rock were noted on the forest floor outside of the elk trails. It is very unusual to find visible archaeological materials in undisturbed areas within the boreal forest. We must conclude, therefore, that the occupational remains here are prolific and concentrated.

We examined the eroding edge of the valley rim very carefully and set up a temporary datum from which to take measurements. This datum is a poplar tree which is located on the east side of a rise (1.5 m) in the central area of the site. We blazed this tree on its east and west sides to allow its

Table 1. Observations of Archaeological Materials		
Distance from Datum	Cutbank Exposure	Elk Trail Exposure
0mE	4 pieces fcr*	1 piece fcr
15mE	scatter of unburned and calcined bone fragments	
18mE	4 pieces fcr	
22mE	1 piece fcr	
24.5 mE	1 fragment clamshell	
33mE	1 piece fcr	
42mE	1 piece fcr,1 unburned bone fragment, 2 SRC** flakes	
45mE	3 small unburned bone fragments	
48.5mE	exposed hearth—2 pieces fcr, ashes, many small fragments of calcined bone	
50mE	many small fragments of calcined bone	
56.5mE	1 piece fcr,1 burned and 5 calcined bone fragments	
61mE	2 large mammal long bone fragments, 1 piece fcr	
64.5–66 m E	2 SRC flakes,1 quartz flake, 1 shale flake,1 bird bone fragment, many small fragments of calcined bone	
70.5–72 m E	1 piece burned limestone, many small fragments of calcined bone	
75 E	major hearth exposed—13 pieces fcr, charcoal fragments, 3 fragments of unburned bone—including one section of large mammal rib	
77.5mE	1 rim sherd,1 basalt flake, 1 fragment unburned bone	
86.5mE	1 SRC uniface,1 burned and 6 unburned bone fragments	
96mE	1 flake SRC,1 flake basalt, 2 fragments burned bone	
108.5 m E	1 flake SRC,1 piece fcr, many small fragments of caldned bone	
115.5mE	numerous small fragments of 1 piece fcr burned and unburned bone	
142.5 m E	10 pieces fcr	
167mE	1 fcr	
9.5 m W	1 fcr	
11.6mW	1 fcr	
41.8mW	1 split phalanx moose, 1 unburned bone fragment	
45mW	1 SRC flake,1 piece beaver mandible, numerous unburned bone fragments	
47.3 m W	1 fcr, numerous bone fragments	
62.5mW	1 shale gouge blade,1 endscraper 2 pieces fcr, numerous calcined bone fragments	
81–85 m W	1 shale core fragment,1 piece schist,1 piece fcr, numerous fragments of unburned and calcined bone	
159mW	4 pieces fcr	
165–166 m W	numerous fragments unburned bone	
197–199 m W	4 SRC flakes,1 burned and several unburned bone fragments, 1 first phalanx deer	
207 m W	1 piece fcr	
*fire cracked rock, **Swan River chert.		

Figure 8. Fire-cracked rocks and ashes eroding from a hearth exposed in the valley top at Pasquatinow.

identification over the next few years. Since the cultural materials in the cut bank tended to occur in clusters, we measured the distance from the datum tree to each of the concentrations, made notes on the materials visible in each concentration and collected some samples.

The materials observed within and beyond each of the clusters are listed in Table 1. Most striking are the major hearths, at 48.5 m east and 75 m east (Figure 8); however, several smaller hearths are represented by smaller concentrations of fire-cracked rock in association with burned and calcined bone fragments.

Of particular interest is a pottery rimsherd which we found at 77.5 m east of datum. This rimsherd (Figure 9a) has a maximum thickness of 10 mm and tapers to a thickness of 4 mm at the narrow, uneven lip. Both the interior and exterior surfaces are essentially smooth, although the interior bears some broad striations, evidently a result of wiping with a coarse material. The exterior does not bear any striations but is not perfectly smooth. The broken edges of the sherd reveal the presence of two fragments of grey rock. These are rounded pebbles which, with some other white flecks, may have been natural inclusions in the clay. There is no evidence of the grit temper which is characteristic of pre-contact pottery in central Saskatchewan. All of the exterior surfaces are yellow-brown to reddish, evidence that this vessel was

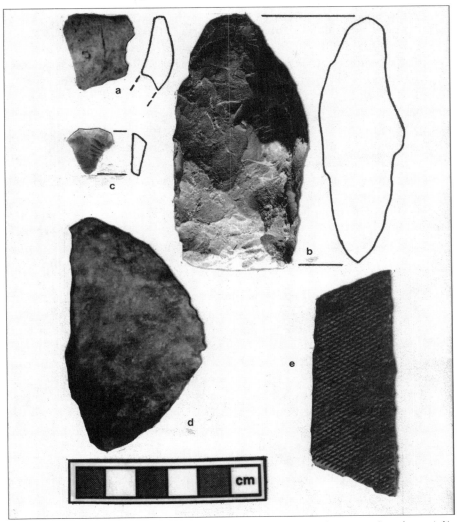

Figure 9. Artifacts from Pasquatinow: a) rim sherd; b) gouge; c) end scraper; d) uniface; e) file fragment.

fired in an oxidizing atmosphere. Generally, the interiors of such vessels, and the interiors of individual sherds, are black (fired in a reducing atmosphere). The fact that the breaks on this sherd are yellow-brown in colour is evidence that this vessel cracked in the course of firing and the surfaces exposed by the cracks were also oxidized.

We also recovered three stone tools. At 62.5 m west of datum we found a gouge and an endscraper, in association with a cluster of calcined bone fragments and two pieces of fire-cracked rock. The gouge (Figure 9b) is of hard, gray-green shale which has been bifacially flaked on all of its margins. One surface is flat, the other convex, resulting in a piano-convex cross section. The working edge was flaked to form a hollow bit which had been lightly ground on the dorsal surface. The cutting bits of these tools are believed to have been periodically reflaked and then ground to a sharp edge. It appears that one last attempt had been made at reshaping the bit on this tool. When it became apparent that this would not be successful, the tool was discarded. This gouge is 81 mm long, 42 mm wide, and 29 mm thick. With the gouge was a tiny endscraper of fine-grained Swan River chert (Figure 9c), 16 mm long, 16 mm wide, and 5 mm thick. The ventral surface is unworked, with all flaking restricted to the working edge which has an angle of 55°.

We found a third stone tool 86.5 m east of the datum. This is a large, relatively thin flake of coarse Swan River chert (Figure 9d), the longest margin of which has been unifacially flaked, as has a portion of an adjacent margin. The ventral surface is not worked and this tool is 77 mm long, 46 mm wide, and 11 mm thick.

Lithic debitage was observed in relatively modest numbers. This totalled eight flakes of Swan River chert, one flake of white quartz, one flake of hard shale, and two flakes of basalt. Also present was a core fragment of hard shale. All of these materials are characteristic of this part of Saskatchewan, as evidenced by the results of the large-scale, multiyear archaeological work which was conducted in the Nipawin area in the first half of the 1980s.[21]

At 61 m east and 6.5 m north of the cutbank edge, we noted two pieces of fire-cracked rock protruding from the surface. We trowelled away the humus and found another three pieces of this rock. Then we dug a small trowel hole, about 20 cm across and 15 cm deep. All that this produced was a section of a broken file (Figure 9e). In width, this fragment tapers from 26 mm to 23 mm and it is 6 mm thick. According to Olga Klimko: "The sides are double cut with about 20 teeth per inch, while one edge has a float or single cut with about 20 teeth per inch. The other edge is too corroded for observations."[22] Because files have changed very little over time, it is not possible to determine the age of this specimen; however, the heavy encrustation of rust present on some parts would be consistent with a date in the nineteenth century or earlier.

With regard to the faunal remains, the larger pieces were sections of ungulate bones which had been smashed, often producing spiral fractures. The faunal remains also included a section of a beaver mandible, the first phalanx of a deer, a split phalanx of a moose, and a fragment of a bone from a large bird (Table 1).[23]

As noted above, the site datum is on the eastern edge of a slight rise on the valley rim. This undulation is about 20 m wide (east-west) and about 1.5 m high. The exposed edge of the valley rim here revealed an almost continuous exposure of bits of burned and calcined bone, along with some pieces of fire-cracked rock. It is possible that this slight rise contains the greatest concentration of occupational remains at this site. In any case, it is evident that archaeological materials are particularly abundant in the area extending east from this rise for about 115 m. To the west of this low rise, the exposed archaeological materials are less frequent, becoming very sparse beyond 85 m west. In short, the main occupation here extends along the valley edge for about 200 m, between 85 m west and 115 m east. However, we found evidence of occupation well beyond this central concentration. Very intriguing is a set of three depressions, around 164 m east of datum. Two of these are 5 m apart and 37 m north of the valley rim. The more easterly is about 1.5 m in diameter, its sides sloping down to a depth of about 40 cm. A stone protruded from the leaf mold on the south side of this depression and upon trowelling away the humus, we found four more stones. As well, a sixth rock was found on the north side of the depression. This is not fire-cracked rock, four being limestone and the remainder Precambrian rocks. The depression on the west is slightly larger but we found no rocks here, despite probing the soil with a trowel tip. Some 10 m to the south is a smaller depression, about 40 cm in diameter and 20 cm deep, with no rocks in association. Even more distant from the central section of the site is a cluster of fire-cracked rock on an elk trail 256 m east of datum and 30 m north of the valley rim.

Looking to the west, in the course of our 1989 visit we followed the elk trail along the valley rim for 1,040 paces, nearly a kilometre west of the datum point. At 546 paces west we encountered a concentration of five pieces of fire-cracked rock while there was a similar cluster on the trail at 624 paces. At 700 paces west we began to ascend the topographic high shown on the topographic map (Figure 4). The valley rim at this point rises over 24 m (75 ft.) above the river; however, the river, at a distance of .4 km, is hidden by trees and one has the sense only of being in the midst of a large forest. At present, therefore, this location is not attractive for camping because the river is not readily accessible.

Archaeological Interpretation

It is apparent that a very large archaeological site is present at Pasquatinow, extending at least .9 kilometres along the valley rim. A central area about 200 m in length appears to contain the greatest concentration of archaeological remains. Most of these remains appear to be pre-contact in age, including lithic debitage, three stone tools and a rim sherd. Many of the hearths, as well, are likely pre-contact. The only evidence of post-contact occupation is the piece of a file.

The most puzzling features here are the three previously described depressions which are grouped 30–40 m north of the valley edge. It is possible that these depressions are natural (for example, uprooted trees); however, the cluster of stones at one of these reflects human involvement as stones do not occur naturally in the dune sand.

On the basis of the limited recoveries, it is difficult to assess either the time period of the pre-contact occupation(s) or its cultural affiliation. The gouge blade is similar in size, workmanship and material to adze and celt blades found in Laurel and Selkirk assemblages in northern Manitoba and Saskatchewan. However, the puzzling aspect of this artifact is the fact that this is the first gouge blade to be recovered from northern Saskatchewan. The potsherd is also puzzling. It narrows to the lip, a characteristic of Laurel (and Avonlea) pottery. However, given the strong curvature of the sherd it is likely that it derives from a small bowl and it is probable that it was simply a quickly made "pinch" pot. This interpretation is supported by the lack of the normal grit temper, suggesting that the usual careful preparation of pottery clay did not occur. Pinch pots need not conform to the usual pottery-making styles, and so this pot could as likely be a Selkirk as a Laurel vessel. In the Saskatchewan River valley, Laurel occupations generally date about A.D. 500–1000, while Selkirk occupations date ca. A.D. 1450–1700.[24]

Although we recovered only a few identifiable faunal remains, these reflect the hunting of birds and a variety of animals, including beaver, moose and deer. These materials are too few to allow a determination of the season(s) during which this site was occupied.

Congregating Centres in the Saskatchewan River Valley

Hunters and gatherers throughout the world employ systematic seasonal rounds by which they endeavour to position themselves appropriately within their territories as food resources become available for harvesting.[25] Through much of the year these peoples live in small social units, often composed of several closely related families (25–40 persons), in relative isolation. These groups are sometimes referred to as "local bands."[26] At least once a year, all or most of the local bands in a particular region may congregate at some location within their territory. This grouping of local bands has been termed the "regional band."[27] These gatherings may involve a few hundred individuals and serve vital cultural and social needs.[28] Major religious ceremonies are celebrated, marriages are arranged, and disputes are settled.

Interior of a Cree lodge near present-day Nipawin, Saskatchewan, March 25, 1820. Original drawing by Lieutenant Robert Hood, a member of the first Franklin Expedition (courtesy of the Glenbow Archives/LAC-1344-3).

The Cree who occupied the Saskatchewan River delta in the 1700s and 1800s were hunters and gatherers whose social organization conformed to the above outline. During some periods of the year, the population was dispersed in small social units; at other times, larger social aggregations occurred. The fur-trade and church-missionary accounts provide evidence that in the late winter/early spring (before breakup) the occupants of various parts of the Saskatchewan River valley moved to gathering places such as Opaskweyaw (The Pas), Nipowiwinihk[29] (Nipawin) and Pehonan (Ft. à la Corne)[30] (Figure 1). In the historic records, these gatherings were sometimes referred to as "rendezvous."[31] At these locations these Cree built new (or refurbished old) canoes and waited for the waterfowl to return. Then, with the onset of the major spring fish-spawning runs, this food resource was harvested.[32] In particular, fish weirs were extensively used within the Saskatchewan River delta.[33] They were often maintained into the summer, when sturgeon became an important food source.[34] Major ceremonies, such as the Goose Dance,[35] were held at these gathering centres. For example, the Reverend Henry Budd described the annual spring ceremonial round at Pehonan.[36] Eventually, the spring aggregation broke up into smaller groups for the latter part of the summer. It should be noted, also, that small numbers of people could be found camping at the congregating centres at almost any season—if local food resources were abundant.

In contrast to Pettipas,[37] we see the various regional bands of the Saskatchewan River valley as oriented to central bases, in both pre-contact and historic times. Indeed, the congregating centres may have been occupied for two months or more, each spring and early summer. A smaller-scale aggregation sometimes occurred at the gathering centres in the autumn, before the winter dispersal.

This contact period seasonal round may be considered a useful analog for pre-contact times. Indeed, archaeological investigations at Nipowiwinihk, Opaskweyaw, and Pehonan provide evidence that the cultural deposits in each case are massive and extensive. Opaskweyaw has been used for at least 3,500 years[38] and Nipowiwinihk for at least 5,000 years.[39] At the latter location, the authors have been involved in extensive excavations of Selkirk sites (ca. A.D. 1400–1700) and found them to have been occupied in the spring. A small amount of archaeological work was conducted at Pehonan in the summer of 1985,[40] sufficient to show that the extent and age of the archaeological remains there are comparable to those at Nipowiwinihk.

Pasquatinow as a Regional Centre

We do not have for Pasquatinow the substantial historical documentation which exists for locations such as Opaskweyaw, Nipowiwinihk and Pehonan, nor the extensive archaeological data which are available for Opaskweyaw and Nipowiwinihk; however, our archaeological observations do confirm it as a major regional camping place. Indeed, aside from the archaeological evidence, the fact that its summit is described historically as bare of trees and covered with grass may be taken as an indicator of intensive camp use. In the boreal forest, trees are largely absent from regularly occupied camp sites—such as those in contemporary use along the Churchill River. The trees are cut down for tent poles and for firewood, or they are simply removed to enlarge the space available for tenting and camp activities. Grasses become established as a result.

We would hypothesize also that, like the other named gathering places, Pasquatinow was occupied primarily during the spring. Indeed, residents of the western part of the Saskatchewan River delta may have found it necessary to move to higher land in late winter/early spring to avoid floods, particularly those associated with ice jams. Beyond this, the fact that Pasquatinow is a sandy valley top would also make it attractive for camp use (at any season). The sandy soil would result in good drainage during

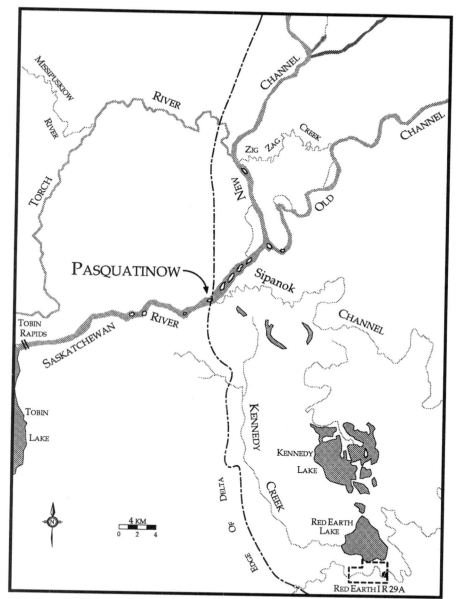

Figure 10. Map of the Pasquatinow region.

rains, providing a relatively dry tenting area. As well, if occupied into the summer, its elevated nature would subject it to breezes and so keep insects at bay.

It is apparent that Pasquatinow was well positioned in terms of travel routes in the four cardinal directions (Figure 10). Of course, people could come to Pasquatinow from the east and the west simply by following the Saskatchewan River, but there was also a route to the site from the north (Figure 10). This involved a 1.5-kilometre portage from the Torch River to Zig Zag Creek[41] and then south to the Saskatchewan River at Mosquito Point (Anderson Island). Similarly, the Sipanok Channel was used for travel from the southeast, while Kennedy Creek (Figure 10) provided access from the region more directly to the south.[42]

These travel routes provide suggestive evidence of the territory which could have been occupied by the peoples who seasonally gathered at Pasquatinow. Stronger evidence in this regard is provided by a consideration of the territory over which the Red Earth Cree hunted and trapped until the early 1900s.[43] Red Earth territory in the late 1800s and early 1900s encompassed an extensive region centred on Red Earth. In part, it extended north up the Kennedy Creek and Sipanok Channel systems and thence across the Saskatchewan River (including Pasquatinow) into the Torch River system.[44]

Summary

Based on the historical accounts, we believe that we have identified the location known as Pasquatinow. It is a well-elevated section of sandy valley summit across from the entrance to the Sipanok Channel. The small meadows which are present here were probably larger in historic and pre-contact times as a result of regular camp use, with associated removal of trees.

Pasquatinow now appears as a large archaeological site, with a 200 m long central concentration, and sparser occupational remains beyond this core. It is likely that several cultural phases are represented at this site. The gouge blade and rimsherd which were recovered relate to either a Laurel or a Selkirk assemblage. Only one specimen, a broken file, provides evidence of post-contact occupation of this site; however, it is very likely that opening an excavation block here would result in the recovery of numerous items dating to the historic period.

Pasquatinow was only one of several major gathering places in the Saskatchewan River valley. All of the members of a particular regional band (perhaps 200–400 persons) would travel to their congregating centre at the end of winter. With breakup they began to hunt returning waterfowl and then took advantage of the spring fish-spawning runs. In many cases, this aggregation lasted into the early summer. Archaeological investigations at several of the aggregating centres have provided evidence that they have been gathering places for thousands of years.

Notes

This article first appeared in *Prairie Forum* 17, no. 2 (1992): 201–24.

Our thanks are extended to Olga Klimko who provided a written opinion on the broken file from Pasquatinow, to Dr. Ernest Walker who examined and identified the faunal remains from Pasquatinow, to Dr. Vernon Harmes who identified the grasses collected at Pasquatinow, and to Leslie Amundson who pointed out geomorphological studies relevant to the Saskatchewan River delta. As well, David Arthurs of the Provincial Archives of Manitoba located late nineteenth century maps produced under the supervision of Edouard Deville. In particular, we must thank Anne Morton, archivist of the Hudson's Bay Company Archives, who very kindly provided an excerpt from Peter Fidler's journal of 1792. We gratefully acknowledge the receipt of permission from the Hudson's Bay Company to quote materials held in the Hudson's Bay Company Archives, Provincial Archives of Manitoba. Archaeological investigations at Pasquatinow (Site FkMs-2) were conducted under Permit 90-54 issued by the Heritage Branch, Saskatchewan Parks, Recreation and Culture.

1. David Meyer, "Cree Ethnography in the Late Historic Period," in D. Burley and D. Meyer (eds.), *Regional Overview and Research Considerations, Nipawin Reservoir Heritage Study*, Volume 3 (Saskatoon: Saskatchewan Research Council 1982), 213–15. Publication No. C-805-25-E-82.

2. Sir John Franklin, *Narrative of a Journey to the Shores of the Polar Sea in the Years 1819, 20, 21 and 22* (Rutland, VT and Tokyo, Japan: Charles E. Tuttle, 1970), end map.

3. Captain John Palliser, *The Papers of the Palliser Expedition 1857–1860*, edited by I.M. Spry, Vol. 44 (Toronto: The Champlain Society, 1968), end map.

4. D.F. Acton, J.S. Clayton, J.G. Ellis, E.A. Christiansen and W.O. Kupsch, *Physiographic Divisions of Saskatchewan* (Map) (Saskatoon: Saskatchewan Soil Survey, University of Saskatchewan, 1960). See also J. Howard Richards, "Physical Features of Saskatchewan," in J.H. Richards and K.I. Fung (eds.), *Atlas of Saskatchewan* (Saskatoon: University of Saskatchewan, 1969), 40–41.

5. William McInnes, *The Basins of Nelson and Churchill Rivers*, Geological Survey of Canada, Memoir 30 (Ottawa: King's Printer, 1913), 101–02.

6. E. Kuiper, *Saskatchewan River Reclamation Project Regime Saskatchewan River*, Interim Report No. 10 (Winnipeg: Canada Department of Agriculture, 1955), 4.

7. Derald D. Smith, "Anastomosed Fluvial Deposits: Modern Examples from Western Canada," in J.D. Collinson and J. Lewin (eds.), *Modern and Ancient Fluvial Systems* (Oxford, London, Edinburgh: Blackwell Scientific Publications, 1983), 155–68.

8. For example, Franklin, *Narrative of a Journey to the Shores of the Polar Sea*, end map.

9. William McInnes, "Saskatchewan River District," in Canada, *Sessional Papers* 26 (Ottawa: King's Printer, 1910), 169–70. See also N.D. Smith, T.A. Cross, J.P. Dufficy, and S.R. Clough, "Anatomy of an Avulsion," *Sedimentology* 36 (1989): 1–23.

10. Otto J. Klotz, "Report on Exploratory Survey to Hudson's Bay, 1884," in Canada, *Sessional Papers* vol. 7, no. 13, part II (Ottawa: King's Printer, 1885), 16.

11. Franklin, *Narrative of a Journey to the Shores of the Polar Sea*.

12. Palliser, *The Papers of the Palliser Expedition, 1857–1860*.

13. Provincial Archives of Manitoba (PAM), Hudson's Bay Company Archives (HBCA), B.239/a/69, 1772 journal and log, Matthew Cocking.

14. Ibid.

15. E.E. Rich (ed.), *Cumberland and Hudson House Journals, 1775–82*, First Series, 1775–79, vol. 14 (London: Hudson's Bay Record Society, 1951), 13.

16. PAM, HBCA, E.3/1,1792 journal of Peter Fidler.

17. Ibid.

18. Ibid.

19. Elliot Coues (ed.), *The Manuscript Journals of Alexander Henry and of David Thompson, 1799–1814*, 3 vols. (1897; Minneapolis: Ross and Haines, 1965), 478.

20. Klotz, *Report on Exploratory Survey to Hudson's Bay, 1884*, 17.

21. For example, J. Michael Quigg, "The Lloyd Site," in D. Meyer (ed.), *Nipawin Reservoir Heritage Study: 1982 Final Excavations*, vol. 6 (Saskatoon: Saskatchewan Research Council, 1983), 107. Publication No. E-903-6-E-83

22. Olga Klimko, personal communication, 1990.

23. Ernest Walker, personal communication, 1990.

24. David Meyer and Henry T. Epp, "North-South Interaction in the Late Prehistory of Central Saskatchewan," *Plains Anthropologist* 35 (1990): 321–42.

25. For example, Bruce Winterhalder and E.A. Smith (eds.), *Hunter-Gatherer Foraging Strategies: Ethnographic and Archaeological Analysis* (Chicago: University of Chicago Press, 1981).

26. For example, June Helm, "Bilaterality in the Sodo-Territorial Organization of the Arctic Drainage Dene," *Ethnology* 4 (1965): 361–85.

27. For example, June Helm, "The Nature of Dogrib Socio-territorial Groups," in R.B. Lee and I. DeVore (eds.), *Man the Hunter* (Chicago: Aldine Publishing Company, 1968), 119–21. See also Richard B. Lee and Irven DeVore (eds.), *Man the Hunter* (Chicago: Aldine Publishing Company, 1968), 245–48. For a Dene overview, see John W. Ives, *A Theory of Northern Athapaskan Prehistory* (Calgary: University of Calgary Press, 1990), 62–65.

28. L. Rodseth, R.W. Wrangham, A.M. Harrigan and B.B. Smuts, "The Human Community as a Primate Society," *Current Anthropology* 32 (1991): 240.

29. In 1977, this toponym, *nipowiwinihk*, was provided to David Meyer by a Red Earth elder, Donald MacKay (Eyistiwan). This place name is usually rendered by Cree speakers as *nipowiwin("standing* place"), but Eyistiwan added the locative *-ihk*. He specifically applied this name to a section of the Saskatchewan River valley in the vicinity of the contemporary village of Codette—and this, indeed, is one of the locations identified as "Nipowiwin" in the fur-trade records. However, during the fur-trade period, the name "Nipowiwin" (or some variant spelling) was, inexplicably, also applied to the Pehonan area, some 70 kilometres upstream; therefore, we have chosen to use the form "Nipowiwinihk", in order to refer explicitly to that section of the Saskatchewan River valley 3.5 kilometres northwest of Codette. For a more detailed discussion, see Arthur S. Morton, "Nipawi on the Saskatchewan River, and its Historic Sites," *Proceedings and Transactions of the Royal Society of Canada* 38 (1944): 117–39.

30. Meyer, "Cree Ethnography in the Late Historic Period," 236–37. See also David Meyer, *The Red Earth Crees, 1860–1960*, Canadian Ethnology Service Paper No. 100, Mercury Series (Ottawa: National Museum of Man, 1985), 60–61, and Henry Y. Hind, *Narrative of the Canadian Red River Exploring Expedition of 1857 and of the Assiniboine and Saskatchewan Exploring Expedition of 1858* (Edmonton: Hurtig, 1971), 403.

31. Paul C. Thistle, *Indian-European Trade Relations in the Lower Saskatchewan River Region to 1840*, Manitoba Studies in Native History II (Winnipeg: The University of Manitoba Press, 1986), 87.

32. Meyer, *Red Earth Crees*, 61.

33. For example, Joseph B. Tyrrell (ed.), *Journals of Samuel Hearne and Philip Turnor*, Vol. 21 (Toronto: The Champlain Society, 1934), 108.

34. Lawrence J. Burpee (ed.), "An Adventurer from Hudson Bay: Journal of Matthew Cocking, From York Factory to the Blackfeet Country, 1772–1773," in *Proceedings and Transactions of the Royal Society of Canada*, Third Series, vol. 2, section 2 (1908): 98.

35. David Meyer, "Waterfowl in Cree Ritual: The Goose Dance," in J. Freedman and J.H. Barkow (eds.), *Proceedings of the Second Congress, Canadian Ethnology Society*, Vol. 2, Canadian Ethnology Service Paper No. 28, Mercury Series (Ottawa: National Museum of Man, 1975). See also David Meyer, "The Goose Dance in Swampy Cree Religion," *Journal of the Canadian Church Historical Society* 33 (1990): 107–18.

36. Hind, *Narrative of the Canadian Red River Exploring Expedition of 1857 and of the Assiniboine and Saskatchewan Exploring Expedition of 1858*, 402–04.

37. Katherine Pettipas, "An Ethnohistory of The Pas Area, Prehistoric–1875: A Study in Cree Adaptation," in L. Pettipas (ed.), *Directions in Manitoba Prehistory* (Winnipeg: Manitoba Archaeological Association, 1980), 169–70.

38. Morgan J. Tamplin, "Prehistoric Occupation and Resource Exploitation on the Saskatchewan River at The Pas, Manitoba" (PhD dissertation, Department of Anthropology, University of Arizona, Tucson, 1977).

39. J.T. Finnigan, D. Meyer and J. Prentice, "Resource Inventory, Assessment and Evaluation," in D. Meyer (ed.), *Nipawin Reservoir Heritage Study*, Vol. 5 (Saskatoon: Saskatchewan Research Council, 1983), 88, 199–204. Publication No. E-903-9-E-83.

40. David Meyer and Olga Klimko, *The James Smith Archaeological Survey* (Saskatoon: Saskatchewan Research Council, 1986). Publication No. E-903-5-E-86.

41. McInnes, *The Basins of Nelson and Churchill Rivers*, 102.

42. Meyer, *The Red Earth Crees, 1860–1960*, 51.

43. Ibid., 11.

44. Ibid., 12.

4. The Western James Bay Cree: Aboriginal and Early Historic Adaptations

Charles A. Bishop

Although a good deal is now known about the Cree Indians who inhabit the region from northwestern Quebec to Alberta, both from ethnological field studies and from ethnohistorical research, Cree culture at the time of European contact remains largely conjectural. Archaeological research which can provide information on subsistence activities, seasonal settlement size and location, and inter-group exchange relationships has barely begun. Likewise, ethnohistorians have been hampered by a lack of data pertaining to the protohistoric period, that important time span when European trade goods and other influences penetrated Cree domains but when there were no Europeans present to provide first-hand accounts of Indian life and the events that were affecting it (Bishop and Ray 1976).

One method of filling this void is to make use of the later, more detailed, written accounts and field-obtained information. Yet, while these data undoubtedly provide useful clues about Aboriginal life, the fact that the Cree being observed were also involved in the mercantile fur trade, and often had been for a considerable time, renders reconstruction hazardous. As Indians adjusted to the fur trade, their social and economic life gradually altered. Thus, by the time that better information is provided, significant changes had already occurred. Traders' accounts, more often than not, describe the consequences. Indians are noted coming to the trading post with furs or food, or to acquire trade items or food donations. Likewise, they are noted leaving to trap or hunt geese for the post, or to hunt for themselves. Clearly, many of these activities reflect modified adaptive strategies, accommodations to the new fur trade economy. Nevertheless, despite such changes, many Cree customs continued on in the new context, indeed continued into the 20th century. The survival of these distinctive Cree customs, however, can create the illusion that other features of Cree culture also persisted unchanged. The degree to which this is so, however, cannot simply be assumed. It requires testing against the limited early evidence. That is the purpose here. Through an analysis of the sketchy evidence pertaining to the western James Bay Cree of the 17th and early 18th centuries, insight can be gained about aboriginal culture and the adaptive modifications that were occurring. Also, given the above methodological caveat, such analysis provides a perspective that can be applied to other regions of western Canada.

The Western James Bay Cree: Circa 1625 to 1725

Almost nothing is known of the Cree prior to the mid-17th century. We can, nevertheless, be confident that they were hunter-gatherers possessing some form of band organization. We can also assume that they didn't engage in trapping to the extent that the historical records indicate was the case in later times. In consequence, adaptive strategies probably maximized subsistence efficiency and social welfare. While some inter-group trade probably existed, it is unlikely that such trade interfered with basic subsistence activities. Different bands, related to each other through kinship ties, likely moved from area to area to exploit seasonally large tracts of land, fissioning and fusing when food was difficult to obtain or abundant. In the lowlands west and southwest of James Bay, an area of some 40,000 square miles, it is doubtful that there were more than ten such bands averaging, perhaps, 50 persons each. Whether Indians occupied the lowlands continuously throughout the year is uncertain, but it is doubtful that they remained near the barren sea coast in winter. Henry Hudson while wintering in James Bay in 1610–11 met only one Indian, suggesting that others had retreated inland. As will become evident, this is in marked contrast to the situation a century later.

The French presence along the St. Lawrence after 1600 no doubt began to have an indirect influence on the Cree. The Cree may have received their first European items by the 1620s or earlier from Montagnais, Algonquins, and Nipissings to the southeast and south. These trade networks, which may have been prehistoric, grew in importance as the demand for furs grew, except when temporarily disrupted by Iroquois raids upon more southerly peoples. By the 1650s and 1660s, French *coureurs de bois* were trading directly with some Cree who visited the Upper Great Lakes. Pierre Esprit Radisson and Medard des Groseilliers described the Cree as being clothed in beaver skins in winter. Expert beaver hunters, they killed only adult animals, leaving the young to mature for future use (Adams 1961: 95). Their seasonal cycle saw them moving via the large rivers of northern Ontario from the coast of the "North Sea" (James Bay) in summer to their inland winter quarters. The apparent richness of their country ultimately led to an

English exploratory venture to the mouth of the Rupert's River in 1668. Returning to England with some 3,000 pounds of beaver pelts in 1669, the English Crown, convinced by this success, granted a charter establishing the Hudson's Bay Company in 1670. The traders returned to Charles Fort at Rupert's River that same year.

We get some first-hand accounts of Indians during these early years on the Bay. Indians were reported to have subsisted on venison, partridges, geese, and fish taken with nets (Nute 1978: 118). Of the several different groups who visited the post, one held a shaking tent ceremony, a Northern Algonkian custom that has continued to this day (Tyrrell 1931: 386). Bands speaking different dialects came to trade, suggesting that they may have come from different directions. During the summer of 1674, the English explored the western shore of James Bay encountering the "Tabittee" (probably the Abitibi from further south), the "Shechittawans" from the Albany River area, and some Indians who had suffered losses from starvation on the coast (Tyrrell 1931: 390–91). Indian groups from different areas were led by "okimahs" who represented their band in their dealing with the English and who annually determined where different families or groups would winter (Tyrrell 1931: 382). There are no explicit data on Cree social structure at this time, but it may be conjectured that they practiced cross-cousin marriage, polygyny, the levirate and sororate, all widespread Northern Algonkian customs. Also, given seasonal, annual, and regional fluctuations in resources, it is doubtful that band territories were exclusively exploited by any single group. Rather, Indians seem to have continued to move seasonally to areas where food and also fur bearers could be obtained. Some additional time and energy, however, were now being devoted to trapping and travelling to the trading post with furs and country foods for the English. Although many Indians continued to trade with the French, the opening of trading posts at the mouths of the Moose and Albany Rivers during the mid-1670s drew many more Indians directly into the trade. The new English posts and the resultant rivalry with the French benefitted the Cree who no longer had to trade at high rates through middlemen, or travel long distances to acquire French materials.

The advantages of rivalry were terminated in 1686 when the De Troyes expedition from New France forcefully took the English James Bay posts. Because the new occupants were unable to supply adequately the captured posts, the James Bay Cree suffered. Thus, when Captain James Knight regained Fort Albany for the English in 1693, the Cree rejoiced, and Knight, to reaffirm their allegiance, gave out lavish presents of guns, powder, shot and tobacco to the Cree leaders.

Thereafter, ritual gift-giving accompanied by speeches became an established pattern at Hudson's Bay Company posts. Indians within a hundred miles of the post became habitual visitors while those further inland came with their pelts when not lured away or threatened by the French and their Indian allies.

The quantity of furs obtained at Fort Albany, the only post operated by the Hudson's Bay Company in the western James Bay area after 1693, fluctuated annually depending mainly upon the conditions of rivalry, but also upon seasonal ecological conditions that affected hunting. Indians nearer to the post and in the James Bay lowlands usually traded a higher proportion of marten, whereas those further inland produced the bulk of the beaver. A high figure of 25,118 "made" beaver (the standard of value) was obtained during 1708–09 and a low figure of 8,907 during 1704–05.

In addition to furs, Indians supplied Fort Albany with various country provisions needed to supplement the limited supply of European foods consumed by the some twenty traders. These included fish, venison, small game, and especially geese. Several Cree families came to hunt geese regularly and others periodically both in the spring and the fall. After gathering at the post in April, Indians received a feast of oatmeal and sometimes other foods and were provided with guns, ammunition and other necessary equipment for the hunt. Transported by canoe from the coastal marshes, geese were packed with salt in barrels. Goose feathers were also kept. The spring hunt usually lasted from late April to early June, and the fall hunt from late August to mid-October. The quantity of geese killed varied with the number of hunters and climatic conditions from no more than a few hundred to over 2,000 in any given season. Later in the 18th century, the numbers increased as more hunters came to participate and techniques became more efficient. Also, in later times, a goose hunt leader came to preside over the hunt. Whether the goose dance held by the Cree was aboriginal or a custom that evolved in the 18th century is uncertain. During these seasons the Cree lived largely on geese and also received trade goods for their services.

At other times Indians traded birchbark canoes and other materials and occasionally provided certain services needed by the Hudson's Bay Company employees. They also supplied information pertaining to the trade and the whereabouts of the French. Since the fort had already been captured once, the English kept a constant vigilance, although many reports were only rumors. Nevertheless, in 1709 a contingent of French and Mohawks that attempted to take the post was driven off, thanks to advance warning by the Cree (Davies 1965: xxxviii–xxxix).

In return for their furs and services, Indians received a wide range of trade goods. For example, in 1694-95 some 396 guns, 288 ice chisels, 5,329 knives, 1,384 awls, 1,146 hatchets, 118 arrow heads, 30 net lines, 634 pounds of twine, 348 kettles, 430 coats, over 1,000 yards of various types of cloth and 2,308 pounds of tobacco, as well as considerable quantities of many other items were traded (HBCA B.3/d/5). In addition, band leaders, the "captains," annually received a captain's coat, tobacco and other presents at gift exchange ceremonies (see Ray and Freeman 1978: 55–59, 66–75). It is to be noted that the above list of goods was received by local "homeguard" Cree as well as "unpaid" Indians. There is no way of determining the proportions different groups received.

To an extent, the band organization of the Cree is reflected in the names of groups that traded at the post. One group headed by captain "Tick-aw-tucky" exploited the Albany River area west of the post. Another group (or perhaps two related groups) called the Salkemies occupied the Moose River region and during the 1690s was led by "Old Noah." Kesagami Lake, fifty miles south of Moose Factory, appears to have been named after this group. Still another band, the "Metlawarith," appears to have wintered northwest of Fort Albany. In addition, a number of other Indians are named in the early records, but whether they belonged to one of these groups or some other unspecified group is uncertain. The names of more distant groups, however, are also occasionally mentioned, including the "PakanaSheas" from east of Moose River, the "Tibitiby" from the Lake Abitibi area, the "Rabbit Indians" from far to the northwest of the post, the "Ta-mishka-mein" from Lake Timiskaming, the "Clisteens" from north of Lake Superior, the "Ka-chi-ga-mien" from the Great Lakes, and the "Rygaga-mees" perhaps from the same area. On occasion a few canoes of Assiniboine from near Lake of the Woods visited the post. Most of these more distant peoples were in the outer orbit of trade at Fort Albany but their visits were no less coveted.

The evidence dating to the early 18th century indicates that Indians in the lowlands experienced periodic food privations. Some actually starved to death, while others ate their furs and a few even turned to cannibalism. Still others who wintered within reach of the post came to receive donations of fish and potatoes. In cases where they were too weak to travel, others carried food to their tents. Such hardships, however, were not experienced every year, or by all groups. Some appear to have lived in a condition of relative abundance while others in a different direction starved. Or the same group might experience both feast and famine at different times during the same winter. Food shortages, then, were a regional and/or temporal phenomena, often the result of adverse climatic conditions that prevented hunting, or local game scarcities.

A basic question is whether similar hardships were experienced by Aboriginal Indians. Although starvation was often attributed to too much or too little snow or radical fluctuations in temperature, both of which made hunting difficult or impossible and which also must have occurred in prehistoric times, there appear to have been other factors that intensified the effects of weather conditions. That is, although starvation may have occurred periodically in prehistoric times, it may have been less frequent and less severe than the records of the early 18th century indicate was then the case. There are three primary and interrelated reasons why post-contact stress may have been greater. These are: 1) the introduction of a new technology for obtaining food and fur; 2) changes in labour patterns involving an intensification and specialization of energy to acquire materials for trade; and 3) a reduction in the total subsistence resource biomass involving beaver and caribou.

The Hudson's Bay Company account book lists of goods traded indicate that many items had gradually come to replace aboriginal ones. It is unlikely that Indians had forgotten how to produce traditional goods at this early date; rather new items were, in some cases, more efficient than stone or bone ones. Still other materials such as tobacco, combs, hawk bells, etc. came to have social and/ or ritual value. But regardless of the function of an item, all trade goods required the expenditure of additional energy because hunters had to devote more time to trapping and women more time to preparing fur pelts. Time devoted to trapping was not time devoted to food hunting, even though the meat of fur bearers was consumed. The quantity of meat from these animals, however, was probably less than would have been the case had Indians focused solely or mainly on food hunting. Also, beaver, which do contain more flesh than most other fur bearers, appear to have been relatively scarcer in the lowlands than further inland. Thus, Indians who tried to survive on the flesh of marten, mink and fisher, supplemented by the periodically unreliable snowshoe hare and a few straggling caribou, indeed would have been vulnerable to the effects of inclement weather.

Not only was more energy being expended in trapping and pelt preparation, the records also suggest that trapping efficiency combined with limited food resources required that families remain spatially separated from each other for lengthy periods in winter. Groups usually no larger than families arrived at the post except when caribou were being killed. Small herds of caribou can be more effectively hunted by several adults, usually belonging to three or four related families, and, in turn, the flesh of these larger animals will support larger social groups as long as it lasts than will the meat of small game. There is, however, some indirect evidence suggesting that both caribou and beaver were declining in the lowland area. Near York Factory, Indians wered draining beaver dams and destroying lodges in winter, practices that would have resulted in the death from exposure of any animals not killed outright (Tyrrell 1931: 235–36). Whether Fort Albany Indians were doing the same thing is uncertain but not unlikely given the value of beaver pelts. Likewise, the caribou herds appear to have been reduced through overhunting. At different times between 1693 and 1705, presents of 36, 40, 80, 105 and even 200 "deer" tongues, as well as smaller quantities of meat on other occasions were given to the Fort Albany post. After 1705, relatively less venison was given. Perhaps Indians were simply consuming the flesh themselves, but more likely there were fewer animals to be killed. It may have been that the caribou population had been sufficiently thinned to make hunting them less reliable and productive, unless there were signs that animals were nearby. Also, by concentrating more on fur hunting, many families may have wintered in areas where there were few big animals. In consequence, they would have been forced to live on what was locally available. In contrast, in prehistoric times when food hunting did not compete with fur trapping, and when there were no traders to feed, the movements of Indians would have been far less restricted. They could have ranged over larger areas, even far inland to the more productive Shield country. But the quest for furs, combined with the relative scarcity of foods nearer the coast, came to intensify food stresses within a mere three decades after Fort Albany was established, creating the numerous instances of starvation reported after 1700.

Families prevented by starvation from acquiring a sufficiency of furs to meet with trade needs, nevertheless, could later earn these by goose hunting. This, combined with the knowledge that food could be obtained from the traders in times of hardship, worked to inhibit some families from travelling beyond reach of the store in winter. Also, unless curtailed early, the fall hunt could be especially disruptive since it conflicted with Indians' ability to lay up a larder of food and prepare for the approaching trapping season. Traders had to allow goose hunters to depart early or promise to feed families should they arrive starving. These same promises may also have had the effect of encouraging hunters to engage in fur trapping at times when they formerly would have been food hunting.

The scattering of families to areas to trap under conditions where survival came, in part, to depend upon the acquisition of certain trade goods was a precondition for changes in property relationships. By 1700, near York Factory, Indians were marking beaver lodges to "be sure no one else will be so unfair as to hunt it" (Tyrrell 1931: 233). Given similar ecological and trade conditions near Fort Albany, it is probable that similar concepts were developing there too. If heeded, such marks designating private ownership by families could, in time, lead to game management.

Conclusions

The reciprocal bond between Indians within a hundred odd miles of Fort Albany and the traders there, involving the production of furs, geese and venison by the former, in exchange for trade goods and periodic food donations, had by the early 1700s generated subtle and important social and economic changes. Regular participation in new economic activities came to alter Cree social organization and the habitat Indians exploited. Although many traditional beliefs and customs persisted in the new context for many more years, scholars, nevertheless, should not be deceived into believing that distinctive Cree traits give evidence that other aspects of their culture remained unaltered, or that the fur trade was simply grafted onto traditional culture. Notwithstanding, the Cree were not passive recipients. Rather, they reacted to the fur trade and modified it. But all the same, the consequence of this reaction was the narrowing of their range of options, a fact reflected by the term "homeguard" applied to those who hunted geese or remained near the post. The changes experienced by these lowland Cree also foreshadow in a general way what other Indians further inland and to the west would later endure. The case of the western James Bay Cree, then, is instructive in two ways. Provided caution is employed, it is possible to upstream from the early records to aboriginal baseline conditions. Second, materials can be used to gain a comparative perspective on Indians involved in the fur trade in other places and at other times.

References

This article first appeared in *Prairie Forum* 8, no. 2 (1983): 147–56.

The author wishes to thank the Governor and Committee of the Hudson's Bay Company for permission to view the extensive archival materials pertaining to Fort Albany and other posts where the Cree traded.

Adams, Arthur T. (ed.). 1961 *The Explorations of Pierre Esprit Radisson*. Minneapolis: Ross & Haines, Inc.

Bishop, Charles A. 1972. "Demography, Ecology and Trade Among the Northern Ojibwa and Swampy Cree," *Western Canadian Journal of Anthropology* 3: 58–71.

———. 1975. "Ojibwa, Cree and the Hudson's Bay Company in Northern Ontario: Culture and Conflict in the Eighteenth Century." Pp. 150–62 in A.W. Rasporich (ed.), *Western Canada Past and Present*. Calgary: McClelland and Stewart West, Ltd.

Bishop, Charles A. and Arthur J. Ray. 1976. "Ethnohistoric Research in the Central Subarctic: Some Conceptual and Methodological Problems," *The Western Canadian Journal of Anthropology* 4: 116–44.

Davies, K.G. (ed.). 1965. *Letters from Hudson Bay: 1703–40.* London: The Hudson's Bay Record Society.

Hudson's Bay Company Archives (HBCA). B. 3/a/1-150 Fort Albany Post Journals, 1705–1845.

——. B. 3/d/1-78 Fort Albany Account Books, 1692–1770.

——. B. 3/e/1-19 Fort Albany District Reports, 1815–1837.

——. B. 3/z/1-3 Fort Albany Miscellaneous Items, 1694–1871.

Nute, Grace Lee. 1978. *Caesars of the Wilderness: Medard Chouart, Sieur Des Groseilliers and Pierre Esprit Radisson, 1618–1710.* St. Paul: Minnesota Historical Society Press.

Ray, Arthur J. and Donald Freeman. 1978. *"Give Us Good Measure": An Economic Analysis of Relations Between the Indians and the Hudson's Bay Company Before 1763.* Toronto: University of Toronto Press.

Tyrrell, J.B. (ed.). 1931. *Documents Relating to the Early History of Hudson Bay.* Toronto: The Champlain Society.

Williams, Glyndwr (ed.). 1975. *Hudson's Bay Miscellany: 1670–1870.* Winnipeg: Hudson's Bay Record Society.

The Fur Trade

5. The Northern Great Plains: Pantry of the Northwestern Fur Trade, 1774–1885

Arthur J. Ray

The expansion of the fur trade into the Athabasca and Mackenzie River drainage basins in the late 18th century had major implications for the trading system that had already been established in the northern Great Plains. Operating a burgeoning network of posts posed serious logistical problems for the competing Hudson's Bay and North West companies. The boreal forests could not provide sufficient food to feed men stationed at the growing number of posts and those who manned the canoe and boat brigades plying the routes between them. European food was too costly to import in large quantities. Even more important, cargo space in canoes and York boats was limited. The proportion of that space devoted to provisions had to be kept to a minimum. Complicating this problem, the transportation season was too short to permit crews to hunt and fish along the way. For these reasons, food had to be obtained in the country and stockpiled at strategic locations along the transportation routes.

The European traders quickly realized that the parkland and prairie areas could serve as the pantry for the western fur trade. This region could produce large food surpluses and it was strategically located beside the main supply line of the northwestern fur trade (Figure 1). In order to collect plains provisions, the Hudson's Bay Company and the North West Company built posts along the North Saskatchewan as well as the Red and Assiniboine rivers between 1779 and 1821. The provisions obtained from the Saskatchewan area were forwarded to Cumberland Lake for use by the Athabasca-bound brigades of the two companies. In the southern Manitoba area, the North West Company sent its foodstuffs to Fort Bas de la Rivière on the lower Winnipeg River for use by its canoe brigades as they travelled between Cumberland Lake and the Rainy Lake-Fort William area. The Hudson's Bay Company forwarded its provisions from southern Manitoba

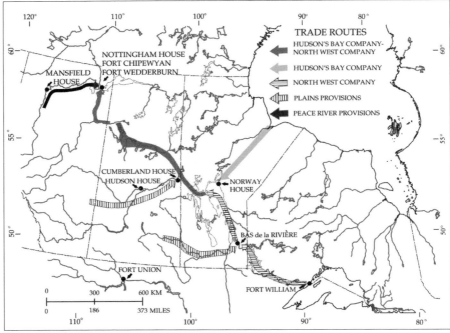

Figure 1. Trade routes.

to Norway House, at the head of Lake Winnipeg, where they were picked up by inland brigades travelling to and from York Factory. Even with these new logistical arrangements a large proportion of cargo space continued to be taken up with provisions (Table 1).

Indians were quick to appreciate the opportunities the new provision market offered to them. For instance, in 1779 the Hudson's Bay Company built Hudson House on the North Saskatchewan River to obtain provisions for Cumberland House. Within a year, the local Indians were burning the surrounding prairies in the autumn to prevent the buffalo (*Bison bison*) herds from approaching the post. By making it impossible for the traders to hunt buffalo themselves, the Indians hoped to increase the prices that they could demand for the provisions they brought to barter. This Native practice became commonplace in the parklands.[1]

The foodstuffs that the Indians supplied consisted almost entirely of dried buffalo meat (jerk meat), pounded (powdered) meat, grease and pemmican. The butchering and processing was done by Native women. Drying meat involved cutting it into long strips about 0.6 cm (0.25″) thick. The strips were then hung on wooden slats supported by tripods of sticks. It took two or three days for the meat to dry. The better quality dried meat was packed

| Table 1. Proportion of North West Company Canoe Space Devoted to Provisions, 1814 ||
Destination from Fort William	% Provisions
Athabasca	34
Athabasca River	39
English River	38
Rat River	42
Upper Fort des Prairies	48
Lower Fort des Prairies	38
Upper Red River	25
Lower Red River	24
Fort Dauphin	28
Lake Winnipeg	37
Based on data in Williams S. Wallace, *Documents Relating to the North West Company* (Toronto: n.p., 1934), 277–79.	

into bundles. The remainder was dried further over a hot fire until brittle. It was then laid out on a buffalo hide and pounded into a powder. This powdered meat was dumped into a kettle containing boiling fat or marrow. As it cooked the mixture turned into a paste. Crushed berries were often added at this time. While still boiling hot, the paste was poured into leather bags which were sealed as tightly as possible. The mixture was then allowed to cool until it was hard. This very nutritious food concentrate was known as pemmican.[2] It was highly stable and could be stored for long periods of time. For these reasons, pemmican was an ideal food for people on the move. It could be eaten right from the bag without any further preparation, roasted in its own fat, or boiled.[3]

The expanded market for buffalo meat products after 1780 had significant implications for the Native suppliers. For example, it is reasonable to suppose that the prehistoric demand for dried provisions by parkland/grassland groups was limited because these groups hunted buffalo to some extent at all seasons of the year. Therefore, a large portion of their food consumption would have consisted of fresh or previously frozen (in winter) meat.[4] Dried provisions were used in emergencies when herds were not present locally, when travelling, or when engaged in raiding expeditions. Pemmican was especially important in the latter circumstances since it did not have to be cooked. Being able to avoid using fires while on the warpath was an important consideration in the open grasslands, where smoke was visible for miles.

Besides domestic use, nomadic hunters probably also traded dried meat and pemmican with horticultural Indians who lived in the Missouri valley during the late prehistoric period.[5] In addition, some exchange undoubtedly took place when local food shortages were common in the forests. However, there is no reason to suppose that this trade was extensive.

In light of these considerations, it is clear that the fur trade provision market would have served to increase the importance of pemmican as an article of commerce. Whether or not this market stimulated the initial commercialization of the hunt is uncertain at this time because there is some archaeological evidence that suggests there may have been an increased output of dried provisions in the late prehistoric era.[6] On the basis of this evidence the archaeologist Thomas Kehoe has argued that the commercialization of the hunt began before European contact.[7] If Kehoe is correct, the development of a fur trade provision market may have simply served as a catalyst which accelerated a trend that had begun earlier. It is unclear why the process would have begun in the prehistoric/protohistoric periods. Possibly the incentive for increased pemmican production in the late pre-contact period was related to the increase in warfare that was associated with the northward spread of the horse. Acquisition of this animal may also have served to increase intertribal trade. Whatever the causes for the increased output may have been, it is clear that in the historic period the expanded output of provisions was aimed at serving a new external market.

While a changing economic climate provided the incentive, technological changes resulting from European contact made it easier for Native groups to expand their production of traditional meat products and to transport them. For instance, historical accounts of pemmican-making indicate that buffalo fat was melted in copper or brass kettles.[8] It is uncertain how fat would have been melted down on a large scale in prehistoric times given the relatively poor quality ceramics that Indians possessed (judged by modern technical standards) and the fact that plains Indians used the buffalo paunch extensively as a cooking container. Being limited to this domestic equipment meant that most foods had to be either stone-boiled or roasted over an open fire. Indeed, when writing about the Métis (descendants of Indians and Europeans) buffalo hunts in the middle of the 19th century, Red River settler Alexander Ross noted that a great deal of meat, fat, and bone marrow was wasted because the Métis hunters lacked a sufficient number of kettles to process it.[9] Ross's observation is of particular interest given the fact that the Métis undoubtedly were better equipped with kettles than their Plains Indian cousins. Thus, although kettles would have offered the prospect of improved efficiency of meat processing, the limited quantity of kettles available as late as the middle of the 19th century was a factor that set limits on the amount of pemmican that groups could make from their kill. In other

An Assiniboine running a Buffalo.
Drawn by an Assiniboine warrior
and hunter. Fort Union, Jan 16, 18 54.

"An Assiniboine running a buffalo. Drawn by an Assiniboine warrior and hunter, Fort Union, Jan. 16, 1854." Plate 70 from 46th annual report, Bureau of American Ethnology, by Edwin .T. Denig, on Indian tribes of the Upper Missouri (courtesy of the Glenbow Archives/LAC-3225-3).

words, food wastage may have been partly a function of the per capita distribution of kettles. It may be that prehistoric pemmican production occurred only on a relatively small scale owing to technological constraints.

Hunting efficiency and transportation capability were affected by the introduction northward of horses from the southern plains where they had been brought by the Spaniards. By the early 1700s horses were found in the southern Alberta region, and by the 1740s they were being adopted by Indians in southern Manitoba. Horses altered summer hunting practices in that the animals enabled Indians, and later Métis, to "run" the herds. This involved having a group of men approach a herd as closely as possible before it took flight. Once the buffalo stampeded, the Indian hunters chased after them on their horses. Being faster than the fleeing buffalo (a buffalo was said to run at two-thirds the pace of a horse), a good buffalo pony enabled Indian hunters to ride up alongside of their prey and kill them at close range with arrows, lances or muskets. The chase usually continued until the horses were tired. As in the past, the Indian women and children followed, often on foot, to butcher the fallen prey. Although not without its hazards, this method of hunting was less risky and probably more efficient than the older walking surround or fire drive. Ross witnessed a Métis "buf-falo run" that lasted two hours and yielded 137 animals. This is a kill rate of slightly more than 11 per minute. In terms of the 40 men involved, howev-er, it is less impressive, giving each hunter an average of 3.5 animals.[10] Perhaps of greater importance, horses gave the plains hunters the potential of carrying larger loads at a faster pace than when dogs were the sole beasts of burden.[11] However, the potential was not fully realized because of limited availability. Many Indian groups in southern Manitoba and eastern Saskatchewan were "horse-poor." They did not have enough mounts for everyone. Therefore, the speed of these groups was limited to their slowest pedestrian members. In contrast, the Métis had a relative abundance of horses. They often travelled with riding horses, buffalo-running ponies (which were used solely for that purpose), cart horses and pack horses.

As the fur traders pushed into the Athabasca and Mackenzie River coun-try, they quickly realized it was necessary to have an advance food supply base to augment meat products obtained in the prairie region. The mainline of the fur trade skirted the edge of the Canadian Shield, where many large lakes (Great Bear Lake, Great Slave Lake, Lake Athabasca, Lake Winni-pegosis and Lake Winnipeg) teemed with fish. The fisheries developed on these lakes supported a number of trading posts. However, even though fish could be smoked, dried or, in the case of sturgeon, processed into pemmi-can, it did not become an important voyaging food.[12] It is unclear why. Perhaps it was related to food preferences. It is also likely that fish pemmi-can would have had a shorter "shelf life" than buffalo pemmican. The fail-ure to exploit the great inland fisheries meant that alternative sources had to be developed. The Nor'Westers were the first to confront this problem and in the late 1870s they turned to the Beaver Indians living in the Peace River valley to supply them with the additional food. By the turn of the century the North West Company was relying on the Peace River area for all of its dried provisions in the region. This meat was sent from the Peace River val-ley to Fort Chipewyan where the Nor'Westers used it to outfit their canoes bound for Cumberland House from Peace River, Great Slave Lake, and Lake Athabasca.

In 1802 the Hudson's Bay Company moved into this area and built Nottingham House on Lake Athabasca, near Fort Chipewyan. It was hoped that the men at this post would be able to feed themselves on fish. Like the Nor'Westers, the Hudson's Bay Company men also realized that they would need to tap the Peace River country for more food. They launched this effort with the construction of Mansfield House on the Peace River in 1802. Realizing the strategic importance of the Peace River supply base and wanting to block the Hudson's Bay Company's push into Athabasca and Mackenzie river country, the Nor'Westers quickly moved to intimidate the Hudson's Bay Company on the Peace River. This venture was successful and the Hudson's Bay Company was forced to withdraw. Having failed to secure a supply base in the Peace River area, the Hudson's Bay Company also found it was necessary to close Nottingham House in 1809 and temporarily abandon the Athabasca country. They did not return again until 1815 when they built a new post, Fort Wedderburn, on Lake Athabasca. Once again the Hudson's Bay Company battled with the Nor'Westers for access to the provision trade of the Peace River country. This time they were successful and secured a toehold in the region by 1819.[13]

The battle for control of the provision trade at this time was not limited to the Peace River country. It erupted in the Red River area also. In 1812 the Hudson's Bay Company established the Selkirk agricultural colony on the banks of the Red River. This posed a strategic threat to the North West Company since the colony lay astride its provision supply line in that quarter. The seriousness of the danger was manifest in the winter of 1814. The colony was seriously short of provisions. In an effort to deal with the problem Miles Macdonell, the autocratic colonial governor, issued his "Pemmican Proclamation" on January 8, 1814, forbidding the export from the area of any provisions that had been secured or grown there. All provisions were to be reserved for the colony's consumption.[14] Macdonell's action provoked the so-called "Pemmican War" in which the Nor'Westers, using the Métis as pawns, sought to destroy the colony.

The struggle for control of shares of the vital Plains provision trade continued in all quarters until the union of the two rival companies in 1821. Although this union temporarily reduced the overall labour force of the fur trade by as much as one-third, thereby temporarily diminishing the size of the provision market, this market rebounded a short while later. But after 1821 a new group emerged as one of the major suppliers—this group was comprised of French (the Métis) and English mixed-blood men. Most of these men were laid off by the Hudson's Bay Company in the early 1820s. Some simply quit. Previously most of them had been stationed at the parkland posts and had Native wives of Parkland Indian ancestry. The mixed-bloods congregated near the Red River colony and around the present town of Pembina, North Dakota, until they abandoned the latter location in 1823. These men and their families combined the older Indian ways with the newer ones of the settlers. They established small farms, but between sowing and harvest they hunted buffalo for dried provisions and hides. From late August until early November many of them left for the plains a second time to secure fresh meat and buffalo robes for the winter. Their hunts were like those of their Plains Indian relatives, but there were also some differences. One was in the mode of transportation that the mixed-bloods used. The Métis employed two-wheeled carts fashioned of local materials (wood, leather and sinew) instead of the travois. These were the famed Red River carts. They were pulled by one horse, or an ox, and carried some 900 pounds of cargo—nearly double that of the travois. The carts gave the mixed-bloods great mobility, enabling them to extend their foraging range as far westward as was necessary to pursue the buffalo herds. Further, Indians tended to follow the herds, hunting them at all seasons. Since the mixed-bloods, who lived in fixed settlements, worked for the Hudson's Bay Company on a seasonal basis, and farmed on a part-time basis they could not hunt all year round. Therefore, their buffalo hunting was confined largely to two hunts annually. These hunts were much like those organized by the Indians, except that Métis hunters skinned the slain buffalo and brought the carcasses back to camp rather than having their women and children follow in their wake. For both groups, the women did the butchering and meat processing.[15]

Recently it has been argued that the mixed economy of the Métis was better suited to the regional economic situation between 1821 and 1870 than was the way of life chosen by settlers who attempted farming on a full-time basis.[16] The farmers were frequently devastated by natural disasters. Colonial observer James Hargrave noted in 1870 that the Red River settlement had been completely flooded in 1808, 1826, 1852, and 1861, and had been plagued with locusts in 1818, 1819, 1857, 1858, and 1864 through 1868.[17] Besides these 13 major calamities in 60 years, droughts and early frosts were also a frequent problem. These recurring misfortunes kept the colony from producing a steady agricultural output sufficient to meet its own provision requirements. Poor storage and handling procedures frequently reduced the size of any surpluses produced.[18] Therefore, the developing colony remained partially dependent on the buffalo hunt to survive. This dependency extended the size of the provision market beyond that provided by the Hudson's Bay Company.

The Métis, as competitors of the Parkland Indians for the provision market, were most successful in southern Manitoba. One can assume that they satisfied nearly all of the colony's needs and a significant portion of the Hudson's Bay Company's requirements in that quarter. Posts situated along the middle and upper reaches of the Assiniboine River and North and South Saskatchewan Rivers and their tributaries supplemented the provisions that the mixed-bloods brought to Red River. Most of these western posts conducted the bulk of their provision trade with Indian groups. As in earlier

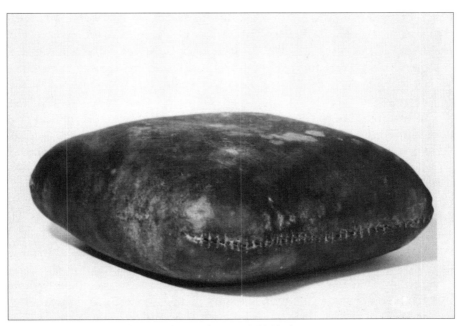

Pemmican bag (courtesy of the Glenbow Archives/LAC-2360-1).

years, these provisions were transported to Cumberland House and Norway House.

The dimensions of the provision market created by the fur trade can be pieced together by employing scattered bits of information that are available. For example, in the first decade of the 19th century the North West Company was obtaining an average of 12,600 lb. of pemmican from its Red River department and 27,000 to 45,0W lb. from the Saskatchewan area.[19] This gives an average annual total of between 39,600 and 57,600 lb. of pemmican for the North West Company from the prairie/ parkland area. Historical accounts provide somewhat contradictory statements about the amounts of fresh meat that were needed to produce a bag of pemmican. James Hargrave stated that the meat of one bull made a 100-lb. bag of pemmican, while Father G.A. Belcourt claimed it took two buffalo cows to produce a 90-lb. bag of pemmican (one cow yielded 45 lb. of pemmican). But he added that experienced hunters reckoned it took eight to 10 cows' meat to fill one cart with pemmican (one cow = 90 to 112.5 lb. of pemmican).[20] There is a discrepancy in these figures of over 100%. Guillaume Charette, a Métis, observed that it took 4,000 cows to fill 500 carts with pemmican, or eight per cart.[21] This suggests that Belcourt's second figure is the more accurate estimate.

Data obtained from the North West Company post of Fort Pembina reveal that the mean dressed weight of 35 bulls killed during the winter was 514 lb. while that of 112 cows was 402 lb.[22] In light of these various sets of figures, it would have taken approximately 350-440 lb. of fresh meat to produce 90–100 lb. of pemmican. This represents a weight loss of between 72% and 80% using cows and bulls. Using cows exclusively the range is 72–77.5%.

All historical sources agree that cow's meat was preferable for all types of consumption. F.G. Roe concluded that this preference was on the order of 10 to one.[23] More bulls would be taken only if there were not enough cows. Given the very strong historical preference for cows, and assuming a 75% weight loss in processing, it is possible to estimate the number of buffalo required to meet the pemmican demands of the fur trade as well as Métis and Indian subsistence requirements. For this reason, the estimates for slaughter will be expressed in "cow equivalents." On this basis it would have taken between 158,400 and 230,000 lb. of fresh meat to yield the quantity of pemmican the North West Company needed annually in the early 19th century. This represented roughly 400 to 575 buffalo cows. If we assume that the Hudson's Bay Company's requirements were the same during this period, the combined demand could have been met by killing fewer than 1,200 animals.

Table 2 gives the provision demand of the Hudson's Bay Company at 10-year intervals between 1830 and 1870. These figures have been translated into equivalents. These data reveal that the size of the company's pemmican and dried meat market increased over two and one-half times between 1840 and 1870. But the numbers of animals needed for slaughter remained relatively low, suggesting that the provision market accounted for only a small percentage of the total output of provisions in the northern plains region.

This conclusion is based on an estimation of the magnitude of the demand for buffalo meat products by the Red River Colony and the Native population. This estimation takes into account census figures for the colony, approximations of the Native population in the mid-19th century, scattered data dealing with food consumption at the beginning of that century, the ration rates employed by the Hudson's Bay Company, and transportation capabilities of the mixed-blood population. During the winter of 1807–08, 41 men stationed at the North West Company post of Fort Pembina consumed 63,000 lb. of fresh buffalo meat over a 213-day period (September 1–March 31). This represents an average of 7.2 lb./man/day or about 5,360 calories. In addition, during the same period the men consumed three red deer (*Cervus elaphus*), five black bear (*Ursus americanus*), four beaver (*Castor canadensis*), three swans (*Cygnus* sp.), one white crane (*Grus americana*), 12

Table 2. Provision Demand of the Hudson's Bay Company

Commodity	1840	1850	1860	1870
Pemmican (lb.)*	90,900	120,375	137,610	202,680
Dried Meat (lb.)**	20,000	16,600	11,000	9,000
Total	110,000	136,975	148,610	211,680
Price (sterling)/lb.****	£ s.d	£ s.d	£ s.d	£ s.d
Pemmican	3d	3d	4d	6d
Dried Meat	2d	2d	3d	4d
Inventory Value**** (sterling)				
Pemmican	£1,136 5s	£1,504 14s	£2,293 10s	£5,067
Dried Meat	£166 13s	£138 7s	£137 10s	£150
Total	£1,302 18s	£1,643 1s	£2,431	£5,217
Equivalent in Red River Cart Loads ***	122	152	165	315
Equivalent in fresh meat (lb.)	482,000	579,870	615,625	864,053
Equivalent number of buffalo cows	1,205	1,450	1,539	2,160

* Ray, *Indians in the Fur Trade*, 200–10.
** According to Belcourt, 1 cow = 67.50 lb. dried meat.
*** Cart load = 900 lb.
**** British Columbia Provincial Archives, Add MS, 220, "Standing Rules and Regulations, Northern Department, Rupert's Land, 1847–67."

outards, 36 ducks, and 1,150 fish of various kinds.[24] This level of consumption was only slightly below the rations that the Hudson's Bay Company provided for its boat brigades. Company boatmen were given eight lb. of fresh meat per day, their wives four, and their children two. Allowances for employees and their families stationed at trading posts were one-half that of the brigades. A variety of other foods was consumed also. Applying the Hudson's Bay Company rates to the population censuses of Red River suggests that the buffalo meat consumption of the colony would have ranged between approximately 2,200,000 lb. and 4,400,000 lb./year in 1831, potentially rising to between 7,500,000 lb. and 15,000,000 lb./year in 1870.[25]

This simple prediction must be modified, however, to account for additional factors besides human population growth. The colony was making slow, if erratic, progress in its agricultural output. Also, transportation capacity did not expand sufficiently to carry the quantity of meat projected by the 1870 estimate. In 1870 Hargrave wrote that an average of 1,200 carts took part in the two annual hunts—roughly the same number as in the late 1840s despite the population increase. This indicates that the Métis hunters could have supplied a maximum of 1,080,000 lb. of pemmican (the equivalent of 4,320,000 lb. of fresh meat) from the August hunt and 1,080,000 lb. of fresh meat in the autumn if all of their cargo space was devoted to provision supplies. Of course, this was not the case given that they also carried hides and robes. Thus, the annual buffalo consumption by the Red River colony in 1870 would have had to be less than the equivalent of 5,400,000 lb. of fresh buffalo meat per year. This indicates a daily ration of meat of less than three pounds of fresh buffalo meat per adult male, or one-quarter less than the post allowance rate of the Hudson's Bay Company.

These calculations indicate that provision demands of the colony in 1831 would have generated a slaughter on the order of between 5,500 and 11,000 buffalo cows, while that of 1870 would have been under 13,500. This suggests that the maximum probable increase would have been less than two and one-half times between 1831 and 1870.

In 1856 Governor George Simpson of the Hudson's Bay Company calculated that the Plains Indians numbered just under 30,000.[26] Using this figure and applying the ration rates of the trading companies, the potential buffalo meat requirements of the Indians would have necessitated the slaughter of between 54,000 and almost 110,000 cows/year. In this case, the mean figure of about 82,000 is more likely, given that this number would closely approximate the size of slaughter that would be generated by a population of nearly 30,000 having a diet very similar to that of the men stationed at Fort Pembina in 1807–08.

As large as it appears, it should be pointed out that a projected kill rate of 82,000 animals per year is probably a conservative estimate bearing in mind that hunts were wasteful. During the summer season Indians sometimes slaughtered herds just to obtain the tongues and bosses for feasts. The rest of the carcass was left to spoil. Even without such profligate behaviour the hunt was wasteful by its very nature. The buffalo being a herd animal that was easily spooked to stampede, it was difficult for the Indians or Métis to kill only those that were needed. The most obvious example would be a cliff drive where it would have been impossible to control the number of animals that stampeded over a precipice. When running buffalo, hunters could not predict how many animals they could successfully skin and butcher. A number of problems could arise that would abbreviate the butchering. These included raiding parties of hostile Native groups, rainstorms which rendered exposed meat useless, and nightfall. Predators, most notably wolves (*Canis lupus*), were effective scavengers after dark and took a heavy toll. According to one Métis hunter, besides these problems, the blinding dust of a run often made it impossible to carefully pick out the choice fat cows and many undesirable quarry were killed.[27] For all these reasons a significant allowance has to be made for wastage. Alexander Ross claimed that 2,500 animals were slain in one hunt by Métis, but the meat of only 750 buffalo was processed—scarcely one-third.[28] Given all of the factors that could influence the ability of a party to process the meat of its hunt, wastage rates would not have been constant. If we assume that Ross's experience represented extreme conditions, then presumably they ranged up to as much as 66%.

Taken together, it is clear that the combined food needs of the Hudson's Bay Company, the Red River Colony and the Indians would have necessitated a slaughter that amounted to the equivalent of just under 100,000 cows (2,160 + 13,500 + 82,000) per year. Considering wastage, a range of 100,000 to 300,000 is a possibility. Of this, just over 2% of the kill would have been generated by the fur trade.

Although a slaughter of this magnitude might appear to represent a serious threat to the survival of the wild buffalo herds, this apparently was not the case if Roe's estimation of the natural rate of increase of the species is correct. Based on data obtained from the captive animals in Wainwright Buffalo Park, Roe concluded the population increased 18%/year.[29] At that rate the combined provision hunt could have been sustained by a herd of between 555,555 (if 100,000 were killed) and 1,666,666 animals (if the slaughter equalled 300,000). Most calculations of the size of the northern herds exceed these figures by a wide margin. Therefore, it seems likely that other economic developments in the 19th century served to accelerate the slaughter beyond the level of a sustainable harvest and eventually destroyed this vital food resource. The first of these developments was the emergence of a strong market for robes. A few robes had been traded ever since the beginning of the fur trade in the area in the late 17th century. However, the volume of this traffic was limited since there were no sizeable markets in eastern North America or Europe. Also, these articles were bulky and heavy and, therefore, it was difficult to transport large quantities of them by canoe. But by the early 19th century the picture began to change. American traders pushed up the Missouri River and established Fort Union at the confluence of the Yellowstone and Missouri rivers. This post became an important hub of trade, drawing Indians from a large surrounding area including the prairies south of the Saskatchewan and Assiniboine rivers. Using bateaux and steamboats the American traders' transportation costs were substantially less than those of the Hudson's Bay Company which continued to depend heavily on the less efficient York boat and canoe. The Americans' cheaper transportation costs enabled them to cater to the growing market for buffalo robes in eastern North America. This market developed to the point where it triggered off a virtual flood of robes down the Missouri River toward St. Louis. It has been estimated that between 1815 and the early 1860s the trade of the Missouri River area fluctuated between 20,000 and 200,000 robes/year.[30] Probably 50% of this trade came from the Canadian prairies north of the upper Missouri.

In the early 1820s Governor George Simpson of the Hudson's Bay Company made a few exploratory efforts to see if the company could take part in this new market, either by making overland shipments to Montreal or by exporting robes via York Factory to London for reshipment from that city to New York. These initial efforts were failures.[31] Somewhat later the company became involved in the robe trade, but its share of the enterprise remained very small (Figure 2). The Company's annual trade never reached 20,000. The Métis also became involved, and in 1844 they began carting robes overland to the St. Paul area of Minnesota. Few data exist concerning the volume of traffic. However, in 1856 it amounted to more than 7,500

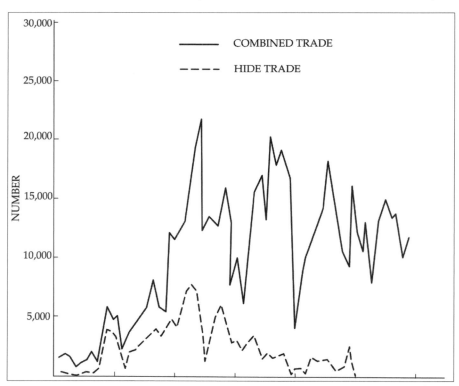

Figure 2. Hudson's Bay Company Northern Department hide and robe trade, 1821–1879.

Cree Chief Sweetgrass in St. Boniface, Manitoba with a bow and arrow and a buffalo robe draped over his arm, June, 1872 (Courtesy of the Glenbow Archives/ LAC-1677-10).

robes.[32] That year the Hudson's Bay Company traded almost 16,000 robes, suggesting that Métis trade comprised about 50% of that of the company's volume.

These sketchy data (in the case of the Métis) suggest that the combined robe trade of the Métis and the Hudson's Bay Company ranged between 10,000 and 40,000/year between 1840 and 1879. Added to the 10,000 to 100,000 robes that probably flowed southward from the Canadian prairies to the Missouri River posts, an annual winter slaughter of 20,000 to 140,000 animals is indicated.

The robe hunt must be considered in relation to the provision hunt to understand the combined impact that it had on the Native economy (Indian and Métis) and on the buffalo resource. Recall that the fur trade provision market consisted entirely of dried produce obtained from the summer hunts; therefore, no robes would have been taken as by-products of the 2,160 cows needed. Almost 11,000 of the 13,500 animals slaughtered for the colony's consumption were killed to produce dried meat products. Therefore, only about 2,500 (perhaps 7,500 if we allow for waste at the maximum rate) would have been killed for food during the robe season. There were about 6,000 Métis in Red River in 1870.[33] Allowing one robe for every man, woman and child per year for personal use, it is clear there would not have been any surplus left for trade. If, for the sake of discussion, we assume that the provision hunts of the Indians were spread out over the entire year, then 66% of the approximately 82,000 buffalo needed would have been slain at a time when robes could have been obtained as a by-product. This amounts to some 54,120 robes (perhaps 135,000 with a maximum wastage allowance). If we allocate two robes per Indian per year for clothing and bedding purposes (probably a conservative figure), it is necessary to subtract some 50,000 robes from the above figure to determine the number available for trading purposes. The result suggests that no by-product robes would have been available if Indian hunts were highly efficient and aimed primarily at meeting their food needs.

Adding together the median values of the estimated ranges of the volume of Canadian Indian robe trade to the Missouri River posts, the Hudson's Bay Company's robe trade, and the Métis traffic to Minnesota territory, it appears that the magnitude of the robe market for the region at mid-century was something on the order of 60,000 robes (40,000 + 13,000 + 6,000 = 59,000). This suggests that the development of the robe market could have had the effect of almost doubling the winter slaughter of buffalo (e.g., increasing it from just under some 56,600 to nearly 110,000). The problem is that we do not know if the Indians were able to take and process robes more efficiently than meat. If this was the case, then the robe trade may not have increased the Indians' winter kill at all if provision wastage was as high as 66%. If this was so, and all of the robes of the wasted animals were collected, then perhaps as many as 85,000 were available for trade. This seems unlikely, however, as robe processing, like meat preparation, was time-consuming although the rapid spoilage of the raw material was less critical.[34] Added to the summer hunt, conservatively estimated at just over 40,000 (27,060 + 2,160 + 11,000), the annual provision and robe slaughter probably ranged between 150,000 (assuming little wastage in the provision hunts), as much as 354,000 (if two-thirds of the provision kill were wasted and no robes were obtained from the carcasses). The latter scenario is unlikely.

The magnitude of the difference in the economic importance of the provision and robe markets is not easy to gauge since we have good data only for the Hudson's Bay Company markets and, as noted earlier, the company took part in only a fraction of the robe trade. As Table 2 shows, the dried meat and pemmican that the Hudson's Bay Company purchased was valued in Sterling at £1,302 18s. in 1840, increasing to £5,217. Considering the number of Métis and Indians involved in the trade, these are very small figures. In contrast, the Company bought between 4,000 and 22,000 robes/year during this period (Figure 2). In 1843, at the height of the company's trade, it valued prime robes at 5s. and common ones at 2s.6d. Using an average price of 2s.9d. (the returns did not specify the quantities of prime and common) the 1843 trade was worth about £3,025 or nearly two and one-half times more than the provision market. In 1870 prime robes fetched 10s. and common 5s. for an average price of 7s.6d. At these prices the approximately 11,500 robes bought by the company were worth about £4,312 10s. to the

Indians and Métis. In other words, the Hudson's Bay Company's robe market was of roughly the same value as its provision market. Since the company's prices for provisions and robes had doubled between 1840 and 1870, the shift in relative value of the markets represented the growing volume of the provision trade (it almost doubled between 1840 and 1870), whereas the volume of the robe trade showed an irregular decline. Thus, for Indians and Métis who traded solely with the Hudson's Bay Company, it would appear that the provision trade was of increasing relative importance. However, few traded exclusively with the company. Given the very large market for robes in the United States until the 1870s, one can speculate that before 1870 most Indian and Métis hunters derived the bulk of their hunting income from selling robes.

In the 1870s technological developments in the tanning industry made it possible to process buffalo hides. This had the effect of creating an extremely large market. Attention very quickly shifted from robes to hides to take advantage of this new economic opportunity. The development of this new trade served to accelerate the buffalo slaughter for a number of reasons. Hides could be prepared more quickly than robes and required less skilled labour. This meant that Euro-Canadians could enter the field on a much larger scale than previously. The hide market was larger than that for robes, although the Hudson's Bay Company played a smaller role (Figure 2). Unlike the robe hunts, the kill was concentrated in a relatively short period. The dried provision needs of the Indians, Métis and the Hudson's Bay Company could have yielded something on the order of 40,560 hides. If the Indian and Métis population used two hides/year, probably a conservative number given the many uses hides served in their cultures, 60,000 hides would have been required for the Native population annually. In short, there was no surplus. Indeed, the need for hides likely led the Native population to slaughter more animals than their provision needs would have dictated, hence the "waste" noted earlier. If the estimates of food and hide needs are in the "ball park," one-third of the meat of the summer hunt could have been wasted as a result of the Native demand for hides which necessitated a higher slaughter rate. In any event, it is clear that the hide trade probably increased the Indian and Métis level of hunting much more sharply simply because there was virtually no surplus available as a by-product of provision hunting. Thus, the robe and hide trade greatly increased the attack on the herds, hastening the day when they would vanish forever.

The tell-tale effects of overkill were manifest as early as the 1820s. By that time buffalo ceased to frequent the Red River valley near the colony. In the late 1850s their appearance in the southern Manitoba area was becoming

Cree buffalo pound near Fort Carlton, Rupert's Land, 1820. Original drawing by Lieutenant George Back, a member of the 1819–22 Franklin Expedition (courtesy of the Glenbow Archives/LAC-1344-2).

irregular and this caused Alexander Ross to comment that the combined attack on the herds, from the north by Canadian groups and from the south by Americans, was forcing the herds to retreat westward.[35] He foresaw the day when they would be totally destroyed. By the 1860s the buffalo were in sharp decline north of the Qu'Appelle and South Saskatchewan rivers. By the late 1870s, the herds were largely confined to southwestern Saskatchewan and southern Alberta areas.

In the early 1880s the buffalo had declined to the point where Native groups could no longer depend upon them for subsistence, much less produce a surplus of provisions, hides and robes for a commercial market. Thus, pemmican, once a staple of the fur trade, became very expensive (Table 2), rising from 3¢/pound in the 1830s to between 9.5 and 10¢/pound in the late 1870s. Also, the quality deteriorated. For these reasons, in 1880 the Hudson's Bay Company's chief factor at York Factory stated he was looking forward to the day when the company's dependence on this commodity would end entirely.[36] This came to pass a very short time later, and brought a great deal of hardship and suffering to the Indians and many of the Métis. Alternative game supplies could not meet their subsistence needs and provide them with a sufficient quantity of marketable products to maintain their former lifestyle. The blow was severe. In the 19th century these groups had become the most economically independent and powerful groups in the west. But their economy and society had a fatal flaw: it was based on the exploitation of a single renewable resource, at a rate that exceeded the level required for a sustained yield harvest. Thus the once-proud Grassland Indians and many Métis were reduced to poverty levels by the 1880s, and found themselves in a much worse socio-economic situation than their cousins in the wooded areas of the plains. The latter had never reached the same economic heights, but were spared reaching the same lows. The local provision market in the Peace River country led to the serious depletion of the wood buffalo population. But the market was organized very differently. Most of the meat was obtained by a relatively few Indians who were hired as post hunters. Therefore, income from this activity was not spread as broadly through the population. Also, since moose (*Alces alces*) was the preferred food animal for most of the local Indians, the assault on the buffalo in this area had very different implications for the Native inhabitants.[37] As this resource declined, the Woodland Indian bands were able to continue to support themselves by hunting, fishing and trapping. Meanwhile their grassland counterparts were reduced to subsisting on ground squirrels ("gophers") (*Spermophilus* sp.), and prairie dogs (*Cynomys ludovicianus*), and to relying increasingly on government assistance. The pantry of the prairie plains was bare and could never be stocked with natural surpluses again. There and then the era of the hunter yielded to that of the farmer and rancher.

Notes

This article first appeared in *Prairie Forum* 9, no. 2 (1984): 263–80.

The author would like to thank the Hudson's Bay Company for permission to consult and quote from its archives. I would also like to thank D.W. Moodie and Keith Ralston for commenting on earlier drafts of this paper. Of course the author is responsible for opinions expressed. Bison have been referred to throughout this paper as buffalo in keeping with historical practices. The term mixed-blood is used for the same reasons.

1. Arthur J. Ray, *Indians in the Fur Trade* (Toronto: University of Toronto Press, 1974), 131–35.

2. Numerous accounts of this process exist. For a recently published observation see G. Charette, *Vanishing Spaces: Memoirs of Louis Goulet*, edited and translated by R. Ellenwood (Winnipeg: Editions Bois-Brûlés, 1980), 55.

3. Ibid., 56.

4. Given this practise, B. Gordon has cautioned against using the hunting schedule of the Métis as a model for the Indians. See, B. Gordon, *Of Men and Herds in Canadian Plains Prehistory* (Ottawa: National Museum of Canada, 1979).

5. Ray, *Indians in the Fur Trade*, 87–89.

6. See, for example, Thomas Kehoe, *The Gull Lake Site* (Ottawa: National Museum of Man, 1973), 22–50.

7. Ibid., 195.

8. Charette, *Vanishing Spaces*, 55, and Alexander Ross, *The Red River Settlement* (Minneapolis: n.p., 1972), 257.

9. Ross, *The Red River Settlement*, 257.

10. Ibid., 256–57.

11. For a discussion of the spread of horses in this area, see Ray, *Indians in the Fur Trade*, 156–62.

12. A.J. Russell, *The Red River Country, Hudson's Bay & North-West Territories Considered in Relation to Canada* (Ottawa: G.E. Desbarats, 1869), 194.

13. L. Ugarenko, "The Beaver Indians and the Peace River Fur Trade, 1700–1850" (MA thesis, York University, 1979), 80–87.

14. For a discussion of this episode, see A.S. Morton, *A History of the Canadian West to 1870–71*, 2nd ed. (Toronto: published in cooperation with University of Saskatchewan by University of Toronto Press, 1973), 537–72.

15. J.J. Hargrave, *Red River* (Montreal: printed for the author by J. Lovell, 1870), 168.

16. C. Sprenger, "The Métis Nation: The Buffalo Hunt vs. Agriculture in the Red River Settlement, ca. 1810–70," *Western Canadian Journal of Anthropology* 3, no. 1 (1972): 159–78.

17. Hargrave, *Red River*, 175–76.

18. Ross, *The Red River Settlement*, 113–14 and 120–24.

19. Ray, *Indians in the Fur Trade*, 132.

20. C.M. Judd, *Lower Fort Garry, The Fur Trade and the Settlement at Red River* (Ottawa: Parks Canada, 1976), Appendix E: 313.

21. Charette, *Vanishing Spaces*, 53.

22. Ray, *Indians in the Fur Trade*, 131.

23. F.G. Roe, *The North American Buffalo*, 2nd ed. (Toronto: University of Toronto Press, 1972), 373–76 and 860–61.

24. Ray, *Indians in the Fur Trade*, 131.

25. Hudson's Bay Company Ration schedules are contained in "Standing Rules and Regulations, Northern Department, 1843–70," Public Archives of British Columbia, Add MSS 220. Red River census data are contained in *Censuses of Canada, 1665–1871*, Statistics Canada, Vol. 4 (Ottawa: Queen's Printer, 1876).

26. Hudson's Bay Company Archives, Public Archives of Manitoba, E 18/8, folio 40.

27. See Ross, *The Red River Settlement*, 258 and P. Erasmus, *Buffalo Days and Nights*, edited by I. Spry (Calgary: Glenbow-Alberta Institute, 1977), 31–33.

28. Roe, *The North American Buffalo*, 404–09.

29. Ibid., 503–05.

30. Ray, *Indians in the Fur Trade*, 210–12.

31. Ibid.

32. Ibid., 212.

33. Hargrave, *Red River*, 174.

34. Robes were processed by the women. The need for this skilled labour prevented large numbers of white hunters from entering into the trade.

35. Ross, *The Red River Settlement*, 267.

36. A.J. Ray, "York Factory: The Crises of Transition, 1870-1880," *The Beaver* (Autumn 1982): 28–29.

37. Ugarenko, "The Beaver Indians and the Peace River Fur Trade, 1700–1850," 117.

6.   Some Logistics of Portage La Loche (Methy)

C.S. Mackinnon

Canadian history is largely the story of transportation. One of the most convenient ways of studying developments is to focus on famous nodal points. The present article chronicles the changes at Portage La Loche during the fur-trade era. As the transportation systems from Montreal and York Factory expanded to transcontinental proportions, great ingenuity and effort were required to resupply distant posts before winter set in.[1] One answer was the celebrated rendezvous of wintering partners and Montreal agents at Grand Portage at the west end of Lake Superior. Somewhat less well known is the later interchange of fur for outfit achieved by the Mackenzie and La Loche Brigades at the top of the Churchill River over Portage La Loche. For over a century this arduous portage was the chief connection between the Hudson Bay drainage area and the Athabasca-Mackenzie, the Eldorado of the fur trade.

Distinguished travellers waxed eloquent at the view from the crest of Portage La Loche looking westward down the Clearwater valley. It became a literary convention to extol it, and Walter Kupsch has compiled a useful annotated anthology of published accounts.[2] Even a busy Chief Trader, James Anderson, paused to write in tiny script in his private diary:

> The view from the "Crête" is magnificent—this crete is a steep Ridge like the roof of some Titanic house—along the top a path 3 or 4 feet wide passes—on either side is a profound dell—well clothed with superb pines whose plume-like tops are seen far below—the sides of the ridge are covered with dwarf willows, bear berries, etc. one sheet of scarlet and yellow and different hues of green—the trees now being tinted with the Dyes of Autumn—opposite and beyond the River is an amphitheatre of conical sand hills—of different sizes, one blending to another—they resemble

the cones of volcanoes—from their distance the individual forms of the trees are lost—and the hills appear as if painted, with scarlet, crimson, Gold and different hues of Green — while here and there a dark line of pines crosses them— below at my feet was a beautiful little prairie, while the "Clearwater" pursues its silvery and devious course through the Valley—it was a lovely scene, and I saw it on a lovely day.[3]

For those sweating under repeated 180-pound loads, the 12 miles of the portage were brutal indeed. Starting from the canoe landing, the first eight miles from the southeast end are level with good footing in dry weather but no drinking water. Across the small Rendezvous Lake, the trail is level, dry and good for three miles before heading down a moderately steep 600-foot hill and through a wet prairie. In addition, the rivers on the approaches, the La Loche and the Clearwater, are subject to low water, a factor which caused further difficulties. Altogether the portage presented a formidable logistical problem.

In piecing together something of the story of the fur traders' attempts to cope, one is helped not only by walking over the trail itself but especially by the extensive records so carefully preserved by the Hudson's Bay Company. Further back still, there is enough archaeological evidence to suggest that Indians had used this route for many hundreds of years.[4] Certainly in historic times some of the Chipewyans came this way en route to trade at Hudson Bay. The name "Methy(e)" is the Cree word for the freshwater fish burbot; later the French version "La Loche" supplanted it.[5]

In 1778 Peter Pond, a forceful "pedlar" from Montreal, was the first recorded Euro-Canadian to cross over the Methy Portage into the fur-rich Athabasca area.[6] To sustain this distant, lucrative enterprise, Pond and others entered, the next year, into the first of a series of partnerships. This famous North West Company and its breakaway rival, the XY Company (1799–1804), pursued the trade around the Athabasca-Peace with great success. Two or three dozen north canoes and their outfits and returns were annually carried back and forth across the Methy.[7] Fired by the profit motive and with voyageurs of great stamina, the Nor'Westers simply treated the Methy like any other portage. However, Alexander Mackenzie admitted that it "discourages the men very much" and asked his cousin Roderick to search out a better route.[8] There was no fit alternative, however, either by the Beaver River or by David Thompson's Reindeer-Wollaston.

The more remote Mackenzie area overtaxed the technological resources of the reunited North West Company. The ice-free season was too short to

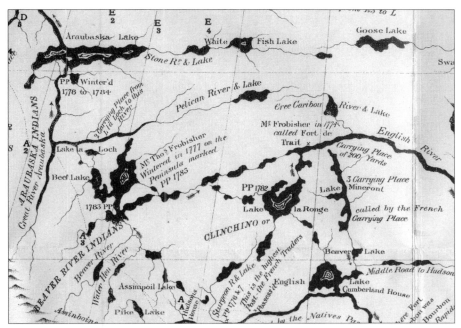

Detail of Peter Pond's 1785 map as it appears in Harold A. Innis, *Peter Pond: Fur Trader and Adventurer* (Toronto: Irwin & Gordon, 1930).

allow annual contact with Grand Portage headquarters on Lake Superior. In this regard, a leading expert on Fort Chipewyan has stated:

> The use of canoes rather than boats was probably a cause of the closure of the Mackenzie River posts in 1814. The frail craft had to be constantly attended and thus no thought was given to organizing two brigades for the Mackenzie River region so that canoes could be left at Portage La Loche.[9]

The North West Company, operating out of Montreal, employed French Canadians who were past masters with canoes and refused to adapt to new methods. Methy Portage called forth maximum exertion and passed into tradition as a badge of manhood.

Meanwhile, the old Hudson's Bay Company was trying to compete with the Canadians in their prime grounds, Athabasca. Peter Fidler, a surveyor, tried to find a new route to Athabasca, but came out via Methy in May 1792. Opposite the north end, he noticed a small provision post where Nor'westers stocked Peace River pemmican. The portage he considered in good shape except for the narrow, steep north end. Even so, 10 years later on his way to establish Nottingham House on Lake Athabasca, Fidler still took

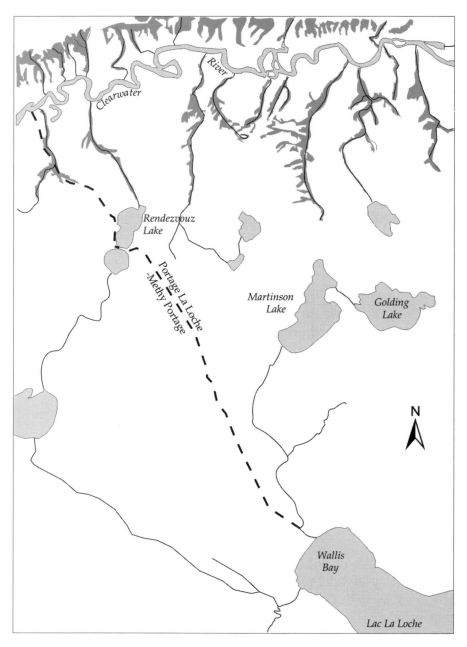

Methy Portage, northwest Saskatchewan.

George Simpson (1786/7–1860) photographed in 1857. In 1841, he was knighted, becoming "Sir George Simpson" (Courtesy of the Saskatchewan Archives Board/R-B3579).

one week to cross.[10] Aggressive Canadians at Fort Chipewyan soon forced the Bay men to retire. After another dozen years, the Hudson's Bay Company sent in more vigorous competitors. One of these, Colin Robertson, noted the need for supporting provisions to be sent from Carlton via Green Lake and the Beaver River to Île-à-la-Crosse. He also considered that "much benefit would result from Horses on this Portage."[11]

In 1820 the decisive figure of George Simpson appeared on the scene. His initial appointment was to the Athabasca area in the last year of competition. On the way in, he respected voyageur Methy tradition which required each new Bourgeois to give a dram of rum to the men or be "subject to the unpleasant process of shaving (as practised on board Ship in crossing the line)…"[12] but he also cast a shrewd eye on the state of the trail, calculating that, after improvements, steady men could take York boats and freight over in a week. Like Robertson before him, Simpson was frustrated by lack of support from the Île-à-la-Crosse depot.[13] However, talk of horses and carts ended when Simpson had digested the full implications of switching from canoes to York boats. In 1821 he was promoted to overall direction of the combined North West and Hudson's Bay companies and reorganized the transport of half a continent. Among other things, he incidentally relieved pressure on Portage La Loche (Methy) by soon opening up a regular route to the Columbia via a trail from Edmonton to Fort Assiniboine on the upper Athabasca[14] and by redirecting the New Caledonia returns to Fort Vancouver via the Okanagan Fur Brigade.

York boats were already in use in much of the Hudson's Bay Company territory.[15] The merger gave an opportunity to extend the system. Freight capacity per man was doubled, cheaper Orkneymen could displace expensive French Canadian canoe experts, and the boats lasted longer. In theory

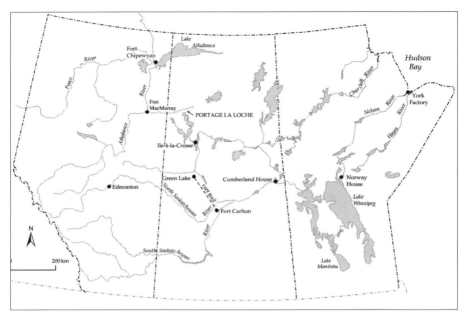

Access routes to the North-West.

or for special arctic expeditions, it was possible to take boats across the portage, at least from south to north. But to ask the men of the Athabasca Brigade to haul their boats to and fro every year made no sense when a two-boat system would allow them to store their craft at one end and simply take their freight over to identical boats at the other end.[16] From management's point of view, York boats were a labour-saving device. Those doing the work knew just the opposite. There might be one or even two more men in a boat, but the number of 90-pound "pieces" increased from 24 to 60 to 70 or more. The implications on Portage La Loche were considerable. Yet Simpson, with his characteristic greater concern for his cargoes than for his men, lost interest in making improvements there.

On May 21, 1823 the first four York boats were saluted by "2 Shotts with our cohorn" as they left Fort Chipewyan to inaugurate the system.[17] These boats would be kept at the west end of Portage La Loche until the crews returned in the autumn. The same men did the round trip from Fort Chipewyan to York Factory. The officer in charge of the returning Athabasca Brigade was instructed "to arrange your [second set of] four Boats at the east end for the Winter." Already in 1824 "a half breed (Beaulieu)" had been put in charge of the boat store "lately built" at that spot,[18] although a surprising number of people insist that at first York boats were dragged back and forth.

Replica of a York boat afloat on the Bigstone River at Cumberland House, August 1993 (courtesy of Greg Marchildon and Sid Robinson).

Isaac Cowie, in charge of the portage in its last days, is the source of this confusion.[19] Considering the slope of the north hill, he must have had too high an opinion of his predecessors. His superior officer, Roderick Ross, remarked of the boats that "once over the portage, they can never come back."[20]

Applying the York boat solution to the Mackenzie River problem required more careful timing. With canoes, two seasons were required before fur returns could reach the London market. Late breakup on Great Slave Lake meant that 30 Mackenzie men had to winter in Fort Chipewyan to take the fur the following spring to York Factory. Simpson calculated on "saving £1200" by getting most of the returns out the same year.[21] The Council of the Northern Department accordingly directed that a special brigade of York boats take in the Mackenzie outfit for 1826 to Portage La Loche and "interchange" for fur returns simultaneously brought thither from the Mackenzie district. The first rendezvous worked well, but the returning La Loche Brigade only just managed to connect with the ship at York Factory. In his anxiety to meet that mid-September deadline, Simpson explained to Chief Factor Edward Smith that his Mackenzie men would have to do most of the carrying on the portage.[22] Moreover, Norway House at the north end of Lake Winnipeg was made the advance depot for Macken-zie district. This permitted the La Loche Brigade, crewed by Red River Métis tripmen, to follow the breakup on Lake Winnipeg to Norway House, pick up the outfit and then ascend the Churchill system for a late July rendezvous at La Loche. Coming back, they would take the fur all the way to York Factory and convey the next season's outfit from York Factory as far as Norway House before returning in mid-fall to their Red River homes. These great distances and intricate timetables required strong leadership. For many years the dependable chief guide on the La Loche Brigade was a French Canadian, Alexis Bonamis *dit* L'Esperance, who had served in Simpson's own canoe to the Columbia, etc.[23] Although he could not even sign his own name, L'Esperance was the vital link between management and men and between supply base and isolated fur trader.

Once the overall strategy was settled, local circumstances governed the actual tactics on the portage itself. In the canoe era, voyageurs themselves had evolved a traditional response to the gruelling 12-mile Portage La Loche. James Keith, on one of the last trips before the shift to boats, noted,

> loaded Canoes of 25 Packages cargo and 5 men usually take 5 days. Each Voyageur contrary to the ordinary routine on the lesser Portages has a fair division of the Public cargo to transport, which if he fails, or is unable through want of strength or health to perform, his comrades will not fail to tax him accordingly at the rate of from 50 to 200 livres per Package. Here the Guides possess and exercise little author-ity or control. Such and such customs and regulations hav-ing tacitly been assented to by the different superintendents and conductors and understood and acted upon by the Voyageurs, from long usage constitute part of the Common Law of the Voyage, and however harsh, arbitrary and unjust in some respects, it is necessary to connive at their operation in order to prevent abuse and imposition from the more indolent and worthless who are very subject to feign or counterfeit disease or incapacity.[24]

Simpson's system did away with carrying craft over the portage. However, as we have seen, the extra capacity of York boats meant four or five or more trips per man. Also they could no longer count on using the lit-tle lake in the centre. The Athabasca men on their annual round trip to York Factory did the outward and return carries across the portage several weeks apart. The Mackenzie men had one ordeal which, as originally planned,

Sir John Franklin (1786–1847). The arctic explorer was knighted in 1829 (engraving courtesy of Library and Archives Canada/C-001352).

would have involved them in moving loads both ways over the whole portage. Very quickly a sensible division of labour was arrived at between the La Loche and Mackenzie Brigades. They exchanged at the south shore of Rendezvous Lake. The hill at the north end made that four miles a rough equivalent of the level southern eight miles of the portage. In addition to the regular fur-trade brigades, there were several British arctic expeditions which had the extra problem of taking in canoes or boats. For his second trip in 1825 Franklin constructed a little "truck" on the spot to carry his largest boat. In 1833 Captain Back and Dr. King were appalled by the severe dehydration suffered by their voyageurs in the dry eight-mile section.[25]

The difficulties of this particular portage were truly so exceptional that unusual solutions were necessary. Even hardened Chief Factors thought that "7 Trips over a distance of 12 miles with loads forming 91 miles" explained the reluctance of men to renew their contracts.[26] Another reported, "I positively saw one of the young hands, altho' lamed by severe cuts in his feet received before reaching the Portage, attempt to carry his share of the pieces, with the skin worn off his back by the friction of his loads..."[27] Assistance from Indians seemed the answer. Surely it was sensible to overlook the men paying for help on the portage? Simpson did not see it this way even though he had hired Indians to speed his crossing in 1828. He became "sick" of the subject.[28] Officers in charge of brigades were either "complaining of delays" or "corrupting the natives." For instance, the Île-à-la-Crosse district suffered because their Indians earned so much on the portage that they did not "sett a snare all Winter." Moreover, the Company's trading monopoly was being violated. The brigade tripmen were indulging in private trade![29] Catholic missionary sources confirm that "the portage was a perfect babel of tongues and tribes" for a whole month.[30] The Council of the Northern Department forbade the hiring of Indians at Portage La Loche, but Chief Factors of the Mackenzie district were anxious to reach Fort Simpson in time to resupply their trappers.[31] The resolve of Council had to be ignored.

The next idea was horses, again unofficially at first. In 1842 a Métis, "Old Cardinal," assisted with 34 pack horses. This saved effort and also damages to the packages because

> the portage La Loche Boys are a sett of rough & terrible fellows caring little for the contents of packages. All their *aim* is to get through the voyage as quick as possible, their cry is the *D—l take the hindermost*, helter, skelter, bing, bang, the pieces here & there on the portage.[32]

There were problems with the horses too. Sometimes the horses could not be harnessed because they were "running wild as Deer through the Woods."[33] They were brought each season from the prairies, many dying en route. At other times they were completely unavailable. The obvious need was for permanent, efficient management. A "freeman Desjarlais" was hired in 1848 to keep horses in the vicinity of the portage. The Company hoped to be able to rely on the service and to see the Indians get back to trapping. But grass was in short supply in the vicinity of the portage. Conditions were harsh. The horses were emaciated and "sorely galled on their backs."[34]

With the increased volume of freight, oxen and carts had to be employed in a systematic way. This reform was overdue. Simpson could not ignore the fact that the Arctic boat expedition of Dr. John Richardson had been delayed when disease killed all the horses. Also, Chief Trader James Anderson reported in 1850 that Indians were on the point of ambushing the brigades. Their women had been abused and their dogs shot by tripmen the previous year.[35] A more reliable method of transport was needed in order to avoid breakdowns, calling for old-fashioned portaging by tripmen or Indians. Accordingly, Chief Trader George Deschambeault was instructed to widen the trail, procure oxen, build carts and set up a post at Lac La Loche as part of Île-à-la-Crosse district.[36] This would also serve to check private trading by portage tripmen.

Although an improvement, oxen did not solve all difficulties. Horses and sleds were still needed for the north hill or Indians would have to be employed there. By the 1860s, 1,600 90-pound pieces were being sent in by 22 boats in several divisions of the La Loche and Athabasca Brigades. True, by holding tripmen and portage workers to about £20 a season, freight costs from York Factory were only 25% higher to Fort Chipewyan than to Île-à-la-Crosse. Moreover, the tariff charged Indians for these trade goods could be adjusted accordingly in Athabasca which thus could still average annual profits of about \$32,000.[37] Other problems remained despite the oxen. Economics were more adjustable than sandbars and tempers. Low water in the La Loche River so distressed the men that a general strike was feared.[38] As a result of the Riel excitement, some Red River tripmen in 1870 abandoned their loads near the mouth of the Saskatchewan River and returned home. Hasty improvisations prevented real distress in the Mackenzie district. Significantly, the Chief Factor there did not act on the suggestion that he send two boats over to Île-à-la-Crosse for provisions.[39] The hill was too intimidating.

Understandably, the search was on for new methods and routes. What is remarkable is the continued use of Portage La Loche with all its shortcomings. To avoid the many portages on the middle Churchill, an increasing part of the Athabasca outfit was first carted, then steam-boated to Carlton on the Saskatchewan River. From there it went overland to Green Lake and down the Beaver to Île-à-la-Crosse. This had been the old pemmican route to supply the northern brigades. However this was simply another approach to the same bottleneck at La Loche. A more daring attempt was made in the mid-1860s to open up a different route via Lac La Biche to the middle Athabasca. The Company had mixed results from these tests with York boats in the Grand Rapids of the Athabasca. A Roman Catholic venture in 1867 had to harness even nuns to drag its boat round that formidable obstacle.[40] With the mountain runoff in midsummer, it would be even more difficult taking the returns out against such a current. There was some consolation in reflecting that the hated free traders would also be prevented from having easy access to the profitable northern fur districts.

In the early 1870s a concerted effort was made to upgrade the Portage La Loche operation. The cart road was rebuilt from Carlton to the south end of Green Lake, where a holding depot was developed for the supplies in transit for the northern districts. The 21 oxen and the few horses working the portage were at first kept at Bull's House on the La Loche River.[41] Due to the harsh conditions, the attrition rate was 20% a year. In 1873 the cattle were shifted to the new post at Fort McMurray where feed was more plentiful. Ironically, two years later a great flood, the water rising 57 feet in one hour, drowned almost all the animals. Henry Moberly showed commendable initiative in rushing to La Biche to purchase more.[42] By using switchbacks, he also realigned the trail on the notorious north hill to its present modest slope. To avoid the portages and low water on the Clearwater he also suggested cutting a road from the middle of Portage La Loche across 20 miles to below the Cascade Rapids. This suggestion was refused but his energies were well employed in any case in maintaining the deeply rutted central

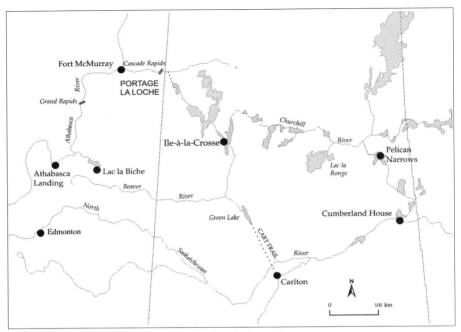

Routes from the Saskatchewan River Delta to the Athabasca River.

section of the portage.[43] By the 1880s a quarter of a million pounds of company and missionary freight were crossed from 31 boats whose arrival was spread out over the season.[44]

The Hudson's Bay Company was well aware of the potential of steam transport but wisely preferred not to become prematurely dependent on it. After the *Northcote* ascended the Saskatchewan to Carlton in 1874, the bulk of the northern outfits went via that route. But York boats were maintained out of Cumberland House, supplemented now by the boats from Lac La Ronge and Pelican Narrows.[45] A similar piecemeal approach was taken to introducing steamboats to the north. The first choice was the lower Athabasca-Peace-Slave section. Some of the machinery needed to build a steamboat at Fort Chipewyan came in by the traditional La Loche way in 1882.[46] This boat, named the *Grahame*, proved to be a success in her first full season of 1884, plying between the landings on the Clearwater and the Slave rivers.[47] Naturally, the relatively large steamboat could not be dragged past the rapids in these rivers as the York boats had been. This involved scows to connect between the north end of Portage La Loche and the bottom of Cascade Rapids. Moberly's road bypass idea was almost sanctioned. Indeed, the main portage was functioning reasonably well, being capable of crossing

[Sir] John Franklin's expedition making camp on Methy Portage, March 15, 1820. Original drawing by Lieutenant George Back, a member of the 1819–22 Franklin Expedition (courtesy of the Glenbow Archives/LAC-1344-4).

200 pieces a day with 30 oxen when transport officers like Moberly or Cowie rode across by horse three or four times a day to expedite matters. The holdup was the constant transshipment from scow to ox cart on the five small portages totalling almost 4.5 miles, especially when low water compounded the problem.[48]

Contemplating the overall system from the Saskatchewan to Great Slave Lake—the hideous melange of the old and the new, tumplines on men's backs, innumerable ox carts and assorted craft from *bateaux* to steamboats—Roderick Ross remarked with restraint: "It is clear that some system and order must be observed in moving freight through such a broken route."[49] So much handling magnified defects in packing, as a less philosophical recipient at the far end of the line protested: "It is wrong to put paint, oil, nails and raisins in the same case—there was a fine mixture and smash-up when I opened it."[50]

Clearly the *Grahame* was only the first stage of an overall plan. Another steamboat, this time for the lower Slave-Mackenzie system, was a logical follow-on. More daring was the testing of a radical change—by railway to Calgary, ox cart through Edmonton to Athabasca Landing and by scow past the Grand Rapids, etc. to connect with the *Grahame* near Fort McMurray.

Hitherto the Athabasca trail, completed a decade earlier, had been used only to supply the Peace River district. Wisely, the old La Loche route was kept up as well. Unhappily, the year was 1885. As an offshoot of Riel's North Saskatchewan River rebellion, some Indians stole a few items from the "pyramid" of supplies at the south end of Green Lake. Actually, the police who arrived to check out the incident took far more! Company officials simply billed the government, realizing that "looting was universal; from the General down to the smallest drummer boy…"[51] The confusion was worse than the actual loss. As usual, great exertions prevented real hardship among the trappers at the northern end of the long supply route.

Even more dramatic was the barge trip down the Athabasca to inaugurate the new route. Captain Smith and Chief Factor Camsell were taking in bulky machinery for the new steamboat to be constructed at Fort Smith. The excitement of the Riel trouble postponed the trip until harvest time when good men were less available. Also, low water made it more dangerous. To Smith's disgust, "the *things* we had in the shape of men" preferred eating to navigating. The steersman was an "*imbecile*" who "hung up" the barge on a rock, whereupon the boiler rolled overboard.[52] The answer seemed to lie in proper timing of the descents, trained crews, a tramway at Grand Rapids and either cheap one-way scows or strong trackers pulling on the return upstream.

In order not to overburden the new route, Portage La Loche was kept operating in 1886. Once again a freakish disaster incommoded the transport system. The *Marquis* half sank on the lower Saskatchewan, the *Northcote* was stopped by shoals, and only the *North West* made it up to Edmonton.[53] It was useful to have both the scows on the Athabasca and the oxen on Portage La Loche to rush in extra supplies. However, by its very nature, the La Loche run could not be operated fitfully at half volume. Oxen and men had to eat. It made sense to shift the cattle from there to the new transshipment bottleneck, the Fort Smith portage around the rapids of the Slave, and thus Portage La Loche was finally abandoned.[54]

Officers and employees, who had long advocated it,[55] all cheered the move away from the detested La Loche route, although they recognized that it had deterred competitors from penetrating their sacred northern fur preserves. Roderick MacFarlane, who had spent his career along the Mackenzie and as Chief Factor at Fort Chipewyan, best summed it up:

> Only those, however, who have had much experience of Inland Boating, of late years, can adequately appreciate the greatness of the Boon conferred by the introduction of Steam into the remote Districts of Athabasca and Mackenzie River.[56]

When change became inevitable, the ancient Company pioneered the real opening of the north to all comers despite thus ending its private, paternalistic empire. Another veteran officer, MacFarlane's successor, Roderick Ross, accurately saw the far-reaching implications:

> The Opposition will now permanently establish itself at Forts Chipewyan and Smith on the high road to McKenzie River District and although in some respects this may not be a desirable thing, yet in view of the needed reforms and change of policy in the conduct of the business, it will certainly help to hasten as well as facilitate action in that direction. With a cheap and efficient transport service and our trading establishments reduced from populous villages with schools and churches to store and shops in the hands of a manager with 2 or 3 assistants each, the Company should easily command the trade of the country in the face of all competition.[57]

Epilogue

Nearly 100 years later, in the sandy soil, the old Portage La Loche trail strangely still has the appearance of a heavily travelled route with even hints of a double track of the ox carts. The chief users now are occasional local Indians with snowmobiles for essential subsistence hunting, and the annual brigade of eight north canoes of St. John's School which believes in doing unpleasant routes the hard way. Also in June 1978 there was a special re-enactment of Peter Pond's historic trip. Nothing seems to have been done yet on the excellent 1969 proposal by Henry Epp and Tim Jones to make the portage a Saskatchewan Historic and Nature Trail.[58] Remoteness is its real protection so far. But a cut-line of the mid-1970s intrudes at Mile Three. A fire tower

Faint ruts left behind by the big wooden wheels of ox carts from the late fur trade era are still visible in a few places on Portage La Loche (Methy Portage), such as on this section photographed in 1986 (courtesy of Greg Marchildon and Sid Robinson).

on a ridge opposite the north end keeps watch over the area. At the south end a recent National Historic Sites monument recounts some of the former significance of the route.

Things seem to have come full circle. It is nice to come across places, in a natural setting, essentially unchanged from another age. One can attempt to pace off the old halting places or "poses" such as "La Vieille" near Mile Five.[59] The "old woman," the wind, was usually his enemy but here a welcome breeze cooled the sweat off the voyageur as he smoked his "pipe" and thought of distant Montreal. One gains insight into the transcontinental unity of the Canadian experience. As Innis said, we are a nation because of geography not in spite of it.[60]

Notes

This article first appeared in *Prairie Forum* 5, no. 1 (1980): 51–66.

1. Eric Morse, *Fur Trade Canoe Routes of Canada: Then and Now* (Ottawa: R. Duhamel, 1968), 17.

2. W.O. Kupsch, "A Valley View in Verdant Prose: The Clearwater Valley from Portage La Loche," *Musk-Ox* 20 (1977): 28–49.

3. Hudson's Bay Company Archives (HBCA), Provincial Archives of Manitoba, E37/1 James Anderson Diary, 18/9/1850. Permission to quote from the Hudson's Bay Company Archives is gratefully acknowledged.

4. D.N. Steer, "History and Archaeology of the Historic Site of La Loche House," *Musk-Ox* 12 (1973): 16, note 9. Also, D.N. Steer, "The History and Archaeology of a North West Company Trading Post and a Hudson's Bay Company Transport Depot, Lac La Loche, Saskatchewan," Manuscript Report Number 280, Parks Canada, 1977.

5. J. Richardson, *Arctic Searching Expedition*, vol. 1 (London: n.p. 1851), 108. C.S. Houston (ed.), *To the Arctic by Canoe 1819–1821: The Journal and Paintings of Robert Hood, Midshipman with Franklin* (Montreal: Arctic Institute of North America, 1974), 115, note 35.

6. H.A. Innis, *Peter Pond: Fur Trader and Adventurer* (Toronto: Irwin & Gordon, 1930), 83.

7. W.S. Wallace (ed.), *Documents Relating to the North West Company* (Toronto: The Champlain Society, 1934), 277.

8. W. Kaye Lamb (ed.), *The Journals and Letters of Sir Alexander Mackenzie* (Toronto: Macmillan, 1970), 437.

9. J. Parker, "The Fur trade of Fort Chipewyan on Lake Athabasca 1778–1835" (MA thesis, University of Alberta, 1967), 66.

10. HBCA E3/1 Peter Fidler's Journals and B 39/a/1 Nottingham House Journal, September 1802.

11. C. Robinson to Governor Williams, 25/1/1820 in E.E. Rich (ed.), *Colin Robertson's Correspondence Book: September 1817 to September 1822* (Toronto: The Champlain Society, 1939), 267. HBCA B190/a/2, September 11, 1819.

12. E.E. Rich (ed.), *Journal of Occurrences in the Athabasca Department by George Simpson, 1820–1821, and Report* (Toronto: The Champlain Society, 1938), 36.

13. Ibid., 248.

14. J.S. Galbraith, *The Little Emperor, Governor Simpson of the Hudson's Bay Company* (Toronto: Macmillan of Canada, 1976). Also, inscription on National Historic Sites monument at south end Methy Portage.

15. J.A. Alwin, "Mode, Pattern and Pulse. Hudson's Bay Company Transport 1670 to 1821" (PhD dissertation, University of Manitoba, 1978).

16. HBCA D4/2 fo. 11, G. Simpson to J.G. McTavish, Île-à-la-Crosse 11/11/1822.

17. HBCA B39/a/21b, fo. 74, Fort Chipewyan Journal, 21/5/1823.

18. HBCA B39/a/22, fo. 3, E. Smith to J. Keith, 5/9/1823. B 39/a/22, fo. 53, 6/6/ 1824. See note 4 above.

19. Isaac Cowie, *Company of Adventurers: A Narrative of Seven Years in the Service of the Hudson's Bay Company During 1867–1874, on the Great Buffalo Plains, with Historical and Biographical Notes and Comments* (Toronto: W. Briggs, 1913), 135. S.C. Ells, Northland Trails (Toronto: n.p., 1956), 190–202. F.J. Alcock, "Past and Present Trade Routes to the Canadian Northwest," *The Geographical Review* (1920): 72. National Historic Sites monument, south end Methy Portage.

20. HBCA D20/37, fo. 92, R. Ross to J. Wrigley, Île-à-la-Crosse, 20/1/86.

21. HBCA B200/4/2, fo. 8, Fort Simpson Correspondence, note by A.R. Macleod, 3/1824 "Inventories and cost of transport." A1271, fo. 179, para 56, G. Simpson to Governor and Committee, 8/1825.

22. R.H. Fleming (ed.), *Minutes of Council, Northern Department of Rupert's Land 1821–31* (Toronto: The Champlain Society, 1940), p. 131. HBCA D4/12, fo. 113, G. Simpson to E. Smith, 20/6/27.

23. J. Turner, "The La Loche Brigade," *The Beaver* (1943). HBCA A32/22, fo. 7, contracts of Alexis Bonamis *dit* L'Esperance. J.J. Gunn, *Echoes of the Red* (Toronto: Macmillan, 1930), Ch. 3.

24. HBCA B39/a/ 22, fo. 24, Journal of James Keith from York Factory 1823.

25. J. Franklin, *Narrative of a Second Journey to the Shores of the Polar Sea in the Years 1825, 1826, and 1827* (Edmonton: n.p., 1971), 3. R. King, *Narrative of a Journey to the Shores of the Arctic Ocean in 1833, 1834 and 1835*, vol. 1 (London: n.p., 1836), 88.

26. HBCA D5/4, fo. 222, E. Smith to Governor, Chief Factors and Chief Traders, Fort Chipewyan, 1/1/37.

27. HBCA D5/5, fo. 371, J. Lewes to G. Simpson, Fort Simpson, 20/11/1840.

28. M. McLeod (ed.), *Peace River: A Canoe Voyage from Hudson's Bay to Pacific by Sir George Simpson in 1828, Journal of the late Chief Factor, Archibald McDonald (Hon. Hudson's Bay Company) Who Accompanied Him* (Toronto: Coles, 1971), 9. W.S. Wallace (ed.), *John McLean's Notes of a Twenty-Five Years' Service in the Hudson's Bay Territories* (Toronto: The Champlain Society, 1932), 309.

29. HBCA D5/6 fo. 83, R. Mackenzie (Senior) to Governor, C.F. and C.T., Île-à-la-Crosse, 1/3/41; ditto fo. 85, (Private) Mackenzie to Simpson, 2/3/41. HBCA D4/58, fo. 156b, G. Simpson to J. Lewes, 28/6/41.

30. P. Duchaussois, *Mid Snow and Ice: The Apostles of the North-west* (London: Burns, Oates & Washbourne Ltd., 1923), 97.

31. HBCA 239/k/2, fo. 124, Northern Department, Minutes of Council, 1836; ditto, fo. 219, Minutes for 1841. D5/4, fo. 222, E. Smith to Governor, D.F. and C.T., Fort Chipewyan, 1/1/37.

32. G.P. de T. Glazebrook (ed.), *The Hargrave Correspondence 1821–1843* (Toronto: The Champlain Society, 1938), 325. (Private) J. Lewes to J. Hargrave, Fort Simpson, 11/1840.

33. HBCA D5/18, fo. 520, C. Campbell to Governor, C.F. and C.T., Fort Chipewyan, 24/12/46.
34. HBCA B239/k/2, fo. 424, Minutes of Northern Council, 1848. D5/22, fo. 415, M. McPherson to Governor, C.F. and C.T., Portage La Loche, 30/7/48.
35. HBCA D5/22, fo. 335, J. Bell to G. Simpson, Portage La Loche, 5/7/48. J. Richardson, *Arctic Searching Expedition*, vol. 1: 108. HBCA E 37/9, fo. I, J. Anderson to G. Simpson, Fort Chipewyan, 29/ 10/50.
36. HBCA B239/k/3, fos. 29, 102, Minutes of Northern Council, 1852, 1855.
37. HBCA B239/k/3, fos. 369, 374, 376, Minutes of Northern Council 1867, 1868. B89/d/161, "Voyaging Expenses at Île-à-la-Crosse 1872." D20/ 31, fo. 264, R. MacFarlane to J. Wrigley, 24/12/84. D20/31, fo. 124, MacFarlane to Wrigley, 2/12/84, enclosing "Returns for Athabasca 1858–1883."
38. HBCA B39/b/18, fo. 10b, A. Christie to Acting Governor, C.F. and C.T., Fort Chipewyan, 24/12/65.
39. HBCA B154/ 6/10, fo. 460, J.G. Stewart to Governor and Council, Norway House, 12/7/70. B200/b/38, fo. 61, Fort Simpson Inward Correspondence, W. McMurray to W.L. Hardisty, 10/10/70.
40. HBCA B89/b/6b, fo. 15, R. Ross to J. Wrigley, 10/3/85. B39/a/45, fo. 23, Fort Chipewyan Journal, 2/11/65. B39/b/19, fo. 8, W. McMurray to Governor, C.F. and C.T. Fort Chipewyan, 31/12/67. P. Duchaussois, *The Grey Nuns in the Far North: 1867–1917* (Toronto: McClelland & Stewart, 1919), 107.
41. HBCA D20/1, fo. 383, H. Moberly to R. MacFarlane, Fort Chipewyan, 15/9/74.
42. H. Moberly, *When Fur Was King* (Toronto: J.M. Dent, 1929), 151.
43. HBCA E23/1, Journal of Inspecting Chief Factor W.J. Christie, Sept. 29, 1872. D20/1, fo. 193, R. MacFarlane to Chief Commissioner J. Grahame, 24/7/74. Geological Survey of Canada, Report of Progress 1875–76, *Report by Professor Macoun*, 174.
44. HBCA B89/b/6b, fo. 4, Ross to Chief Commissioner J. Wrigley, Île-à-la-Crosse, 10/2/85, "Transport Estimates for 1881." B167/a/4, Portage La Loche Transport Journal 1885. B89/b/6a, fo. 88b, R. Ross, "Transport Memorandum Season 1885," Île-à-la-Crosse, 20/1/85. D20/30, fo. 119, W.J. MacLean to J. Grahame, 5/9/84.
45. HBCA D20/30, fo. 198, H. Belanger to J. Wrigley, Cumberland House, 27/9/84. HBCA B89/b6A fo. 23b, E. Macdonald to Grahame, Île-à-la-Crosse, 6/8/82.
47. J.G. MacGregor, *Paddle Wheels to Bucket Wheels on the Athabasca* (Toronto: McClelland & Stewart, 1974), 87–89.
48. HBCA D20/1, fo. 355, H. Moberly to R. MacFarlane, Portage La Loche, 15/8/74. H. Moberly, *When Fur Was King*, 151. D20/33, fo. 88, "Sketch Plan of Clearwater," by W.S. Simpson (1884).
49. HBCA B89/b/6a, fo. 90b, R. Ross to J. Wrigley, Île-à-la-Crosse, 20/1/85.
50. HBCA D20/31, fo. 280, Extracts from J. Flett (Fort Resolution) to R. MacFarlane (Fort Chipewyan), 13/12/84.
51. HBCA D20/35, fo. 85, L. Clarke to J. Wrigley, 14/7/85.
52. HBCA D20/36, fo. 198, John M. Smith to Wrigley, 8/ 10/85.
53. B. Peel, *Steamboats on the Saskatchewan* (Saskatoon: Western Producer, 1972), 196, 198. HBCA D13/8, fo. 75b, J. Wrigley to W. Armit, Secretary, London.
54. HBCA D20/43, fo. 259, Fortescue to J. Wrigley, Île-à-la-Crosse, 27/ 12/86. B 307/a/3, fos. 75, 76, Fort McMurray Journal, 23/6/87, 9/7/87.

55. HBCA D20/ 1, fo. 674, W. Hardisty to Chief Commissioner Grahame, Fort Simpson, 1/12/74. D20/20, fo. 229, R. MacFarlane to Grahame, Fort Chipewyan, 23/10/81.

56. HBCA D20/36, fo. 142, R. MacFarlane to J. Wrigley, Fort Chipewyan, 22/9/85.

57. HBCA D20/40, fo. 130, R. Ross to J. Wrigley, 19/6/86.

58. Henry T. Epp and Tim Jones, "The Methy Portage-Proposal for a Saskatchewan Historic and Nature Trail," *The Blue Jay* (June 1969).

59. J. Richardson, *Arctic Searching Expedition*, vol. 1: 111, note.

60. H.A. Innis, *The Fur Trade in Canada: An Introduction to Canadian Economic History* (1930; Toronto: University of Toronto Press, 1956), 393. But see also W.J. Eccles, "A Belated Review of Harold Adams Innis, *The Fur Trade in Canada*," *Canadian Historical Review* (1979): 440.

7.   **"Victuals to Put into our Mouths": Environmental Perspectives on Fur Trade Provisioning Activities at Cumberland House, 1775–1782**

George Colpitts

This article appraises provisioning activities at the Hudson's Bay Company (HBC) post, Cumberland House, between 1775 and 1782. By analyzing the post's initial eight years of operation, it offers a quantitative assessment of the nature of provisioning in the North American fur trade. While historians, ethnologists and geographers have noted the important roles Indians played in providing country food to posts and have identified specialization among some provisioners like the Assiniboine and Cree,[1] few studies have fully assessed the extent of these activities, the size of provisioning hinterlands, and other factors such as resource exhaustion that might have influenced the "victualling" of individual posts.

This shortfall in the historiography of the fur trade deserves more attention. An examination of several 19th-century post journals[2] reveals that posts often traded more for food than furs. As well as buying provisions from visiting or Home Guard Indians, many employees daily maintained gardens, fished, mended nets, hunted, and—in season—left their posts to live and hunt with Indians. The numbers of post employees dedicated to foraging activities represented a formidable operating cost for the HBC and other fur-trading companies.

A quantitative analysis of Cumberland House's provisioning activities sheds further light on these features of post life. It also raises questions about a number of assumptions regarding Indian hunting behaviour during the fur trade, behaviour linked to resource depletion. A culmination of ruthless competition between rival trading companies and traders' long-term meat requirements is believed to have caused Indians to deplete the beaver and game resources of northern Ontario, central and southern Manitoba, and Saskatchewan by 1821.[3] To explain this apparently destructive behaviour,

A sketch of Cumberland House from the *Canadian Illustrated News*, published in Montreal, June 12, 1875 (courtesy of the Archives of Manitoba/N21477).

scholars have suggested that an ecological "disequilibrium" was achieved—that Indians fell out of traditional, harmonious relationships with nature into *unnatural* trapping and provisioning—or that economic profit motives existed and shaped Indian activities.[4] Our present understandings of such issues might benefit from a fuller historical analysis of the hunting effort required to deplete forests and watersheds,[5] and of the extent to which Indians significantly altered their seasonal activities to participate in the trade. Furthermore, food shortages periodically marking post life, raising the price of provisions, slowing the trade and threatening the existence of Indian and trader alike, can find a meaningful and informative context within a local environment and ecological setting.[6]

Cumberland House journals show that post employees collected their provisions seasonally and often according to wildlife population cycles. Periodic food shortages which became apparent almost immediately after the post was constructed can be attributed to the local environment and the post's social organization. Cumberland employees, after all, were members of a semisedentary society. They were required to seek alternative provisions when nearby meat resources could not sustain their needs. At Cumberland House, food scarcities forced employees to specialize in fishing and widen the post's provisioning hinterlands. In short, they changed their eating habits and got their food from farther afield. These changes can be recognized in a quantitative analysis of post journals over an eight-year period, when employees periodically consumed less fresh, or "green," meat and replaced it in their diets by eating more dried meat from ever more distant hunting grounds. Records are not explicit, but the buffalo seems to have played an increasingly important dietary role at Cumberland House by 1782.

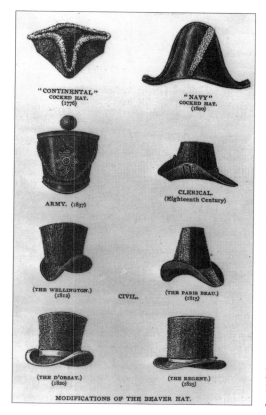

"Modifications of the Beaver Hat." The huge European demand for hats such as these in the late 18th and the early 19th centuries caused the fur trade to boom in British North America (courtesy of the Archives of Manitoba/N8318).

This assessment has wider implications for fur trade studies. From its beginnings the trade clearly was burdened with a costly and onerous provisioning challenge that not only affected post life, but determined some of the post's interaction with Indians and tested some of the commercial viability of the fur trade itself.[7]

Cumberland House was established in 1774, the first HBC post on the Saskatchewan River. The company had sent Samuel Hearne to establish the house in response to the prior incursions and effective competition of Montreal pedlars.[8] Constructed in 1775 on Pine Lake in present-day Saskatchewan, the trading post constituted the furthest step inland by the company after its construction of Henley House on the Albany River. It also marked the beginnings of an intensive trade rivalry between Canadian traders and the HBC that would extend along the North Saskatchewan and up the Athabasca Rivers. This trade rivalry resulted in the building of more posts and the placement and of more men. It also increased food requirements.[9] Transporting provisions to the interior—corn, wild rice, oatmeal and flour—constituted a staggering expense, as did buying food from Indians. Alexander Henry the Younger's reference to "the vast quantity of provision we require yearly to carry on the trade in the northwest," included not only the thousands of pounds of meat required at posts, but the massive quantities vital for the success of canoe brigades going in and out of trading areas.[10]

Although strategically situated to tap both western and northern fur

Samuel Hearne, the founder of Cumberland House (courtesy of Library and Archives Canada/ C-020053).

regions,[11] Cumberland House was less fortunate with respect to food resources. Unlike the posts situated in "Buffalo Country," Cumberland was located in the boreal forest, between the Precambrian Shield to the north and the edge of the Great Plains to the south. Philip Turnor's late-18th-century map shows a conspicuously empty game region surrounding Cumberland House, unlike the abundant "southern Indian country" along the South and North Saskatchewan Rivers.[12] At Cumberland House, conifers, especially white and black spruce, were dominant. Wildlife such as moose (*Alces alces*) were fairly abundant and Pine Lake held whitefish (*Coregonus clupeaformis*), sturgeon (*Acipenser fulvescens*), pike (*Esox lucius*), and perch.[13]

Indians had adopted seminomadic lifestyles to compensate for an environment noted for cyclical and seasonal food availability.[14] A.J. Ray has studied the seasonal migrations of the Cree and Assiniboine in this light. The Cree inhabited woodland areas where they hunted moose and beaver during the summer and early fall, and moved to the parkland belt during the winter. The Assiniboine spent the warmer months in the grasslands and moved into the parkland belt during winter.[15] This "exploitation" cycle allowed Indians to take advantage of the hunting opportunities of both environments.

Cumberland House employees did not enjoy such mobility. As a social organization the post was quite different from Native bands and the small, highly mobile groups of pedlars who operated extensively to the north, west and south of the house.[16] When Matthew Cocking replaced Hearne as the post's chief trader in 1775 and had to oversee the dietary requirements of fifteen employees, he immediately set out to exploit fish populations in Pine Lake, encouraged trade in provisions, and built up a meat surplus sufficient to withstand privations.[17] A "victualling shed" was built and a garden planted. Cocking's intention was to compensate for the sedentary nature of the post's social organization by stocking a surplus of food and exploiting nearby resources.

The strategy might have succeeded had nearby game resources not been susceptible to depletion. Country food was marked by seasonal availability and sometimes dramatic natural population cycles. Wildfowl was available only in spring and fall. Rabbits and pheasants also followed population fluctuations. Within a year of arriving at Cumberland House, Cocking heard from Indians that lynx (or "inland cats") were unavailable due to the scarcity of rabbits, this explaining why HBC men had no success snaring hares that winter and the next.[18] Even fish populations moved within Pine Lake according to seasonal water temperatures and oxygen levels.[19] Post employees set out virtually year-round with nets, but sturgeon, trout, perch and whitefish were abundant only in specific periods of the year, when schools were within reach. The catch generally fell off by January and remained poor until March.

During late winter, meat provisions began dwindling when weather conditions prevented trading Indians from travelling. While in summer and fall moose moved to watered areas where they could be hunted with relative ease and transported by canoe, by late October rivers and lake systems were beginning to ice over. A master learned that any significant stores of meat had to be collected by fall, "when the Buck Moose are Fat, and the Indians have the convenience of Canoes."[20] By January, with northern winds howling outside and few visitors likely to arrive, house rations were often cut in half.

Traders, then, faced periodic, if not predictable provisioning constraints throughout the year. As at all trading posts, a seasonal cycle dominated the provisioning activities at Cumberland House (Figure 1).

This provisioning cycle, however, raises a number of questions. The extent to which changing game populations affected traders is not fully known. This is of critical importance when considering big game. The primary meat resource at Cumberland House was moose, still relatively abundant in the lakes region of present-day Saskatchewan and Manitoba. Indians delivered moose in a variety of forms: fresh ("green"), "beat" (Indians pounded it between rocks and sometimes added dried fish to the composite), dried and "half-dried."[21] Of these, green meat was a favoured trade commodity, especially after long periods of rationing and dried meat consumption. It fetched higher prices for trading Indians.[22] The extent to which forests nearby were depleted of moose over time is not known, but a close examination of the post's green meat consumption ought to show whether numbers of moose killed locally, and sold fresh for higher prices, changed over time.

An expanding provisioning hinterland might also indicate local resource

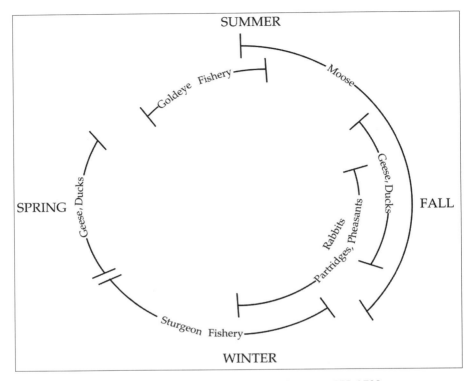

Figure 1. Major seasonal provisioning activities, Cumberland House: 1775–1782.

exhaustion. A growing scarcity in moose might have encouraged provisioning Indians from further west to trade. If that was the case, post records ought to indicate the arrival of more Indians from distant game regions and different meat being introduced, particularly buffalo.

Quantitative analysis of the post journals helps shed light on these issues. Few of Cumberland House's account books, which would have indicated changing prices of country food, have survived.[23] However, the HBC Archives preserved the post's journals of daily occurrences from 1775 well into the 19th century. The present study analyzes the first eight years of these journals in an attempt to find the *relative* amounts, description and origins of country foods reaching the post. At the end of the period studied, Hudson House was supplying Cumberland with more quantities of provisions, notably buffalo, and the complex relationship between these two posts beyond this period requires further investigation.[24] The Cumberland House journals which have been analyzed nevertheless provide valuable information about the size of fish catches, the numbers of rabbits snared and partridges shot—commodities often collected by employees which, because no trade items were exchanged for them, would not appear in account ledgers. These journals offer, then, a rich source of information for estimating the total effort directed towards stocking provisions at the post as well as the volume of the food trade taking place with Indians.

Seasonal and cyclical changes in game and fish resources have been assessed by comparing monthly totals of species reaching the post and appearing in the journals' daily entries. The sturgeon, geese, swans, ducks, partridges (known also as "pheasants"), and rabbits brought back to the post were frequently enumerated explicitly. Sturgeon, unlike smaller lake fish, attracted the attention of journal writers, possibly due to the species' size which ranged from 15 to 85 pounds in weight. The specific number of this type of fish, therefore, was usually well recorded.

A number of problems arise, however, in the assessment of moose and of fish other than sturgeon. Often expressions such as "a few fish," or "three canoes arrived with moose," were used by the journal writers. For purposes of comparison, meat has here been measured by the numbers of canoes bringing it to the post. The total weight of meat carried in canoes obviously varied. It was sometimes as high as 250 pounds,[25] often the amount of meat taken from a killed moose. Difficulties with this unit of measure are encountered in winter entries, when the few provisions arriving at the post were listed by the number of sleds or the number of Indians arriving to trade. In these cases, the study has converted two "sleds" to equal one "canoe," for the sake of comparison. Likewise, individuals occasionally arrived at the post carrying between 45 to 80 pounds of meat.[26] For the purpose of these estimates, four trading individuals have here been represented as carrying the equivalent of one canoe of provisions. As for daily fish catches described as "a few," "a great success at the nets," "not much success at the nets," and "a middling success at the nets," the values of three, ten, two and five, respectively, have been assigned to these occurrences in the journals.

Many of these figures, then, will not show real quantities of food resources. Only occasionally do the post journals clearly list inventories of meat (see Figure 2).[27] The journals rarely list the total number of pounds of provisions traded by Indians. What has been assumed is that expressions such as "a few" were used consistently, and just as wildlife population surveys are presently conducted with margins of error, it is expected that errors will occur consistently in the survey. The survey's value, then, lies not in its ability to show the actual number of moose and fish collected, but in its ability to indicate change in provisioning over time.

A final note on methodology is required. Post journals were often

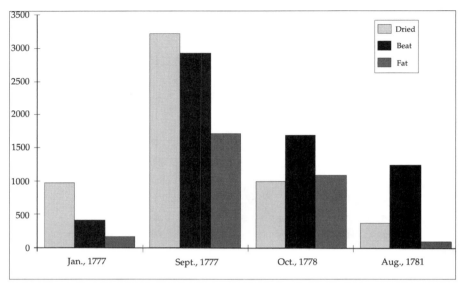

Figure 2. Inventories of provisions in Cumberland House, 1777, 1778, 1781 (in pounds).

explicit about the canoes of fresh meat arriving at the post, possibly because they brought food more costly in terms of trade goods, and also because employees preferred fresh meat to dried meat. On several occasions the expression "a canoe of provisions" was used by a journal writer to describe a cargo of green meat, its freshness identifiable only when men were assigned to smoke or dry portions of it the day after it was traded. These cargoes have been counted as "green." Furthermore, since the purpose of the green meat survey is to see nearby population cycles,[28] moose that were killed near the post by Home Guard Indians and post employees have been assumed to be green, even though portions of this meat were likely dried for future use.

The post journals show that the total amount of meat arriving at Cumberland House varied according to the season. Canoes of provisions arrived in greatest frequency in August and September, while much smaller numbers of canoes reached the post in May (Figure 3). The meat trade ended abruptly in October, when rivers and streams finally froze over and Indians could bring only small amounts of meat by sled. Chief trader Cocking was quite surprised by the arrival in March 1777 of four Sweet Herb Lake Indians with a "trifle" of provisions, but "according to their Number [they had brought] much more Provisions than I could have expected at this Time of the Year such a Distance."[29] Fish (Figures 4 and 5), wildfowl (Figure 6), partridges and rabbits (Figures 7 and 8), meanwhile, display an availability

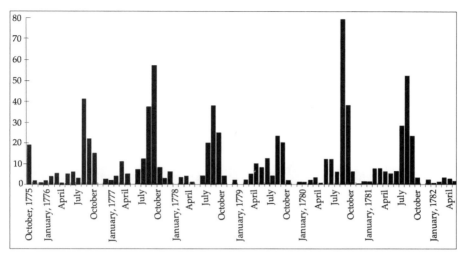

Figure 3. Meat, dry and green, reaching Cumberland House, 1775–1782 (by number of canoes).

in specific seasons of the year. The figures also display peaks and lows in natural population cycles: for instance, an abundant year for pheasants is clearly discernible in 1780, while rabbits were reaching their cyclical peak in 1778.

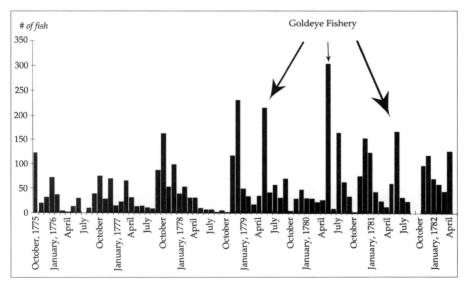

Figure 4. Fish, all species, Cumberland House, 1775–1782.

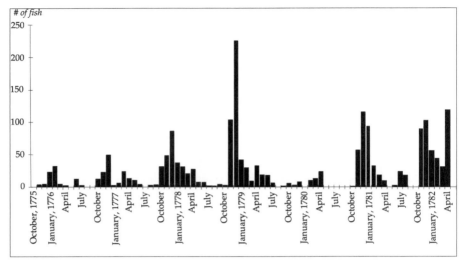

Figure 5. Sturgeon Fishery, Cumberland House, 1775–1782.

William Cocking adapted his post's sedentary organization to such seasonal and cyclical population changes in a number of ways. In October of the first year inland Cocking sent William Walker, one of the post's employees, to winter with Indians at Cranberry Portage, "to be supported" by the Indians and aid in hunting. In late December, Walker returned with two

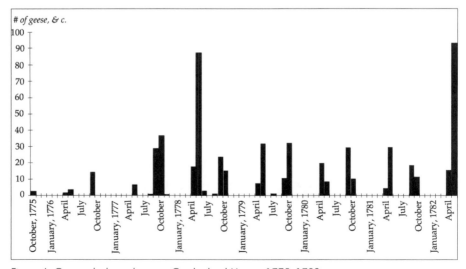

Figure 6. Geese, ducks and swans, Cumberland House, 1775–1782.

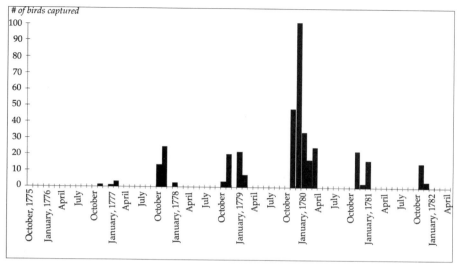

Figure 7. Total "pheasants" and "partridges," Cumberland House, 1775–1782.

sleds of moose and beaver flesh.[30] Sending post employees away "to be sup-ported" became a common strategy, especially when nets were falling off by January and provisions were scant. In those cold, hungry months in 1779, for instance, Nicholas Wishart was sent "away with Indians to be supported" and to "assist in bringing in provisions, when they may kill a moose."[31]

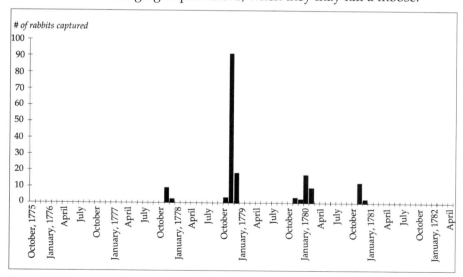

Figure 8. Rabbits captured at Cumberland House, 1775–1782.

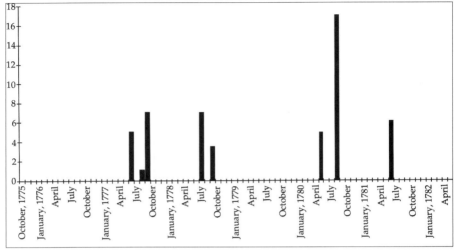

Figure 9. Buffalo provisions reported, Cumberland House, 1775–1782.

The post also drew provisions from Home Guard "hunter" Indians living nearby in camps. Some provided considerable food for the post, such as one unnamed individual described by Cocking as "the only Indian that has continued by us this Winter" and who supplied the post with 740 pounds of

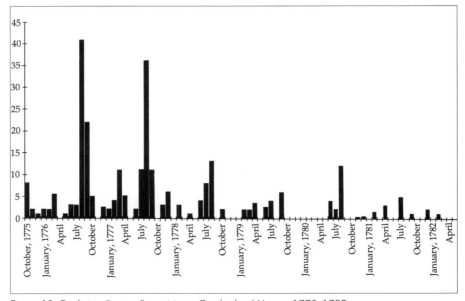

Figure 10. Declining "moose" provisions, Cumberland House, 1775–1782.

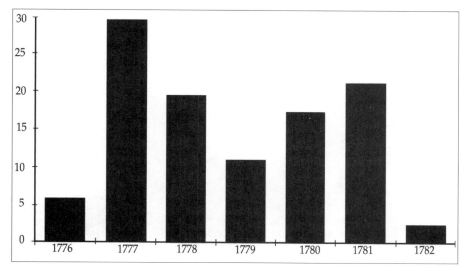

Figure 11. Canoes of "green" meat supplying Cumberland House, 1776 to May 1782.

fresh moose meat.[32] Often encamped nearby in the late summer to trade furs, some Indians were persuaded to stay on to hunt geese and, later, meat for the post in the winter. From their "wooder" camps, these hunters often sent for rum and ammunition, and shared portions of their animal kills with the post.

The limited returns of this local hunting, however, are apparent in the journals. The Basquio Indians who stayed on during the first winter to hunt for the post complained that "no moose are about,"[33] echoing the hunter Indians in 1778 who pointed out that there were "no moose stirring" in local forest.[34] Even when a hunter occasionally killed a moose that provided upwards of 300 pounds of meat, given the number of mouths to feed, one moose could be expected to serve only eight days of provisions.[35]

During inevitable periods of scarcity, post masters reduced rations accordingly and saw to it that food remained well preserved in the victualling shed. The shed itself was frequently upgraded, rotting floors replaced and provisions frequently "turned."

But always supplementing the pantry at Cumberland House was its "everlasting resource of fish."[36] It is apparent that the post modified both its fishing technology and technique in the face of meat shortages. At first, the post's fishermen used regular fishing twine, susceptible to damage, for their sturgeon nets. In fact, for every day that nets were being used, another was often spent repairing them. By 1777, the post had acquired "Italian" twine

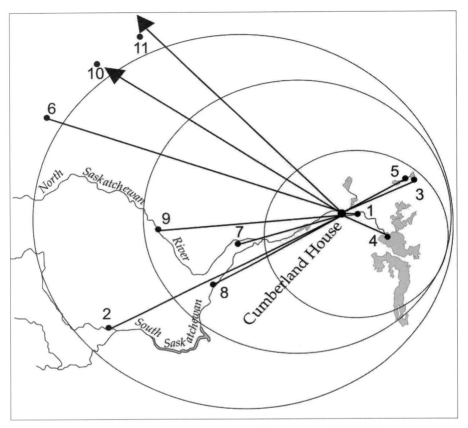

Figure 12. An expanding provisioning hinterland, Cumberland House, 1775–1782.

that proved better for sturgeon but tended to swell in the water. Jack twine, too rigid for the smaller species of fish, was eventually used exclusively for sturgeon. Together with these technological improvements, post fishermen adapted their techniques. Journals are not explicit but it seems that fishermen no longer fished at random in Pine Lake: they chose proven locations and netted individual species. The expression "sturgeon nets" was used more frequently after 1780, almost always in reference to the fishing taking place in late November and December; fishermen by then had found locations under the ice favourable to that species. Cocking, meanwhile, often sent men upriver to specific locations, and by 1779 the post had obviously discovered local runs of goldeye, with spring catches sometimes numbering eighty to ninety fish per day. By the third year, whitefish were netted more consistently in November.

The best evidence of changing technique can be seen in a significantly improved sturgeon fishery. As Figure 5 indicates, December 1778 was a record year for sturgeon, with some 225 fish netted that month alone. Although the following seasons declined, all winters after 1777 had more efficient fishing than the winters of 1775 and 1776. Indeed, in the early years most references to the fishery state that two or three sturgeon had been netted daily during favourable seasons—whereas, by 1781, fishermen were netting between 10 and 30 per day. This was probably due to increased knowledge of the habits of these fish under the ice and to the introduction of deeper-sunk nets.

However, the post's men required more than fish. Desperate for meat to survive the winter, employees often traded significant quantities of goods, especially liquor and tobacco, to provisioning Indians and occasionally cut off the fur trade altogether to purchase food instead.[37] Even with these efforts, food was rarely abundant. In 1778, the post diarist noted that hunters were having no luck finding game, and "our whole dependence must be now intirely [*sic*] on a few Buffalo Indians who used to come down in the fall."[38] The next year, the post journal lamented the few provisions reaching the post; in August, the writer pointed out that "if it had not been for netting a few fish, we should not have had a mouthful to have puten [*sic*] in in our mouths."[39] Between September 1779 and January 1780, the post received almost no green meat stores, except for partridges and one deer.[40] Finally, in 1782, William Tomison, then in charge of Cumberland House, noted that he had never seen such scarcity. That winter he had seen no more than six sides of moose; rabbits and partridges were scarce; and fish were not "plentiful."[41]

Such scarcity likely had many causes. Smallpox struck Indians around Cumberland and its outpost, Hudson House, in 1781, severely reducing the furs brought in by these disease-stricken people. Provisioning also dropped: strong competition from the pedlars also meant that provisions were often traded before they reached Cumberland.[42]

Whatever the causes for such scarcity, Figure 11 shows that green meat stores rose and fell dramatically. Rather than suggesting that local game populations were being depleted, the figure communicates a number of possibilities: that nearby moose underwent cyclical population change, or that local Indians and Home Guard "hunters" experienced variable success in finding moose. A third possibility is that local Indians participated inconsistently in the provisioning trade, took their goods elsewhere, or had little surplus to trade with the HBC. The important implication of Figure 11, however, is that moose seem to have been periodically available to the post, and periodically *unavailable*. The winter of 1776, for instance, had the greatest scarcity of fresh meat, while in 1777 the post enjoyed almost 30 canoes of green meat before a downward trend reached another low in 1779. At that point it is possible that moose populations in nearby forests began building up numbers by 1780, or else Indians began participating in the trade more frequently. A growth in the green meat trade can be discerned until 1782, when the numbers of canoes carrying fresh provisions dropped drastically once more.

Figure 10 suggests that moose were not available consistently and for that reason Cocking frequently encouraged Indians from further away to furnish the post with provisions. Initially the post journals record provisioners from The Pas, Red Deer River, Sweet Herb Lake, Cedar Lake and Grass River, all of whom probably supplied moose (see Figure 12). Evidently this provisioning hinterland was not great enough. In 1777 Cocking encouraged a Sweet Herb Lake Indian to bring provisions, and expressed the hope "that these [people] he came from or any others that he might meet with, would be diligent in Collecting Provisions and bring in Here."[43]

Cocking's call for Indian provisions was evidently answered. Although small groups of Pigogamew,[44] Beaver, and Eagle Hills Indians arrived in 1775, by 1777 many more Indians were bringing food from much further afield. In 1778 and 1780 they arrived in impressive numbers. In late June 1781, six canoes of "Athopuskow" Indians arrived, likely from Lake Athabasca, a few days before the arrival of eight canoes from the "Barren Grounds," possibly Chipewyan or Plains Indians. These groups, it should be pointed out, arrived with both provisions and furs. When sixteen canoes from the "Barren Grounds" arrived in late August "with provisions," what seems to be a significantly widened provisioning hinterland was in place, connecting Cumberland House to Lake Athabasca, Beaver Indian territory, and the buffalo grounds along the North and South Saskatchewan Rivers where, by 1778, Assiniboine Indians were staking a monopoly in the buffalo trade.[45]

More provisions probably arrived from these buffalo regions as time passed. The journals first mention the pounding of buffalo by Assiniboine Indians near Alexander Henry's (the Elder) Upper Settlement in March 1775; little, if any, of that buffalo was brought to Cumberland House, however. Trading expeditions were started the following year by the post's employee, Robert Longmoore (eventually establishing Hudson House), but the distance was too great and the hands too few to bring back much buffalo meat. In 1777, Longmoore's inland expedition returned with some pemmican, although he stated that "they were obliged to eat it up" on the canoe trip back to Cumberland House.[46] The post's first reported trade in buffalo meat took place in September, when four canoes from "Buffalo Country" arrived. Out of nearly 6,000 pounds of dried and beat meat, the post's inventory of food lists 100 pounds of pemmican after this visit.[47] As Figure 9 shows, reports of buffalo provisions arriving at the post had become more commonplace by 1778; and it is likely that with the arrival of many Pigogamew, Eagle Hills and "Buffalo Country" Indians, many provisions traded were dried buffalo, without being reported as such. Figure 9 should possibly be read in light of Figure 10, which shows a decline in reports of "moose" provisions arriving at the post; what these two trends suggest is that dried buffalo and pemmican stores were replacing moose as a primary food source of the post.

This article suggests that quantitative analysis helps illuminate features of the provisioning trade at Cumberland House. The post's garden, probably an important source of food, has not been analyzed because of the scarcity of references to the amount of garden produce grown and used by the post. Emphasis has been placed on the source and availability of meat provisions and the important changes in their supply over time. Country food was subject to significant seasonal availability, as well as dramatic natural population cycles. Rabbits, pheasants, and possibly even moose, showed short-term population cycles; geese were available only in season; even fish had migratory movements that clearly determined the success of nets in specific seasons of the year.

Indians had adapted to the seasonal and cyclical constraints of country food by adopting seminomadic lifestyles. Cumberland House employees engaged in a semisedentary post lifestyle and adapted in other ways: they specialized in fishing and became more efficient in sturgeon and goldeye netting through technological and technical improvement. To gain other sources of meat, the post had to ever widen its provisioning hinterland. Local moose populations, as indexed by the trade in green meat, showed inconsistent availability; even when local hunting was successful, it often could not provide the post with enough meat. The post employees, as a consequence, welcomed and traded meat from ever more distant hunting grounds. By 1781, Cumberland House's provisioning hinterland had increased dramatically, and finally tapped into distant buffalo grounds and even Beaver Indian hunting territory. By then, dried buffalo possibly constituted a greater proportion of the fur traders' diet.

At the beginning of this study, aspects of ecological and economic explanations for Indian behaviour in the fur trade were briefly discussed. Widening provisioning hinterlands have not been fully incorporated into studies of wildlife depletion and the Indian's role in over-hunting. The local environment at Cumberland House was never abundant enough to fully feed post employees; much of their food was drawn from other game areas, regions themselves likely susceptible to depletion. Some aspects of the issue of depletion, then, do not reflect destructive behaviour on the Indians' part as much as the collective effort of widely scattered Indians who had chosen on a particular year to provision distant posts. Certainly more research will identify the hinterlands which supplied posts with food after trade competition intensified. The periodic shortage of green meat also suggests that local Indians were making decisions, perhaps on a year-to-year basis, as to whether or not to supply the post with meat. Disease and pedlar competition obviously affected the quantities brought to the post, but the very fact that Indians were not bringing food to the post consistently, demanded larger provisioning hinterlands.

Possibly the most significant by-product of such a provisioning system was increased cost. Many Indians were well aware of a post's dependence on wild meat, despite York Factory's stem edict to chief traders to keep such information secret.[48] Indians clearly exacted higher prices when posts had few provisions. At Hudson House, Cumberland's outpost, Assiniboine Indians burning off grazing grounds (possibly to improve pasturage, possibly to monopolize the resource) made buffalo scarce around the post. William Tomison reported that he had procured a month of provisions from Indians there, but "that had been purchased at a very dear rate."[49] Waiting for Assiniboine Indians to bring in meat constituted, as he said, "a great Expence for Provisions."

Cumberland House provisioning problems, in turn, have relevance for discussions of the later fur trade. Although the post system extended into parkland, grassland and woodland regions, each with unique game resources, the feature of widening provisioning hinterlands added significant costs to the trade and determined how it was to be undertaken. Duncan M'Gillivrey's journals, kept at Fort George on the Saskatchewan in 1794, share many of the same concerns as Cocking's at Cumberland House. While closer to buffalo grounds, Fort George employees experienced periodic problems gathering enough food and witnessed Assiniboine Indians burning grazing grounds to heighten their provisioning roles.[50] Moreover, when beaver were quickly depleted and the country around the post was "ruined," another post was built further up the Saskatchewan to trade furs while the original was maintained to continue the trade with the *gens du large*—the provisioning Indians who were unwilling to travel to the other post with their vital food supply. What was established was a significantly larger provisioning area and the maintenance of an expensive victualling post, later commonplace when a complex pemmican service for much of the fur trade had been established.[51]

Provisioning became all the more costly as the 19th century unfolded: big game animals were reduced in numbers, and such key resources as the buffalo began to disappear. At that time, the HBC had monopoly over a vast fur-trading region and had inherited a prohibitively expensive provisioning responsibility. By the 1860s, the cost of feeding both post employees and Indians trapping in barren game regions mounted significantly in London accounts.[52]

A close analysis of account ledgers would help determine the real cost of provisioning and whether its price increased over time. In the meantime, the feature of expanding provisioning hinterlands might have enabled posts like Cumberland House to exist; but when the interior trade flourished, posts multiplied and employee numbers increased. This strategy had a marked impact on the fur trade as a business endeavour; and, in time, it seriously undermined its commercial viability.

Notes

This article first appeared in *Prairie Forum* 22, no. 1 (1997): 1–20.

The author would like to acknowledge the comments and research suggestions of the late John Foster, Professor of History, University of Alberta.

1. Ray identifies the seasonally changing roles of these groups: Arthur J. Ray, *Indians in the Fur Trade: Their Roles as Trappers, Hunters and Middlemen in the Lands Southwest of Hudson Bay, 1660–1870* (Toronto: University of Toronto Press, 1974.) Ray also addresses the importance of Great Plain provisioning in the expansion of the fur trade: Arthur J. Ray, "The Northern Great Plain: Pantry of the Northwestern Fur Trade, 1774–1885," *Prairie Forum* 9, no. 2 (Fall 1984): 263–80. Morantz has pointed out post employees' dependency on Home Guard goose and "deer" hunters: Toby Morantz, *An Ethnohistoric Study of Eastern James Bay Cree Social Organization, 1700–1850*, National Museum of Man Mercury Series, Paper No. 88 (Ottawa: Canadian Ethnology Service, 1983). See also Dale Russell, "The Effects of the Spring Goose Hunt on the Crees in the Vicinity of York Factory and Churchill River in the 1700s," National Museum of Man Mercury Series, Paper No. 28, *Proceedings of the Second Congress, Canadian Ethnology Service*, Vol. 2: 420–32 (Ottawa: National Museums of Canada, 1975).

2. This study draws upon a number of late 18th and 19th century journals including: George Simpson, *Journal of Occurrences in the Athabasca Department, 1820 and 1821* (Toronto: Champlain Society, 1938); Frederick Merk (ed.), *Fur Trade and Empire: George Simpson's Journal* (Cambridge: Harvard University Press, 1931); Glenbow Archives (hereafter GA), M941, Diary of Murdoch McPherson, 1834; GA, M272, Fort Resolution Post Journal, 1861; GA, M889, Qu'Appelle Lake Post Journal, 1857–1858; GA, M165, McLeod's Lake Post Journal, 1845–48; *Fort Pelly Journal, 1863* (Regina: Regina Archeological Society, 1987); Duncan M'Gillivrey, *The Journal of Duncan M'Gillivrey of the North West Co. at Fort George ... 1794–5* (Toronto: Macmillan Co., 1924); A.N. McLeod's Journal, Fort Alexandria, 1799, in Charles Gates (ed.), *Five Fur Traders of the Northwest: Being the Narrative of Peter Pond and the Diaries of John Macdonnell, Archibald N. McLeod, Hugh Fades, and Thomas Connor* (Minneapolis: University of Minnesota Press, 1933).

3. See Arthur J. Ray, "Some Conservation Schemes of the Hudson's Bay Company, 1821–50: An Examination of the Problems of Resource Management in the Fur Trade,"

Journal of Economic History 1, no. 1 (1975): 49–68. Charles Bishop examines the depletion of ungulates leading to changes in social organization among Northern Ojibwa: Charles A. Bishop, *The Northern Ojibwa and the Fur Trade: An Historical and Ecological Study* (Toronto: Holt Rineholt and Winston, 1974).

4. For ecological perspectives, see Rene R Gadacz, "Montagnais Hunting Dynamics in Historicoecological Perspective," *Anthropologica* 17, no. 2 (1975): 149–68; David V. Burley, "Proto-Historic Ecological Effects of the Fur Trade in Micmac Culture in Northeastern New Brunswick," *Ethnohistory* 28, no. 3 (1981): 203–16. Martin presented crises in religious cosmology as another motivation: Calvin Martin, *Keepers of the Game: Indian-Animal Relationships and the Fur Trade* (Berkeley: University of California Press, 1978).

5. Carlos and Lewis' work applies carrying capacity estimates within their quantitative analysis of beaver harvests: Ann M. Carlos and Frank D. Lewis, "Indians, the Beaver and the Bay: The Economics of Depletions in the Lands of the Hudson's Bay Company, 1700–1763," *Journal of Economic History* 53, no. 3 (1993): 465–94.

6. Some of the complex issues related to starvation reports are addressed by Mary Black-Rogers, "Varieties of 'Starving': Semantics and Survival in the Subarctic Fur Trade, 1750–1850," *Ethnohistory* 33, no. 4 (1986): 353–83.

7. Arthur J. Ray, "Periodic Shortages, Native Welfare, and the Hudson's Bay Company, 1670–1930," in Shepard Krech III (ed.), *The Subarctic Fur Trade: Native Social and Economic Adaptations* (Vancouver: University of British Columbia Press, 1984), 1–19.

8. See E.E. Rich's Introduction to the post journals: E.E. Rich (ed.), *Cumberland and Hudson House Journals 1775–1782*, 2 vols. (London: The Hudson's Bay Record Society, 1951), hereafter, *Cumberland*.

9. Ernest Voorhis, *Historic Forts and Trading Posts of the French Regime and the English Fur Trading Companies* (Ottawa: Department of Interior, 1930).

10. A.S. Morton cites this quotation in his introduction to M'Gillivrey's diaries, *Journal of Duncan M'Gillivrey*, viii. Henry had stated that each canoe brigade consumed four 90-pound bags of pemmican en route to Cumberland House.

11. "Cumberland House Historical Park," Government of Saskatchewan Museum's Branch, 1978. Also, J.E.M. Kew, *Cumberland House in 1960*, Report No. 2. Economic and Social Survey of Northern Saskatchewan, March 1962 (Saskatoon: University of Saskatchewan, 1962).

12. A reproduction of Turnor's map is appended to *The Journals of Samuel Hearne and Philip Turnor, 1774–1792* (Toronto: Champlain Society, 1934.)

13. It is not clear what species of perch dominated in Pine Lake. Robins et al. provide common and scientific names for fish in Canada. C.R. Robins et al., *Common and Scientific Names of Fishes from the United States and Canada*, 5th ed. (Bethesda, MD: American Fisheries Society, 1991). Special Publication #20.

14. Bruce Cox, *Cultural Ecology: Readings on the Canadian Indians and Eskimos* (Toronto: McClelland and Stewart, 1973), 56.

15. Ray, *Indians in the Fur Trade*. Theodore Binnema is presently investigating related issues.

16. Cocking noted that pedlars divided themselves into groups of six men during the winter and supplied themselves with nets and ammunition. See Rich, *Cumberland* 1: 28.

17. Rich cites the gifted "patience" and skills of Orkney fishermen. "Introduction," *Cumberland* 2: liv–lv.

18. On December 11, 1775, Cocking noted that both pheasants and rabbits "were scarce, particularly Rabbets [*sic*]." See Rich, *Cumberland* 1: 24. By July Indians attributed a lack of "cats" to declining numbers of rabbits: see ibid., 67.

19. Martin J. Paetz and Joseph S. Nelson, *The Fishes of Alberta* (Edmonton: Government of Alberta, 1970), 8–15. In 1777, post employees fished 140 days of the year; days not fishing were often spent mending nets.

20. Rich, *Cumberland* 1: 110.

21. Graham describes these meat preparations in ibid., 1: 77n. Cocking pointed out to York Factory officials that "half-dried" meat at Cumberland was the same as "dried" meat at York; half-dried meat was further dried to better preserve it, ibid., 1: 28. Ray also provides detail of these various meat productions: Arthur J. Ray, "Fur Trade Pantry," 265.

22. On September 26, 1779, William Tomison, then chief trader at Cumberland House, noted that he purchased two canoes of green meat from Indians, even though the post had sufficient fresh geese. He did so not to "affront" the trading Indians: "me haveing it dried made it some little more Expences." See Rich, *Cumberland* 2: 16.

23. Accounts appear in the post's journals for the years 1796 and 1827. The post's account books are preserved in the HBC Archives for the years 1796–1797, 1804–1805, 1810–1816, and frequently for years between 1821 and 1870.

24. See the journals of Robert Longmoore and William Tomison at Hudson House, 1778–1782, HBC Archives, B/87 a/1-5.

25. This is likely a high estimate. More often, canoes arrived with about 150 pounds of moose–see September 26, 1777. Two canoes often arrived with 200 to 250 pounds of green moose—see July 3 and 14, 1778. Similarly, September 20, 1781, two canoes arrived with 265 pounds of green and dried meat.

26. The journals record eight Sweet Herb Lake Indians arriving with 375 pounds of meat, an average of 45 pounds per person on March 8, 1777. Four men were often sent to collect meat from a killed moose. See December 23, 1777, when four men returned with 290 pounds of moose meat, an average of 72 pounds per person. On February 17, 1778, one man and three women arrivedat the post with 334 pounds of provisions, an average of 83 pounds each.

27. These should not be confused with the winter's total stock. The post went through staggering amounts of meat. For instance, on January 23, 1777, when Cocking made out that year's inventory of stock as 1,566 pounds total (represented in Figure 2), he lamented that it would last the post only 37 days.

28. The post rejected green meat brought from too great a distance or after it went bad. One canoe brought to the post meat that "had been too long kept for some part of it was running over with maggots." See Rich, *Cumberland* 2: 109. On July 7, 1777, a canoe carried "tainted" moose and was refused.

29. Cocking to Marten, March 8, 1777, Rich, *Cumberland* 1: 126–27.

30. October 18, 1775, December 22, 1775. See Rich, *Cumberland* 1.

31. Ibid., February 18, 1779.

32. Ibid., 1: 214.

33. Ibid., April 7, 1776.

34. October 13, 1778.

35. Cocking slotted 2.5 pounds of meat per man, in a post of fifteen men.

36. Rich, *Cumberland* 1: 67.

37. In August 1778, Cocking could not trade five canoes of furs because "my stock [of liquor] is so small I am obliged to preserve it for Provisions, for as yet I have but small stock considering the season of the year." See ibid., August 19, 1777.

38. Ibid., 1: 255.

39. Ibid., 2: 9.

40. Ibid., 2: 27.

41. Ibid., 2: 136.

42. Robert Longmoore wrote Cocking in 1779 from Hudson House, stating that "the Canadians are now so numerous that many are left inland, all the summer. These buy up all the food they can and hinder the Indians from carrying furs or food to your settlement." See Longmoore's Journal, Rich, *Cumberland* 1: 309. In 1779, Cocking noted that Le Pas Indians often promised to return with green meat, "but they having so many houses to go to they like to be near and there and everywhere." Ibid., 2: 29.

43. Ibid.,1: 129.

44. Many of the names for Indians are identified in the synonymy section of "Western Woods Cree," *Handbook of North American Indians*, Vol. 6: *Subarctic* (Washington: Smithsonian Institution, 1981). My thanks to John Foster for pointing out that "Beaver" may have been Sarcee from the Elk Island area, and "Eagle Hills," possibly Blackfoot. "Barren Grounds" Indians might refer to prairie Indians.

45. Both Canadian peddlars and HBC men at Hudson House noted that Assiniboine Indians were burning forage grass around their posts to ensure they could not hunt buffalo themselves. See Arthur Ray for more details on the Assiniboine trade in provisions and their seasonal lifestyle shared between plains and parkland belt environments.

46. Rich, *Cumberland* 1: 157–58

47. September 22, 1777 in Rich, *Cumberland* 1.

48. See Cocking's instructions in ibid., September 12, 1776.

49. December 31, 1779 in ibid., 2: 27.

50. M'Gillivrey, *The Journal of Duncan M'Gillivrey*, 33.

51. GA, M889, Qu'Appelle Lake Post Journal, 1857–1858; *Fort Pelly Journal of Daily Occurrences, 1863* (Regina: Regina Archaeological Society, 1987).

52. "Country food," and "goods imported" to posts in the many districts rose significantly between 1874 and 1877. By then, the Northern Department was supplying Indians with provisions to survive while trapping. See "Report of the Governor and Committee of the Hudson's Bay Company, June 27, 1882," and "Report on the Fur Trade Accounts, 1879," CIHM no. 07873.

8. Home, Away from Home: Old Swan, James Bird and the Edmonton District, 1795–1815[1]

Tolly Bradford

His Death may be of more than ordinary consequence in this river.

James Bird reporting the death of Old Swan
Fort Edmonton, October 17th 1814.[2]

Siksika leader Old Swan had long been an active participant in the fur/provisions trade of the North Saskatchewan River.[3] He, unlike the other Siksika bands further west, had chosen to pursue a policy of cooperation with European traders. That James Bird, chief trader for the Hudson's Bay Company (HBC) in the region, recorded his death so exactly is evidence of the influence of Old Swan's policy of cooperation. While historians have looked at what the consequences of these two men were, none have looked at the space, "this river" (the North Saskatchewan), where they lived, or, more precisely, the way "this river" was perceived by these men.[4]

Showing that Old Swan and James Bird saw the physical landscape of the North Saskatchewan and surrounding plains differently, and that they perceived or imagined the resources and "races" of people in the space before 1815 in a different way, is an important focus of this study. What is argued here is that Old Swan saw the space of the Edmonton District as being fairly fluid in meaning and prone to change, while James Bird saw the district as a static space with two clear and separate parts, only one portion of which—the area along the North Saskatchewan River itself—he knew. Beyond showing how these two people imagined the space of the Edmonton District, I also want to suggest that it was each man's location of "home"—more than simply material or economic considerations—that informed their imaginings. It was because the Edmonton District was "home" to Old Swan and not "home" to James Bird that the space of the district was imagined, used and lived in differently by each man.

Why "Home"?

This examination of the Edmonton District picks up where Theodore Binnema's study of Old Swan left off. Binnema's narrative explained how Old Swan, as opposed to another Siksika chief, Big Man, chose a policy of cooperation and conciliation with fur traders in the Edmonton District between 1794 and 1814. Although Binnema's point is well stated, and he does well to show that decisions to participate in the fur trade were being made at the individual, not the tribal, level, he remains vague on two points: what, exactly, motivated Old Swan to trade, and what, materially and culturally, were the outcomes of this trade from Old Swan's perspective.[5] This chapter engages directly with these questions by arguing that Old Swan's location of "home" was a key force shaping how he imaged the space and thus a central factor informing how and why he participated in the fur trade.

Unlike Binnema's article, what is examined here are not Old Swan's actions in the Edmonton District, but how he perceived or imagined the space of the district. If, as Derek Gregory argues, landscape is at the "heart of the social process," understanding how Old Swan imagined the landscape of the Edmonton District gives us a glimpse, however slight, into Old Swan's "social process" and world view.[6] Reading Old Swan's imagination of the space tells us, for example, how he used the resources of the district, what motivated him to cooperate with the fur traders in the district, and how he may have changed his culturally constructed view of the district because of the fur trade. Driving my argument about Old Swan is the fact that, because the district was "home" to him, he was able to integrate the fur trade into his imagination of the space but not become dependent on it: thus, Old Swan constructed the district as a fluid space in which fur posts were important—but not central—elements. In taking this approach I am supporting Paul Thistle's model of cultural change in the fur trade, and arguing that the "core" cultural values of Old Swan were not changed because of the trade: there was change for Old Swan in the contents but not the concept of the space—the space was always his "home."[7]

Unlike Old Swan, James Bird, the most senior Hudson's Bay Company trader in the Edmonton District, was not at "home" in the district. Also unlike Old Swan, Bird never saw the space as fluid. To Bird, the space was rigidly divided in two: there was the area inside the palisade walls and along the North Saskatchewan River; and there was the other world—the space beyond the palisade walls and north and south of the river. By examining Bird's imagination of the space alongside Old Swan's, it becomes clear that the Edmonton District was used and perceived differently by different people and that the district did not, to say the least, represent a single "fur

View of Fort Edmonton, 1863. Sketch from The North-west passage by land : being the narrative of an expedition from the Atlantic to the Pacific, undertaken with the view of exploring a route across the continent to British Columbia through British territory by one of the northern passes in the Rocky Mountains by Viscount Milton and W.B. Cheadle, 1865 (courtesy of the Glenbow Archives/LAC-1240-6).

trade society." This characterization of the Edmonton District as a space without a unitary "fur trade society" reflects, and follows from, what Jennifer Brown has observed about the fur trade generally. Michael Payne, in summarizing Brown's thoughts, writes:

> [Brown] suggests the existence of multiple fur trade societies [across space and time] or alternately no society at all but rather sets of social ties and exchanges that gave the fur trade a socio-cultural dimension but stop well short of any sociological definition of society.[8]

Certainly, it is unlikely that James Bird and Old Swan saw themselves as members of the same "society." Despite this disconnectedness, however, Old Swan and James Bird did share a common element in how they lived in the space: they each used their respective locations of "home" to inform how they imagined, and thus how they used and moved through the space of the Edmonton District. In choosing to focus on James Bird and Old Swan I am also suggesting that defining "home" was a personal experience, and that the historian of the fur trade should pay close attention to individual voices and choices. As Binnema has revealed about Siksika bands, it is inappropriate to talk of "tribes" as having a single identity or set of strategies; likewise,

James Bird, I would stress, was only one person at Fort Edmonton. This present study does not explore other HBC personalities, and it should not be assumed that all HBC employees at Edmonton shared Bird's vision of the Edmonton District.

Home Not Home

The concept of "home," writes Ilan Magat, "can help us identify the order people try to impose on experience in the course of shaping their own behaviour."[9] Although Magat's interest is the experiences of immigrants in 20th-century Canada, his observations are useful for understanding how Old Swan and James Bird experienced the Edmonton District and how they used their "home" to impose order on, and inform their actions in, the district. Magat distinguishes between two types of "home." First, he writes, there is "'home'—the commonly accepted usage of the term where one resides," then there is "'Home'—the metaphysical usage of the word to illustrate a much larger concept."[10] It is this second concept—the metaphysical Home where one belongs but might not reside—that is the more powerful of the two. This is a useful distinction; for, as I will show, although James Bird may have made his home at Fort Edmonton, his Home was not located there. Conversely, Old Swan, it is clear, saw the Edmonton District both as his home and as a portion of his Home. Thus, when I stated above that it was the location of "home" that accounted for how and why Bird and Old Swan imagined the district in a certain way, I meant—more specifically—that it was where each man located Home, not home, that informed them.

The discussion that follows is broken into three thematic areas, each addressing a different element Old Swan and James Bird had to confront in the space of the Edmonton District. These three areas are the physical and seasonal elements of the space, the resources of the space, and the "races" of people in the space.

The Physical *Space*

In 1809 North-West Company (NWC) trader Alexander Henry (the younger) recorded what he deemed to be a description of Slave (or Blackfoot) space.[11] "The Tract of land which they call their own Country at present," wrote Henry,

> commences by a due south direction from Fort Vermilion to the south branch of the Saskatchewoine and up that stream to the foot of the Rocky Mountains, then in a northern direction along the mountain [sic] until it strikes upon the North branch of the Sakatchewoine again and down that stream to the Vermillion River.[12]

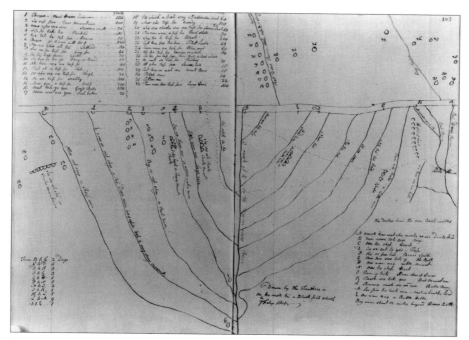

Figure 1. Old Swan's 1801 map (as transcribed by Peter Fidler). Chesterfield House is halfway up the right side of the map. The "Rocky Mountains" are represented by parallel lines running left to right near the top of the map. *Source:* Hudson's Bay Company Archives (HBCA), Provincial Archives of Manitoba (PAM) E.3/2 (N4348).

Henry further specified that Old Swan's band is "the most eastward" of the Slave. This description somewhat matches how Old Swan had seen the space eight years earlier. At that time (1801) he had been trading at Chesterfield House at the east end of the South Saskatchewan River. Peter Fidler, a skilled cartographer and the Chesterfield House postmaster, was well acquainted with Old Swan. In early 1801, after a 49-day excursion to the upper Missouri, Fidler had asked Old Swan to describe both his journey and the landscape it went through. Old Swan agreed to do this. And, as Old Swan described the journey, Fidler transcribed it into a map. This map is a textual representation of the space. It describes a space dominated by what were assumed to be the Rocky Mountains and the Missouri River (see Figure 1).[13] Because Old Swan was at Chesterfield house, and because Fidler had asked about his trip to the south, Fort Edmonton does not appear on the map. The Red Deer River is the most northerly reference point on the map.

What the map does show is that Old Swan and other Blackfoot groups were, or reported to be, the most powerful military force on the plains north of the Missouri, and that rivers—the Missouri, the Red Deer, the South Branch—were not central to Old Swan's definition of the space. Unlike the European maps of the time, a detailed understanding of the rivers would not have been needed for Old Swan. Binnema's careful study of the map shows, for example, that Old Swan's map was drawn for simplicity and usefulness, or for what Siksika people like Old Swan deemed to be useful. As a pedestrian/equestrian people the Siksika would have conceived of the space for land-based travel; the rivers would have been merely borders or lines on the large surface area of the space. The rivers were important for sources of water, but the details of the bends and flow of the rivers were not deemed relevant.[14] This depiction reflects Henry's 1809 reportage—a main difference being, perhaps, that by 1809, the space known or frequented by Old Swan had shifted slightly. Although the emphasis remained on land and surface area, by 1809 Old Swan had been in the North Saskatchewan River district on and off for at least four years.[15] It was the "Edmonton district," then, not the more southerly Chesterfield House that became his new position from which to launch war parties, plan buffalo pounds, and frame his idea of Home.

One gets the feeling that James Bird never ventured far beyond the valley of the North Saskatchewan River, although he did recognize that there were peoples and spaces beyond the river. Bird's definition of the Edmonton District in 1815 explains that, at least in part, "the limits of this district are formed by the extent to which the Indians who trade here occansionally [sic] removed their tents in search of food or Furs..."[16] After this disclaimer— readable as a partial dependency on the "Indians" to describe the borders of the space—Bird gives a more concrete, fur trade-centric, description:

> The District is bounded on the North by the Athapuskow
> River, Red Deer Lake, and the Beaver River; on the East by
> a line running from the Pack lake to the Missouri; and on
> the west to the Rocky Mountains.[17]

The next section of the report, entitled "Of the Rivers," gives detailed descriptions of the main water channels, most of which Bird describes as "quite safe"—with only one having rapids, although even these were "unattended with danger."[18] Unlike Old Swan, the intricacies and usefulness of the rivers were central to Bird. Juxtaposing Old Swan's map with the HBC's 1802 map by Arrowsmith gives a pictorial representation of Bird's river-centric vision of the space (see Figure 2). Bird also describes the plains, the surface that I have here identified with Old Swan. Certainly Bird did know that the plains south of the river existed, but before this 1815 report he does not discuss them in any detail. In 1812, for example, having been back from York

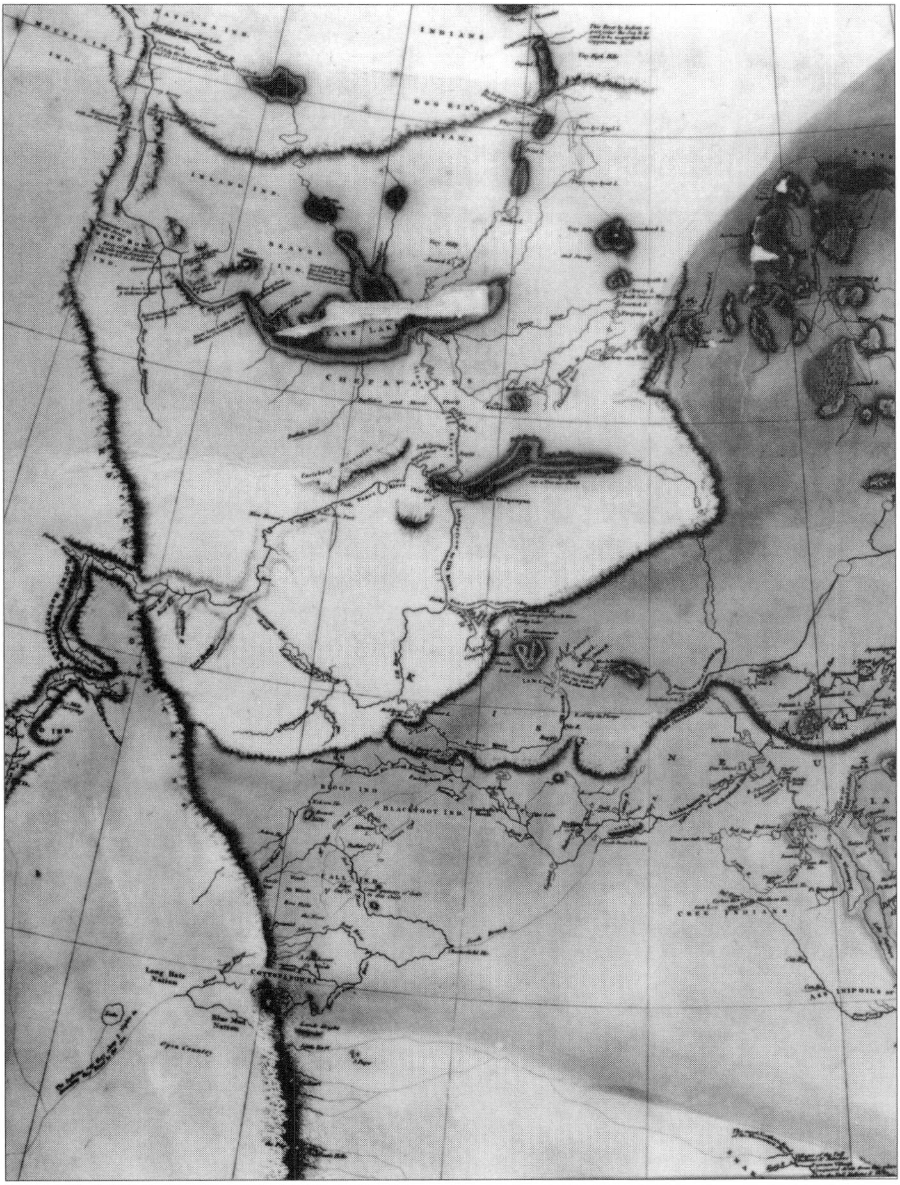

Figure 2. A detail of Arrowsmith's 1802 map of the "Interior parts of North America." This map, which was drawn based on information gathered from people like Old Swan, emphasizes the Rocky Mountains and the details of the water channels used by the HBC. The bottom half of this map is part of the area described in Old Swan's 1801 map in Figure 1. *Source:* HBCA, PAM G.3/672 (N4836).

Factory two weeks, Bird wrote that because the "sun is obscured with smoke" the plains must be burning. He further extrapolates that "the plains must be burnt to such an extent as to preclude all Hopes of our getting a large supply of dry provisions," although, because he does not seem to leave the river valley, he can never say for sure.[19] In fact, Bird's journals are all written either at Fort Edmonton or en route to and from York Factory. Any movement he does record occurs along the strip of waterways from York Factory to Fort Acton, and hardly ever above or below this river-based line.[20] For information about the burning plains in 1814, for example, he relies on "a band of blood Indians…"[21] And in 1811, even with starvation apparently threatening the fort, he declares that a four-day journey is "too great [a distance] to be able to fetch meat…"[22] He was at home in the fort, but not at Home in the space of the plains.

Although the river dominated Bird's space while the plains was the focus of Old Swan's space, both men did to some extent agree on the role of the Rocky Mountains within the district. Bird had a love-hate relationship with the mountains. Pushing to the western extent of the Saskatchewan River in 1799 he wrote, "nothing can be seen but the gloomy tops of pines till the Rocky Mountain [sic] (whose icy summits seem to pierce the sky) intercepts the view."[23] Bird offsets this view of the mountains with what he describes as the "fairly agreeable plains below."[24] Leading up to 1815, Bird's opinion of the Rockies as something aesthetically interesting though not very "agreeable," changes little. In 1808 he describes crossing the mountains to trade as "impossible."[25] In 1811, due to rising tension between Salish and Blackfoot groups, he sees a traverse as "too dangerous,"[26] and in 1813 he thinks lucrative trade via the mountains to be "extremely improbable."[27] By 1814 he clarifies these beliefs, saying that because the "road … across the mountains is long and extremely bad" because there is a "scarcity of Food…" to supply such a journey, and because, even if successfully crossed, the "beavers are not numerous nor the Indians industrious," such an endeavour would be of little point.[28] These imaginations or constructions of the Rocky Mountains were based on Bird's position as a trader, not his position as a person at Home in the space or at Home in the mountains. To James Bird, the mountains were a physical obstacle that slowed the HBC's trading plans. David Thompson of the NWC and Bird's own man Joseph Howse had crossed the mountains by 1810, yet in Bird's mind the mountains still represented a barrier to economically viable trade. By 1815, thus, Bird was happy to recognize the mountains as an important aesthetic component of his space, as "one of the grandest prospects in Nature" even, but he remained sceptical of the possibility of cross-mountain trade.[29]

To Old Swan the mountains were also a kind of border in his space, though not, perhaps, the barrier Bird saw. A careful examination of Old Swan's 1801 map reveals that what Fidler labelled the "Rocky Mountains" were actually what Old Swan would have called the *mistakis*, the foothills or the front range of the Rocky Mountains.[30] Old Swan's inclusion of the *mistakis* in his map was not simply for aesthetic reasons but because, to him and to his band members from their vantage point on the plains, these foothills were points of reference. Binnema is again invaluable on this. His analysis reveals that the specific "mountains" on the map were not necessarily the highest peaks, but rather those most distinguishable from the plains—those that, because of their shape or position, could be seen from the plains and used as reference points for Blackfoot heading west.[31] More correctly, then, the mountains and foothills were signposts—not obstacles to cross over. Because the space was Home to Old Swan, the mountains had a different meaning and played a clearly different role than they did for Bird.

The other thing Old Swan's 1801 map reveals, and that the Fort Edmonton journals support, is that Old Swan, and certainly the members of other Blackfoot groups, saw the Mountains not as a barrier for their movement west, but as a way to stop Kootenay and Salish from coming east—a positive barrier to the trade James Bird was trying to pursue. The mountains were beneficial to the Siksika because, with Bird's apparent apathy about crossing the mountains, the Kootenay and Salish would not have direct access to trade goods. The mountains, in this sense, helped maintain Blackfoot dominance over the trade on the east side of the mountains, and thus helped protect Old Swan's Home on the plains.

Seasoned *Space*

An important variable contributing to how each man imagined the space of the Edmonton District was seasonal change. In the fall, Bird would arrive back from York Factory, evaluate the situation of provisions, do some small trading, and prepare for the winter ahead. Old Swan's movements in the fall are more difficult to track. Reports from Chesterfield House and Fort Vermillion suggest that Old Swan was often around the posts throughout the fall; he was probably among those waiting for Fidler to arrive in September 1801, for example.[32] In the late fall Old Swan either set up a buffalo pound or set off on a war expedition to the west. This seasonal pattern of movement suggests that Old Swan was to some extent continuing what had been done for years by Blackfoot groups: using the high concentration of buffalo found on the plains in the late fall and early winter to set up pounds for mass harvesting during December.

Bird was indirectly dependent on this harvesting of buffalo. By December, Edmonton House needed to acquire buffalo meat either through trade or hunting; and during a difficult winter Bird became more dependent than usual on these outside provisions. The years 1811, 1812, 1813, and 1814 were all difficult for Bird. Because of the "extreme severity of the winter & [the] extraordinary Depth off [sic] snow" in 1811, hunting, especially if using horses, was nearly impossible.[33] In 1814, the problems of procuring provisions continued: "The Plains for sixty Miles round this place were entirely ravaged by Fires last fall [i.e., 1813] and the consequence has been that we have neither seen an Indian from that quarter nor heard of a Buffalo since that Time."[34] Between fire, snow and cold, Bird's life and the way he lived in the space were shaped by what the seasons brought him in weather, and by his dependency on provisions from Native groups around him. The other seasonal pattern he had to respond to was that of doing business within the large system of the HBC. By mid-May, after surviving these winters and doing some spring trading, Bird would begin his trip out to York Factory. Reaching York Factory in July or August, he would stay at the bay-side post for up to two weeks before returning to Edmonton to start the cycle again.

In these spring and summer months, Old Swan's movements are nearly impossible to pin down. Drawing on Alexander Henry's (the Younger) report that "in the summer, they [Old Swan's band] chase the Buffalo on horse back and kill them with bow and arrow," we might assume that a certain continuity with pre-contact Blackfoot society was maintained and that the summer buffalo hunt was still important to the space. The other major activity Old Swan probably undertook in the summer, and one again reflecting how he imagined the space of the northern plains as his Home, was warfare. In the fall of 1807 and 1808 Henry and Bird both report that Blackfoot and Cree had been at war over the summer, although Old Swan himself may not have been directly involved in these incidents.[35] Throughout seasonal changes, therefore, Old Swan's Home continued to be located on the plains. Conversely, locating a long-term, trans-seasonal Home for James Bird is a difficult task for the historian.

Resource *Space*

While we cannot know how Old Swan dealt with the prairie fires of 1812 to 1814, we know that Bird was constantly complaining about the "scarcity" of buffalo during these years.[36] Bird, of course, was being pressured to supply not only his own community at Fort Edmonton but also the outlying areas of Swan River and Acton House.[37] Bird viewed the buffalo as a resource not needed just by the local Fort Edmonton population, but also by a wider group of people. Likewise, Bird viewed the trees of the district as a resource needed by the HBC. Trees were needed to build boats, to construct the posts and the palisades, and to supply the fort with firewood. By 1815, Bird happily declared that "trees ... grow in favourable situations to a size sufficiently large for any purpose they can be requested," and that the area around the fort could "afford subsistence to a much greater number of inhabitants" than were presently at the fort.[38] And, despite his apparent difficulty in the winters between 1812 and 1814, by 1815 he believed that "large quantities of Meat and Fish [could] be procured in all seasons and the ground [could] yield abundantly Barley, Potatoes, Turnips, Cabbages and all other hardy vegetables."[39] This 1815 report, of course, was written to the HBC committee and Bird was necessarily putting a positive spin on the district and his role in it. However, there also seems to be another story evolving here. If Bird, from his initial time of entry into the Edmonton District, had seen the river not as a Home but as a space to build the HBC trade from, then by 1815 his comments about the plentiful resources may be a continuation and an amplification of this theme: Bird was becoming more willing to procure and exploit the resources of the surrounding environment in order to benefit the HBC. The 1815 report about the plentiful resources of the region and the ability of the region to support "almost any number of men" suggests that Bird and/or the HBC officials in London were coming to see Edmonton as more than just an isolated post to be visited and to trade through.[40] Edmonton seemed to be becoming a more fixed and sedentary idea, a fort that would have a life after the trade was over as well as a space where the environment could be controlled and used and reshaped for these interests. As of 1815, however, Edmonton was still not Home to either James Bird or the HBC.

While Bird saw the natural resources of the space as useful, Old Swan was concerned with how these things—the buffalo especially—could allow him access to other resources: namely, how the buffalo could be used to acquire the manufactured goods Bird was bringing into the space from England. When Old Swan and his band started trading at Chesterfield House in 1800, they seemed to be vying to become the home-band of Chesterfield. Although Chesterfield House was abandoned in 1802, Old Swan's actions clearly show his interest in adding the fur trade post to his ideal image of the space as Home. Peter Fidler, the senior HBC official at Chesterfield, was cognizant of the need to maintain Old Swan's support. He, like the NWC six years previously, had a coat (a uniform) made for Old Swan; this coat was a symbol of Fidler's and the HBC's, and perhaps even the British Empire's, interest in and respect for Old Swan as an important trading ally. But this gift had not come without Old Swan's persistent help to Chesterfield House, and to Fidler in particular. The 1801 map mentioned earlier would have been part of this exchange of things beyond simply furs and buffalo. Blackfoot guides provided by Old Swan were also vital to Fidler's success at this isolated post.[41] Old Swan and other Blackfoot groups were not only part of the trade at the post, but were vital actors in the operation of the post—an interesting observation when placed alongside the lesser role of the Gros Ventre and the violence they instigated before the post's closure in 1802.[42] Old Swan, then, seemed to have made a conscious decision not only to allow the post to be constructed, but also to encourage his Siksika band members to trap, to hunt and to work with the HBC officials in operating the post.

With Old Swan's help, Chesterfield House was able to accumulate an impressive 12,000 Made Beaver (MB) in 1801, compared to Edmonton's 2,087 MB.[43] The exact reason for this kind of enthusiasm on the part of the Siksika at Chesterfield is unclear, although much of the existing fur trade historiography has tended to place a primacy on economic motivations when describing the actions of Aboriginal traders.[44] While not ignoring this historiographic trend, I want to add the dimension of Home to these economic analyses by arguing that Old Swan's location of Home informed the way he dealt with the European traders and the goods they introduced to the district. Old Swan, to be sure, needed to maintain access to trade in order to keep guns coming to him. It was guns, as Arthur Ray has shown in his study of the trade further to the east, which often separated trading and non-trading groups.[45] Without guns military pursuits were weakened, and groups like the Salish and Kootenay would threaten Blackfoot dominance on the plains.

Beyond guns, there were the other so-called "necessities" Old Swan and his band saw as resources: especially, although not exclusively, alcohol and tobacco.[46] On the second day back at Chesterfield House in the fall of 1801, Fidler exclaimed that "upwards of forty men came here in the night for tobacco," Blackfoot among them.[47] In the same year Fidler points out the need to keep well-stocked supplies of Brazilian tobacco but not the carrot tobacco, which "the Indians will not trade."[48] Not only did the Blackfoot want tobacco, but—much like the HBC's own interest in specific kinds of furs and resources—they would only trade for a specific type of tobacco. Of alcohol, Fidler notes that in November "Two blackfeet came in with a few furs which they trade[ed] only for liquor."[49] As Old Swan himself, trading in 1807, explained to James Bird, "his countrymen … [have] been long accustomed to be[ing] supplied with Brandy, tobacco &c. These article are become objects of primary necessity to them."[50] As with guns and blankets, these materials seem to have been integrated into the Siksika definition of Home.

Old Swan's band, then, had a mixture of resources in mind when they traded, but what of Old Swan personally, and of the "Chiefs coats and other things" which Fidler "rigged" him with in the spring of 1802? The sources suggest that this incentive did not hurt relations between the HBC and Old Swan.[51] These gifts may have been viewed, from the perspective of the HBC, not only as a thank-you gift to a "friendly Indian," but also as a way to inscribe an identity on Old Swan which privileged Europeanized materials and fashions, thus trying to bring him into the cultural (as well as economic) sphere of the trading company. To Old Swan this coat was probably less culturally intrusive than Fidler might have hoped, and was more likely a way to further his own status within his community and Home. More to the point, the presentation of the coat was Fidler's way of inviting the Siksika to follow him back to the North Saskatchewan as well as a way to maintain a trading relationship between the HBC and Old Swan's band.

Race *Space* (?)

I do not want to ignore the fact that the space of the Edmonton District was Home or home for many different people: there were men and women in the space, each with their own experience and relationship to it. In the language of today, the Edmonton District and its immediate vicinity were actually fairly cosmopolitan spaces. That said, my focus now is on how Old Swan and James Bird imagined men in the space, and specifically how they each perceived men who were from outside their own communities: how Old Swan saw the "white men" in the space, for instance, and how James Bird saw the "Indian" men in the space. Again, it is clear that each man's location of Home dictated his ideas of "outsiders." While Bird saw people outside the fort walls as inherently different from himself—as not part of his Home—Old Swan integrated the different people in the district to construct a vision of the space in which various "races" overlapped and interacted. Old Swan imagined his Home, in fact, as multi-racial.

In his 1815 report James Bird explains that while "the disadvantage with regard to trade [in the south-west of the district] are the indolence and independent and cruel treacherous disposition of great part of the inhabitants," many of the bands in the immediate vicinity of Fort Edmonton are "independent and alive to their own interests" regarding the trade.[52] By 1815, then, Bird sees the populations outside the fort walls as different from himself, yet he also sees a complex network of Native societies, and he recognizes differences between distinct bands and "tribes." This recognition of differences between Aboriginal peoples was based on how Bird regarded each group's, or each individual's, proficiency to trade. Those who were most helpful to the fort and to Bird's aims were "friendly," those who were not helpful were "indolent" or "useless." These categorizations, then, were not biological-based racial categories but linked rather to the apparent economic usefulness of a particular "Indian" or band.

In 1813 Bird recorded that "an Indian arrived at our Neighbours who informed me that one of our very best Indians is so ill that his life is despaired of."[53] About two weeks later this "very best Indian," or "our very best Indian" as Bird had called him, died. Bird's entry of the death is again marked with his preoccupation of its economic impact, lamenting: "This is the second very good Trader we have lost since July."[54] Likewise, upon the death of Old Swan, who had long been an important trader, Bird acknowledged: "This Chief was imminently instrumental in preserving peace…[and] was also the firm friend of the white Men."[55] These two "very best" or "firm friends" were "Indians" that Bird saw as helpful and useful to the trade, and as they are the only "Indians" so described by Bird, their stories are the exception in Bird's journal up to 1815.

Equally as scarce in Bird's journal are statements that describe Aboriginal people as "indolent" or as being "useless and … troublesome"[56]; these kinds of observations, like those of "friendly Indians," are few in Bird's journal. Of the overwhelming majority of Aboriginal people who come to trade, Bird passes few editorial comments, simply saying, for example, "Three Muddy River Indians arrived who brought a few beavers,"[57] or, most commonly, "The Indians of yesterday traded and went away." In fact, even when there was alcohol-related violence in the camps near the fort, Bird does not seem to invoke racial stereotyping or racial discourse. On January 3, 1811, for example, Bird writes:

> A woman arrived from the crees of yesterday and informed us that a quarrel had taken place amongst them last night which terminated in the Death of one man, and another man receiving two stabs in the back.[58]

Yet Bird leaves no qualifying statement. Of a similar incident in 1814, Bird writes: "An Indian woman arrived… She informed me that a quarrel had taken place among the Indians in consequence of which two Men are killed…" Explaining that this incident accounted for the sixth and seventh such deaths in the past year, Bird only editorializes the incident in reference to its impact on the trade: the dead men, he explains, were "unfortunately, our traders."[59]

The question of whether Bird's imagination of the space was "racialized" is complex. He did recognize that in the space of the Edmonton District there were "White men" and there were "Indians," and that it was the latter that posed not only an opportunity but also a threat to the trader.[60] We see this image of the "Indian" as a threat in the October 19, 1808 entry where Bird reports that the Stoney Indians have "long secretly determined on the kind of revenge … [where] all white men were equally satisfactory Object for their Vengeance…"[61] Likewise the April 11, 1813 entry explains that the men of the fort must "endeavour to get up the Stockades Before the Indians arrive," fearing, one supposes, an invasion into the "white man's" home-space of the fort.[62] Although there is certainly an element of "race" here—that the space was divided into (at least) two "races"—this is not the discourse of the later 19th century. That there is the absence of this later discourse is perhaps because the operation of the fort, especially during the winters of 1811–14, was too dependent on these "others" to allow for knowledge to be manufactured about them.[63] Since Bird did not hold real power and knowledge in the space, using racial discourse from the metropolitan centre would have to wait. Also, so long as Bird was in the space only to trade, not to create a sense of Home, it follows that besides discussing how people like Old Swan participated, or disrupted, the HBC's commerce, Bird would have had no need to racialize and categorize the inhabitants of this space.

Old Swan, however, was at Home in the space and seemed to deal with "race" slightly differently. For him, of course, there were several other people besides the "white man" to imagine or work with inside this space. There were the members of his own band, those of the Cree and Assiniboine bands around Fort Edmonton, as well as members of the Salish bands to the west. Each group, and each person within each group, would have presented a considerable challenge to the way Old Swan perceived the space and constructed his Home. In essence, he wanted to negotiate between these people and between their competing interests. He wanted to maintain access to trade and access to the buffalo, and also respond to the needs and ideas of his own band members. Chief among these needs would have been his band's interest in having a well-defined Home.

His time with Peter Fidler—making maps, getting coats, acquiring tobacco—gives insight into why Old Swan wanted to trade; but understanding how he viewed the person or people providing these trading goods is more difficult to grasp. In the most straightforward terms, he probably approached the white man like most Native traders did: having "very little attachment to a particular house" and choosing the "House where the greatest value is set on the commodity [he] may have…"[64] This pragmatism suggests that Old Swan would have seen the white man as an economic partner and explains why, according to Alexander Henry (the Younger), Old Swan believed that without "white people" the Blackfoot would be "pitiful indeed."[65]

Henry's account of his visit to a Siksika buffalo pound in 1809 gives us further insight into how Old Swan viewed the "white people." Writing five days before Christmas, Henry explains how "The Black feet have repeatedly sent for ... me to go to their Camp which [is] near at hand [to] see the Buffalo enter the pound."[66] This visit lasted three days. During the visit, Henry and his men were treated to food and tent space; they were encouraged, in a way, to come into Old Swan's "fort" and be integrated into *his* definition of the river valley as a fluid space. Henry also observed that, although

> they [the Siksika] were very civil and kind to us ... like all Indian tribes, their principal object was to get what they could from us, and once they perceived there is nothing more which they can expect to get ... they then become careless about us.[67]

Old Swan ultimately saw Henry and his men as trading allies, not as members of a different "race."

In a long passage of ethnographic information apparently given by Old Swan to Henry in 1809, another clue about Old Swan's perception of the "white man" is revealed. In this passage we see Old Swan apparently comparing a Creator-like figure to the/a "white man":

> He [Old Swan] says at first the world was one large Body of Water, inhabited by only one Great White man and his Wife but they had no children. This man in the course of time made the earth, divided the water into Great Lakes and Rivers and formed the great range of Rocky Mountains after which he made all the Beasts, Birds and Fish and every other living creature.[68]

Reading the layers of transmission here is crucial. The question of who in fact said/wrote "Great White man" is not clear: was it Alexander Henry (who had apparently recorded the story)? Or was it Old Swan? Or was it, perhaps, the publisher of Henry's journal?[69] We know that in contemporary oral tellings of this story the Old Man figure is not connected to a "white man"—"great" or otherwise. It is true that Blackfoot in the mid-18th century had associated the "white man" with *Napi*, or *Napikwan*, which means "old Man person," but, according to one historian, this association had fallen out of use by Old Swan's time.[70] If this is true, why does Henry's journal record Old Swan referencing "one Great White man" as a creator-like figure?

It must be stressed that the authorship of this creation story is hard to pin down. If we assume, however, that Old Swan did in fact tell Henry that initially the world was "inhabited by only one great White man" we should question his motives. Perhaps Old Swan was consciously recasting or redeploying the idea that *white people—those men inside the post—hold power over special resources.*[71] Put another way, because Old Swan recognized that the "white men" were an important element in the space around him, he may have taken one of "his own" myths and reworked it to suit the realities of this new context: he may have reformulated the creation story for a new set of white ears—ears that would probably appreciate seeing the "white race" in the position of "creator." Later in Old Swan's telling (or Henry's writing) of the story, this "one Great White man" goes on to make

> a man out of clay … [and] a wife … [who] in course of time had a [sic] numerous offspring that again intermarried and from them originated all the White men. The Indians were made afterwards, by the Great White man, and out of the same material as he had made the first.[72]

The existence of "race" seems to be understood by Old Swan here, and is hence woven into the story. But, as suggested above, Old Swan was probably not responding to the Eurocentric discourse of "race" or "racialization" that was to pervade the later 19th century. One historian of the British Empire, C.A. Bayly, has suggested that it wasn't until the 1820s that the British Empire had a clear vision of how to "invent" (or construct a discourse about) the indigenous populations of the realm.[73] The above discussion of James Bird's imagination of the "Indians" at Edmonton supports Bayly's theory. Certainly, it seems that any racial discourse being manufactured by Bird probably meant little to Old Swan: "race," to Old Swan, was linked to material culture, nothing more.

The two passages from the creation story quoted above can be read in a number of ways. I, referring back to earlier observations, see Old Swan's decision to reconstruct the creation myth as a way to appease the white ears of Henry. This action is suggestive of Old Swan's vision of this space as fluid and as Home: it was a space where "old myths" about the meaning of Home could even be re-oralized to include a role for the new "race" of men inside the space. As the contents of the space changed for Old Swan, so to, it seems here, did the contents of his Home. Alternatively, the way this creation story was told may have been nothing more than a bit of jovial leg-pulling by Old Swan—a laugh at Henry's (earnest) expense.

Going Home

Old Swan died sometime before October 17, 1814.[74] According to his testimony to Henry, his "spirit [would have] instantly [gone] to a great Hummock of Wood that is situated between the Red Deer River and the South branch of the Saskatchewan within sight of the Rocky Mountains."[75] That this afterlife "location" was set within the space of the district is significant: the space, the surface of the northwestern plains, was part of his Home even in death. It was in this space that he had grown up; had hunted buffalo in both pounds and from horseback; had gone to war with, and—in the river valley area—made peace with the Cree; had participated in the trade with Europeans; had invited the "white men" operating this trade to his pound; had become "accustomed" to the "necessities" provided by their trade; and had continued using the resources of the plains to both live and get the materials of this trade. Because this space was his Home he was able to imagine and re-imagine this space; he was able to allow for the overlapping of these activities and the changes and continuities they wrought. He was also able to—and had to—shape his own vision of how he could use this trade system and this space in the best way possible to make and remake his Home.

James Bird, on the other hand, died a "pretentious and insensitive" man in the Red River Colony over ten years later. He ended his time as chief factor at Edmonton in 1816, although he was still employed by the HBC until his death. Bird was never at Home in Fort Edmonton; he had always been there as a trader and an employee, not as a settler. And, although he travelled to England in 1822–23, even this trip was probably not the "leave home" that John Foster describes it as.[76]

Unlike Old Swan, locating Bird's Home is difficult. He had left England at age fifteen and had lived and worked all of his adult life in Rupert's Land, making no visits east of York Factory until he was 49.[77] He did, however, in 1815 still list his home parish as Acton (unlike, for example, his sons who were from the parish of "Hudson Bay").[78] And Bird did keep fragments of Britishness with him at the fort. In 1795 he obtained a violin from England, and by 1799 he had in his library the 21-volume Ancient Universal History among his books.[79] An 1801 letter to Bird explained that "The Honourable Company" had given him "permission to send [his] son to England," although Bird does not seem to have followed through with this plan.[80] Although it is possible, then, that England was once Home for Bird, by 1822, after 34 years away from it, his "leave home" was probably very jarring, and probably not very "Home-like" at all. Bird seems to have been an early victim of the global world; his was a life that exemplified what Homi Bhabha has called the "'unhomeliness' inherent in … cross-cultural initiation."[81]

The HBC committee, and their rules and ideas of status, were his strongest, most concrete tie to England, although even these were flexible due to geographic distance. At least twice during his time at Edmonton Bird recognizes the need to bend the rules on the valuation of furs, explaining that he would "follow [the valuation] as far as Prudence will permit."[82] This flexibility of the frontier, yet attachment to London, was an important tension shaping Bird's imagination of the space around him at Edmonton.[83] Bird may have seen Fort Edmonton as attached to London, but also as a place over which he had some autonomous control. Because his entire journal, especially after 1811, clearly shows his deferential treatment towards the readers—the committee in London—we have trouble seeing/hearing what James Bird the person, as opposed to James Bird the status-conscious HBC employee, thought about the Edmonton District. Bird's journal was in fact a kind of performance for London, drawing on the reality of Fort Edmonton for its material.

An examination of Bird's life and career, then, reveals that Bird was "unHomely": the Edmonton District, and the river Bird seemed to pin himself to, was not Home, though neither was Britain. He was in Edmonton to trade, to take resources from the space. He was not at Edmonton to, like Old Swan, integrate together the different elements of the space or to find a new, fluid, Home-like definition of it. If Bird had any identifiable Home it was the "Honourable Company," the HBC itself; if this was the case, Bird, unlike Old Swan, lived in a Home tied to a set of rules and expectations—not to a space. Because Old Swan and Bird had such dissimilar Homes, it is little wonder that they each imagined and used the space of Edmonton and the plains differently.

Home

More than simply pointing to the economic and material motivations involved in the fur trade at Edmonton, this study has argued that it was where James Bird and Old Swan located Home that informed how they used the Edmonton District and how they saw their role in the space of the district. Much of the historiography about the fur trade has tended to place a primacy on economic factors alone to explain why Aboriginal people traded, and how HBC officials acted. This study has added nuance to this trend. Because Old Swan was at Home in the district it was a logical decision for him to trade and to integrate the new materials and people of the trading posts into his definition of Home; for Old Swan, at least, the trade at Edmonton was a boon to his Home. Likewise, James Bird, not at Home in the space of the Edmonton District, organized his actions in the space to benefit his Home—the HBC—and his own position in this Home. Constructing the story of James Bird and Old Swan at Edmonton around the theme of Home has revealed, therefore, the context in which each man made economic decisions.

This study also suggests something else: the power to define the space of the Edmonton District did not—at this point in history—rest with James Bird and the HBC. At least before 1815, to James Bird the Edmonton District was always just a space to do business in by taking resources from it. To Old Swan, however, the district was place, a Home into which resources from industrial Britain could easily be integrated with the resources from the fall buffalo hunt. It is worth questioning, of course, what happened to Home at the end of the 19th century after the "Great Transformation" of Western Canada.[84] Where was Home for Siksika people and HBC officials in 1880? How had the construction of the reserve system changed the definition of Home for all people living on the plains? Had Home—and a changing definition of it—informed the way treaties were negotiated and reserves established? Western Canadian historiography has often relied on economic analyses to describe this "transformation" and to describe the fur trade era before it; investigating the role of Home is a way to write a history that, although cognizant of economic factors, stresses the intellectual and cultural forces in this history and in the history of cross-cultural interaction generally. Thus, Home is a basic feature organizing human actions that is deserving of considerable historical inquiry.

Notes

This article first appeared in *Prairie Forum* 29, no. 1 (2004): 25–44.

1. For valuable feedback on early drafts of this paper I'd like to thank Gerhard Ens, Michael Payne, Ted Binnema, and my fellow students from the Fort Edmonton seminar at the University of Alberta, Fall 2002. Portions of this paper were presented at, and appear in the proceedings of, the Culture and State conference, University of Alberta, May 2003.

2. Hudson's Bay Company Archives (HBCA), Provincial Archives of Manitoba, Winnipeg, B.60/a/13, October 17, 1814.

3. In my own text I use labels Aboriginal peoples self-identify with, such as "Siksika." When quoting primary sources, however, I have kept the original terminology used by James Bird and other Europeans; Bird, for example, labels "Siksika" people as "Blackfoot" or "Blackfeet." During the 1794–1814 period Old Swan traded at a number of Forts. He mostly traded in and around the North Saskatchewan except between 1800 and 1802 when he based his trade at Chesterfield House on the South Saskatchewan just inside present day Saskatchewan.

4. For a study of Old Swan see Theodore Binnema, "Old Swan, Big Man, and the Siksika Bands, 1794–1815," *Canadian Historical Review* 77 (1996): 1–32. For a biography of James Bird see John Foster, "James Bird, Fur Trader," in Bob Hesketh and Frances Swyripa (eds.), *Edmonton: The Life of a City* (Edmonton: New West Publishers, 1995), 12–20.

5. On the questions of motivation for Old Swan's participation in the trade, Binnema suggests only that the decision to trade was motivated by the "complex reality in which individual and communal choice were made." Of the outcomes of this trade, Binnema suggests: "direct trade ... had more than economic consequences, for it allowed the Blackfoot to reconsider a whole array of established relationships and behaviours." See Binnema, "Old Swan, Big Man and Siksika Bands," 32 and 11.

6. Derek Gregory, *Geographic Imaginations* (Cambridge, MA: Blackwell), 145. For an example of how spatial analysis has already been thought about in the context of the fur trade see Arthur Ray, *Indians in the Fur Trade: Their Role as Trappers, Hunters, and Middlemen in the Lands Southwest of Hudson Bay, 1660–1870* (Toronto: University of Toronto Press, 1974), and Arthur Ray and Donald Freeman, *"Give Us Good Measure": An Economic Analysis of Relations Between the Indians and the Hudson's Bay Company Before 1763* (Toronto: University of Toronto Press, 1978), 257. More recently, James Carson has argued that Ray's spatial analysis of the fur trade, although sophisticated, is too economic in nature. Carson argues that a spatial analysis of an event like the fur trade must see land as being a "physical" as well as a "moral place." See James Carson, "Ethnography and the Native American Past," *Ethnohistory* 4 (2002): 769–88

7. Paul Thistle, *Indian-European Trade Relations in the Lower Saskatchewan River Region to 1840* (Winnipeg: University of Manitoba Press, 1986), 34–35.

8. Michael Payne, "Fur Trade Historiography: Past Conditions, Present Circumstances and a Hint of Future Prospects," in Theodore Binnema, Gerhard Ens and R.C. Macleod (eds.), *From Rupert's Land to Canada* (Edmonton: University of Alberta, 2001), 9. See also Jennifer Brown, "The Blind Men and the Elephant: Fur Trade History Revisited," in Patricia A. McCormack and R. Geoffrey (eds.), *The Uncovered Past: Roots of Northern Alberta Societies* (Edmonton: Canadian Circumpolar Institute, University of Alberta, 1993).

9. Ilan Natan Magat, "Home As the Meeting of Heaven and Earth" (Ph.D. dissertation, University of Alberta, 1995), 2. Thanks to Tosha Tsang for her ideas on "Home" and for drawing my attention to this source.

10. Magat, "Home As the Meeting of Heaven and Earth," 6.

11. Slave also means Blackfoot Confederacy or the combined "nation" of the Piegan, Siksika and Kainai Indians. There was, as several historians have pointed out, no formal political structure uniting these three groups. See Binnema, "Old Swan, Big Man and Siksika Bands," 3.

12. Barry Gough (ed.), *The Journal of Alexander Henry the Younger, 1799–1814*, vol. 2 (Toronto: Champlain Society, 1992), 376–77. Henry's journal provides extensive information about Old Swan. Henry was a North-West Company (NWC) trader who lived along the North Saskatchewan River between 1808–1810. See Barry Gough, "Alexander Henry" in *Dictionary of Canadian Biography*, vol. 5, (Toronto: University of Toronto Press, 1983), 418.

13. See Binnema, "How Does a Map Mean?: Old Swan's Map of 1801 and the Blackfoot World," in *From Rupert's Land to Canada*, 214–16. As Binnema shows, the "Rocky mountains" in Fidler's drawing of the map was probably in fact the , the front-range hills most noticeable from the plains.

14. Ibid., 216–17. Binnema, however, never raises the possibility that the map was a piece of propaganda about the military superiority of the Blackfoot: it may have been that Old Swan was trying to impress Fidler with the map and its meaning.

15. HBCA B.60/a/6, April 7, 1807.

16. HBCA B.60/e/1, District Report, 1815.

17. Ibid.

18. Ibid.

19. HBCA B.60/a/11, October 12, 1812.

20. One exception was a journey Bird took on horse back in 1812 to the new Factory site—although even this trip was along the riverbank. See HBCA B.60/a/11, October 9, 1812.

21. HBCA B.60/a/13, October 20, 1814.

22. HBCA B.60/a/9, February 18, 1811,

23. Bird, "Sept. 25 1799," in Alice Johnson (ed.), *Saskatchewan Journals and Correspondence 1799–1802* (Toronto: MacMillan, 1967), 210–11.

24. Ibid, 211.

25. Bird to McNab, HBCA B.60/a/7, August 8, 1808.

26. HBCA B.60/a/9, July 30, 1811.

27. HBCA B.60/a/12, October 15, 1813.

28. HBCA B.60/a/12, February 28, 1814.

29. HBCA B.60/e/1, District Report 1815.

30. Binnema, "How Does a Map Mean?," 214.

31. Ibid., 215–18.

32. For movements in the early fall see Peter Fidler, "September 27 1801," in *Saskatchewan Journals*, 293. See also Gough, *Journal of Alexander Henry*, 366. For record of a fall war-trip see Fidler, "November 1, 1800," *Saskatchewan Journals*, 274. For movement to plains for winter buffalo hunts see Theodore Binnema, *Common and Contested Ground: A Human and Environmental History of the Northwestern Plains* (Norman: University of Oklahoma Press, 2001), chapter 2.

33. For the difficulty of using horses see HBCA B.60/a/9, January 31, 1811.

34. Bird to Captain MacDonald, HBCA B.60/a/1, February 28, 1814.

35. See Gough, *Journal of Alexander Henry*, 381 and 358. See also Bird's reaction to Old Swan as a peacemaker between Cree and Siksika: HBCA B.60/a/6, April 7, 1807; and HBCA B.60/a/13, October 17, 1814.

36. HBCA B.60/a/10, February 17, 1812; HBCA B.60/a/11, December 29, 1813; HBCA B.60/a/12, September 28, 1814.

37. HBCA B.60/a/12.

38. HBCA B.60/e/1, District Report 1815.

39. Ibid. For another discussion of the gardens see HBCA B.60/a/10, October 18, 1811.

40. HBCA B.60/e/1, District Report 1815. Bird's perception of the space as a cornucopia characterizes what may have become the HBC's approach to land and resources at Edmonton later in the 19th century. See Terence O'Rierdon, "Straddling the 'Great Transformation': The Hudson's Bay Company in Edmonton during the Transition from the Commons to Private Property, 1854–1882," *Prairie Forum* 28, no. 1 (Spring 2003): 1–26.

41. See *Saskatchewan Journals*, 272, 277, 286.

42. Binnema, *Common and Contested Ground*, 170.

43. See Johnson, *Saskatchewan Journals*, Appendix A. The Made Beaver (MB) was used to describe the value of furs and trade goods in the North West. The Made Beaver was equal in value to one prime beaver skin.

44. Two important works that emphasize economic/material motivations are Arthur Ray and Donald Freeman, *"Give Us Good Measure,"* and Arthur Ray, *Indians in the Fur Trade*.

45. Arthur Ray, *Indians in the Fur Trade*, 73–75.

46. A list of trade items in 1813 also includes blankets, cloth, beads and hatchets. See HBCA.60/z/1. For reference to these as "necessities" see B.60/a/6, April 7, 1807.

47. Fidler, "September 27, 1801," *Saskatchewan Journals*, 293.

48. Fidler, "November 9, 1801," *Saskatchewan Journals*, 300.

49. Fidler, "November 15, 1801," *Saskatchewan Journals*, 300–301.

50. HBCA B.60/a/6, April 7, 1807.

51. See the initial letter from Fidler to Edmonton House in December 1800 asking for supplies: Fidler asks for "cloth for Chiefs coats and other things to rig the chiefs…" These may not have been the actual materials used to make Old Swan's coat, but it reveals that chiefs were "rigged" with more than just "a coat." Old Swan was actually "rigged" with the coat in April 1802. See Fidler, "December 2, 1800" and "April 3, 1802," *Saskatchewan Journals*, 278 and 320.

52. HBCA B.60/c/1, District Report, 1815.

53. HBCA B.60/a/12, November 24, 1813.

54. HBCA B.60/a/12, December 14, 1813.

55. HBCA B.60/a/13, October 17, 1814.

56. HBCA B.60/a/7, December 20, 1807.

57. HBCA B.60/a/12, October 20, 1813.

58. HBCA B.60/a/9, January 3, 1810.

59. HBCA B.60/a/12, March 21, 1814.

60. It is difficult to say where Bird placed people of mixed descent (including his own sons) as he never comments directly on this. However, in 1811 Jimmy "Jock" Bird (James's son) is labelled as a "native" in Edmonton House documents. See "Men's Debts," Edmonton House Account Books, HBCA B.60/d/2a 1811.

61. HBCA B.60/a/7, October 19, 1808. This was in response to Stoney horse raiding and conflict between the Stoney and traders to the east.

62. HBCA B.60/a/11, April 11, 1813. See also Bird's subsequent decision to post guards at the fort.

63. See Edward Said, *Orientalism* (1978; New York: Random House, 1994), 1–15. Said's seminal work gives an explanation of what might be the knowledge/power paradigm in the colonial context and how "race" and racialization are associated with this process. See also C.A. Bayly's discussion of this process in the global context of the Empire. Bayly points to the 1820s as the time after which the Indigenous people in the Empire were, in Bayly's words, "invented." C.A. Bayly, "The British and Indigenous peoples, 1760–1860: Power, perception and identity," in Martin Daunton and Richard Halpern (eds.), *Empire and Others: British Encounters with Indigenous People 1600–1850* (Philadelphia: University of Pennsylvania Press, 1999), 21–33.

64. HBCA B.60/e/1, District Report, 1815.

65. Gough, *Journal of Alexander Henry*, 401.

66. Ibid., 421

67. Ibid. 421–22

68. Ibid., 379.

69. To see why I've included the publisher's (potential) role in this transmission process

see I.S. Maclaren, "Paul Kane and the Authorship of Wanderings of an Artist," in *From Rupert's Land to Canada*, 225–48.

70. See Ella Clark, *Indian Legends: From the Northern Rockies* (Norman: University of Oklahoma Press, 1989), 235. See also Binnema, "Old Swan, Big Man and Siksika Bands," 12.

71. For the theoretical ideas employed here see Jean and John Comaroff, *Ethnography and Historical Imagination* (San Francisco: Westview Press, 1992), 5.

72. Gough, *Journal of Alexander Henry*, 379.

73. C.A. Bayly, "The British and Indigenous Peoples, 1760–1860," 33.

74. HBCA B.60/a/1B, October 17, 1814.

75. Gough, *Journal of Alexander Henry*, 380.

76. Foster, "James Bird," 20.

77. Bird's leave to England in 1822 seems to be his first time east of Hudson Bay since arriving in Rupert's Land. See Johnson, "Introduction," in *Saskatchewan Journals*, passim.

78. HBCA B.60/f/I, "List of Servants [1815]."

79. See Johnson, "Introduction," *Saskatchewan Journals*, xcviii. Included here is a long list of books owned by James Bird.

80. William Tomison to Bird, April 4, 1801, quoted in Johnson, "Introduction," *Saskatchewan Journals*, lxxxiii.

81. Homi Bhabha, *The Location of Culture* (London: Routledge, 1994), 9.

82. Bird to Mr. Prudens, HBCA B.60/a/7, December 14, 1807. In another instance, Bird explains why he is choosing to ignore the rules about not taking in wolf skins. See HBCA B.60/a/12, October 8, 1813.

83. Examples of how this tension informed Bird's life include his endorsement and practice of inter-racial marriage, an act technically outlawed by the HBC. Also, Bird did not always follow the Company protocol for discipline and social control. See Elizabeth Burly, *Servants of the Honourable Company: Work, Discipline, and Conflict in The Hudson's Bay Company, 1770–1879* (Don Mills, ON: Oxford University Press, 1997), 147.

84. For discussion of the "great transformation" of Western Canada see Irene Spry, "The Great Transformation: The Disappearance of the Commons in Western Canada," in R.A. Allen (ed.), *Man and Nature on the Prairies* (Regina: Canadian Plains Research Center, 1976), 21–45.

Rupert's Land and Red River

9. The 1857 Parliamentary Inquiry, the Hudson's Bay Company, and Rupert's Land's Aboriginal People

A.A. den Otter

In 1857 the British Parliament appointed a Select Committee to review the activities of the Hudson's Bay Company, which had possessed a chartered fur trading monopoly in Rupert's Land since 1670.[1] Sitting for over 40 days, the committee took testimony from nearly two dozen witnesses. The transcript of their evidence furnishes an extremely detailed snapshot of how these observers viewed ecological and cultural conditions in the region at mid-century. In particular, the committee's report offers a unique glimpse into the attitude of Europeans towards the Aboriginal nations in the northwestern interior of British North America and portrays what they perceived to be the long-term future of those peoples.

The portrait of the indigenous peoples[2] that emerges from the pages of the Select Committee's report reflected the context of the time. Witnesses and questioners alike believed that over the past two centuries, the powerful combination of science, technology, and capitalism, flourishing under increasingly free political and economic institutions, had created the great and wealthy British Empire. To sustain the pace of economic growth and an improving standard of living, Britain's leaders scoured the globe for raw materials for the nation's machines, food for its workers, and employment for its surplus populations. They believed that the country's mandate was to develop the natural and human resources of the entire world. Thomas Carlyle, the Victorian essayist, angrily lamented the lingering remnants of poverty in industrial Britain when there was "a world where Canadian Forests stand unfelled, boundless Plains and Prairies unbroken with the plough ... green desert spaces never yet made white with corn; and to the overcrowded little western nook of Europe, our Terrestrial Planet, nine-tenth of it yet vacant or tenanted by nomades, is still crying, Come and till me, come and reap me!"[3] Carlyle thus eloquently articulated a powerful civilizing mission, an expansionist creed that urged western Europeans to tame the world's remaining wilderness regions and manage them for the desires of humanity. At the same time, Victorians believed that this civilizing task also included the mandate to share with other people in the world the knowledge that had produced this unprecedented wealth. Thus, a host of civil servants, entrepreneurs, teachers, and missionaries spread across the globe to bring the gospel of liberalism to uneducated people everywhere. The whole world must be civilized, they assumed; that is, peoples everywhere must be raised to the level of enlightened, Christian, industrial, and urbanizing Victorian Britain.[4]

The theme, that the enormous resources of Rupert's Land must be opened to private enterprise, that its indigenous peoples must be educated, and, in other words, that the days of the Hudson's Bay Company's hegemony over its resources and peoples were numbered, echoes throughout the Select Committee's report. While contemporary observers likely saw two distinct points of view emerging from the evidence placed before the committee, a modern historian, reading the manuscript a century and a half later, may notice a remarkable similarity in the statements concerning Rupert Land's resources and its Aboriginal nations. Seemingly, one perspective encouraged the continuation, for as long as possible, of the monopoly and the preservation of the supposedly traditional (but post-contact) indigenous lifestyles; the other view, advocated the commencement, as soon as feasible, of the colonization of the territory's arable lands and the integration of the Native peoples into this new society. This polarization, however, mirrored specific objectives; in actual fact, both perceptions were remarkably similar as each was based on an imperialist view of the environment and the Aboriginal nations.[5] All witnesses, as well as committee members, assumed that the resources of the vast interior were to be exploited for the benefit primarily of Europeans. While Hudson's Bay Company officials and their friends seemed more sympathetic to maintaining the lifestyles of the Native peoples, and while their economic objectives differed from their opponents, all witnesses believed that the Aboriginal people were uncivilized, culturally homogenous, and that their fate was to be decided in London. All the participants adopted a paternalistic attitude towards the Aboriginal prairie peoples, believing that in their supposed ignorance they could not cope with either the fur trade or impending settlement without the guidance of the European newcomers. In fact, no one thought it necessary to invite anyone of the First Nations to testify at the hearings.

Not unexpectedly, the Hudson's Bay Company welcomed neither the Select Committee nor the impending settlement of the North-West. While the former would likely cast unfavourable light upon the company's activities, the latter would inevitably and unfavourably affect the company's business. Yet, the future course of events was quite clear to the company's governors and they acknowledged they must accommodate themselves to the new reality. In the meantime, they would do all in their power to persuade the committee to preserve the status quo. The governors informed their Canadian representative, Sir George Simpson, that "our great object before the Committee of the House of Commons will be to shew that all our regulations for the administration of the country and the conduct of our trade, have been such as were calculated to protect the Indians and prevent their demoralization, and that, as far as can be reasonably expected, we have been successful."[6] By demonstrating their good stewardship, company officials thought, they could, by implication, be trusted to retain the monopoly and ensure the welfare of the Natives.

The star witness defending the company's position was its Canadian governor, Sir George Simpson. Born in February 1786 or 1787, Simpson joined the Hudson's Bay Company in 1820 just prior to its merger with the North West Company. Renowned for his many incredibly fast journeys across the vast territories, he devoted most of his time capitalizing on the company's monopoly, economizing its operations, and imposing a stringent discipline on all employees. Dynamic and aggressive, Simpson was a fast learner and a very capable, shrewd manager, keeping himself well informed on all aspects of the business and adapting it quickly to new environments. Although he forbade his low-ranked employees to form relationships with the Natives, Simpson himself had short liaisons with at least three Métis women and sired four children. These associations, his sojourn in the territories, and his incessant, restless travels, gave Simpson a comprehensive knowledge of Rupert's Land and its peoples.[7]

Despite his relations with the Métis women, Simpson nurtured a prejudice against North America's indigenous people. Obsessed with the early Victorian ideal of the beautiful, pure, cultured, and genteel lady, he refused to marry any woman born in Rupert's Land and in 1829 abruptly ended a relationship to wed his 18-year-old Scottish cousin, Frances.[8] Even though Frances lived in Red River for nearly four years, at Simpson's insistence she socialized only with the few white women in the settlement and thus met no Native females and only Métis servants.[9] In 1833, she returned to Scotland, and in 1838 settled into Simpson's permanent residence in Lachine, Canada East.

George Simpson's testimony before the Select Committee reflected that of his Montreal and London peers. As an investor, not only in the fur trade,

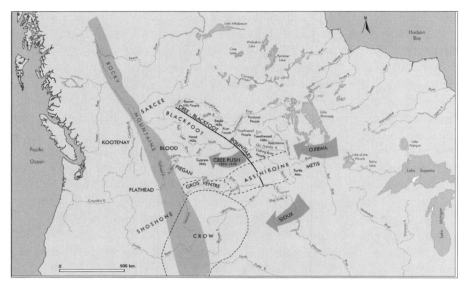

Plains Indian tribal boundaries, c. 1850 (courtesy of the Canadian Plains Research Center Mapping Division/Adapted from Milloy, *The Plains Cree* [1988]).

but also in banking, mining, and railways,[10] Simpson understood the mid-19th-century resource development mentality. Like many of his peers, he was glad to have escaped the so-called wilderness, had cultivated a condescending antipathy to the Native people, especially their women, and had attuned himself to the restless energy of Canada's emerging technological culture and looming expansionist ambitions.[11] Although his testimony advocated the preservation of the traditional fur trade and the Aboriginal way of life, he consciously participated in business endeavours that were central to the new order.

Sir George Simpson's contention, that the Hudson's Bay Company was best suited to protect the prosperity of Rupert's Land's Natives, was challenged by the Aborigines Protection Society, a humanitarian association, deeply concerned about the well-being of the indigenous nations. Founded in 1837 to fight the dispossession, massacre, and enslavement of Aboriginal people by invading colonists, the society took a special interest in North America and persistently lobbied the imperial government to protect, educate, and integrate its First Nations into the newcomer society. From its humanitarian platform, the Aborigines Protection Society valiantly attempted to persuade church and state to shield indigenous inhabitants from the whites: it advocated that British North America's Native peoples be regarded as British subjects, that their lands not be further alienated without proper compensation, that they be educated into British culture and religion, and then integrated into the new white society.[12] Athough the society professed itself not to be an opponent of the Hudson's Bay Company, in a pamphlet it published a year prior to the Select Committee's hearings, it accused the firm of impeding "the progress of civilization and religion," and of violating what it considered to be the "universal benefits of free trade and free communications.[13] Mixed in its altruistic position, the society also appealed to practical concerns by arguing that teaching the indigenous peoples the principles of contemporary industrialized society would stabilize and settle them thus creating a much larger market for British manufactures instead of, what it perceived to be, a declining, nomadic population of savage hunters.[14] In any case, the society assumed that the British should develop and settle the vast North American continent and that, therefore, its Native people must accommodate themselves to the new order.

The Aborigines Protection Society took a close interest in the Select Committee and placed before it a comprehensive brief which it hoped would help the committee devise measures for the "future improvement and preservation" of the Aboriginal populations.[15] In its submission, the society charged that the activities of the Hudson's Bay Company had adversely affected British North America's Aboriginal people. Even though the Natives were the real producers of corporate wealth, they had suffered under the company's rule and their numbers had declined precipitously.[16] Although the society believed that alcohol abuse and disease were contributing factors to the problem, dwindling food supplies were the primary and most worrisome cause of the declining Aboriginal population. The society acknowledged that vaccinations and prohibitions against the use of alcohol in most districts had already greatly mitigated the impact of those difficulties.[17] What concerned the society was that the fur trade by its very nature continued to contribute to the precipitous drop in animal numbers.[18] Meanwhile, the demand for furs and provisions was increasing and the company was reducing expenditures on trade goods. The society believed the future appeared harsh and starvation was a grim reality. The paramount question, according to the society, therefore, was whether the Natives could survive the end of the fur trade and prospective settlement. "What is to become of the Indians," the society asked, "when their lands can no longer furnish the means of subsistence?"[19]

The society's penetrating question laid bare the two fundamental considerations before the Select Committee. Simply put: should the Hudson's Bay Company's monopoly be continued and should Rupert's Land be opened for settlement? In 1857, with the Canadas becoming increasingly interested in expanding into the North-West, the answers to these two queries were intricately intertwined and their answers would have enormous implications for the territories' indigenous people. On the surface, the responses that the witnesses provided appeared to be clearly and mutually exclusive, with a distinct fracture line running between the pro- and anti-company camps. Yet, coursing beneath the surface of their testimonies was a consensus, which the committee, itself divided into defence and opposition, also shared. Whether they believed in free trade or the monopoly, in colonization or a fur preserve, explicitly or implicitly questioners and respondents based their arguments on the common and erroneous assumption that the Natives were part of the uncivilized wilderness and that their savagery could not withstand the onward march of Europe's supposedly superior civilization. No one suggested that the Aboriginal nations formed complex, differentiated societies and controlled their own destinies.[20] All the participants at the committee's hearings saw the issue only as one of timing and responsibility: how quickly could the British government permit the civilizing of the wilderness and its inhabitants to proceed and who would assume the task of educating the Natives for the civilization process?

Opening Rupert's Land to European civilization, that is, to settlement and resource development, immediately raised the question of a competitive fur trade and its impact on the Aboriginal populations. While those who sided with the company neatly side-stepped the issue of profits, they pointed to the era of rivalry between the Hudson's Bay and the North West companies at the turn of the century as an example of all that could go wrong in a free trade regime. They recalled an era of violence, widespread lawlessness, general disorder, and flagrant alcohol misuse. Sir J. Richardson, who had made three journeys through the territories, one with John Franklin, testified that in 1819, when the North West and Hudson's Bay companies were at war, both firms supplied the Natives with liquor. "The Indians were spending days in drunkenness" going from fort to fort for liquor "and a contest altogether shocking to humanity was carried on," Richardson asserted, adding, "At that time it scarcely appeared that the Indians had any capability of being civilised at all."[21] On his second trip, the Hudson's Bay Company had re-established its monopoly and had greatly reduced liquor imports. There was a manifest improvement in life in the North-West Richardson noted, although he expressed disappointment that no Aboriginal persons had become Christian, which he considered an essential step in the civilization process. Open trade, he believed, would reproduce the violent rivalries of the first decades of the century. "At present the Hudson's Bay Company's influence over the Indians is beneficial," he observed, "the natives are dependent upon the Hudson's Bay Company for supplies: but if they could get supplies elsewhere, and if spirits were brought in (for there is nothing which will prevent the introduction of spirits but the resolution of the Company not to take them in), I think itwould require a strong military force to keep the Indians in subjection."[22]

Several witnesses bolstered Richardson's testimony.[23] Competition in the fur trade, they conceded, might lead to an immediate increase in prices and living standards but eventually, they added, it would destroy the indigenous people. The rivalry would lead to the re-introduction of alcohol, to an increase in crime and intertribal warfare, to starvation and hardship among the Natives, and eventually to their demoralization and decimation. It would, said David Anderson, the Anglican bishop of Assiniboia, ruin the Natives' way of life before they could be civilized.[24]

Not only would a competitive fur trade destroy the Aboriginal people, according to Edward Ellice, the grizzled veteran of the fur trade, it would also ruin their habitat. In areas where the company did not face competition, it urged the Natives to preserve "the animals just as you do your pheasants and hares in this country. [It] … encourage [d] the Indians only to kill a certain number of animals when in good season for their furs, and not to kill so many as to interfere with the breed."[25] But, in territories where the company did not have complete control over traders and Aboriginal hunters, it could not impose quotas. Where two or more tribes hunted, if one preserved animals, the other would take more, Ellice explained, unless the company refused to take the fur, something it could not do if a rival would take the surpluses. To make his point, he noted that the company was able to practice conservation only north of the 60th parallel where the Natives had fixed hunting grounds. In the south, where the Plains tribes wandered over vast territories and could sell their furs to American competitors, management was impossible.[26] Competition, he predicted, would lead to massive over-hunting and the destruction of the trade within 10 years, leading to widespread starvation among the Aboriginal people.

As far as Alexander Isbister, a Rupert's Land-born critic of the Hudson's Bay Company residing in England, was concerned, these were all self-serving arguments. Having lived the first 20 years of his life in Red River and served a three-year stint as a company clerk, Isbister felt that the company's only interest in the indigenous hunters was to "procure furs at the cheapest rate" it could. All that needed to be done to end the liquor trade, Isbister stated, was to adopt the American system of licensing. While enforcement of prohibition might be difficult, he argued, it was not impossible nor need it hamper the settlement of the fertile portions of the northwestern interior. Free trade would be a good inducement to settlers, he continued, attracting immigrants to the North-West by the possibility of extra earnings. Although increased settlement in Red River would inevitably lead to greater participation in the fur trade, he believed that the violence and debauchery of the Natives, alleged to have occurred during the period of rivalry between the North West and Hudson's Bay companies, would not redevelop because of the presence of missionaries in the region and public opinion in eastern Canada.[27]

Other witnesses agreed that an open fur trade would not lead to a bitter life-and-death struggle as had occurred at the turn of the century. Although no one made the specific reference, a growing number of Métis had already been trading in furs, pemmican, provisions, and other articles for a number of years, particularly after 1849 when four of them had been found guilty in court of violating the company's charter but were not sentenced.[28] With this experience in mind, some witnesses asserted that free trade would greatly benefit the Natives economically and culturally. "It is only by competition, of course, that the Indians will receive anything like fair play," argued John McLaughlin, a company critic who had lived in the North-West for about five years in the late 1840s as a private settler and merchant.[29] Donald Gunn, a free trader in the Lake Superior area, agreed and added that the Natives would shake off their dependence upon the Hudson's Bay Company for their supplies; they would become more self-reliant. Competition would allow them to obtain necessities like clothing and provisions more easily and more abundantly; it would lessen privation and suffering due to shortages of supplies. Referring to specific examples from the Sault Ste. Marie and Lake Superior region, Gunn demonstrated that under company control, the Aboriginal peoples suffered hardship and hunger but once freed from its grip they earned more for their hunting efforts or they diversified into farming, including cattle raising and wild fruit gathering, or they worked in the mining, lumbering, or fishing industries. Exposed to "all the various industrial pursuits of civilised life," competition would "at the same time advance them to civilisation."[30] All these new opportunities, therefore, meant that the Natives would "no longer [be] obliged to roam over the country in search of a livelihood, families would congregate together, become fillers of land, and their condition be thus greatly improved."[31] Thus, in Gunn's opinion, free trade was part of the civilization process. Specifically, he and other critics charged, the monopoly, where it still existed, had created an impoverished society. By using an outdated credit system and excessive markups, the Hudson's Bay Company, they censured, not only exploited the Natives, causing periodic famines, but also thwarted their education and civilization.[32]

The Aborigines Protection Society elaborated on this theme. Committed to the *laissez-faire*, free enterprise, capitalist economy that had reached a zenith in mid-19th century Britain, the society viewed the problem not as a question of pricing or methods of exchange but as the presence of a state-sponsored monopoly. "We have given unlimited scope to the cupidity of a company of traders," the society chided, "placing no stint on their profits, or limits to their power."[33] Since it did not operate for the benefit of the Natives, the monopoly was an injustice. Not only did it deprive the hunter of fair value for his work but, from its humanitarian, paternalistic, and British supremacist perspective, the Aborigines Protection Society imputed that it barred him from contact with civilized man and the supposedly ameliorating influences needed for his advancement on the scale of humanity. The company, whose monopoly had been virtually unchallenged for the past 30 years, had squandered the opportunity to civilize the Aboriginal people. at was the result, the society asked: an unhappy race of people toiling for the company's profit; a people who were perishing in frequent famines. While the Hudson's Bay Company was rich, prosperous, and powerful, the indigenous hunter was a slave, wandering about without a home, with little clothing, "as much a stranger to the blessings of civilisation as when the white man first landed on his shores." Although the society did not censure individual Hudson's Bay employees, seeing most as benevolent, humane, enterprising, and intelligent, it charged that the corporate character, the habits and the policies of the company were "unfavourable to that progressive settlement and civilisation of the country which has been going on in so remarkable a manner to the south of the British and American boundary."[34] In this surprising lack of understanding of the fate of many Natives in the United States, the Aborigines Protective Society expressed its fundamental faith in 19th-century culture; it believed that free enterprise United States had made much greater progress in civilizing the wilderness and its indigenous human inhabitants than mercantilistic Great Britain; obviously, in its view, redemption lay not with a monopolistic company but with the state, the church, and the school. These institutions would bring the Natives to the technological level of European civilization.

Not surprisingly, company officials countered that they treated the Natives justly and paid them fairly. They pointed out that company policy required its employees [servants in the contemporary term] to treat the Aboriginal hunters equitably. The governor and his council as well as the imperial government, they said, closely supervised the behaviour of the company's servants in the interior and dismissed officers who were indolent or exploitive or took sexual advantages of Aboriginal women. As Edward

Ellice made clear, the company encouraged a sympathetic understanding of indigenous traditions, yet fostered the adoption of European customs when suitable. The most valuable servant was one "who, by proper means and humane attention, and attempts to civilise the Indian, established an influence with the Indians."[35] To prove his point, he cited the fortieth standing rule of the fur trade:

> That the Indians be treated with kindness and indulgence, and mild and conciliatory means resorted to in order to encourage industry, repress vice, and inculcate morality; that the use of spirituous liquors be gradually discontinued in the very few districts in which it is yet indispensable; and that the Indians be liberally supplied with requisite necessaries, particularly with articles of ammunition, whether they have the means of paying for it or not and that no gentleman in charge of a district or post be at liberty to alter or vary the standard or usual mode of trade with the Indians, except by special permission of council.[36]

As the fortieth rule implied, the company's trade policy was based on a paternalistic system in which company executives assumed the Natives to be relatively immature in business, economic, and political acumen and thus required management and protection. Except in Canada and near the United States boundary—where there was competition—the company conducted the trade entirely on credit, exchanging fur for clothing, robes, blankets, traps, guns, and ammunition. In practice, this meant that the traders were perpetually in debt to the company, which, in itself, may not necessarily have been detrimental to the hunters and their families. While they may have accumulated significant, long-term debts, most appeared to have preferred the system. As Eleanor Blain has observed in the case of the Ojibwa, the company tried on several occasions to abandon the debt system because periodically it had to forgive unreasonably high debt loads. The Ojibwa, Blain notes, always rejected such overtures.[37]

In somewhat legalistic terms, Governor George Simpson also explained that the company did not actuall' trade goods but "gave" them to the Natives and they repaid the company with fur.[38] Simpson's carefully drawn, legalistic distinction between trading and giving illustrated his paternalistic and often patronizing attitude. Since the giving of gifts had a long history among North America's Aboriginal people and was an integral part of any commercial transaction,[39] the use of this concept showed that Simpson understood an ancient tradition, but it also demonstrated the power the company had over the hunters. By calling trade goods gifts, the company felt, for example, it need not differentiate among fur species and did not have to pay a premium for more highly valued furs. Simpson argued that "the Indian[s] would never understand our varying the prices of the fur according to the prices here [in London]," and that they would concentrate on the more valuable species and hunt them to extinction. Moreover, as former trader, John Rae, opined, "the Indian is so improvident that if he were paid in the spring he would waste everything before winter."[40] To what extent, one might ask, were Simpson and Rae's assumptions, that the Aboriginal hunters could not appreciate the value of cash, any different than the Aborigines Protection Society's belief that they could not survive the onslaught of European culture?

Despite Simpson and Rae's paternalistic justifications for the credit system, some contemporary observers noted that Native hunters fully comprehended the concept of trading. Although they may not have adequately grasped the intricacies of the market and margins, they "understood the value of every skin they had, and they had in mind everything they wanted."[41] They were "perfectly shrewd" in their dealings and knew their rights; they fathomed the concept of pricing and, if feasible, would go to the outpost which offered the best prices.[42]

Modern historians confirm the contemporary evidence. Running through Arthur Ray's groundbreaking analysis of the fur trade in Rupert's Land is the theme that the Natives were active partners in the trade.[43] In a more specific way, Eleanor M. Blain suggests that the northern Ojibwa knew how to manipulate white traders into giving them better prices by shopping at various posts, coming back for more "essential" goods, and refusing to hunt for fur.[44] Similarly, John S. Milloy demonstrates compellingly that over generations the Plains Cree, as go-betweens, had developed complex trading relationships covering the Plains and had established a reputation as shrewd traders.[45]

In the final analysis, however, by 1857, the impact of the fur trade on the lives of the Aboriginal people of still unsettled Rupert's Land's may actually have been relatively slight. Governor Simpson testified that the company supplied only a small portion of the Natives' annual needs. He suggested that they did not require supplies for the summer and that even in winter their wants were limited. As hunters, they supplied most of their own food and made most of their own clothing out of fur and hides. Although he could provide no specific figures on the amount of goods traded to the Natives, he estimated that the company landed annually at York Factory, Moose, and East Main about £60,000 worth of British manufactures, such as blankets, fabrics, arms, ammunition, iron works, and axes. With about two-thirds of that amount designated as trade goods, Simpson estimated that the company distributed less than £1 per Aboriginal person in Rupert's Land.[46] Even if his calculations were based on imprecise and high population figures, the logic of Simpson's argument is compelling.

Recent scholarship on this issue seems to suggest that Governor Simpson's assertion may have been simplistic. Most historians would agree that on a macro level, and over several centuries, the fur trade contributed to altered tribal boundaries, to shifted seasonal migrations, and to specialized economic activities. Arthur Ray, for example, argues that today's Aboriginal welfare syndrome has deep roots in fur trade history.[47] Hunting for commercial purposes encouraged Natives to concentrate on killing only certain species or to become traders only; it definitely altered their seasonal movements. Moreover, by the mid-19th century, when game was becoming increasingly scarce, the Hudson's Bay Company had appropriated considerable control over food supplies in Rupert's Land. It made survival possible for its servants and many of its hunters in marginal areas by imposing sophisticated logistics on the territories, replete with fixed depots and rigid transportation schedules over set routes.[48] The company's labour policies, wage schedules, and trade standards, while they ensured comfortable profits, returned marginal benefits to the Natives and made credit and frequent gratuities essential to the welfare of the hunters and their families. Without losing sight of human agency in this complex process, the fur trade had been instrumental in significant economic and demographic changes in the territories. Moreover, as Calvin Martin has so eloquently argued, fur traders, along with missionaries and disease, contributed to the erosion of indigenous religious beliefs and values and thus profoundly affected Native culture and society.[49]

Case studies, focussing on limited regions and time periods, suggest that alterations in economic patterns and social institutions were subtle, multifarious, and geographical.[50] Using the Cree of eastern James Bay, for example, Toby Morantz argues for a continuous time line from pre-contact to at least the end of the 19th century in which few significant changes occurred in the economic and social life of her subjects. Her inland Natives, who did not specialize in hunting for the fur trade and retained their reliance on local food sources, did not materially change their subsistence lifestyle and social relationships. "In sum, given the state of historical knowledge now available for the James Bay region, one would have to favour characterizing Cree society as one of cultural and social continuity reaching back into pre-European times," Morantz writes, "The contact period and the early fur trade did not drastically or even dramatically alter their overall cultural and social configurations."[51] Similarly, Shepard Krech challenges the idea that the fur trade had a great impact on the Kutchin who lived along the lower Mackenzie, Yukon, and Porcupine Rivers. Although the fur trade integrated them into a global fur market, they did not become subjugated to this intruding economic system, they did not lose their economic autonomy, nor did they depend on the Hudson's Bay Company for their survival. In fact, Krech argues that the European traders could not likely have maintained their northern posts without help from Aboriginal hunters, fishers, labourers, and interpreters. Conversely, while the Kutchin desired European commodities because they were technologically superior to their own indigenous tools, they did not purchase food items. The fur trade, then, changed their material culture; it also instigated some hostilities with neighbouring tribes, turned some Natives into go-betweens, and killed many through imported diseases. But, Krech concludes, the Kutchin continued to hunt and fish as they did before the white trader had reached their grounds and they traded fur only as an extra activity. In fact, many of them did not participate in the trade at all.[52] Obviously, the Cree, the Kutchin, and, as Eleanor Blain argues convincingly, the northern Ojibwa, were quite capable of living for years without acquiring European trade goods.[53]

Contemporary observers, however, doubted whether the indigenous hunters could live indefinitely without European commodities. Both sides of the debate before the committee assumed that the Natives had become dependent upon white traders and could not survive without their products. Sir George Back, a member of two Franklin expeditions and one on his own in 1833 to 1835, thought the Natives could no longer live without the Hudson's Bay Company. Before the arrival of the company, "they were accustomed to rely upon their own exertions; they used the bow and arrow; they knew nothing of fire-arms, and consequently were self-dependent," Back claimed, "and being self-dependent, they maintained themselves at that time."[54] Once the Natives abandoned their traditional way of life, he insisted, they lost their ability to survive in the wilderness. Should the company leave the territories, they would die, he concluded. Sir J. Richardson, an equally inveterate traveller through the territories early in the century, agreed entirely and told the committee that the Natives could no longer live without ammunition. Lastly, Lieutenant-Colonel William Caldwell, Governor of Assiniboia until 1855, went further than Back and Richardson, arguing that the Natives had enjoyed the protection of the company's rule:

> I think that the management of the Company, with the Indians, has been the means of keeping them longer than would have been the case if they had been without the aid

and assistance of the Company. If there had been free trade,
if the trade had been thrown open, I think that there would
not have been the number of Indians which they at present
have in the territory.[55]

Simpson's testimony also raised the question as to what extent his paternalism translated into fair prices and justice for the indigenous hunters.
Under the credit system, the standard of exchange was the beaver skin; in
other words, prices, set down in written scales, were expressed in terms of
beaver skins; one blanket, for example, being equivalent to four beaver
skins. The markup for company employees anywhere in the territories
ranged from one-third to one half, depending upon rank. For white customers it approached 50%, but for the Natives it varied from 200 to 300%
depending on location, local conditions, and transportation costs.[56] John Rae
thought the company's prices reasonable and recalled that company servants could sell Hudson's Bay Company merchandise privately in the
United States and still make a profit. He also explained that even though the
tariff in the Mackenzie district was marked up relatively high to pay for
transportation cost, it was still less than half of Russian prices. But even Rae
could not escape the paternalism inherent in the fur trade by suggesting that
the Natives had sufficient to clothe themselves, and, in fact, admitted that
one time he had not lowered prices because they were so well dressed.
Moreover, Rae, like many of the other witnesses, skirted the just price issue
by concentrating on fair treatment instead. Hudson's Bay Company traders
were respectable men who treated the Natives kindly and with humanity,
said one witness; they "are men of simple primitive habits, leading the most
hardy lives; generally speaking, contented, doing their duty faithfully to
their employers, and in many instances taking sincere interest in the welfare
of the Indians around them, and doing all they can to benefit them, but the
Indian is a very difficult subject."[57] Of course, as John Rae admitted, company officers had considerable self-interest for treating their customers fairly.
"It is their object both to clothe the Indians well and to give them plenty of
ammunition, because the better they are fed, and the better they are clothed,
the better they will hunt."[58] In sum, Rae thought that the Aboriginal people
had benefited from the commercial relationship because they received supplies from England, including "the luxury of tobacco."[59]

If the Hudson's Bay Company, with the support of friendly witnesses,
could argue with some conviction that it treated its Aboriginal partners with
a measure of fairness, it had greater difficulty persuading the commissioners that starvation was not becoming a common occurrence in Rupert's
Land. The most alarmist evidence of wide-spread hunger came from the

Aborigines Protection Society. Citing Alexander Simpson, a disgruntled chief trader formerly posted in Hawaii,[60] the society claimed that Rupert's Land contained vast areas in which the means of subsistence was scanty. From Lake Superior to Lake Winnipeg, for example, Simpson wrote that Natives found it difficult to survive in the winter. To the north of Canada game was more abundant, but subsistence was hard and famine frequent. Fish was scarce, according to Simpson, and, during the winter, inhabitants of the region had to survive entirely on rabbit, considered a wretched food. When that supply failed, the people were in real trouble. In fact, he had heard of parents who killed and ate their children. Gradually, he warned, famine was extending over the entire territory, except the Prairies. He and the Aborigines Protection Society doubted that the Hudson's Bay Company could avert imminent disaster because they thought the cause of hunger was the decline in animals rather than the company's abuses.[61] Nevertheless, some witnesses accused the company of being niggardly with supplies.[62]

Company officials dismissed the allegations of widespread starvation. They asserted that game was still plentiful in certain regions and that elsewhere the Natives could supplement their diets with agriculture or in extreme cases by relief supplies. Governor Simpson emphatically denied suggestions of extensive hunger among the Naskapi in Labrador specifically and dismissed the claims of cannibalism of children as totally exaggerated. He similarly discounted the stories of A.G.B. Ballatyne, a strong opponent of the company, that starving people north of the Arctic Circle were eating beaver skins. Ballaryne had never been north of the circle, Simpson snorted, and years ago, while he served as his secretary, "his judgment was [not] very sound upon many points."[63] When questioned further, Simpson denied any specific recollections of cannibalism but admitted there might have been some cases in the Athabasca district in the recent past.

Contemporary witnesses defended Simpson's contention that food supplies in Rupert's Land were still sufficient. Bishop David Anderson believed that the Prairies still supported an abundance of buffalo, fish, and fowl most of the year. He did note, however, that food shortages occurred because the Plains Natives did not store any food. "They are improvident as regards the rest of the year," he observed.[64] He also reminded the committee that wherever Natives adopted farming methods their food supplies were plentiful and their populations increased, but where they refused, they suffered hunger and declining numbers. John McLaughlin believed that the isolated cases of starvation were a consequence of the monopoly. In fact, he believed hunger would be worse if it was not for smuggling and illicit trading among the Natives. It provided supplemental income for many.[65]

Current historiography seems to support Simpson's assertion that starvation was relatively rare and limited to isolated regions. Although she does not provide a quantitative answer to the question, Mary Black-Rogers argues that historians must place their analysis of fur trade terminology in a cultural context. She identifies three levels for the word "starving": a literal usage implying an actual shortage of food and going without eating; a technical function suggesting that the search for scarce food did not allow time for fur hunting; and a manipulative meaning where starving included "metaphorical, deliberately ambiguous, or untruthful statements."[66] More specifically, Irene M. Spry suggests that, despite occasional shortages and incidents of begging, food resources were relatively plentiful until the end of the 1860s.[67] Inferentially, however, both arguments imply that food shortages, even if sporadic, were a reality and were probably becoming increasingly frequent by the late 1850s. Quite possibly, then, the supply of game was diminishing in some parts of the territories; and that fact alone would place the Aboriginal nations in a weak position when the agricultural frontier approached Rupert's Land.

If the extent of the company's responsibility for the decline of animal populations in the North-West remains an open question, its role in the relatively peaceful character of the territories went unchallenged. All witnesses agreed that the company and its employees had minimized animosity among the inhabitants of Rupert's Land and kept crime to insignificant levels. Under the company's protection, some noted, it was possible to travel anywhere in the region safely and securely.[68] This was true in part because company officials, they agreed, were respected and they supervised their employees closely.[69] To be sure, their task was eased by two important conditions. In the first place, they admitted, the sparseness of the white population was crucial. Hudson's Bay personnel comprised a small minority scattered across a vast territory. On the one hand, they did not crowd the indigenous people out of traditional hunting grounds; on the other hand, their survival and their ability to maintain a profitable trade rested entirely on their ability to create a friendly, symbiotic alliance with the overwhelmingly larger Native population. As Governor Simpson put it, "They look to us for their supplies, and we study their comfort and convenience as much as possible; we assist each other."[70] At the same time, this amicable relationship rested on the peaceful character of the northern tribes.[71] Pointing to the incessant warfare among indigenous peoples and newcomers in the United States, most witnesses concurred that the congenial nature of the northern, woodland Natives was a prime factor in the peaceful relationship.

If the company officials took credit for the tranquility in the northern woodlands, they could not do so for the Plains. A few of the witnesses admitted that the Blackfoot were a particularly fierce and warlike tribe and did on occasion cause trouble.[72] This testimony presented almost as an aside, like so much of the evidence about the Native peoples, greatly oversimplified a complex reality. In fact, since the beginning of the decade, intricate cultural and economic pressures, largely caused by the fur and buffalo hide trade, were shifting traditional hunting ground boundaries. The decline of all animal populations, but especially the buffalo, impelled a slow but relentless westward movement of all the indigenous Plains hunters, including the Métis. While the Cree were pushing into Blackfoot territory, the latter were squeezing tribes to their west and north and fighting back the invaders from the east. Violent clashes over control of the resource became increasingly common and, in fact, in the spring of 1857 a marauding band of young Cree stole a large number of Blackfoot horses from an encampment on the South Saskatchewan River. In the resultant chase the Blackfoot killed 17 of the Cree.[73]

Most committee members and witnesses, however, were interested primarily in the incidence of natural resources in Rupert's Land and the extent of arable land; they paid only scant attention to the history of the Native peoples. They were ready to accept the evidence that conditions in Rupert's Land were comparatively stable and somewhat satisfactory. Moreover, any concerns the committee may have had were with the future of the Native peoples rather than their past. And, with the supply of game diminishing, the outlook was bleak. "What is to become of the natives when their lands can no longer furnish the means of subsistence?" the Aborigines Protection Society asked.[74] Others worried that the company's sudden withdrawal, whether voluntary or forced, would spell disaster for all inhabitants of the territories.[75] In either case, everyone recognized that the inevitable settlement of the arable sections of the North-West would likely bring considerable hardship to the Natives and significant changes to their society. The problem, all agreed, was how to prepare the Aboriginal people for these far-reaching transformations. But, because all the witnesses and committee members were white and no Natives were asked or expected to testify, the answer inevitably was one-sided and simplistic: the civilization of the Natives.

Equally clear was that no one expected the Hudson's Bay Company to play a significant role in this civilization process. To be sure, some critics charged the company for having failed its obligations to educate and Christianize the Natives. Rev. Griffith Owen Corbett, a Church of England clergyman at St. Andrew's, the largest parish in Red River, from 1852 to

1855, observed that the Hudson's Bay Company had actively opposed the establishment of Aboriginal settlements and missionary activities. He told the commissioners that he had tried to establish a mission at Portage la Prairie but the bishop had informed him that the company objected because it wanted to restrict settlement to the Red River region, thinking it too difficult to govern people outside that community.[76] Corbett did admit, however, that the Hudson's Bay Company had recently withdrawn its objections. Nevertheless, he believed that company policies still practically prohibited the establishment of missions even if Natives desired them, citing an aborted mission at Fort Alexander, near Lake Winnipeg, where the company ordered a missionary to confine himself to the fort and "not to civilise and evangelise the heathen; not to form a locality or permanent dwelling for the Indians." When asked, Corbett charged that the company opposed settlement because "if missionaries and missionary settlements increase, chief factors and fur trading posts must decrease."[77]

Meanwhile, Sir George Simpson vigorously denied the charge that the Hudson's Bay Company had thwarted "the settlement of Amerindians as agricultural labourers or as a Christian community."[78] The Natives could occupy any piece of land [except that which had been purchased by Lord Selkirk] without payment to the company, he added gratuitously; moreover, the company had encouraged agricultural pursuits at its Rainy Lake, Cumberland, Swan River, and Norway House posts as well as at various missions by supplying the Natives with tools and seed potatoes and grain. "We are exceedingly anxious that … [the Natives] should give their attention to agriculture,"[79] he asserted, quickly appending that the conspicuous lack of success was due not to company policy but to the Aboriginal people's distinct distaste for field labour. As for the criticism that the company discouraged the task of instructing the Natives in European ways, Simpson argued that "as a Company [we are not] charged with the education or civilization" of the Natives.[80] Yet, the company had voluntarily assisted the Church Missionary Society because "we are anxious to improve the condition of the Indians."[81] It had built schools at York Factory, Norway House, and other posts; it had provided free passage to missionaries, their goods, and their school supplies; and, it had paid salaries for some schoolmasters and missionaries. The evident lack of success was due not to company recalcitrance but to the isolation of the posts, the sparse populations, and the reluctance of parents to leave their children at the schools.

Despite the differing opinions on the amount of effort the Hudson's Bay Company had put into the education and evangelization of the Aboriginal nations, the members of the Select Committee could sense the elements of a consensus in the testimony placed before them. All parties agreed that if the Hudson's Bay Company were forced to withdraw from the territories quickly or if the region were opened to free trade completely, the Native people would not be able to cope with the resultant settlement process. A rapid, unchecked flow of white colonists, they believed, would be devastat ing and likely lead to bloody confrontations. "If you take a very large extent of territory, and by doing so take away the employment which the Hudson's Bay at present give to tribes of Indians, and leave them in want," John Ross, a Canadian representative warned, not without some self-interest, "they may perhaps find means of helping themselves, and they may come down upon the border settlements."[82] Instead, many of the witnesses agreed that the company and the Aboriginal hunters should withdraw gradually and in stages from the fertile southern plains and river valleys to the northern forests. John McLaughlin, who expressed perhaps the most advanced of the apartheid schemes, suggested that settlement would extend no further than the northern limits of arable land. "There is a certain portion of the country which, of course, is so inhospitable that it would be impossible to colonize or cultivate it," McLaughlin declared. The far northern reaches of the territories should remain as a fur trade preserve he thought, but he too accepted the notion that once the Natives were prepared they should gradually move back into the newly settled areas and be integrated into the new society. In time, he believed, "the Indians ... might be all drawn down to the more habitable portions as they are such a race that they might amalgamate with others."[83] Judiciously handled and carefully controlled, the gradual settlement of the North-West, most witnesses echoed McLaughlin, could occur without the bloodshed witnessed in the United States. "Any settlement from Canada must come up naturally, and very gradually indeed."[84]

Meanwhile, the opinion surfaced, that church and state should devise policies to prepare the remaining Natives for the encroaching white society. As Bishop David Anderson put it, there should be programs "which might at once be sound and salutary, and in accordance with the spirit of the present age; such as may tend to the good of all committed to ... [the company's] care, whether Europeans or Indian; their temporal advantages in the present world, and their higher interests as immortal beings, to be trained for another and an unending state."[85] Although his experience in Red River caused him to believe that the "brown man can resist the encroachments of the white man," Anderson hoped "that the Indian may be raised in the interval before ... civilization sweeps westward, as it must."[86] By "raised" he meant not merely Christianizing but also integrating the Aboriginal peoples into the advancing western European, mid-19th-century lifestyle. With rhetorical hyperbole, Anderson painted a Utopian vision. "The perfection of work is a European and an Indian together," he suggested, but added with some feelings of superiority "that there should be the European head, and the Indian as the mouthpiece."[87] In other words, despite all their humanitarian compassion, the advocates of settlement believed that there was no room in the proposed agrarian society for what they perceived to be an inferior savage way of life. The Native inhabitants of Rupert's Land had to accommodate themselves to the new order.

Bishop Anderson's opinion reflected current belief among many expansionists, missionaries, and humanitarians that the indigenous inhabitants of the region should be educated into accepting the newcomer's culture because the agrarian settlement of the Plains was inevitable and desirable. Not only was the civilization of the Natives appropriate but as witnesses were eager to demonstrate, it was possible. Some noted that limited progress in training Natives to be farmers had been achieved already in Red River, at The Pas, and at some posts like Norway House and Moose Factory. The Aborigines Protection Society forwarded a letter from a Peguis, a Saulteaux chief, as proof of the "Indian capacity" to adapt to the agrarian way of life. The society's secretary observed that the Red River settlement was a "remarkable example of the improvement of which the Indian race is capable."[88] In addition to becoming farmers, one Native had become a harness maker and another a tinsmith. Moreover, the secretary noted with obvious pride, the fact that in a settlement with considerable poverty there was not a locked door was clear proof that the moral standards of the Natives could also be improved.

When pressed, those witnesses before the committee who had lived or travelled in the North-West were not as sanguine in their hopes for farm training. John Rae, for example, very much approved "of settling and attempting to civilise" the Aboriginal people but observed that agricultural settlements "would be beneficial" only as a supplement to the winter's hunt. The Natives will "never become great farmers" because of their fondness for hunting and their opposition to "civilised life," he thought.[89] At best, then, cultivation would be an additional income to the fur trade, only complementing it "because the time when … [the Natives] would be employed in the settlements is not the time when they hunt."[90] Rae, therefore, did not expect the Natives to become full-time farmers.

Similarly, Rev. Griffith Corbett also expressed some reservations. Even though he thought that those who had turned to farming had improved their lives remarkably, converting an entire independent, hunting people into a sedentary agrarian society would be extremely difficult. Corbett noted that while some Indian tribes had been agriculturalists in the past, they had never grown sufficient vegetables to sustain themselves nor would they ever want to live on vegetables. By way of illustration, he noted that most Chippewas and many Natives at Red River inhabited fertile lands and had received training and assistance; nevertheless, the vast majority refused to adopt agrarian lifestyles, preferring to fish, hunt, and harvest wild rice. When asked, Corbett could not explain why some settlements were success-ful and others not but speculated that those Natives who were most inde-pendent of the Hudson's Bay, who had plenty of fish and rice and who did not need ammunition and clothing, were least likely to adopt farming. On the other hand, he predicted that the Swampy and Saskatchewan Cree were the most likely to accept "habits of civilised life" because they had long been dependent upon the company and needed their supplies. Thus, he reasoned, they would be more ready to accept "civilisation."[91]

The debate, whether or not the indigenous hunting society could adapt to an agricultural economy, was framed in the common 19th-century assump-tion that North Americans had a mandate to colonize the continent by culti-vating the soil, or more specifically, that the Prairies were an expansive, non-productive wilderness that needed to be civilized through agriculture. As Frieda Knobloch has argued, agriculture, as its name implied, meant bring-ing culture to the wilderness.[92] In Red River, for example, Alexander Ross, a prominent leader, felt a divine calling to toil in the fields as the vanguard of civilization in a vast wasteland and he criticized those Métis who preferred "indolence to industry, and their own roving habits to agricultural or other pursuits of civilized life."[93] In other words, farming was a superior econom-ic endeavour to hunting because it was part of a civilizing process. More to the point, Rupert's Land's Native hunters had to become part of this civiliz-ing strategy. All the participants in the Select Committee's hearings—none of whom were Native—agreed on this point; they only quarrelled about timing and procedures.

Turning the Aboriginal citizens of the North-West into agriculturalists, all witnesses agreed, was only one aspect of the required civilizing process. The strategy also required a general education, which in turn was closely connected with evangelization. In other words, the Select Committee, its speakers and listeners, enamoured by the perceived glory of mid-19th-century British culture, sought to spread its mentality to the farthest reach-es of the empire.[94] Swept by the euphoria of the economic and social progress that the industrial revolution apparently had brought, Victorian Britons wanted to propagate their successful achievements across the globe. The free-trade doctrine that accompanied industrialization was not simply about the unfettered exchange of commodities, it also included the unhampered transmission of ideas, the message that Britain's industrial, technological, and Christian culture was the pinnacle of human civilization.[95] From this supposedly lofty perspective, the notion that the vast North American interior should be preserved to sustain an Aboriginal way of life and yield only furs instead of agricultural crops, minerals and precious metals seemed absurd. Humans were destined to dominate the wilderness, to civilize it, to remove its natural cover and inhabitants, and to prepare its soil for profitable, cultivated crops. The Natives, according to this view, were savages: like the wilderness, they needed to be civilized; they had to be separated from unredeemed nature and inducted into the marvels of the industrializing, urbanizing civilization.[96]

Working from this model, the criticism directed against the Hudson's Bay Company was more than a tirade against an outdated monopolistic enterprise; it considered the company to be a representative of an outdated culture, an obsolete way of life. Various critics charged that the Hudson's Bay Company had not only failed to inculcate modern European ideals into North America's Aboriginal societies but had actively opposed settlement and evangelization.[97] The latter charge was contradicted by church officials who noted that the company provided adequate subsidies to missionary efforts.[98] In fact, Bishop David Anderson believed that the company's "disposition latterly has been to do much more for the Indians in carrying out civilization"; but he was quick to point out, "of course the direct object of the Company would not be to colonise or to settle."[99] By the dictates of its corporate mandate, its activities would not be conducive to settlement, nor to "the civilisation and improvement of the inhabitants."[100]

Bishop Anderson's position, set between the extremes taken by the supporters and detractors of the Hudson's Bay Company, exemplified the well-intentioned, yet patronizing position of many Victorian contemporaries. He suggested that without the company the Natives would not have advanced much "beyond that state of nature which may have existed for a very lengthened period."[101] By using the phrase, "state of nature," Anderson alluded to more than the sinful condition of the Aboriginal tribes. He also implied that they were an integral part of the wilderness, which was still untamed and uncivilized. Both the landscape and its indigenous inhabitants needed to be redeemed, that is, to be civilized. Speaking from his European-centred platform, the bishop firmly believed in the objective of turning the territory into a rural English countryside and he wanted the Aboriginal inhabitants to be a part of this British society. "My own desire and endeavour would be to raise and rescue them as a people, and to prepare them to be able to stem the current when civilisation, as it gradually must, spreads westward from Canada over this mighty territory."[102] Although he reluctantly admitted that the saying "the brown population dies out as the white population advances" was likely true, he optimistically hoped that "the experiment [of Anglican missions] may yet save the Indian."[103] Bishop Anderson, therefore, was concerned not only with the souls of the Natives, but also their society, culture, and life.

Ever the optimist, Bishop Anderson observed with some satisfaction that the church had already experienced some success in this endeavour, particularly in Red River. There, he claimed, many Natives "have been induced [by missionaries] to adopt settled and industrious habits" and some of their settlements were like English parishes with little farms and all the comforts of life. Obviously, Anderson added with regret, in more northern, isolated regions, the harsh climate, low temperatures, and poor soil were less likely to yield satisfactory results. Moreover, seasonal migrations would also make missionary work more difficult. Nevertheless, he concluded, wherever Native people had settled in communities and converted to Christianity, the results had been dramatic. "Wherever they are Christianised and settled," he observed, the population had increased. Even as hunters, Christian Aboriginal people "socially, as regards their position in life ... are much improved"; their moral and social character had advanced from their "primitive state."[104] They had become like Victorian families, conducting family worship twice daily and attending church regularly.[105] Noting with considerable pride that two of the missionaries under his jurisdiction were Natives and that another was a Métis, Bishop Anderson, therefore, believed that civilizing the Native through missionary activity had already met with considerable success.

Anderson's optimistic assessment received support from Peguis, the Saulteaux chief who in 1817 had signed a treaty with Lord Selkirk supposedly releasing title to a large parcel of land straddling the Red River. Subsequently, Peguis assisted the early colonist and even settled some of his people at Netley Creek on the river. Eventually, however, he came to realize that the treaty favoured the newcomers and not the indigenous people and he claimed that the four Native signatories to the treaty did not have the authority to extinguish Aboriginal title to the land.[106] Peguis' evidence, obtained indirectly through a letter attached to the Aborigines Protection Society's written submission, was the only statement from an Aboriginal inhabitant of the North-West.

Unwittingly, the sole voice for several First Nations, Peguis condemned the fur traders for robbing him and his fellow Natives and keeping them

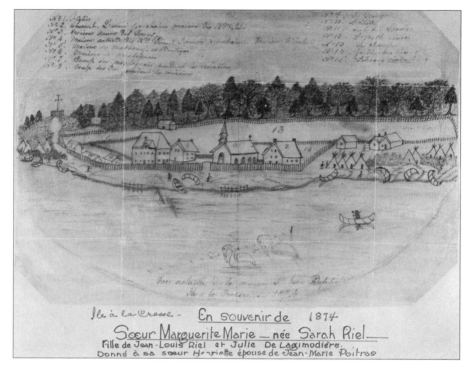

Ile-à-la-Crosse in 1874, based upon the memories of Sister Marguerite Marie (née Sarah Riel, Louis Riel's sister). In 1846, Father Alexandre-Antonin Taché (later Bishop) and Father Louis-François Richer Laflèche (for whom the southern Saskatchewan town is named) arrived from St. Boniface to establish the first Roman Catholic mission in what is present-day Saskatchewan. In 1860, Sisters Agnes, Pepin, and Boucher founded a convent, bringing medical services, education, and Western culture to the community (courtesy of the Archives of Manitoba/N3964).

poor; but he praised the settlers and missionaries for teaching them agricultural techniques and the values of Christianity. On the one hand, the colonists had taught them how to cultivate the soil and raise cattle; on the other hand, the missionaries had shown them how to pray, to be industrious, honest, sober, and truthful; they had explicated the truth and peace of Christ. Many of his fellows, he explained, wanted to practice this religious ideal. While his commendation of farmers and missionaries may have been obsequious and fawning, it may also have been driven by a pragmatic trait and a dawning under-standing of the implications of European settlement. He and his fellow Natives were not against further settlement, Peguis insisted, but before more white settlers would be permitted to take lands, a fair and mutually advantageous treaty must be negotiated. The indigenous inhabitants of the territories expected to be paid for the alienated lands. Moreover, they asked that the imperial government appoint a fair-minded person as their advocate in the bargaining. Since the Select Committee had not bothered to invite any Natives to express their opinions and feelings, Peguis' letter was but a footnote, a passing reminder that the Aboriginal people understood the value of the land which they inhabited."[107] Moreover, it indicated a willingness to adapt to changing conditions and adopt an agricultural economy.

Canadian expansionists, who had their eyes on the enormous northwestern plains and contiguous forest, assured the committee that they understood that the Natives would have to be compensated for the loss of their property. William Henry Draper, chief justice of the Common Pleas of Upper Canada and official Canadian delegate, assured the committee that the Aboriginal people would have to be recompensed. "I do not think they can be plundered with impunity."[108] Although Draper appealed to the British tradition of treating North America's Aboriginal nations as diplomatic equals, he did not mention that more recently his province had departed on a different course. While the Select Committee was sitting, the colonial legislature passed the Gradual Civilization Act with the express purpose of Christianizing and civilizing the Natives by taking them from their communal reserves and placing them on smaller individual, freehold plots near white communities. Here they supposedly could observe at firsthand industrious, civilized life. For the first time, however, legislation allowed the government to erase any legal distinctions between Native and non-Native peoples, to appropriate reserve lands, to intervene in tribal affairs, and to actively promote the integration of Natives into white society. In short, the 1857 Canadian legislation, based on the belief that Aboriginal leaders were strengthening rather than eroding indigenous culture, legalized a new policy of forced civilization and assimilation.[109] Although the act did not in any way anticipate the future annexation of Rupert's Land, it did indicate the civilizing and assimilating intentions of government policy.

The expansionists also believed that violence could be prevented by a gradualist approach. John McLaughlin, for example, believed that Canada could avoid the violence experienced in the United States with proper planning. Suggesting that northern Natives were not as warlike and easily insulted as those in the United States, McLaughlin believed that proper legislation and the establishment of law and order could mitigate disputes and prevent violence.[110] Similarly, supposing that the fur trade had kept the Natives in helpless dependency upon the company for many goods, like guns, ammunition, and blankets, Justice Draper argued that the Hudson's

Bay Company could not be ejected suddenly nor replaced easily. Returning to the segregationist argument, he proposed that settlement be limited to the southern, arable territories and the fur trade be preserved in the northern regions. Separation, he believed, would prevent the violence seen in the United States; it would ensure peaceful relations with the Indians.[111] Bishop Anderson, who believed that the greatest obstacle to the assimilation of the Native was alcohol, also advocated secluding the Natives in the northern territories while permitting free trade and settlement in the south. The Aboriginal peoples were threatened, he opined simplistically, not because "a more energetic, a more civilized, and in fact, a more intellectual man would come in competition with him," but because the Native, as a less civilized being, was more subject to the temptation of alcohol. In other words, until liquor could be eliminated entirely from the North-West and until the indigenous tribes could be elevated to the bishop's British standards, he hoped the government would limit settlement to the southern portion of the territories and allow the Natives to live a protected existence in the northern forests.[112]

Company officials took a realistic attitude, which did not differ much from that of the bishop. Having lived among the Natives in the North-West for decades, their perspective was perhaps less sanguine. It would not be the fur trade that would destroy Aboriginal culture Edward Ellice suggested, but the "the march of civilisation."[113] Thus, he and Governor Simpson recommended the preservation of the indigenous way of life as long as possible. Simpson, an investor in modern transportation technologies and conscious of the rapid advance of the railway across the North American continent, understood that the settlement of the southern plains and Saskatchewan River valley was inevitable. Based on past experience, he argued, the result would be intemperance and disease for the First Nations and "little or no progress in education or civilisation." In other words, like Bishop Anderson, he had no confidence in the Natives' ability to adapt to new circumstances. But, for him personally, the issue was simply a business proposition. Limited by its mandate to conduct a profitable fur trade, the Hudson's Bay Company was able to administer a sparsely peopled fur empire but was not equipped to govern a large, heavily populated colony. A private company, he was quick to point out, did not have the financial resources nor bureaucratic experience to direct a colonizing effort. Thus, he had no objections to Canada annexing the southern, apparently arable, portion of Rupert's Land and providing for its settlement and administration, granted the Hudson's Bay Company received compensation for the loss of trade and territory. "I think there would be no objection to it, provided the Company were satisfied," he stated tersely but reminded the committee that the shareholders "consider themselves lords of the soil, proprietors of the country, in their own special territory."[114] In the end, the company was interested only in sufficient compensation for the land and business it would be asked to surrender and the retention of a trading monopoly in the remaining regions.

As far as the Aboriginal people were concerned, Simpson privately argued that if the British government's objective was "the preservation of the Indian race," then he believed "that it can only be attained by preserving them from the contaminating influence of bad example and the use of ardent spirits, and by allowing them to retain their primitive habits, following the occupations for which alone they appear to be suited by nature—that of hunters."[115] Personally, he believed that assimilation was a dubious prospect. Whenever they had integrated among settlers, the Natives had "cast aside their simple habits of life," he suggested, "and follow[ed] the, by no means beneficial example of whites and half-castes." To save the Aboriginal way of life, Simpson recommended that the imperial government limit settlement to the southern portion of Rupert's Land and set aside a northern fur reserve, where the company could continue a profitable business and meanwhile maintain what it considered to be the traditional way of life of the original inhabitants of the territories. This did not mean, said Simpson, that the Natives were "to be left in a state of ignorance and barbarism." Indeed, it was the European's "duty to instruct and civilize them." Simpson's approach, as condescending in its supposed superiority as the other witnesses, was not, however, as thorough-going as that of the expansionists. "Without attempting to force upon them white man's habits and feelings," company employees, with the help of missionaries must prepare the Natives for the impending change by "a gradual development of their mental faculties, naturally almost dormant." But, the intent of this education would not be to alter their basic lifestyles, but to cope with the new technological culture. Still, this corporate manager, personally involved in the exploitation of the territories' resources, be they fur or minerals, understood the virtual inevitability of the settlement and development process and he was but proposing a temporary reprieve for an old way of life.

In the end, the Select Committee accepted the obvious compromise. It decided that it was in the imperial interest that, when it was ready, Canada should be permitted to annex all the lands it needed for colonization. At that time, the imperial government should make equitable arrangements with the Hudson's Bay Company and Canada for the surrender of the designated lands. Meanwhile, the committee recommended that in the interim it was important to maintain law and order in the region, to curb the liquor trade, and to stop "the indiscriminate destruction of the more valuable fur-bearing animals"; therefore, the company should retain its exclusive trading rights. This, according to the committee, was best "to the prosperity and content-ment of our North American fellow subjects; and especially in the mode which is best calculated to add strength to the great colony of Canada."[116] The committee also believed that action in the North-West must be quick and decisive to demonstrate to the United States that Great Britain had a determined interest in the region. "The rapid extension of settlement which had been going on in so remarkable a manner to the south of the American boundary line, renders it a matter of great importance to establish within our own territory a counterpoise favourable to British interests, and mod-elled upon British institutions."[117] To the committee, then, the settlement of the southern portion of the North-West was imperative and the Native peo-ples had to be fitted into the mould.

The Select Committee's recommendation and the Hudson's Bay Company's ready acquiescence demonstrated how closely all the partici-pants in the process had followed the same score. While every witness and member had played their distinctive and at times discordant parts, they had all rendered the same theme. Rupert's Land was a vast, isolated and untamed wilderness. Modern scientific knowledge, consummated in cur-rent farming and transportation technologies, would enable European new-comers to turn the still hostile wasteland into a productive landscape. The great expanse, which so far had only spawned fur, could generate much more valuable cash crops. The unorganized territories must be subdivided, fenced, and hedged in; they must nourish millions of people. Trees must be planted and bogs drained, minerals mined, and soils cultivated.

Viewed from this perspective, the original human inhabitants of the northern expanse were but components of an uncivilized nature. They, like the wilderness, needed to be redeemed, that is civilized. That assumption was predicated on the notion that the First Nations, living in Rupert's Land, were a homogenous people with a simple, undiversified culture. The testi-mony before the Select Committee over-looked the complexity of the many different nations that lived on the prairies and in the woodlands. It did not recognize that the Native peoples were more than savage hunters, but that their movements also accorded with the ripening of fruits and the availabil-ity of tubers, and, that in some cases, tribes engaged in agriculture.[118] Since the Aboriginal nations had no written history, the witnesses disregarded the rich diplomatic and cultural relations between the various tribes; since they did not share the capitalist ideology, the testimony ignored the trade and commerce among the indigenous peoples that pre-dated the arrival of the white fur traders. Most importantly, the participants in the committee's hearings did not recognize that the Natives were active participants in the history of Rupert's Land. Thus they resorted to a paternalism, which despite its arguably good and humanitarian intentions, sought to manage and control the future of the original citizens. In short, the committee failed to accept them as equals, as people whose participation in the development of the North-West was important.

Despite its obvious flaws, the committee's report is an important document because it mirrored the Victorian attitude to Aboriginal people and because it was an omen of what was in store for Rupert's Land's first citizens. The directors of the Hudson's Bay Company, like many of their critics, may not have fully appreciated the rich cultural heritage of Rupert's Land's Native people, but they, and particularly their North American governor, understood the expansionist ideology. As shrewd, literate businesspeople, they were active participants in their emerging technological society. Closely connected to government circles, they were fully cognizant of the new realities and of imperial ambitions. As they explained to the colonial secretary,

> We are convinced, notwithstanding the hostile agitation of parties in Canada against our Company, that our prosperity is not opposed to that of Canada, neither is the advancement of Canadian interests incompatible with ours, but, on the contrary, that in all matters of essential importance our joint interests are mutual and identical. It requires but a small degree of knowledge of the existing state of British North America, and more particularly of the policy which guides the adjoining Government of the United States to perceive that the honor and reputation of Great Britain and the interests of her subjects can be best preserved by the cordial union of all those in that locality who are bound to it by the ties of birth and affection.[119]

This appeal to an imperialist duty, that equated a commercial mandate with an implied ecological as well as territorial mission, did not preclude a strong dedication to trade and profit. Although the Hudson's Bay Company was ready to accept the recommendations of the Select Committee, it expected to be compensated for the loss of its territories. Provided Canada paid appropriate compensation, the company was prepared to withdraw from the arable portions of their enormous holdings and leave the civilization of that portion of the wilderness to settlers and the state. Meanwhile government, school, and church could attend to the refinement of the Aboriginal nations. Thus the company and the Canadian government of the day accepted the report of the Select Committee as a prelude, an articulation of a theme that would dominate the impending settlement of western Canada.

Notes

This article first appeared in *Prairie Forum* 24, no. 2 (1999): 143–69.

1. Under a 20-year license granted in 1839, the Hudson's Bay Company also controlled trade in areas west of Rupert's Land, known as the Indian Territory. In fact, it was the end of the license that inspired the establishment of the Select Committee.

2. The Select Committee did not discuss the Métis at all, considering them not as indigenous people but as British citizens in no need of special attention.

3. Cited in Michael Adas, *Machines as the Measure of Men: Science, Technology, and Ideologies of Western Dominance* (Ithaca: Cornell University Press, 1989), 218.

4. Ronald Hyam, *Britain's Imperial Century 1815–1914: A Study of Empire and Expansion* (New York: Barnes and Noble Books, 1976), 31–36.

5. The concept of an "imperial" view of nature is developed in Donald Worster, *Nature's Economy: A History of Ecological Ideas* (Cambridge: Cambridge University Press, 1994), 29–30. Worster argues that in the imperialist schema a mechanistic, rational, and technological nature was considered to be the domain of humans, to be altered and rearranged for their purposes and needs. Alfred W. Crosby, *Ecological Imperialism: The Biological Expansion of Europe, 900–1900* (Cambridge: Cambridge University Press, 1986) suggests that bacteria, viruses, weeds, domesticated seeds and animals as well as rodents imported from the Old to the New World partly explain the success of Europe's conquest of the American continent. John S. Galbraith, *The Hudson's Bay Company as an Imperial Factor, 1821–1869* (New York: Octagon Books, 1977) uses imperialism in the more traditional but still very useful sense.

6. Hudson's Bay Company Archives, Provincial Archives of Manitoba, [hereafter cited as HBCA/PAM] , A7/2, Shepherd to Simpson, January 2, 1857.

7. John S. Galbraith, "Sir George Simpson," *Dictionary of Canadian Biography, 1851–1860*, Vol. 8 (Toronto: University of Toronto Press, 1985), 812–18; J.S. Galbraith, *The Little Emperor: Governor Simpson of the Hudson's Bay Company* (Toronto: Macmillan, 1976); A.S. Morton, *Sir George Simpson, Overseas Governor of the Hudson's Bay Company: A Pen Picture of a Man of Action* (Toronto: Dent, 1944).

8. Sylvia Van Kirk, *Many Tender Ties: Women in Fur-Trade Society, 1670–1870* (Norman: University of Oklahoma Press, 1983),183–86.

9. Frances' first-born, a son, died at eight months. See Jennifer S.H. Brown, *Strangers in Blood: Fur Trade. Company Families in Indian Country* (Vancouver: University of British Columbia Press, 1980), 129–30.

10. See Montreal Mining Company, *Report of the Trustees of the Montreal Mining Company* (Montreal: n.p., 1846) for Simpson's active participation in this Lake Superior mining company.

11. Works that discuss the expansionist resource development attitude are: A.A. den Otter, *The Philosophy of Railways: The Transcontinental Railway Idea in British North America* (Toronto: University of Toronto Press, 1997); Doug Owram, *Promise of Eden: The Canadian Expansionist Movement and the Idea of the West 1855–1900* (Toronto: University of Toronto Press, 1980) ; and Frederick Turner, *Beyond Geography: The Western Spirit against the Wilderness* (New York: Viking Press, 1980). Simpson's prejudices against Native women are described well in Brown, *Strangers in Blood*, and Van Kirk, *Many Tender Ties*.

12. Standish Motte, *Outline of a System of Legislation for the Securing of Protection to the Aboriginal Inhabitants of all Countries Colonized by Great Britain* (London: n.p., 1840).

13. Aborigines Protection Society, *Canada West and the Hudson's-Bay Company* (London: n.p., 1856), introduction. The society's name is spelled in various ways, often with an apostrophe. This article will use the more common non-possessive form.

14. Aborigines Protection Society, *Report on the Indians of Upper Canada, 1839* (London: n.p., 1839), 21.

15. Aborigines Protection Society to Labouchere, undated [1857], in Great Britain, House of Commons, *Report from the Select Committee on the Hudson's Bay Company; Together with the Proceedings of the Committee, Minutes of Evidence, Appendix and Index, 1857*, 441 [hereafter cited as Report].

16. Shifting tribal territories and a lack of solid reference points made population estimates highly problematic. In 1844, Lieutenant-Colonel John Henry Lefroy, of the Royal Artillery, who made a two-year scientific journey through the Hudson's Bay territories for the Royal Society, compared his figures with those of Sir John Franklin 20 years previously. Lefroy concluded that the Aboriginal population was decreasing rapidly. He noted the greatest decline in the north but also in the south near Lake of the Woods, Rainy Lake, and all around Lake Superior. In the Saskatchewan district, where resources were greater, he believed the decrease was the least [*Report*, 24].

Just prior to the Select Committee's inquiry, the Hudson's Bay Company conducted its own census. Taking the figures to the committee, Governor George Simpson estimated the population of indigenous people in company controlled territories east of the Rockies at approximately 55,570 [*Report*, 57, 366–67]. The Aborigines Protection Society argued that if Governor George Simpson's estimate was correct, the population was "wasting away." It claimed that travellers were confirming this dismal reality. Moreover, citing John McLaughlin, a former resident of Red River, the society estimated that seven-eights of the Indian population west of the Rockies had disappeared [*Report*, 442].

Arthur J. Ray, *Indians in the Fur Trade: Their Role as Trappers, Hunters, and Middlemen in the Lands South of Hudson Bay, 1660–1870* (Toronto: University of Toronto Press, 1974), 187–91, estimates that in the 19th century Aboriginal numbers increased quite rapidly until the late 1830s when the smallpox epidemic decimated the Assiniboine. Their numbers never recovered. The Cree population, less touched by the epidemic, continued to expand. Ray's findings corroborate Governor Simpson's view that the population of the northern, forest Natives was increasing rather than decreasing as some supposed [*Report*, 85].

17. On the question of disease, see Ray, *Indians in the Fur Trade*, 187–91. Virtually all witnesses, hostile and friendly, agreed that alcohol was not used in competition-free and only sparingly in contested areas, mainly in regions bordering the United States. See for example, the testimony of John Rae, Sir George Simpson, Alexander Isbister, Reverend Griffith Corbett, Sir J. Richardson, John McLaughlin, and Richard King [*Report*, 37, 41, 58, 60–61, 65, 85, 88, 91, 122, 146–47, 154–56, 163, 272–74, 316, and 369–70]. In addition, the company's land deed, several standing rules and resolutions, as well as official correspondence, prohibited the use of alcohol as an article of trade [*Report*, 78, 79, 361, 368, 373]. Arthur Ray, *Indians in the Fur Trade*, 198, concludes that the Hudson's Bay Company made a diligent effort to end the alcohol trade. John Galbraith, *Hudson's Bay Company*, agrees.

18. The society readily admitted that the Natives shared the blame for the dangerously reduced number of animals. They had willingly over-hunted and wantonly destroyed small game. On the general topic of over-hunting among Natives before Europeans

arrived in North America see, Richard White and William Cronon, "Ecological Change and Aboriginal-White Relations," in Wilcomb E. Washburn (ed.), *Handbook of North American Indians*, 4, *History of Indian-White Relations* (Washington: Smithsonian Institution, 1989), 417–27. See also, William Cronon, *Changes in the Land: Indians, Colonists, and the Ecology of New England* (New York: Hill and Wang, 1983); Charles A. Bishop, *The Northern Ojibwa and the Fur Trade: An Historical and Ecological Study* (Toronto: Holt, Rinehart & Winston, 1974), 197–206 discusses the consequences of hunting techniques in Rupert's Land.

19. *Report*, 443.

20. Daniel Francis, *The Imaginary Indian: The Image of the Indian in Canadian Culture* (Vancouver: Arsenal Pulp Press, 1992) argues that the "disappearing Indian" is one of the prevailing images of Native people in the 19th century. For a harsh and emotional assessment of the ideological underpinnings of the destruction of Aboriginal cultures in North America see Turner, *Beyond Geography*. Arthur Ray, *Indians in the Fur Trade*, cites numerous examples of Native hunters controlling aspects of the fur trade.

21. *Report*, 154.

22. Ibid., 156.

23. See the testimony of John Ross, John Henry Lefroy, John Rae, John Ffolliott Crofton [ibid., 1–23, 23–26, 26–44,169–84, respectively].

24. Ibid., 231–47.

25. Ibid., 327.

26. Outside the committee room, Governor Simpson explained that the company's organization in the interior assisted the conservation effort. As shareholders in the firm, the factors had a long-term stake in the trade. "It is their interest to preserve the fur-bearing animals from wanton destruction, to lessen the burdens on the business, and to increase the natural resources of the country, so as to render it independent of foreign supplies of provisions." HBCA/PAM, A12/8, Simpson to Shepherd January 26, 1857. Arthur J. Ray, supports Ellice's assertion that the company practiced conservation when feasible but "without a monopoly it was not possible to manage the fur trade on an ecological sound basis since the primary supplier of fur pelts, the Indians, did not readily support the Hudson's Bay Company's conservation programme." See his, "Some Conservation Schemes of the Hudson's Bay Company, 1821–50: An Examination of Resource Management in the Fur Trade," *Journal of Historical Geography* 1, no. 1 (1975): 58. Calvin Martin, *Keepers of the Game: Indian–Animal Relationships and the Fur Trade* (Berkeley: University of California Press, 1978), blames the erosion of indigenous spirituality for the high incidence of over-hunting.

27. Ibid., 120–37, 353–56.

28. Provincial Archives of Manitoba, District of Assiniboia, Court Records, May 17, 1849; Irene M. Spry, "The 'Private Adventurers' of Rupert's Land," in John E. Foster (ed.), *The Developing West: Essays on Canadian History in Honor of Lewis H. Thomas* (Edmonton: University of Alberta Press, 1983); A.A. den Otter, "The Sayer Trial: An Ecological Perspective" (unpublished paper presented at the Canadian Studies Conference, Edinburgh, May 1999).

29. *Report*, 276.

30. Gunn to Vankoughnet, March 6, 1857, in ibid., 388, 389.

31. *Report*, 393.

32. The only witness to bringing specific examples of price gouging was John McLaughlin [ibid., 262–85]. All the others spoke only in generalities.

33. Ibid., 443.

34. Ibid., 444.

35. Ibid., 342.

36. Ibid., 368. In a letter to the secretary of the board of governors, Simpson reiterated the company's paternalistic, yet self-centred policy. "Above all it is an object to secure the well-being and good-will of the natives, to encourage them to industry and to prevent the operation of those causes which in other countries have led to their degradation and the decrease of their numbers." This policy, Simpson believed, had won the company a respect which was necessary so a few men could govern and keep order in a large territory. The policy had also resulted in an increase in population in the northern regions of Rupert's Land and therefore more hunters, an increase in furs trapped and supplies bought. In sum, Simpson concluded, the relationship with the Natives went beyond trade: "We befriend and assist the native to the utmost of our ability; we come to their aid in every difficulty and emergency, we afford relief in times ofsickness and want, we settle their quarrels and exercise a general guardianship over them." HBCA/PAM, A12/8, Simpson to Shepherd, January 26, 1857.

37. Eleanor M. Blain, "Dependency: Charles Bishop and the Northern Ojibwa," in Kerry Abel and Jean Friesen (eds.), *Aboriginal Resource Use in Canada: Historical and Legal Aspects* (Winnipeg: University of Manitoba Press, 1991), 101–02.

38. *Report*, 64, 81.

39. Ray, *Indians in the Fur Trade*, 196, argues that at various times the company attempted to abandon gift giving.

40. Report, 35. See also the testimony by non-Hudson's Bay witnesses such as Sir J. Richardson, Colonel John Ffolliott Crofton, Sir George Back, Lieutenant-Colonel William Caldwell, and Richard King [ibid.,150–69, 169–84, 184–90, 298–312, 312–20].

41. Ibid., 37.

42. Ibid., 282.

43. Ray, *Indians in the Fur Trade*.

44. Blain, "Dependency and the Northern Ojibwa," 93–105.

45. John S. Milloy, *The Plains Cree: Trade, Diplomacy and War, 1790 to 1870* (Winnipeg: University of Manitoba Press, 1988).

46. *Report*, 62–63, 81.

47. Arthur Ray, "Periodic Shortages, Native Welfare, and the Hudson's Bay Company 1670–1930," in Shepard Krech (ed.), *The Subarctic Fur Trade: Native Social and Economic Adaptations* (Vancouver: University of British Columbia Press, 1984), 1–20.

48. In 1849, for example, Sir George Simpson increased inventories of supplies and ordered that in addition to regular supplies, the London office ship enough goods so that the company would have on hand at its York and Norway House depots a one-year reserve on all essential items, two-thirds of a year on those that could be curtailed without serious inconvenience, and one-half on those that traders and Natives could do without in an emergency. In addition, Simpson insisted that the country have a two-year supply of ammunition and twine. See, HBCA/PAM, A12/4, Simpson to Barclay, June 30, 1849.

49. Martin, *Keepers of the Game*.

50. Shepard Krech (ed.), *Indians, Animals, and the Fur Trarde: A Critique of Keepers of the Game* (Athens: University of Georgia Press, 1981) offers a series of articles that question Calvin Martin's conclusions.

51. Toby Morantz, "Old Texts, Old Questions: Another Look at the Issue of Continuity and the Early Fur-Trade Period," *Canadian Historical Review* 73 (June 1992): 185. See also

Morantz, "Economic and Social Accommodations of the James Bay Inlanders to the Fur Trade," in Krech, *The Subarctic Fur Trade*, 55–79; and Paul C. Thistle, *Indian European Trade Relations in the Lower Saskatchewan River Region to 1840* (Winnipeg: University of Manitoba Press, 1986). In Krech, *The Subarctic Fur Trade*, Carol M. Judd, "Sakie, Esquawenoe, and the Foundation of a Dual-Native Tradition at Moose Factory," 81–97, and Charles A. Bishop, "The First Century: Adaptive Changes Among Western James Bay Cree Between the Early Seventeenth and Early Eighteenth Centuries," 21–53 are that at certain times and upon various people the trade did have a significant impact.

52. Shepard Krech, "The Early Fur Trade in the Northwestern Subarctic: The Kutchin and the Trade in Beads," in Bruce G. Trigger, Toby Morantz and Louise Dechène (eds.), *"Le Castor fait Tout": Selected Papers of the Fifth North American Fur Trade Conference, 1985* (Montreal: La Société historique du lac Saint-Louis, 1987). In an earlier article, "The Trade of the Slavey and Dogrib at Fort Simpson in the Early Nineteenth Century," in Krech, *The Subarctic Fur Trade*, 142, Krech had cautioned, "The effects of the trade surely varied from one individual to the next, from one band to another, and one ethnic group to the next." Yet, he maintained the thesis that the trade at Fort Simpson had not led to significant dependency.

53. Blaine, "Dependency and the Northern Ojibwa."

54. *Report*, 188.

55. Ibid., 311.

56. Ibid. 34, 393.

57. Ibid., 25–26.

58. Ibid., 29.

59. Ibid., 187.

60. Galbraith, *Hudson's Bay Company*, 319.

61. *Report*, 443.

62. George Gladman, a long-time company employee, charged that shortages of supplies, usually caused by local managers, were not uncommon and that the Natives frequently suffered hunger. "The treatment of the Indians, whether humane or otherwise, depends entirely on the officers in charge of posts;" Gladman noted, "his liberality governed by his outfit" [ibid., 393].

63. Ibid., 85. Privately, Simpson explained to the board of governors that he believed the company had managed the Natives well, that the period since 1821 was characterized by the absence of crime, the gradual development and knowledge of trade, and an increase in the Aboriginal population. More specifically, he argued that the Natives and environment had benefited from the fur trade. Through careful preservation of the resource, the company had been able to increase the fur trade, a fact of great benefit to the indigenous hunters as they were better able to purchase clothing, ammunition, and other necessities. In those rare cases of scarcity, the company could supply relief to all Indians at times of scarcity. But that happened only as a "result of the proverbial improvidence of the Indian race" or illness. HBCA/PAM, A12/8, Simpson to Shepherd, January 26, 1857.

64. Ibid., 242.

65. Ibid., 264.

66. Mary Black-Rogers, "'Starving' and Survival in the Subarctic Fur Trade: A Case for Contextual Semantics," in Trigger, Morantz and Dechene, "Le Castor Fait Tout," 618–49.

67. Irene M. Spry, "Aboriginal Resource Use in the Nineteenth Century in the Great Plains of Modem Canada," in Abel and Friesen, *Aboriginal Resource Use in Canada*, 81–84.

68. *Report*, 22.

69. Ibid., 59.

70. Ibid., 92. The governor neglected to mention that without the provisions of pemmican and meat which the Natives supplied, the Hudson's Bay could not operate as efficiently in the North-West as it did.

71. Ibid., 284.

72. Ibid., 22–23, 117, 284.

73. Milloy, *The Plains Cree*, 103–10; Robert A. Church, "Blackfeet and Fur Traders: Storm on the Northwestern Plains," *Journal of the West* 36 (April 1997): 79–84.

74. *Report*, 443.

75. Alexander Isbister argued that the denser populations of both white and Native people in the United States was a crucial factor in that country's more violent history. Beginning with relatively sparse populations, government could carefully control the rate of settlement and avoid wars between Indians and whites [ibid., 122].

76. Lieutenant-Colonel William Caldwell, commander of a pensioner corps in Red River, confirmed that he had discouraged the establishment of a mission at Portage la Prairie because it would be outside his jurisdiction [ibid., 309]. See also the testimony of Alexander Isbister and the letter of an Aboriginal chief, called Peguis [ibid., 120–37, 353–56, and 445].

77. Ibid., 139. The attitude of the company to missionaries was ambivalent. While it supported a number of missionaries of various faiths with free transportation and board and room, it exerted a measure of control over their expansion and actively opposed competition among the faiths. See, for only one example, Gerald M. Hutchinson, Introduction and Notes, *The Rundle Journals, 1840–1848* (Calgary: Alberta Records Publication Board, Historical Society of Alberta, 1977), xiv–xvi.

78. Ibid., 63.

79. Ibid., 58.

80. Ibid., 105.

81. Ibid., 64.

82. Ibid., 285.

83. Ibid., 275.

84. Ibid., 285.

85. Ibid., 239.

86. Ibid., 245.

87. Ibid., 235.

88. Ibid., 444.

89. Ibid., 30, 42.

90. Ibid., 41.

91. The assumption that the Natives were unwilling to take up farming, held by many authorities even to the present, is challenged by Sarah Carter, "'We Must Farm to Enable us to Live': The Plains Cree and Agriculture to 1900," in R. Bruce Morrison and C. Roderick Wilson (eds.), *Native Peoples: The Canadian Experience* (Toronto: McClelland and Stewart, 1995).

92. Frieda Knobloch, *The Culture of Wilderness: Agriculture as Colonization in the American West* (Chapel Hill: University of North Carolina Press, 1996), 5.

93. Alexander Ross, *The Red River Settlement: Its Rise, Progress, and Present State...* (1856; Minneapolis, 1957), 194; see also 78–80, 84–85, 98–99,193–96, 203–23.

94. Walter E. Houghton, *The Victorian Frame of Mind 1830–1870* (New Haven, 1957).

95. John Gallagher and Ronald Robinson, "The Imperialism of Free Trade," *The Economic History Review* 6, no. 1 (1953): 1–15. This seminal article has launched a furious debate among historians. A dated, but useful, introduction to the discussion is Roger Louis, *Imperialism: The Robinson and Gallagher Controversy* (New York: New Viewpoints, 1976). An excellent overview of Britain's cultural expansionism is Ronald Hyam, *Britain's Imperial Century 1815–1914*, 31–36. As its title implies, Alfred Crosby's *Ecological Imperialism* argues that disease, plants, and animals acted as shock troops preparing the way of Europe's invasion of North America and other New World continents.

96. Adas, *Machines as the Measure of Men*; Turner, *Beyond Geography*.

97. See testimony of Alexander Isbister and John McLaughlin, *Report*, 127 and 264.

98. *Report*, 157–58, 231, and 237.

99. Ibid., 240.

100. Ibid., 237.

101. Ibid.

102. Ibid., 237–38.

103. Ibid., 246.

104. Ibid., 240.

105. Lieutenant-Colonel William Caldwell supported Anderson's view. He was very pleased with the progress of the Aboriginal mission in Red River. He complimented the Natives on their mode of Sunday worship observances, adding that "they were as devotional in appearance as any congregation I ever was in" [ibid., 309].

106. W.L. Morton, *Manitoba: A History* (Toronto: University of Toronto Press, 1957), 55, 72; Olive Patricia Dickason, *Canada's First Nations: A History of the Founding Peoples from Earliest Time* (Toronto: Oxford University press, 1997), 213, 239.

107. *Report*, 446.

108. Ibid., 225.

109. John S. Milloy, "The Early Indian Acts: Developmental Strategy and Constitutional Change," in Ian A.L. Getty and Antoine S. Lussier (eds.), *As Long as the Sun Shines and Water Flows* (Vancouver: University of British Columbia Press, 1983), 58–59; John L. Tobias, "Protection, Civilization, Assimilation: An Outline History of Canada's Indian Policy," in ibid., 42.

110. *Report*, 285.

11.1 Ibid., 216, 227–28.

112. Ibid., 252–54.

113. Ibid., 342.

114. Ibid., 87. See also HBCA/PAM, A7/2, Shepherd to Labouchere, July 18, 1857.

115. HBCA/PAM, A12/8, Simpson to Shepherd, January 26, 1857.

116. *Report*, xi.

117. Ibid., xiii.

118. Carter, "Plains Cree and Agriculture," 447.

119. HBCA/PAM, A8/8,Shepherd to Labouchere, March 16, 1857.

10. The Red River Settlement: Lord Selkirk's Isolated Colony in the Wilderness

Barry Kaye

When the fur trader-historian Alexander Ross wrote that "the remote colony of Red River may be said to be as far from England as any colony or people on the habitable globe," he was taking literary license to emphasize what were perhaps the most remarkable geographic features of the Red River Settlement—isolation and its relative location.[1] Founded in 1812 by the Scottish nobleman Thomas Douglas, fifth Earl of Selkirk, the colony was located almost at the geographical centre of the North American continent. It was separated on the east from the British settlement frontier in Upper Canada by one thousand miles of nearly empty Canadian Shield, and on the north from York Factory, its maritime connection to Europe, by almost as many miles of difficult and often dangerous water navigation. To the south stretched the seemingly endless and essentially unexplored grasslands of the interior Great Plains of North America which, on the borders of the colony, were controlled by the powerful and largely hostile Sioux Indians. The colony was established at the junction of the Red and Assiniboine Rivers and, between 1812 and 1821, Selkirk placed emigrants from Europe at this location on the southern flanks of Rupert's Land, the chartered lands of the Hudson's Bay Company.

Historical tradition has been that Selkirk's decision to found the Red River Settlement at this location derived from the sanguine descriptions of the agricultural potential of the Red River valley, contained in the writings of the fur trader Alexander Mackenzie. Closer scrutiny reveals, however, that this fundamental, and perhaps most important locational decision in the settlement history of Western Canada, derived not from Mackenzie's descriptions but from a complex of factors that had coalesced in Selkirk's mind, and in Hudson's Bay Company affairs, about this time.

An Inland Colony in British North America

Prior to his association with the Hudson's Bay Company, which began in 1807, Selkirk had submitted two proposals to the British Colonial Office outlining settlement schemes in British North America. The proposal of 1802 contains his earliest ideas about North American colonization. He initially urged that a settlement expressly for Irish Catholics be established in North America and he declared himself "willing to devote his exertions to the service of his country in conducting the proposed Colony to America, if a situation can be procured possessing such natural advantages as are requisite for the success of the plan."[2] He wished to see the colonists located in a situation possessed of a "favourable" climate, fertile soil, and access to navigable waterways, so that the settlers could direct their attention to "objects of cultivation not only useful to the Commerce of Britain, but for which at present she depends chiefly on the territories of her habitual enemies." From the start, Selkirk clearly had in mind a colony for which a mercantile, commercial agriculture would provide the economic justification. It was his belief, at this time, that the wilderness lands of British North America did not have, for climatic reasons, the characteristics necessary for a successful colony. As a result, Selkirk eliminated these lands from consideration in his initial proposal and instead suggested Louisiana as the best location for his prospective colony. There it would be possible to find "a situation in which every advantage would be united; in which there would be the fairest prospects both of the internal prosperity of the Colony and of its becoming a valuable acquisition to the Commerce of Britain."

Louisiana was a curious choice, for this territory lay outside British possessions in North America. It was also vaguely defined, since Louisiana at that time embraced much of the valleys of the Mississippi and the Missouri. In 1880 New Orleans and Louisiana west of the Mississippi were retroceded by Spain to France. Selkirk was aware that the British might be able to persuade the French to give up Louisiana during the ongoing negotiations (1801–02) between Britain and France preliminary to the Peace of Amiens (1802). However, the British did not press the French for the transfer and Louisiana remained in French hands until its purchase by the United States in 1803.

The failure of his first proposal caused Selkirk to draw up another one, "Observations Supplementary to a Memorial Relative to the Security of Ireland," dated April 3, 1802, which he submitted to the Colonial Office.[3] Again, Selkirk discussed possible locations for his proposed colony in North America. No mention was made of Louisiana, for by April 1802 Selkirk's mind had become fixed on the distant interior of British North America,

Thomas Douglas, 5th Earl of Selkirk, date unknown (courtesy of the Archives of Manitoba/N8755).

particularly on the upper countries west of Lake Superior, the "Northwest" of the Montreal fur traders and the most important fur preserve of the continent.

Selkirk's second document began by justifying his choice of an interior rather than a coastal location for a colony. His argument was that "no large tract remains unoccupied on the Sea Coast of British America, except barren and frozen desarts."[4] In order "to find a sufficient extent of good soil in a temperate climate," it would, therefore, be necessary to "go far inland."[5] Such an inland situation would be an inconvenience, but "not however an unsurmountable obstacle to the prosperity of a colony," while advantages to be found in certain "remote parts of the British Territory" would more than compensate for its distance from the sea.[6] Selkirk then pinpointed the "remote area" he had in mind. He wrote that, "At the western extremity of Canada upon the waters which fall into Lake Winnipeck [Winnipeg], & uniting in the great River of Port Nelson fall into Hudson's Bay, is a country which the Indian traders represent as fertile, & of a climate far more temperate than the shores of the Atlantic under the same parallel, & not more severe than that of Germany & Poland. Here, therefore the Colonists may with a moderate exertion of industry be certain of a comfortable subsistence; & they may also raise some valuable objects of exportation."[7] Selkirk believed that an interior location might preclude the export of grain. However, such a location would compensate by turning "the attention of the colonists to articles of greater value in proportion to their weight; & of these none can be more promising than hemp, which has been neglected in the maritime settlements, chiefly perhaps because the sure & ready market for grain has encouraged the inhabitants to persevere on the simple culture to which they had of old been accustomed."[8]

Selkirk's proposal for hemp cultivation was based on what he believed to be the similaries of climate and soil between parts of the Canadian Northwest and Russia, at that time the major hemp supplier in Europe. Interference with these supplies during the Napoleonic Wars made it imperative that the British establish alternative centres of hemp production, preferably in their overseas colonies.[9] The lands of the Northwest, however, might be more than another Russia. According to Selkirk, they had the potential, because of their suitability for vine cultivation, to be another France. It was his information that "some of the British Canadians have extended their discoveries into a climate apparently well adapted even to the vine, the successful cultivation of which would save immense sums, that go every year from this Kingdom into the hands of its enemies [France]." Selkirk tried to win over the British Government to his scheme for a colony in the interior of British North America by pointing out what he believed to be the favourable conditions of the area he had in mind. He anticipated no problems in moving agricultural products to the coast for export to Europe. The colony might make use of the well-established Nelson-Hayes fur trade route to York Factory to facilitate passage to the Bay. "To a colony in these territories, the channel of trade must be the river of Port Nelson, which from the Lake [Winnipeg] to its discharge is between 3 & 400 miles, & a navigation interrupted by considerable obstructions- these however may probably be remedied." Selkirk surmised that if the British were to acquire territory on the Upper Mississippi in the future, settlements there would be able to take advantage of the same outlet to the Bay, since the southward flowing waters of the Upper Mississippi were separated by only a short, level divide from streams flowing north into Lake Winnipeg and Hudson Bay.

Selkirk also suggested that colonization would stimulate commercial developments other than those based on agriculture. In some unexplained manner agrarian settlement would initiate the exploitation of the fishery resources of Hudson Bay and Hudson Strait. Once the "now so imperfectly known" Rupert's Land was opened up for settlement, hitherto unsuspected resources would quickly be revealed and developed.

His final argument in favour of an inland colony concerned the broader imperial and commercial strategies in North America. "It appears particularly, that the branches of the River of the West, or Columbia, interlock not only with the heads of the Missouri, but with the waters of Lake Winnipeck [Saskatchewan River]. A communication might therefore be opened, and a post established on the Pacific Ocean, from which many of the advantages would be derived, which were formerly expected from the discovery of a North West Passage." In Selkirk's scheme, a settlement located on one of the streams draining into Lake Winnipeg would form one link in a great transcontinental water route to the Pacific. A port would establish Britain's relations with Asia and the Pacific trade, a real alternative to the elusive Northwest Passage.

The question that might be posed is what caused Selkirk to reverse his opinions about the possibilities for colonization in the short time that elapsed between his initial "Proposal" and his later "Observations." In his "Proposal" he excluded from consideration for settlement all of the empty lands of British North America for climatic reasons whereas, in his "Observations," parts of these same lands were described as "temperate" and suited to the cultivation of hemp and the vine.

The few geographical considerations that Selkirk presented to the government, in making his case for a colony in interior British North America, were a mixture of known fact, distortion, and pure fantasy. Most scholars concerned with the source of these ideas have concluded that Selkirk derived most of his information about the Canadian Northwest and its agricultural potential from reading Alexander Mackenzie's *Voyages*, published in London in 1801.[10] The great explorer-fur trader had reached the Arctic Ocean in 1789, via the Slave and Mackenzie rivers, and four years later reached the Pacific Ocean, via the Peace River and present-day British Columbia. His book, based in part on these epic journeys, became available about the time Selkirk submitted his colonization proposals to the British Government and sought facts to bolster his belief that a colony in the interior of British North America would be viable. Scholars have frequently suggested that Selkirk read Mackenzie's book sometime between submitting his "Proposals" and writing his "Observations." The historian J.P. Pritchett, for example, has written that, "it was probably after a reading of Sir Alexander Mackenzie's account of his northern and western explorations, as published in 1801, that Selkirk conceived the idea of planting a colony in the distant interior of British North America."[11] It was also his view that Selkirk wrote his "Observations" of 1802 with Mackenzie's book close at hand, and subsequently selected the Red River valley as the location of his colony on the basis of information it afforded.

Mackenzie's book may well have aroused Selkirk's interest in the Canadian Northwest but, contrary to what has become standard interpretation,[12] nothing in the historical record supports the belief that it was through reading Mackenzie that Selkirk settled upon the Red River valley

Sir Alexander Mackenzie (1764–1820) c. 1800. Engraving based upon the oil on canvas portrait painted by Thomas Lawrence (courtesy of the Glenbow Archives/LAC-1733-1)

as the best location for a colony. Indeed, the Red River is not mentioned in the "Observations." In 1802, Selkirk wrote only of "the waters which fall into Lake Winnipeck, & uniting in the greater River of Port Nelson fall into Hudson's Bay…" There is no reason to assume, as have most reading this quotation, that Selkirk had the Red River valley specifically in mind for his inland colony. Almost all of the prairie and parkland region of the western interior of Canada drains into Lake Winnipeg.

Furthermore, there is nothing in Mackenzie's *Voyages* to support the frequent claim that he considered the Red River country to be outstanding for agricultural development. In fact, Mackenzie failed to mention agricultural possibilities in his short description of the Red River country. Of the Red River he wrote that

> The country on either side is but partially supplied with wood, and consists of plains covered with herds of the buffalo and elk, especially on the Western side. On the Eastern side are lakes and rivers, and the whole country is well wooded, level, abounding in beavers, bears, moose-deer, fallow-deer, etc., etc.[13]

He described the country between the Red and Assiniboine valleys as

> almost a continual plain to the Missisoury. The soil is sand and gravel, with a slight intermixture of earth, and produces a short grass. Trees are very rare; nor are there on the banks of the river sufficient, except in particular spots, to build houses and supply fire-wood for the trading establishments, of which there are four principal ones. Both these rivers are navigable for canoes to their source, without a fall; though

in some parts there are rapids, caused by occasional beds of limestone, and gravel; but in general they have a sandy bottom.[14]

There is nothing in these accounts that would generate visions of a great agricultural future for the Red River valley. Quite the opposite; references to sand, gravel, short grass, and timber scarcity would more likely have raised the spectre of sterility and low agricultural potential. The glowing account of the Red River country which Selkirk supposedly found in his reading of the *Voyages* is not present. Perhaps Selkirk was influenced by Mackenzie's statement that "there is not, perhaps, a finer country in the world for the residence of uncivilised man... It abounds in everything necessary to the wants and comforts of such a people. Fish, venison, and fowl, with wild rice, are in great plenty; while, at the same time, their subsistence requires that bodily exercise so necessary to health and vigour."[15] But it would have been supreme folly for Selkirk to have presumed what Mackenzie considered a land of abundance for native hunters and gatherers might be a land of similar abundance for European agriculturalists. Elsewhere in the *Voyages*, it is made clear that rock and water predominated in the region west of Lake Superior and that soil was scarce.

Mackenzie's most positive comment on the agricultural possibilities of the lands draining into Lake Winnipeg referred to the large stretch of highly varied country between Lake Winnipeg's western shore and the South Branch of the Saskatchewan. He wrote of this area that "the soil is good, and wherever any attempts have been made to raise the esculent plants, etc. it has been found productive."[16] If Mackenzie was Selkirk's sole authority for his "Observations," then this is the only statement in the *Voyages* that could have reasonably formed the basis for Selkirk's contention. The *Voyages* are less positive about the North Saskatchewan country, saying only that on the north and west side of the river, the country "is broken by the lakes and rivers with small intervening plains, where the soil is good, and the grass grows to some length."[17]

Neither did Mackenzie's summary remarks on the settlement possibilities of Rupert's Land offer encouragement for anybody seeking information about the area in order to support plans for an agricultural settlement in the western interior. Of the section of the continent between Hudson Bay and the Pacific Ocean, Mackenzie wrote that

> The whole of this country will long continue in the possession of its present inhabitants, as they will remain contented with the produce of the woods and waters for

their support, leaving the earth, from various causes, in its virgin state. The proportion of it that is fit for cultivation is very small, and is still less in the interior parts; it is also very difficult of access; and whilst any land remains uncultivated to the South of it, there will be no temptation to settle it. Besides, its climate is not in general sufficiently genial to bring the fruits of the earth to maturity."[18]

If, as is widely believed, Selkirk relied heavily on Mackenzie for the information in his "Observations," he either ignored the opinions and facts he found there or distorted them out of all recognition.[19] In suggesting the possibility of hemp and vine cultivation in the interior of British North America, Selkirk was clearly telling the British government what he thought it wanted to hear. Cultivating hemp and vine in the British colonies was considered a desirable national objective, so Selkirk created, on very flimsy evidence, a physical geography that would support these crops in the lands he wished to colonize.[20]

Although there is no evidence that Selkirk read an earlier publication by Edward Umfreville, it is worth noting that the ideas expressed in the "Observations" coincide more closely with those in Umfreville's *The Present State of Hudson's Bay* (published in London in 1790) than they do with Mackenzie's.[21] Umfreville had worked for both the Hudson's Bay and North West companies and had seen service at Bayside posts as well as on the North Saskatchewan. He says nothing about the Red River but comments on the agricultural potential of the North Saskatchewan country, an area of which he had firsthand knowledge:

> How far the soil of this boundless country may be favourable to the culture of vegetables, I am not enabled to advance. Experiments, which should be our only guide to knowledge in these matters, never having been made use of; but if the opinion of an unexperienced person, could be of any weight, I think I may venture to say, that many parts would admit of cultivation.[22]

Umfreville compared the climate of the North Saskatchewan favourably with that of Canada:

> It is true we are situated a few degrees more to the Northward, and about fifty degrees to the Westward of Quebec, but in four years experience I have had, I have not yet found a winter so severe, as one I passed near Montreal,

where the weather is generally something milder than about Quebec. The cold sets in, and the river ice breaks up, much about the same time as it does here.[23]

In comparing the Bayside and the interior of Rupert's Land, Umfreville described the North Saskatchewan valley as "temperate and healthy, the land is dry, pleasant, and fertile in spontaneous productions, and the animal creation is various and excellent for the support of man: in it, a person who could live retired, might pass his days with ease, content, and felicity, and if he did not enjoy an uninterrupted state of health, it would not be the fault of the air he lived in."[24] This was the type of material out of which one could build a reasonable case for the viability of an agricultural settlement. Given Umfreville's sanguine views on the settlement possibilities of the parkland region of the Canadian Northwest, one must wonder if Selkirk was familiar with these views when he wrote his "Observations" in 1802. Certainly, along with Mackenzie's *Voyages*, it was at the time one of the few published works containing information on the geography of the Canadian Northwest.[25]

Whatever the merits of Selkirk's case for encouraging Irish emigration to North America, or the accuracy of his information about Rupert's Land, nothing came of the proposals put forward in the "Observations." In May 1802 Lord Pelham, Secretary of State for Ireland, declared himself against the proposal; the government was opposed to "colonizing at all en masse" and saw "great difficulties & objections to Government undertaking to Transport & settle people from Ireland or elsewhere."[26] The government also declared its opposition to any interference with the trade and monopoly of the Hudson's Bay Company in Rupert's Land. This put an end to any immediate plans for an agricultural settlement in the Company's territories. In an audience on June 11, 1802, Lord Hobart, Secretary for War and Colonies, made clear to Selkirk "that at this state of events the section of the 'Proposal' which dealt with a colonization site in the interior of British North America met with most objection. The Secretary hinted at this interview that the government would probably be more willing to grant lands for settlement in Prince Edward Island than in the West."[27] Once it became evident that the government was unwilling to back his plan for an Irish colony in interior Rupert's Land, Selkirk dropped the scheme and began to pursue his colonizing ambitions elsewhere in British North America. "To bring his plans as nearly as possible in line with the wishes of the government Selkirk now turned his attention from the Hudson's Bay Company's territories to Prince Edward Island and Upper Canada."[28] In February 1803, Selkirk was granted land on the eastern peninsula of Prince Edward Island and soon after received a tract in western Upper Canada, between Lakes Erie and Huron, known as the Baldoon colony. For the next five years most of his attention was directed towards organizing the settlement of Scottish Highlanders on Prince Edward Island and at Baldoon.[29]

The Choice of the Red River Country

If Selkirk's hopes of a British colony in Rupert's Land were put aside for a number of years, they were not forgotten. By about 1807, matured by his colonizing experiences in Prince Edward Island and Upper Canada, Selkirk's interest was renewed in the affairs of the Hudson's Bay Company and in the possibilities of establishing a colony in the Winnipeg basin. It had been made clear to Selkirk that it was the charter of the Hudson's Bay Company, as much as the Government's opposition, that presented the major impediment to his colonization plans in Rupert's Land. Independent legal opinion had informed Selkirk that the Company's charter of 1670 "made the Hudson's Bay Company sole proprietor of all the territories granted, with full powers of government, including the appointment of sheriffs, the trial of lawbreakers, and the leasing or alienation in fee simple, of any part of its domain."[30] Selkirk could only conclude from this that he must get the support of the Hudson's Bay Company if he wished to implement his plans for an agricultural settlement on its chartered lands. Consequently, he commenced to buy himself into a position of power and influence within the Company. In the summer of 1808 he began buying Company stock and continued to do so for the next few years. In 1810 he presented to the Company's directors his scheme for a settlement colony in the Winnipeg basin.

Selkirk's intrusion into the affairs of the Hudson's Bay Company was timely. The relentless competition of the Nor'Westers in Rupert's Land and the exclusion of British goods, including furs, from Europe with the imposition of Napoleon's Continental System (1806) had brought the Company to insolvency. "In 1809 the company could not pay a dividend; its trade was being financed on credit, with Committee members often having to provide ready cash; and it had a heavy overdraft of £50,000 at the bank."[31] However, the years 1809 and 1810 were marked by the emergence of a new determination on the part of the Company to improve its competitive position. These measures were known collectively as the Retrenching or New System and Selkirk's plans fitted well with this scheme for reorganization. One area in which the London committee wished to economize was in the cost of sending provisions to Rupert's Land. In a lengthy statement, the Company later explained to the colonial office its reasons for supporting Selkirk's third colonizing venture:

The servants of the Hudson's Bay Company employed in the fur trade, have hitherto been fed with provisions exported from England. Of late years this expense has been so enormous, that it has become very desirable to try the practicability of raising provisions within the territory itself; notwithstanding the unfavourable soil and climate of the settlements immediately adjacent to Hudson's Bay, there is a great deal of fertile lands in the interior of the country, where the climate is very good, and well fitted for the cultivation of grain. It does not appear probable that agriculture would be carried on with sufficient care and attention by servants in the immediate employ of the company; but by establishing independent settlers, and giving them freehold tenures of land, the company expected to obtain a certain supply of provisions at a moderate price. The company also entertained expectations of considerable eventual benefits from the improvements of their landed property by means of agricultural settlements. Having a due regard to the implied conditions of their charter, they deemed it a duty incumbent on them (as soon as the practicability of agricultural improvements was demonstrated) to give a liberal degree of encouragement to an experiment, which, independently of the advantages, promised to have the most beneficial effects on the civilization of the Indians.[32]

The idea of an agricultural settlement in Rupert's Land was not new. Indeed, as E.E. Rich has noted, there was in the Company's charter "provision for a colony to be established and even for the whole direction of the Company to be taken out to such a colony; but the Company had never seriously engaged in colonization."[33] The Company had not colonized its lands[34] but, nevertheless, it had long encouraged its officers in Rupert's Land to increase gardening activities, as far as circumstances and the environment would allow, at the posts under their charge.[35] The establishment of an agricultural settlement was a logical extension of the Company's earlier policies and intentions.

In cooperating with Selkirk in his plan for a settlement in Rupert's Land, on June 12, 1811 the Hudson's Bay Company granted him a vast area of land, known as the Assiniboia Grant, for the purposes of agricultural colonization (Figure 1). Selkirk was apparently well-satisfied with the area granted, for he later claimed that it included land which, "in point of soil and climate," was "inferior to none of equal extent in British America." In

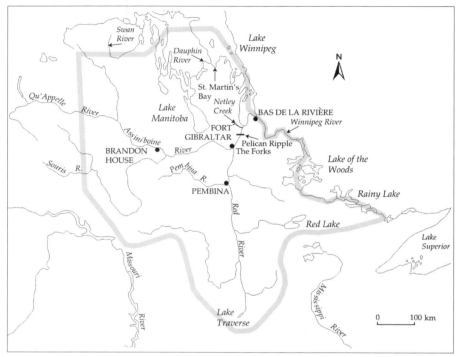

Figure 1. The Assiniboia Grant, 1811.

reality, Assiniboia comprised land of varying agricultural potential. To the east it included areas of the Laurentian Shield, to the west the wooded heights of the Manitoba escarpment, with adjacent parts of the second prairie level, and to the north a swampy and stony plain. Assiniboia centred on the low-lying, flat corridor of the Red River valley draining north to Lake Winnipeg, with "the Forks," the junction of the Red and Assiniboine rivers, as its focus. Before the departure of the first Rupert's Land settlers in 1811, it had been agreed that they should establish the colony on the Red River somewhere close to the strategic Forks.

It is impossible to determine precisely when the decision was made that the Red River country was the best choice for the location of an agricultural settlement in the Northwest. The evidence suggests that the decision was made either in 1809 or, more likely, in 1810, after Selkirk became a major shareholder in the Hudson's Bay Company and made the acquaintance of its directors. Most likely the crucial choice of the Red River country was not Selkirk's alone, but was made in close consultation with the directors after he had put forward his scheme for an agricultural settlement on the

Company's lands. As a Company shareholder, Selkirk gained access for the first time to a new body of information about Rupert's Land—the journals and letters sent annually to London by the Company's officers. From references and information in his later writings, we know that Selkirk spent time perusing these detailed documents. W.L. Morton has remarked that Selkirk's 1811 Instructions to Miles Macdonell were "written with the precision of a man who had pored over every description of his new domain [Assiniboia] until he had fixed every feature in his mind's eye."[36] In these "instructions" Selkirk acknowledged his debt for much of his knowledge of the geography of the Red River country to the travel journals of Peter Fidler, the Hudson's Bay Company trader and surveyor.[37] Selkirk also increased his familiarity with the Red River and other parts of the Northwest by interviewing the Company's officers and servants retired from service or on leave in Britain. When Hugh Heney, a Hudson's Bay Company trader stationed at Pembina, discussed the Northwest with Selkirk in London he found "he [Selkirk] was uncommonly well versed in the Topography of this part of America..."[38] Whatever his sources of information about the Northwest, Selkirk had sufficient confidence in them to allow him to ignore the advice of University of Edinburgh philosopher, Dugald Stewart, that "whatever pains you may have taken to collect information, nothing short of a personal examination and survey of the place of your destination could justify you in forming arrangements of so gigantic a magnitude, involving not only your own dearest interest but the fate of all such as may follow your fortunes."[39] Selkirk did not visit Red River until 1817, five years after the beginnings of settlement.[40]

There is no way of knowing what facts were communicated orally to Selkirk, or what images of the Red River area he built up from reading the letters and journals deposited in the Company's headquarters. No doubt the information they contained was varied and contradictory. What few indications there are suggest that by the early 19th century there was a body of opinion amongst both Hudson's Bay Company and Canadian traders that the Red River country, of all the areas in the Northwest, offered the greatest advantages for agricultural settlement.

Hudson's Bay Company Trader John Sutherland, who travelled along the Assiniboine on his way back to Brandon House, commented on the "beautiful plains which only wants the hand of industry to make this one of the finest countries in the universe no clearing of the ground wanted, but the plow to till and the scythe to cut the finest hay; the woods along the river is still large and thick..."[41] A month later at Brandon House Sutherland noted that "it is a known fact that anything will grow in this country."[42] Archibald

Mason, a Scots farmer from Invernesshire turned fur trader, who considered himself "a good judge of land," had this to say of the Red River valley:

> from Nattli [Netley] creek or below it, to the Forks of the Red River from Red River, to Pabin [Pembina] House or Sumer berry River, all the way to Red Lake, and to the Shoe [Sioux] country for hundreds of miles to the westrd. & south west of Pabina a remarkable rich soil of marl and black mold.[43]

He described the Red River country as "that famous Lands" and as "that Rich Fertile spontaneous Country." It was Mason's view that the Red River country had no equal elsewhere. "A Mason has seen much fine lands between Britian [sic], & America but Red River Hudson Bay is so far in head of all he ever have seen no strangers can form an idea thereof."

North West Company traders were equally optimistic about the agricultural potential of the Red River lands. John Macdonell, a North West Company employee, informed his brother Miles that "from the Forks of the Assiniboine and Red Rivers the plains are quite near the banks, and so extensive that a man may travel to the Rocky Mountains without passing a wood, a mile long. The soil on the Red River and the Assiniboine is generally a good soil, susceptible of culture, and capable of bearing rich crops... The buffalo comes to the forks of Assiniboine, besides in these rivers are plenty of sturgeon, catfish, goldeyes, pike and whitefish—the latter so common that men have been seen to catch thirty or forty apiece while they smoke their pipes."[44] The Forks of the Red and Assiniboine was described by Daniel Harmon, who had travelled widely in the Northwest, as appearing to have "a richer soil than at any other place I have observed in this part of the World—and is covered with Oak, Basswood, Elm, Poplar and Burch etc., also are here Red Plumbs & Grapes etc."[45] Although the Nor'Westers' opinions were not available to Selkirk, they indicate the generally favourable view of the region that was impressed on those who had spent all or part of their years of service there.[46]

The preliminary evaluation of the Red River country carried out by Selkirk and the Company judged it for agriculture and its overall position in the fur trade of the Northwest. The Red River lowlands had never been a rich fur preserve, but a variety of animal pelts were still being taken out of the valleys of the Red and the Assiniboine during the first decade of the nineteenth century. However, the fur returns were by that time the remnants of a trade carried on with little interruption since the 1730s. As far

1, 2. A Swiss colonist with wife and children from the Canton of Berne. 3. A German colonist from the disbanded De Meuron Regt. 4. A Scottish Highland colonist. 5. An immigrant colonist from French Canada.

TYPES OF LORD SELKIRK'S SETTLERS IN 1822.

From a photo of black and white drawing of a Swiss Colonist, touched up by Mr. Lawson, artist of the *Manitoba Free Press.*

Courtesy of Dr. Doughty, Dominion Archivist.

"Types of Lord Selkirk's Settlers in 1822." Depicted are a Swiss colonist and his wife and children, a German colonist, a colonist from the Scottish highlands, and an "immigrant colonist from French Canada" (courtesy of the Archives of Manitoba/N13832).

as the fur trade companies were concerned, the Red River lowland was exhausted of prime furs by the early 19th century. The valuable beaver, in particular, had become scarce. In 1818 Bishop Provencher described the economic role of the Red River country as follows:

> Red River is by no means a place for trade. There are no furs here. The largest trade would be in buffalo robes, but the Companies do not take them. ... All that the North West Company and Hudson's Bay Company obtain from this area is provisions, which consists of dry meats, for their voyageurs along the route to their scattered posts in the North and elsewhere.[47]

Although Provencher was incorrect in claiming that no furs came out of the Red River area, his estimate of the region's significance in the Northwest fur trade was basically correct. As MacLeod and Morton have stated, "it was its buffalo plains rather than its fur forests that made the Red River country significant to the fur traders in 1812."[48]

The depletion of furs in the Red River country was a major factor in its choice as the location for the colony. In his most direct comment about the choice of the general location for the colony, Selkirk wrote in 1819 that "the Red River country was selected, as a place where the natural resources of provisions were abundant, & where at the same time beaver and other valuable fur bearing animals had been so much exhausted, that the district was of little consequence for the fur trade."[49] Four years earlier the Company had provided Lord Bathurst, Secretary of the Colonies, with similar reasons:

> In entering upon this transaction [granting of Assiniboia to Selkirk], the Hudson's Bay company had no reason to suppose that the intended establishment would meet any peculiar difficulties. The country on Red River, where it was to be formed, had been frequented by the servants of the company for a long course of years [since 1793]; and they were in the habits of the most friendly intercourse with the natives. The district had been much exhausted of valuable furs, so that the trading posts in it had proved of late years unprofitable, and doubts had been entertained whether they ought to be continued; and the Indians had, on various occasions expressed much anxiety, lest the Hudson's Bay company should abandon the posts from which they had so long been accustomed to receive their supplies of British manufacturers.[50]

Colonization attempted at this time in the Northwest would inevitably have had a disruptive influence on the fur trade. However, by 1810 or 1811 it seems that the directors of the Hudson's Bay Company were persuaded that the advantages of any agricultural colony would more than compensate for any injury it might cause the trade. The relative absence of furs in the Red River valley meant that such injury would be minimal there.

This was sound reasoning as far as it went. But in evaluating the Red River's position in the trade solely on the basis of its fur production, Selkirk and the Company ignored the crucial provisioning role that the posts on the Red, Assiniboine and Qu'Appelle rivers played in the trade, especially for the North West Company. The proposed settlement on the Red would lie astride the river routes by which the Nor'Westers carried pemmican, the food staple of the fur brigades, to their depot at Bas de la Rivière, near the mouth of the Winnipeg River. Moreover, the whole east-west transcontinental water route of the North West Company would be seriously threatened if Bas de la Rivière was cut off from its annual pemmican supplies from the Red River country. It was the fear of such an interruption of their trade and transport that caused the Nor'Westers to oppose the colony strenuously, both before and after its establishment. This opposition eventually led to the Pemmican War and the breakup of Selkirk's Red River Settlement in 1815 and 1816.

A Site on Red River

The first important decision confronting Macdonell after his arrival at Red River in 1812 with the founding settlers was "the choice of a situation for the colony." In deciding this important question, Macdonell was to apply a number of basic criteria outlined by Selkirk.[51] These included good drainage on a level site above a river where the banks were backed by an expanse of fertile soil, yet close to supplies of timber; the site of the colony should also be dry and airy "for the sake of health." Specific suggestions found in Selkirk's correspondence with his governor included the examination of the Red River at Stony or Pelican Ripple (later St. Andrew's Rapids). This was the location of the first "plain" going up the river, as well as the first break in navigation, and a place of possible future importance. Selkirk cautioned Macdonell that information from Peter Fidler's survey suggested that the site at the rapids might be too low and, consequently, subject to flooding.[52] Macdonell was also advised that if it was necessary to go beyond the Forks "to the edge of the great plains," he should examine both the Assiniboine and the upper Red in his search for a site.

From the information he was able to collect, Macdonell thought "the tract of the country below the Forks" as the most likely to provide a suitable loca-tion.[53] He spent three days early in September examining "the different points and bays" along that stretch of the Red, searching for a site that met the requirements he had in mind. Macdonell was seeking a spot which could be cleared quickly, tilled, and sown with wheat before the onset of the win-ter. The colonists planned to spend the winter months at Pembina, some sixty miles south of the Forks, living off the hunt. After examination, the site at the rapids was judged inadequate. Macdonell's choice as "the most eligi-ble spot" to locate the first settlers was "an extensive point of land" a little below the Forks.[54] The place chosen was the promontory formed by a mean-der of the Red, about a mile below the Forks, known for a short time as Point Sherbrooke (later Point Douglas, commemorating Lord Selkirk's family name). Macdonell was informed of the suitability of this point of land for settlement by an old freeman named Peltier, whom he encountered during his travels along the lower Red.[55] Macdonell's original choice had been a location somewhere below the point.

Macdonell made clear the reasons for his final choice. A fire had recently swept through the point and destroyed the timber and underbrush, leaving it with only a light cover of "weeds, brush & under-wood." As "these could be easier overcome than woods or grass," the land could readily be put into cultivation. Furthermore, in Macdonell's judgement the soil was excellent, and nearby there were stands of timber for initial building operations. The proximity of the Forks, dominated by the recently erected North West Company post of Fort Gibraltar, might have seemed like an additional recommendation. During the early weeks of colonization, when relations between the North West Company and the settlers appeared friendly, Macdonell received considerable aid and advice from the men at the fort. There was no important Hudson's Bay Company settlement at the Forks at this time.

The major disadvantage of Macdonell's choice of the site just north of the Forks was spring-melt flooding, as events in 1811 had shown. William Auld, writing from Churchill, had informed the Governor and Committee of serious flooding along the Red River then. "The Red River down thro' its whole course particularly to its junction with the Assiniboine River had 50 feet of water above its usual level of 5 feet the average width of the river was 8 miles instead of 80 or 100 yards."[56] This information was conveyed to Selkirk, for he wrote to Macdonell in December 1811 that flooding was "a serious consideration notwithstanding the rarity of the occurrence."[57] In proposing a settlement on the Red, Selkirk had been under the mistaken impression that what he called "the upper banks" were quite out of reach of any flood waters. In the same communication Selkirk proposed a possible alternate location for the colony, although he claimed that the 1811 flood was not the reason for doing so. The alternate location was near the northern edge of the Assiniboia Grant, on the western shores of Lake Winnipeg at, or near, the mouth of the River Dauphin. This stream flows out of Lake St. Martin, reaching Lake Winnipeg in what was then called St. Martin's Bay (present-day Sturgeon Bay).[58]

It was Selkirk's belief that a location on the River Dauphin would offer several advantages over one on the Red provided that "plains" could be found in its vicinity. Included amongst these advantages would be access to good harbours on Lake Winnipeg and greater proximity to Hudson Bay. This latter advantage would largely offset any handicaps arising out of the

The Governor of the Red River Settlement and his wife being transported in a light canoe, c. 1824 (courtesy of the Archives of Manitoba/N7554).

fact that the River Dauphin was 2° farther north than the Red. Selkirk understood, correctly, that the bedrock along the western shores of Lake Winnipeg was limestone, a material that in itself would be useful to a settlement and which was also a reliable indicator of "good land" and fertile soil.[59] Any disadvantages stemming from the distance of a River Dauphin location from the Company's posts on Red River would be offset by its closer proximity to the fur posts of the Saskatchewan.

Selkirk, however, seems to have been ignorant of the most important fact: that for climatic reasons the agricultural potential of the western shore of Lake Winnipeg is very low, and an agricultural colony founded there would be only a futile venture. On learning of Selkirk's proposal, Auld wisely cautioned him that a settlement on the River Dauphin would have serious difficulty in obtaining country provisions, although, being further from the United States, it would be "less exposed to the inroads of the Americans or Indians instigated by them."[60] But Selkirk was not to be dissuaded. He again raised the possibility of a River Dauphin settlement in a letter of June 20, 1813, by which time colonization was already underway on Red River.[61] A decision about the location of the settlement had already been made by Macdonell, yet Selkirk still urged that the vicinity of the

River Dauphin "be well examined." In addition, Selkirk advised that the extreme northwestern shore of Lake Winnipeg, from the Grand Rapids of the Saskatchewan River to the Limestone River, be considered. Selkirk wrote that "the good land of the interior country may be more easily accessible from the sea than at any other point." This area lay well outside the Assiniboia Grant.

Once settlement was underway, however, Macdonell made no attempt to relocate the colony and Selkirk's suggestions about the River Dauphin and the north shore of Lake Winnipeg were wisely disregarded. The advantages of access to the Red and the belt of woodland along its banks seem to have been more than enough to cancel out the disadvantages arising from periodic spring flooding.[62]

The colonists themselves challenged Macdonell over his selection of the site for initial settlement.[63] In the spring of 1814 they informed him of their reluctance to settle at the Forks, asking instead for land at Pembina, a location which they believed presented superior opportunities for agriculture because of its slightly milder climate. In response, Macdonell promised them land at Pembina in three years if their efforts at the Forks during that time proved "unproductive."

In the same letter in which he informed Selkirk of this request, Macdonell also justified his choice of the Point Douglas site, which he compared favourably with Pembina.[64] There a small settlement of freemen and half-breed hunters, as well as renegade colonists, was emerging about Fort Daer, erected in 1812. Macdonell expected a "fine settlement" to develop at Pembina, but, everything considered, he judged the location at Point Douglas in no way inferior for an agricultural colony. Pembina's more southerly location may have given it the edge climatically, but the soil at Point Douglas was, in Macdonell's opinion, potentially as fertile as that at Pembina, and the Forks had the crucial advantage of freedom from "troublesome Indians." This meant that the Point Douglas colonists would be able to toil in comparative safety and, unlike the people gathering at Pembina, would be able to herd cattle with little chance of theft or slaughter. Macdonell's experience during winters spent at Pembina had made him aware that the Pembina hunters and settlers lived under constant threat from the Sioux. As early as June 27, 1812, Macdonell had been advised by his brother John that "the safest places from the incursions of these barbarians [the Sioux Indians] and the best lands lay between our post [Fort Gibraltar] of the Forks or junction of the Red and Assinbouan and Lake Winipick, a distance our canoe men reckon twenty leagues."[65]

The outbursts of violence between the Nor'Westers and the colonists in

1815 and 1816, and the resulting dispersal of the settlers, provided opportunities for relocating or even abandoning the colony. Nevertheless, the surviving settlers made their way back to the Red River valley and re-established the colony just below the Forks.

Notes

This article first appeared in *Prairie Forum* 11, no. 1 (1986): 1–20.

The author thanks the Hudson's Bay Company for granting permission to consult and quote from the Company's archives.

1. Alexander Ross, *The Fur Hunters of the Far West* 2 (London: Smith, Elder and Co., 1855), 259.

2. Lord Selkirk, "A Proposal tending to the Permanent Security of Ireland," Provincial Archives of Manitoba, Selkirk Papers (hereafter cited as SP) 52, p. 13, 893.

3. Selkirk, Observations Supplementary to a Memorial Relative to the Security of Ireland by the E. of S., SP 52, p. 13, 913.

4. Ibid.

5. Ibid.

6. Ibid.

7. Ibid.

8. Ibid., p. 13, 914.

9. Also Selkirk to Lord Pelham, April 4, 1802, SP 52, p. 13, 908: "Expectations have often been held out, of a supply of Hemp from other colonies, & these have been so repeatedly disappointed, that perhaps a positive engagement to furnish from that now proposed, a specific quantity annually might be considered a sufficient ostensible motive for the expense of the settlement."

10. Alexander Mackenzie, *Voyages from Montreal on the River St. Laurence, through the Continent of North America to the Frozen and Pacific Oceans in the Years 1789 and 1793 with a Preliminary Account of the Rise, Progress, and Present State of the Fur Trade of that Country* (London: T. Cadell, jun. and W. Davies, etc., 1801).

11. J.P. Pritchett, *The Red River Valley 1811–1849: A Regional Study* (Toronto: Ryerson Press, 1942), 26.

12. An exception is the early historian of Manitoba, F.H. Schofield, who believed that it was the fur trader Colin Robertson, at a meeting in Montreal during the winter of 1803–04, who advised Selkirk to locate his inland colony in the West at the junction of the Red and Assiniboine. But modern historians appear to lend little credence to this view. See J.M. Bumsted, "The Quest for a Usable Founder: Lord Selkirk and Manitoba Historians" *Manitoba History* No. 2 (1981): 6.

13. W. Kaye Lamb (ed.), *The Journals and Letters of Sir Alexander Mackenzie* (Toronto: Macmillan of Canada, 1970), 111.

14. Ibid., 112.

15. Ibid., 111.

16. Ibid., 113.

17. Ibid., 118.

18. Ibid., 411.

19. The intent here is not to deny that Selkirk read Mackenzie's Voyages. In his diary for January–February 1804 Selkirk makes a reference to Mackenzie's book. See Patrick C.T.

White (ed.), *Lord Selkirk's Diary 1803–1804. A Journal of his Travels in British North America and the Northeastern United States* (Toronto: Champlain Society, 1958), 204.

20. The opinions about Mackenzie and Selkirk expressed by the author in the preceding paragraphs are an attempt to elaborate upon a brief but suggestive comment made several years ago by the geographer Gary Dunbar, who wrote that "It has been said that Selkirk's interest in the Northwest was aroused by reading Mackenzie's Voyages (1801), but Mackenzie's book made no great claims for the settlement possibilities of the Northwest, and Selkirk was then investigating several other regions as well." G.S. Dunbar, "Isotherms and Politics: Perceptions of the Northwest in the 1850s" in A.W. Rasporich and H.C. Klassen (eds.), *Prairie Perspectives* 2 (Toronto: Holt, Rinehart and Winston of Canada, 1973), 83. Dunbar seems to be the only scholar to have questioned the extent of Mackenzie's influence on the thinking of Selkirk.

21. Edward Umfreville, *The Present State of Hudson's Bay Containing a Full Description of that Settlement, and the Adjacent Country; and Likewise of the Fur Trade* (London: Printed for C. Stalker, 1790).

22. Ibid., 151.

23. Ibid., 152.

24. Ibid., 156.

25. The only other accounts of the Company's territories based upon personal observation that would have been available to Selkirk were Joseph Robson's *An Account of Six Years Residence in Hudson's Bay, From 1733 to 1736, and 1744 to 1747* (London: Printed for J. Payne and J. Bouquet, etc., 1752), and Samuel Hearne's *A Journey from Prince of Wales's Fort in Hudson's Bay to the Northern Ocean, in the Years 1769, 1770, 1771 & 1772* (London: A. Strahan and T. Cadell, 1795). The report of the Parliamentary Enquiry of 1749 also contained testimony of men who had lived and worked on Hudson Bay. See United Kingdom, *Report from the Committee appointed to Enquire into the State and Conditions of the Countries Adjoining to Hudson's Bay and of the Trade Carried on There* (London: n.p., 1749).

26. Pritchett, *The Red River Valley*, 28.

27. Ibid.

28. Ibid., 28–29.

29. Selkirk's settlement plans in Prince Edward Island are discussed in J.M. Bumsted, "Settlement by Chance: Lord Selkirk and Prince Edward Island" *Canadian Historical Review* 59 (1978): 170–88.

30. Pritchett, *The Red River Valley*, 37.

31. Glyndwr Williams, "Highlights of the first 200 years of the Hudson's Bay Company," *The Beaver* outfit 301 (Autumn 1970): 37.

32. United Kingdom, *Papers relating to the Red River Settlement* (London: n.p., 1819), 4.

33. E.E. Rich, *The Fur Trade and the Northwest to 1857* (Toronto: McClelland and Stewart, 1967), 205.

34. As early as the 1680s, the London Committee had put forward plans for the establishment of an agricultural colony on Charlton Island in James Bay. The plan never came to fruition. See D.W. Moodie, "An Historical Geography of Agricultural Patterns and Resource Appraisals in Rupert's Land 1670–1774" (PhD dissertation, University of Alberta, 1972), 34–43.

35. For an examination of the role of agriculture in the operations of the Hudson's Bay Company see, Barry Kaye, "The Historical Geography of Agriculture and Agricultural Settlement in the Canadian Northwest 1774–ca. 1830" (PhD dissertation, University of London, 1976).

36. W.L. Morton, *Manitoba: A History* (Toronto: University of Toronto Press, 1957), 47.

37. Selkirk's Instructions to Miles Macdonell, 1811, SP 1, p. 174.

38. Pembina post journal, March 25, 1813, Hudson's Bay Company Archives, Provincial Archives of Manitoba (hereafter HBCA, PAM), Winnipeg. B 160/a/4, p. 22.

39. Stewart to Selkirk, Observations on American Plan, SP 52, pp. 13, 905–13, 906.

40. He had, however, toured areas of eastern North America in 1803–04 and several accounts of the origins of the Red River Settlement state that during the time he spent in Montreal, Selkirk increased his knowledge of the basic geography of the Canadian Northwest through his conversations with fur traders who had first hand experience of that region.

41. Brandon House post journal, August 31, 1796, HBCA, PAM B/22/a/4, fo. 13.

42. Ibid., fo. 14, September 27, 1796. Similarly, Alexander Kennedy, also stationed at Brandon House, wrote in 1812 of the Red River country as "one of the finest countries and the richest soils to be found in the upper country." John Bellanden to Selkirk, June 17, 1813, quoting a letter from Alexander Kennedy, dated August 10, 1812, SP 3, p. 737.

43. A description of Hudson's Bay in North America by Archd. Mason, February 23, 1812, SP 2, pp. 522–23.

44. Quoted in Pritchett, *The Red River Valley*, 56. Pritchett does not date this communication.

45. D.W. Harmon, *Sixteen Years in the Indian Country: (His) Journal, 1800–1816* (edited by W. Kaye Lamb) (Toronto: Macmillan Co. of Canada, 1957), 91. Harmon's journal was not published until 1820 so his comments would not have been available to Selkirk.

46. It is relevant to note that Ian Alexander Bell Robertson, the imaginary author created by Eric Ross to expedite his survey of the Canadian Northwest in 1811, also considered the Red River country "to be much richer than other parts of the Northwest." Eric Ross, *Beyond the River and the Bay* (Toronto: University of Toronto Press, 1970), 141.

47. G.L. Nute (ed.), *Documents Relating to Northwest Missions, 1815–1827* (St. Paul: Minnesota Historical Society, 1942), 141.

48. M.A. MacLeod and W.L. Morton, *Cuthbert Grant of Grantown* (Toronto: McClelland and Stewart,1963), 13.

49. M.S. by Lord Selkirk Relating to Red River, 1819, SP 47, p. 12, 641.

50. United Kingdom, *Papers relating to the Red River Settlement*, 4.

51. Selkirk's Instructions to Miles Macdonell, 1811, SP 1, pp. 173–75.

52. Fidler mentions the Pelican Ripple in his journal of Exploration and Survey, 1794–1808, entry for May 24, 1808. "Pelican ripple when the water or heavy winds from NE in Lake Winnipeg the waters dam up the water to this ripple." HBCA, PAM, E3/3, fo. 58.

53. Macdonell's journal of his first trip along the lower Red to the Forks in late August 1812, contains several references to the excellent quality of the soil and of land "fit for tillage."

54. Miles Macdonell's journal, September 7, 1812, SP 62, p. 16, 747; Macdonell to Selkirk, July 17, 1813, SP 3, pp. 765–66.

55. This was probably Joseph Peltier, a leading Métis of the Red River country at this time. See Marcel Giraud, *Le métis canadien; son role dans l'histoire des provinces de l'Ouest* (Paris: Institut d'ethnologie, 1945), 608.

56. W. Auld to Governor and Committee, August 24, 1811, HBCA, PAM, A 11/16, fo. 15. See also W. Auld to A. Wedderburn, October 5, 1811, SP 1, pp. 86–87.

57. Selkirk to Macdonell, December 23, 1811, SP 1, p. 125.

58. Ibid. It is difficult to determine why Selkirk had his mind so strongly fixed on the River Dauphin as an alternate location to Red River for his colony. Most likely it came out of reading the writings of Alexander Mackenzie and Peter Fidler. There is nothing in their writings, however, to suggest that the western side of Lake Winnipeg would be a good location for an agricultural settlement.

59. Limestone of Ordovician age forms the bedrock throughout much of the Interlake area of Manitoba. In 1819 Selkirk reaffirmed his belief that "The Western Shores of this Lake [Winnipeg] are formed of limestone covered in general with a fertile soil." Selkirk, M.S. by Lord Selkirk Relating to Red River, 1819, SP 47, p. 12, 819.

60. W. Auld to Selkirk, September 12, 1812, SP 2, p. 492.

61. Selkirk to Macdonell, June 20, 1813, SP 3, p. 726. In raising the possibility of a settlement at River Dauphin there is an echo of Selkirk's decision prior to establishing his Baldoon colony to investigate the agricultural potential of the Sault Ste. Marie area.

62. Macdonell soon had firsthand experience of Red River flooding as parts of the colony were under water in the spring of 1815.

63. Macdonell to Selkirk, July 25, 1814, SP 4, p. 1, 195.

64. Ibid., 187.

65. Quoted in Chester Martin, (Lord) *Selkirk's Work in Canada* (Oxford: Clarendon Press, 1916), 44, n. 3.

11. The Historiography of the Red River Settlement 1830–1868

Frits Pannekoek

A great deal has been written on the Selkirk years of Red River and even more on its annexation to "the Empire of the St. Lawrence" in 1869. The years between have received less attention. These were not only critical years of intermittent crises, but also years of relative stability, prosperity and consolidation—years which nurtured a community with a unique identity and sense of purpose. Since Alexander Ross published *The Red River Settlement* in 1856, historians have tried to come to grips with the character of this exotic mixture of Scottish peasants, half-breeds and fur traders. Ironically, only Alexander Ross succeeded. Other historians have imposed interpretations contrived from central Canadian, British or American environments; while they have unearthed quantities of detailed information, they have been able to assess it only from the perspective of London, Montreal or St. Paul, not Red River itself. They perceived that the dynamics that shaped Red River were externally rather than internally generated and lost their most important analytical tool in the process. Only in the last decade have historians again begun to write Red River's history from a uniquely western Canadian viewpoint, thereby offering the promise of a new synthesis.

Alexander Ross, the most prolific writer and holder of offices in the pre-1870 West, was Clerk to the Pacific Fur Company, the North West Company and Hudson's Bay Company, Sheriff of Assiniboia, Councillor of Assiniboia and member of its Committee of Public Works and Finance, Commander of the Volunteer Corps, Magistrate of the Middle District, Governor of Gaol, Collector of Customs, *ex-officio* President of the Court in the Upper District and Elder of the Presbyterian Church at Frog Plain. He authored three books at Colony Gardens, his home in Red River. His first two books were based on careful and detailed journals written during his years in the Pacific North-West; his third book, *The Red River Settlement*, appeared in 1856 shortly before

The Red River cart, which played a prominent role in the development and settlement of the North-West Territories (courtesy of the Saskatchewan Archives Board/R-A3278).

his death. The best single piece of writing on Red River, the history clearly illustrates Ross's belief that the motley, quixotic settlement at the forks of the Red and Assiniboine had a predestined purpose. To Ross, Red River was a nucleus of Christian civilization. Through Selkirk the settlement had been ordained to bring this civilization to the heathen. But in this Red River had failed. Its sons did not comprehend their divine purpose and their colony was smothering under the weight of its own ignorance.

Despite his pessimism, Ross was tireless in his devotion to his community, his church and especially his mixed-blood children. He attempted to ease them through the brutal shock of civilization when he could, but he suspected that neither they nor the other mixed bloods had the skills to survive. In Ross's opinion, the feuding and incompetence of the missionaries rather than the Hudson's Bay Company or the environment were to blame for this sorrow. Convinced that the Company's monopoly was necessary, Ross felt that complete free trade would be ruinous to Rupert's Land. He argued further that the Métis' ill-considered cry for free trade could have been contained had it not been for the oppressive racism of Adam Thom, the first Recorder of Rupert's Land.

Other historians who share Ross's methodology and his general observation that Red River was moribund also saw Red River from the inside. Joseph James Hargrave (1841–1894), was a Red River fur trader and son of James and Letitia Hargrave; Alexander Begg (1839–1897) was a journalist, merchant, civil servant and immigration agent; and Donald Gunn (1797–1878) was a Smithsonian Institute Corresponding Secretary, fur trader and leading citizen. Their histories, Hargrave's *Red River*, Begg's *The North West* and Gunn's *Manitoba* all fail, however, to acknowledge the mission that Ross assigned to the settlement.[2] In the later 19th century when Hargrave, Begg and Gunn were writing, Red River had already been seduced by the prosperity that union with Canada offered. Immigration, railroads and wheat soon supplanted the missions and the fur trade as the focus of Red River society.

Gunn was particularly happy to see the end of the Red River Settlement and the dominance of the Hudson's Bay Company. A staunch defender of the Selkirk colonists, he believed that the Company's every move was a conspiracy to destroy the vitality of the settlement. Hargrave's views, if indeed he can be said to have any, were those of a Company employee and a member of the Red River elite. He supported the Company, and despised the malignant Canadians and their newspaper, the *Nor'Wester*. Nevertheless, he too was a pragmatist and he looked longingly toward union and prosperity.

The 20th century marked a re-orientation of Red River historiography and witnessed the first efforts at academic analysis. R.G. MacBeth (1854–1934) was a native of Kildonan, a lawyer and a clergyman; George Bryce (1844–1931) was corresponding secretary to the Manitoba Historical, Literary and Scientific Society, a Presbyterian clergyman and the founder of Manitoba College. To both writers Red River became an arcadian Utopia:

> The primitive history of all the colonies that faced the Atlantic—when the new-found continent first felt the abiding foot of the stranger—from Oglethrope to Acadia, reveals, alas! no Utopia, a transplant of elder habitudes, where the rancor of race, caste and rule was found to be too ingrained to yield to even the softening influence of such a sylvan paradise as Virginia. It remained for a later time,—the earlier half of the present century, amid every severity of climate, and under conditions without precedent, and incapable of repetition,—to evolve a community in the heart of the continent, shut away from intercourse with civilized mankind—that slowly crystallized into a form beyond the ideal of the dreamers—a community, in the past, known

faintly to the outer world as the Red River Settlement which
is but the by-gone name for the one Utopia of Britain.[3]

Above all, the Selkirk colonists were glorified for their struggles to preserve
the West for Confederation, for it was "the opening of the West (that made)
Canada complete."[4] The function of the Selkirk settlers as seen by Ross was
augmented by MacBeth. They were now not only God's instrument of civilization but also his instrument for preserving the West for Canada. In
MacBeth's mind the two were not mutually exclusive.

Father A.G. Morice (1859–1938), British Columbian missionary and
founder of Le Patriote de L'Ouest, and A. de Trémaudan, a French Canadian
teacher, real estate agent, lawyer and newspaper editor, can also be grouped
with Bryce and MacBeth, despite their vicious feud over a number of specific issues in Métis history. Where MacBeth and Bryce emphasized the Selkirk
influence, Morice and Trémaudan dwelt on Métis nobility and the Métis
emerged as unblemished as the Selkirk settlers:

> Il avait d'excellentes qualités. Gai et expansif avec les liens,
> strictement honnête et sans souci de l'avenir, hospitalier
> pour les étrangers et généreux jusqu'à l'imprudence, il
> passait sa vie aventureuse soit à la pêche, comme guide de
> caravanes, ou bien à la chasse au bison. Par ailleurs ilt était
> naturellement religieux et respectueux de l'autorité.[5]

Morice and Trémaudan argued that Riel thwarted American annexation and
brought self-government first to Manitoba and then to the Northwest.
MacBeth and Bryce had established the place of Selkirk's contribution.
Morice and Trémaudan hoped that the Métis contribution would gain a sim-
ilar recognition through the establishment of a dual Northwest both
Catholic French-speaking, mixed-blood, and white English-speaking
Protestant.

The reasons for the glorification of the Red River's past by these historians cannot conclusively be established without a great deal more research,
but Carl Berger's The Sense of Power (Toronto, 1970) is helpful. Berger argues
that the Canadian nationalism of the 1880s emphasized historical
antecedents, stimulated an interest in history, and most important,

> depended for its credibility upon the assumption that the
> past contained principles to which the present must adhere
> if the continuity of national life was to be preserved.[6]

In 19th-century Canadian terms it was the Loyalists who embodied all the
past virtues of the new nation. The Selkirk settlers and the Métis were the
Loyalists' western counterparts. The myth that they were the distilled

essence of what the West had become was fostered by early Red River Canadian settlers like Frank Larned Hunt, and Kildonan descendants like MacBeth. Morice and Trémaudan also would have been susceptible to the nostalgic myth because of the disasters that had befallen the Métis in the decades after Confederation. A didactic perception of the western past that extolled idyllic agrarian life, Canadian and Imperial connections, and (in Morice's and Trémaudan's case) ethnic duality, was imperative if the new west of the 20th century was to achieve an acceptable identity within the Canadian historical tradition.

When Harold Innis, in Toronto, A.S. Morton, a Saskatchewan history professor and archivist, and E.E. Rich, the editor of the Hudson's Bay Record Society and Professor of History at Cambridge University, trained their attention on western Canada, the history of Red River became a footnote to their more pressing interest in the fur trade. To Innis, Red River was merely a convenience that absorbed the fur trade's cast-offs while serving as the transportation and provisioning hub for the Saskatchewan and Athabasca hinterlands. Because of the St. Paul influence he also saw Red River as the weakest link in the east-west economic and geographic chain that bound the Canadian nation, a nation that had emerged "not in spite of geography, but because of it."[7]

On the other hand, the westerner A.S. Morton, in his *The History of the Canadian West to 1870–71* (Toronto, 1939), saw the fur trade as a sub-regional, rather than national or even western, unifying force. It was not Canada, but each of the four sub-regions of the Northwest—the tundra, the shield, the prairies and the Pacific mountains—that was united by the fur trade. The west was fractured because of its disparate geography and only unified by the administrative structure of the Hudson's Bay Company. While Morton cannot be labeled as an adherent of any one school of history, his great concern with geography does place him very loosely with those who would see the environment as history's principal motive force. Yet in spite of these differences, Morton's interpretation of Red River between 1830 and 1868 differed little from Innis's analysis. His examinations of political and social detail were only embellishments on Innis's rather disjointed and thoroughly unsatisfactory study of the pre-1870 West. The impression given by Morton's manuscript footnotes to *The History of the Canadian West to 1870–71*, in the University of Saskatchewan Archives, is that Morton was exhausted by the last chapters and that much of his writing on Red River was done with less than his usual care.

Morton divided the history of Red River into three chronological periods: 1817–40, 1840–59 and 1860–69. The first period was one of stability, and the last, one of growing political polarization. This was a departure from the commonly accepted Red River chronology. Previously 1827, the year after the great flood which drove many of the undesirable elements from the settlement and consequently set the ethnic mix for Red River; 1849, the year of the Sayer trial which saw the "breaking" of the Company's abhorrent monopoly; and 1869, the year of the great Riel uprising which finally "freed" Red River from the Company's tyranny, were the common dividing dates.[8]

In the end, Morton's major contribution to Red River historiography was not his moderate and credible environmentalist interpretation, or his slight alteration of the traditional periodization of Red River history, but his

Authur Silver Morton (1870–1945), pictured in 1942 (courtesy of the Saskatchewan Archives Board/S-B858).

minute consideration of the formidable Hudson's Bay Company archives. Unfortunately, he had failed to consult the supplementary material in the missionary archives and many of his statements regarding the Red River clergy, the settlement's most important element of social control, were overgeneralized and misleading. The critical importance of William Cockran, who almost single-handedly founded and ruled St. Andrew's, the most important English-speaking mixed-blood settlement, is altogether ignored. Having neglected the Church of England half-breeds of the Upper Red River parishes in favour of the more flamboyant Métis, Morton was prompted to make the false generalization that Red River was a "little Quebec."[9] Red River was rather a community equally influenced by Indian, Scot, Métis, Half-breed, Canadien and Canadian.

From the work of A.S. Morton a logical historiographical step would have been the production of a series of detailed scholarly studies on various aspects of pre-1870 western Canadian history, with at least one on Red River

1830–69. Another monographic history of the West to 1870 was hardly needed and E.E. Rich's three-volume *Hudson's Bay Company* (Toronto, 1960) became little more than a paraphrase of segments of the Company's archives. It is as muddled as the Innis volume and, in many areas, duplicates Morton's spadework of the 1930s.[10]

Rich's major theme, the maintenance of the Company's charter through prosperity and adversity, did not merit his thousand pages and failed to allow for a smooth integration of Red River history into that of the fur trade. Only four of 31 chapters dealt with the settlement. The major social conflicts, the Presbyterian-Anglican burying yard controversy or the Ballenden scandal, so important to explaining the disintegrative forces at work in Red River, are artificially inserted into an uninspired narrative. Rich fails to see that the conflict over the Presbyterian right to bury in Anglican consecrated ground or the alleged sexual improprieties of Mrs. Ballenden, a mixed-blood, fractured the community once and for all amongst its white and mixed-blood, its Métis and halfbreed, its Catholic and Protestant and its Anglican and Presbyterian parts. Basically Rich contended that Red River was the source of an agricultural and free trade threat to the Company's rights as granted by the Charter. But these threats were met and in 1849, while the Company may have abandoned its "legal defences," it certainly did not lose economic control. The Company now would not use the courts to enforce its hegemony; rather, it would ruthlessly exercise its considerable economic power to eliminate the free traders—prices were cut in areas of competition and furs trapped to extermination.

This concentration by Innis, Morton and Rich on Red River in the context of the fur trade was not as great a departure from the themes in the works of Hargrave, Begg, Bryce, MacBeth, Morice and Trémaudan as might be thought. They sought to justify union with Confederation by events in the romantic Red River past where Innis, Morton, and to a lesser extent Rich attempted to justify Confederation by geography. Red River, the focus of the fur-trade hinterland, provisioned the staple trade that welded the Saskatchewan, Columbia, Nelson and Mackenzie river systems to that of the St. Lawrence. Whatever the nuance in argument, or however scholarly the research, Confederation was seen as the millennium for the pre-1870 Canadian West.

With the appearance of John Perry Pritchett,[11] Alvin Gluek[12] and J.S. Galbraith,[13] Red River became the concern of the frontier historian. Pritchett saw Red River at the heart of the North American continent. It lay at the junction of three drainage basins, the St. Lawrence, the Nelson and the Mississippi, controlled respectively by Canada, the Hudson's Bay Company

RETURN OF THE HUNTERS.

Métis hunters with Red River carts returning to camp on Red River, 1859. Sketch published in *Harper's Monthly*, October, 1860 (courtesy of the Glenbow Archives/LAC-1406-8).

and the United States, but the Nelson basin capitulated to the indigenous Red River Métis in 1849. They retained virtual independence until annexation by the "Empire of the St. Lawrence" in 1869. To Pritchett this fate was not final:

> What the next or the most permanent outcome of this triple tug will be, no one knows. Will the West become independent, as Riel seemed to wish, and trade by way of the Nelson drainage basin? Will it form with the Mississippi drainage basin an economic union?—a political union? Or will it resist the pressure from both the Nelson and the Mississippi systems and remain indefinitely, both politically and economically a vassal of the St. Lawrence?[14]

The struggle of the river basins masked an equally important internal struggle. Pritchett imposed a frontier-tainted, Whig interpretation on the Red River past. One of the "nurseries of democracy," Red River fought the traditional battle against "vested autocratic interests," in this case the Hudson's Bay Company. Effective "self government" was seen by Pritchett as an achievement of the Sayer "insurrection" of 1849, but no conclusion could have been more absurd![15] The Company did not capitulate in 1849 and the Council of Assiniboia remained under the Company's influence after this date. Furthermore, Red River society could not be construed as democratic. The clergy and fur-trade aristocracy, for the most part adherents to the Company's society, lost their dominance only during the social disruptions of the 1860s.

Gluek, in his *Minnesota and the Manifest Destiny of the Canadian Northwest* (Toronto, 1965), provided a well documented and researched addition to Pritchett's river-basin thesis. The Red River valley, Gluek asserted, was a geographic extension of Minnesota. The natural tendency to political absorption by Minnesota failed because of Minnesota's economic collapse in 1857, the Sioux and the Civil Wars of 1861–66, the Hudson's Bay Company, the activities of Canada, and the preference of the people of the Red River. Gluek was not as hostile to the Company as was Pritchett. Instead he sympathetically documented the Company's continuing battle for that most important fur-bearing northern district.[16] To him the struggle for Red River was a commercial one, not a territorial struggle of conflicting political powers.

Gluek, unlike Pritchett, revealed little of the inner workings of Red River society. He accepted A.S. Morton's view that 1840 was the year Red River acquired its permanent character, though he studiously avoided footnoting Morton.[17] Perhaps more disconcerting is the impression that Gluek was uninfluenced by M. Giraud's *Le Métis Canadien* and that his conclusions

A Métis cottage at the Red River settlement, c. 1870 (courtesy of the Archives of Manitoba/N461).

regarding the English parishes of Red River were based on a few documents appended to W.L. Morton's edition of Begg's *Red River Journal*.[18] Most important, he over-emphasized the American impact on Red River while the English, though not the Canadian, impact was ignored.

While Gluek concentrated on the American connection, Galbraith in his *The Hudson's Bay Company as an Imperial Factor 1821–1869* (Toronto, 1957) was concerned with the Hudson's Bay Company and the Imperial government policies toward the monopoly, free trade and the settlement frontier. While the volume is invaluable as a comment on British policy, the sections dealing with Red River had been, for the most part, superseded by Gluek's and Rich's more extensive though by no means definitive works.[19]

The major contribution of the frontier school of Red River historiography has not been its insight into the Red River past, but rather its questioning of Innis's argument that Canada was a nation because of geography. Red River's major overland connections were southward and only political and military factors ensured that Red River would be Canadian.

It was through the imaginative labours of Marcel Giraud, the French ethnologist, that Red River history broke from the historiography of competing river basins, commercial powers and imperial designs. His monumental work, one of the milestones in Canadian history, still provides the most exciting interpretation of the Red River settlement and serves as the impetus for much recent study. His most famous western Canadian exponent has been W.L. Morton. The change Giraud produced in Morton's work on Red

River is startling. Morton's first essay, "The Red River Parish" written in 1936, reflected the grip of the fur-trade school: "The Settlement was an adjunct, not of civilization but of the fur trade."[20] It was a suggestive article and posed a still unanswered question about the allegiance of the Red River inhabitant to his parish, ethnic group or the settlement at large. But, based as it was on a fur-trade thesis, the article was antithetical to the Giraud paradigm which Morton first clearly accepted in his "Agriculture in the Red River Colony" (*Canadian Historical Review*, 1949) and in his appreciative review of Giraud's *Le Métis Canadien* (Paris, 1945) in *The Beaver* (1950).

Giraud traced the history of the Métis in thirteen hundred well-researched, impeccably footnoted pages; three hundred concerned Red River. The Red River past was divided into two periods: "les années d'incertitude" (1818–27) and "les années de stabilisation" (1828–69). These latter forty years were, for the Métis, "les années les plus heureuses." Yet it was a life of precarious equilibrium, balanced between the hunt, the trip, the river lot, and the fisheries, a life symbolic of Red River itself:

> In the Red River colony civilization and barbarism met and mingled. On the one hand was the sedentary agricultural economy of the colony, on the other the nomadic hunting economy of the plains… The result was a society quaint and unique, in which were reconciled the savagery of the Indian and the culture of Europe.[21]

Giraud and Morton argue that civilization failed to bridle the Métis; that their nomadism was self-perpetuating and inescapable. Indeed, how could it be otherwise, given the attitude of the clergy, the needs of the Hudson's Bay Company, the economic stagnation of Red River and the Company's continued opposition to an always faltering agriculture? The constant intercourse with the Indians and the never-ceasing influx of Métis from the plains further reinforced the tendency to "barbarism." The clergy and "la bourgeoisie," the only elements of stability, could hardly be other than ineffective counterpoints. It was a way of life, "as swiftly transient as a prairie cloud," and it could exist only

> dans un pays dont l'économie prédominante respecte la nature primitive et dont le gouvernment est animé d'une mentalité statique, réfractaire aux innovations profondes.[22]

The Métis tendency to free trade weakened the very government that protected their existence. In 1869,

> civilization (would triumph) over barbarism, the sedentary over the nomadic way of life, and the Métis who were

intermediaries between the two—the personification of the equipoise of the Stone Age and the Industrial Revolution which was the fur trade—(would be) shattered.[23]

Yet, the Giraud/Morton hypothesis only accounts for half of Red River society and assumes that the values in conflict within this half were in conflict within Red River society as a whole. The English-speaking half-breed, the Kildonan settler, and the agents of the Church Missionary Society were nowhere satisfactorily examined. But the religiously and ethnically distinct parishes may not have been as interconnected as Giraud and Morton believed. Was there, in fact, a delicate balance between the two Red Rivers, the "civilized" and the "barbaric," as Morton and Giraud assumed?

Recently, historians have begun to look at Red River as a complex entity, a community. Unfortunately, while interest in Selkirk and Riel continues unabated, interest in Red River *per se* is waning. Only the frontier school, within its constant attempt to justify Confederation, continues to dote on Red River. There are always the graduate students, but they have tended to offer marginally researched narrative histories devoid of complex interpretation. The Red River past must be attacked with sophisticated weapons. Demographic studies of each parish and the internal dynamics of the community must be undertaken. Sylvia Van Kirk's work, *Many Tender Ties* (recent PhD dissertation), is very provocative, determining as it does the role of white women in the disintegration of Red River society.[24]

Van Kirk proves without a doubt that the white women who came to Red River in the 1830s as the wives of the missionaries and of a select few chief officers of the Hudson's Bay Company precipitated serious racial conflicts within the settlement. Where before the mixed-blood wives of the officers had ruled supreme, they now were challenged by intruders who had no doubt as to the inferiority of those with Indian blood. Because Van Kirk is more concerned with the fur trade than with Red River, she does not investigate the impact these schisms may have had on Red River more generally. In fact, there is sufficient evidence to suggest that the racial conflict precipitated by the coming of these white women may have aggravated the landmark crises of Red River: the 1849 free-trade troubles and the Riel uprising. The deep schisms within English-speaking Red River that prevented any effective opposition to Riel can in fact be traced to the racism of the 1830s. If racism is indeed the central theme in Red River's history, rather than geography or economics, then perhaps the old historic time markers like the Riel Rebellion may, upon closer investigation, not be as relevant as tradition dictates. Perhaps the racial flashpoints like the Ballenden scandal, which divided the community along racial lines, or the Corbett scandal of 1863, which divided the settlement between Métis and Halfbreed and Halfbreed and European, are more important. Only future research will tell.

Jennifer Brown's *Strangers in Blood* (Vancouver, 1980) provides similar unique insights which require further clarification with regard to Red River.[25] She suggests that the Northwest Company and the Hudson's Bay Company had two separate and unique social and family structures. This of course could lead to the conclusion that the divisions between the Métis and Halfbreeds within Red River were the result of cultural antecedents unique to Rupert's Land rather than a conflict imported from Ontario.

The most promising enquiries to date have been undertaken by the Métis Federation of Manitoba in their efforts to analyze the community quantitatively.[26] The results are still preliminary and conclusions indefinite, but their findings are tending to reinforce the directions hinted by Van Kirk and Brown that Red River was an increasingly highly stratified and divided community. In fact, Red River provides a unique laboratory from which to explore the dynamics of closed, isolated single-industry communities.

What more recent historians all have in common is their emphasis on the internal dynamics of the community. Their basic question is not "How Was the West Won for Confederation?" but rather, "Why Did the Red River Community Change?" Why could this peculiar community not survive the immigrations from the Canadas? This inward reflection is an indication that western scholars are no longer looking to Eastern Canada or London as the metropolitan centres which directed historical change. Rather, they are saying that it is time Western Canada looked at itself, its people and its geography for historical causation. While many of these new reflections are somewhat rough and uncut, they do promise new directions, and for that they are welcomed.

Notes

This article first appeared in *Prairie Forum* 6, no. 1 (1981): 75–86.

1. George Bryce, "Alexander Ross," *The Canadian Magazine* 44 (1917): 163–68. Other biographies of Ross are listed at the end of the introduction to the 1957 Ross and Hains Inc. edition of Alexander Ross, *The Red River Settlement* (London: n.p., 1856).

2. Donald Gunn, *History of Manitoba from the Earliest Settlement to 1835* (Ottawa: Maclean, Roger, 1880), 156. The second half of the volume is written by Charles R. Tuttle (b. 1848), journalist, author and census commissioner for Manitoba. He arrived in Manitoba in the late 1870s and can be regarded as a member of the Bryce-MacBeth school. The biography of Gunn at the beginning of the volume is by Frank Larned Hunt.

3. Bryce has apparently lifted entire sections of his volume from Frank Larned Hunt, "Britain's One Utopia," *The Historical and Scientific Society of Manitoba* 61 (February 1902): 1–12. See for example George Bryce, *The Romantic Settlement of Lord Selkirk's Colonists* (Toronto, 1909), 240.

4. Ibid., 318.

5. A.G. Morice's most important work is *History of the Catholic Church in Western Canada* (Toronto: Musson Book Co., 1910). His *Histoire abrégée de l'Ouest canadien* (Saint-Boniface: n.p., 1914) is however representative. The quotation is from p. 45.

6. Carl Berger, *The Sense of Power: Studies in the Ideas of Canadian Imperialism, 1867–1914* (Toronto: University of Toronto Press, 1970), 89–90.

7. H.A. Innis, *The Fur Trade in Canada: An Introduction to Canadian Economic History* (Toronto: University of Toronto Press, 1970), 393. W.J. Eccles' "A Belated Review of Harold Adams Innis, The Fur Trade in Canada," *The Canadian Historical Review* 60 (December 1979): 419–41, is the single best critique of Innis's work. His conclusions are that "the work contains a great mass of information, much of it presented in chapters that lack cohesion, and frequently the evidence presented contradicts the book's conclusions. The end result has been the establishment of myths as conventional wisdom" (441).

8. A.S. Morton, *The History of the Canadian West to 1870–71: Being a History of Rupert's Land (The Hudson's Bay Company's Territory) and of the North-west Territory (including the Pacific Slope)* (New York: T. Nelson, 1939). Morton has offered some basic re-interpretations of La Vérendrye, Radisson, Groseilliers and Thompson but offers little startling for Red River 1830–1868.

9. Ibid., 802. By 1860 the population was almost equally divided between French and English. It was the mixed-blood (Métis and Half Breeds) who were predominant.

10. While E.E. Rich, *History of the Hudson's Bay Company, 1670–1870* (London: Hudson's Bay Record Society, 1958–59) contains no footnotes, a foot-noted copy has been placed in the National Library of Canada.

11. J.P. Pritchett, *The Red River Valley 1811–1849: A Regional Study* (New Haven: Yale University Press, 1942), ix.

12. A.C. Gluek, *Minnesota and the Manifest Destiny of the Canadian North West: A Study in Canadian-American Relations* (Toronto: University of Toronto, 1965), 292.

13. J.S. Galbraith, *The Hudson's Bay Company as an Imperial Factor 1821–1869* (Toronto: University of Toronto Press, 1957), 10.

14. Pritchett, *Red River Valley 1811–1849*, 271.

15. Ibid., 263–66.

16. Gluek, *Minnesota and the Manifest Destiny of the Canadian North West*, 76, 77, 118.

17. Ibid., 25.

18. Ibid., see footnotes pp. 252–61.

19. Compare for example Gluek, *Minnesota and the Manifest Destiny of the Canadian North West*, 46–77 and Galbraith *Hudson's Bay Company as an Imperial Factor 1821–1869*, 312–32 on the struggle for free trade.

20. W.L. Morton, "The Red River Parish; Its Place in the Development of Manitoba," *Manitoba Essays* (Winnipeg: n.p., 1937) p. 90.

21. W.L. Morton, "The Canadian Métis," *The Beaver* 281 (September 1950): 3. Giraud, *Le Métis canadien: son rôle dans l'histoire des provinces de l'Ouest* (Paris: Institut d'ethnologie, 1945), 630.

22. Morton, "The Canadian Metis," 7.

23. Sylvia M. Van Kirk, "The Role of Women in the Fur Trade Society of the Canadian West, 1700–1850," (PhD dissertation, University of London, 1975), and *Many Tender Ties: Women in Fur Trade Society in Western Canada, 1670–1870* (Winnipeg: Watson & Dwyer,

1980). Jennifer S. H. Brown, *Strangers in Blood: Fur Trade Company Families in Indian Country* (Vancouver: University of British Columbia Press, 1980).

24. D.N. Sprague and R.P. Frye, "Fur Trade Company Town: Land and Population in the Red River Settlement, 1820–1870" (unpublished manuscript, University of Manitoba, 1981).

12. Forming Civilization at Red River: 19th-Century Missionary Education of Métis and First Nations Children

Jonathan Anuik

In the early 1820s, a number of Protestant and Roman Catholic missionaries developed school systems in Red River that transmitted European civilization to the settlement in Hudson's Bay Company (HBC)–controlled Rupert's Land. The settlement was rife with tension between the indigenous First Nations and Métis peoples and the new Canadian, British, and continental European colonizers. The development of denominational schooling, designed by the missionaries to educate a next generation of "civilized" children, exposed the cultural differences. The missionaries believed Christianity to be the main pillar of European civilization, and also held that agriculture was essential to a civilized economy; they also believed that children would be most receptive to their teachings of British civilization. Consequently, the missionaries concentrated their efforts on establishing denominational school systems, and used then-current pedagogical theories to form the civilized child. The different denominations hoped that this educated child would then grow up to "civilize" the settlement. Overall, the formed child was, to the missionaries, Christian, educated, and agrarian; but not all parents saw the need for this type of education. Consequently, all parents did not agree. This fundamental lack of consensus thus created two formidable challenges to education when its foundations were being laid, in the period between 1820 and the late 1850s.

Civilization was the goal of the missionaries, but the ideal and the term itself are problematic. By civilizing, the missionaries hoped to transplant 19th-century British culture—with its accumulated scientific and technical knowledge, its capitalist, industrializing and urbanizing economy, its literature and Christian religion—into the Red River settlement. The missionaries perceived that children, especially the cross-cultured Métis children, would be the best recipients and transmitters of civilization, and thus erected churches and schools to disseminate the principles of civilization. Civilization implied European superiority, and civilizing was the act of introducting British "superior" education, religion, industry, and economics into an "inferior" Aboriginal culture and settlement. For the missionaries, a "productive" Aboriginal society would result from their teachings. They considered working for the HBC freight brigades or buffalo hunting to be antithetical to their concept of civilization; but transplanting their favoured mode of economic production brought poor results for those who followed their religious and educational plans.

From 1820 to 1870, the population of Red River was composed of a variety of ethnic and religious groups. The four most prominent ethnic groups were the Métis, the Scots, the Canadiens, and the First Nations. The Métis formed the majority of the population at the settlement, but where members of this group lived depended on their ethnic parentage and religious affiliation. Persons of different religious affiliations clustered in particular areas; most historians refer to these different areas as parishes with a particular religious affiliation. The majority of anglophone and Anglican Métis settled on the west side of the Assiniboine and Red rivers, while the francophone and Catholic Métis settled in the central area of the settlement, at St. Boniface and White Horse Plain, later known as Saint-François-Xavier.[1] The divisions in ethnicity and religion were a result of tension between Anglicans and Catholics from the 1840s to the 1860s; the pedagogues differed in their opinion about what constituted the principles of civilization for children.[2]

The missionary ideal of civilization for Métis children was that of a structured becoming: they perceived that undisciplined, disobedient, and uneducated children should be formed into Christian, literate, industrious, sedentary, polite, and obedient adults. To the missionaries, this formative process would consist of instruction in scriptural and doctrinal knowledge as well as in basic academic and industrial subjects.[3] In order to mold children into the perceived ideal, the pedagogues would implant a more conditioned personality.[4] Ideally, as civilized adults, the children would pursue activities such as agriculture, and would also spread the faith of God both to their children and to the non-Christian bands into which they were born.

The one group whose attitudes about childhood conflicted most with the missionary ideal of the civilized child was the francophone Métis. In the first three decades of Red River, the HBC and the governing Council of Assiniboia encouraged the francophone Métis to abandon the hunt and become farmers. However, the hunt and the HBC freight brigades proved

Anglican Church at Red River settlement, 1860. Sketch published in *Harper's Monthly*, August, 1860 (courtesy of the Glenbow Archives/LAC-1406-11).

more profitable for the francophone Métis—especially after 1849, when the monopoly of the HBC on trade declined. From 1850 to 1870, the settlement relied on imports for food, a need the francophone Métis helped to fill through the hunt; as a result, the economic demands of these industries kept many of the children from becoming civilized.[5] In order to educate these Métis children, the missionaries believed they would have to remove them from territory where their "heathen" behaviour was encouraged and isolate them at Red River.

To ensure that students would learn virtue and good moral conduct, the teachers of civilization would have to instill discipline early, or all instruction that children had received would run the risk of being lost. According to the missionaries, children were inherently undisciplined, especially orphan Métis children who wandered around the fur trade posts and Red River without purpose,[6] or Métis children who travelled with the hunt. For the missionary societies, civilized children would have to learn order and virtue early so that ideas like discipline would not be foreign to them.[7] Part of discipline was good moral conduct: throughout the years of Red River, good moral conduct was an important goal of civilization, because it enforced discipline and conformity in the rural British Christian and agricultural landscape.

In order to Christianize and educate children, teachers were to provide them with religious instruction and to ensure that they understood religious teaching; they would also teach children basic academic skills such as reading and writing. These two objectives were intertwined: the teachers would use the Bible to facilitate the development of reading and writing; once a child was Christianized, disciplined, and literate, teaching topics such as agriculture would be simple. While teaching students to be agriculturalists, instructors would also reinforce the value of attendance and obedience: only by attendance and obedience would children be educated to fulfill a role in the civilized society, as farmers, clergy, teachers, HBC officers or servants, or their wives.

According to the missionaries, civilized male and female children would have different roles; children would thus be prepared for these distinct roles in the classrooms of Red River. Gender separation in the classroom was the 19th-century British way of preparing male and female children for their adult roles. The same picture developed at Red River. Civilized male children would learn agriculture, husbandry, carpentry, and weaving, or would receive an academic education; both industrial and agricultural instruction would allow these adult men to financially support their families. Civilized male children would also spread the word of God and the habits of industry to their Aboriginal families. Civilized female children would become domestics, learning trades such as spinning, knitting, sewing, milking, and making butter; in the home, civilized women would also be the providers of comfort for their families.[8] In the domestic sphere, civilized women would be the transmitters of morality and discipline to their children, and would be the upholders of a good moral standard.[9] Therefore, women would teach discipline and obedience to children, who then would be willing participants in the Christianization and education provided at the schools.

The majority of the male and female children who would be Christianized, educated, and agrarian were Métis, and both genders were being reared for the mission of transmitting civilization to future generations. The missionaries thought of Métis children as the bridge between the First Nations, or "heathen" orders, and the European or civilized society: in sum, they hoped that their civilized Métis children would grow into adults and parents who would demonstrate to their First Nations communities and children the principles of a sedentary existence on a British cultural landscape.[10]

In order to rear the first generation of Christianized, educated, and agrarian Métis children, the missionaries had to convince three different types of parents of the value of education. The first group was the elite parents, or those adults who were retired HBC and North West Company (NWC) officers and, in some cases, discharged servants. These individuals made up the new middle class evolving in the settlement in the 1820s, and were often adults who served on the governing Council of Assiniboia or worked as merchants or farmers. The new middle class parents supported the missionaries in their plans for civilization, as they desired that their Métis children be educated as Europeans, and distanced from their First Nations and Métis cultural ties as well as from economic activities like the hunt. These parents had the financial means to ensure that their children received at least an elementary education, and to often send them to Canada or Britain for secondary and post-secondary education. The second group consisted of settler parents who came from Europe to engage in agricultural pursuits. These parents appreciated the opportunities that education brought their children, but due to their economic circumstances could not send their children to school on a regular basis—nor could they afford the education that the missionaries provided. They did want their children to become farmers, however, and owned land on which their children could learn industry. Finally, there were the hunter, gatherer, and trader parents. This group of adults looked to these activities rather than to agriculture for subsistence, and they relied on their children's help for survival. When they were not hunting, they squatted in shacks and engaged in subsistence agriculture; they were often illiterate, and in some cases saw no benefit from the education that the missionaries proposed for their children: instead, they taught their children the practical skills they needed to survive on the plains. Consequently, they were the individuals who co-operated the least with the missionaries, and their children were the least likely to attend school. The missionaries met all three groups of parents at Red River, and the attitudes about child-rearing and education from each group both advanced and stalled missionary plans to civilize the children.

The agricultural parents could not afford to educate their children, so the children usually received education financed by the missionaries. In 1833, the Church Missionary Society (CMS) granted £100 to the regular day schools at Upper Church, Frog Plain, Image Plains/Middle Church, and Grand Rapids. The schools were established to instruct the poor of the settlement, who were usually anglophone Métis, Scottish, or central European. Funding problems plagued these schools, and administrators could often not afford qualified teachers. The CMS continually attempted to reduce costs, looking to HBC Governor Sir George Simpson for extra funding or reducing teacher wages to better provide education.[11] The children were not the best students: Reverend William Cockran, at Grand Rapids, noted that they were undisciplined and "read & play according to their own weight & measure."[12] He believed that parents were to blame for the lack of academic appreciation of their children in school[13]; however, in the 19th century, education for most children would be partial and incomplete.[14]

Anglican missionary and schoolmaster Cockran disliked the economic pursuits of the hunter, gatherer, and trader parents:

> The Females being Natives & Half-Breeds, and consequently entirely ignorant of the economy and industry necessary to make a family comfortable in civilized life. And they are Naturely, so, indolent, … and licentious, that it requires a great deal, both of instruction and grace, to make them honest and virtuous Christians.[15]

For Cockran and other missionaries, fur trade children and parents were of the most concern, because nothing had conditioned them to absorbing the principles of civilization and becoming either farmers or future missionaries.

The missionary societies planned to transmit their idea of the civilized child through a curriculum that involved obedience, discipline, religion, reading, rote memorization, writing, arithmetic, and industry. The attempt to form a civilized child through education contradicted the undisciplined and roving education of the First Nations and Métis societies. While some First Nations and Métis welcomed the chance for their children to be taught subjects such as reading, writing, and arithmetic, as well as industrial pursuits like agriculture, the two groups did not want this form of education to change the personality and culture of their children. The parents wanted to help themselves and their children adapt, but they did not want to assimilate into a 19th-century Victorian British cultural terrain.[16] The missionaries, especially the Anglican missionaries, hoped to convert Indian Schools into Schools of Industry, where First Nations children would learn weaving, carpentry, agriculture, and any other pursuits the missionaries thought were civilized.[17] Consequently, while parents welcomed the chance for education and were reasonably co-operative, the implementation of the denominational system of education and the plan for forming a civilized child met several challenges.

Two major factors seriously affected denominational civilization programs. First, parents and guardians influenced their children; if they either did not initially support denominational education, or withdrew their children from the program, then the potential for rearing civilized children was lost. Parents and guardians needed the help of their children in industries like farming, hunting, gathering, and trading; as well, Métis hunter, gatherer, and trader parents who were squatters during the off-season and often illiterate saw little benefit from education. Secondly, financing the tools required for civilization—schoolrooms, schoolbooks, and schoolmasters and schoolmistresses—was a continual challenge. Parents and guardians rarely had the funds available, so missionary societies usually had to finance most or all of the education provided to children. Overall these two factors would always plague denominational efforts at civilizing the child.

As a community remote from trade, Red River was suitable for the evolution of a system of denominational education that imposed the 19th-century European model of the civilized child on what the missionaries perceived as a primitive Métis society. The Anglicans and the Catholics developed this denominational system, and key individuals in each group were responsible for its formation. The education contained religious, academic, and industrial components, and its implementation resulted in divisions based on race, class, and gender. All education would begin with lessons from the Bible, which would allow children to acquire spoken and written English and would serve as the basic textbook of instruction. Once Christianized and literate, these children could embark on a path of academic and industrial instruction.

The Reverend John West laid the foundation for the CMS's program of civilization.[18] West came to Rupert's Land from his native Britain after the HBC appointed him chaplain and the CMS appointed him as a missionary. He arrived at Red River in October 1820. Prior to his arrival, West lived at York Factory, where he used his British training to come up with a plan for educating the children at the post. West's philosophy of educating First Nations and Métis children focused on removing them from the fur trade, the industry that in his view had negatively changed their culture. West planned to remove First Nations and Métis children from York Factory to Red River, where they would "be educated in white man's knowledge and religion."[19] He planned to educate a generation of agriculturalists who could return to their families and teach them the value of agriculture.[20] The children would be taught to read the Bible, or "Book which the Great Spirit had given to White people ... which would show them how to live well and die happy."[21] The First Nations and the Métis seemed to like what West proposed, as he noted that "the Indians were willing to part with their children for the purpose of their being instructed."[22] At Red River, West established a day school in November 1820 in the area of what would later be known as Kildonan, and instructed children taken from trading posts in Rupert's

Mr. West taking leave of the Indians at Beaver Creek, before stepping into his Cariole.

Reverend John West of the Church Missionary Society bidding farewell to Assiniboine family before stepping into a carriole, c. January–February, 1821 (engraving, courtesy of the Glenbow Archives/ LAC-3421-1).

Land. The children were educated at the expense of the CMS at a cost of £12 per annum.[23]

To better carry out his plans for civilization, West would soon receive a helper. Reverend David Jones arrived at Red River in January 1822. Prior to his arrival, he had studied for two years at the Lampeter Seminary in Wales, and after completing his studies there, was accepted by the CMS as a missionary candidate. Jones was ordained deacon in December 1822 and became a priest in April 1823. He assumed West's position as HBC chaplain in 1823 after serving as West's assistant for one year. Upon assuming West's position, he commenced a large-scale project of schoolroom erection. Jones attempted to increase the number of students attending schools by including the Métis in the Anglican school system. He also initiated the first recorded schools for First Nations and Métis children, as well as a training school for future missionaries. In 1824, he established a day school at Middle Church in St. Paul's parish, a few miles down the river from St. John's parish. He also formalized religious and industrial instruction in the schools, and developed schools that segregated groups of students.

From 1822 to 1823, Jones worked to expand the number of individuals the CMS reached in its mission efforts. Jones and his schoolmasters went door to door in parish or settler communities, and obtained almost 50 children.[24] By going door to door, Jones recognized the importance of educating "a numerous race of Half-caste children, [who] equally claim the attention of the Christian Philanthropist."[25] He was especially concerned about orphaned or abandoned anglophone Métis children at HBC posts, and wanted to remove them to the settlement[26] or to one of the HBC posts.[27] For the francophone Métis, Jones hoped that failures in the hunt would motivate them to receive instruction in agriculture and separate them from what he considered "uncivilized" and "semi-nomadic" pursuits.[28] Overall, education was very important for Jones, especially the education of Métis children left orphaned by the 1821 merger of the HBC and the NWC, or by fur trader fathers.

Jones quickly became frustrated with the HBC, a company which he thought ignored his plans for a formal solution to the civilization problem of Métis children.[29] Consequently, by the end of the 1820s he had done little to remove the orphan children from the HBC posts or the hunt. Jones was not alone in his pleas, as all CMS personnel, from missionaries to teachers, advocated that at least orphaned Métis children be removed from the HBC posts and placed at Red River. The question of how to civilize them was not answered until 1829, when the CMS officially decided to include amongst its students orphan Métis children who drifted around the settlement.[30]

Jones' system of education paralleled 19th-century British educational principles: although education in Britain was becoming more accessible, students in school were still separated by gender and social status. Male and female children were thus to be trained for different roles in the civilized agricultural landscape. In 1827, Jones entered into "an engagement with some of the gentlemen of the Compy's Service, [to] commence a Female School under the charge of Mr. Cockran," with female students to arrive in the summer of 1827.[31] If female children were educated in the same classroom as male children, they were segregated. For example, in CMS schoolmaster Reverend Alfred C. Garrioch's schoolhouse, "the chimney end of the building was reserved for the girls, of whom in the school's best days, there were from twenty-five to thirty. The other and more frigid zone, was allocated to the boys, of whom there were about an equal number."[32] In the schools, male children were educated as the next generation of family providers, learning trades like husbandry and carpentry; the female students were taught to transmit morality, obedience, and discipline to their children, as well as domestic subjects like spinning, knitting, sewing, milking, and making butter.[33] Jones thought that "the bearing ... which female education is calculated to have on the moral and spiritual improvement of a country, will urge us to prosecute this object [the education of female children] with unremitting attention."[34] In accordance with British principles of education, students were separated not only by gender, but also by social status.

Jones responded to the request from HBC officers that their children receive an elementary and high school education superior to that of other children at the settlement: he proposed that their children needed to be educated separately from the other Métis and non-Métis groups at the settlement. From 1832 to 1833, he established a respectable seminary for the sons and daughters of Chief Factors of the HBC. The seminary was known as the Red River Academy,[35] and its teachers had the goals of moral improvement, religious instruction, and general education for the sons and daughters of settlers in the fur trade. The Academy was the first high school in Red River. In an attempt to discourage individuals who were socially unqualified from attending, Jones charged £30 per year per student; he also hired a schoolmistress to instruct all children in the ornamental branches of education, such as music and drawing. Overall, the school was Jones' response to the fear of fur trade officers that their sons and daughters would associate with their First Nations ties. Former traders hoped that their children, if distanced from their First Nations and Métis ties at a young age, would forget their First Nations or Métis ancestry. For Jones, the Academy was the institution to prevent cultural contact.[36]

Throughout the 1830s and 1840s, the Anglicans continued to use education to separate groups on the basis of social status. Inevitably, these forms of class separation resulted in the separation of racial groups: the poorer Métis, especially anglophone Métis elements and continental European settler children, were separated from the affluent anglophone Métis children of the retired HBC officers. CMS-educated Peter Garrioch, former NWC officer John Pritchard, principal settler Donald Gunn, and CMS missionary Reverend William Cockran taught the poorer anglophone Métis at Upper Church, Frog Plain, Middle Church, and Grand Rapids respectively. Those who taught poorer anglophone Métis and settler children often had less education than schoolmasters at the Academy established by Jones.[37] Therefore, the Academy or Boarding School served to separate the Europeans from the First Nations and Anglican Métis of the settlement.[38]

Jones was a motivator for civilization who found a follower in Alexander Ross and a teacher of religion and industry in his successor, Cockran. Cockran arrived at Red River in 1825 and was initially a co-worker of Jones. The two men modified their liturgy to attract the settlement's Presbyterian and Gaelic-speaking settlers. Jones and Cockran also ran the Academy, and after the departure of Jones in 1838 Cockran assumed complete responsibility for the

Reverend David Jones saying farewell at Red River, 1838. Engraving by T. Gilleed (courtesy of the Glenbow Archives/LAC-3421-8).

Academy and for Jones' ministry. Through instruction and examination in religion, academics and industry, as well as in discipline and obedience, Cockran formalized the curriculum for the schools that Jones had established.

Cockran employed harsh discipline to ensure the compliance of his students. This practice was in accordance with 19th-century pedagogy. As historians of education such as Ellen Key and Alice Miller have observed, a will and wickedness common in all young children had to be eradicated before children participated in learning; Key and Miller both agree that physical discipline, laced with concern for conformity and discipline in children, was a form of "poisonous pedagogy."[39] In the 1820s and 1830s, the missionaries perceived themselves as not only responsible for the education of children, but also as teachers of discipline and obedience—roles usually fulfilled by parents. Cockran believed in the use of corporal punishment to enforce conformity and discipline in children; he thought that children would conform to the civilized society by becoming virtuous adults who maintained and developed the community.[40] While West removed children from their parents and Jones provided the first curriculum and increased the number of schools, Cockran had the clearest vision of what defined the civilized child and used a combination of discipline, industry, and religious instruction to accomplish this task.

Cockran also thought that industrial instruction was necessary for rearing self-sufficient adults. Like his predecessors, West and Jones, Cockran continually advocated the founding of a school of industry that would train students to fulfill industrial roles in the growing settlement[41]: he wanted to convert the existing Indian School at the Rapids into a school of industry, where there would be "5 distinct apartments, for the boys and girls to learn to read and write in, one to weave in, and one to learn the trade of carpenters."[42] At the proposed school, children would learn farming by practice and the agricultural products they produced, such as grain, potatoes, and hogs, would feed them while they learned to farm.[43]

Like West and Jones, Cockran combined religious and secular objectives with his curriculum of industry. He hoped that through religious instruction teachers and students would learn to worship God together, and that students would be faithful to the lessons of the Scriptures.[44] He observed that through instruction in the Bible, the schools "afford them [the students] the means of obtaining a scriptural education… [and one] embraces the whole bible, thus by its precepts, they are taught their duty to God … [and] are allured to a willing obedience."[45] The full integration of spiritual and practical objectives was illustrated by the regular visitations and examinations that Cockran and other missionaries conducted. An example of such an examination was one conducted at the Middle Church School on October 3, 1842. The examiner, schoolmaster John Roberts, reported that "after examining the first and second class in Arithmetic, Geography, History & c. I directed their attention to the sacred Scriptures and told them to read in the books of Liviticus [sic]."[46]

For Cockran, providing religious instruction was a challenge. He had not failed in teaching the rudiments of religion to children, as they could read, write, sing psalms, hymns, spiritual songs, and say prayers; but he noted that the students made little progress in the knowledge they acquired. He blamed Aboriginal mothers for the lack of comprehension in children, noting that these women had no use for the lessons of the Sunday schools and therefore did not encourage their children to remember the lessons they learned.[47]

From 1820 until 1850, the Anglicans laid the foundations for a system of education that became firmly implanted. West first removed children from what he perceived made them "uncivilized," the fur trade; then Jones followed West and established the schools that West had envisioned; finally, Cockran worked with Jones' curriculum of obedience, discipline, religion, basic academics, and industry to train a generation of virtuous adults. The Catholics followed a similar plan, and by the end of the 1850s had developed an education system similar to that of the Anglicans.

Several individuals contributed to the formation of Catholic education at Red River. Joseph-Octave Plessis, Bishop of Quebec, brought the Catholic Church to the settlement. In the late 1810s, Plessis requested that Joseph-Norbert Provencher, Sévère Dumoulin, and William Edge bring religion and schools to Red River. As well, Plessis wanted the three men to legitimize European marriages to First Nations wives through Christian instruction, erect schools, and develop catechism classes for children. Subsequently, Georges-Antoine Belcourt came to Red River in 1830 as an assistant to Provencher. The two Nolin sisters, Angélique and Marguerite, provided female children with

Alexandre-Antonin Taché (1823–94), c. 1890 (courtesy of the Archives of Manitoba/N2959).

primary education and separated them from the male children. The Grey Sisters, who arrived in the late 1850s, continued this gender-separated education. Other important Catholics were Reverend L. Laflèche, who established year-round schooling at Saint-François-Xavier, and Provencher's successor, Alexandre-Antonin Taché, who focused on agricultural instruction. Overall, all of these Catholic missionaries saw the Métis as the bridge that connected European and First Nations societies at Red River.

Plessis established a mission at Red River around 1818. He wanted to educate the First Nations at the settlement, as well as French Canadians and Métis Christians who lived amongst the First Nations. For Plessis, instructing potential converts and converts in marriage customs, family life, and the education of children sowed the seeds for growing cultural change.[48]

Ordained Bishop of Juliopolis, and coadjutor Bishop of Quebec in 1822, Provencher made several contributions to Catholic education. He became a schoolmaster at St. Boniface, a parish on the east side of the settlement, composed of French Canadian families who travelled with the Catholic missionaries from Montreal to Red River.[49] However, his attempts at education were informal at best, and focused on training in industry. He brought in two weaving instructors from Quebec to teach Métis women; the students attended class in an older chapel that he provided. However, a fire destroyed this quasi-school of industry and the industrial machinery in March 1839 and left him without a residence for the schoolmistresses and the children.[50] Provencher also instructed a Latin class geared toward preparing six male children for the priesthood. However, none of them succeeded when they went on to Montreal or Quebec for higher education. Provencher's initiatives were costly, and moreover the Catholic ideologies for education, which involved taking their mission and their education to the Métis, conflicted with the theory of civilization: to rear a sedentary generation of Métis child industrialists and missionaries.

As an assistant to Provencher, Belcourt was very involved in the education of Catholic children. In 1834 he was stationed at Baie St. Paul, where he acted as a pastor, teacher, advisor, and confidant to the First Nations and the Métis there and at various other missions from Lake Winnipegosis to Fort Francis. Finally, Belcourt wrote textbooks that he used as curriculum in the schools.[51] When Belcourt commenced his school at Baie St. Paul, he hired the Nolin sisters as teachers. The francophone Métis daughters of former NWC officer Louis Nolin, they had been educated in Quebec as teachers, and in 1825 arrived at St. Boniface to teach school. In 1829, the two sisters opened the first girls' school in St. Boniface,[52] providing the first Catholic education to female children.

Two other individuals and one group also played roles in the development of Catholic education during the foundation years. Laflèche established a school at Saint François-Xavier in the early 1850s for the boys; the school operated throughout the year, but was suspended during the bi-annual hunts, when Laflèche left to educate and minister to adults and children who travelled with the hunt. Taché arrived in the Catholic parish of St. Boniface on August 25, 1845; he was ordained deacon on August 31, and priest on October 12 of the same year. On October 13, 1845, he entered the Oblate order.[53] As a member of the Oblate order, Taché ministered to the French-Canadian and Métis population at Saint-François-Xavier.[54] In the late 1850s, he succeeded Provencher as the Bishop of St. Boniface; in this capacity he proposed that the reason why Anglican missions experienced success in the 1840s was that they provided food and clothing for the students they educated. He wanted to establish a model farm similar to the Anglican one in order to educate children in agriculture and different branches of industry.[55] He, like Provencher, also wanted to train francophone Métis children for the priesthood; in 1858, he sent Louis Riel and two other students to Quebec for classical education.[56] Finally, the Grey Sisters at Saint François-Xavier established a convent school; they were well received at Saint François, and in their first year of operation their school had 80 students.[57]

After 1845, the Catholics too concluded that the only way that students could be civilized through education was by being removed from their parents. The Catholics had allowed the Métis to continue with their ancestral pursuits, and consequently had not attained much success with projects of Christianization and education in religion and industry. The missionaries wanted First Nations and Métis children to interact, so that First Nations children could pattern their behaviour after the more civilized Métis children.[58] However, even post-1845 missionaries like Laflèche, Taché, and the Grey Sisters were not very successful in rearing civilized children: their lack of success was caused by their habit of bringing education to the Métis hunters, gatherers and traders, and their reluctance to remove them to the mission schools on a permanent basis.

Overall, Anglicans and Catholics contributed significantly to the development of civilization at Red River. The mission groups provided academic and industrial instruction, directed toward rearing a generation of civilized individuals who farmed and worshiped God, and spread the example of civilization to other First Nations and Métis groups. However, two factors conspired to interfere with each missionary group's plan for civilization: attendance and funding. As a result, educators became convinced that only with compulsion would the program of civilization function properly, and a Christian and agricultural Red River take shape.

Attendance fluctuated in the schools: attitude of parents, place of residence, illness, whether children were fed and clothed, the availability of textbooks, and children's participation in the rural economy all played a part. In the first place, parents had the option not to send children to school, as education was not compulsory. Second, many children lived far away from the schools: isolation affected attendance, especially during the winter months, when many children did not have warm enough clothing for travel. Third, illness affected attendance: one of the epidemics that plagued the settlement in the early years was scarlet fever, and when such an epidemic afflicted students, attendance declined,[59] not only because of fatalities but also because parents refused to send healthy children to school.[60] Fourth, the Anglicans recruited several of their students by promising parents that their children would be fed and clothed. However, parents sometimes took advantage of the CMS's promise: many children attended only to receive food and clothing, and then left the schools.[61] The only type of education that children and families received was Sabbath School instruction, where attendance numbers, on average, were higher than in the day schools.[62] Consequently, the fluctuation in student attendance resulted in marginal student success, primarily because of the remunerative work their parents performed and the apathy of these parents to their education.

The occupations of parents was another factor that greatly affected attendance of children. Only the discharged fur trade officers, and servants and the individuals connected to the governing Council of Assiniboia, really encouraged school attendance. These children attended the school regularly because their parents did not need them to survive.[63] Although the settler parents valued missionary education, most were farmers who needed the assistance of their children on their farms[64]: seeding and harvesting took precedence over education. In 1848, Anglican missionary Reverend Robert James, who had arrived in Red River in 1845, allowing Cockran to retire temporarily to Toronto, reported that by the age of 12 to 14 years children had left school because their help was required in the home. Gunn thought that the need for child labour during the months of August and September, in conjunction with the cold weather of the winter months, contributed to a drastic decline in student success.[65] However, the Anglicans were not as concerned about the settler children, some of whom were anglophone Métis, because they knew that agricultural parents would be good role models to their children and would ensure that they grew into sedentary and civilized farmers who attended church.[66]

The occupations of the third group of parents, the hunters, gatherers and traders, also affected student attendance at school. In this case, the Anglicans believed that these children were being led astray from civilization, and quickly became frustrated with a group of children whom they could not civilize. The Catholics, who were most often responsible for educating this group of Métis, were very concerned about their children. Unlike anglophone parents, francophone Métis parents demonstrated less regard for Catholic schools.[67] When the Catholic Church arrived at Red River, the francophone Métis were totally dependent on the hunt, whose migratory nature complicated education. In addition, the HBC's demand for furs and provisions meant that parents were unwilling to settle.[68] Finally, after 1849 the francophone Métis looked to the hunt as a profit-generating business, and as less of a means of feeding their families[69]; this resulted in the removal of children from school for long periods of the year. As in agriculture, in this traditional economy children were an economic asset whose help was required; the only difference was that the missionaries looked down on the participation of children in this traditional pursuit.[70]

Although parental attitudes toward education were a major problem with the success of civilization, financial pressures always undermined the civilizing attempts of the CMS and the Catholic Church, primarily because parents could not afford to educate their children. Schoolhouses required maintenance and stretched the budgets of missionary societies. Throughout the 1850s, missionaries and schoolmasters appealed to the CMS for increases in their grants so that they could afford to maintain their buildings, but the grants provided were never enough.[71]

For the Catholics, funding was also an ongoing problem. Frustrated by the cost of educating poor children, Provencher asked the Grey Nuns to erect an English-language school that took both Catholic and non-Catholic students. Provencher hoped that he would be able to use the school fees paid by the wealthy fur traders to cover the expense of educating children who could not afford school.[72] Although Taché hoped to establish a model farming school, he thought that the plan would be impossible because of money[73]; consequently, for the Catholics, keeping the schoolrooms operational while paying for the education of children proved to be a challenge.

Although attendance and funding were significant problems for denominational education, by the 1840s and 1850s the problems were growing pains of a system that was, for Anglicans and Catholics, planted firmly. Problems such as attendance, student isolation, and epidemics represented continuous social issues in education that would take years to overcome. Each missionary group provided at least a partial education in classrooms ranging from 10 to 120 students. However, the over-arching goal of forming civilized children continued to be a challenge, regardless of how developed the curriculum was, how many textbooks were in the schoolroom, and how many schoolrooms were erected. The missionary societies failed to convince many Métis that their ancestral economic activities, and the involvement of their children in these enterprises, were antithetical to their being civilized. Most francophone Métis never shared the missionary goal of civilization or perceived the benefits that the missionaries thought civilization had for their children most likely because throughout this period, hunting, gathering, and trading remained more profitable than agriculture.

For 20 to 30 years, the missionaries transmitted a concept of civilized childhood through their burgeoning system of education. However, the civilization of children had only been partially accomplished by 1870, because the missionary societies could not compel children to remain away from their traditional culture. While many Métis children attended school, the missionaries believed that the effectiveness of the lessons depended on how long and how often the children stayed in missionary schools and away from their ancestral economy.

The missionaries experienced trouble transmitting their concept of childhood because the traditional economy prevented the regular attendance of children at school. The francophone Métis hunters, gatherers, small-scale agriculturalists, and traders saw their children as participants in their subsistence family economy, not as large-scale farmers, a pursuit the missionaries equated with civilization. However, the HBC officer, servant, and settler parents were more inclined to accept the teachings of civilization through Christianity and agriculture. According to the missionaries, many students did not become civilized because their parents or guardians did not understand or did not want to understand what the missionaries wanted to accomplish.[74] In response, the missionaries wanted to completely remove students from First Nations and Métis communities and place them in an environment where missionary principles of discipline, obedience, Christianity, academics, and industry predominated over trading, hunting, and gathering. The missionaries thought that cultural confusion would be alleviated only if the removal of children from First Nations and Métis communities was mandatory and permanent.[75] However, the post-Confederation period proved the civilizing missionaries wrong: the federal government justified missionary education and politicians would develop legislation that compelled children to attend schools designed to disassociate them from their Aboriginal cultural ties. However, Aboriginal children would resist these systematic attempts to erode their culture and identity, and reject the ideology of Victorian civilization.

Notes

This article first appeared in *Prairie Forum* 31, no. 1 (2006): 1–16.

1. A.A. den Otter, "The 1849 Sayer Trial: An Ecological Perspective," in Derek Pollard and Ged Martin (eds.), *Canada 1849: A Selection of Papers Given at the University of Edinburgh Centre for Canadian Studies Annual Conference May 1999* (Edinburgh: University of Edinburgh Centre for Canadian Studies, 1999), 31.

2. Frits Pannekoek, "The Anglican Church and the Disintegration of Red River Society," in Carl Berger and Ramsay Cook (eds.), *The West and the Nation: Essays in Honour of W.L. Morton* (Toronto: McClelland and Stewart Limited, 1976), 81.

3. Berry Mayall, *Children, Health, and the Social Order* (Philadelphia: Open University Press, 1996), 5, 19–21, 54.

4. Ellen Key, *The Century of the Child* (New York: G.P. Putnam's Sons, 1909), 113. Priscilla Robertson, "Home as a Nest: Middle Class Childhood in Nineteenth-Century Europe," in Lloyd deMause (ed.), *The History of Childhood* (New York: Psychohistory Press, 1974), 407–8, 421.

5. den Otter, "The 1849 Sayer Trial," 130, 135, 146.

6. National Archives of Canada (NA), CMS, Jones' Journal, August 22, 1822, A-77, 36–37 and ibid., Clockhouse in Fairham, December 3, 1823, A-77, 64.

7. Alice Miller, *For Your Own Good: Hidden Cruelty in Child-Rearing and the Roots of Violence*

(trans. Hildegarde Hannum and Hunter Hannum) (New York: Farrar Straus Giroux, 1983), 11–13, 27, 45–46. Alice Miller referred to childhood theorist J. Sülzer, who, in 1748, wrote that willfulness in children would have to be eliminated early so that the educational process could take over.

8. NA, CMS, Cockran to Woodroffe, August 3, 1831, A-77, 438.

9. Mayall, *Children, Health, and the Social Order* 5, 19–21, 54.

10. Raymond J.A. Huel, *Proclaiming the Gospel to the Indians and Métis* (Edmonton: University of Alberta Press, 1996), 104.

11. NA, CMS, Cockran to the Secretaries, August 5, 1833, A-77.

12. Ibid., Cockran to the Secretary, Grand Rapids, December 16, 1833, A-77.

13. Ibid.

14. Bruce Curtis, *Building the Educational State: Canada West, 1836–1871* (London: Althouse Press, 1988), 72, 169–70, 184–85, 187, 201, 299, 311. Education in Red River and in Canada West was resisted by agricultural adults who did not understand the benefit their children would receive from completing or fully participating in education. Bruce Curtis, in his monograph *Building the Educational State*, noted that many male students withdrew from education around the age of 12 to 14 years because many parents did not understand the value of discipline and the need to keep their children in school from 9 am to 3:30 pm daily year-round.

15. NA, CMS, Cockran to Rev. T. Woodroffe, Red River Settlement, August 3, 1831, Private, A-77.

16. J.R. Miller, *Skyscrapers Hide the Heavens: A History of Indian-White Relations in Canada* (Toronto: University of Toronto Press, 2000), 129–30, 135, 142.

17. NA, CMS, Rev. Mr. Cockran to the Secretaries (Private), Grand Rapids, July 30, 1833, A-77.

18. Robert J. Coutts, *The Road to the Rapids: Nineteenth-Century Church and Society at St. Andrew's Parish, Red River* (Calgary: University of Calgary Press, 2000) 14.

19. John West, *The Substance of a Journal During a Residence at the Red River Settlement* (New York: Johnson Reprint Corporation, 1966), 14.

20. NA, CMS, Rev. David Jones's Journal from June 1 to August 1, 1823, A-77, 37.

21. Ibid., Jones's Journal from June 1 to August 1, 1823, 37.

22. NA, CMS, Minutes of Benjamin Harrison, Esq. on the formation of a Mission Among the Indians in the Hudson's Bay HBC's Territories, A-77. However, West's plans for education were not well received by the HBC, and in 1823, while in England on a brief leave of absence, the HBC decided not to renew his contract as their chaplain. Richard A. Willie, "West, John," *Dictionary of Canadian Biography*, vol. VII (Toronto: University of Toronto Press, 1988) 900–902.

23. Willie, "West, John," 900.

24. NA, CMS, Jones to the Secretaries, January 31, 1827, A-77, 234.

25. Ibid., Jones's Journal from June 1 to August 1, 1823, August 22, 1822, A-77, 36.

26. Ibid., 36–37.

27. Ibid., Clockhouse in Fairham, December 3, 1823, A-77, 64.

28. Thomas F. Bredin, "The Reverend David Jones: Missionary at Red River 1823–38," *Beaver* 312, no. 2 (1981): 48–49.

29. NA, CMS, Clockhouse, December 23, 1823, A-77, 64.

30. Ibid., D.T. Jones, G. Harbidge, and Mrs. Harbidge, Particulars respecting the Schools at Red River Settlement during the Summer of 1824, A-77.

31. Ibid., Jones to the Secretaries, January 31, 1827, A-77, 227.

32. Rev. A.C. Garrioch, *First Furrows: A History of the Early Settlement of the Red River Country, Including That of Portage La Prairie* (Winnipeg: Stovel Company Limited, 1923) 121.

33. NA, CMS, Cockran to the Secretaries, July 30, 1833, A-77, 539.

34. Ibid., Jones to the Secretaries, January 31, 1827, A-77, 235.

35. Wayne K.D. Davies, "A Welsh Missionary at Canada's Red River Settlement, 1823–38," *National Library of Wales* 27, no. 2 (1991): 223. The Bishop of Rupert's Land, David Anderson or David Rupert's Land, changed the name of the Red River Academy to St. John's Collegiate School when he became Bishop of the newly formed diocese of Rupert's Land, in 1849. In 1867, St. John's Collegiate School became St. John's College, and is now a part of the University of Manitoba in Winnipeg, Manitoba.

36. Pannekoek, "Anglican Church," 67, 69–70.

37. Ibid., 69, 79.

38. Davies, "Welsh Missionary," 223.

39. Key, *Century of the Child*, 108. See Miller, *For Your Own Good*, 11–12, 14–15, 27, 31, 45–46, 59, 65–66, 70, 76. According to Key and Miller, the administration of corporal punishment facilitated resentment and fear in children, and did not inspire obedience and enthusiasm for education. In the 20th century, educational theorists discouraged the use of corporal punishment and advised teachers to instill respect and not fear in their students.

40. George van der Goes Ladd, "Father Cockran and his Children: Poisonous Pedagogy on the Banks of the Red," in Barry Ferguson (ed.), *The Anglican Church and the World of Western Canada, 1820–1970* (Regina: Canadian Plains Research Center, 1991). Van der Goes Ladd's analysis is limited, in that he failed to observe specific instances of corporal punishment. However, van der Goes Ladd found evidence to support the claim that the students of Cockran respected him, especially the future Reverend Garrioch.

41. NA, CMS, Cockran's Journal, September 1831 to August 1832, November 17, 1831, A-77, 463.

42. Ibid., Cockran to the Secretaries, July 30, 1833, A-77, 539.

43. Ibid., Smithurst's Journal from August 1, 1842 to November 8, 1842, A-78.

44. Ibid., Cockran to the Secretaries, July 30, 1827, extract from journals, January 21, 1827, A-77, 271.

45. Ibid., Cockran to the Secretaries, August 4, 1841, A-78, 539–40.

46. Ibid., Robert's Report from August 1842 to July 1843, October 3, 1842, A-78, 255.

47. Ibid., Cockran to the Secretaries, Parsonage House, Red River Settlement, August 11, 1828, A-77.

48. Martha McCarthy, *To Evangelize the Nations: Roman Catholic Missions in Manitoba 1818–1870*, Papers in Manitoba History Report Number 2 (Winnipeg: Manitoba Culture Heritage and Recreation Historic Resources, 1990), iv, 3–6, 25.

49. Andrée Désilets, "Hout, Marie-Françoise," *Dictionary of Canadian Biography*, vol. VII (Toronto: University of Toronto Press, 1988), 431–32.

50. *Bulletin de la Societe Historique de Saint-Boniface: Lettres de Monseigneur Joseph Norbert Provencher, Premier Evêque de Saint Boniface* 3 (Société Historique de St. Boniface, MB), J.N. Ev. de Juliopolis A Monseigneur J. Signay, Eveque de Quebec St-Boniface de la Rivière Rouge (Rivière Rouge, juillet 1839), 181.

51. *Georges-Antoine Belcourt* (Winnipeg: Manitoba Culture, Heritage, and Recreation, 1984), 1.

52. McCarthy, *To Evangelize the Nations*, 26.

53 Henry Youle Hind, *Narrative of the Canadian Red River Exploring Expedition of 1857 and of the Assiniboine and Saskatchewan Exploring Expedition of 1858*, vol. 1 (New York: Greenwood Press, Publishers, 1969), xi.

54. Huel, *Proclaiming the Gospel*, xii–xiii, 17–18, 24–25, 100.

55. McCarthy, *To Evangelize the Nations*, 41, 44.

56. Robert Gosman, *The Riel and Lagimodiere Families in Métis Society 1840–1860, St. Vital, Manitoba* (Parks Canada, Department of Indian and Northern Affairs, July 1975), 28.

57. Margaret MacLeod, W.L. Morton, and Alice R. Brown, *Cuthbert Grant of Grantown: Warden of the Plains of Red River*, The Carleton Library No. 71 (Toronto: McClelland and Stewart Limited, 1974), 141.

58. Huel, *Proclaiming the Gospel*, 104.

59. NA, CMS, Hunter's Journal from May 13 to July 28, 1845, A-78.

60. Ibid., Pembrum's Report, A-78, 314.

61. Ibid., Cowley's Journal, October 19, 1845 and January 1, 1846, A-78.

62. Ibid., Memoranda respecting the Settlement at Red River, A-77.

63. Gosman, *Riel and Lagimodiere Families in Métis Society*, 28–29, 34.

64. Curtis, *Building the Educational State*, 185.

65. NA, CMS, Gunn to Cockran, July 6, 1843, A-78 165.

66. Ibid., Cowley to the Secretaries, July 31, 1843, A-78, 165.

67. Gosman, *Riel and Lagimodiere Families in Métis Society*, 28, 34.

68. McCarthy, *To Evangelize the Nations*, 15, 20; Heather Devine, personal communication, Wednesday, February 26, 2003.

69. den Otter, "The 1849 Sayer Trial," 146.

70. Gerhard J. Ens, *Homeland to Hinterland: The Changing Worlds of the Red River Métis in the Nineteenth Century* (Toronto: University of Toronto Press, 1996), 28, 37.

71. NA, CMS, Cowley To Hon. Lay Secretary, August 8, 1854, A-79, 558.

72. McCarthy *To Evangelize the Nations*, 28.

73. Ibid., 44.

74. NA, CMS, Cockran to Secretaries, August 11, 1828, A-77, 314.

75. Ibid.

13. Aboriginal Rights Versus the Deed of Surrender: The Legal Rights of Native Peoples and Canada's Acquisition of the Hudson's Bay Company Territory

Frank J. Tough

Introduction

On June 23, 1870, some 2.9 million square miles of British North America—Rupert's Land and the North-Western Territory—were incorporated into the Dominion of Canada.[1] This vast area, composed largely of boreal forest, tundra and prairie, now amounts to nearly 75% of Canada's land mass (Figure 1). Despite the geographical magnitude of this event in the history of nation-building, Canada's acquisition of this territory from the Hudson's Bay Company (HBC) has been left unexamined. Traditional constitutional history has focussed on political evolution in those areas of British North America settled by Europeans.[2] The transfer agreement or Deed of Surrender has been used by conventional fur-trade historians merely as a means to conclude accounts of 200 years of Company history.[3] The more recent work on Native-white relationships has largely excluded the post-1870 fur trade.[4] Again, the Deed of Surrender is seen as an insignificant event in Native history. Because the question of Indian title enters into the transfer, legal scholarship has examined the published documents associated with the surrender of the HBC territory and the subsequent union with Canada.[5] These specialized approaches have not led to a general view of the long-term importance of the Rupert's Land transfer to the history of Native people. An analysis of the events surrounding the transfer of Rupert's Land will provide insights about Indian title.

Brian Slattery provides useful direction for pursuing research on Native legal issues: "yet if the historical role of Native peoples is now widely recognized, it has not yet been accommodated by the standard intellectual framework that influences legal thinking."[6] This problem is evident in the

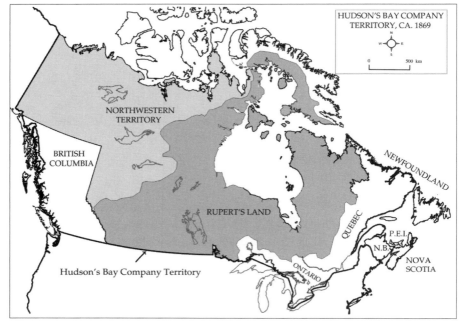

Figure 1. The Hudson's Bay Company Territory: Rupert's Land and the North-Western Territory.

discussion on Indian title and the surrender of Rupert's Land. Most published research looks for meaning in the "Address to Her Majesty the Queen from the Senate and House of Commons of the Dominion of Canada," December 16 and 17, 1867 (hereafter Address of 1867); the "Address from the Senate and House of Commons," May 29 and 31, 1869 (hereafter Address of 1869); term 14 of the draft of surrender, which is synonymous with the HBC's Deed of Surrender; and term 8 of the "Memorandum of the Details of Agreement between the Delegates of the Government of the Dominion and the Directors of the Hudson's Bay Company," March 22, 1869 (hereafter Memorandum of March 22, 1869). These documents are reproduced in the "Order of Her Majesty in Council admitting Rupert's Land and the North-Western Territory into the Union," June 23, 1870 (hereafter the Rupert's Land Order).[7] In the Rupert's Land Order the Crown accepted the surrender of Rupert's Land from the HBC and then transferred Rupert's Land and the North-Western Territory to the Dominion of Canada. Term 8 of the Memorandum of March 22, 1869 provides the original source for the Aboriginal-title concept which emerged during the negotiations of 1868–69.[8] It states:

8. It is understood that any claims of Indians to compensation for lands required for purposes of settlement shall be disposed of by the Canadian Government, in communication with the Imperial Govemment and that the Company shall be relieved of all responsibility in respect of them.

Term 14 of the Deed of Surrender states:

14. Any claims of Indians to compensation for lands required for purposes of settlement shall be disposed of by the Canadian Govemment in communication with the Imperial Govemment; and the Company shall be relieved of all responsibility in respect of them.[10]

On the surface, this is a clear recognition of Indian title, but since Indians were not party to the surrender talks, it is not immediately clear which of the parties—the HBC, the Canadian government or the Colonial Office—sponsored this term concerning Indian title. Interpretations of the meaning of the particular conceptualization of Aboriginal title, which emerged during the surrender negotiations, can be better appreciated by considering the political and economic context of the events which led up to Canada's annexation of the region.

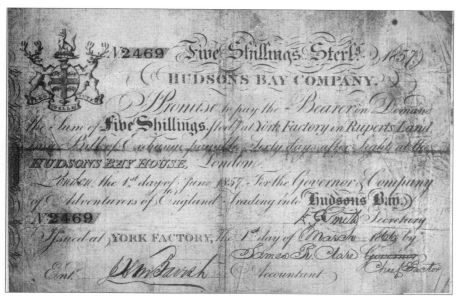

A Hudson's Bay Company promissory note for five shillings issued at York Factory (courtesy of the Archives of Manitoba/N479).

By discussing the leading Canadian court cases in an historical context, Slattery has outlined a general theory of Aboriginal rights.[11] The transfer of Rupert's Land merits specific attention. An historical analysis of the Rupert's Land Order contributes to an understanding of the legal principles surrounding the extension of Canadian sovereignty into Indian lands under the control of the HBC. For some Indians, the terms by which the HBC surrendered its claim to Rupert's Land were a contentious issue during the western or numbered treaty negotiations.[12] Thus, research on the Aboriginal-title concept embodied in term 14 of the Rupert's Land Order has implications for ongoing comprehensive and specific Native land claims. Given the importance of the Rupert's Land Order to the Constitution Act 1982 (more specifically, the British North America Act 1867, the Manitoba Act 1870, and the BNA Act 1871), the meaning of term 14 has a bearing on comprehending section 35 of the Constitution Act 1982, which recognizes and affirms the existing Aboriginal and treaty rights.

A broader interpretation of Indian title as conceived by the Rupert's Land Order has not developed for several reasons. By and large, legal research has focussed on term 14 and has excluded an examination of the other terms of the surrender agreement. In specific terms, we do not know exactly why and how the HBC ended up with one-twentieth of the surveyed lands of the Prairies. An examination of the terms of surrender might cause one to ponder the legal implications of the Crown granting lands to the HBC prior to treaty-making between the Canadian state and the Indians. Does the inclusion of a recognition of Indian claims make the surrender consistent with the Royal Proclamation of 1763, or could other terms, such as the HBC land grants, actually make sections of the Rupert's Land Order repugnant to the Royal Proclamation of 1763? The history of the development of the Aboriginal-rights doctrine[13] should consider the Rupert's Land Order by evaluating the terms of surrender as a package. McNeil has shown that the Canadian government in the Address of 1867 was supposed to deal with Indians on the basis of "equitable principles."[14] The meaning of the expression "equitable principles" can be considered by comparing the compensation that the HBC received for its claims to Rupert's Land to the compensation that Native people obtained for their interest in Indian title. Methodological biases are responsible for some of the limitations on our knowledge of the Aboriginal-rights concept which emerged during the transfer. Generally, the existing legal research has focussed on printed documentation, in particular "The Report of Delegates appointed to negotiate for the acquisition of Rupert's Land and the North-West Territory."[15] Although the Delegates' Report contains a sizable selection of correspondence between August 8, 1868 and April 10, 1869, it mainly represents the Canadian position. Manuscript sources from the Hudson's Bay Company Archives (HBCA) not only present the HBC's viewpoint, but also provide some vital documentary evidence. In *R. v. Sioui*, extrinsic historical evidence was vital to the judgement.[16] New archival evidence which reflects on the meaning of term 14 is presented in this article.

Finally, a close look at the negotiations leading to the HBC's surrender of Rupert's Land, and a brief summary of Native reactions to this, will provide insights about the formulation of Indian policy. Purely legalistic approaches cannot evaluate Mr. Justice Mahoney's decision in the Baker Lake case that term 14 "merely transferred existing obligations from the Company to Canada."[17] What were the HBC's obligations to Indians prior to the cession of Rupert's Land to Canada in 1870? Certain obligations were embodied in the practices of two centuries of trade relations between the HBC and the Natives.[18] Does term 14 create a fiduciary obligation? For some, a political-economy approach is too unorthodox and unnecessary. However, and by analogy, what sort of understanding of any of the Aboriginal-rights sections of Constitution Act 1982 would exist without some awareness of the positions of various federal and provincial governments and the state of land claims in their respective jurisdictions?

Dual Claims to Rupert's Land: Mercantile and Aboriginal

The HBC's Royal Charter of 1670 not only incorporated the HBC but also established this mercantile firm on a monopoly basis. Of importance to Native people, the charter granted monopoly trading rights on the "whole and entire trade and traffic."[19] Also, the HBC was given possessory rights. This 1670 document stated:

> and grant unto them and their successors the sole trade and commerce of all those seas, straits, bays, rivers, lakes, creeks and sounds, in whatsoever latitude they shall be, that lie within the entrance of the straits, commonly called Hudson's Straits, together with all the lands, countries and territories upon the coasts and confines of the seas, straits, bays, lakes, rivers, creeks and sounds aforesaid, which are not now actually possessed b any of our subjects, or by the subjects of any other Christian Prince or State...[20]

In effect, title was granted at the pleasure of the Crown. The all-encompassing territorial claims were stressed because the Company

> at all times hereafter shall be, personable and capable in law to have, purchase, receive, possess, enjoy and retain lands,

> rents, privileges, liberties, jurisdictions, franchises and
> hereditaments, of what kind, nature or quality soever they
> be, to them and their successors; and also to give, grant,
> demise, alien, assign and dispose lands, tenements and
> hereditaments…[21]

The Charter granted a variety of proprietary rights and benefits to the HBC and its successors; as well, the capacity to give up its proprietary rights was granted. The Charter made several references to the HBC's proprietary rights to the lands in the Hudson Bay basin.[22] In practice, the HBC was not in the habit of making territorial claims to the exclusion of Aboriginal land tenure.[23] The Charter also granted the HBC judicial authority, and the HBC thus had the status of a proprietary government. The authority of the HBC in Rupert's Land, with its governing powers, possessing land entitlements and monopoly trade rights, generated political opposition; nonetheless, the Charter was never challenged in court by the HBC's opponents.[24] In 1857, a legal opinion for the HBC tended to reinforce early European concepts of possession:

> I am of the opinion that the Grant of soil of the Territory
> embraced within the limits mentioned in the Charter of
> Incorporation of the Hudson's Bay Company is in itself
> good newly discovered and unoccupied lands taken pos-
> session of by British subjects in the name of the Crown of
> Great Britain became the property of the Crown and there-
> fore may be granted by it to anybody it pleases. The
> Territory of Hudson Bay was unoccupied by Christians
> until it was taken possession of by the English and was first
> settled by the Company and their Servants.[25]

Such arguments and the unchallenged Charter of 1670 provided the basis for a longstanding mercantile claim to Rupert's Land. The HBC's territorial claims were advanced in the European sphere of diplomacy, and were based on "discovery." Because the HBC's relationship with Natives emphasized trade, there was little effort in the first 200 years of its operations to challenge Native use and occupancy of land.

The doctrine of Aboriginal title substantiates a claim to Rupert's Land by Native people.[26] The basic concept of Aboriginal title, that Indians had a valid title that could only be surrendered by proper legal procedures, arose out of some of the earliest interactions between Europeans and Indians. In Canada, a legal foundation for the acknowledgment of Aboriginal rights is found in the Royal Proclamation of 1763. This constitutional document indicated and summarized the preexisting British policies on Aboriginal rights. The proclamation restricted European encroachment on Indian lands by closing off a large area (designated as the Indian Territory) to settlement and by establishing a means for surrendering Indian title. Brian Slattery argued that the Proclamation "is one of those legal instruments that does simple things in complicated ways." He simplified the Proclamation's means for defining Aboriginal title by stating, "colonial governments are forbidden to grant any unceded Indian lands, British subjects to settle on them and private individuals to purchase them."[27] But the Royal Proclamation outlined a system of public purchases "as the official mode of extinguishing Indian title."[28] Indians could surrender their lands only to the Crown. Slattery concluded, "In technical terms, the Indian interest constitutes a legal burden on the Crown's ultimate title until surrendered."[29] Significantly, the Proclamation also declared that "the Trade with the said Indians shall be free and open to all our Subjects whatever."[30]

One of the complexities of the Proclamation pertains to an ambiguous geographical designation of limits of the Indian Territory; this in turn obscures the status of Indian title in those areas excluded from the Indian Territory. In its definition of the Indian Territory, the Proclamation excluded Rupert's Land by stating the Crown did "reserve under our Sovereignty, Protection, and Dominion, for the use of the said Indians, all Lands and Territories not included … within the Limits of the Territory granted to the Hudson's Bay Company…"[31] Under the terms of its Charter of 1670, the HBC was, in effect, a proprietary government and notwithstanding the exclusion of Rupert's Land from the area designated as the Indian Territory, there is an implicit recognition of Indian title in the HBC Territory. The Proclamation also provided:

> that no private Person do presume to make any Purchase from the said Indians of any Lands reserved to the said Indians ... and in the case they [Indian Lands] shall lie within the limits of any Proprietary Government [HBC's Rupert's Land], they shall be purchased only for the Use and in the name of such Proprietaries, conformable to such Directions and Instructions as We or they shall think proper to give for the Purpose…[32]

Thus the Proclamation laid down a means for surrendering title in areas such as Rupert's Land. Legal scholarship has shown that the Proclamation applies to Rupert's Land; Slattery stated, "the document's main measures are not confined to the Indian Territory; they apply throughout British North

America."[33] The Royal Proclamation's provision to open up trade was not consistent with the monopoly terms granted by the Charter of 1670. The exclusion of Rupert's Land from the designated Indian Territory must be seen as an effort to accommodate the Proclamation's open trade provision with the existing HBC monopoly in Rupert's Land.

Aboriginal title as a legal doctrine means that Native people's rights have survived the advent of the Crown's sovereignty, but such rights may be limited, as Slattery noted, "insofar as these [rights] were incompatible with the Crown's ultimate title, or were subsequently modified by statute or other lawful acts."[34] The original customs and practices of Aboriginal people have been enmeshed in the politics and law of European sovereignty. Slattery has provided a lucid explanation for the reasoning behind the Crown's involvement in the surrender of Indian title:

> Even if we suppose that a discovering state gained an exclusive right against other European states to appropriate the region discovered and thereby gain territorial title, it does not necessarily follow that a subject of the discovering sovereign could not purchase private title from the native peoples and hold it under the sovereignty of the incoming monarch. Clearly a subject could not, under the principle, obtain international title to any portion of the discovered territory and set himself up as an independent potentate. But why could he not secure a private title? The answer must lie, not in the principle of discovery, but in the domestic law of the European state concerned. If that law stipulates that the sovereign is the sole source of private title for subjects settling in colonial acquisitions, then private purchases from native peoples are ruled out.[35]

Moreover, the concept of Aboriginal rights is not restricted to land rights but also includes Aboriginal "customary laws and governmental institutions."[36] The HBC territorial claims cannot be easily reconciled with Slattery's definition that Aboriginal title "imported full rights of possession and use."[37] For analytical purposes, the negotiations and legislative steps leading up to surrender of the HBC's Charter and the transfer of Rupert's Land to Canada should be considered by examining both the mercantile and the Aboriginal claims to the region. Such an approach does not concede the validity of claims made on the principle of discovery or argue that Rupert's Land was "legally vacant."[38]

Political and Economic Erosion of Hudson's Bay Company Rule

The fate of the Native inhabitants of Rupert's Land was closely tied in with proposals and schemes of railroad financiers. Even the geographical isolation of Rupert's Land could not protect the HBC's mercantile rights from laissez-faire thought and the export of British capital. In the 1840s people of mixed blood (both French- and English-speaking) challenged the HBC monopoly in Rupert's Land. By 1849, the HBC's monopoly in the Red River district had effectively ended. In the 1850s, English-speaking mixed bloods opposed the HBC's political rule, advocated Crown colony status for the Red River Settlement and made common cause with Canadian expansionists. The 1857 British parliamentary Select Committee on the HBC, established because of pressure from English-speaking mixed bloods and Canadian expansionists, and the need to consider the extension of the HBC's exclusive license to trade, provided no clear political direction for the region. The monopoly license to trade in those areas outside of Rupert's Land controlled by the HBC was not renewed. However, the HBC Charter remained a barrier for Canada's westward expansion, and a self-governing mixed-blood Crown colony was not realized.[39]

By 1863, a coalescing of various political and financial interests led to a buyout of the HBC. This put the HBC's Charter rights into the hands of those interested in colonizing the fertile belt.[40] Edward Watkin was the key player in promoting transcontinental railway and telegraph schemes, which required the acquisition of Rupert's Land. Watkin was heavily involved in the management of the Grand Trunk Railway, and was closely allied with the Duke of Newcastle, the influential colonial secretary. Rich outlined the interlocking nature of their political and economic objectives by 1861: "the statesmen and the railway magnate were of one mind on the need to complete the Intercolonial line and to reach out towards the Pacific with railways which would be a preliminary necessity to the union of all provinces and territories into 'one Great British America'."[41] A great deal of financial and political interest was generated by Watkin's plans to alleviate the existing railway financial problems by extending railways, telegraphs, or even wagon roads across the HBC's territory, thereby connecting British Columbia with the pre-Confederation Canadian provinces. A variety of commercial and political concerns, backed by influential individuals, supported Watkin's proposals: the North West Transportation Company, Grand Trunk Railway, Atlantic and Pacific Transit and Telegraph Company, and the London lobby of the British North American Association.[42]

From 1859 the HBC held the position that its monopoly could be bought out, but the imperial government would not purchase the HBC; mercantile interests were more than willing to give railway financiers access to Rupert's Land.[43] Concerning a proposal for a partial surrender of the fertile land and a right of way, HBC governor Berens responded: "If these gentlemen are so patriotic, why don't they buy us out?"[44] Watkin eventually agreed to Berens's price of £1.5 million for the HBC, although HBC stock was valued at £500,000. The real assets of the HBC were worth £1,081,000, but another £1 million was added to the actual worth of the HBC in order to account for its lands. The market price of a £100 share was £190, but annual profits were only £35,000 and the undervalued stock would make the dividend rate appear good. The buyout arrangement settled on the selling of the £100 old stock for £300, thereby raising the Company's stock to £1.5 million. The buyout also meant that the control of the HBC would pass to Watkin and his backers. Watkin managed the buyout of the HBC through the newly established International Financial Society (IFS). The old stock of £500,000 was raised to £1.2 million, and new stock was raised to £2 million through a public issue.[45] The details of this stock-watering have never been clear, and in 1869 Canadian government representatives described the situation with obvious frustration: "The stock of the old Company, worth in the market about £1,100,000, was bought up, and by some process which we are unable to describe, became £2,000,000."[46] Mitchell notes that IFS made a profit, and Watkin recalled that the IFS took "a profit to themselves and their friends who had taken the risk of so new and onerous an engagement."[47]

The IFS buyout of the HBC forebode a changing political economy for Rupert's Land. The takeover of the HBC had a furtive quality, and as Rich noted, Berens "did not even know distinctively who the parties were with whom he was negotiating."[48] Apparently, when the Duke of Newcastle learned of the takeover of the HBC he had "believed that a new era was about to open in the north-west, and the wild animals and fur traders [would] retreat before the march of 'European' settlers."[49] The new stockholders that bought into the reconstructed HBC were investing in land; the prospectus stressed that the Company lands would be opened up for European colonization and mining grants would be available.[50] Moreover, as a result of the IFS takeover, the HBC was now under the control of men whose priority was "to realize the values of the southern parts Rupert's Land rather than to manage a trade to the north."[51] The objectives of the IFS suggest the reasons for a financial interest in Rupert's Land: "undertaking, assisting, and participating in financial, commercial, and industrial operations, both in England and abroad, and both singly and in connection with other persons, firms, companies and corporations."[52] The directors of the IFS included directors of important English and European merchant banks. The

IFS's first purchase was the HBC, but it also financed railways, land companies, foreign banks and trading companies; indicative of this era of British capital exports, the IFS converted the public debt of Mexico.[53] At Red River the buyout, which occurred without consultation with the residents, created the belief among the fur-trade elite that "they had all been sold 'like dumb driven cattle'."[54] Nonetheless, the acquisition of the HBC by a modern financial enterprise did not result in either the expeditious transfer of Rupert's Land to Canada or the sudden displacement of fur trader by settler. A period of difficult negotiations followed.

Negotiating and Legislating the Transfer

Despite the fact that the new owners of the HBC wanted to realize a value on their assets through colonization and that Canadians wanted to annex the fertile belt, there was no quick resolution to the Company's territorial claims. The legal status of the Charter was still a block: the HBC could not promote colonization of land with unclear title, the imperial government could not initiate litigation against its own Charter, and the Canadians were unwilling to test in court their position that the Charter was invalid. Consequently, neither the HBC nor the Canadians could proceed with colonization plans. The opening up of western Canada required a negotiated agreement. The Colonial Office acted as an intermediary, but the imperial government would not assume any of the costs of compensating the Canadians for a buyout of HBC claims or assume the burden of administrative costs of a Crown colony at Red River. Negotiations dragged out between 1863 and 1868. The period between October 1868 and the end of March 1869 was crucial for affecting the transfer.

The HBC wanted a large cash payment, a large grant of land, and royalties from mineral wealth. The Company claimed that the land was worth a shilling per acre. Eventually the principle developed that the HBC interest in Rupert's Land would be accommodated by future revenues from land sales. By May 1868, the Company was holding out for one shilling per acre from land sold by the government and one quarter of all gold and silver revenues, although these revenues would cease once £1 million had been paid out. The HBC wanted an ongoing stake in land, asking for 6,000 acres around each post and 5,000 acres for each 50,000 acres disposed of by the government. The HBC also sought confirmation of land titles it had issued at the Red River Settlement, and it wanted no exceptional taxation of the fur trade. Before surrendering Rupert's Land, the HBC wanted to ensure a large cash payment, ongoing revenues from future development, and protection of its fur-trade operations. The Company's bargaining position was constrained by the new speculative shareholders. This group had bought in after the HBC was reconstructed and had expected £5 million for Rupert's Land.[55]

The imperial government, through the Colonial Office, favoured political union of British North America, but the Royal Charter of 1670 had to be respected. Newcastle's position only admitted that the HBC could expect compensation for its claim to Rupert's Land. He agreed with the appraisal of one shilling per acre but opposed the granting of large blocks of land; a negotiated settlement awaited Confederation. Confederation was not just a political idea, it sponsored a new economic strategy which sought a western hinterland for Ontario and a transcontinental railway. Certain legislative steps reflected the urgency to acquire Rupert's Land. The westward expansion of Canada was provided for in section 146 of the British North America Act 1867, since an address from the Canadian Parliament would "admit Rupert's Land and the North-western Territory, or either of them, in the Union, on such Terms … as the Queen thinks fit to approve…"[56] Canada followed up on section 146 with the Address of 1867, which argued that the transfer of the HBC territory "Would promote the prosperity of the Canadian people, and induce to the advantage of the whole Empire."[57] Furthermore, the Address of 1867 outlined the economic objective of union:

> That the colonization of the fertile lands of the Saskat-
> chewan, the Assiniboine and the Red River districts; the
> development of the mineral wealth which abounds in the
> region of the North-west; and the extension of commercial
> intercourse through the British possession in America from
> the Atlantic to the Pacific, are alike dependent on the estab-
> lishment of a stable government for the maintenance of law
> and order in the North-western Territories.[58]

The Canadian position argued that section 146 and the Address of 1867 were all that was required to bring about the transfer, after which the dominion government could legislate in both areas and the HBC's territorial claims to Rupert's Land could be decided in a Canadian court. This bargaining strategy was partially undermined when the British Parliament enacted the Rupert's Land Act of 1868. This act facilitated the transfer of Rupert's Land, but it also acknowledged that the Charter of 1670 had "granted or purported to be granted" land and rights to the HBC.[59] This act, upon reaching agreed terms, permitted the surrender of the HBC's Charter to the queen, and with an address from the Canadian Parliament, the queen would admit Rupert's Land into the Dominion. With the passage of the Rupert's Land Act, the problem was reduced to arriving at terms of surrender acceptable to the HBC.

The period between October 1, 1868, when George E. Cartier and William MacDougall were delegated to represent Canada at the negotiations, until the end of March 1869, entailed complicated, three-way negotiations. In the end, one of the largest real-estate deals in history was concluded. Colonial secretary Granville and his undersecretary, Sir Frederick Rogers, acted as intermediaries between the Canadian delegates and the governor of the HBC, the Earl of Kimberley (during this period, Northcote replaced Kimberley as governor). The HBC directors and the Canadian delegates negotiated from separate rooms but the purpose, unencumbered by politics, was clear. Rogers stated: "It is of course obvious that this negotiation for the purchase of the Hudson's Bay Company Territory is really between the seller and buyer, the Company and the Colony [Canada]..."[60] Little progress had been made by the close of 1868. The HBC's claim on a share of future revenues from land sales would have financially deprived the future government of the territory. The Colonial Office suggested that the HBC might receive the following terms: land around posts (between 500 and 6,000 acres, but only 3,000 acres in the fertile belt), one quarter of land receipts and one quarter of various gold and silver revenue up to £1 million, all previous land titles alienated by the HBC confirmed by the imperial government, grants of lots of not less than 200 acres in each township, no exceptional taxes on the HBC, liberty to carry on the trade, similar land grants for the posts in the North-Western Territory, the boundary between Canada and the HBC Territory to be defined once £1 million had been paid over, the selection of lots and payment of royalties and land receipts cease, and finally, lands set aside for Native Indians were not included in the payment of receipts from land sales.[61] At this point in the negotiations, the most significant suggestion, with long-term implications, was the granting of lots to the HBC in each township. With no large, up-front cash payment, this offer was unacceptable to the speculative stockholders.

The Canadian position was articulated in a letter from Cartier and MacDougall to Rogers in early February 1869. A long argument was made to support Canada's claim that the Charter did not cover the fertile belt and that the Charter itself was not valid, but they left it for the Colonial Office to determine "whether this Company is entitled to demand any payment whatever, for surrendering to the Crown that which already belong[ed] to it."[62] The Canadians suggested that the HBC's claim amounted to a "nuisance suit," but the HBC occupation of Rupert's Land obstructed "the progress of Imperial and Colonial policy, and put in jeopardy the sovereign rights of the Crown."[63] The principle of compensating the Company through future revenues was unacceptable.[64] Cartier and MacDougall provided calculations for fixing a monetary value to the territorial claims of the HBC. They argued that the HBC's assets had been worth £1,393,569 and that the buyout of the old company in 1863 had cost £1.5 million; thus "£106,431 was the amount which the new purchasers actually paid for the 'Landed Territory'."[65] This the Canadians were willing to concede, and they once again asked that the Address of 1867 be acted upon and that, at the very least, the North-Western Territory be transferred to Canada.

Clearly all three parties were far apart: the Canadian delegates offered a fixed payment of £100,000, the Company and the Colonial Office were considering various forms of ongoing compensation, and, as well, the HBC shareholders wanted a large cash payment. To resolve the years of dispute, Lord Granville proposed a series of terms to the HBC and the Canadians on an accept or reject basis. The essential terms provided the following: the HBC would surrender rights to Rupert's Land and other areas of British North America as directed by the Rupert's Land Act, Canada would pay the HBC £300,000 when Rupert's Land was transferred to the Dominion, the HBC would select blocks of land around posts, up to 50,000 acres (the number of acres selected at Red River was left blank), and would select, within fifty years, one-twentieth of the land set out for settlement in the area defined as the fertile belt, all land titles of land conferred by the HBC before March 8, 1869 would be confirmed, and the HBC would be free to carry on trade without exceptional taxation.[66] These terms were not proposed as a basis of negotiations, and a rejection by either party would lead Granville to recommend that the Judicial Committee of the Privy Council examine the rights of the Crown and the HBC.

Although the HBC attempted to effect some substantive changes, the governor and committee had displayed enough interest in the terms that a deal could be fashioned through face-to-face negotiations between the Canadians and the HBC. At this point the Colonial Office pulled out of the negotiations and the HBC and Canadian delegates effected an agreement, specifying more detailed terms in memoranda of March 22 and 29, 1869. The Memorandum of March 22 provided that the HBC would retain posts in the North-Western Territory, made a number of provisions for the HBC land around its posts, allowed the HBC to defer selected land in townships, established a charge for surveying HBC land, and held the Canadian government responsible for Indian claims. The Memorandum of March 29 allowed the HBC to select lots in townships adjacent to the north bank of the North Saskatchewan River and made it possible for the Canadian government to expropriate for public purposes land allocated to the HBC.[67]

The correspondence after Granville laid down the terms on March 9,

1869 elucidates some aspects of the HBC's strategy for dealing with the changes that would follow the transfer of Rupert's Land. Most of the points raised by Northcote were discussed in great length, and many became terms in the memoranda of March 22 and 29. The HBC attempted to increase its allocation of land from one-twentieth to one-tenth of the fertile belt but the Canadian delegates rejected this proposal. In keeping with a desire to be rid of its long-established social obligations to fur-trade society, the HBC unsuccessfully attempted to get the Canadian government to pay the salary of the bishop of Rupert's Land. Northcote also alluded to the HBC's desire for usufructuary rights:

> Regarding the Country lying outside the Fertile Belt as a hunting ground alone, we presume 1st that we shall be at liberty to hunt over it freely, and without being subject to any licenses[,] tax or other similar import [duties]—2nd That we shall be granted a title to our posts and to such joining land as may be necessary for their maintenance and for supplying pasture and wood—3rd That we shall be allowed to cut wood as we may require in any part of the Territory.[68]

Clearly, the HBC was attempting to protect the established land-use patterns following a change in political jurisdiction. The allusion to the idea that the area outside of the fertile belt would remain as a "hunting ground alone" is relevant to understanding the Aboriginal-title concept that developed during the transfer arrangements. Northcote also suggested that

> it would be for the interest of the Company and still more for that of Canada, that Canada should give us for a limited period some special control over the importations made into the hunting Country so as to enable us to keep spirits from the Indians.[69]

Again there is a reference to the idea of a hunting country. With this proposal the Company was intending to maintain its control over the fur-trade country.

By the end of March, a deal had been arranged which was acceptable to the parties responsible for negotiating the terms. Nonetheless, a number of legislative steps, some of which got bogged down, had to be taken, which, along with unexpected political activity by the population of Red River, meant that no quick transfer of Rupert's Land occurred. On April 9, 1869, a meeting of the HBC resolved "to surrender to Her Majesty's Government all this Company's territorial rights in Rupert's Land, and in any other part of British North America not comprised in Rupert's Land, Canada or British

Columbia."[70] There was considerable opposition from shareholders who had invested £2 million to a deal that returned only £300,000 and some vague prospects about potential returns from future land sales.[71] On May 20, 1869 the Company's solicitors prepared a Deed of Surrender. Canadian acceptance of the transfer arrangements were indicated by resolutions and an Address to the Queen on May 29 and 31, 1869. Some differences in wording between the HBC's Deed of Surrender and the terms listed in the Canadian 1869 Address to the Queen, the need for imperial legislation guaranteeing the loan for £300,000, and Canadian difficulties in arranging the financing delayed the planned date of transfer from October 1 to December 1, 1869.[72] Even still, the Rupert's Land Order was further delayed until June 23, 1870, since it had to wait for the provisional government of Louis Riel to accept the terms of union which had been negotiated with the Canadian government. The outcome of these negotiations was the Manitoba Act, section 34 of which acknowledged the deal made for transferring the HBC territorial claims, stating: "Nothing in this Act shall in any way prejudice or affect the rights or properties of the Hudson's Bay Company, as contained in the conditions under which that Company surrendered Rupert's Land to Her Majesty."[73] Thus, the arrangements made with the HBC were enclosed within the Canadian Constitution, beginning with section 146 of the British North America Act 1867 and closing with section 34 of the Manitoba Act, which was validated by the British North America Act 1871.

Traditionally, it has been assumed that tension existed between the HBC and Canadian expansionists, and that the transfer arrangements were hindered by the legacy of fur trader/settler conflict. From a political-economy perspective, the Deed of Surrender resolved the transfer of Rupert's Land harmoniously. In April 1869 Rogers wrote Northcote, conveying Granville's sentiment

> that no long period may elapse before the conditions of settlement thus accepted by the Company will be adopted by the Parliament of Canada, and that the transfer which Her Majesty will then be authorized to effect will prove a source of increasing prosperity both to the inhabitants of that Dominion and to the proprietors of the Hudson's Bay Company.[74]

The Rupert's Land Order stipulated a list of terms which were based on the terms laid out by Granville on March 9, 1869 and agreements made in the memoranda of March 22 and 29. As far as understanding the long-term situation of Natives and the prosperity of the HBC were concerned, the most

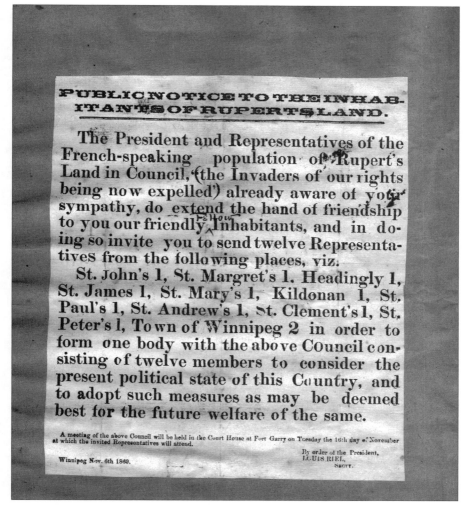

PUBLIC NOTICE TO THE INHAB-
ITANTS OF RUPERTS LAND.

The President and Representatives of the
French-speaking population of Rupert's
Land in Council, (the Invaders of our rights
being now expelled) already aware of your
sympathy, do extend the hand of friendship
to you our friendly Inhabitants, and in doing so invite you to send twelve Representatives from the following places, viz.

St. John's 1, St. Margret's 1. Headingly 1,
St. James 1, St. Mary's 1, Kildonan 1, St.
Paul's 1, St. Andrew's 1, St. Clement's 1, St.
Peter's 1, Town of Winnipeg 2 in order to
form one body with the above Council consisting of twelve members to consider the
present political state of this Country, and
to adopt such measures as may be deemed
best for the future welfare of the same.

A meeting of the above Council will be held in the Court House at Fort Garry on Tuesday the 16th day of November at which the invited Representatives will attend.

Winnipeg Nov. 6th 1869.

By order of the President,
LOUIS RIEL,
Secty.

"Public Notice to the Inhabitants of Ruperts [sic] Land," by Order of the President; Louis Riel, Secty. Winnipeg, November 6, 1869 (courtesy of the Glenbow Archives/LAC-4273-1).

crucial terms provided the following: a payment of £300,000 to the HBC, along with 50,000 acres of land around its posts, and over a 50-year period selection of one-twentieth of the lands of the townships surveyed in the fertile belt, titles conferred by the HBC before March 8, 1869 to be confirmed, and Indian claims for compensation for lands required for settlement were to be disposed of by the Canadian government.[75] Despite the protracted bargaining, the complementary backgrounds of some of the key decision makers contributed to a resolution of the difficult political and economic problems that the transfer of Rupert's Land required. In the early 1860s, Watkin and Newcastle worked closely together and pulled off a deal which Rich referred to as "machinations on behalf of the Grand Trunk, the Intercolonial and Transcontinental Railway."[76] The governors of the HBC between 1863 and 1874 had careers which included important positions with the state: Sir Edmund Walker Head had been governor general of Canada before taking over as governor of the HBC; the Earl of Kimberley (governor of the HBC from 1868 to 1869) had had a career in the Foreign Office and had been a member of the cabinet as Lord Privy Seal; and Sir Stafford H. Northcote, the Earl of Iddesleigh (governor from 1869 to 1874), had also been in the cabinet as president of the board of trade and secretary of state for India. Nor was the movement between the state and the HBC one way—after the transfer, Sir John A. Macdonald's government would look to the Company's experience for assistance in developing an Indian policy in the North-West.[77]

Indian Title and the Transfer of Rupert's Land

For the negotiators, the question of Aboriginal rights was never central to the surrender agreement, but Indian title entered the talks in several curious ways. For example, the Canadian delegates refer to the North-Western Territory as the Indian Territory.[78] This acknowledgment of Indian title is relevant to the problem of the geographical ambiguity of the Royal Proclamation of 1763. An aspect of Indian title was raised when proposals were made to appraise the Company's claim. Kimberley informed the Colonial Office that HBC officials

> also admit that it is proper that a similar exception [as with the lands for schools, roads or churches] should apply to land set apart as Indian reserves, on the understanding that these reserves will be made by Her Majesty's Government, as they are reinforced it is Its Graces' intentions they shall be, and that, if at any time before the million sterling is paid to the Company, such lands shall be used or granted for other purposes, it shall be liable to the payment of a shilling an acre in common with other land.[79]

The reference to Indian reserves indicates that the London committee of the HBC had anticipated the future direction of Indian policy. The fact that the HBC willingly offered to exempt Indian reserves from the estimates of its claim to Rupert's Land indicates that mercantile interests were attempting to stay well clear of any complications from Indian title. The Colonial Office agreed to this separation of lands from which the HBC could and could not obtain compensation:

> Such lands as Her Majesty's Government shall deem necessary to be set aside for the use of Native Indian population shall be reserved altogether from this arrangement, and the Company shall not be entitled to the payment of any share of receipts thereof, under previous Articles [stipulating compensation schemes], unless for such part, if any, of these lands as may be appropriated with the consent of the Crown to any other purposes, than that of benefit of the Indian Native.[80]

Indian lands were a unique category during the discussions of the principles and terms of compensation for the HBC claim.

Overall, the negotiations for the transfer did not take a hard look at Indian title or demonstrate much interest in Indian policy. On April 10, 1869, Granville notified the governor general that the proprietors of the HBC had accepted the terms of surrender, but most of this communique was directed at Indian policy and the expectations of Her Majesty's government. He urged the Canadian government to consider the HBC's relationship with Indians because "the Indian Tribes who form the existing population of this part of America have profited by the Company's rule."[81] He stated:

> They have been protected from some of the vices of civilization, they have been taught to some appreciable extent, to respect the laws and rely on the justice of the white man, and they do not appear to have suffered from any causes of extinction beyond those which are inseparable from their habits and their climate. I am sure that your Government will not forget the care which is due to those who must soon be exposed to new dangers, and in the course of settlement be dispossessed of the lands which they are used to enjoy as their own, or be confined within unwontedly narrow limits.[82]

Clearly, the colonial secretary had anticipated that the transfer of Rupert's Land would affect Indians, and foresaw the dispossession of their lands.

Granville did not let his concern for Indian interests distract from the negotiations. On April 10, 1869 he wrote:

> This question had not escaped my notice while framing the proposals which I laid before the Canadian Delegates and

the Governor of the Hudson's Bay Company. I did not however even then allude to it because I felt the difficulty of insisting on any definite conditions without the possibility of foreseeing the circumstances under which those conditions would be applied, and because it appeared to me wiser and more expedient to rely on the sense of duty and responsibility belonging to the Government and people of such a Country as Canada.[83]

By reducing Indian title to a sense of duty, the negotiations did not have to reconcile the two differing claims to Rupert's Land. During the negotiations, serious consideration of Indian title would have led to a comparison of the HBC claim to Rupert's Land and Indian entitlement. Clearly, the question of Indian title was not a mere oversight; there was a deliberate effort by the imperial government to confine Indian entitlement to a policy status.

With the transfer of Rupert's Land, the Aboriginal-title concept can be traced back to the Address of 1867. It called for the annexation of the territories and the resolution of the HBC claims in court. The question of Indian title was raised in the third term of the Address of 1867:

And furthermore that, upon the transference of the territories in question to the Canadian Government, the claims of the Indian tribes to compensation for lands required for purposes of settlement will be considered and settled in conformity with the equitable principles which have uniformly governed the British Crown in its dealings with the aborigines.[84]

The Canadian delegates reiterated the terms of the Address of 1867 during the negotiations and added that these three points "were the only terms and conditions which, in the opinion of the Canadian Parliament, it was expedient to insert in the Order in Council, authorized by the 146th section."[85] Clearly, the Canadian position acknowledged compensation for Indian title. Later the address of May 29 and 31, 1869 stated Canadian intentions:

That upon the transference of the territories in question to the Canadian Government it will be our duty to make adequate provision for the protection of the Indian tribes whose interests and well-being are involved in the transfer…[86]

Although this second address acknowledged the importance of the transfer to Indians, its definition of Indian interests really reflects Granville's policy recommendations of April 10, 1869 and not the commitment of the Address of 1867. In fact, this later address did not indicate the Aboriginal-title concept expressed by term 14 of the Deed of Surrender. A shift in emphasis from Indian legal claims to a protectionist policy occurred. The notion of compensation for a property right gave way to "care which is due."

Term 14 of the Deed of Surrender is often cited as recognition of Aboriginal rights. It stated:

> 14. Any claims of Indians to compensation for lands required for purposes of settlement shall be disposed of by the Canadian Government in communication with the Imperial Government; and the Company shall be relieved of all responsibility in respect of them.[87]

McNeil has considered some of the legal questions this provision entertains, such as what territory the term applies to, whether only land required for settlement could be traded for, and whether communication with the imperial government was required.[88] It is a difficult problem.

A deeper understanding of the intent of term 14 can be developed by considering its meaning within the context of the transfer negotiations; on its own, textual exegesis is insufficient. An interpretation of term 14 requires the use of extrinsic records. What is the origin of term 14? What party sponsored it? A consultation of extrinsic records is aided by an understanding of the fur trade. Clearly the term relieves the Company of any costs associated with Indian title, for there is no direct burden of Indian title on lands granted as HBC lands.[89] This concept of Aboriginal title did not enter into the talks until the face-to-face negotiations between the HBC and the Canadian delegates, appearing only after the Colonial Office ceased to participate actively as an intermediary. Moreover, Granville clearly stated that he decided not to raise Indian claims in the March 9 list of terms, and he did not raise the issue of Indian interests until April 10, 1869. Since the imperial government was not directly responsible for term 14, either the Canadians or the HBC sponsored it—possibly both parties initiated different aspects of it. As far as Native interests were affected directly by the transfer negotiations, the imperial government had abjured its responsibilities for the Indian peoples.

Other documents elucidate the concept of Aboriginal title that emerged during the transfer talks. Drafts of the Memorandum of March 22, 1869 were found in the HBC London correspondence with Her Majesty's government (see Figure 2). The correspondence leading up to the memoranda of March 22 and 29 contains considerable discussion about the details of various terms. Term 14 is not expanded upon in this record; apparently, neither party committed to paper an argument on the issue of Indian claims.

However, the draft of term 14 (term 8 of the Memorandum of March 22,

1869) indicates that it went through two stages before the final wording was set down (Figure 2). The first version reads:

> It is understood that any arrangements which should be made for the satisfaction of Indian claims on the land shall be made by the Canadian Govt. in communication with the Colonial Office, and that the Company shall not be considered to be responsible for them.

In this version the Canadian government acknowledged sole responsibility for Indian title. Only one change is made between the first and second version. The second version reduces the commitment to Indian title; "maybe necessary" is substituted for "should be made." Between these drafts (Figure 2) and

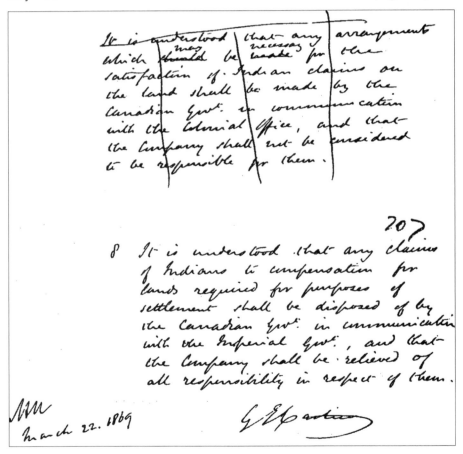

Figure 2. Draft versions of Term 8, Memorandum of March 22, 1869. Source: HBCA, A.13/16/3, ff. 206–207.

the final version used in the Memorandum of March 22, 1869 some important rewording occurred. The idea of Indian title is tied to the concept of compensation; thus, "satisfaction of Indian claims on the land" is substituted for "claims of Indians ... for lands required for the purposes of settlement." This change in wording indicates there was a conscious effort to link Indian compensation to a specific change in land use. Another change in wording substituted the imperial government for the Colonial Office. The final change broadened the Company's expectations in the post-1870 period. The use of "them" is ambiguous, possibly meaning "compensation" or "Indians"—or both. The indirect expression "shall not be considered" is replaced with the more direct "shall be relieved." The term "all responsibility" broadens the disengagement of the HBC from any obligations to Indians.

These drafts of term 14 provide no direct indication of which party desired a term on Aboriginal title in the Memorandum of March 22. Clearly the HBC gained, and in the post-1870 period it reduced its social obligations to Natives, which it subsequently argued were a government responsibility.[90] It seems unlikely that the Canadians felt a need to indicate their intentions towards Indian claims. Their intentions were already outlined in the Address of 1867, and certainly the imperial government did not force the Canadians to commit to Indian claims. In fact, Granville's correspondence of April 10, 1869 makes an argument for a protectionist Indian policy, and he does not seem to be aware of term 14. While it is not entirely clear how this term was arrived at, the HBC benefited. Ultimately, term 14 may have had the effect of reconciling the ambiguous HBC claim to Rupert's Land with Indian title. The text of this term in itself does not provide an obvious meaning.

Conclusion and Retrospect

The transfer of Rupert's Land in 1870 marked a fundamental shift in the nature of Indian/white relations. Under HBC rule, the relationship between Indians and whites was primarily economic. The relationship became largely political with the decline of the fur trade and because the recognition of Aboriginal title resulted in treaties between Indians and the Canadian state. In April 1869, colonial secretary Granville had communicated the "expectations of Her Majesty's Government," not the least of which was that the responsibilities for the Indian population were to shift from the HBC to the Canadian government. On the question of responsibility, Kent McNeil has considered the difficulty of a legal interpretation of the expression "equitable principles," wording used in the Address of 1867. He suggests that "although the requirement is that the principles rather than the settlements be equitable, it is suggested that an application of equitable principles should lead to an equitable result."[91] The outcome of the settlement of HBC claims could provide a comparative reference for determining whether Indians received "equitable results." How does the compensation that was paid to the HBC compare with the compensation negotiated for Natives?

The IFS takeover of the HBC in 1863 fundamentally changed the society that had existed in the fur-trade country. The Rupert's Land Order was the first step towards dispossession of Native people's lands. In a laconic fashion, the Deed of Surrender acknowledged Indian title, but the two claims to Rupert's Land were not given equal consideration. In 1869 and 1870, the HBC's claim to territorial rights was given priority, and the compensation that the HBC received was significant. Whether term 14 of the Deed of Surrender is a weak recognition of a property right or whether the wording should have reflected inherent rights has not been an historical debate during the last 120 years. The legal strength of the Aboriginal title acknowledged by term 14 was not significant in determining the extent of compensation. In reality, the HBC had more economic power, and it was therefore able to extract greater compensation for its claim. Yet term 14 and the Address of 1867 are a significant counterbalance to the protectionist policy thrusts of the Address of 1869.

Native peoples never gave much credence to the Company's claim to Rupert's Land. When the state eventually dealt with Aboriginal title, knowledge of the deal made between Canada and the HBC complicated the efforts to establish the Canadian state in the North-West. Louis Riel, president of a provisional government that represented the general interests of the Red River population, and more particularly the mixed-blood middle class, stated: "Again, on a late occasion they tried to sell us. There never was a parallel case. A Company of strangers, living beyond the ocean, had the audacity to attempt to sell the people of the soil."[92] Riel specifically objected to the term which granted one-twentieth of the lands of the surveyed townships and he argued that "We in this settlement must get control of all the lands in the North-West."[93] Essentially, he objected to the basis of the surrender: "the transfer of country should be carried on between Canada and the people of Red River and not between Canada and the Company."[94] Opposition to the terms of the surrender were not confined to the mixed bloods at Red River. During treaty talks, Indians made government treaty negotiators aware of the fact that they disputed the HBC's claim to Rupert's Land and that they wanted the £300,000 that had been paid to the HBC. The HBC's claim to Rupert's Land was a major issue at the Treaty 4 talks in 1874; an Indian by the name of The Gambler stated, "The Company have stolen our land. ... I hear it is true."[95] Moreover, he wanted to restrict the Company's position: "I want them to remain here to have nothing but the trade... The Indians want the Company to keep at their post and nothing beyond."[96] The Native perspective of their rights did not allow for HBC claims to territory.

Indian title was not ignored. After recognizing the HBC claims, the Canadian state turned its attention to Native claims. Those known as Métis or "halfbreeds" were dealt with by issuing land and money scrip on an individual basis. Métis scrip quickly passed into the domain of land speculators, and thus public or Crown lands which still had the burden of a Métis claim to Indian title passed into the hands of a commercial elite. This approach to the Métis neither satisfied the legal aspects of Aboriginal title nor provided them with the means to adjust to a changing economy. Treaties with Indian tribes were the most important mechanism for dealing with Aboriginal title. The terms of these treaties varied, but the essential compensation provided by them included land for reserves, subsistence rights, annuities amounting to $5 per person, treaty supplies to support subsistence activities, and relief during deprivation. Yet Granville's expectation that Indian land interests would not "be confined within unwontedly narrow limits" was not borne out. Small reserves, unfulfilled treaty land entitlements, reserve surrenders, pass laws and the imposition of game and fish protection legislation in opposition to treaty and Aboriginal rights had the effect of confining Indians. They were prevented from exercising some of their rights. Unlike the HBC, Indian claims were not compensated by future revenues from land sales. Basically, the terms of the treaties allowed only a bare survival for Indians. Retrospective views by Native leaders indicate that the surrender was a turning point in the history of western Canada. In their submission to the Ewing Commission of 1935, Malcolm Norris and James Brady began by stating: "We will undertake to show the depths of poverty to which the Métis people have been reduced since the surrender of Rupert's Land."[97]

During the transfer arrangements between 1863 and 1870, two interrelated processes were at work. The legal and legislative processes permitted a reorientation of the political economy of Rupert's Land, but they were preceded by a change in the ownership of the HBC. Hence the importance of railroad financiers to the Rupert's Land transfer. Eventually, the settler replaced the fur trader, but the owners of the HBC realized their interest in the fertile belt. Between 1905 and 1922, the Company's dividend rate ranged from 20% to 50%.[98] These large dividends were supported by land sales. Although Native peoples were kept at a subsistence level, the HBC accumulated capital. Between 1891 and 1930 the HBC's land earnings netted profits of $96,366,021, a far cry from the £2 million invested in 1863.[99] Ultimately,

HBC land sales were greater than the £1 million that the Colonial Office had agreed to in 1869 as the value of the HBC's claim to Rupert's Land. The actual amount of land granted is another measure of the compensation due to these two claims to Rupert's Land. In the case of Manitoba, the Department of the Interior calculated that by 1930, some 559,301 acres had been set aside for Indians (2.6% of the land that had passed from the Crown), but 1,279,965 acres had been granted to the HBC (6.1% of the land that had passed from the Crown).[100] The outcome of these very different claims was not equitable.

The complexity of Canada's acquistion of the HBC territory reflected the interplay of political economy and law. As the history of the Rupert's Land transfer demonstrates, Aboriginal title is not only a relevant approach to understand pressing legal issues, it also provides new avenues to interpret Canadian history.

Notes

This article first appeared in *Prairie Forum* 17, no. 2 (1992): 225–50.

This article is a revised version of a paper presented to the 26th Congress of the International Geographical Union entitled "Aboriginal Title, Indian Treaties and Halfbreed Scrip: The Political Economy of Changing Colonial Relations in Rupertsland," Sydney, Australia, August 1988. I would like to acknowledge the assistance I received from the staff of the Hudson's Bay Company Archives. Keith Bigelow, Department of Geography, University of Saskatchewan, provided cartographic assistance. I would also like to thank Peter Kulchyski, Winona Stevenson, John Thornton, Jim Waldram and Norm Zlotkin for feedback on this topic; the interpretation is my responsibility.

1. This calculation includes the Arctic islands, which were transferred officially in 1880. Arctic islands outside of the Hudson Bay drainage were not part of the HBC territory. Rupert's Land, which corresponded to the drainage of the Hudson Bay basin, amounts to 1,490,000 square miles. The Arctic and Pacific drainage referred to as the North-West Territory (induding the Arctic islands) totals 1,406,255 square miles. These data were derived from Canada, *The National Atlas of Canada* (Ottawa: Department of Energy, Mines and Resources, Information Canada and Macmillan Company, 1974).

2. For example, Trotter did not consider the HBC's negotiations with Canada and he made no reference to Indian title in the transfer. Reginald George Trotter, *Canadian Federation: Its Origins and Achievement: A Study in Nation Building* (London: J.M. Dent and Sons, 1924).

3. On the term "aboriginal title," Rich simply stated "and the Canadians agreed that the Company should be exempt from responsibilities for claims by Indians who alleged that they owned the lands." E.E. Rich, *The History of the Hudson's Bay Company* (London: The Hudson's Bay Record Society, 1959), 88 and 89. Morton's treatment of the terms of the transfer are also cursory, see Arthur S. Morton, *A History of the Canadian West to 1870–71*, 2nd ed. (edited by Lewis G. Thomas) (Toronto: University of Toronto Press and University of Saskatchewan, 1973). Giraud's encyclopedic study of the Métis paid little attention to the surrender. See Marcel Giraud, *The Métis in the Canadian West* (translated by George Woodcock) (Edmonton: University of Alberta Press, 1986).

4. An important exception is Arthur J. Ray, *The Canadian Fur Trade in the Industrial Age* (Toronto: University of Toronto Press, 1990). Ray's research on the business strategies of

the HBC in 1871, relations between the state and HBC in the immediate post-treaty period, and Native and HBC relations are relevant to any appreciation of Native history following the transfer of Rupert's Land.

5. Although Narvey's research is a major study on aboriginal title in Rupert's Land, his discussion of the terms of surrender is laconic, see Kenneth M. Narvey, "The Royal Proclamation Of 7 October 1763, the Common Law and Native Rights to Land Within the Territory Granted to the Hudson's Bay Company," *Saskatchewan Law Review* 38, no. 1 (1973–74): 123–233. See also Kent McNeil, "Native Rights and the Boundaries of Rupert's Land and the North-Western Territory," *Studies in Aboriginal Rights* No. 4 (Saskatoon: University of Saskatchewan Native Law Centre, 1982) and Kent McNeil "Native Claims in Rupert's Land and the North-Western Territory: Canada's Constitutional Obligations," *Studies in Aboriginal Rights* No. 5 (Saskatoon: University of Saskatchewan Native Law Centre, 1982).

6. Brian Slattery, "The Hidden Constitution: Aboriginal Rights in Canada," *American Journal of Comparative Law* 32 (1984): 363.

7. The "Order of Her Majesty in Council admitting Rupert's Land and the North-Western Territory into the Union," June 23, 1870, is printed in E.H. Oliver, *The Canadian North-West: Its Early Development and Legislative Records*, 2 vols. (Ottawa: Government Printing Bureau, 1914 and 1915), 939–63. A handwritten manuscript of the Rupert's Land Order can be found in the Provincial Archives of Manitoba, Hudson's Bay Company Archives (hereafter HBCA), A.13/16/5. A galley proof of this address can be found in A.13/16/5, and a printed copy of this address in A.12/L 121/1.

8. The term "Aboriginal-title concept" used in this article refers to an interpretation deriving explicitly from the documents transferring Rupert's Land. Hence the published and unpublished documents from the negotiations which transferred Rupert's Land to Canada are necessary sources.

9. Memorandum, "Details of Agreement between Delegates of the Government of the Dominion, and the Directors of the Hudson's Bay Company," March 22, 1869, Oliver, *Canadian North-West*, 950.

10. Found in Rupert's Land Order, ibid., 959.

11. Brian Slattery, "Understanding Aboriginal Rights," *Canadian Bar Review* 66 (1987): 727–83.

12. During Treaty 3 and 4 talks, Indian opposition to the terms of the transfer were expressed. See Alexander Morris, *The Treaties of Canada* (1880; Toronto: Coles Publishing, 1979), 73, 99–106.

13. Brian Slattery, "Ancestral Lands, Alien Laws: Judicial Perspectives on Aboriginal Title," *Studies in Aboriginal Rights* No. 2 (Saskatoon: University of Saskatchewan Native Law Centre, 1983).

14. McNeil, "Native Claims," 13–21.

15. Canada, *Sessional Papers*, 1869, no. 25, Report of Delegates appointed to negotiate for the acquisition of Rupert's Land and the North-West Territory, pp. i–ii, 1–39 (hereafter Delegates' Report).

16. *R. v. Sioui*, [1990] 1 S.C.R. at 1049–50. This judgement is also published in Native Studies Review 6, no. 2 (1990): 151–93. On the question of extrinsic evidence see Franklin S. Gerber and Peter W. Hutchins, "Introduction: The Marriage of History and Law in R. v. Sioui," *Native Studies Review* 6, no. 2 (1990): 115–30.

17. McNeil, "Native Claims," 31, citing *Hamlet of Baker Lake v. Minister of Indian Affairs and Northern Development*.

18. For an important discussion of the HBC's social and economic obligations to Natives see, Arthur J. Ray, "Periodic Shortage, Native Welfare, and the Hudson's Bay Company, 1670–1930," in Shepard Krech III (ed.), *The Subarctic Fur Trade: Native Social and Economic Adaptations* (Vancouver: University of British Columbia Press, 1984), 1–20. For a sense of change following the transfer of Rupert's Land see, Arthur J. Ray, 'The Decline of Paternalism in the Hudson's Bay Company Fur Trade, 1870–1945," in Rosemary E. Ommer (ed.), *Merchant Credit and Labour Strategies in Historical Perspective* (Fredericton: Acadiensis Press, 1990), 188–202; and Ray, *The Canadian Fur Trade*, 30–49, 199–221.

19. "The Royal Charter Incorporating the Hudson's Bay Company, 1670," Oliver, *Canadian North-West*, 146.

20. Ibid., 136.

21. Ibid., 137.

22. The Charter was repetitious on this point, stating "WE HAVE given ... together with all the lands and territories upon" the basin and made the HBC "the true and absolute lords and proprietors of the same territory..." and again "TO HAVE, HOLD, possess and enjoy the said territory..." It granted resource rights, such as "the fishing of all sorts of fish, whales, sturgeons, and all the other royal fishes in the seas, bays, inlets and rivers within the premises, and the fish therein taken, together with the royalty of the sea upon the coasts within the limits aforesaid, and all mines royal, as well discovered as not discovered, of gold, silver, gems and precious stones..." Furthermore, the Charter granted to the HBC "all lands, islands, territories, plantations, forts, fortifications, factories or colonies, where the said Company's factories and trade are or shall be..." Ibid., 143–44, 149.

23. The clearest example of this is the Selkirk Treaty of 1817, which acknowledged Indian title so that agricultural settlement of Assiniboia could proceed.

24. To the extent that Métis free traders were prosecuted in courts in Assiniboia, some legal consideration of the Charter rights occurred. The trial of Guillaume Sayer in 1849 was something of a legal victory for the Métis, because no penalty was imposed.

25. HBCA, A.3917, fo. 310.

26. Cumming and Mickenberg provided a limited definition of aboriginal rights stating: "are those property rights which inure to Native people by virtue of their occupation upon certain lands from time immemorial." See Peter A. Cumming and Neil H. Mickenberg, *Native Rights in Canada*, 2nd ed. (Toronto: The Indian-Eskimo Association of Canada and General Publishing Co., 1972), 13. Increasingly, Aboriginal rights are defined as inherent rights.

27. Slattery, "Hidden Constitution," 369.

28. Ibid.

29. Ibid., 370.

30. Royal Proclamation 7th of October 1763 (hereafter, Royal Proclamation), excerpted in Cumming and Mickenberg, *Native Rights in Canada*, 292.

31. Ibid., 291.

32. Ibid., 291–92.

33. Slattery, "Hidden Constitution," 370. For a very detailed account of Rupert's Land and the Royal Proclamation, see Narvey, "Royal Prodamation and Common Law."

34. Slattery, "Hidden Constitution," 387.

35. Slattery, "Ancestral Lands," 37.

36. Slattery, "Hidden Constitution," 373.

37. Ibid.

38. Changes in international law, which have a bearing on aboriginal title, are beyond the scope of this artide. See Brian Slattery, "Aboriginal Sovereignty and Imperial Claims," in Frank Cassidy (ed.), *Aboriginal Self-Determination* (Lantzville, BC: Oolichan Books, and Halifax: Institute for Research on Public Policy, 1991): 197–217. On the question of inherent Aboriginal rights, see Michael Asch and Patrick Macklem, "Aboriginal Rights and Canadian Sovereignty: An Essay on *R. v. Sparrow*," *Alberta Law Review* 29, no. 2 (1991): 498–517.

39. For background on this period of instability see Morton, *A History of the Canadian West*, 802–69; John S. Galbraith, "The Hudson's Bay Company Under Fire, 1847–62," *Canadian Historical Review* 30, no. 4 (1949): 322–35; and Elaine Allan Mitchell, "Edward Watkin and the Buying-out of the Hudson's Bay Company," *Canadian Historical Review* 34, no. 3 (1953): 219–44.

40. This was a prairie/parkland belt which was deemed to have adequate moisture for agriculture. The area south of the fertile belt was thought to be too arid.

41. Rich, *History of the Hudson's Bay Company*, 826.

42. A number of individuals had overlapping interests. Some of the colonial and imperial connections to Watkin included: Thomas Barring (banker), Robert Benson (London investment house and North-West Transportation Co.), Viscount Bury (North-West Transportation Co.), R.W. Crawford (Crawford, Colvin and Co.), George Carr Glyn (Glyn Mills and Co.), George Grenfall Glyn (North West Transit Co.). The British North American Association included: Howe, Tilley, Barring, Crawford and Benson. For details, see Rich, *History of the Hudson's Bay Company*, and Mitchell, "Edward Watkin."

43. Galbraith, "Hudson's Bay Company Under Fire," 333.

44. Rich, *History of the Hudson's Bay Company*, 832.

45. For details see, Mitchell, "Edward Watkin"; and Rich, *History of the Hudson's Bay Company*, 816–49.

46. Delegates' Report (Cartier and MacDougall to Rogers, February 8, 1869), 19.

47. Mitchell, "Edward Watkin," 241; and Trotter, *Canadian Federation*, 275.

48. Rich, *History of the Hudson's Bay Company*, 835.

49. Delegates' Report (Cartier and MacDougall to Rogers, February 8, 1869), 19.

50. Rich, *History of the Hudson's Bay Company*, 841.

51. Ibid., 848.

52. Ibid., 836.

53. Ibid.

54. Joseph James Hargrave, *Red River* (1877; n.p.: 1971), 299.

55. For details of the negotiations, see Rich, *History of the Hudson's Bay Company*.

56. Section 146, British North America Act 1867, Oliver, *Canadian North-West*, 871.

57. "Address to Her Majesty the Queen from the Senate and House of Commons of the Dominion of Canada," December 16 and 17, 1867, ibid., 945.

58. Ibid.

59. Rupert's Land Act, 1868, 31–32 Victoria, Chapter 105, ibid., 937.

60. HBCA, A.13/16/2, Rogers to Northcote, February 7, 1869, fo. W.

61. HBCA, A.8/12, Adderley to Kimberley, December 1, 1868, ff. 38–40.

62. Delegates' Report (Cartier and MacDougall to Rogers, February 8, 1869), 23.

63. Ibid., 24.

64. Ibid., 25. Cartier and MacDougall used the rate of investment in Upper Canada to assess the payout of £1 million and asked "What is the present value of an annuity of £3,575 per annum for 280 years?"

65. Ibid., 26. In another calculation the Canadian delegates indicated that the marketvalue of the stock had fallen to £1,350,000 which was "£43,569 less than the value ... in 1863, of the Company's assets, exclusive of the 'landed territory'."

66. Delegates' Report (Granville to Northcote, March 9, 1869), 32. The terms also defined the fertile belt and disposed some of the telegraph material the HBC had purchased.

67. Memorandum of March 22, 1869 and Memorandum of March 29, 1869, Oliver, *Canadian North-West*, 949–51.

68. HBCA, A.8/12, Northcote to Cartier, March 22, 1869, fo. 95.

69. Ibid., fo. 69

70. HBCA, A.13/16/4, Northcote to Rogers, April 10, 1869, fo. 207.

71. Arthur J. Ray, "Adventures at the Crossroads," *The Beaver* 62, no. 2 (1986): 4–12.

72. HBCA, A.13/16/5; A.13/16/6.

73. The Manitoba Act, 1870, 33 Victoria, Chapter 3, Oliver, *Canadian North-West*, 970.

74. HBCA, A.13/16/4, Rogers to Northcote, April 17, 1869, fo. 292.

75. Rupert's Land Order, Oliver, *Canadian North-West*, 941–44.

76. Rich, *History of the Hudson's Bay Company*, 848.

77. See Ray, *The Canadian Fur Trade*, 4–5.

78. Delegates' Report (Cartier and MacDougall to Rogers, February 8, 1869), 21, 23.

79. HBCA, A.8/12, Kimberley to Adderly, October 27, 1868, fo. 32.

80. Ibid., Adderly to Kimberley, December 1, 1868, ff. 39–40.

81. Delegates' Report (Granville to Governor General of Canada, Sir John Young, April 10, 1869), 38.

82. Ibid. On the question of Indian policy, Granville stated: "That Government I believe has never sought to evade its obligations to those whose uncertain rights and rude means of living are contracted by the advance of civilized men. I am sure that they will not be so in the present case, but that the old inhabitants of the Country will be treated with such forethought and consideration as may preserve them from the dangers of the approaching change, and satisfy them of the friendly interest which their new Governors feel in their welfare."

83. Ibid. There is nothing in this letter to suggest that the colonial secretary was aware of term 8 of the Memorandum of March 22, 1869.

84. Address of 1867, Oliver, *Canadian North-West*, 946.

85. Delegates' Report (Cartier and MacDougall to Rogers, February 8, 1869), 17.

86. Address of 1869, in Rupert's Land Order, Oliver, *Canadian North-West*, 954.

87. The Deed of Surrender, in Rupert's Land Order, ibid., 958.

88. McNeil, "Native Claims," 21–25.

89. In a legal opinion for the HBC's land commissioner in 1917, S.J. Rothwell cited correspondence from Donald A. Smith in the 1870s which suggest that a retrospective viewpoint of the HBC's intentions were to safeguard its land grants from Indian We. But Rothwell also stated: "The correspondence between the Company and the Government leading up to the surrender indicates that at that time there were a great many Indians under the care of the Company and it was necessary that provision be made in the surrender for the compensation of the claims of the Indian to the lands required for

settlement." Rothwell connected the HBC's social and economic responsibilities to the legal title of Indians. HBCA, RG2/2/109, fo. 14.

90. See the Company's position in the Library and Archives Canada (LAC), RG 10, vol. 3708, file 19,502 pt. 1. The shift in responsibility from the HBC to the Canadian government is discussed in Frank Tough, "Buying Out The Bay: Aboriginal Rights and the Economic Policies of the Department of Indian Affairs after 1870," in David R. Miller, Carl Beal, James Dempsey and R. Wesley Heber (eds.), *The First Ones: Readings in Indian/Native Studies* (Piapot Reserve #75, Saskatchewan: Saskatchewan Indian Federated College Press, 1992), 398–408.

91. McNeil, "Native Claims," 21.

92. Riel argued this position in "The Proceedings of the Convention, February 3 to February 5, 1870," in W.L. Morton (ed.), *Manitoba: The Birth of a Province* (Winnipeg: Manitoba Record Society Publications, 1984), 20.

93. Ibid.

94. Ibid., 21.

95. Morris, *The Treaties of Canada*, 101.

96. Ibid., 110–11. A comparison of Morris's presentation of the terms of surrender of the HBC claim to Rupert's Land before the Indians assembled at Qu'Appelle in September 1874 with the documentary evidence indicates that either the lieutenant governor was unaware of the actual terms or he knowingly misled the Indians.

97. Cited by Murray Dobbin, *The One-And-A-Half Men* (Vancouver: New Star Books, 1981), 89.

98. Douglas MacKay, *The Honourable Company*, 2nd ed. (Toronto: McClelland and Stewart, 1949), 349.

99. HBCA, A.1 2/L 77; A.86/1-11; and RG 1, series 1. This figure is derived at from annual data between 1891–92 and 1930–31. It is based on balance statements showing net revenue, deposits to the capital reserves, and net profits.

100. LAC, RG 33/52, vol. 1, file 7. In fact more land was set aside as road allowances (997,244 acres) than for Indians.

Resistance and "Rebellion"

14. "Conspiracy and Treason": The Red River Resistance from an Expansionist Perspective

Doug Owram

In the autumn of 1869 a group of Métis under the leadership of Louis Riel forcibly prevented William McDougall from entering Red River. McDougall was Canada's governor designate for this territory, which was expected to soon become a part of the Dominion, and the Métis refusal to let him enter marked the beginning of what was to become known as the Red River resistance. It would take nearly nine months, the creation of a new province and the presence of a military force before the North West truly became a part of Canada. Through the intervening period the Métis continued by force of arms to assert their right to be consulted on their own future, while the Conservative government of John A. Macdonald sought to repair past carelessness and to find a compromise solution. Standing between these two parties and working to prevent any agreement was an informal coalition made up of expansionists and nationalists in Ontario and the pro-annexation "Canada Party" in Red River.

History has not been kind to these men who were most extreme in their opposition to the Métis. They have been assigned much of the blame both for the outbreak of the rebellion and for increasing the problems in the way of a solution.[1] Even more seriously, they have been accused of bringing unnecessary racial and religious prejudices to the surface, thereby undermining the understanding between French and English Canada that was essential to national unity.[2] Descriptions of their tragi-comic military efforts in Red River and their paranoid rhetoric in Ontario have ensured that the image presented to successive generations has been of a dangerous and slightly ludicrous group of fanatics.

Much of the criticism is justified. The economic designs of Canadians on the Red River settlement and their arrogance in assuming the right to impose these designs encouraged the Métis resistance to the transfer. Emotional

meetings in the East and attempts to arrest delegates from Red River aggravated an already tense situation and brought forth the spectre of racial conflict. Even if the main points of these traditional interpretations are accepted,
however, two questions arise. First, what provoked these men to take such an
extreme position? What distinguished the analysis of men like George
Brown, Charles Mair and John Christian Schultz from that of other English
Canadians, including John A. Macdonald, who saw the Métis action as a
political problem and acted accordingly? Second, how was it that a rebellion
on the banks of the Red River became a major threat to French-English relations in Canada? French Canadians had never closely identified the Métis
with their own culture, and when the rebellion began the French-language
press differed little in its reactions from its English counterpart.[3] Yet within a
few months the resistance of the Métis became a symbol to many in both
French and English Canada of their own position in the young Dominion.

In order to answer these questions, it is useful to view the Red River
resistance through the eyes of those who most opposed it. In retrospect it is
apparent that many of their attitudes were the result of misconceptions and
prejudice. Nevertheless, given the assumption from which they operated,
their actions were fairly consistent throughout. They were motivated not by
a vindictive desire to obliterate a weaker culture in the West, but by a fear
that others were manipulating these people for conspiratorial ends. They felt
it their duty to unmask the true conspiracy that lay behind Métis actions. In
attempting to do so, they transformed and aggravated the whole nature of
the rebellion.

The reaction of those who took the hardest line during the rebellion was
largely predetermined by their enthusiastic acceptance of the twelve-year
campaign for annexation of the North West to Canada. Since 1857 groups in
English Canada had been calling for the immediate transfer of the Hudson's
Bay Territories, and those who figured prominently in the events of 1869-
1870 were among the most ardent supporters of this movement.[4] From the
beginning, Canadian expansionism had been predicated on the assumption
that the inhabitants of the Hudson's Bay Territories were unhappy with
Company rule. The petitions presented to the Colonial Secretary by
Alexander Isbister in the 1840s and the resistance of the Métis to Hudson's
Bay Company rule in the Sayer trial had been factors in stirring Canadian
interest.[5] By 1857, when the expansionist movement in Canada came into its
own, the links between Canadian desires and supposed discontent in Red
River had grown even stronger. The assumption had developed that there
was a community of interest between Canada and Red River.[6] It was truly, if
conveniently, believed that, as Isbister said, "the unanimous desire of the

inhabitants of the Hudson's Bay Territories is to have the entire region annexed to Canada."[7]

During the expansionist campaign this belief was reinforced by numerous petitions from Red River. The pattern was set in the summer of 1857 when a petition with some 574 signatures was sent to Canada praying for the development of the region.[8] From then until 1869 numerous other petitions flowed eastward to Canadian and British authorities. Resolutions such as the one of January 1867 asking "to be united with the Grand Confederation of British North America" encouraged the idea that the extension of Canada's frontier was a two-way process.[9] Of course, a good many of these petitions were of a questionable nature, having the support of but a relatively small segment of Red River's population. Expansionists were not aware of this, however, and few in Red River who opposed the resolutions made their concerns known in the East. Canadian expansionists had neither reason nor the desire to doubt their authenticity, and the impression thus continued to grow that the settlers of Red River wanted annexation.

Actively encouraging this assumption were those expansionists who migrated west in the wake of the expansionist campaign and settled in Red River. They were to become known both by contemporaries and by history as the "Canada Party." This group's membership was succinctly defined in 1869 as being "those who favor annexation to Canada."[10] These individuals, centred around the young Dr. John Christian Schultz, had been the force behind many of the petitions that had originated in Red River. It is not surprising that these men, having made a material and personal commitment to the development of the North West, attempted to encourage annexation.

The Canada Party had an especially strong influence in shaping the Canadian image of Red River because it controlled the *Nor'Wester*, the only newspaper published in the North West. In 1859 two English-born journalists, William Buckingham and William Coldwell, arrived in Red River from Canada. Both had previously worked for George Brown at the *Globe*, and when they moved west they took not only their type and their practical experience in journalism but also a set of attitudes formed in Canadian expansionist circles. They founded Red River's first newspaper in order to further spread their expansionist views. Over the next several years the editorship of this paper would change hands many times, but it would remain a consistent advocate of the idea of Canadian expansion.

It is questionable whether the *Nor'Wester* did much to encourage support for Canada among the inhabitants of Red River. The *Nor'Wester*, like the Canada Party itself, proved a disruptive addition to the already unstable social structure of Red River in the 1860s and may have served to alienate rather than promote support for annexation to Canada.[11] Even if such was the case, the influence of the *Nor'Wester* on Canadian expansion cannot be discounted. As every editor of the paper sensed, as much could be accomplished in the name of Canadian expansion in the East as in the West. The real impact of the paper was not among its readers in Red River but in a constituency thousands of miles away. As John Schultz said, "by it we are not only influenced here but judged abroad." The *Nor'Wester* was "the light-house on our coast—the beacon that lets men know we are here."[12]

From Buckingham and Coldwell through James Ross, Schultz and W.R. Brown, the editors of the *Nor'Wester* realized that their paper could act as a spur to the eastern expansionists, and their style reflected that

[Dr.] John Christian Schultz, c. 1860s. Schultz practised medicine in Fort Garry in 1860s, and later became the Lieutenant Governor of Manitoba from 1888 to 1895. Although he claimed to have medical credentials, there is no evidence that he was ever licenced to practice medicine or that he had received a medical degree as he had claimed (courtesy of the Glenbow Archives/LAC-933-1).

realization. As the only newspaper in the North West between 1859 and annexation, the *Nor'Wester* had a near monopoly on the interpretation of events in that region. Expansionists in the East, in turn, welcomed the information which the *Nor'Wester* provided as reliable and interesting. Editorials and opinions of the *Nor'Wester* were frequently printed in the Canadian papers and often served as the basis for their own editorial stance. Among Canadian expansionists a subscription to the *Nor'Wester* became a badge of membership in the campaign for annexation.[13] At times it even seemed as if the paper's real readers were not the inhabitants of Red River at all but the eastern expansionist community. When the *Nor'Wester* ran a special supplement on the formation of a Scientific Institute in Red River, none of the supplements reached the local populace for, as the paper unapologetically pointed out, "the whole impression [has] been mailed to foreigners."[14]

The *Nor'Wester* and the Canada Party worked consistently to convince their eastern audience not only of the potential of the land but of the urgent desire of the people to cast off the yoke of the Hudson's Bay Company. Attacks on Company rule were a consistent part of the paper's policy and, by at least the latter 1860s, it repeatedly argued that the best solution was annexation to Canada.[15] Further, many of the petitions which reached the East from Red River had their origins, and much of their support, in the group surrounding the paper. The petition presented by Sandford Fleming to the Canadian and British governments in 1863 was a case in point.[16] The meetings which led to this petition were headed by none other than the two current editors of the *Nor'Wester*, James Ross and William Coldwell.[17]

Thus, if the Canada Party was less than successful in its attempt to convert the people of Red River to annexation, the same cannot be said for its mission to convince Canadians that the settlement was ready and willing to join with them. The fictional and malicious character, Cool, in Alexander Begg's *Dot-It-Down* summed it up when he said that "Canada has had an eye to the North West for some years past, and is only too ready and willing to swallow anything that is said against the Honorable Company, whether true or not."[18] Expansionists had long believed that by bringing British progress and liberties to the North West they were a "ray of light" in a dark region, and when the *Nor'Wester* confirmed their opinions they found no reason to doubt it.[19] As the time for the transfer approached they confidently assumed, in the words of Charles Mair, that it was the unanimous desire of the people of Red River to possess "the unspeakable blessings of free Government and civilization."[20]

A second factor determining the expansionist attitude was the fact that the rebellion was primarily a movement of the French half-breed population. The men who had prevented McDougall's entry into the North West had all been French-speaking, Catholic, half-breeds. Throughout the rebellion McDougall and those who shared his outlook saw the Métis as acting alone. It was believed, whether accurately or not, that the Canadians, English half-breeds and Europeans in the settlement were opposed to Riel. In other words the expansionists were convinced that the resistance had its origin and support in only one section of the population of Red River.

Until the rebellion, neither the Canadian government nor the expansionists had paid much attention to the Métis. The Sayer trial and the appearance of French names on various petitions had encouraged the assumption that their opinions were indistinguishable from those of the other segments of Red River's population. This is hardly surprising, given eastern reliance on the Canada Party and the *Nor'Wester* for information. Nevertheless, the failure to recognize this powerful and distinct community in Red River proved to be a costly blunder.

Contributing to the lack of understanding was the prevailing lack of knowledge concerning the Métis in Canada. Aside from the buffalo hunt, which drew general comment from tourists and writers before 1870, little was written on the Métis. Even in the case of the buffalo hunt, writers had consistently failed to follow the implication of such organization through to its logical conclusion. Those who wrote of the North West did not relate, or did not themselves perceive, the powerful sense of identity and ability to work in concert which was a part of the Métis tradition. Rather, when the Métis were mentioned at all, it was in a manner that portrayed them as rather quaint and undisciplined individuals whose habits and character were drawn from their wilderness environment.[21] It was a composite portrait that served to accentuate their Indian background rather than their French language or Catholic religion. Even among French Canadians, where the identity of religion and language produced some sympathy for the Métis, there was a general belief that these people were a poor semi-nomadic group whose only link to civilization was through the church.[22] English Canadians, while they noted the French language and Roman Catholic religion, saw the Métis character as distinct and separate from that of French Canada.

With such characteristics it was generally believed that the future of the Métis within a European framework was, at best, limited. The assumption was that they would only partly adapt to the on-rushing civilization and would thus be relegated to the bottom end of the socio-economic scale. They "will be very useful here when the country gets filled up," Mair noted shortly before the transfer, for they are "easily dealt with and easily controlled."[23] The image of the Métis, and their role for the future, thus resembled that of peasant as much as it did Indian. Strong but manageable, able to cope with European civilization but unlikely to thrive on it, they were expected to passively accept their new lot.

Even such a limited prospect was regarded by expansionists as an improvement on the life which the Métis had led under the rule of the Hudson's Bay Company. For both political and economic reasons, Canadians expected to receive the gratitude of these people in the same way they expected the gratitude of all Red River. At the same time, it was hardly to be expected that the Métis, as either peasants or Indians, would be consulted in such a major transaction as the transfer of the North West. They were at best a "wretched half-starved people" whose comprehension of such matters would be feeble.[24] Even in the face of armed resistance, William McDougall could not understand that this image of the Métis was distorted and incomplete. "The Canadian Government," he maintained, had "done nothing to injure these people but everything to benefit them." There was thus no reason for the rebellion, except perhaps that "they—3 or 4000 semi-savages and serfs of yesterday—will not be trusted with the government and destiny of a third of the American continent."[25] With such an image of the Métis and such an underestimation of their sense of identity, it is not surprising that the expansionists were never able to comprehend the real reasons for the decisive resistance in Red River.

The first reaction of expansionists to this seemingly meaningless resistance was one of ridicule and contempt. McDougall initially predicted that the "insurrection will not last a week."[26] The *Globe*, on hearing of the activity, scornfully commented on November 17, 1869, that "it is altogether too much of a joke to think of a handful of people barring the way to the onward progress of British institutions and British people on the pretence that the whole wide continent is theirs." As autumn moved into winter, however, and Louis Riel's provisional government gained rather than lost strength, such offhand comments dwindled in number. Gradually expansionists were forced to take the whole issue more seriously.

In attempting to analyze the situation and thereby reach a possible solution, the expansionists were at a disadvantage. Their image of the Métis and their continued belief that the majority of Red River was in favour of annexation made them unable to accept the arguments of the rebels at face value. Only by portraying the Métis as puppets in the hands of artful manipulators, whose real purpose was not being revealed, were they able to find an explanation satisfactory to their own presuppositions. The *Nor'Wester*, in its last issue, maintained that the Métis had been "imposed upon" and led into rebellion.[27] McDougall concurred and wrote to Macdonald that "the half-breeds were ignorant and that parties behind were pushing them on."[28] The *Globe* referred vaguely but pointedly to "certain persons in their settlement, who are hostile to the Dominion" as the ones who "have made it their business to stir up discontent among the most foolish and ignorant of the population."[29] As expansionists, and those who agreed with them, developed this conspiratorial interpretation of the rebellion they began to focus on three individual but interrelated groups as the real instigators of the Métis resistance.

The conspirators who figured most prominently in expansionist thoughts came from south of the border. "It was well known at Fort Garry," McDougall commented in the fall of 1869, "that American citizens had come into the country." Ostensibly they were traders, but that was merely a mask for their plans to "create disaffection, and if possible, a movement for annexation to the United States." These men and their allies "had been actively engaged in circulating stories, absurd as they were unfounded, to alarm the fears of the half-breeds, and excite their hostility against the Canadian government."[30] It was not surprising that American designs on Red River should be seen as a force behind the Métis resistance. Canadian expansionists had long worried about American pretensions to the North West. The *Nor'Wester*, throughout its existence, had urged Canada to act quickly before Red River was forced into "annexation with the United States."[31] Also, as those interested in the North West were well aware, Canada was not the only home of expansionists. The effective monopoly which the State of Minnesota exerted over trade and transportation with Red River gave its own expansionists some hope that the North West would drift into the American political orbit.

The activities of American expansionists, such as Oscar Malmros, the U.S. Consul in Red River, Enos Stutsman and James Wickes Taylor, gave some reality to the charges of American encouragement of the Red River resistance. What Canadians, and particularly expansionists, failed to realize, however, was that these annexationist forces were auxiliary rather than basic to the Métis resistance.[32] The presence of some annexationists in Riel's provisional government and the creation of the *New Nation* gave the American party some influence in Red River in December 1869 and January 1870. Thereafter, however, this influence rapidly declined. Ironically, these Americans were as unable to understand the purpose of the Métis as were Canadian expansionists. The Americans assumed that their dislike of Canada could be transformed into American annexationism, while the Canadians feared that such a goal was all too probable.

The second force which expansionists perceived behind the rebellion was the Hudson's Bay Company. When McDougall met resistance his first reaction, besides perplexed surprise, was to warn William McTavish, Governor of the Council of Assiniboia, that "you are the legal ruler of the country, and responsible for the preservation of the public peace."[33] It was, however, not as simple as that. As McTavish well knew, the Hudson's Bay Company had no force with which to assert its authority. This had been apparent as far back as the Sayer trial, and it would have been both impossible and dangerous for the Company to have attempted to face such a determined group as the Métis. Canadian expansionists, however, had a different explanation. "The Hudson's Bay Company are evidently with the rebels," Schultz wrote in November, 1869. "It is said the rebels will support the Government of the Hudson's Bay Company as it now exists."[34] The member of Parliament for

Brant North, J.Y. Bown, passing on the opinions of his brother, the deposed editor of the *Nor'Wester*, warned Macdonald that before the rebellion "certain parties then in the pay of the Company and holding office under it made threats of what they would do."[35] McDougall, perhaps because he was an official representative of Canada, was more circumspect but did point to "the complicity of some of his [Governor McTavish's] council with the insurrection."[36] However circumspect McDougall's letter, the message remained the same. The current government of the North West had actively encouraged opposition to the lawful transfer of the territory of Canada.

Though a few individuals in the Company showed some sympathy for the Métis, the

William McTavish (also MacTavish), Hudson's Bay Company factor and the last governor of Rupert's Land (1864–70), c. 1860s (courtesy of the Glenbow Archives/LAC-1010-14).

expansionists had little evidence to support their charges. The expansionists had proclaimed for so long that the Company exerted an oppressive tyranny over the people of Red River that they could not now accept the fact that it was powerless. Those more detached from the expansionist perspective tended to have a more realistic analysis. John A. Macdonald sharply disagreed with McDougall's condemnation of McTavish, and at no time did the Canadian government accept the theory that there was any Hudson's Bay involvement in the rebellion.[37]

The third conspiratorial force perceived behind the rebellion was to prove the most dangerous in its implications for Canada. The Roman Catholic church, or at least its representatives in Red River, were also accused of aiding the Métis in their resistance. "The worst feature in this case," McDougall told Macdonald, "is the apparent complicity of the priests." Rather than support constituted authority they had openly supported rebellion. "It appears certain that at least one of them has openly preached sedition to his flock and has furnished aid and comfort to the parties in arms."[38] On December 9, 1869 the Toronto *Globe* singled out Father J.N. Richtot as the "head and front of the whole movement by the French half-breeds." The Catholic clergy joined the rapidly swelling ranks of those who were seen as the instigators of rebellion, having "worked upon the ignorance and fears of the French speaking portion of the people to such an extent as to lead them to armed resistance."[39]

Expansionist perceptions of the relationship between the Métis and the clergy made it natural for them to suspect the priests. The Métis were viewed as a superstitious and ignorant people and, as every good Ontario Protestant knew, the Roman Catholic church exercised totalitarian control over its membership. It followed that had the clergy wished to stop the rebellion they could have. Further, no individual priest would dare work in opposition to his own church hierarchy. Thus the ultimate conclusion had to be, as the *Globe* decided in the spring of 1870, "that Bishop Taché holds the whole threads of the affair in his hand."[40] At any time he could have commanded the Métis to cease resistance, but he consistently refrained from doing so. This was the best proof of all that the church was in league with the rebels. "A word from their Bishop," McDougall charged, "would have sent them all to their homes and re-established the lawful Government of Assiniboia, but that word was not spoken."[41]

These accusations against the clergy were an almost instinctive reaction to a body which was viewed with extreme suspicion. The expansionist movement and its nationalist allies consisted largely of English-speaking Protestants. French-Canadian Roman Catholics had played little part in the effort to acquire the North West and thus had no spokesmen within the ranks of the movement. Moreover, many expansionist leaders, such as William McDougall, had long viewed the Catholic church as some sort of hostile foe conspiring against Canada. The religious and political controversies of Canadian history had paved the way for the expansionist reaction to the clergy in 1869. Many English Canadians were all too ready to implicate the Catholic church in any activity directed against the Canadian nation or British Empire.

Such conspiratorial explanations enabled the expansionists and nationalists to reconcile the rebellion with their belief that the population of Red River favoured entry into Canada. The rebellion was not a popular uprising at all. The majority of the people opposed the resistance, but as Mair theorized, "the Yankee, the Company and the Priests had a fair field; whilst the loyal English natives, comprising about two thirds of the population, without arms and ammunition, cursed their own helplessness and shrunk from the guns at Fort Garry."[42] The rebellion was the fault neither of Canada nor

mrs dougall DC.

William McDougall, first Lieutenant Governor of the North-West Territories, 1869 (courtesy of the Glenbow Archives/LAC-826-2).

of the Canadian expansionists, and was not supported by the people of Red River. Foreign elements had manipulated an ignorant segment of the populace in order to gain their own nefarious ends.

The analysis of the rebellion had obvious implications for the policy to be pursued in bringing it to an end. For John A. Macdonald, who saw expansionist arrogance and Métis suspicions behind the outbreak, the best solution seemed to be "to behave in as patient and conciliatory a fashion as possible."[43] The rebellion was essentially a movement aiming at political guarantees; to Macdonald, that implied a political solution. Compromise with the Métis would allay their fears and allow the peaceful acquisition of the territory before American expansionists could exploit the situation. He even suggested bringing Riel into the police force which was planned for the region as "a most convincing proof that you are not going to leave the half-breeds out of the law."[44]

In contrast to Macdonald, those who saw the rebellion as a conspiracy felt it dangerous to assume that the matter could be resolved by conciliation. They perceived the ultimate goal of the rebellion to be the disruption of Canada and perhaps the whole British Empire. Attempts to reconcile the Métis were pointless, for they were not at the base of the rebellion. The problem went much deeper and had much more important consequences. Given these beliefs, the expansionists thus felt that the only possible response to continued rebellion was the use of force. Moreover, as the *Globe* concluded, the rebellion was not a popular uprising, and the use of troops would thus not put Canada "in the unpleasant position of oppressors forcing an unpopular government upon a protesting people." Military action would simply ensure the wishes of the majority of people of Red River were carried out while, at the same time, stopping those who "for merely selfish purposes"

PROCLAMATION [april 9, 1870]

To the People of the North-West.

LET the Assembly of twenty-eight Representatives which met on the 9th March, be dear to the people of Red River! That Assembly has shown itself worthy of great confidence. It has worked in union. The members devoted themselves to the public interests and yielded only to sentiments of good will, duty and generosity. Thanks to that noble conduct, public authority is now strong. That strength will be employed to sustain and protect the people of the country.

TO-DAY the Government pardons all those whom political differences led astray only for a time. Amnesty will be generously accorded to all those who will submit to the Government, who will discountenance or inform against dangerous gatherings.

FROM this day forth the public highways are open.

THE Hudson's Bay Company can now resume business. Themselves contributing to the public good, they circulate their money as of old. They pledge themselves to that course.

THE attention of the Government is also directed very specially to the Northern part of the country, in order that trade there may not receive any serious check, and peace in the Indian districts may thereby be all the more securely maintained.

THE disastrous war which at one time threatened us, has left among us fears and various deplorable results. But let the people feel reassured.

ELEVATED by the Grace of Providence and the suffrages of my fellow-citizens to the highest position in the Government of my country, I proclaim that peace reigns in our midst this day. The Government will take every precaution to prevent this peace from being disturbed.

WHILE internally all is thus returning to order, externally also, matters are looking favorable. Canada invites the Red River people to an amicable arrangement. She offers to guarantee us our rights and to give us a place in the Confederation equal to that of any other Province.

IDENTIFIED with the Provisional Government, our national will, based upon justice, shall be respected.

HAPPY country, to have escaped many misfortunes that were prepared for her! In seeing her children on the point of a war, she recollects the old friendship which used to bind us, and by the ties of the same patriotism she has re-united them again for the sake of preserving their lives, their liberties, and their happiness.

LET us remain united, and we shall be happy. With strength of unity we shall retain prosperity.

O MY fellow-countrymen, without distinction of language or without distinction of creed—keep my words in your hearts! If ever the time should unhappily come when another division should take place amongst us, such as foreigners heretofore sought to create, that will be the signal for all the disasters which we have had the happiness to avoid.

IN order to prevent similar calamities, the Government will treat with all the severity of the law those who will dare again to compromise the public security. It is ready to act against the disorder of parties as well as against that of individuals. But let us hope rather that extreme measures will be unknown, and that the lessons of the past will guide us in the future.

LOUIS RIEL.

"Proclamation To the People of the North-West," issued from Fort Garry, April 9, 1870. In the text Riel pardoned "all those whom political differences led astray for a time." He also declared the public highways open, and stated that the Hudson's Bay Company was free to resume business (Courtesy of the Archives of Manitoba/N5413).

Members of a delegation that travelled to Ottawa in the winter of 1870 to report on conditions at Red River. They were bitterly critical of Louis Riel. Left to right: John Christian Schultz; William Drever; Charles Mair; J. Letter (Courtesy of the Glenbow Archives/LAC-741-3).

sought to overthrow "British authority and British freedom."[45] At a meeting of some 5,000 citizens in April 1870, the mayor of Toronto warned that the British Empire might employ troops to "put down that miserable creature … who attempts to usurp authority at Fort Garry."[46] As the months went by, the rhetoric of expansionism indicated a growing willingness, even enthusiasm, for the use of military force.

The official government approach remained much more conciliatory. Further, many government officials blamed leading expansionists, especially William McDougall, Charles Mair and John Schultz, for their provocative actions.[47] The expansionists replied with their own increasingly harsh criticisms. Macdonald was blamed for his abandonment of McDougall and his refusal to accept the transfer of the territory from Britain until peace was restored.[48] Joseph Howe, the Nova Scotian cabinet minister and former anticonfederationist, was suspected of secretly encouraging the rebellion during his visit to the settlement shortly before it began.[49] In this climate of bitterness and mutual recrimination, expansionists began to feel increasingly estranged from the government and to perceive themselves as an unjustly vilified minority within the nation. It seemed that only Ontario had enough national patriotism to create a forceful demand for the suppression of the rebellion. Other parts of the Dominion and the government itself delayed and hesitated while Canada's future remained in danger.

The charges that began to circulate in the spring of 1870 gave this sense of bitterness more concrete form. In the wake of the execution of Thomas Scott by Riel, the Canadian government reluctantly decided that a military expedition to the North West was necessary. From the expansionist perspective such an expedition was of the utmost importance. They had called for a show of force from the beginning, and Scott's death added a new emotionalism to these demands. Scott had been martyred for his loyalty and "humble though his position was—yet he was a Canadian; his mental gifts may have been few—yet he died for us."[50] As preparations were undertaken for the expedition, however, many individuals began to suspect that there was an element in the government working to hamper it. Singled out were prominent French-Canadian politicians, including George Cartier, Minister of Militia. Those who supported the use of force saw in Cartier and his allies a "party which opposed in every possible manner the departure of the expedition."[51]

Complicating matters was an increasing public opposition in French Canada to the use of such force. As attitudes in Ontario grew increasingly militant in the wake of Scott's death, many French Canadians became wary of the motivation which lay behind such vehemence. Naturally sensitive to the intolerance often exhibited by English-Canadian Protestantism, they had little difficulty in accepting the Métis rationale for the rebellion at face value. The Métis were, with good reason, simply seeking guarantees that their religious and linguistic rights would be protected under the new order. A military expedition seemed both unnecessary and oppressive, and many French Canadians protested against the decision to send one.

To the expansionists and to a good many other English Canadians, however, such a position was treasonable. More and more, the wrath of Ontario public opinion turned its attention from Fenians and foreign agents to those within Canada who would oppose their militant brand of expansion. French-Canadian opposition to the expedition, the *Globe* warned, contained within it an ominous principle:

> If British troops cannot go on British territory wherever the authorities desire to send them without being denounced as butchers and filibusterers by fellow subjects, things must be in a poor way. If that can't be done in Red River, it can't in Quebec, and if the latter doctrine is held, by all means let it be advanced, but it is just as well to have it understood that a good many pounds will be spent, and a good many lives lost before it will be acquiesced in.[52]

Expansionists believed that Howe and others, for personal reasons, might have worked to thwart the interests of Canada. In the growing hostility of French Canada, however, they perceived a movement of much larger proportions and much greater significance.

The racial and religious implications of the Red River rebellion had never been far below the surface. The priests, accused of participation in the insurrection, had brought the issue of the Catholic religion into the question from the beginning. The Métis had often been rather loosely referred to as the "French party" and that term, in turn, was used as a description of the rebellious elements in the settlement.[53] On the other hand, expansionists had tried to play down the popular support for the rebellion by portraying the rebels as a small segment of even the French half-breeds. John Schultz, for instance, made a point at the public rally in Toronto of distinguishing between the rebels and the loyal French half-breed elements in Red River.[54] Also, William McDougall had initially seen the clerical involvement in the rebellion as a result of the fact that most of them were foreign born.[55] Thus, if religious and racial undertones were present throughout the rebellion, they were muted.

The debate over the military expedition brought these undertones to the surface. The process was a dialectic one. French Canada objected to Ontario demands for the use of force against a people which it felt was, whether in a correct manner or not, simply trying to protect itself. Ontario expansionists, seeing the complaints of the Métis as a subterfuge for more malignant ends, took the French-Canadian opposition to the expedition as a sign of disloyalty. The muted racial friction increased until it became a dominant ingredient of Canadian politics.

By July 1870, it was being argued not only that French Canada opposed the expedition but that, unless loyalists acted quickly, the force would never reach Red River. Canada First members George Denison and R.G. Haliburton saw a devious plot on the part of Cartier and his cohorts to give Riel an amnesty and recall the force before it reached Red River. Warning was given by these "loyalists" that any such attempt would meet massive resistance from Toronto and that Cartier and Taché, scheduled to arrive in Toronto, would be confronted by hostile crowds. Shortly afterwards another huge rally was called, and there the honour of the Empire and the suppression of rebellion were again demanded.[56] Once again the cry of treason had been raised but in this case the traitors were identified as French-Canadian cabinet members rather than the rebels themselves.

The slightly ludicrous hysterics of Denison and Haliburton indicate the change which had taken place in the analysis of the rebellion by the summer of 1870. Between March, when news of Scott's death first created widespread support for the use of force, and July, the focus in the conspiratorial analysis of the rebellion shifted. Fenians and Hudson's Bay Company officials remained involved but it was the role of the priests that was assuming the greatest significance. Their role in the rebellion became much clearer once it was believed that French Canada was also involved. The two forces, linked through their common language and religion, were in league. Their joint goal was, as McDougall warned his constituents after his return to Canada, to have "the North-West made into a French Catholic Colony, with special restrictions on all their inhabitants."[57] The Toronto *Globe*, replying angrily to criticism of Ontario's militancy in the Quebec press, charged that "the fanatics are the French Canadians, who are striving to obtain for themselves peculiar and exclusive privileges."[58]

In a complex psychological process brought on by French-Canadian opposition to Ontario militancy, the conspiratorial figures of Red River were transferred from the North West to Canada. It was the story of the established church, clergy reserves and anti-democratic privileges for the minority all over again. French Canada had allied itself with the priests of Red River in order to prevent the natural development of British civilization and to preserve autocratic rule. And the expansionists argued that rule by the Catholic church, as surely as by the Hudson's Bay Company, would "lock up the splendid country under a more odious tyranny than that which has long ruled it."[59] French Canada had come to be considered as much of a danger as the Hudson's Bay Company to the sort of Protestant commercial culture which the expansionists envisaged for the North West.

The expansionists' fears concerning the West were reinforced by the government's proposed Manitoba Act, first introduced to Parliament on May 2, 1870. The boundaries of the new province, the educational system and those clauses which set aside land for the Métis were seen as further evidence of a conspiracy to create a French Catholic province in the North West. The Act prompted McDougall to bring his view of the rebellion to the floor of the House of Commons. Over shouts of opposition he charged that "the rebellion in the North West originated with the Roman Catholic priesthood" and that "the priesthood desired to secure certain advantages for themselves, their Church or their people."[60] Captain G. L. Huyshe, a member of the Red River expedition, envisaged dire consequences were the Act to succeed and warned that if any land were given to the Métis "it is probable that a large portion of it will eventually fall into the hands of the Roman Catholic church." It would thus gain "an undue preponderance of wealth and power" in Manitoba.[61] To many the overall implications of the Manitoba Act were clear enough. Its designs threatened by Wolseley's advancing troops, French

Canada had attempted one final time to gain what it had sought from the beginning. The Manitoba Act was nothing more than "a Bill to establish a French half-breed and foreign ecclesiastical supremacy in Manitoba."[62]

Two implications flowed from the shift of attention from conspiracies in Red River to those in Ottawa and Quebec. First, the French Catholic nature of the Métis was emphasized. Previously, as has been argued, the Métis tie to the wilderness was seen as the dominant factor in shaping their character. During the controversy surrounding the rebellion, however, this changed. As agents, whether wittingly or unwittingly, of French Canada and the Catholic church, the Métis' connection with French Canada began to be stressed. This shift was apparent in both French and English Canada. The continual references in the Ontario press to the "French party" had led French Canadians to identify with the Métis to an extent unknown before the resistance.[63] The year 1870 was only the beginning of a period which would see French Canadians increasingly associate the cause of the Métis and their leader, Louis Riel, with the rights of French Canadians.

The second implication for the expansionists was that only Ontario possessed the true spirit of Canadian nationalism. After all, they argued, only in Ontario had there been strong support for annexation of the North West and forceful suppression of the rebellion. If necessary, that province would have to abrogate to itself the development of the North West in the name of Canada, in the same way that Canada had claimed it in the name of the Empire. It was Ontario, as Schultz pointed out, from which "this movement to add Red River to the Dominion commenced; it was in Ontario this expression of indignation was expressed." It was therefore, he concluded, "to Ontario the Territory properly belonged."[64] The rebellion made explicit what had been implicit all along: the regional nature of Canadian expansionism.

While the arrival of the expeditionary force in Red River in August 1870 ended the actual rebellion, its legacy was to be felt for many years to come. The soldiers of that force and those immigrants who followed them brought to Manitoba a set of suspicions which continually threatened to destroy the racial and religious balance which the Canadian government had recognized in Manitoba.[65] Contributing to this tension was the tendency of the Canadian volunteers stationed in Winnipeg to assume the right to mete out justice to those associated with the rebellion. The tragic climax of such vigilante action occurred when a former supporter of Riel drowned in the Red River while attempting to flee pursuing militiamen. Thereafter violence declined, but there were sporadic outbreaks as religious and racial frictions prompted individuals to refight the rebellion of 1870.

Such individual violence was only a symptom of a general suspicion that

French-Canadian attempts to turn Manitoba into a Catholic province had not ended with the collapse of the rebellion. Expansionists and nationalists continued to watch for signs of government or individual activity against English Canadians in Manitoba. Typical was Denison's warning to Schultz that the Ontario troops would be sent back east on some pretext rather than be allowed to disband in Manitoba and thus contribute to the permanent English population there.[66] Haliburton, not to be outdone, wrote Macdonald angrily when he heard that a French Canadian was to be appointed to the bench in Manitoba. Such an appointment, he argued, would simply aid Quebec in its attempts "at making Manitoba a New Quebec with French laws."[67] Suspicions of racial bias in Manitoba, distrust of the federal government and the question of amnesty for Riel perpetuated and deepened the attitude created by the rebellion itself. In the process eastern politics and prejudice were not only taken West, but found there an ultimate test of the strength of the various factions:

> Manitoba has been to us on a small scale what Kansas was to the United States. It has been the battle-ground for our British and French elements with their respective religions, as Kansas was the battleground for Free Labour and Slavery. Ontario has played a part in the contests there analogous to New England, Quebec to that of the southern States.[68]

While the specific analogy may have been inappropriate, the comment was a perceptive one for it revealed how the resistance had been transformed by expansionist perceptions of it. The argument has been made that "the most persistent social theme of the Prairies has been the struggle for cultural dominance."[69] If so, then the events surrounding 1870 mark a decisive stage in the development of that theme. Expansionists saw in the resistance and its aftermath a contest between French and English in Canada for a dominant position in the West. Moreover, the events of the rebellion had proven to their satisfaction that French Canada had been willing to sacrifice or distort the development of the region for its own ends. It was thus impossible, expansionists believed, to entrust a heritage as important as the West to such a group. Not only was it necessary to have an eastern agricultural order dominant in Manitoba, but it also had to be English and Protestant. And as Kansas became a testing ground for dominance in the American West, so Manitoba became one for the Canadians. "Prairie culture," it has been noted, "developed from a Manitoba base."[70] Expansionists seem to have sensed this would be the case and they were thus determined to assert their dominance there in order to ensure their influence over the rest of the Prairies.

The racial strife which marked Manitoba's entry into Canada gradually subsided. The settlement of the question of amnesty for Riel, whether satisfactory or not, removed this contentious issue from the daily papers. In the same period legal and political institutions were firmly established under the governorship of Adams Archibald and his successor, Alexander Morris. Most importantly, the continuing inflow of population from Ontario gave assurance to English Canada that its culture would dominate in the new province and thus eased fears of a French-Canadian plot.[71] It was perhaps symbolic of the triumph of the Canada Party in old Red River that as early as 1872 Morris recommended that John Schultz, implacable enemy of the Métis, should be appointed a member of the North West Council.[72] The Manitoba "base" was, within a few years of 1870, increasingly English Canadian and Protestant.

The triumph of one order meant the collapse of the other. While the Province of Manitoba was able to incorporate many elements of old Red River into its social order, the French half-breed was not one of them. In increasing numbers the Métis sought refuge from the civilization of Red River and the intolerance of its new inhabitants. Moving to the still empty banks of the North Saskatchewan, they remained separate representatives of the old order and of a French Catholic tradition. Their respite was to be temporary, however, for the agricultural frontier continued to spread westward and would soon threaten their distinct existence once again. Nor did either side seem to learn much from the experience of 1870. Alexander Morris's warning to Macdonald in 1873 that "the Saskatchewan will require prompt attention, or we will have the same game over again there" went unheeded in the same way as had the warnings of the 1860s.[73]

Notes

This article first appeared in *Prairie Forum* 3, no. 2 (1978): 157–74.

1. G.F.G. Stanley, *The Birth of Western Canada: A History of the Riel Rebellions* (Toronto: University of Toronto Press, 1961), 44–143; W.L. Morton, *Manitoba, A History* (Toronto: University of Toronto Press, 1957), 109–20, and *The Critical Years: The Union of British North America, 1857–1873* (Toronto: McClelland and Stewart, 1964), 235–44; A.C. Gluek, *Minnesota and the Manifest Destiny of the Canadian North West* (Toronto: University of Toronto Press, 1965), 254–61; Pierre Berton, *The National Dream: The Great Railway, 1871–1881* (Toronto: McClelland and Stewart, 1970), 29–30.

2. Morton, *The Critical Years*, 237; Mason Wade, *The French Canadians, 1760–1967*, Vol. 1 (Toronto: Macmillan, 1968), 402.

3. Arthur Silver, "French Quebec and the Metis Question, 1869–1885," in Carl Berger & Ramsay Cook (eds.), *The West and the Nation: Essays in Honour of W.L. Morton* (Toronto: McClelland and Stewart, 1976), 91–113, 92.

4. For a more complete description of the nature of Canadian expansionism and the personnel behind it see D. R. Owram, "The Great North West: The Canadian Expansionist

Movement and the Image of the West in the Nineteenth Century" (PhD dissertation, University of Toronto, 1976). For convenience the term expansionist will be used henceforth to describe members of the Canada Party, Canada First movement and individuals like Brown and McDougall who strongly opposed the rebellion.

5. A.K. Isbister, *A Few Words on the Hudson's Bay Company* (London: n.p., 1847). For an account of Isbister's efforts see E.E. Rich, *History of the Hudson's Bay Company, 1670–1870*, Vol. 3 (London: Hudson's Bay Record Society, 1958–59), 545–47.

6. See, for instance, Toronto *Globe*, December 13, 1856; Montreal *Gazette*, June 6, 1857.

7. Toronto *Globe*, March 5, 1857. Letter from Isbister.

8. Great Britain. Parliament. *Select Committee on the Hudson's Bay Territories*, Appendix 15 (London: n.p., 1857), 439.

9. *British Parliamentary Papers*. Colonies. Canada. Vol. 27, 485. "Resolution Adopted at a Public Meeting of the Inhabitants of the Red River Settlement," dated January 17, 1867.

10. *Nor'Wester*, January 12, 1869.

11. Alexander Begg, *Dot-It-Down: A Story of Life in the North-West* (Toronto: Hunter, Rose, 1871) portrays the *Nor'Wester* as the voice of a few self-interested men.

12. *Nor'Wester*, November 28, 1864.

13. Public Archives of Manitoba (PAM), Schultz Papers, Box 16, Mair to Schultz, May 14, 1866; B. Chewitt and Co., to Schultz, December 30, 1867 (for a subscription for S.J. Dawson).

14. *Nor'Wester*, March 5, 1862.

15. Ibid., September 22, 1865; December 1, 1866; July 13, 1867; August 4, 1868.

16. Sandford Fleming, *Memorial of the People of Red River to the British and Canadian Governments* (Quebec: n.p., 1863).

17. *Nor'Wester*, January 24, 1863.

18. Alexander Begg, *Dot-It-Down*, 107.

19. *Nor'Wester*, December 14, 1862.

20. Toronto *Globe*, May 28, 1869. Letter from Mair.

21. Paul Kane, *Wanderings of an Artist among the Indians of North America: From Canada to Vancouver's Island and Oregon through the Hudson's Bay Company's Territory and Back Again* (London: Longman, Brown, Green, Longmans and Roberts, 1859), 51; Province of Canada, *Sessional Papers* (1859), Number 36; Daniel Wilson, "Displacement and Extinction Among the Primeval Races of Man," *Canadian Journal* (January 1856): 12.

22. A.I. Silver, "French-Canadian Attitudes Towards the North-West and North-West Settlement 1870–1890" (MA thesis, McGill University, 1966), 106.

23. Toronto *Globe*, December 4, 1868; February 16, 1869. Letters from Mair.

24. Queen's University Library, Mair Papers, Denison to Mair, March 29, 1869.

25. Library and Archives Canada (LAC), Macdonald Papers, Vol. 102, McDougall to Macdonald, November 13, 1869.

26. Ibid., McDougall to Macdonald, October 31, 1869.

27. *Nor'Wester*, November 23, 1869.

28. LAC, Macdonald Papers, Vol. 102, McDougall to Macdonald, October 31, 1869.

29. Toronto *Globe*, November 13, 1869.

30. Dominion of Canada, *Sessional Papers* (1870), Number 12, McDougall to Howe, November 5, 1869.

31. *Nor'Wester*, February 5, 1862. See also, July 28, 1860; September 28, 1860; May 28, 1862; July 13, 1867; January 12, 1869.

32. Gluek, *Minnesota and the Manifest Destiny of the Canadian North West*, 263–94, discusses American aims in Red River and the impact of these aims on the resistance.

33. LAC, Macdonald Papers, Vol. 102, McDougall to McTavish, November 2, 1869.

34. Dominion of Canada, *Sessional Papers* (1870), Number 12, Schultz to McDougall, November 1869; see also Mair to McDougall, November 8, 1869.

35. LAC, Macdonald Papers, Vol. 102, J. Bown to Macdonald, November 26, 1869.

36. Dominion of Canada, *Sessional Papers* (1870), Number 12, McDougall to Joseph Howe, November 13, 1869.

37. LAC, Macdonald Papers, Vol. 516, Macdonald to McDougall, December 8, 1869.

38. Ibid., Vol. 102, McDougall to Macdonald, October 31, 1869.

39. Toronto *Globe*, January 4, 1870.

40. Ibid., April 15, 1870.

41. William McDougall, *The Red River Rebellion: Eight Letters to the Hon. Joseph Howe* (Toronto: n.p., 1870), 44.

42. G.T. Denison, *Reminiscences of the Red River Rebellion*, "Letter by Charles Mair," (Toronto: n.p., 1873), 6.

43. D.G. Creighton, *John A. Macdonald: The Old Chieftain* (Toronto: Macmillan, 1955), 47.

44. LAC, Macdonald Papers, Vol. 516, Macdonald to McDougall, November 20, 1869.

45. Toronto *Globe*, January 24, 1870.

46. Ibid., April 7, 1870.

47. LAC, Macdonald Papers, Vol. 516, Macdonald to McDougall, December 8, 1869.

48. Toronto *Globe*, December 31, 1869.

49. Canada, House of Commons, *Debates*, 1st Parliament, 3rd Session, February 21, 1870, 111–16. Also, McDougall, *Red River Rebellion*, 5–6.

50. W.A. Foster, *Canada First, or, Our New Nationality* (Toronto: n.p., 1871), 33.

51. G.L. Huyshe, *The Red River Expedition* (London: n.p., 1871), 23.

52. Toronto *Globe*, May 2, 1870.

53. Dominion of Canada, *Sessional Papers* (1870), Number 12, "Proclamation by J.S. Dennis, December 9, 1869," 101.

54. Toronto *Globe*, April 7, 1870.

55. LAC, Macdonald Papers, Vol. 102, McDougall to Macdonald, October 31, 1869.

56. Norman Shrive, *Charles Mair: Literary Nationalist* (Toronto: Universitiy of Toronto Press, 1965), 112–15.

57. *Carleton Place Herald*, February 9, 1870.

58. Toronto *Globe*, April 14, 1870.

59. *Carleton Place Herald*, February 9, 1870. Speech by McDougall.

60. Canada, House of Commons, *Debates*, 1st Parliament, 3rd Session, May 2, 1870, 1302.

61. Huyshe, *The Red River Expedition*, 212. See also *Globe*, April 23, 1870.

62. McDougall, *The Red River Rebellion*, 46.

63. Stanley, *The Birth of Western Canada*, 157.

64. Toronto *Globe*, April 7, 1870.

65. W.L. Morton, *Manitoba*, 146–50.

66. PAM, Schultz Papers, Box 16, Denison to Schultz, January 28, 1871.

67. LAC, Macdonald Papers, Vol. 342, Haliburton to Macdonald, October 7, 1870. See also, ibid., Haliburton to Macdonald, October 6, 1870, and R.G. Haliburton, "The Queen and a United Empire," *St. James Magazine and United Empire Review* (January 1874).

68. "Current Events," *Canadian Monthly and National Review* (September 1874), 250.

69. J.E. Rea, "The Roots of Prairie Society," in David Gagan (ed.), *Prairie Perspectives* (Toronto: Holt, Rinehart and Winston of Canada, 1970), 46–55, 46.

70. Ibid., 47.

71. W.L. Morton, *Manitoba*, 159.

72. LAC, Macdonald Papers, Vol. 252, Morris to Macdonald, October 1, 1872.

73. Ibid., Morris to Macdonald, January 25, 1873.

15.   Thomas Scott and the Daughter of Time

J.M. Bumsted

"Truth is the daughter of time"—an old proverb

In 1951 the Scottish author Elizabeth MacKintosh, writing under the pseudonym of Josephine Tey, published one of the most celebrated detective novels of all time, *The Daughter of Time*. In this novel Tey's Scotland Yard detective Allan Grant becomes fascinated by an historical mystery while recovering in hospital from a serious illness. This work has long fascinated historians. Unlike most historical detection, Tey's book does not attempt imaginatively to re-create either the historical personalities or the time period involved, but rather focusses on a modern detective re-examining a mystery from the historical past. This investigation proves very much like the research done by the historian, since it involves working with old books and documents. The mystery Grant investigates in the mid-20th century is the deaths five centuries earlier of two princes of the realm in the Tower of London, an evil deed attributed to their uncle, King Richard III. Grant quickly discovers that Richard III was a character with an ambivalent reputation, a curious mixture of many positive attributes and the villainy in the Tower. As Grant's research continues, he learns that the evidence on which posterity has convicted Richard of the death of the princes is extremely dubious, consisting of a combination of hearsay assumptions and the assertions of his worst enemies. Grant reads the documents looking for the "one unqualified fact" buried within them, and is a sworn enemy of "Tonypandy," which an associate describes as "someone blowing up a simple affair to huge proportions for a political end."[1] Grant himself adds that the point is not simply that the story involved was nonsense, but that everyone there knew it was nonsense and it was never contradicted.[2]

Thomas Scott, who was executed in Red River in 1870, was hardly Richard III. But the historical problem of Scott's reputation has much in

Thomas Scott photographed in Belfast in 1863 (Courtesy of the Archives of Manitoba/N16492).

common with that of the English king. The Scott execution is unquestionably the most notorious public killing in Canadian history—a mixed jury of Francophones and Anglophones in Manitoba unanimously found that it was "murder." Unquestionably the Scott affair is surrounded by "Tonypandy" on all sides. Most of what we think we know about Scott comes to us in two ways. In the first place, there are unwarranted extrapolations by historians (professional and amateur) from very limited hard evidence. Scott was a young man, and apart from his unexpected involvement in stirring events, was quite an obscure figure. Alexander Begg initially referred to Scott in his journal without giving his first name, and it is likely that some of what little we think we know about Thomas Scott is really information about Alfred or James Scott, both of whom were also in Red River in 1869. Both Thomas Scott's arrival in Red River and his social origins probably help account for his victimization. To a considerable extent, extrapolations from insufficient data are repeated and even improved upon by subsequent historians, as well as influenced by our information from the second source: the evidence about Scott's character and behaviour in captivity as presented by his executioners, particularly by Louis Riel. If we stop and think about this captivity evidence itself for a minute, it presents a number of problems. For the most part, it cannot be substantiated from other sources since Scott's fellow prisoners did not actually witness many of the events which led to his trial, and the trial itself was conducted in camera by a small group of Métis without any outside observers. The details of the tribunal's actions themselves are the subject of considerable confusion, despite its centrality in the subsequent murder trial of Ambroise Lépine in 1874.[3]

From the beginning, anything involving Louis Riel has been the subject of enormous controversy. The contemporary disputatiousness of the death of Scott—a highly partisan business—has helped obscure the fact that much of what we know about Thomas Scott comes mainly from those who executed him. The reasons for that execution have always been shrouded in mystery, and under normal circumstances we would appreciate that it would be in the best interests of those responsible to make their victim out to be as villainous as possible, in order to justify their actions. Why this appreciation appears never to have happened with Scott is an interesting question. For some reason, both contemporaries and subsequent historians seem to have accepted without question the Métis account of Scott's behaviour which served as an explanation for his death, questioning mainly the severity of the response to the charges rather than the charges themselves.

The final problem Scott presents is in the very nature of the assertions about his character and behaviour. Louis Riel described the behaviour of Scott which led to his execution not once, but a number of times over many years. These explanations were not always the same. The charges against Scott that were accepted by his contemporaries in 1870 were certainly not the same accusations levelled against Scott in later years by Riel and then by others. In short, the Métis case against Scott escalated. As the years went by, the charges became progressively more detailed, and Scott became an increasingly nastier character. Many of the secondary accounts of Scott's life and death became based, not on the original 1870 version of his misdeeds, but on the subsequent elaborations, some of which entered the oral traditions of the Métis. Even when the assessment of Scott was based on contemporary evidence, more than one historian has managed to make it sound worse.[4] Overstatement passing well beyond the limits of the evidence is characteristic of much of the writing about both Scott and Riel.[5]

The present study is in the spirit of Josephine Tey's novel. It attempts to untangle the surviving evidence about Thomas Scott's life, fully conscious that much of what we think we know about Scott has been influenced by unsubstantiable accounts of his behaviour in the days and weeks before his execution, as well as by partisanship. It is not concerned with explaining why Scott died; that is a separate study involving the psychology of Louis Riel, among others. It seeks to strip Scott from the legend, to establish the facts of Scott's life and to offer some reassessment of his character. In the process, we may discover a good deal about a variety of related matters. To begin, let us examine what we know about Thomas Scott apart from the evidence of his captors and executioners.

The principal impression to be gained from the testimony of Thomas Scott's anglophone colleagues is that he was a gentle, well-mannered and personable individual, although as we shall see, there was also a minority view that he could be outspoken. Admittedly, most of this testimony was recorded after Scott's death. Whatever its import, this evidence has frequently been neglected or discounted, probably because it has been regarded as part of the closing of ranks of the Canadian Party after the event and in response to the Métis charges at the time of Scott's execution that he was a bad man who deserved to die. Such evidence may well be biased, but it is entitled to as much attention as that of those who killed him. It certainly sets up Scott as a potential dual personality, with one face shown to his friends and another to his enemies.

Scott According to His Anglophone Contemporaries

Thomas Scott's Irish origins are obscure. He was apparently born sometime in the early 1840s in County Down. Lord Dufferin, governor general of Canada in 1874, wrote that Scott "came of very decent people—his parents are at this moment tenant farmers on my estate in the neighbourhood of Clandeboye." Dufferin then added, "but he himself seems to have been a violent and boisterous man such as are often found in the North of Ireland."[6] These two assertions need to be separated. Dufferin undoubtedly knew first-hand that the Scotts were his tenants, but the statement about violence and boisterousness is qualified with the give-away verb "seems," suggesting that the governor-general has extrapolated a stereotyped character from what he had heard about Scott rather than from personal knowledge. There was a good deal of such extrapolation with Scott. In any event, Scott came to Canada in the early 1860s, probably to join his brother Hugh in Toronto.

One of the few surviving records of Scott's Ontario sojourn is a testimonial from one Captain Rowe, of Madoc, Ontario, of the Hastings Battalion of Rifles at Stirling. In a letter to the commanding officer after Scott's death, Rowe wrote:

> I have to inform you that the unfortunate man, Scott, who has been murdered by that scoundrel, Riel, was for a time a member of my company, and did duty with the battalion at Sterling in 1868. He was a splendid fellow, whom you may possibly remember as the right-hand man of No. 4, and I have no hesitation in saying, the finest-looking man in the battalion. He was about six feet two inches in height, and

twenty-five years of age. He was an Orangeman, loyal to
the backbone, and a well-bred gentlemanly Irishman.[7]

The Reverend George Young, who attended Scott in his last hours, reprinted this testimonial in his 1897 memoir, noting that after the execution he had
forwarded Scott's papers to his brother, Hugh. These papers included
"many commendatory letters of introduction, with certificates of good character, from Sabbath-school teachers and the Presbyterian minister with
whose church he had been connected in Ireland, as well as from employers
whom he had served faithfully."[8] Among the material forwarded to Hugh
Scott were savings of $103.50.[9] Young also quoted from a journal kept by
Scott in 1869. It noted that he and his brother had rowed on Belleville Bay,
and wondered "where we shall both be ten years from to-day."
Unfortunately, Young apparently did not copy the full texts of all the documents before returning them to the family, and could only refer to most of
them in the most general of terms. Nevertheless, Young's evidence indicates
that Scott had a Presbyterian upbringing and connection, as well as some
education. The presence of substantial savings do not suggest a riotous
lifestyle.

The letter from Captain Rowe is also one of the few first-hand pieces of
evidence that Scott was not only a northern Irishman or Ulsterman, but "an
Orangeman," a term used by contemporaries both to refer to all Protestant
Ulstermen who were of anti-Catholic persuasion and to those who were
actually members of the Orange Order founded in 1795 to defend the British
sovereign and the Protestant religion. In 1989 George Stanley reproduced a
resolution of the Orange Lodge of Toronto, which supposedly came from the
Toronto *Globe* of April 13, 1870. I have been unable to find the resolution
anywhere in the *Globe* or in other contemporary newspapers, but have no
reason to doubt that Stanley unearthed it somewhere, probably in another
Toronto newspaper unavailable to me. It read:

> Whereas Brother Thomas Scott, a member of our Order, was
> cruelly murdered by the enemies of our country and reli-
> gion, therefore be it resolved that while we sympathise with
> the relatives of our deceased Brother, we, the members of
> L.O.L. No 404 call upon the Government to avenge his
> death, pledging ourselves to assist in rescuing the Red River
> Territory from those who have turned it over to Popery, and
> bring to justice the murderers of our countrymen.[10]

Note that the Toronto Lodge does not claim Scott as a member of L.O.L. no.
404, but only that Scott was "a member of our Order"; the local lodge to

which Scott belonged never stepped forward, however, perhaps because it was in Ulster.

At the same time that the Orange Order claimed Scott, there is no evidence that he ever claimed the Orange Order. Despite the massive response of Orange Ontario to the death of a "brother," orchestrated by the Canada First movement, Scott has left no record—even in the Métis-inspired accounts—of anti-Catholic sentiment. Even if Scott had been a fervent anti-Catholic, of course, there is no reason to regard him as any more a "bigot" than millions of other Americans, Canadians, and Britons who shared with him an antipathy to "Popery" in the 18th and 19th centuries. According to Linda Colley, extreme Protestant anti-Catholicism was part of the glue that held the "British nation" together in the early years of the 19th century.[11] There was no reason to expect such sentiments to disappear by 1870. Whatever Scott's attitude toward Catholicism, as we shall see there is some evidence to support his brother's assertion that "where principle and loyalty to his Queen & country were at stake" he was "a thoroughly brave and loyal man."[12] Loyalty to monarch was another Orange attribute, of course, perhaps as important as hostility to the Pope.

In 1869 Thomas Scott decided to head west. He collected up his papers, doubtless including the introductions and testimonials later left by him with Reverend Young. According to an 1870 private letter of S.H. Harvard, reprinted by Young in 1897, he and Scott travelled from St. Cloud by coach in the summer of 1869.[13] Since St. Cloud was the head of the railway at the time, Scott presumably had gotten there by train. Harvard described Scott as "a fine, tall, muscular youth of some twenty-four years of age," who "behaved properly" and whose bearing was characterized by "inoffensiveness" to "those with whom we came in contact." Harvard made such observations in full appreciation of Scott's execution. The two men shared a bed at a roadside inn outside Abercrombie. Scott told Harvard that he was heading toward the Cariboo to try his luck at the gold mines. If what Scott told Harvard really revealed his plans, his sojourn in Red River may have been intended to be brief.

Shortly after his arrival in Red River in the summer of 1869, Scott took a job with the Canadian road-building crew headed by John Allan Snow. Snow had experienced considerable trouble over the construction of the road from Lake of the Woods to Upper Fort Garry, both within the settlement and on the site. Residents in the settlement were unhappy that the road was being built by the Canadians in advance of the transfer, under the cloak of providing work for famine-ravaged Red River. The settlers were also restive over Snow's efforts to buy land from the Natives. The labourers

Louis Riel and associates, c. 1869. Back row, left to right: Tom Laroque, Pierre Delorme, Thomas Bunn, Xavier Page, Andre Beauchemin, Baptiste Beauchemin, Thomas Spence. Middle row, left to right: Pierre Poitras, John Bruce, Louis Riel, W. B. O'Donoghue, Francois Dauphinais. Front row, left to right: Bob O' Lone, Paul Prue (Courtesy of the Archives of Manitoba/N5396).

themselves were unhappy both over their wages and their provisioning. Alexander Begg in his journal had earlier reported that Snow was charging more for provisions than he was paying for them in the settlement, and in 1874 Charles Nolin testified that Scott and other workmen did not like the food they were given, speculating this was perhaps because it was being improperly prepared.[14] According to Nolin, Scott led a three-day strike against Snow, which concluded with the strikers—Scott at their head—marching seventeen miles to Snow's office on October 1 to demand pay both for the time they had worked and for the time they had been on strike. Snow was prepared to pay the former, but not the latter. The men seized Snow and threatened to "duck" him. Snow paid up, but then had warrants issued against four of the men for aggravated assault.

The subsequent court case, the Queen *v.* W.I. Allan, Thomas Scott, Francis Moggridge, and George Fortnay, was heard before Mr. Justice John Black at the quarterly court of the District of Assiniboia on November 19. The court record is tantalizingly brief. It merely notes that Moggridge and Allan were found not guilty, while Fortnay and Scott were given 30 days to pay a fine of 4£ sterling each, their counsel Joseph Coombes acting as security for the payment.[15] Alexander Begg observed in his journal that the case had been

334 | THOMAS SCOTT AND THE DAUGHTER OF TIME

badly handled by the defence, suggesting that, given a better presentation by defence counsel Coombes, all four men would have been found innocent. He also added that Scott was overheard commenting before leaving the court "that it was a pity they had not ducked Snow when they were at it as they had not got their money's worth."[16] This comment is interesting both for the use of the term "duck," which suggests something different than "drown," and for the evidence that Scott had something of a dry sense of humour. We will see further evidence of the sense of humour later.

Much has been made of the Snow incident, particularly by Riel and the Métis, as an illustration of Scott's "troublemaking" and general willingness to employ violence and intimidation to gain his ends. Perhaps so. But it seems fairly feeble evidence on which to brand a man either a troublemaker or a bully. Scott was part of an organized worker protest against an employer regarded as having been exploitative and oppressive. He went to some lengths to confront that employer, and while he may have issued threats, no violence was actually employed. From what little is known of the affair and Scott's reaction to his court appearance, it would appear likely that he threatened John Snow with nothing more than a dunking, hardly a serious offence on the 19th-century frontier.

Scott presumably ended his employment with John Snow on October 1. According to Charles Mair, who regarded himself as a friend of Scott, the young man returned to Winnipeg and took up employment as a bartender.[17] If Scott did work as a bartender in Winnipeg, there was bound to be some confusion between himself and the American Alfred Scott, who was also employed as a bartender and was known to be a drinker. There is certainly no real evidence that Scott drank heavily, if at all. A large part of the supposed evidence for Scott's drinking is in testimony by one of his fellow prisoners in the Lépine trial that Scott was on one occasion "apparently half drunk." George Stanley uses this testimony—Scott was even drinking in confinement!—as the only evidence to support his assertion that Scott "drifted into Winnipeg where he drank and fought."[18] Apart from the fact that Stanley attributes the evidence to the wrong prisoner—William Chambers instead of Alexander Murray—it is clear from Murray's statement that he was referring to Alfred Scott, who was visiting Fort Garry with Hugh McKenny and Bob O'Lone for electioneering purposes. The only other contemporary reference to Thomas Scott and drink comes in the Lépine trial testimony of Alexander McPherson on October 15, 1874. He and Scott were taken prisoners together in February 1870, said McPherson, and when they arrived at the Fort, "Scott spoke to me, said it was very cold, let us go down and have a glass; started to go out, when we came near the gate we were pressed back by men of the Fort, Riel's men." This little incident tells us more about Scott's insouciance and sense of humour, however, than it does about his relationship with alcoholic beverages, since Scott must have known full well how unlikely it was that the Métis would let the two men saunter off to the saloon.

If there is little hard evidence to label Scott a drinker, there is even less to substantiate the story that he and Riel had, in 1869, come to blows over a woman. This tale first makes its appearance in 1885, in a little work written by Toronto journalist Joseph Edmund Collins entitled *The Story of Louis Riel the Rebel Chief*. Opposite the title page in this book is an engraving of an Indian attack on a log cabin, clearly showing stereotyped eastern rather than western Indian warfare. Thus is the tone set for the account that follows. The female, a métisse named Marie but given no surname, had supposedly been rescued from flooding waters by the brave Scott, who subsequently helps the girl and her family to hide from Riel and his clumsy courtship of her. After Scott is condemned to death, Riel attempts to get him to reveal the whereabouts of Marie. Scott refuses, of course, and Riel turns on him. "'She shall be mine!' he hissed, 'when your corpse lies mouldering in a dishonored traitor's grave'."[19] There is no contemporary evidence to support any part of this story.

In December of 1869 Thomas Scott joined a number of other residents of Red River, most of them Canadians or members of the so-called "Canadian Party," in an armed defence of the home and storehouse of Dr. John Schultz. In some quarters Scott has been regarded as a henchman or bully boy of Schultz, so it is important to emphasize that there is no contemporary evidence outside the accounts of his executioners to suggest that Scott and Schultz were even acquainted, much less close collaborators. That Scott gravitated to Schultz's house in December of 1869 does not particularly mark him out as under the influence (evil or otherwise) of the good doctor. Schultz was the acknowledged leader of the Canadian Party in Red River. All Canadians gravitated to him as the Métis stepped up their military activities, and the December 1 date was chosen for the Canadian takeover of Red River (the postponement by Ottawa of this event was not known in the West). Some Canadians, like the Graham brothers, apparently did not know Schultz at all when they "enlisted" to guard the stores and provisions stored at his house.[20] Others of the party, like J.H. O'Donnell, obviously did not like Schultz very much.[21] The party of defenders were buoyed up by the circulation by John Dennis of Governor William McDougall's proclamation of the Canadian takeover dated December 1, 1869. McDougall, of course, had jumped the gun, but the Canadians at Red River were not to know this fact for several weeks. In early December they could legitimately see themselves as the local supporters of the Canadian government and opponents of Louis Riel as a rebel leader.

Scott only emerged out of the crowd at Schultz's house when he was appointed by the band of loyalists on December 7, 1869 as one of the delegates in a "deputation to Riel under a flag of truce, to endeavour to make terms."[22] The Reverend George Young subsequently wrote that these delegates bore "a request to Riel that the ladies then resident in Dr. Schultz's besieged buildings should be permitted to retire therefrom, as they were suffering from prolonged excitement and alarm."[23] According to the account in the *Globe* of April 15, 1870, Scott and "Mr. McArthur" were the two chosen. Peter McArthur in 1934 recalled that the two delegates were Scott and his brother Alex McArthur.[24] According to A.W. Graham's diary, however, the delegates were Scott, McArthur, and William Hallett.[25] Whoever the delegates, the Canadians had no bargaining power whatsoever. Riel had the house surrounded with armed Métis, backed up by cannon from the fort trained at the flimsy wooden structure, and he felt no need to make a deal. All three sources agree that Riel held Scott and sent McArthur back to report that the only terms were total surrender. The sort of spin that could be put on such actions is demonstrated by Major Boulton's account in 1886. Although Boulton appears to confirm Young's account of Scott's peace mission, he probably heard the story from the Methodist clergyman in the first place: "Scott, it ought to be said, was not taken prisoner with arms in his hands. On the first occasion, before the prisoners were captured in Dr. Shultz's house, he had gone boldly down to the Fort to ask Riel to give safe conduct to the ladies and children who were in danger there, and Riel's only answer to his peaceful mission was to thrust him into prison."[26]

After the unsuccessful negotiations, a party from the town headed by A.G.B. Bannatyne met with the Canadians to advise unconditional submission. What happened to Scott is a matter of some disagreement among the sources, however. Both Graham and McArthur suggest simply that Scott had been made prisoner a few minutes earlier than the remainder of the Canadian party. The account of Coombes and Allan is far more detailed, however. "Aha! says the sneaking Louis" to Scott, "'you are just the man I was looking for,' and with deep malice gleaming from his treacherous and sinister eyes, he ordered his men to seize him. Scott was a man of great stature, six feet two inches in height, of goodly symmetry, and of an ardent and rather impetuous nature, freely expressing his opinions. The act of the despot was prompted by the pettiest motives of personal revenge. Scott had always treated him with marked contempt. Once in the town of Winnipeg he [Scott] got into an altercation with him [Riel], in a saloon, and threw him by the neck into the street."[27] Scott's service as a "bartender," an occupation that often included "bouncer" duties, might explain this contretemps. But the confrontation must have occurred between early October (when Scott left Snow's employ) and early December, a period in which Riel, who was not a drinking man under any circumstances, would have been unlikely to have spent much time in Winnipeg saloons. Indeed, the constant alcoholic consumption of Riel in the account of the Red River uprising according to Allan and Coombes leads one to suspect that they were already engaging in their own version of myth-making and character assassination. Nonetheless, another version of this story had been reported unattributed to anyone by the *Globe* a few days earlier: "Mr Scott, we are told, was a quiet and inoffensive, but at the same time, very powerful and determined man. Before his arrest, Riel stopped him on some road he was going and Mr. Scott with a strong arm thrust him aside and told him to mind his own business."[28] Like the later story of rivals in love, more obviously a total fabrication, these accounts seek to provide an explanation for the later behaviour of Riel towards Scott, which might otherwise appear inexplicable. But these stories are contemporaneous—the tale of Allan and Coombes coming from men who were imprisoned for six weeks with Scott—and therefore cannot be totally ignored.

In any event, Scott became a prisoner at Upper Fort Garry. Incarcerated with the great crowd of Canadians in an upper-storey flat normally used by Hudson's Bay Company clerks, Scott had no opportunity for contact with Dr. Schultz, who was imprisoned in one of the officer's houses below along with his wife, and who subsequently escaped separately from the others. Scott does not appear in any of the first-hand contemporary accounts of prison life until January 9, 1870, when he was one of a number of prisoners who escaped from the Fort. Several of his fellow prisoners subsequently commented on Scott's first incarceration in Upper Fort Garry. In 1914 George Winship sent a manuscript account of the first imprisonment to James Ashdown for comment. In it Winship had characterized Thomas Scott as a "pugnacious fellow" who "believed in the arbitration of violence to settle disputes," although how much such a description owed to Scott's subsequent reputation is open to question. In any case, Ashdown commented, "I do not consider that Scott was very 'Pugnacious': he was a big strong fellow and used language somewhat freely, but was not a bad fellow in any sense of the word."[29] Twenty years later, Peter McArthur in his "Recollections" of 1934–35 wrote that "Scott's death was a great shock to us; he had said loudly and openly what the rest of us quietly thought."[30] Unfortunately,

Upper Fort Garry (left background), May 1873. Situated at the junction of the Red and Assiniboine Rivers ("the Forks"), the fort stood in what is today the centre of the city of Winnipeg. Today, only the north gate of the fort remains standing, a heritage site in a small park (Courtesy of the Archives of Manitoba/N14017).

McArthur was not more specific about what either Scott said or the other prisoners thought. On the other hand, A.W. Graham, in the course of reporting the death of Scott as a reason for his family's hasty departure from Red River in 1870, recorded in his diary somewhat closer to the event: "Let me say here that I was over four weeks in Scott's company in Fort Garry jail and I found him quiet, civil and always gentlemanly. Why Riel should say he was a bad man I could never learn."[31]

We do have an account of Scott's escape from Upper Fort Garry in the journal of Henry Woodington, who accompanied him out of the window that cold January night. According to Woodington, the sound that night of the wrenching of a window frame out of the wall in the prisoners' room was covered by the noise of the prisoners "piling on" Joseph Coombes. "Piling on" was, along with chess, cards, and checkers, one of the principal games played by the prisoners in confinement. It was indeed their special favourite. "It begins," explained Woodington, "with one catching hold of another and throwing him down or against the wall, yelling 'pile on.' Then there is a general rush to the scene, and pity the poor fellow that gets under."[32] The popularity of such schoolboyish antics in captivity reminds us that most of the prisoners at Upper Fort Garry were, like Scott, young men with their hormones in full flight. Apart from going down the hall to relieve themselves, this was apparently the only exercise the prisoners got. What the Métis guards made of "piling on," which must have happened so frequently that they did not bother to check on the noise the night of the escape, is another matter. The game may well have produced a general Métis perception that the prisoners were all crazy men of violent proclivities.

In any event, Scott and Woodington by prior arrangement started a brisk trot to Headlingly upon their escape from the Fort. The snow was deep and they were weak from confinement, but they hurried on. They called at the home of William Hallett about two and one half miles from the Fort, and then raided a stable for horses. But they could find no tack. Scott tried to ride without saddle, harness, and reins, but was pitched off the horse into a deep snowbank. "Just imagine the sight," recalled Woodington. "Scott is over six feet in height, with a short body and very long legs, sticking in the snow, with his legs almost straight up in the air." The two men lost the horses and resumed walking. The impression Woodington leaves of the affair is one of great jocularity. The majority of the 12 escapees were easily recaptured, and one of them (Walton Hyman) was badly frostbitten. Thomas Scott was one of the five who remained at large.

Scott eventually made his way to Portage la Prairie. This village was technically outside the jurisdiction of the Council of Assiniboia and beyond the reach of Métis armed authority. It had originally been settled mainly by Canadians, and many other Canadian refugees, including Major Charles Boulton, had gathered there after the imprisonment of the party at Dr. Schultz's house. Another escapee from Upper Fort Garry, Charles Mair, had ended up in Portage at about the same time as Scott, although independently of him. In his 1886 memoirs of the North-West Rebellions, Boulton offers us a glimpse of Scott at Portage. "He gave graphic accounts of his imprisonment and escape, and once more the question was raised to organize a party to effect the release of the other prisoners," wrote Boulton.[33] Boulton's words give us no reason to conclude that Scott was particularly active in organizing the rescue operation; the use of the passive mood in the second part of the sentence on Scott is instructive. There is corroboration on this point. In the 1874 trial of Ambroise Lépine, William Chambers testified that Scott had come to Portage after the question of liberating the prisoners had already been raised.[34]

Nor does Boulton suggest in any way that Scott was a leader of the Portage expedition. In fact, he specifically lists the expedition's "officers," a roster that does not include Scott. Several of the witnesses at the Lépine trial emphasized that Scott was not a leader of the Portage party. According to William Chambers, for example, "Scott had no position in the force, was a full private."[35] Alexander McPherson recalled that the Portage party "seemed to act spontaneously"; he added, "Thomas Scott was with us; he was not a principal actor; there were none."[36] Alexander Murray testified of the Portage expedition: "there was not much commanding by any one."[37] Boulton did record that it was Scott who—on the party's passage through the vil-

Charles A. Boulton, pictured here as a Lieutenant-Colonel at the time of the North-West Resistance in 1885. From *The Illustrated War News*, Volume 1, Number 10, June 6, 1885 (Courtesy of the Glenbow Archives/LAC-1480-26).

lage of Winnipeg on its way to Kildonan—helped him call at a house looking for Louis Riel: "Thinking we might make a timely capture, we surrounded the house, and Scott and I entered to search for Riel; but the host assured us he was not there; so we passed on without disturbing the family."[38] As we shall see, this incident became an important part of the Métis indictment of Scott.

None of the contemporary Anglophone evidence even mentions Thomas Scott's presence at Kildonan, where Norbert Parisien was badly beaten after he had shot Hugh John Sutherland. The only eye-witness glimpse we have of Scott at Kildonan comes from Donald McLeod, in a memoir of 1942 written when he was 84 years old. Born in 1858, McLeod in 1870 had carried bread to the soldiers at the Kildonan schoolhouse. Scott was among them. "As clothing he wore a Pea Jacket, Beaver cap and leather britches and a gold ring in his left ear," Mcleod recalled.[39] This is the only place where the gold earring appears. It is such an odd recollection that one wants to believe it. Although hundreds of Anglophones gathered at Kildonan in mid-

February of 1870, the assemblage quickly dispersed when it was announced that Riel was already releasing the prisoners held at Upper Fort Garry. The Portage party, including Thomas Scott, decided to make its way back to its point of origin. Unfortunately, it returned via a route that took it all too near Riel's stronghold at Upper Fort Garry, and it was easily captured by Riel's forces. Many of the party insisted that Riel had promised them safe passage, but whatever the reason for the blunder, Thomas Scott found himself once again a prisoner of Louis Riel. Apart from Alexander McPherson's story about Scott's jocular walk for a drink, there were no other anecdotes told about Scott at this particular juncture. According to William Farmer, at the moment of capture "Scott offered no resistance."[40]

Anglophone evidence from Scott's second incarceration is both limited and confused. Two points stand out. First, the time period between the capture of the prisoners and the court-martial of Scott—especially after the time taken up with the threatened execution of Charles Boulton is excluded—was relatively short, less than two weeks. Secondly, none of the fellow prisoners or clergymen whose testimony has survived appear to have spent much time with Scott over the course of his captivity, and none, except Alexander Murray and George Sanderson in a much later oral account, offered much account of his behaviour. Sanderson claimed that Scott had been offensive to everyone, including his fellow prisoners, but from what vantage point in Upper Fort Garry he made these observations is not clear.[41] According to Alexander Murray, Scott was initially kept in a room in the same range as the other prisoners, but he was eventually put in another room on the opposite side. Certainly Scott ended up in solitary confinement. Murray added, "I heard that Scott had difficulties with the guards more than once, but never saw it."[42]

Few of the Anglophone prisoners witnessed any persistent confrontations between Scott and his guards. George Newcombe dated Scott's troubles from only the day before his execution.[43] So Alexander Murray, who offered one of the most detailed fellow-prisoner accounts of Scott's confrontation with his guards:

> I saw Riel, Lépine and O'Donolme on the night previous to Scott being shot; they were in the guard-room; Riel came and asked me if I was a Canadian; I told him no! but I belonged to that party; I went back to my room; he followed me up and apparently looking [*sic*] in my room; I closed the door and said, "Boys, keep quiet, for Riel, O'Donohue and Lépine are in the guard-room." I knelt on my knees and looked through the key-hole; I heard a knock on the door

where Scott was confined; the door was opened slightly by one the guards; Scott said, "I want to get out"; the door was opened a second time; Riel stepped up to Scott, and Scott said he wished to be treated civil; Riel said he did not deserve to be treated civil and called him a dog; Scott asked for his book, I think a pocket-book; Riel said he hadn't it; the door was then shut; I understood it to be a call of nature.[44]

Charles Boulton told a similar story in his memoirs. Although the events he describes happen over a shorter time frame, there are several confrontations between Scott and his guards. About a fortnight after the capture, Boulton recognized Scott's voice in the guardroom, demanding his pocket-book. A considerable scuffle ensued and Scott was locked up in a room. Boulton investigated, and learned that Scott had just advised the prisoners to have nothing to do with Alfred Scott and others who had solicited their votes. The visit of Alfred Scott dates this confrontation in late February. Later Scott asked leave to go outside (presumably to the lavatory) and was refused, which led to another altercation. Riel and O'Donohue visited Scott that same afternoon and evening, "and used violent language against Scott." According to Boulton, he did not manage to visit with Scott until the court-martial had been completed. "I found that similar questions had been put to him as had been put to me, and the same mode of passing sentence had been passed upon him as had passed upon me. I told Scott to be very careful what he said, as I felt sure that Riel meant mischief and would take his life if he could. By then such advice was too late."[45]

The evidence of the several Protestant clergymen who dealt with Scott's final hours was potentially quite confusing. The Reverend John McLean testified at the Lépine trial that he "saw Scott one day, found him handcuffed and his legs ironed; asked him how he was and why he was there; he said he had some trouble with the guards; had some conversation with him about his spiritual wants and when I was coming away I asked permission to call upon him again, but that night he was brought up, and on the following day he was shot; I was totally ignorant of his danger; I afterwards learned that that was the last day of his life."[46] In the wake of the threatened execution of Charles Boulton, McLean told the court he had spoken to the prisoners about the deal he and Donald Smith had made with Riel to save Boulton's life (to visit the Anglophone parishes and convince them to send representatives to the new provisional government). He wanted to gain their consent, and admitted he did so by telling the prisoners "that I thought they were in danger of their lives."[47] But this warning was not particularly directed at Scott. McLean's recollections are quite compatible with (although not identical to) Donald Smith's report of his meeting with Father Joseph Jean-Marie Lestanc on March 4, at which Lestanc had commented on the bad behaviour of the prisoners. According to Smith, "I expressed much surprise at the information he gave me, as the prisoners, without exception, had promised to Archdeacon McLean and myself, that seeing their hopeless condition they would endeavour to act so as to avoid giving offence to the guards, and we encouraged them to look forward to being speedily released, as fulfilment of the promise made by Mr. Riel." Smith added that a prisoner named Parker had been described as quite obnoxious, but not one word had ever been said to him about Scott.[48]

The Reverend George Young in his 1874 trial testimony insisted that he had no conversation with Scott before March 3, by which time he had been tried and was out of irons, but added that when he had visited Scott the previous Saturday—presumably without exchanging any words worthy of the label "conversation"—the young Irishman had been in irons.[49] Young's account in 1897 was quite different: "On Sabbath, February 27th, while visiting the various prisons, I was pained to learn that Scott had been sent into solitary confinement, and going at once to his room, found him in a most pitiable condition—a dirty arid fireless room, a single blanket to rest on or wrap himself in, and with manacles on both wrists and ankles. No marvel that he shivered and suffered under such circumstances. On my asking if he knew the reason of this increased severity, he assured me that he did not, and readily promised to carefully avoid, in action and utterance, whatever might be offensive to the guards."[50] These clerical accounts (and that of Alexander Murray) can be more or less reconciled by assuming that Scott's first confrontation with his guards (as reported by Murray and Boulton) had occurred on Saturday, February 26, and that Scott was in irons from at least the Saturday to the Thursday, when he was tried and then unshackled in preparation for his execution. But the chronology never entirely hangs together.

In any event, Thomas Scott was brought before a military court on the evening of March 3 and tried for his life. At the 1874 trial of Ambroise Lépine, the adjutant general's private secretary Joseph Nolin was the star prosecution witness, offering the only eye-witness account of that trial available. Why Nolin testified in 1874 is not clear from the court records, although the Nolin family had been opponents and critics of Louis Riel for many years. None of the other participants in the event, including Ambroise Lépine, testified in 1874, presumably for fear of self-incrimination. Because it remains the fullest account, and because there is so much confusion in the secondary literature over the details of the trial, Nolin's evidence (as given by unofficial court reporters) must be quoted in full.[51] He was reported as testifying:

> Scott was tried on the evening of the third of March; at the council that tried him Lépine presided; the other members of the council were Janvier Richot, André Nault, Elzear Goulet, Elzéar Legemonière, Baptiste Lépine, and Joseph Delorme; I was secretary of the council; Scott was not present at the beginning; some witnesses were examined to state what evil Scott had done; these witnesses were Riel, Ed Turner, and Joseph Delorme; don't recollect any other witnesses; do not recollect nature of the evidence; Scott was accused of having rebelled against the Provisional Government and having struck the captain of the guard; Riel made a speech, I think against Scott; after the evidence had been heard Scott was brought before the council; Riel asked me to read to Scott what had passed before the council; did not, as I had written nothing; Rid then explained the evidence to Scott, and asked him if he had any defence to offer? Scott said something but I forget what; Riel did not ask Scott whether he had any witnesses; there was no written accusation against Scott; the work of the Council was done in about three hours; the Council sat about 7 o'clock; took some notes of the evidence; wrote them out regularly and gave them to the Adjutant General; Richot moved and Nault seconded that Scott deserved death; Lépine said he would have to be put to death—the majority want his death and he shall be put to death; that closed the business of the council; Riel explained to Scott his sentence; and asked him if he had any request to make or wanted to see a minister? I do not remember what answer Scott made; Riel said if the minister was at the Stone Fort he would send for him; Riel said he would send Scott up to his room, that his shackles would be taken off, and that he would have pen, ink, and paper to write what he wished to; Riel then told Scott he would be shot next day at 10 o'clock; I do not know what Scott said; he was then taken to his room; when the vote was taken Baptiste Lépine objected to taking the life of Scott; he said they had succeeded so far without shedding blood and he thought it better not to do so now; Ed Turner took Scott to his room; saw Lépine the next morning about

> 8 o'clock; Lépine told me to write a verbal report of the pro-
> ceedings of the Council; Riel came to see the report and said
> it was not formal; Riel then dictated the report; it was made
> from notes of the evidence; don't remember what Riel
> changed; gave it to Lépine when written.[52]

Under cross-examination by defence attorney Joseph Chapleau, Nolin
observed that during the entire trial he heard Lépine say nothing against
Scott. Nolin testified:

> After the vote had been taken on the execution of Scott, by
> the words Lépine used and his demeanor during the whole
> trial, I understood him to be against the death of Scott, but his
> words were "the majority being for his death, he must die."

The witness then added,

> the prisoner [Lépine] did not order me to write the sen-
> tence, nor did he write judgment then; Riel was the person
> who explained what was the sentence, and where and when
> it was to he performed; Riel was Scott's accuser; Scott was
> accused of having taken up arms against the Provisional
> Government, after taking an oath not to fight against it; he
> was also accused of striking one of the guards, and Riel
> himself; Edmund Turner one of the witnesses was an
> Irishman; Turner and Joseph Delorme were witnesses,
> Joseph Delorme was also one of the Council; do not know
> what position Turner held; believe Riel was first accusator
> and also witness; Riel made the charges against Scott ver-
> bally; Riel was sworn to prove his charge by me; Riel was
> the only accuser; don't think Scott asked to examine wit-
> nesses; I think he said something, but do not know what he
> said; Riel was speaking English; Turner was speaking
> English. The charge of striking Riel and the guard referred
> to the scuffle in the guard room.

Nolin then told the chief justice that he was "not sure that evidence was produced to show that Scott had taken the oath to the Provisional
Government," adding: "I do not know if any book was produced; the 'taking up arms' referred to his coming down with the Portage party." At the
close of his testimony, Nolin also told the chief justice that escaped prisoners had never taken any oath.[53] The impression he left in his testimony was
that there had been one or two incidents involving Scott rather than a
persistent pattern of offensive and insulting behaviour. However, Scott's

behaviour toward Riel and his guards was only part of the indictment against him.

Leaving aside all questions about the legal propriety of or possible legal models for these proceedings, exactly what—according to Joseph Nolin—had happened there? Before attempting to answer this question, two points must be made about Nolin's account of Scott's trial. One is that Nolin was a key witness for the prosecution in a murder trial of 1874. The second, however, is that he was under oath and subject to full cross-examination. While what we have of his testimony are unofficial reports rather than an official verbatim transcript, it is clear from these that defence counsel Chapleau cross-examined Nolin extensively, and the chief justice himself asked questions of clarification as well. Nolin is not necessarily the definitive witness on Scott's trial, but his testimony must be accepted as credible as far as it goes. His account is quite clear that Scott was not present for a most important part of the proceedings, the presentation of the evidence in support of the charges against him.[54] Those charges and the evidence for them (emanating partly from Louis Riel) were subsequently summarized to Scott in English by Louis Riel. Later commentators such as A.H. de Trémaudan, who have tried to insist that Riel was not present at all at the trial, must contend with Nolin's evidence.[55] On the other hand, whether Nolin's account fully supports George Young's assertion that "Riel acted as prosecutor, witness, and judge" is for the reader to decide.[56] Certainly Nolin emphasized that it was Riel who had written up the report of the tribunal, although this official account has not survived.

Scott was not condemned entirely unheard. He was offered some opportunity to respond to the charges, although not to examine the witnesses. According to the Reverend Young in 1874, Scott said afterwards he had "objected to the trial as it was conducted in a language he did not understand, but was told it made no difference; he was a bad man and had to die."[57] Scott's objection was only partially correct. While he was present before the tribunal Scott was dealt with in English, but he was not present the entire time, and especially had not heard any of the testimony against him, at least some of which was given in French. A better objection would have been that much of the trial had been conducted in his absence. Scott certainly had no legal advice at any point and was, according to subsequent reports, quite stunned by the entire proceedings. Whether the young Irishman was actually present for the vote on his case, which was not unanimous, is not clear from Nolin's statements, but the sentence was subsequently "explained" to him by Riel and he was offered what amounted to "last requests" of the condemned, including the services of a clergyman.

The Métis Evidence of Scott's Character and Conduct

Métis explanations for Scott's death began before the firing squad had begun its work. The chief Canadian commissioner to Red River in 1870 was Donald A. Smith, who had been kept under virtual house arrest at Upper Fort Garry since his arrival in the settlement several months earlier. On March 11, Smith was visited by the Reverend George Young about 11 A.M., and informed of the intended execution of Scott at noon. Young then went to plead with Riel, unsuccessfully, first for Scott's life and then for delay on the grounds that the young Irishman was not prepared to die. The minister sent a messenger to inform Smith of his failure. Smith, accompanied by Father Lestanc, then called on Riel himself. The Métis leader turned to Smith and said, "I will explain to you." In his report to Ottawa, Smith transcribed what Riel then said. According to Smith, Riel

> said in substance, that Scott had, throughout, been a most troublesome character, and had been ringleader in a rising against Snow, who had charge of a party employed by the Canadian Government during the preceding summer in road making, that he had risen against the Provisional Government in December last, that his life was then spared; that he had escaped and had been again taken in arms, and once more pardoned (referring no doubt to the promise he had made to me that the lives of the prisoners were secured), but that he was incorrigible, and quite incapable of appreciating the clemency with which he had been treated; that he was rough and abusive to the guards and insulting to him (Riel), and that his example had been productive of the very worst effects on the other prisoners, who had become insubordinate to such an extent that it was difficult to withhold the guards from retaliating.[58]

Riel further told Smith that Scott had admitted to him that he and the Portage party "intended to keep you [Riel] as a hostage for the safety of the prisoners." Smith, who had never met Scott, argued that the worst case Riel had made out was that the Irishman was a "rash, thoughtless man, whom none could desire to have anything to do with." This statement represented Smith's summary of what Riel had recounted, rather than his own assessment, and was hardly evidence of Scott's character or personality.[59] The charges Riel raised against Scott, Smith more than implied, did not deserve a death sentence. In this assessment it is difficult not to concur. The Snow affair was irrelevant, the searching of the Winnipeg house a natural by-product of the internal conflict of the time, and Scott had never taken an oath of good conduct. Obviously prisoners should be well-behaved, docile, and easily manageable, but prison authorities might well expect other behaviour, especially in the course of a civil war.

At the end of this lengthy interview, which delayed the execution beyond its appointed time, Donald Smith noted that the insurrection had to this point been bloodless, and that bloodshed might make the negotiations with Canada more difficult. To this Riel replied, "We must make Canada respect us." Riel then offered one more example of Scott's offensive behaviour. When Alfred Scott, at Riel's behest, went to see the prisoners to look for their vote in the Winnipeg election for councillor to the provisional government, it was Thomas Scott who had come forward to advise against such support, saying "My boys, have nothing to do with those Americans."[60] Riel and Smith then jousted about the Americans. Why Riel thought Scott's comments and actions here could serve as part of the indictment against him was not clear from the conversation as reported by Smith. Charles Mair, who was not present at the second incarceration, reported an alternate version of this incident, based on a later account he received from Murdoch McLeod. Alfred Scott had been accompanied by the Fenian Dan Shea in the solicitation of the prisoners' votes. According to McLeod, Thomas Scott had shouted, "Boys, you can do what you like, but I won't consent." He was thereupon "ironed with irons which had been taken off Boulton."[61] In any event, Riel closed the discussion by observing to Smith, "I have done three good things since I have commenced. I have spared Boulton's life at your instance, and I do not regret it, for he is a fine fellow; I pardoned Gaddy, and he showed his gratitude by escaping out of the bastion—but I do not grudge him his miserable life; and now I shall shoot Scott." The impression Riel left with Donald Smith was that Scott had been condemned as much for defying Louis Riel as for his behaviour with his guards.

The explanations given to Smith were quite compatible with Joseph Nolin's 1874 testimony in the Lépine trial about the charges levied at the military tribunal against Scott. They were also more or less compatible with two subsequent statements emanating from the friends of the provisional government at the time of the execution. The first appeared in the Red River newspaper controlled by Riel, *The New Nation*, dated the very day of Scott's death. *The New Nation* described the deceased as "Private T. Scott," giving him (and the Portage party) formal military standing and turning the affair into a proper military execution. It reported that from Scott's second capture, he was "very violent and abusive in his language and actions, annoying and insulting the guards, and even threatening the President." It then provided a more detailed discussion of Scott 's threats against Riel: "He

[Scott] vowed openly that if ever he got out he would shoot the President; and further stated that he was at the head of the party of the Portage people who, on their way to Kildonan, called at Coutu's house and searched it for the President, with the intention of shooting him."[62] Donald Smith had reported Riel's assertion that Scott had admitted he would have held him to ransom if he had managed to capture him, but there had been no mention of further violence. Now, according to *The New Nation*, Scott actually had threatened to shoot Riel on several occasions! The emphasis of this newspaper account seemed to be on Scott's threats against Louis Riel.

The second contemporary statement appeared in the Quebec clerical newspaper the *Courrier de St. Hyacinthe* in March, and was translated and reprinted in the *Globe* on April 7. The correspondent began: "I send you the following details so that you may be able to use them in reply to the attacks which will doubtless be made." According to this account, Scott had "led the conspiracy against Mr. Snow," whose life had been saved by the Métis. When the Portage people "rose in insurrection against the Provisional Government, he was a strong partisan and entered a house in Winnipeg, where the President often passed the night, while others surrounded it, doubtless with the intention of killing Mr. Riel." Reimprisoned, he had "insulted the President, attacked a captain and a soldier, his insolence was so great that one day Capt. Boulton asked to be admitted to his room so as to make him quiet."[63] The *Courrier* letter insisted that Scott's behaviour had negatively affected the other prisoners. The execution was both to give an example and to "certainly prevent a great loss of life."[64] The correspondent went on to claim that although Scott had been allowed to see a clergyman, he had told Reverend George Young "that he did not belong to any religion." Riel thereupon ordered all the soldiers in the Fort to pray for Scott's change of heart. This letter was very probably written by Father Lestanc, who, according to the text, had interceded for this unfortunate man "who had rebelled and taken up arms against an authority recognized by the two populations." It did not claim that Scott had actually threatened Riel with shooting, however. Scott's prison behaviour was only a part of his offence against the provisional government: his real problem was that he was neither religious nor a Catholic. The *Globe*'s editorial writers had a field day with this letter, particularly with the collective prayers by the rebels that Scott would experience a last-minute conversion.

As for Louis Riel, he turned again to Scott in 1872, when he drafted "Mémoire ayant trait aux difficultés de la Rivière-Rouge."[65] In this document Riel associated Scott with "Schultz et Co." Riel reported the searching of the house of Henri Coutu with the intention of capturing him, but did not here claim that Scott had threatened to shoot him. He noted the deaths of Sutherland and Parisien, but did not attribute blame to anyone for these occurrences. Scott was very violent in his second incarceration, wrote Riel, who focussed on the Irishman's prison behaviour in this document. On the last day of February Scott had really upset the guards, wrote Riel, beating on the "prison gates" and insulting them. The guards had taken him outside and were preparing to "sacrifice him" when a French councillor saved him. Riel quietened the guards a day later, but Scott continued to be offensive and the guards continued to demand a council of war, which they finally got on March 3. The impression Riel left in this document was that he had been pressured into acting against Scott by the insistent demands of his guards and Scott's refusal (or inability) to cease being offensive to them. The exact nature of Scott's offensive behaviour was never specified. Riel and Ambroise Lépine presented a slightly different argument in their famous memorial to Lieutenant-Governor Morris in January 1873, although the focus was still on Scott's prison behaviour.[66] Scott and "Mr [Murdoch] McLeod" had "beat their prison gates and insulted, and went so far as to strike their guards, inviting their fellow-prisoners also to insult them." Only a punishment could "restrain these excited men," and so, said Riel and Lépine, "we had recourse to the full authority of Government."

The same themes reappeared in an 1874 account by Riel entitled "L'Amnistie. Mémoire sur les causes des troubles du Nord-Ouest et sur les négotiations qui ont amené leur règlement amiable," which he probably wrote while in exile in New York State.[67] This document rehearsed the events of the entire rebellion from the perspective of both Riel and the Métis. Here Scott was described as "one of the most dangerous partisans of Dr. Schultz, McDougall, and Dennis." His involvement in the search for the president of the provisional government in Winnipeg was clear evidence that he was in arms against that authority. Once again imprisoned, he and fellow prisoner Murdoch McLeod "forcèrent les portes de leur prison, se ruèrent gardes, invitant leurs compagnons à faire comme eux." "Tous" demanded that Scott be brought before the "conseil de guerre," and when the Irishman persisted in his "mauvaise conduite" he was finally summoned, against a background of rising new troubles which were not specifically described. Scott was examined on "témoignages assermentés," was convicted and condemned to death. On March 4 the authority of the provisional government, which had the goodwill of the Anglophone colonists, was used to "disarm our enemies."

"L'Amnistie" was published by *Le Nouveau Monde* of Montreal as a pamphlet early in 1874, and quickly drew a response—in the form of a lengthy letter published by various newspapers—written by Dr. James Spencer Lynch, one of the most extreme of the Canadian Party in Red River during the rebellion.[68] Lynch was one of the prisoners taken at Dr. Schultz's house in December of 1869, and he played an active role in the anti-Métis and anti-provisional government campaign in Ontario in the spring of 1870. Lynch's letter objected to Riel's interpretation of the events of 1869–70 on a variety of fronts, including the execution of Thomas Scott. Lynch's principal complaint about the trial of Scott was that it had been quite improper, conducted as it was in French, a language that the accused did not understand. He also criticized the manner and timing of the execution. Riel responded to Lynch's rambling critique in an equally rambling document that was printed in *Le Nouveau Monde* on March 12, 1874.[69] Regarding Scott's trial, Riel denied categorically that it had been conducted in French: "Durant le procès, tout ce qui a été dit en francais, a été traduit en anglais: et tout ce qui a été dit en anglais a été traduit en français." Given Joseph Nolin's subsequent description under oath of the proceedings of the tribunal, this categorical denial may have been a bit disingenuous.

Riel also denied that Lynch had managed to rehabilitate "le caractère de Scott" by asserting that Scott was a decent man of steady habits. Riel's response was noteworthy for the introduction of a new level of attack on the character of Scott. Riel brought several new charges against Scott. "It is said" ("il est dit"), he wrote, that Scott had tracked down Norbert Parisien after the shooting of Hugh John Sutherland, attached a belt ("une ceinture") to his neck, and dragged him behind a horse for a quarter of a mile. Scott was now well set on his way to becoming "the bad man who had to die." That the young Irishman had sought to assassinate ("voulu assassiner") Mr. Snow in 1869 at Pointe de Chênes was an old accusation. What appeared now for the first time about Pointe de Chênes was the assertion that the community still recalled the disorder created by Scott and his companions during riotous evenings. While the men were away, the women and children had guarded their doors and windows against the Canadians. Riel closed his text: "Here is what the entire parish of Pointe de Chênes knows. Scott was reasonable? He was of regular habits? Let the reader decide."[70]

Over the next few years, Riel returned more than once in his writing to the Scott execution, which he appeared to realize full well had been a disastrous misjudgement. In one fragment of 1874–75, for example, he wrote, "Si j'ai mal fait de faire exécuter Th. Scott, ô Divin esprit, daignez me le faire connaître parfaitement afin que je vous en demande pardon, que j'en implore contrition parfaite et que j'en fasse penitence; afin que j'en demande pardon aux hommes; afin que j'avoue hautement cette faute, si je l'ai faite."[71]

But nothing new was introduced by Riel on the Scott front until, on a return visit from Montana to Winnipeg, he gave an interview with a reporter from the Winnipeg *Daily Sun* in June of 1883.[72] It is difficult to know what to make of this interview, which in its frankness was quite different from another Riel gave a reporter from the Winnipeg *Daily Times* only a day later.[73] In the *Sun* interview Riel categorically included the execution of Thomas Scott among those acts he would do again. He insisted that Archbishop Taché's presence would not have stopped the execution, "because I was really the leader, and whenever I believe myself to be right no man has ever changed my opinion." In the *Daily Times* interview, on the other hand, he insisted, "I don't like to speak about political matters at all, and only do so because I do not like to refuse to answer your questions."

Louis Riel, c. 1873 (courtesy of the Archives of Manitoba/N5732).

Riel insisted that Scott was an important loyalist leader "in influence and prominence, among Métis opponents behind only Schultz, Dennis, and Bolton [*sic*]. Schultz and Dennis were beyond the reach of the government, Riel admitted. "They were more guilty, too," thought Riel, "although Scott was guilty enough." Riel told the *Sun* reporter that Scott came close to being killed by the Métis for trying to murder his guard. The Irishman had "seized a bayonet that was in the room and endeavoured to slay the guard by plunging it into him through an opening in the door of the guard room. He was always hot-headed and violent." As an example of one of his "crazy acts," Riel repeated the story of Scott's dragging Norbert Parisien with a horse, one end of a scarf tied around Parisien's neck and the other tied to the tail of the horse. When Riel pleaded with Scott to be quiet in the Fort, Scott had replied, "You owe me respect; I am loyal and you are rebels." From Scott's perspective, of course, this observation was indisputable. From Riel's, it was apparently another illustration of Scott's insulting attitude.

According to a third-hand report reprinted in many Canadian newspapers in 1885, Riel purportedly told his confessor, Father Alexis André, shortly before his execution that he now saw the death of Scott as a "political mistake" but not a crime.[74] Riel added that Sir John A. Macdonald was executing Louis Riel for the same reason that Riel had executed Scott, "because it is necessary for the country's good." He continued, "I admit Scott's shooting was mismanaged, but I commanded it because I thought it necessary. He tried to kill his guards. They came to me and said they could do nothing with him. The rebellion was on the eve of breaking out all over the country, but as soon as Scott was killed it subsided."

Further stories about Scott's bad behaviour, mainly drawn from the oral traditions of the Métis community, appeared in the years after Riel's death, often in work produced within the Manitoba Francophone historiographical tradition. A.H. de Trémaudan recounted in a footnote of great detail Scott's mistreatment of Norbert Parisien, based on an interview of 1923 with André Nault, who sat on Scott's court martial and voted for his execution. Nault gave as his source "Parisien himself, while he was lying on his sick bed."[75] Trémaudan also reported a story told him by Paul Proulx, a councillor of the provisional government in 1870 and a frequent visitor to Upper Fort Garry, about an interview between Riel and Scott, after the guards had told Riel that if Scott was not executed, they would shoot Riel himself.[76] "Riel went to warn Scott, who sneeringly said: 'The Métis are a pack of cowards. They will never dare shoot me.' Then Rich asked him again, 'Ask me anything at all for a punishment.' 'I want nothing,' retorted Scott, 'you are nothing but cowards'."[77] A.G. Morice, without giving a source, wrote in 1935 that "such was the fury which the very sight of the Métis chief could arouse in his [Scott's] breast that, having one day seen him pass by the half-open door, he sprang at him as would a wild beast and, knocking down in his excitement the stool on which he had been sitting, cried out to him with a significant gesture: 'Ah! son of a b—, if I ever recover my liberty, it is at these my hands that you shall perish!'"[78] This is one of the few instances where Scott is recorded as using obscenity, and it is not documented to a first-hand source. In none of Riel's accounts does Scott employ a single swear word, although it is true that Riel may have been too prudish to reproduce any.

There was an Anglophone oral tradition about Scott as well, some of which was reported by George MacBeth in his *The Romance of Western Canada*: "In their cold quarters in Fort Garry, the prisoners used to keep themselves warm by wrestling and sparring. Scott is said to have taken a few rounds out of the guards, and Riel treated that as contempt of his high authority; and so a kind of trial was held…"[79] MacBeth also reported that Scott's body had been dumped in the river, weighted down with chains, "as I learned in later years from one who was there when it was done."[80] Another local story dealt with the failure to find Scott's body. It had Scott released by the Métis at the last minute, and paid to disappear into the United States, as the authorities hoped to do with Riel and Ambroise Lépine a year later. The execution was then faked.[81]

The tendency to view the killing of Scott as a political act, although not everyone would agree on the politics involved, has dominated the historical treatment of Scott since 1870. While on one level such a perspective is quite legitimate, what has gotten lost in the process is the question of the character of Thomas Scott himself. While not everyone has accepted the propriety or legitimacy of Scott's execution, few have come forward to question the Métis characterization of him as a "hard case," at the very least "hot-headed and violent" and at the worst a singularly villainous man.[82] We shall never be able to get at the unvarnished truth: what we can do, however, is to appreciate the nature of the problem of evidence regarding Scott, and seek to avoid some of the worst excesses of the treatment of Scott's character resulting largely from the ongoing partisanship of the events in which he found himself enmeshed.

What can we say about Scott's character? Many of our conclusions must be negative, rejecting features that have most often received attention from the secondary literature. No contemporary first-hand evidence exists to suggest that he was a heavy drinker. The stories from Pointe des Chênes are about all the Canadian workmen, not about Scott. No evidence survives that he was a henchman of John Schultz, that he was a leader of the "Portage Boys" or the Canadian Party, or even in Riel's many statements, that he was either an extreme anti-Catholic or a master of profanity. Ironically enough, given his subsequent enshrinement as Orangist martyr, Scott's Red River contemporaries never mentioned his Orange Order affiliation. Apart from the stories about his treatment of Norbert Parisien— which are not substantiated in any of the many Anglophone eye-witness accounts of affairs at Kildonan in mid-February 1870, including that of Charles Boulton, who claimed to have saved Parisien from his tormenters after he shot Sutherland—there is precious little evidence that Scott was a bully. Aside from his ducking of John Snow—which could well have been an instance either of frontier justice or boyish high spirits—and the dubious tales of his early confrontations with Riel, there is little evidence from the Anglophone side of Scott's use of physical violence. Alexander Begg wrote

LIST OF RIGHTS

1. That the people have the right to elect their own Legislature.

2. That the Legislature have the power to pass all laws local to the Territory over the veto of the Executive by a two-thirds vote.

3. That no act of the Dominion Parliament (local to the Territory) be binding on the people until sanctioned by the Legislature of the Territory.

4. That all Sheriffs, Magistrates, Constables, School Commissioners, etc., be elected by the people.

5. A free Homestead and pre-emption Land Law.

6. That a portion of the public lands be appropriated to the benefit of Schools, the building of Bridges, Roads and Public Buildings.

7. That it be guaranteed to connect Winnipeg by Rail with the nearest line of Railroad, within a term of five years ; the land grant to be subject to the Local Legislature.

8. That for the term of four years all Military, Civil, and Municipal expenses be paid out of the Dominion funds.

9. That the Military be composed of the inhabitants now existing in the Territory.

10. That the English and French languages be common in the Legislature and Courts, and that all Public Documents and Acts of the Legislature be published in both languages.

11. That the Judge of the Supreme Court speak the English and French languages.

12. That Treaties be concluded and ratified between the Dominion Government and the several tribes of Indians in the Territory to ensure peace on the frontier.

13. That we have a fair and full representation in the Canadian Parliament.

14. That all privileges, customs and usages existing at the time of the transfer be respected.

All the above articles have been severally discussed and adopted by the French and English Representatives without a dissenting voice, as the conditions upon which th. people of Rupert's Land enter into Confederation.

The French Representatives then proposed in order to secure the above rights, that a Delegation be appointed and sent to Pembina to see Mr. Macdougall and ask him if he could guarantee these rights by virtue of his commission ; and if he could do so, that then the French people would join to a man to escort Mr. Macdougall into his Government seat. But on the contrary, if Mr. Macdougall could not guarantee such right, that the Delegates request him to remain where he is, or return 'till the rights be guaranteed by Act of the Cana., n Parliament.

The English Representatives refused to appoint Delegates to go to Pembina to consult with Mr. Macdougall, stating, they had no authority to do so from their constituents, upon which the Council was dissolved.

The meeting at which the above resolutions were adopted was held at Fort Garry, on Wednesday, Dec. 1, 1869. Winnipeg, December 4th, 1869.

"List of Rights" drawn up by Louis Riel and his supporters in early December of 1869 (Courtesy of the Archives of Manitoba/N5402).

sympathetically of Scott in the Snow affair; and certainly nothing from the Métis side suggests that Riel and Scott had ever met before December 1869. George MacBeth, who was a young man in Kildonan in 1870 but not personally acquainted with Scott, summarized the Anglophone memory when he wrote in 1898: "There is no need now to canonize Scott, nor to claim that he possessed all the virtues and none of the vices of life; but so far as we can gather from those who knew him well, he was a young man of rather quiet habits, indisposed, as most men of Irish blood are, to be trodden upon, but not given to aggressive and unprovoked offending."[83]

As MacBeth's comments suggest, most of his Anglophone contemporaries saw Scott as a well-mannered young Irishman, who had a sense of humour and may perhaps have had a bit too much of a tendency to speak his mind. James Ashdown was the only one who suggested that Scott might have made frequent use of profanity, if we assume that was what was meant by being "free with his language." Although the Scott of the later secondary literature often employed foul language, Louis Riel himself never suggested that this was what Scott's "insults" were about. It is possible that Riel's objections to profanity meant he could not bring himself to repeat what Scott had actually said, although such a position seems too puritan even for Riel. Scott was certainly fearless: there are hints that some of the actions that brought him to the forefront—the negotiations with Riel in early December, the searching of the Winnipeg house in mid-February, perhaps even the standing up to his Métis captors—were the result of his willingness to do things that others were afraid of doing. Scott was also a loyal Canadian, critical of the Americans and an acknowledged opponent of the provisional government of Riel and the Métis. Perhaps—as much of the secondary literature suggests—Scott had nothing but contempt for half-breeds. But insofar as the actual language he used can be substantiated from first-hand testimony, it suggests that he was chiefly contemptuous of rebels. The lionization of Riel has tended to obscure the fact that loyalty to Canada was quite legitimate in the context of the Red River of 1869–70, and that Riel and the Métis could indeed be perceived as rebels against the Queen. Scott ought not to be made out a villain simply because he opposed Louis Riel and the provisional government, or because many Anglophone contemporaries rather simplistically saw his loyalty as the sole cause of his execution.[84]

Nor ought Scott to become a martyr solely because of the poignancy of his last few hours. The details of the death of Scott were, from the very beginning, the stuff of legend, particularly since it was never clear who actually had been an eyewitness to the event. Most of the written accounts came years later from men who had not been present at the time. There were approximately 150 eyewitnesses to the actual execution, however, mostly residents of the village of Winnipeg. The testimony of many of them, taken at the 1874 murder trial of Ambroise Lépine, demonstrated mainly how lacking in precise observational powers and memory most eyewitnesses could be; they even disagreed over exactly what the time was when Scott was shot.[85] George Young was certainly present at the execution, but his detailed account of it, written years later, was hardly definitive.[86] Much of it was confused with Donald Smith's 1870 report to Ottawa, which Young had obviously read.

The execution of Thomas Scott outside of the walls of Upper Fort Garry on March 4, 1870. From a sketch by Roland Price Meade, an artist and editor with the *Nor'-Wester* newspaper, who had also been imprisoned by Riel (courtesy of the Archives of Manitoba N5953).

Among the various eyewitnesses, there was general agreement that Scott was led out of the east-side gate at Upper Fort Garry and shot against the wall there. Reports varied as to whether he emerged blindfolded or was blindfolded later. Scott apparently prayed continually while in the open air. According to Donald Smith, who was inside the fort and heard an account from others, the condemned man told Reverend Young, "This is a cold-blooded murder." Young's much later report was that Scott had said, "This is horrible! This is cold-blooded murder. Be sure to make a true statement." Scott then knelt in the snow and said, "Farewell." A firing squad of six men, according to some witnesses intoxicated, then shot him. Reports of the number of shots varied, although several narratives (including Young's) agreed that the Irishman did not die instantly after the initial volley. Some said he was dispatched on the spot by a revolver bullet through the head.[87]

As we have seen, there was a bad Thomas Scott; he was almost entirely a product of Métis evidence, however, especially that of Louis Riel. That testimony is almost entirely unsubstantiated on the Anglophone side, either in specifics or in tone. It is possible that Scott turned into a monster around the Métis, and especially under confinement. But as was pointed out earlier, it would seem fairly problematic to accept without question the executioners' unsubstantiable accounts of the victim's bad character and behaviour when this bad character and behaviour was mainly what was used to justify his execution. Moreover, the evidence of Scott's bad character did become progressively blacker and more detailed as time progressed, especially in the later Métis oral tradition and in the burgeoning secondary literature. Louis Riel, for example, saw Scott as a man of incorrigibly violent behaviour, but never suggested that Scott used profanity, was contemptuous of Métis, or was bigoted against Roman Catholics. André Nault, who had been tried and acquitted of Scott's murder, was the source for several of the later stories, recounted to earnest researchers after an afternoon or evening of conviviality.[88]

One of the many mysteries surrounding the execution of Thomas Scott was what had become of his body, which had supposedly been buried in a plain wooden coffin within the walls of Upper Fort Garry. The question took on special piquancy because of the insistence of several witnesses, mainly Métis guards, that the firing squad had not actually killed him. Noises and talking were heard from the coffin by several passers-by after the execution. Moreover, when the grave was finally dug up after the arrival of the Wolseley expedition in the autumn of 1870, it was found to be empty. The defence in the trial of Ambroise Lépine made much out of this absence of a body, although most contemporaries were satisfied with trial testimony which suggested that the corpse had been disinterred in the middle of the night a few days after the execution and dumped in the Red River.[89] Louis Riel went to his grave without disclosing the final whereabouts of Scott's body, which was one of the last questions asked him.[90]

Instead of becoming obsessed with the disposition of Scott's physical remains, however, it might have been more useful if more of his contemporaries had been concerned with his reputation. Thomas Scott was not only a victim, he was also a perfect illustration of the way historians, or the twists of history, can blame the victim. That he was young, a stranger to Red River, and without social connections, all contributed to the unfortunate end result.

Notes
This article first appeared in *Prairie Forum* 23, no. 2 (1998): 145–70.
1. Josephine Tey, *The Daughter of Time* (1951; London: Harmondsworth, 1974), 94. Tonypandy is a place in the South of Wales where—according to Tey—a riot which was stopped by unarmed London police was built up as a massacre by armed troops of Welsh miners striking for their rights.
2. Ibid., 95.
3. There are two reports of this trial: one in a publication entitled *Preliminary Investigation and Trial of Ambroise Lépine for the Murder of Thomas Scott, Being full report of the proceedings in this case before the Magistrates' Court and the several Courts of Queen's Bench in the Province of Manitoba* (Montreal: Burland-Desbarats, 1874), which was based on the court reports of various reporters for eastern Canadian newspapers; and one in Winnipeg's

Free Press, which was based on the work of local reporters. The two sets of reports have much in common, particularly because the various participants distributed their set speeches in advance to the press, but also probably because the reporters often pooled their resources. But there is some significant new material in the *Free Press* accounts which has not often been used by historians. In addition to the published accounts, the trial notes of Judge Edmund Burke Wood also survive, in the Provincial Archives of Manitoba. These provide over 160 pages of crabbed judge's notes, often illegible, on the testimony.

4. Easily the most blatant example of such malpractice occurs in Dr. Peter Charlebois, *The Life of Louis Riel in Pictures* (Toronto: NC Press, 1978). He quotes from Mrs. Black's account of her brother's death in William Healy's *Women of Red River* (Winnipeg: Women's Canadian Club, 1923) that his killer Parisien was "lying half-unconscious with the blood streaming from a wound in the side of his head which Thomas Scott had given him with a hatchet." In Healy's text, the original quotation read "which someone had given him with a hatchet."

5. W.B. Osler in *The Man Who Had to Hang: Louis Riel* (Toronto: n.p., 1952), for example, described Thomas Scott as an "obscure young man" who "cursed himself into eternity." Osier continued: "First there was the time—it was months before Riel and his men turned back McDougall at the frontier—when they [Riel and Scott] met on the street in Winnipeg and Scott, cursing, furiously attacked Riel with his fists. Louis, no fighter, was rescued by onlookers. No one ever found out what caused this outburst. Even Riel apparently did not know. Later, when Scott was first captured and imprisoned at Fort Garry, he screamed curses at his guards and beat upon his cell door. Then he escaped, and in the raid on Coutu's home he informed the indignant householder and anyone else within hearing that when he caught Riel he would kill the bastard. Recaptured, he renewed his abuse of the guards. And one day when his cell door was opened as the President walked past he leaped into the corridor, flung himself upon Riel, and screamed: "You son of a bitch! If I'm ever free I'll kill you with my bare hands!'" (182–83).

6. Quoted in Frances G. Halpenny (ed.), *Dictionary of Canadian Biography*, IX, 1861–1870 (Toronto :and Buffalo: University of Toronto Press, 1976), 707.

7. Quoted in Rev. George Young, *Manitoba Memories: Leaves from My life in the Prairie Province, 1868–1884* (Toronto: William Briggs, 1897), 145.

8. Ibid. What survives of this material is in the United Church Archives (Toronto), George Young file.

9. George Young file. W.L. Morton in his introduction lo W.L. Morton (ed.)*Alexander Begg's Red River and Other Papers Relative to the Red Rivet Resistance of 1869–70* [hereafter *Begg's Journal*] (Toronto: The Champlain Society, 1956), argues from these savings that Scott was "obviously neither a wastrel nor a drinker" (p. 111). This money may have played an important role in Scott's behaviour during his second imprisonment. According to Alexander Murray in his 1871 Lépine trial testimony, he and Scott were taken prisoner together in February. The two were searched and Murray had his pocketbook containing £60 taken from him. According to Murray, Scott asked for his pocketbook in the course of the final contretemps with Riel.

10. G.F.G. Stanley, *Toil & Trouble: Military Expeditions to Red River* (Toronto and Oxford: Dunburn Press, 1989), 78.

11. Linda Colley, *Britons: Forging the Nation 1707–1837* (New Haven and London: Yale University Press, 1992).

12. Hugh Scott to John A. Macdonald, April 6, 1870, quoted in Morton, *Begg's Journal*, 111n. His brother also described Thomas as "a very quiet and inofensive [sic] young man," an assessment which has traditionally been ignored, presumably because of its source.

13. Young, *Manitoba Memories*, 144. If Scott got to Red River by coach, then he could not have been the "James Scott" who arrived on board the steamer *International* in late June in company with "Wm. A. Allen" and "F.J. Mogridge"' *Nor'Wester*, June 26, 1869. It is also possible that the newspaper got the surname wrong; James Robb is a likely alternate candidate.

14. Nolin insisted that the food itself was good, since he had supplied it. Charles Nolin Testimony, October 21, 1874, at Lépine Trial.

15. Provincial Archives of Manitoba (PAM), MG 2 B4-1, District of Assiniboia Minutes of Quarterly Court, Sheriff's Court Book.

16. *Begg's Journal*, 173.

17. Norman Shrive, *Charles Mair, Literary Nationalist* (Toronto: University of Toronto Press, 1965), 94. According to the diary of P.G. Laurie in the Saskatchewan Archives Board, E.L. Storer Papers, Scott was living at "Garrett's" while awaiting trial. According to the *News-Letter* of February 1, 1871, he helped collect funds about this time for the welcome of Governor McDougall to the settlement.

18. Stanley, *Louis Riel*, 111 and note 52.

19. *The Story of Louis Riel the Rebel Chief* (Toronto/Whitby: I.S. Robertson and Brothers, 1885), 117.

20. "Diary of A.W. Graham," *The Elgin Historical and Scientific Institute Proceedings* (1912).

21. John H. O'Donnell, *Manitoba as I Saw It. From 1869 to Date* (Toronto: Clarke, 1909), esp. 30 ff.

22. Report of William Allan and Joseph Coombes, in Toronto *Globe*, April 15, 1870.

23. Young, *Manitoba Memories*, 131–32.

24. PAM, MG 11 A1, "Recollections of Peter McArthur 1934–5."

25. "Diary of A.W. Graham," p. 75.

26. Charles Arkoll Boulton, *Reminiscences ofthe North-West Rebellion, with a Record of the Raising of Her Majesty's 100th Regiment in Canada, and a Chapter on Canadian Social & Political Life, by Major Boulton, Commanding Boulton's Scouts* (Toronto: Grip Printing anti Publishing Co., 1886), 133.

27. Report of Allan and Coombes.

28. The *Globe*, April 4, 1870.

29. PAM, MG 3 B15, James Ashdown notes on Winship Manuscript (1914).

30. PAM, NG11 Al, "Recollections of Peter McArthur 1934–5."

31. "Diary of A.W. Graham," 82.

32. PAM, MG; 3 B11, "Journal of Henry Woodington, 22 September 1869–17 February 1870.

33. Boulton, *Reminiscences*, 101 ff.

34. Testimony of William Chambers, *Free Press*, October 15, 1874.

35. Ibid. In his unpublished thesis, Neil Allan Ronaghan argues that after Scott's death, the Canadian Party conspired "to leave the impression that Scott had played almost no part in their affairs." He offers no evidence for this assertion, nor does he explain why such action made Scott a better martyr. In any event, the result, argues Ronaghan, is that "the researcher must regard everything written about Scott after April of 1870 with caution,

and everything written after 1885 with suspicion." Ronaghan, "The Archibald Administration in Manitoba—1870–1872" (PhD dissertation, University of Manitoba, 1986), 211–12.

36. Testimony of Alexander McPherson, *The Trial of Ambroise Lépine*, October 14, 1874.

37. Testimony of Alexander Murray, *The Trial of Ambroise Lépine*, October 16, 1874. Nor was Scott one of the fourteen members of the "general council for the force" chosen at Kildonan and listed in the *St. Paul Daily Pioneer*, April 2, 1870.

38. Boulton, *Reminiscences*, 105.

39. PAM, P733 f 110, Memoir of Donald McLeod.

40. Testimony of William Farmer, *Free Press*, October 14, 1874.

41. Irene Spry (ed.), "The Memoirs of George William Sanderson," *Canadian Ethnic Studies* 17 (1985): 115–34.

42. Testimony of Alexander Murray, *The Trial of Ambroise Lépine*, October 16, 1874.

43. Testimony of George Newcombe, *The Trial of Ambroise Lépine*, October 15, 1874.

44. Testimony of Alexander Murray, *The Trial of Ambroise Lépine*, October 16, 1874. Murray continued this testimony by dating this contretemps at nine p.m. on the evening of March 3. We know from other evidence that Scott had already been tried and convicted by this time, so something must be wrong with Murray's chronology.

45. Boulton, *Reminiscences*, 126–27.

46. Testimony of John McLean, *Free Press*, October 20, 1874.

47. Testimony of John McLean, *The Trial of Ambroise Lépine*.

48. Donald Smith to Joseph Howe, April 28, 1870 (no source given)

19. Testimony of George Young, *Free Press*, October 15, 1874. The evidence about the previous Saturday does not appear in the *Free Press* report, however, but only in *The Trial of Ambroise Lépine*.

50. Young, *Manitoba Memories*, 132–33.

51. Donald Gunn and Charles Tuttle, in their *History of Manitoba* (Ottawa: Maclean, Roger, 1885), 396–97, were the only early historians who quoted Nolin's testimony at length, although their earlier discussion of the Scott "court-martial" made clear that they did not entirely understand what Nolin had said.

52. Testimony of Joseph Nolin, *Free Press*, October 17, 1874; *The Trial of Ambroise Lépine*.

53. Ibid.

54. A.G. Morice ignored this point when he cited Nolin's sworn evidence as part of an impassioned demolition of the subsequent "English" criticism of the trial in *A Critical History of the Red River Rebellion* (Winnipeg: Canadian Publishers, 1935).

55. Trémaudan asserted in *The Canadian Historical Review* 6 (1925), "I have it from some of the men who sat on that trial that Riel had nothing whatever to do with the proceedings taken, the decision arrived at, and the execution performed, beyond, of course, the appointment of the tribunal itself, and except, before and after the verdict was rendered, to plead with his people for mercy" (p. 233n).

56. Young, *Manitoba Memories*, 133.

57. Testimony of George Young (no source given).

58. Smith to Joseph Howe, April 28, 1870, reprinted in Morton, *Begg's Journal*.

59. A.G. Morice, in his *Critical History*, wrote in a footnote, "As we have seen, even D.A. Smith called him [Scott] in his Report 'a rash, thoughtless man, whom none cared to have to do anything with'." A number of other writers repeat Smith's remark without noting that it was not Smith's assessment.

60. Smith argued that this was a trifling business, but Riel insisted, "Do not attempt to prejudice us against Americans, for although we have not been with them they are with us, and have been better friends to us than Canadians."

61 Quoted in Shrive, *Charles Mair*, 103.

62. *The New Nation*, March 4, 1870.

63. According to Boulton, this visit occurred only after Scott had been sentenced to death. See Boulton's *Reminiscences*, 127.

64. Letter from Fort Garry in the *Globe*, April 7, 1870.

65. G.F.G. Stanley et al. (eds.), *The Collected Writings of Louis Riel/Les Ecrits Complets de Louis Riel* (Edmonton: University of Alberta Press, 1985), vol. 1: 198–200. This document was originally reprinted as "The Execution of Thomas Scott" with a translation and extensive notes by A.H. de Trémaudan in *The Canadian Historical Review* 6 (1925): 222–36. In these notes, the editor introduced a good deal of information based on recent inteiviews with Métis involved with Riel in 1869–70.

66. Ibid., 243–57, especially 247.

67. Ibid. 298–319, especially 308–11.

68. See the Montreal *Gazette*, February 18, 1874, and the Montreal *Herald*, February 19, 1874.

69. It has been reprinted in Stanley et al., *The Collected Writings of Louis Riel*, vol. I: 323–49.

70. The original document was written in French. This translation is mine. It is entirely possible that the Scott involved in the drinking bout was James Scott, who according to the *Nor'Wester* of June 26, 1869 arrived in Red River in late June with Francis Moggridge and William A. Allen aboard the steamer *International*. If it was James Scott who helped terrorize the community, then Thomas Scott was once again being blamed for alcoholic activities not really his fault.

71. Ibid., 421.

72. Reprinted in Stanley, *The Collected Writings of Louis Riel*, vol. II: 413–23.

73. Ibid., 424–26.

74. Ibid., vol. III: 583–84.

75. Trémaudan, "The Execution of Thomas Scott," 228–29n.

76. Ibid., 231n.

77. The Anglophone witnesses concur that Scott could not believe that he would actually be executed. These witnesses suggest that Scott's disbelief was a product of his sense that he did not deserve death for his behaviour, rather than because of his contempt for his captors.

78. Morice, *Critical History*, 283n.

79. R.G. MacBeth, *The Romance of Western Canada*, 2nd ed. (Toronto: William Briggs, 1920), 156–57.

80. Ibid.

81. PAM, MG3 B23, W.M. Joyce Papers.

82. "Issued from a low social stratum," wrote A.G. Morice, "he was of a naturally rough disposition which, in captivity, bordered on actual ferocity," in *Critical History*, 283.

83. R.G. MacBeth, *The Making of the Canadian West: Reminiscences of an Eyewitness* (Toronto: William Briggs, 1898), 82.

84. Captain George Huyshe in his *The Red River Expedition* (n.p., 1871), 20, insisted that Scott's "only crime had been loyalty to his Queen and country."

85. Scheduled for noon, the execution occurred nearly an hour later, partly because of the time taken by Donald Smith pleading for Scott's life.

86. Young, *Manitoba Memories*, 131–37.

87. Witnesses at Lépine's trial could not agree on who had fired the revolver shot.

88. See, for example, Trémaudan, "The Execution of Thomas Scott" for an account of the interviewing process.

89. A.G. Morice in 1935 wrote that he had learned from André Nault, who claimed to be one of those who had helped Riel remove the body from the Fort, that it had been buried in an unmarked spot in St. John's Protestant cemetery. Morice, *Critical History*, 293–95.

90. Stanley, *The Collected Writings of Louis Riel*, vol. IV: 583.

16. The Battle of Batoche

Walter Hildebrandt

The Battle of Batoche has been the subject of numerous scholarly and popular studies.[1] This interest, however, has been focussed on the significance of the battle, its consequences, and its importance as a watershed in
Canadian history and as a symbolic victory of Anglo-Canadian forces over
those resisting the new economic order. The earliest publications, Major
Boulton's *Reminiscences of the North-West Rebellion*, and C.P. Mulvaney's *The
History of the North-West Rebellion of 1885*, were based on first-hand accounts
of North West Field Force participants anxious to explain their victory.
Immediately after the appearance of the official account of the rebellion,
published in the Canada Sessional Papers in 1886, little analytical work was
attempted.[2] Early accounts made almost no reference to sources that might
have provided perspective to the Métis actions.[3] This to some extent has
been corrected by George Stanley and, more recently, Desmond Morton, but
the overall result of past histories of the Battle of Batoche has left the military actions of the Métis and the Indians vague. The impression that the outcome of the battle was inevitable still remains.[4]

Traditionally, the last day of the battle, when the North West Field Force
suddenly and surprisingly broke through weakened Métis lines at the
southeastern end of the battlefield, has been emphasized. Yet a detailed narrative shows that the first day had by far the most military action, which
included the *Northcote* incident and at least two nearly successful attempts
by the Métis and the Indians to outflank the North West Field Force. On this
first day the Métis and the Indians put such pressure on Middleton's men
that some accounts suggest that only the highly mobile and rapid-fire
Gatling gun prevented a serious setback. In fact, according to Reverend G.
Cloutier's diary, the Métis considered the first day a victory.[5] They believed
that their actions caused Middleton to withdraw into the zareba on the
evening of May 9.

GENERAL MIDDLETON

Major General Charles F.D. Middleton (courtesy of the RCMP Historical Collections Unit/33.20.CXLIV).

One other noticeable imbalance exists in the historic record. The tactics adopted by Middleton bore the brunt of considerable criticism, especially by the Canadian officers, many of whom felt slighted because Middleton preferred British officers. Similar criticism from military historians has been made without reference to contemporary military handbooks such as Garnet Wolseley's *A Soldier's Pocketbook*.[6] Furthermore, none of the well-known accounts of the military actions cite the military manuals of the day, such as Captain Callwell's *Small Wars: Their Principle and Practice*.[7] This last book makes frequent reference to Middleton's actions during the 1885 campaign. Indeed, they are held to be exemplary, given the conditions he encountered. The ten maps which illustrate my article are based on the documents and maps of the period and on many trips to the site to examine the terrain over which this battle was fought.[8] (In this endeavour I am indebted to Jack Summers, who tramped the site with me on numerous occasions over the past two years. Without his insights, much of what is detailed here could not have been accomplished.)

In 1885 there were approximately 48,000 Native westerners in the Assiniboia, Saskatchewan and Alberta territories.[9] Politically, many grievances of these people had been ignored, and fears of an Indian uprising were widespread.[10] The dangers of an uprising by Native westerners were denied by P.G. Laurie of Battleford, editor of the *Saskatchewan Herald*, whose columns frequently contained diatribes against reports from eastern newspapers, whose editors claimed the Western frontier was a lawless and dangerous territory.[11] Laurie thought that such reports might slow the settlement he so desperately wanted. Also known to many was the recent catastrophe at the Little Bighorn. Such factors lent credence to the preconceived but basically irrational notion of a hostile, wild frontier.[12] It was largely for this

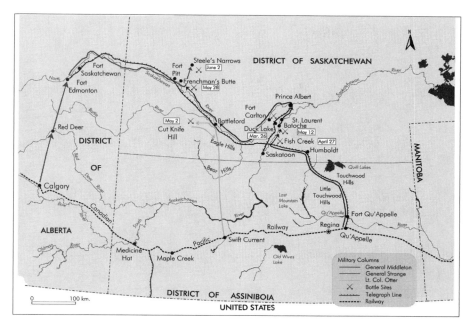

Troop movements and battles of the 1885 North-West Resistance (courtesy of the Canadian Plains Research Center Mapping Division. Adapted from the 1999 *Atlas of Saskatchewan*).

reason that the North West Field Force organized a careful well-ordered strategy to move into this unknown territory.

Major General Charles F.D. Middleton, CB, Commander of the Canadian Militia and leader of the North West Field Force, was uncertain about the exact number of "savages" his men would be fighting. The experience of British contingents in small wars throughout the Empire showed that caution would have to be exercised. When fighting native forces, there was always the fear that a small group could easily gain momentum with a few early successes against a regular European-type army.[13]

Not all Canadian leaders were confident of a clear early victory. The obstacles of geography, transportation and supply were enormous. Middleton, though armed with a brash confidence, initially showed disregard for the fighting prowess of the Métis and forged ahead to confront them as soon as he could. Only after Fish Creek, the first encounter and a setback for the North West Field Force, did Middleton grudgingly acknowledge that he had underestimated the Métis.[14]

To move against Prince Albert and, later, Batoche, identified as the Métis stronghold, Middleton and his officers agreed to a three-pronged movement

Burial site of the victims of the 1885 "Frog Lake Massacre." Names are inscribed on the large cross in the middle, which is surrounded by smaller unmarked wooden crosses. Photograph by Geraldine Moodie (courtesy of the RCMP Historical Collections Unit/941.9.52).

into the Northwest. Columns were to march towards what were considered to be potential trouble spots. Middleton would proceed north from Qu'Appelle (Troy) along the South Saskatchewan; Otter from Swift Current towards Battleford; and Strange from Calgary towards Edmonton. Of these columns only two were to be engaged in any serious fighting, and only Middleton's column was involved in more than one battle with the Métis in which any lives were lost.

Essentially there were five significant battles or confrontations during the suppression of the insurrection in the West. The North West Field Force was involved in four of them: Fish Creek, Cut Knife Hill, Batoche and Frenchman's Butte. At Duck Lake the skirmish was between the Métis and the North West Mounted Police, under Superintendent Crozier. One other major event occurred during the campaign: the Frog Lake Massacre, where whites and Métis in the community were killed and the remainder taken hostage by Big Bear's Cree insurgents. Only the Battle of Batoche gave the government forces a decisive victory. The sole clear victory for the Métis came at Duck Lake. The other three conflicts—Fish Creek, Cut Knife Hill and Frenchman's Butte—were all stand-offs in one form or another. At Fish Creek, the Métis retreated after an indecisive battle; at Cut Knife Hill, Otter withdrew pursuant to the resistance of Poundmaker's Cree; and at Frenchman's Butte, Big Bear's Cree retreated from the barrage of fire into their defensive alignment, although the militia were unable to pursue them through the muskeg.

Perhaps more significant than the battles which were fought, were those which were not. Although the newspapers of the time indicate that many whites feared reprisals from Indians during the rebellion, very few took place. At Battleford, some 500 men, women and children were allegedly besieged in the North West Mounted Police fort by Poundmaker's Cree, but the fort was not directly attacked, although the stores of the town, momentarily abandoned by a frightened population, were looted.[15] In Prince Albert, residents protected by the North West Mounted Police were not threatened by Indians or mixed bloods. Trouble was anticipated from the large number of Indians comprising the Blackfoot Confederacy. Crowfoot, their war chief, had received an invitation from Riel to join the resistance, but did not respond. The presence of the North West Mounted Police and the trust the Indians had was certainly partially responsible for their reluctance to participate alongside Riel.[16] A general attack was feared by many whites in the West, however.

The Governor-General and Adolphe Caron, the Minister of the Militia, differed with Middleton over the course of action that would most quickly end the campaign. The target for the first attack remained uncertain. Governor-General Lansdowne clearly believed that after Fish Creek, Prince Albert would be the objective for the North West Field Force. He had written to Lord Derby in London stating that he hoped Middleton would join forces with Otter at Prince Albert and would then advance on Batoche: "Middleton will probably have to fight again on his way to Prince Albert. He would, I gather, prefer not to fight if he could avoid doing so, until after he had reached Prince Albert and perhaps effected a junction with Otter."[17] Lansdowne, who was in touch with Caron on an almost daily basis, appeared to be under the impression that a greater number of troops would finally advance on Batoche.[18]

The correspondence between Lansdowne, Derby and Melgund (later Earl of Minto and Governor-General of Canada) leaves the impression that there were reservations over Middleton's ability to conduct the campaign from the field. Lansdowne intimated these concerns to Melgund. On one occasion he wrote, "The Fish Creek affair has troubled me very much—Even

Middleton's column proceeding though the Qu'Appelle Valley (courtesy of the Saskatchewan Archives Board/R-B2845).

without your private telegrams I could read something very like the word disaster between every line of the General's other accounts. I have thought all along that he and the experts quite underrated the difficulty of the task before him."[19] Other observers saw Middleton as a general too old and reluctant to engage in combat and to advance on Batoche:

> During this tedious delay General Middleton gave all sorts of excuses for his reaction. One day it was want of supplies then he had not sufficient medical staff to take with him after having a suitable force to look after the wounded. Then the excuse was that the wounded could neither be left where they were nor removed up the river to Saskatoon. The truth was that he was afraid to advance on the rebels' position at Batoche until he was materially reinforced.[20]

Whether Middleton actually had a clear plan of attack in mind for Batoche after Fish Creek is not known. According to Boulton, Middleton seldom communicated his intentions even to those in his immediate staff. What is known is that up to April 29, Middleton was heading towards Prince Albert and that he was reluctant to engage his men too hastily after Fish Creek: "Find it would be better to push on to Prince Albert by Hudson's Bay Crossing. Troops behaved well but are raw, officers same. Would not be safe to risk defeat so shall relieve Prince Albert and join with Otter in attacking rebels.

Shall send courier to Humboldt or Clark's Crossing … am engaged in bringing column to this side. Will march tomorrow."[21] It was a rather optimistic
prediction the day after Fish Creek and it was in fact to be over two weeks
before he would march again. Three days later, on April 28, Middleton again
reasserted his conviction to move to Prince Albert first. Middleton had
mixed reactions to the battle; in his communications to Caron there was only
a cautious optimism. "I think we have taught the rebels a lesson and am
pretty sure that I would march to Batoche, but their men would harass me
all the way, and I lose a great many men and I am very averse to that and do
not think it would be politic."[22]

The arrival of the *Northcote* on May 5, with its supplies and two companies of the Midland Battalion on board, coincided with Middleton's change
of plans. Middleton's confidence seemed renewed with the appearance of the
Northcote, and Batoche now became his objective. Reasons for changing tar-
gets from Prince Albert to Batoche are unclear, and no evidence exists to suggest that he discussed his change in plans with any of those around him or
with Caron in Ottawa. Even those at the front believed he would first move
on to Prince Albert. Major Boulton, Commander of Boulton's Scouts, wrote:

> On the 5th of May General Middleton completed his
> arrangement for a further advance on Batoche. At the time
> he was, I believe, urged to advance directly on Prince
> Albert, in order to effect a junction with Colonel Irvine and
> his corps of Mounted Police, leaving Batoche for future
> attack; but no doubt feeling that this would be a sign of
> weakness, the General determined to march on to Batoche,
> and to attack Riel in his stronghold without further delay,
> sending a message to Colonel Irvine to cooperate with him
> from the North.[23]

A new determination now pervaded Middleton's communications and
he no longer expressed concern over his shortage of manpower—he certainly dropped the idea of joining forces with Otter for an attack on Batoche.
This might have been due, at least partially, to Otter's fall from favour after
his battle with Poundmaker's Cree at Cut Knife Hill on May 2. Otter had
embarked on his mission to Cut Knife Hill against Middleton's orders but
with the approval of Lieutenant-Governor Dewdney. These two events—the
arrival of the *Northcote* and Otter's encounter at Cut Knife Hill—coincided
with Middleton's determination to move against Batoche. A two-pronged
attack was still planned, but Otter would no longer be part of it.

The arrival of the *Northcote* significantly strengthened Middleton's
marching capacity. On board the boat were 80 men of the Midland Battalion,

together with Colonel Van Straubenzie and Captain Howard of the United States Army. Howard, a representative of the American gun manufacturer, had with him the Gatling gun which was to provide the important fire power on the first day of fighting at Batoche. The cargo also contained the desperately needed food supplies and some ammunition. The steamer itself was also to be used in the attack.[24]

Alterations to the *Northcote* were made by Major Smith of "C" School of Infantry who was placed in command of the steamer. Middleton ordered the upper deck to be made "bullet proof" and placed the following somewhat motley crew on board:

> Thirty-one rank and rifle, two officers C Company School Corps, Captain Bedson, my aide-en-camp, Captain Wise, who, though better, was to my great loss, incapacitated from walking or riding, three sick officers, Mr. Magre and Mr. Pringle, medical staff, several men of supply and transport services, Mr. Gottam, a newspaper correspondent, and some settlers returning to their homes, amounting with some of the crew to about fifty combatants.[25]

Then Major Smith was ordered "to anchor the first night abreast of our camp, remain there the next day, and on the morning of the ninth drop down and meet the column at about 8, just above Batoche."[26]

These tactics were not without critics:

> the commander had conceived the rather ludicrous idea of converting the *Northcote* into a gunboat. She was furnished with clumsy barricades, which were to serve as bulwarks, and as she had no cannon to counter against, the task of rendering these barricades bullet proof was a difficult one. The utter folly of equipping and arming her in the manner described was seen when she passed down the river and began the fight on May 9.[27]

Obviously, loading down a steamer that had already experienced serious navigational difficulties with sandbars downstream was considered impractical. However, no other sources were critical of this phase of Middleton's strategy for Batoche.

Finally, on May 7, Middleton was prepared to move on from the site of his first battle with the Métis and the Indians. The General had estimated the strength of his force to be 700 but, according to Melgund, 886 men made up his ranks.[28]

Middleton chose to advance with an infantry force which included

Boulton's Scouts and French's Scouts (the Dominion Land Surveyors were to arrive on May 11). There was no trained cavalry at the front even though it was available. Middleton's decision not to include Denison's cavalry was one part of his plan for which he later received much criticism.[29]

Four guns or cannon were in the Field Forces' arsenal, two with the Winnipeg Field Battery and two with "A" Battery. All four were RML nine-pounders and were put to extensive use by Middleton, especially at Batoche. Their effectiveness against the elusive Métis and their well-hidden rifle pits has been questioned by some. But it has also been argued that they were effective in psychologically demoralizing the enemy over the four days of fighting.[30]

The more publicized piece of artillery during the campaign was the Gatling gun carried to the front by the *Northcote*. Operated by Captain Howard throughout the campaign, the Gatling gun's effectiveness at Batoche has been the source of some controversy, judging from the reports following the fighting. For many, it was the first time they had ever seen a rapid-fire gun in action and, as a novelty, it attracted considerable attention and commentary both during and after the campaign. Major Boulton, in his reminiscences, was cautious in assessing the contribution the Gatling made to the success of the North West Field Force. While admitting that it was a significant weapon, particularly on the first day of the fighting, he was less effusive than most. Boulton felt that the success attributed to the Gatling detracted from what he considered the brave and solid role played by the infantry and artillery companies.[31]

The Gatling gun's primary advantage was its rapid-fire capacity—it was advertised as being able to fire 1,000 shots per minute. It was also relatively light to transport and easily adjustable for both elevation and direction. Of the gun's ten barrels, five were fired in succession while the other five were being loaded. When the crank which fired the gun was turned, firing, loading and extraction all took place synchronically without interruption.[32]

The entire combat contingent which was to move against Batoche was thus assembled. On the afternoon of May 7, the troops marched from Fish Creek to Gabriel's Crossing, which they reached by 6:00 P.M. Here they met the *Northcote*, which had landed that afternoon. A scouting mission was undertaken to decide on the safest approach to Batoche. Middleton wrote:

> As I had learned there were some nasty places to pass on the river trail, I rode out with some scouts to the east, accompanied by Mr. Reid, the Paymaster of the Midlanders, etc., in this very neighbourhood. With his assistance I marked out a route for next day's march which would bring

us on the Humboldt trail to about five or six miles from Batoche.[33]

On the morning of Saturday, May 9, reveille was sounded at 4:00, breakfast was taken at 4:15 and the men were ready to march at 5:00, each with 100 rounds of ammunition.[34] As the column advanced on Batoche, it encountered sporadic rifle fire from two houses along the road. The two houses, not far from the church and rectory and belonging to Ludger Gareau and Jean Caron Sr., were barricaded. One report has the building about 400 yards from the church and rectory.[35] The first house was fired on by the Gatling gun, which caused the men in and around the two buildings to scatter. Boulton's Scouts then fell back and a gun from "A" Battery shelled the second house: "Some rebels immediately ran out of a ravine behind the house into the bush. The two houses took fire and were soon in ashes."[36]

The coordinated attack on Batoche was to take place at 8:00 A.M. with the *Northcote* moving downriver from the south and Middleton coming across land from the east. It is clear that 8:00 A.M. had been agreed upon as the time for the two-pronged advance to begin (see map 1).

The steamer was to remain just downstream from Batoche until bombardment from Middleton's guns was heard. But the *Northcote* was engaged by the Métis before Middleton's troops reached the village defense. As Middleton wrote: "As we got near the river, much to my annoyance we heard a rattling fire and the steamer's whistle, showing the latter was already engaged."[37]

According to Major Smith, the *Northcote* was progressing as planned until shortly before 8:00 that morning. At 6:00 A.M., the *Northcote* had moved to a point just south of Batoche, where she anchored because she was slightly ahead of schedule. The sources describing the progress of the *Northcote* agree that she was fired on immediately after her advance up river resumed. There is disagreement, however, over when this advance commenced. One source had it at 8:10, while Major Smith reports it as being 7:40—a difference of some 30 minutes, and enough to spoil the plan.

As the *Northcote* struck out towards midstream she immediately came under heavy fire from both banks. In his reports, Smith indicated that the men on board did not return the fire at first, but as the hail of bullets became heavier his men began "independent and volley firing."[38] The Métis appeared to be lying in wait:

as we rounded the bend a moment or so later we were raked fore and aft by a fierce storm of bullets coming from both banks. From almost every bush rose puffs of smoke, and from every house and trees on the top of the banks came bullets buzzing. The fire was steadily returned by the troops on board, consisting of C Company School of Infantry; and notwithstanding that the rebels were protected by the brush and timber which covers the banks, apparently some injury was inflicted upon them. Volley after volley was fired and several of the lurking enemy were seen to drop headlong down the sloping bank.[39]

Father Fourmond, who was housed in the rectory throughout the fighting, also remembered the activities surrounding the arrival of the *Northcote*:

Vers 8 hs. A.M. nous étions sortis… Tout à coup, un … sifflement affreux se fit entendre à nos oreilles, venant du côté haut de la rivière… C'est le bateau à vapeur… C'est le bateau arrivant et sifflant la guerre… L'attaque commença par un parti de Sioux campés proche de la mission… Aussitôt prennent fusils et se précipitent vers le bateau à travers les buissons… La bataille était engagé.[40]

Philippe Garnot recalled Dumont telling him that almost all of the Métis had left their rifle pits along the Jolie Prairie to fire on the *Northcote* as it moved by the village. Garnot himself remembered sending about 20 men to join the assault.[41]

One of the more spectacular events was the decapitation of the steamer's smoke stacks when the ferry cable crossing the river was lowered—sending them crashing to the deck. Major Smith's report suggested that he was unaware of the loss of the stacks and whistle until after the *Northcote* had anchored again downstream, even though he wrote: "As we passed Batoche the fire was especially heavy, and I heard a crash as if a portion of the upper deck had been carried away."[42] This decapitation was engineered by the ferryman, Alex P. Fisher, who was assisted by Pascal Montour. The consequence of this tactic might have been greater had the Métis been able to corral the steamer at this crossing.

On board the *Northcote* only three minor injuries were reported, including the shot to the heel suffered by Macdonald, the carpenter. Major Smith concluded his report to Middleton by praising the zeal and coolness of his soldiers, while placing the blame for the disastrous fate of the *Northcote* on the near-mutinous crew. "Our weakness lay in the fact that the master, pilot and engineer were aliens, and that the crew were civil employees and not enlisted men."[43] The final assessment published in Mulvaney's history of the North-West Rebellion was less circumspect: "General Middleton's navy

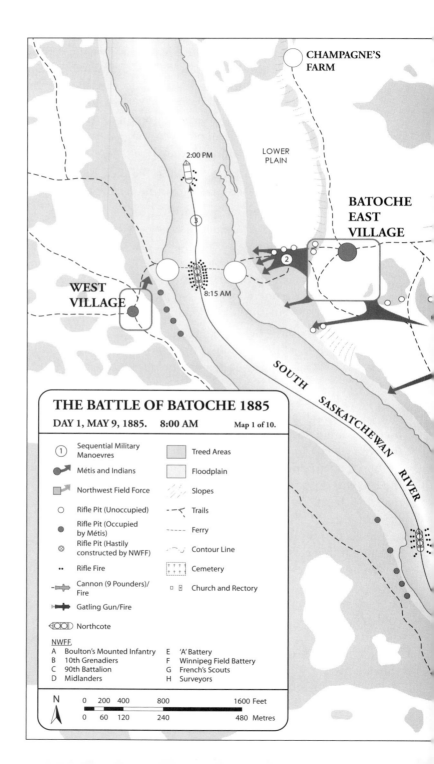

CHAMPAGNE'S FARM

LOWER PLAIN

2:00 PM

BATOCHE EAST VILLAGE

WEST VILLAGE

8:15 AM

SOUTH SASKATCHEWAN RIVER

THE BATTLE OF BATOCHE 1885

DAY 1, MAY 9, 1885.   8:00 AM   Map 1 of 10.

① Sequential Military Manoevres	Treed Areas
Métis and Indians	Floodplain
Northwest Field Force	Slopes
○ Rifle Pit (Unoccupied)	Trails
● Rifle Pit (Occupied by Métis)	Ferry
⊗ Rifle Pit (Hastily constructed by NWFF)	Contour Line
∙∙ Rifle Fire	Cemetery
Cannon (9 Pounders)/ Fire	Church and Rectory
Gatling Gun/Fire	
Northcote	

NWFF.
A   Boulton's Mounted Infantry
B   10th Grenadiers
C   90th Battalion
D   Midlanders
E   'A' Battery
F   Winnipeg Field Battery
G   French's Scouts
H   Surveyors

N

0   200   400   800   1600 Feet

0   60   120   240   480 Metres

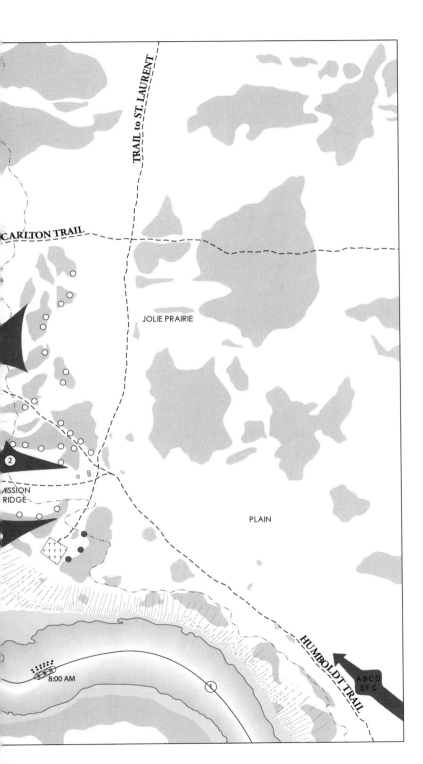

Gabriel Dumont (courtesy of the Saskatchewan Archives Board/R-A6277).

project did little more than imperil many valuable lives and withdrew from his forces a considerable number of men who were badly needed on Saturday, Sunday and Monday."[44] This last condemnation perhaps does not take into account the effect the *Northcote* had in distracting the Métis and the Indians away from the eastern front where Middleton's advance took place. The Métis expended much energy and ammunition on the *Northcote*, even after it had been incapacitated. It is remarkable that on May 9, Middleton reached the church and rectory, which he was unable to do the following day—in fact he would not reach this point again until the final day.

The organization of the Métis facing the troops who were advancing towards Batoche is less well known that that of the North West Field Force, though some evidence was collected by W.B. Cameron from Patrice Fleury and Charles Laviolette later.[45] Two scout detachments were formed, one under Fleury and the other under Ambroise Champagne. Fleury was on the west side of the river, while Champagne patrolled the east side. Both had chosen a few good riders to accompany them. Dumont, who was Commanding General, had nine or ten captains who were responsible to him—each of them, in turn, responsible for a troop of men. A Board of Strategy, headed by Louis Riel and Charles Nolin (who had left before the fighting had started), also was formed to advise Dumont. The first secretary of the board was William Jackson, who was later replaced by Philippe Garnot. Remaining members were Albert Monkman, Napoléon Nault (brother of André Nault), John Boucher, Philippe Gariépy, Pierre Gariépy, Old Man Parenteau (father-in-law of Xavier Batoche), Moise Ouellette, Maxime Lépine and Joseph Arcand.

As the *Northcote* floated downstream beyond Batoche the infantry neared the church and rectory. Within 100 yards of the church two rounds were fired from the Gatling gun. Immediately following this burst of fire a white flag, or handkerchief, was noticed and the firing was halted by Middleton (see map 2). He had apparently given "strict injunctions to the force to spare non-combatants as far as possible."[46] From Middleton's recollections the flag was seen being waved by a priest from the opened door of the church. He then approached the church: "I stopped the fire and rode up to the house which I found to be full of people; three or four Roman Catholic priests, some Sisters of Mercy, and a number of women and children, the latter being all half-breeds. They were naturally alarmed, and having reassured them we continued our advance."[47] According to Boulton, only the corner of the rectory had been struck by the bullets. Some of the bullet marks can still be seen in its woodwork.

Fourmond recorded this encounter in some detail:

> En même temps, nous voyons les habits rouges se dévelop-per en ligne de bataille tout autour de la mission; profitant des divers accidents du terrain, pour cacher leur marche en avant... Sortons, dit P. Fourmond, ils vont nous reconnaître, et ne pas tirer sur nous... PP. Fourmond et Vegreville sortent et s'adossent au pignon de la maison, faire face aux soldats pour titre reconnus... A peine là, qu'une détonation retentit et une balle frappe au-dessus de nos têtes... Rentrons, il y a danger. A peine entrés ... on entend la mitrailleuse cribler le toit de la maison.[48]

There a decision was made to try to raise a white flag:

> P. Moulin saisit un morceau de coton donné par les Mères et entrouve la porte ouverte et l'agite en face des soldats avan-cant en ordre de bataille. Au même instant on entendit ce cri retentir de leur côté. "Don't fear! Don't fear!"[49]

After the encounter at the church, Boulton's Scouts advanced. Only a short distance past the church, Boulton's infantry were fired upon from "a sort of low brush about 200 yards or 300 yards ahead."[50] Two companies of the 10th Grenadiers were then ordered to advance in skirmishing order, and these men reached the edge of the ravine on the left; another two companies moved forward on the right near the church. "A" Battery was now ordered forward to the crest of the hill overlooking Batoche with both its nine-pounders and the Gatling gun. The former began to shell the houses at Batoche while the latter was directed at the west bank, "from where a galling fire was being kept up by a totally invisible enemy."[51] This was the farthest

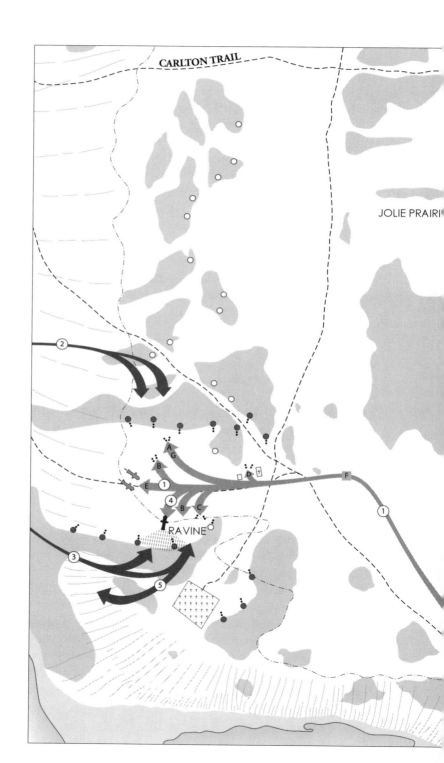

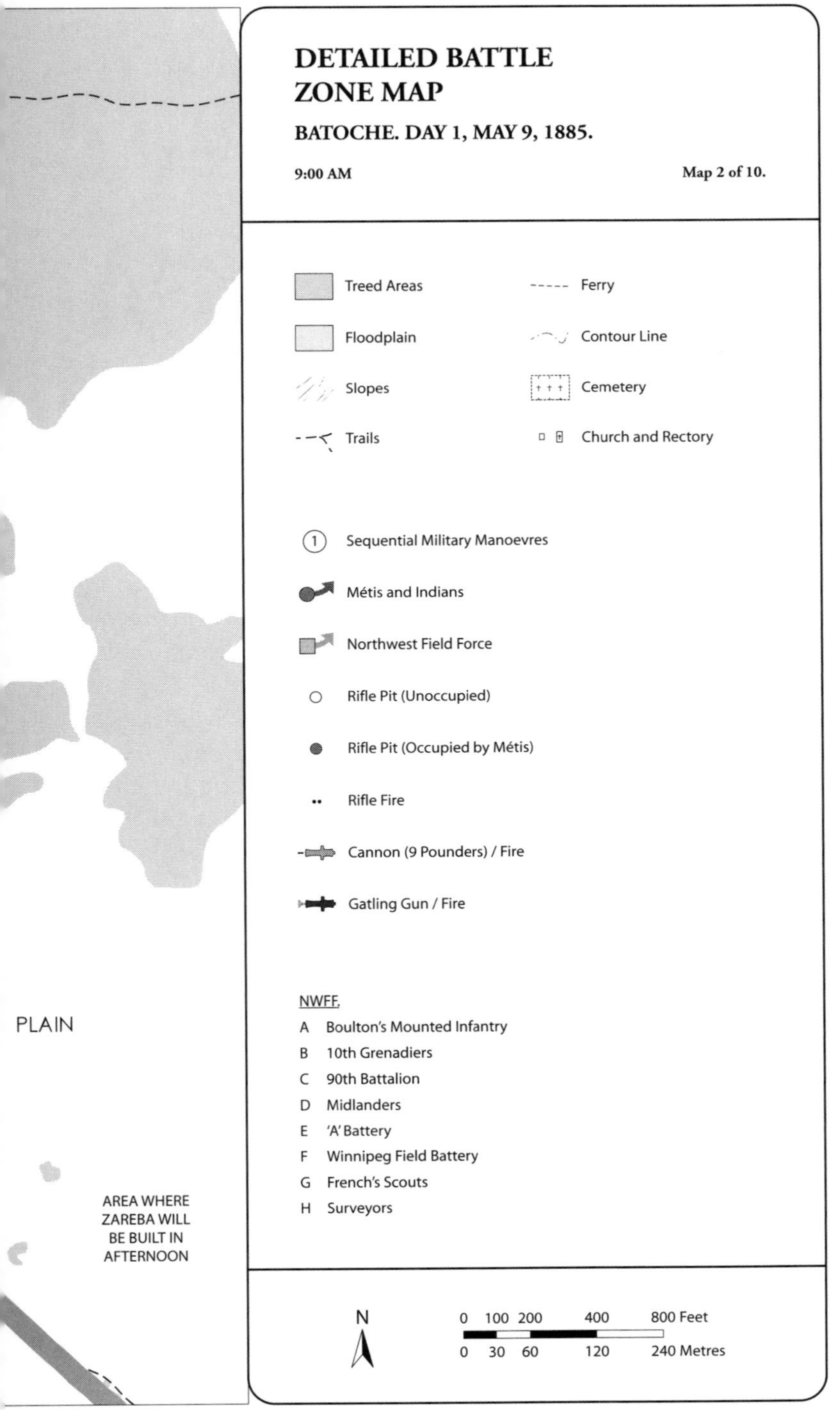

**DETAILED BATTLE
ZONE MAP**

BATOCHE. DAY 1, MAY 9, 1885.

9:00 AM   Map 2 of 10.

Treed Areas	- - - - Ferry
Floodplain	Contour Line
Slopes	Cemetery
Trails	Church and Rectory

① Sequential Military Manoevres

Métis and Indians

Northwest Field Force

○ Rifle Pit (Unoccupied)

● Rifle Pit (Occupied by Métis)

‥ Rifle Fire

Cannon (9 Pounders) / Fire

Gatling Gun / Fire

NWFF.
A   Boulton's Mounted Infantry
B   10th Grenadiers
C   90th Battalion
D   Midlanders
E   'A' Battery
F   Winnipeg Field Battery
G   French's Scouts
H   Surveyors

PLAIN

AREA WHERE
ZAREBA WILL
BE BUILT IN
AFTERNOON

N

0	100	200	400	800 Feet
0	30	60	120	240 Metres

Louis Riel's Council, 1885 (courtesy of the Archives of Manitoba/N14354).

the Field Force was able to advance, and it was not until May 12 that they would reach the crest of the hill overlooking Batoche again. Having reached this ridge by the mission, the Grenadiers and "A" Battery came under a shower of bullets. Recalling this moment, Boulton wrote, "We had now received a decided check. Immediately in our front lay thick bush, beyond which we could not penetrate. We had been driven by a heavy fire of the enemy from the position which the guns occupied overlooking the village, which was within easy range of the rifle pits that were covered by the bush."[52] At this point Middleton ordered the Gatling gun ahead.

This initial clash has been estimated by some to have been just before 9:45 A.M. As the Grenadiers moved forward the heaviest fire was felt from the left, "and desperate efforts were made to turn our left flank by their men in the bush under the high river bank and on the slope, who fired with great vigour."[53]

Having reached the crest of the hill overlooking Batoche, Middleton noted that "the gun detachments and horses were suffering,"[54] and ordered them to pull back. At this point the heaviest of fire was felt from, as Middleton wrote, "a bluff just below."[55] By all accounts it was here that the Gatling gun made its most memorable contribution by holding off the enemy fire until the Grenadiers could make an orderly retreat. It looked as though the Métis were trying to pinch off the Grenadiers, leaving them cut off from an easterly retreat.

The Grenadiers had previously been ordered to fire from a lying position, but now as they stood up to retreat, drawing the Métis fire,

> The Gatling, which was being worked for a second time and was just getting into action, with Captain Howard at the crank, turned its fire on the concealed foe, and for a moment silenced them.[56]

Although the fire from the Métis was intense, no one was killed during these clashes. At this time the Field Force occupied a position just back from the top of the ravine. The Métis held two positions: one lay immediately to the front and centre in rifle pits and to the left on the heavily wooded crest of the river bank. The right as yet was not defended, and it would not be until May 11 that it became necessary for the Métis to deploy greater numbers to the north.

The Gatling gun was now moved from the left flank towards the lines extending to the church (see map 3). This could be considered the second of three attempts to break through the enemy lines. As Middleton, reported, "I brought the gatling round the church and Captain Howard made a dashing attempt to flank the bluff, but could not succeed, as the enemy was ensconced in well made rifle pits."[57] The time was now estimated by one source to have been approximately 9:45 A.M. The Winnipeg Rifles occupied the left flank along the river and graveyard; the 10th Grenadiers were next (going left to right) to the front and centre, while "A" Battery, along with Boulton's and French's mounted infantry, lined the right flank. "The Midlanders were in reserve near the church, near which the General and staff took a position, while the remaining companies of the 90th, aided by the Winnipeg Field Battery and dismounted detachments, were deployed on our right centre, right and right flank."[58]

The Métis made two attempts at encirclement during this early action. The first was made on the left flank. The second attempt came after the Gatling had to save the troops following the initial advance:

> The Grenadiers advanced to the edge of the wood in rear of the school house, and a little to the right of the spot where we first felt the rebel fire… The rebels detected the movement, and desperate efforts were made to turn our left flank by their men in the bush under the high river bank and on the slope, who fired with great vigour; but they had nothing but shot guns, and their fire fell short. Some rebels with rifles on the other side of the river also took a hand in, but the Gatling silenced them.[59]

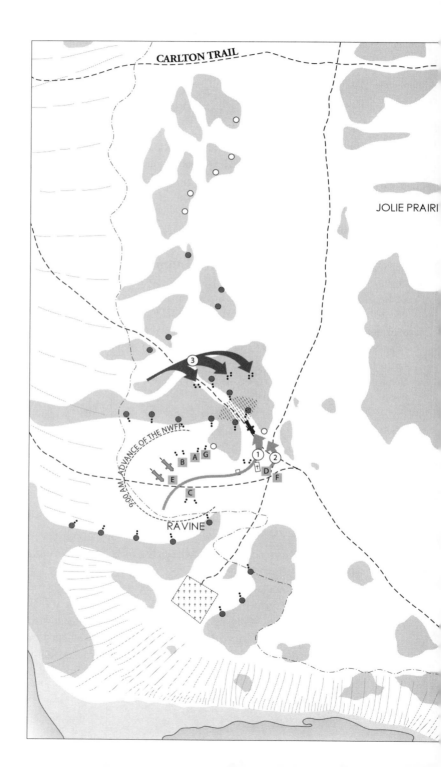

DETAILED BATTLE ZONE MAP

BATOCHE. DAY 1, MAY 9, 1885.

11:00 AM   Map 3 of 10.

Treed Areas	----- Ferry
Floodplain	Contour Line
Slopes	Cemetery
Trails	Church and Rectory

① Sequential Military Manoevres

Métis and Indians

Northwest Field Force

○ Rifle Pit (Unoccupied)

● Rifle Pit (Occupied by Métis)

.. Rifle Fire

Cannon (9 Pounders) / Fire

Gatling Gun / Fire

NWFF.
A   Boulton's Mounted Infantry
B   10th Grenadiers
C   90th Battalion
D   Midlanders
E   'A' Battery
F   Winnipeg Field Battery
G   French's Scouts
H   Surveyors

PLAIN

AREA WHERE
ZAREBA WILL
BE BUILT IN
AFTERNOON

N

0	100	200	400	800 Feet
0	30	60	120	240 Metres

A planned manoeuvre to capture the Gatling gun on the first day failed. It was described by Elie Dumont as they moved from right to left for their aborted attack:

> Tout droit où mettaient le gatling [*sic*], on se trouvait dans les petits trembles… Alors, Philippe tire et Bap. Boucher tire aussi. Gens du gatling ont commencé à tourner la machine. Le gatling tire sur nous. Quand fini la décharge, je me sauve en descendant les côtés… Une partie de nos gens étaient là et voulaient aller au bord de la riviere … on était comme une 30ne. On a suivi la Rivière à l'abri des écarts pour remonter le courant vis-à-vis le gatling… Voulait ramasser du monde assez pour aller prendre le gatling sur la côte en face de nous … restait encore 100 vgs pour aller au gatling: on n'était pas assez de monde. … On a resté 1/2 hs. là, et retourne par même chemin en courant vite au bord de la rivière pour éviter à nos gens de tirer sur nous… On a été auprès du cimetière. Soldats déjà reculés. On ne pouvait pas tirer les soldats étaient trop loin déjà.[60]

After the first line of skirmishers ran into resistance and retreated a short distance, Middleton ordered the two nine-pounders of "A" Battery forward. No. 1 gun, under Captain Drury, fired a few shells a distance of fifteen hundred yards across the river, and No. 2 gun, under Lt. Ogilvie, also fired at buildings across the river. The fire from the Métis was not particularly intense at this time, and an almost unencumbered shelling by the nine-pound guns was continuing. Dumont was on record as stating later that the initial resistance was less than it might have been since "Those in the pits near the river could not resist the excitement of following the 'Northcote' down stream, otherwise the General and the guns would not have advanced to the position from which they shelled Batoche on the 9th, before clearing out the rifle pits along the river bank, in the cemetery coulee, and on either side of the trail from where it descended the hill."[61] In the intervening time after the *Northcote* had floated downstream, the Métis were again manning the rifle pits along the entire front. During this lull Middleton ordered one of the guns further forward. Unfortunately for Middleton, the gun misfired and Middleton ordered a retreat,

> when with a startling suddenness of a thunderbolt from a cloudless sky, a crashing fusillade, it could almost be called a volley, swept through the wooden slope at the right front … the bushy slope, which hitherto appeared to be perfectly

deserted, appeared suddenly to be infested by coyotting savages. The guttural 'ki-yi-ki-yi,' the sweeping fusillade, and above everything, the startling suddenness of the eruption, combined to make the new situation a trying one for the nerves of the bravest.[62]

At approximately 12:00 noon, after Captain Howard's attempt to outflank the Métis on the right had failed, Middleton moved back to the left flank where he had left Melgund in command. When he arrived he found Captain Peters had attacked the Métis lines to the west attempting to reach the rifle pits: "I found Captain Peters had made a gallant and vigorous attempt, with a few of the garrison artillery, to drive the enemy out of the bluff below, but had failed and had retired, leaving a wounded man behind [Gunner Philips]."[63]

Shortly after Philips was shot (one source had it at 2:00 P.M.), an attempt to rescue him was organized under the direction of Captain Peters (see map 4). It was believed at first that Philips had only been wounded, and perhaps that was the case. One participant recalled Philips crying out after he was hit: "Captain French, my leg is broken. For God's sake, don't leave me here."[64]

Shortly after Philips was rescued, a second encirclement of the Field Force was attempted, this time from the right flank of their line of defense (see map 5). Middleton makes almost no mention of these threats of being cut off from supplies, but they are detailed at some length in numerous other accounts. Earlier, the Gatling had been effective in repelling an attack on the left flank, but the Métis now employed distracting tactics by taking advantage of the northwesterly wind blowing towards the church. A prairie fire was lit upwind, and it was expected that the Métis would try to attack under the cover of the smoke. The tactic managed to unsettle some of the senior officers; Melgund described the effects of this unanticipated tactic:

> Enemy … lighted bush fire on our right front, behind smoke
> of which we expected them to advance, things looked awk-
> ward we got wounded out of church into waggons, and had
> ordered them to fall back to camp. I found that the ammu-
> nition waggons were also retiring, and I stopped them,
> much to Disbrowe's relief, who was in charge of them and
> had done well all day.[65]

The smoke and fire appears to have alarmed the men sufficiently that the wounded were moved out of the temporary hospital which had been set up in the church. According to another source, however, the troops were never in danger of panicking:

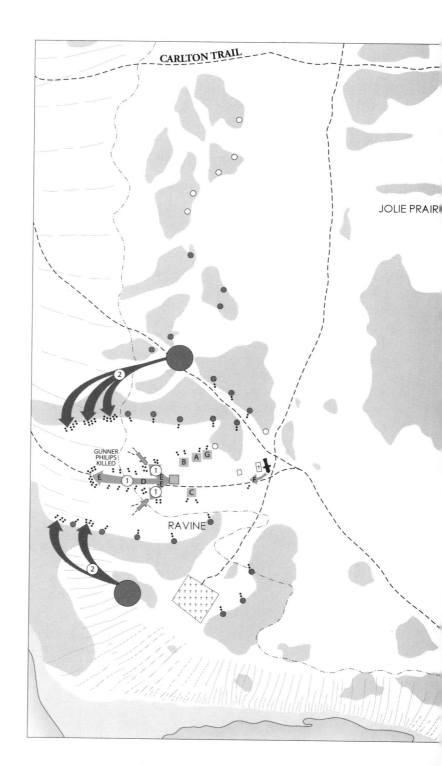

CARLTON TRAIL

JOLIE PRAIR

GUNNER
PHILIPS
KILLED

E

B A G

D E

C

RAVINE

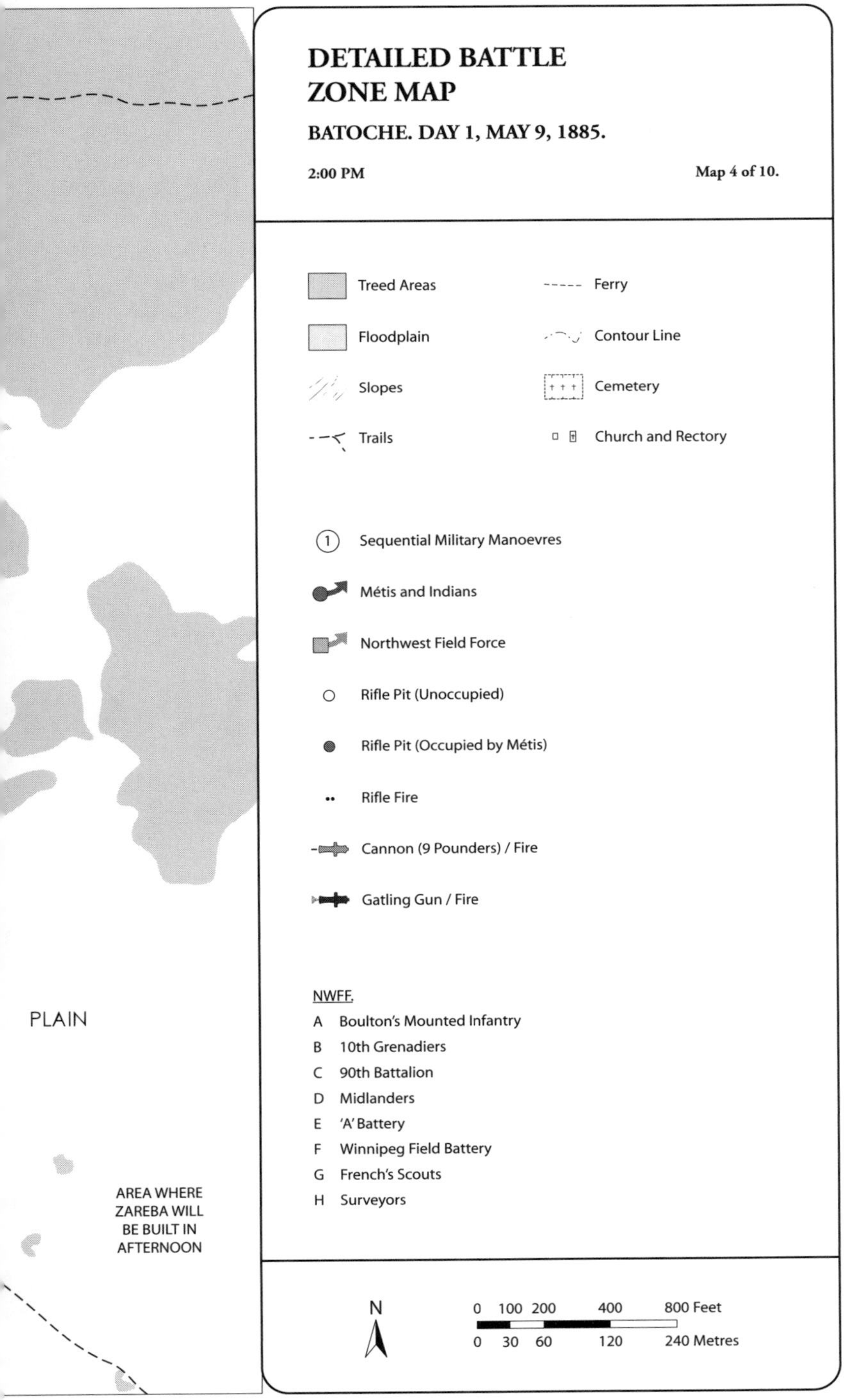

DETAILED BATTLE ZONE MAP

BATOCHE. DAY 1, MAY 9, 1885.

2:00 PM   Map 4 of 10.

Treed Areas	----- Ferry
Floodplain	Contour Line
Slopes	Cemetery
Trails	Church and Rectory

① Sequential Military Manoevres

Métis and Indians

Northwest Field Force

○ Rifle Pit (Unoccupied)

● Rifle Pit (Occupied by Métis)

•• Rifle Fire

Cannon (9 Pounders) / Fire

Gatling Gun / Fire

NWFF.
A   Boulton's Mounted Infantry
B   10th Grenadiers
C   90th Battalion
D   Midlanders
E   'A' Battery
F   Winnipeg Field Battery
G   French's Scouts
H   Surveyors

PLAIN

AREA WHERE ZAREBA WILL BE BUILT IN AFTERNOON

N

0   100 200   400   800 Feet
0   30   60   120   240 Metres

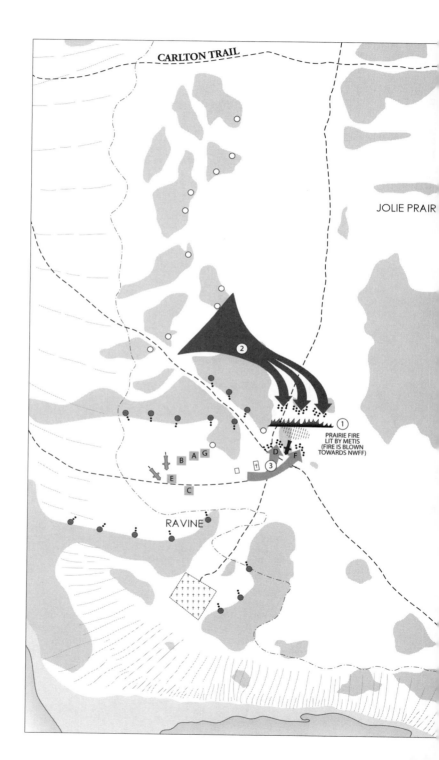

CARLTON TRAIL

JOLIE PRAIR

PRAIRIE FIRE
LIT BY METIS
(FIRE IS BLOWN
TOWARDS NWFF)

RAVINE

DETAILED BATTLE ZONE MAP

BATOCHE. DAY 1, MAY 9, 1885.

3:00 PM   Map 5 of 10.

Treed Areas

Floodplain

Slopes

Trails

Ferry

Contour Line

Cemetery

Church and Rectory

(1) Sequential Military Manoevres

Métis and Indians

Northwest Field Force

○ Rifle Pit (Unoccupied)

● Rifle Pit (Occupied by Métis)

.. Rifle Fire

Cannon (9 Pounders) / Fire

Gatling Gun / Fire

NWFF.

A   Boulton's Mounted Infantry
B   10th Grenadiers
C   90th Battalion
D   Midlanders
E   'A' Battery
F   Winnipeg Field Battery
G   French's Scouts
H   Surveyors

PLAIN

AREA WHERE
ZAREBA WILL
BE BUILT IN
AFTERNOON

N

0   100   200   400   800 Feet
0   30   60   120   240 Metres

> For a time we were surrounded by fires from the sloughs, the smoke of which rolled along the ground like fog. It was a tight place, but the troops never for a moment flinched. They simply looked to their officers who in turn patiently waited for orders from the chief.[66]

The fire, then, was the cause of some anxiety for the right flank but it appears that it was not followed by any sustained advance from the Métis.

After Philips's rescue and the perceived encirclement had been withstood, the heavy firing on both sides subsided. It was now mid-afternoon: "Towards three o'clock the fire slackened somewhat, though a head shown by either party was a target for a score of bullets."[67] At 3:00 P.M., Middleton decided to send Lord Melgund, his chief of staff, to Humboldt, ostensibly to send a private message to Caron. The documentary sources remain ambiguous, so that the real purpose of the mission remains clouded with controversy. Later, some innuendo appeared in the eastern press to the effect that Middleton was panicking and was anticipating a desultory battle which he feared might be lost by the Field Force. The telegram was never found and, therefore, the issue cannot be definitely settled. In his own account, Middleton states that he sent Melgund simply as a precautionary measure. The order to send Melgund in fact was tied to Middleton's larger problems. The first of these was that he was retreating and he was concerned over the effect this would have on the enemy; second, he did not know how far to retire. His concern over whether the Métis would interpret the withdrawal as a retreat from weakness (to which the Métis could respond by an attack) was paramount with Middleton.

Melgund's account of this event does not relate any of the atmosphere surrounding the order, or any of the underlying reasons for it. He simply stated:

> About 3 P.M. General told me he wished me to go to Humboldt and send some telegrams for him. He also wished me for several reasons to go to Ottawa. I accordingly started, and found our camp on prairie breaking up in order to move up to General.[68]

By approximately 3:00 P.M. the fighting had subsided. Middleton had sent Boulton and Secretan to strike camp and move it to within a mile of Batoche (about one-quarter mile from the church). Three and one-half hours later the transport carrying the camp forward was arriving and a zareba was formed. The zareba consisted of a transport pulled into a "zareba" shape, with earth and poplar branches filling the space underneath the wagons; a small trench was also dug around the outside of the enclosure.

Zareba warfare is recommended when a long column of transport needs to be guarded and when fighting guerillas. Major Callwell also advocated the use of these tactics, especially when approaching an enemy of unknown strength. It was seen as a defensive tactic within an overall offensive campaign:

> The principle [zareba warfare] is an excellent illustration of defensive tactics superimposed upon offensive strategy. The regular troops invade hostile territory, or territory in temporary occupation of the enemy, and they maintain strategically the initiatives; but when they find themselves in presence of the irregular forces prepared for battle, they form the laager or zareba as the case may be, and either await attack or else leave their impediments in it and go out to fight without encumbrances. In any case they have a secure bivouac and adequate protection during the hours of darkness.[69]

In fact, Callwell recommended such tactics in the terrain of South Africa and North America. The precedent for the use of such tactics originated with pioneers, who came to the frontier in wagons, and used circling formations in face of hostile natives. In regular military strategy this tactic stems from the square. A similar tactic was actually used by the Métis against the Sioux at the battle of Grand Coteau. In North America, pioneers "when operating against Red Indians often formed laagers, or corrals as they were called."[70] Callwell specifically cited the use of zarebas: "During the suppression of Riel's rebellion in 1885, laagers were generally established after each march by the government troops."[71] He furthermore cited Middleton's tactics as an example of a proper use of these tactics: " in the campaign against Riel … the regular army has adopted it to varying circumstances with great success."[72] And as such Callwell concluded:

> Some think it to be derogatory, some fear its evil moral effect upon the troops. But if kept within limits, and employed only when clear necessity arises, if not permitted to cramp their energies or to check judiciously applied offensive action on the part of the troops there is much to be said for a military system which safeguards the supplies of an army and which grants it temporary repose.[73]

Coinciding with the withdrawal of the troops to the zareba, at approximately 6:30 P.M., was a renewed advance from the Métis. Middleton wrote: "Towards evening the troops were gradually withdrawn, some of the enemy following them up until checked by a heavy fire from the zareba."[74] The Gatling gun was again heavily relied upon to cover the retreat to the zareba (see map 6). From all accounts the retreat was an unpleasant one: "The rebels, well aware of our retirement, took advantage of their safe route under the brow of the cliff, and rising over the brow fired into the zareba."[75] Both the 90th and the 10th Grenadiers were deployed to meet the Métis' pursuit and, as one source noted, "the wonder is that our loss was not heavy. The only reasonable explanations are poor ammunition, poor and hurried marksmanship, greater caution on the part of our forces, and a kind Providence."[76] One man was killed during this final skirmish of the day, however: Private Moor, 3rd Company of the Grenadiers, was shot through the head while defending the zareba.

At dusk, around 7:00 P.M., the fire lessened; "A few of them kept up a desultory long-range fire for a short time, killing two horses and wounding a man."[77] As the fighting waned, fires were lit and men ate supper and prepared for the night. Only the wounded were allowed to sleep in tents, the remainder made do under the open sky. The night was ominous for many, and one man recorded his feelings:

> Night came at length, but tired as we were it was scarcely welcome. We were cooped up, and had the extreme satisfaction of furnishing a good mark for pot shooters. In the corral were more than six hundred mules and horses, and eight cattle. Men were busy throwing up hasty entrenchments; teamsters, nervous and frightened, were yelling at equally nervous animals; around the hospital tents the doctors were busy dressing wounds, probing for bullets, etc. The bullets were whizzing and pinging overhead, and occasionally one remembered that a favorite trick among the reds is to stampede the cattle and horses of the enemy. Hoofs would be apt to deal worse wounds than balls, and against afrighted animals, cooped up within a small space, we had absolutely no defense. The anticipations of a mean night were largely realized, though thus far we have escaped a stampede. Few, if any, slept five hours consecutively, and the firing kept up almost all night.[78]

To prevent a surrounding manoeuvre by the Métis during the night, trenches had been dug around the zareba, and the Midland Battalion and one company of the 90th took up positions on a height of land overlooking the river. This did not prevent the dropping fire which the Métis and Indians kept up throughout the night, however.

According to Elie Dumont, the Indians did much of the firing during the first evening:

> Grosse gagne se sont assis. On tire des plans pour la soirée. Sauvages disaient on va les tirer ce soir dans leur camp, toute la nuit: vous autres vous travaillerez dans la journée, les métis. Métis disent oui. Au commencement de la veillée, les sauvages ont commencé à tirer, sur le camp, une 10ne de minutes entres les coups, toute la nuit jusqu'au jour.[79]

The resistance of the Métis and the Indians on the first day appears to have momentarily stunned Middleton. His decision to move the camp up to the front showed that he had not entirely lost confidence in the ability of his men to break through the defenses at Batoche—but in spite of this, Middleton's actions during the next few days were cautious and deliberate. Even though his intelligence reports were showing that the Métis were fewer in number than he had estimated and that they were low on ammunition, Middleton was taciturn, unwilling to embark on a bold offensive.[80] He chose this tactic even though he had lost only two men and a few wounded. In effect, he was imposing a partial seige on Batoche. His caution was shown when, according to Boulton, he ordered reinforcements to the front, although Middleton himself did not admit this in his official account published in the *Sessional Papers*.

By the end of the first day of fighting at Batoche, Middleton and the North West Field Force were in a defensive encampment; the men and animals huddled in the zareba spent a fretful night. While the Métis and the Indians by contrast were in an almost victorious mood: having witnessed the uniformed army in retreat, they showed an audacious confidence by keeping up a constant fire into the corral throughout the night. Fourmond recalled that the Métis were in a jubilant mood that evening. As he wrote: "On eut dit l'armée mise en fuite. Et la victoire gagnée par les métis qui alors poursuivit l'ennemi d'aussi près que pouvait le permettre le gatling gun."[81]

The priests who occupied the church through most of the fighting made a number of perceptive observations. The first was that the Canadians appeared to be somewhat disorganized on this first day (a weakness that Middleton himself acknowledged): "Parmi les diverses impressions de la journée, il en est une qui regarde la tenue de l'armée canadienne. Fûmes surpris de son triste accoutrement aussi bien que de son peu de discipline. Nous disions: où sont nos troupes françaises. Quel contraste! Il nous semblait voir des enfants jouant au soldat."[82] Fourmond also noted the shortage of ammunition among the Métis even after the first day: "on voyait Sioux,

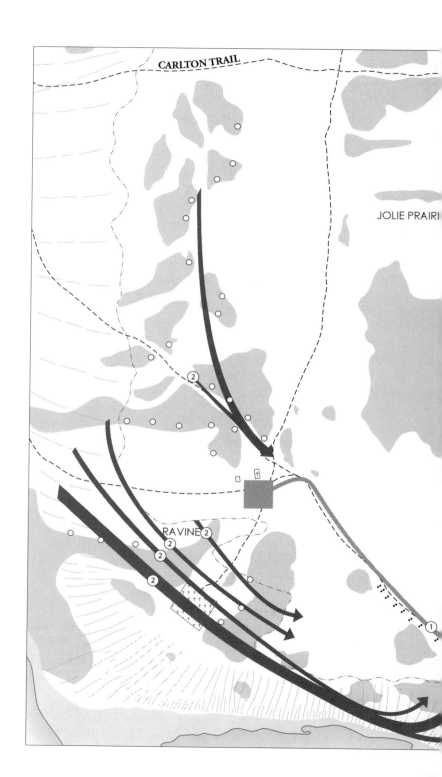

DETAILED BATTLE ZONE MAP

BATOCHE. DAY 1, MAY 9, 1885.

6:00 PM

Map 6 of 10.

Treed Areas

Floodplain

Slopes

Trails

Ferry

Contour Line

Cemetery

Church and Rectory

(1) Sequential Military Manoevres

Métis and Indians

Northwest Field Force

○ Rifle Pit (Unoccupied)

● Rifle Pit (Occupied by Métis)

•• Rifle Fire

Cannon (9 Pounders) / Fire

Gatling Gun / Fire

NWFF.

A Boulton's Mounted Infantry
B 10th Grenadiers
C 90th Battalion
D Midlanders
E 'A' Battery
F Winnipeg Field Battery
G French's Scouts
H Surveyors

PLAIN

ZAREBA

F G D E A
3

N

0	100	200	400	800 Feet
0	30	60	120	240 Metres

rôder sur le champ laissé par les soldats, les cartouches abandonnées ou per-
dues, s'approvisionnant ainsi pour le lendemain."[83] After a cannon ball was
fired on the house holding the prisoners, it too was used for ammunition:
"Le fils de Michel Trottier ramasse le boulet, va au bas de la côte porter la
poudre de dedans et ramasse les balles des soldats et va les faire fondre pour
faire des balles pour Métis."[84] One other observation made by the priests
was that the Métis may have gained a false sense of security from the
method of firing used by the Field Force: "Les Métis souvent induits en
erreur sur les morts des soldats par la manoeuvre qui fait coucher le premier
rang avant le second tire."[85] The recognition by the Métis that they were
killing fewer men than they believed could have demoralized them after the
apparent victory of May 9.

The next day, May 10, was a Sunday; the North West Field Force was
unable to reach the position left the day before, "as the enemy was in greater
force, and now held the high ground about the cemetery and the ground in
front of the church. Some of them, apparently Indians from their war cries,
had taken post at the end of the point of land below the cemetery…"[86] (see
map 7).

Middleton had apparently decided to attempt to demoralize the enemy
with heavy artillery fire during the day. Shortly after 5:00 A.M., he began to
fire on positions which he had held the previous day: "Two guns were
directed against the houses in the basin-shaped depression along the river.
A few rebels lay behind three log shanties just below the river bank, and the
artillery soon drove them out."[87]

On May 11, Middleton appeared more anxious for a direct engagement
with the Métis and the Indians (see map 8). But he approached this strategy
with caution. Most of the day was spent in reconnaissance, exploring all the
possibilities available for a major attack. On this penultimate day of the
Battle of Batoche, the fighting escalated, as a consequence of the reconnaissance carried out by Middleton.

It had been reported to Middleton that a space of open prairie, overlooking the village of Batoche, lay just to the north of the zareba. Boulton, whose
men accompanied Middleton, described the purpose as follows:

> We marched out about ten o'clock under the command of
> the General himself, leaving (Alone) Montizambert,
> Colonel Grasset, Colonel Williams, Major Jarvis, Colonel
> Mackeand and Colonel Van Straubenzie all discussing the
> position, and studying a plan of the ground which had been
> drawn by Captain Haig, R.E. with a view of preparing an
> attack.[88]

Middleton, accompanied by the Gatling gun, proceeded north through a small swamp, under the cover of bushes lying to the north of the zareba (see map 9). They emerged on an irregularly-shaped clearing "about two miles long and 1,000 yards in the broadest part, with a sort of slight ridge running down the centre and some undulations."[89] As they moved northward they attracted a sporadic fire from the rifle pits which ran along this ridge. In response to the sniper fire, Middleton ordered the Gatling gun to direct two or three rounds into the rifle pits. Middleton then rode further to the north, where he pursued two men he spotted riding across the prairie on ponies and captured another, later discovered to be one of Riel's men, who came out of the bush. According to Middleton, "We also captured some cattle and ponies which we took back to camp with us."[90] Boulton wrote: "Before leaving this point we burned down some log houses that might offer shelter to the enemy, in case further operations were needed here."[91]

Middleton had been receiving intelligence reports which indicated that the Métis were almost out of ammunition. Now that he could see the Métis thinly spread out along their line of rifle pits, he discovered what he needed to know in preparation for his final attack on Batoche: "We could see with our glasses that the enemy had a series of rifle pits all along the edge of those woods, and numbers of them were running up between the woods and disappearing into the pits. Evidently they were prepared for an attack in this direction."[92] It was clear that the Métis had responded to Middleton's manoeuvre of pulling men away from their right flank to reinforce the left where the Field Force "drew a smart fire."[93]

Further evidence that the Métis had followed the Gatling gun to the north awaited Middleton when he returned to camp. There he found that the infantry were able to regain the ground they had held on the first day of fighting: "A party of Midlanders, under Lieutenant-Colonel Williams' command, finding the fire slacken from the Indians' post below the cemetery, and led by him, gallantly rushed it, the Indians bolting leaving behind them some blankets and a dummy which they had used for drawing our fire."[94] Middleton now knew that the Métis could not be certain how many men he might deploy in a manoeuvre to the north because of the cover offered by the intervening bushes. As a consequence of the advances made by the infantry, the artillery were again able to draw up in the vicinity of the graveyard to open fire on the village and on the houses on the opposite bank: "shelling the opposite bank we [observed] that the shells created great consternation among the rebels, making them scatter and get well beyond range, and silenced the long range rifles which were a constant source of annoyance."[95]

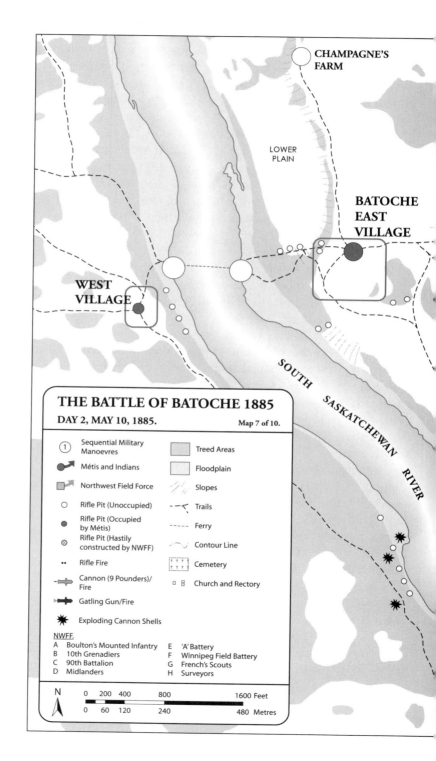

CHAMPAGNE'S
FARM

LOWER
PLAIN

BATOCHE
EAST
VILLAGE

WEST
VILLAGE

SOUTH SASKATCHEWAN RIVER

THE BATTLE OF BATOCHE 1885

DAY 2, MAY 10, 1885.

Map 7 of 10.

①	Sequential Military Manoevres
	Métis and Indians
	Northwest Field Force
○	Rifle Pit (Unoccupied)
●	Rifle Pit (Occupied by Métis)
⊗	Rifle Pit (Hastily constructed by NWFF)
••	Rifle Fire
	Cannon (9 Pounders)/ Fire
	Gatling Gun/Fire
✸	Exploding Cannon Shells

	Treed Areas
	Floodplain
	Slopes
--⌐	Trails
-----	Ferry
	Contour Line
	Cemetery
□ ⊟	Church and Rectory

NWFF.
A   Boulton's Mounted Infantry
B   10th Grenadiers
C   90th Battalion
D   Midlanders

E   'A' Battery
F   Winnipeg Field Battery
G   French's Scouts
H   Surveyors

N

| 0 | 200 | 400 | 800 | 1600 Feet |
| 0 | 60 | 120 | 240 | 480 Metres |

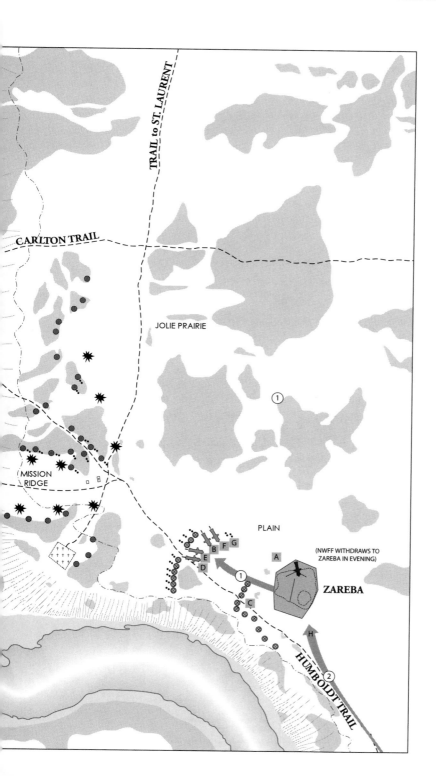

TRAIL to ST. LAURENT

CARLTON TRAIL

JOLIE PRAIRIE

MISSION
RIDGE

PLAIN

(NWFF WITHDRAWS TO
ZAREBA IN EVENING)

ZAREBA

HUMBOLDT TRAIL

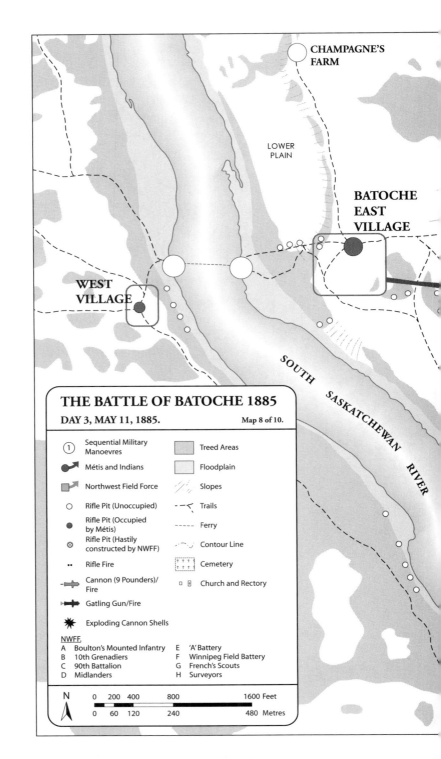

CHAMPAGNE'S FARM

LOWER PLAIN

BATOCHE EAST VILLAGE

WEST VILLAGE

SOUTH SASKATCHEWAN RIVER

THE BATTLE OF BATOCHE 1885

DAY 3, MAY 11, 1885.

Map 8 of 10.

(1) Sequential Military Manoevres		Treed Areas
Métis and Indians		Floodplain
Northwest Field Force		Slopes
○ Rifle Pit (Unoccupied)		Trails
● Rifle Pit (Occupied by Métis)		Ferry
⊗ Rifle Pit (Hastily constructed by NWFF)		Contour Line
•• Rifle Fire		Cemetery
Cannon (9 Pounders)/ Fire		Church and Rectory
Gatling Gun/Fire		
✳ Exploding Cannon Shells		

NWFF.
A   Boulton's Mounted Infantry
B   10th Grenadiers
C   90th Battalion
D   Midlanders

E   'A' Battery
F   Winnipeg Field Battery
G   French's Scouts
H   Surveyors

N

0	200	400	800	1600 Feet
0	60	120	240	480 Metres

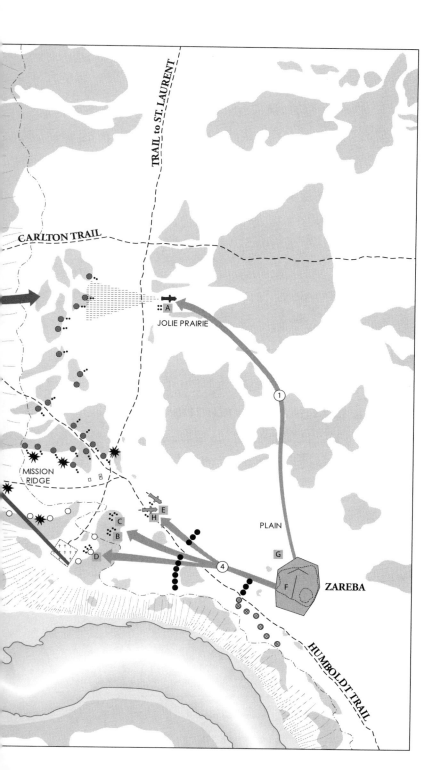

TRAIL to ST. LAURENT

CARLTON TRAIL

JOLIE PRAIRIE

A

MISSION
RIDGE

E

H

C

B

D

PLAIN

G

F

ZAREBA

HUMBOLDT TRAIL

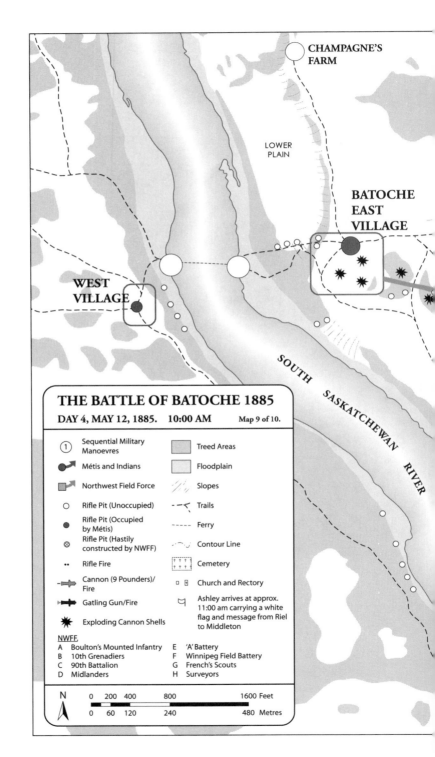

CHAMPAGNE'S
FARM

LOWER
PLAIN

BATOCHE
EAST
VILLAGE

WEST
VILLAGE

SOUTH SASKATCHEWAN RIVER

THE BATTLE OF BATOCHE 1885

DAY 4, MAY 12, 1885.   10:00 AM   Map 9 of 10.

① Sequential Military Manoevres	Treed Areas
Métis and Indians	Floodplain
Northwest Field Force	Slopes
○ Rifle Pit (Unoccupied)	Trails
● Rifle Pit (Occupied by Métis)	Ferry
⊗ Rifle Pit (Hastily constructed by NWFF)	Contour Line
·· Rifle Fire	Cemetery
Cannon (9 Pounders)/ Fire	Church and Rectory
Gatling Gun/Fire	Ashley arrives at approx. 11:00 am carrying a white flag and message from Riel to Middleton
✸ Exploding Cannon Shells	

NWFF.
A   Boulton's Mounted Infantry
B   10th Grenadiers
C   90th Battalion
D   Midlanders
E   'A' Battery
F   Winnipeg Field Battery
G   French's Scouts
H   Surveyors

N

0	200	400	800	1600 Feet
0	60	120	240	480 Metres

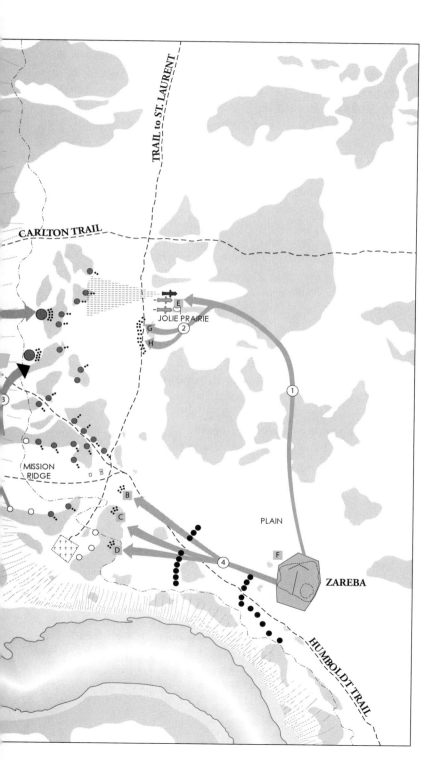

It was clear to Middleton that the resources of the Métis and Indians were running low and that his men were gaining confidence.[96] The Métis hardly pursued the Field Force as it retired for the night and there was no fire into the camp that evening; a parapet had been built around the zareba that day to protect against bullets fired into the camp. Late that evening Middleton made his decision: "Our men were beginning to show more dash, and that night I came to the conclusion that it was time to make our decisive attack."[97]

Convinced that the Métis and the Indians would follow his manoeuvre accompanied by the Gatling gun, Middleton again reconnoitred to the open plain north of the zareba. Middleton then told Van Straubenzie to proceed to the original front, and "that as soon as he heard us well engaged he was to move off, and, having taken up yesterday's position, push on towards the village."[98] This manoeuvre engineered by Middleton was commemorated in a major military study of the 19th century, which examined warfare against what were referred to as "savages" throughout the British Empire. Major Callwell cites Middleton's feinting action as particularly successful in the situation confronting him:

> General Middleton found the half-breeds holding a long line of rifle pits; this stretched across the land enclosed by a wide salient angle formed by the Saskatchewan. The Government forces encamped opposite one end of this line of defence and formed a zareba, and they remained facing the enemy four days engaged in skirmishes. On the third day the mounted troops made a demonstration against the hostile centre, and it was observed that a part of Riel's followers were withdrawn from the end of the line opposite the zareba to strengthen the threatened point. On the following day this demonstration was repeated by the mounted men with two guns, and these then returned quietly to camp. In the afternoon the whole Government force attacked the end of the rebel line in front of the zareba where it had been greatly weakened, and broke through and reached Batoche. The undulating nature of the ground patched with woods and copses enable the feint to be carried out in very effective fashion.[99]

The strategy was straightforward and simple, even though it failed initially. The attack from the left flank was to be led that morning by Colonel Van Straubenzie's brigade. The men making up the party intended to participate in the feinting manoeuvre were "Captain Dennis' corps, my own corps

[Boulton], and Captain French's, in all numbering about one hundred and thirty men, one gun of 'A' Battery, under Captain Drury and the Gatling under Lieutenant Rivers, accompanied by Captain Howard, marched off under General Middleton…"[100] The nine-pounder which accompanied Middleton's expedition was pulled up into firing position, and the Land Surveyors, under Captain Dennis, dismounted and advanced in skirmishing order. The Gatling gun was then stationed to the north of this point, and Middleton rode out to within 400 yards of the Métis rifle pits to order the advance of the dismounted surveyors. The rest of the infantry was kept hidden behind the advancing skirmishers. According to one surveyor's reminiscences, it appeared that the Métis were anticipating an attack from the basin where Middleton assembled his men: "The Rebels evidently expected us, for we had only advanced a few yards when they must have caught sight of one of us over the rise, and a volley was fired into our ranks, at the report of which we dropped our faces in the brush, one of us never again to rise again, for poor Kippen fell dead with a rifle bullet in his brain."[101] The nine-pounder and the Gatling also opened fire and there was a brief, but from most accounts, intense exchange. Perhaps the Métis, in fact, had expected the main attack to come from this front.

During the morning's action, another event occurred which suggests that the Métis position was weakening. It also showed that Riel, by sending his message to this front, believed that it was where the main attack would take place. Just as the Gatling was ready to move to a position further to the north, Middleton saw a man riding towards him with a white flag. It turned out to be a Mr. Astley, a surveyor captured by Riel just after the battle at Duck Lake. "He told me he had just come from Riel, who was apparently in a great state of agitation, and handed me a letter from him in which he said, apparently referring to our shelling the houses, that if I massacred his women and children they would massacre their prisoners."[102] Middleton replied that he had no intention of deliberately injuring women and children and suggested that they be placed in a building marked by a white flag. Astley, after having explained Riel's condition for surrender, returned with Middleton's reply. Shortly after this, another man emerged on foot carrying a white flag. He turned out to be Thomas Jackson, later found to be sympathetic to Riel. Jackson was carrying the same note as Astley; however, he refused to go back to Riel's camp and Middleton allowed him, for the time being, to go free.

It was now about 11:30 A.M. and Middleton was prepared to move back to camp. His deployment of troops in the morning seemed to confuse the men in the rifle pits, according to Boulton, "keeping us for a while just out of sight of the enemy, occasionally showing a mounted man or two to puzzle the rebels as to our movements, which always drew a volley from them."[103] Following this, the men returned to camp having lost only one man in what was to be an all-out advance against the Métis and Indians.

That morning Van Straubenzie had ordered the Midlanders and Grenadiers out in quarter column ready for an attack on the left flank. Due to a strong east wind he was however unable to hear any of the artillery or rifle fire from Middleton's contingent. According to a number of accounts, Middleton was furious when he returned to camp at lunch to find that no attack had been made. Middleton himself wrote: "I am afraid on that occasion I lost both my temper and my head."[104] Later, in retrospect, Middleton seemed to believe that it was fortuitous that the charge had been aborted:

> On regaining the camp I was much annoyed at finding that, owing to a misconception of my orders, the advance parties had not, as I had directed, been sent forward to hold the regained position and press forward, as I drew the enemy from their right by my feint; but now I am inclined to think it was a fortunate thing that they had not, for I believe the total silence and absence of fire from my left only strengthened the belief of the enemy that I was going to attack from the prairie ground.[105]

The men of the Grenadiers and Midlanders were just completing their meal, which one man described as "munching the bulletproof discs of that indescribable compound known as Government biscuit that formed our lunch..."[106] Middleton was sitting down to his when he gave a rather vague order to Van Straubenzie to "take them as far as he pleased."[107] It is believed that the order was simply intended to send the men back to the positions they held that morning although it might have been taken as a signal to advance further against the Métis positions.

Conflicting accounts over exactly what happened and who was responsible for the charge at this point are numerous (see map 10). Much of the conflict was motivated by those who sought personal glory, and also by those who either hated or admired Middleton. One observer noted:

> one of the Midland men on the slope of the hill near the cemetery was hit by a volley from the west side of the river, and the ambulance men going to his relief were also fired upon. This seemed to infuriate the men, and their officers saw that there was no holding them any longer. Colonel Williams therefore decided upon charging, and with only

two companies of the Midland, he led the way counting on the 90th and the Grenadiers for support.[108]

Others also gave credit to Williams for leading the final charge, though it is not clear whether he proceeded on his own or under orders. Colonel Denison, who was not at the front but stationed at Humboldt, acknowledges Williams as the leader of the final charge. Captain Peters gives credit for the charge to Van Straubenzie, while Boulton tends to credit Middleton and Van Straubenzie with issuing the string of orders which led to the final charge.[109] Middleton's own description, which he wrote closest to the time of the action, indicates that the breakthrough merely happened and was not actually ordered as an advance:

> After the men had had their dinners they were moved down to take up old positions and press on. Two companies of the Midland, 60 men in all, under Lt. Col. Williams, were extended on the left and moved up to the cemetery, and the Grenadiers, 200 strong, under Lt. Col. Grassett prolonged the line to the right beyond the church, the 90th being in support. The Midland and Grenadiers, led by Lt. Cols. Williams and Grassett, the whole led by Lt. Col. Straubenzie in command of the Brigade, then dashed forward with a cheer and drove the enemy out of the pits in front of the cemetery and the ravine to the right of it, thus clearing the angle at the turn of the river.[110]

One theory suggests that because of the turn in the river it was necessary for the line of advance to be equidistant from the rifle pits all along the front and that, consequently, the extreme left had to be ordered slightly forward. When so commanded they advanced without resistance, possibly due to weakly manned or vacant rifle pits (men being now located to the north, where attack was anticipated). Gaining confidence and momentum and encountering little resistance, they broke into a run. Seeing this movement, the rest of the front, extending to the right from the river past the church, now followed suit. This advancing front, made up from left to right of the Midlanders, Grenadiers and 90th, was now joined by men ordered by Middleton to extend the line to the right. This was done by sending out the gun of "A" Battery and by "B" and "F" of the 90th; Boulton's Mounted were then sent to lengthen the line even further. The Surveyors were ordered out to the right of Boulton's men. The artillery were now firing both at the village and at the Métis in rifle pits across the river, whose fire was pouring down on the Midlanders closest to the river. The gun from the Winnipeg

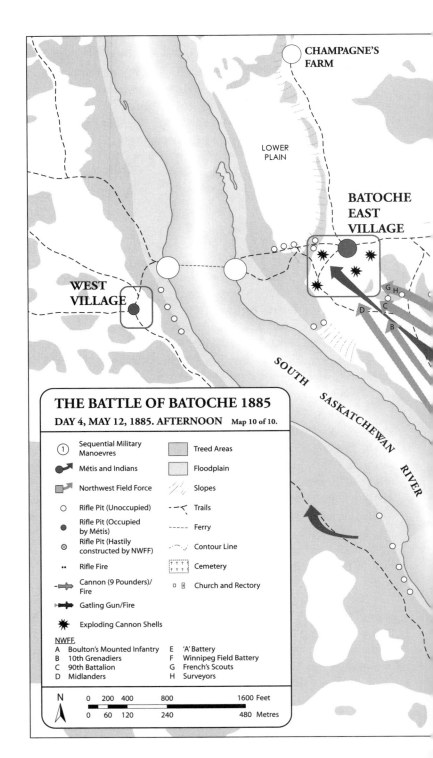

CHAMPAGNE'S
FARM

LOWER
PLAIN

BATOCHE
EAST
VILLAGE

WEST
VILLAGE

G H
D
C
B

SOUTH SASKATCHEWAN RIVER

THE BATTLE OF BATOCHE 1885

DAY 4, MAY 12, 1885. AFTERNOON   Map 10 of 10.

① Sequential Military Manoevres	Treed Areas
Métis and Indians	Floodplain
Northwest Field Force	Slopes
○ Rifle Pit (Unoccupied)	Trails
● Rifle Pit (Occupied by Métis)	Ferry
⊗ Rifle Pit (Hastily constructed by NWFF)	Contour Line
•• Rifle Fire	Cemetery
Cannon (9 Pounders)/ Fire	Church and Rectory
Gatling Gun/Fire	
✳ Exploding Cannon Shells	

NWFF.
A Boulton's Mounted Infantry   E 'A' Battery
B 10th Grenadiers   F Winnipeg Field Battery
C 90th Battalion   G French's Scouts
D Midlanders   H Surveyors

N

0	200	400	800	1600 Feet
0	60	120	240	480 Metres

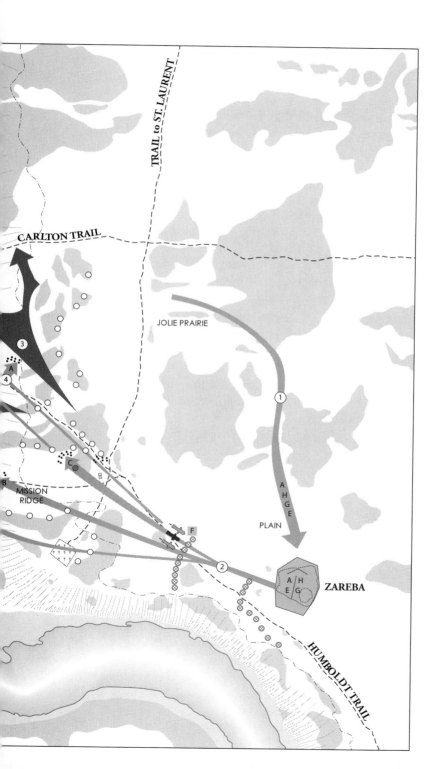

Field Battery and the Gatling were ordered to fire at the village from the right extreme on the front.

Loud cheers were heard as the men now broke towards the village. One reporter wrote:

> with a rush and a cheer they were down on the rebels with the fierceness of Bashi-Basouks, the Midland on the left, the Grenadiers in the centre, and the 90th on the right. The advance came sweeping round until a few minutes saw the line of direction at right angles to the original line of attack. The cheering was that of satisfied and contented men, and the enthusiasm was intense. Nothing could have withstood the pace, the force, and the dogged determination of the men. The cheering attracted the General, and, taking in the situation at glance, he came on with the Winnipeg artillery, Gatling and three companies of the 90th.[111]

Just as Middleton heard cheers from the men as they broke through the first line of rifle pits, Astley, Riel's messenger, again appeared. He carried with him a note from Riel which read, "General,—Your prompt answer to my note shows that I was right mentioning to you the cause of humanity. We will gather our families in one place and as soon as it is done we will let you know."[112] It was signed Louis David Riel. On the outside another missive, reflecting a more agitated state of mind, appeared. "I do not like the war, and if you do not retreat and refuse an interview, the question remains the same concerning the prisoners."[113] The message on the envelope, which contained a veiled threat, was in fact a contradiction of the note inside, an indication of Riel's instability. Middleton ignored both the note and the message:

> Of course no answer was sent, and soon, with the officers well in front, a general advance of the whole line was made with rousing cheers, the place was captured, the prisoners released, and the fighting was over, except for some desultory long-range firing, which was soon put down by two or three parties sent in different directions.[114]

The final offensive did not run as smoothly as Middleton described, and a number of sources indicate that some stiff resistance was met as they moved down the slopes towards the village. One skirmisher recalled the action: "The enemy poured in a hot fire when we started, but I don't think any of our men were hit until we got into the bush. Here many of the men were struck."[115] Most were hit by shots fired from the camouflaged rifle pits.

The well-constructed rifle pits discovered after the attack by the Field Force were praised by Middleton:

I was astonished at the strength of the position and at the ingenuity and care displayed in the construction of the rifle pits ... In and around the pits were found blankets, trousers, coats, shirts, boots, shoes, food, oil, Indian articles of sleep, one or two damaged shot guns and one good rifle. It was evident that a detachment of Rebels had lived in these pits, day and night, and it was easily understood, by an inspection of them, how perfectly safe the holders of these pits were from the fire of our rifles and especially from the Gatling and artillery.

These pits were also judiciously placed as regards repelling a front attack, but by attacking their right (which was their weakest point) and driving it in, we turned and took in reverse all their entrenchments, along the edge of the prairie ground, and thus caused a rout which ended in a "sauve qui peut."[116]

The Métis, as is now well known, were short of ammunition and fighting men on this last day. Of the original 320 to 350 combatants, Lépine recalled that only 50 to 60 men were fighting during the final battle[117]: "40 environ métis, avaient des carabines, le reste avaient des fusils à canard (2 coups)."[118] Nails were being fired by some in the rifle pits when the metal bullets manufactured from the last of the melted down cannon balls had been exhausted. In addition to the fact that they were poorly armed and lacked ammunition, the Métis, it appears, were also misled by appearances on this last day. Vandale remembered thinking that the peace had been won when Middleton withdrew his men from their left flank in the morning. The Métis, it seems, believed that Riel's messages had succeeded in winning a cease-fire. Vandale wrote: "Le canon arrête et Champagne se sauve et dit c'est la paix... Les Métis se lèvent, s'assient sur le bord des trous ... puis se relèvent et se retirent au camp des familles, une douzaine environ, pensant que c'était la paix."[119] As was evident, however, it was a terrible misunderstanding: "On était à se laver, quand Gabriel vient nous renvoyer aux trous du vieux chemin—s'y sont rendus, et grand bruit dans le camp et coups de fusil—10 minutes plus tard, bataille générale. Quand la bataille recommence, il y en avait 18 qui tenaient bon, et plusieurs se sauvaient un à un quand ils avaient une chance."[120] It is clear that the state of disarray the Métis found themselves in on the last day was greater than has previously been believed. Indeed, the orders under which the Métis were acting were confused and contradictory. The final attack by the Field Force was decisive, therefore, even from the perspective of the Métis:

414 | THE BATTLE OF BATOCHE

> On voit l'armée déboucher de tous côtés en ordre de
> bataille. Infantrie, artillerie, cavalerie, tout à la fois. Avec un
> ordre et détermination, une rapidité de mouvement que
> nous n'avions pas vue les autres jours. Du 1er coup d'oeil, on
> comprit que l'heure decisive était venue; que c'en était fait
> de Batoche.[121]

At dusk, Middleton ordered that the camp be formed into a zareba.
Trenches were dug, but they were not as extensive as before. These precautions turned out to be unnecessary as no other shots were fired at Batoche.
The zareba was located just to the north and east of Batoche's houses.

During the period after the fighting and throughout the following days,
the men with the Field Force, and the reporters accompanying them, made
a number of observations about the Métis and recorded statements made by
them. While these statements were accurately recorded, whether they were
factual remains questionable. One recurring observation was that the Métis
and their families were forced to take up arms against their will.[122]

Almost ten years later, when he was reflecting over the events of 1885,
Middleton was generous in his praise of the fighting ability of the Métis and
Indians. Of the combat on May 12, in particular, he wrote:

> Needless to say, I was well satisfied with the result of the
> day's fighting, which proved the correctness of my opinion
> that these great hunters, like the Boers of South Africa, are
> only formidable when you play their games, "bush fight-
> ing," to which they are accustomed, but they cannot stand a
> determined charge.[123]

This seems to be an accurate assessment, but begs the question in that the
Métis and Indians were prevented by their own leader from fully engaging
in guerilla warfare. A bold frontal attack was possible not through anything
Middleton or the Field Force did, but through Riel's determination to decide
their fate at Batoche.

For the Westerners who rose or were tempted to rise in arms, there was
a subtle irony in the presence of these Eastern soldiers. Many who had come
obediently and with preconceived notions of the savagery of the Wild West
came to sympathize with the problems of their former foes. The problems of
the administration of the Northwest was apparent to those who marched
into the territory—they too suffered from privations on the frontier. Only
after receiving reports from the distant Northwest did many of the officials
in the East become aware of Western discontent and discover that there was
substance to the complaints.

Melgund, on whose observations both Lansdowne and Derby relied, believed that there was general discontent in the Northwest among all groups as a result of inadequate administration and neglect. As he wrote after the fighting had ended:

> Riel and Gabriel Dumont were not counting only on their half-breed and Redskin rifles, but on the support of white men who they had been lulled into believing would stand by them. Riel put his fighting men in his first line, but in his second we may perhaps find the disappointed white contractor, the disappointed white land shark, the disappointed white farmer.[124]

The tragedy of Batoche was that those mentioned by Melgund, and especially the Métis and Indians who fought in the last battle, relied too heavily on Riel to win redress for their grievances.

Notes

This article first appeared in *Prairie Forum* 10, no. 1 (1980): 17–64.

The maps for this chapter were redrafted, based on earlier samples, by Anne Krahnen, University of Regina, Department of Geography/HS Karlsruhe–University of Applied Sciences, Germany.

1. See among others, Captain Ernest Chambers, *The Royal Grenadiers. A Regimental History of the 10th Infantry Regiment of the Active Militia in Canada* (Toronto: E. L. Ruddy, 1904); Charles Boulton, *Reminiscences of the North-West Rebellion* (Toronto: Grip Printing, 1886); W.B. Cameron, *The War Trial of Big Bear (or Blood Red the Sun)* (Toronto: Ryerson, 1926); Joseph Kinsey Howard, *Strange Empire: Louis Riel and the Métis People* (New York: William Morrow, 1952); Desmond Morton, *The Last War Drum: The North-West Campaign of 1885* (Toronto: Hakkert, 1972); Desmond Morton and R.H. Roy (eds.), *Telegrams of the North-West Campaign of 1885* (Toronto: Champlain Society, 1972); C.P. Mulvaney, *The History of the North-West Rebellion of 1885* (Toronto: A.H. Havey, 1885); G.H. Needler, *Suppression of Rebellion in the North-West Territories* (Toronto: University of Toronto Press, 1948); C.P. Stacey, "The North-West Campaign, 1885," *Canadian Army Journal* 8 (1954): 10–20; G.F.G. Stanley, *The Birth of Western Canada: A History of the Riel Rebellion* (Toronto: University of Toronto Press, 1936); G.F.G. Stanley, *Louis Riel* (Toronto: McGraw Hill, 1963); P. B. Waite, *Arduous Destiny 1874–1896* (Toronto: McClelland and Stewart, 1971). Although not all of these sources are quoted directly, they were consulted in both the writing of the text and in the preparation of the maps.

2. Canada. *Sessional Papers*, 1886, no. 5, "Report upon the Suppression of the Rebellion in the North-West Territories, and in Matters in Connection Therewith in 1885."

3. One of the earliest analytical pieces was an article by Colonel C.F. Hamilton, "The Canadian Militia: The Northwest Rebellion, 1885," in *Canadian Defence Quarterly* (January 1930): 220.

4. Stanley, *The Birth of Western Canada*; Morton, *Last War Drum*; and Morton, *Telegrams*.

5. Journal de l'abbé G. Cloutier, Archives Archiepiscopales de Saint-Boniface, 1886.

6. Major General Sir Garnet J. Wolseley, *The Soldier's Pocketbook for Field Services* (London: Macmillan and Co., 1869).

7. Captain C. E. Callwell, *Small Wars: Their Principle and Practise* (n.p., 1896).

8. The manoeuvres and positions on these maps are based on both documentary sources and on period maps. The period vegetation as it appears on these maps was based on R. Coutt's study Batoche National Historic Site Period Landscape," MRS 404 (Parks Canada, 1980).

9. Waite, *Arduous Destiny*, 149.

10. For an interesting argument on this topic, see Richard Drinnon, *Facing West: The Metaphysics of Indian-Hating and Empire Building* (Toronto: New American Library, 1980).

11. P.G. Laurie was editor of the *Saskatchewan Herald* from its founding in 1878 until 1902.

12. The etiology of these fears that many whites had of the Indians is explored in the introduction of Drinnon's book and also in Roy Harvey Pearce, *Savagism and Civilization: A Study of the Indian and American Mind* (Baltimore: The John Hopkins Press, 1953) and, most recently, Frederick Turner, *Beyond Geography: The Western Spirit Against the Wilderness* (New York: Viking Press, 1980).

13. Callwell, *Small Wars*, chapter 2.

14. Morton, *Telegrams*.

15. See, for example, Robert Jefferson, "Fifty Years on the Saskatchewan," *Canadian North-West Historical Society Publications* 1, no. 5 (1929), especially Part III. In Part III Jefferson indicates that the dangers anticipated by those beseiged were exaggerated by them.

16. John Jennings, "The North-West Mounted Police and Indian Policy, 1874–96" (PhD dissertation, University of Toronto, 1980).

17. Derby Papers, April 28, 1885, Public Archives of Canada, microfilm A-32.

18. Public Archives of Canada, Minto Papers, Lansdowne to Melgund, April 30, 1885, microfilm A-129.

19. Minto Papers, Lansdowne to Melgund, April 30, 1885.

20. Mulvaney, *North-West Rebellion*, 193–94.

20. Morton, *Telegrams*, April 26, 210.

21. Morton, *Telegrams*, 216.

23. Boulton, *Reminiscences*, 252–53.

24. "Melgund Diary" in *Saskatchewan History* 23, no. 3, (Autumn 1969), 97.

25. Needler, *Suppression*, 44.

26. Ibid.

27. Mulvaney, *North-West Rebellion*, 194.

28. See "Melgund Diary," 91, and Mulvaney, *North-West Rebellion*, 198.

29. In discussing this matter with Jack Summers, he suggested that Middleton may have had more than his personal dislike of Denison in mind when he decided to leave the cavalry at Humboldt. Summers thought that the willful tendency of the calvary to confront every situation by head-on attack might have made them difficult to handle for what Middleton anticipated facing at Batoche.

30. The tactic to use the artillery to demoralize the enemy can be directly traced to Wolseley's recommendation in *The Soldier's Pocketbook* that "Its [the artillery's] moral effect is powerful; it frightens far more than it kills," 225.

31. Boulton, *Reminiscences*, 262.

32. Mulvaney, *North-West Rebellion*, 252.

33. Needler, *Suppression*, 44.

34. Minto Papers, May 9, 1885.

35. Boulton, *Reminiscences*, 260.

36. Mulvaney, *North-West Rebellion*, 199.

37. Needler, *Suppression*, 45.

38. Boulton, *Reminiscences*, 491.

39. Mulvaney, *North-West Rebellion*, 225.

40. Journal de l'abbé G. Cloutier, 5084–85.

41. Ibid., 5111.

42. Boulton, *Reminiscences*, 491.

43. Sessional Papers, 1886, no. 5, 41.

44. Mulvaney, *North-West Rebellion*, 231.

45. Saskatchewan Archives Board, A.S. Morton Manuscript Collection—W.B. Cameron Papers, C550/1/281.

46. Mulvaney, *North-West Rebellion*, 200.

47. Ibid., 199.

48. Journal de l'abbé G. Cloutier, 5085–86.

49. Ibid.

50. Needler, *Suppression*, 46.

51. Ibid.

52. Boulton, *Reminiscences*, 262–63.

53. Mulvaney, *North-West Rebellion*, 200.

54. Needler, *Suppression*, 46.

55. Ibid.

56. Boulton, *Reminiscences*, 262–63.

57. Needler, *Suppression*, 46.

58. Mulvaney, *North-West Rebellion*, 205.

59. Ibid., 200.

60. Journal de l'abbé G. Cloutier, 5123–24.

61. Chambers, *The Royal Grenadiers*, 62.

62. Ibid., 64, and also "Melgund Diary," 104–05.

63. Needler, *Suppression*, 46.

64. Mulvaney, *North-West Rebellion*, 206.

65. "Melgund Diary," 105.

66. Mulvaney, *North-West Rebellion*, 206–07.

67. Ibid.

68. "Melgund Diary," 103.

69. Callwell, *Small Wars*, 240.

70. Ibid., 244.

71. Ibid., 264.

72. Ibid.

73. Ibid., 246.

74. Needler, *Suppression*, 48.

75. Mulvaney, *North-West Rebellion*, 207.

76. Ibid.

77. Needler, *Suppression*, 48.

78. Mulvaney, *North-West Rebellion*, 208.

79. Journal de l'abbé G. Cloutier, 5125.

80. Mulvaney, *North-West Rebellion*, 202–04.
81. Journal de l'abbé G. Cloutier, 5089.
82. Ibid., 5088.
83. Ibid., 5095.
84. Ibid., 5113.
85. Ibid., 5111.
86. Needler, *Suppression*, 48 and also Journal de l'abbé G. Cloutier, 5092.
87. Mulvaney, *North-West Rebellion*, 210.
88. Boulton, *Reminiscences*, 270–71.
89. Canada, *Sessional Papers*, 1886, no. 5, 30.
90. Needler, *Suppression*, 80.
91. Boulton, *Reminiscences*, 272.
92. Needler, *Suppression*, 50.
93. Ibid.
94. Ibid.
95. Boulton, *Reminiscences*, 273.
96. Canada, *Sessional Papers*, 1886, no. 5, 31.
97. Needler, *Suppression*, 50.
98. Ibid., 50–51.
99. Callwell, *Small Wars*, 204–05.
100. Boulton, *Reminiscences*, 275.
101. Mulvaney, *North-West Rebellion*, 257.
102. Canada, *Sessional Papers*, 1886, no. 5, 31.
103. Boulton, *Reminiscences*, 277–78.
104. Needler, *Suppression*, 51.
105. Canada, *Sessional Papers*, 1886, no. 5, 31.
106. Mulvaney, *North-West Rebellion*, 257.
107. Morton, *Telegrams*.
108. Mulvaney, *North-West Rebellion*, 257.
109. Boulton, *Reminiscences*, 259.
110. Canada, *Sessional Papers*, 1886, no. 5, 33.
111. Mulvaney, *North-West Rebellion*, 221.
112. Ibid., 216.
113. Needler, *Suppression*, 52.
114. Ibid., 52–53.
115. Mulvaney, *North-West Rebellion*, 292.
116. Ibid., 292–93.
117. Journal de l'abbé G. Cloutier, 5120.
118. Ibid., 5111.
119. Ibid., 5114.
120. Ibid., 5106–109.
121. Ibid., 5097.
122. Mulvaney, *North-West Rebellion*, 275.
123. Needier, *Suppression*, 53.
124. "Melgund Diary," 314.

17. Parks Canada and the 1885 Rebellion/Uprising/Resistance

Alan McCullough

If each generation writes its own history, it is equally true that each generation creates its own heritage. In Canada, national historic sites are a visible and public part of the Canadian heritage, identified by the Historic Sites and Monuments Board of Canada and administered and interpreted by Parks Canada. Some sites, such as those associated with the 1885 Northwest Rebellion or Resistance, have been a part of the national historic sites system since it was organized in the 1920s. Although the sites have remained the same, the way in which they have been interpreted by Parks Canada and the meanings assigned to them have changed dramatically.

It might be more accurate to say that each generation writes its own *histories*. Although most nation states strive to produce a single, unifying account of their past, subordinate, competing versions of the past often survive beneath the dominant or official version. Sometimes the subordinate versions rise to modify or supplant the dominant story. In *The Past in French History*, Robert Gildea examines how different political cultures in France have supported different versions of the past as a means of defining their vision of France and of strengthening their own identity. Each group has struggled to make its interpretation the universally accepted history, thereby legitimizing its claim to power and strengthening its identity. Equally, each culture has sought to control the commemoration—"the sacralization of its triumphs and defeats, its heroes and martyrs…"—of historic events as a means of defining the collective memory, establishing consensus and legitimating its claims to direct the destiny of France.[1] The identities which the different groups have promoted have not been static, but have been modified to take account of new situations and to maintain their legitimacy.

Gildea holds that political cultures are not defined by sociological factors such as race or class but by collective memory, "the collective construction of the past by a given community." Collective memory is based on the common experiences of a lived history, not a learned history. The past preserved by the collective memory "is constructed not objectively but as a myth, in the sense not of fiction, but of a past constructed collectively by a community in such a way as to serve the political claims of that community."[2] Different communities within the same state will have different, often conflicting, collective memories of the same events which they experienced from different perspectives.

In Canada, as in France, there are many contrasting versions of the past—French/English, newcomer/native, and centre/region—to name only the most obvious. Each of these competing interpretations may be viewed as an attempt by a specific community to define its identity in Canada, and, so far as it is within its power, to have its version of the Canadian past accepted as the dominant version. The contest to define the collective memory is typically presented in terms of a search for historic truth or for greater understanding of the Canadian character, but the interpretation adopted clearly affects the competing political claims of different communities in Canada. In the case of western Canada, the debate over whether the events of 1885 were an unjustified rebellion against lawful authority which threatened the future of Canada or a justified resistance by Aboriginal nations against a distant, unresponsive, and illegitimate government is linked to political, legal and emotive issues—regional autonomy, land claims, Aboriginal rights, and the bilingual, multicultural nature of Canada—which are still current.

Gildea writes that commemoration, which he defines as "remembering in common," is central to the formation of collective memory.[3] Not surprisingly there is often lively competition to control the messages conveyed by commemoration and incorporated in the collective memory. In Canada, the Historic Sites and Monuments Board of Canada (HSMBC) has played a leading role in the formal commemoration of Canadian history and, consequently, in the creation of Canada's collective memory.

The Board was established in 1919 to identify and commemorate events, people and places of national historic significance. In its current incarnation, it is primarily an advisory body; its recommendations must be approved by the minister of Canadian Heritage and are implemented by Parks Canada, an agency of the federal government. The interpretations put forward by the Board and implemented by Parks Canada are sometimes viewed as an authorized version of Canadian history, but they have seldom been uncontested. The most common form of commemoration is by the erection of a bronze plaque. Although bronze plaque texts may have the appearance of a final and authoritative statement on any subject, they have proven surprisingly malleable and subject to change.

This article will focus on the evolving interpretation of a number of sites associated with the events of 1885 in western Canada which have been identified by the Board and interpreted by Parks Canada. It will argue that the events, known to successive generations as the Second Riel Rebellion, the 1885 North West Rebellion, the Uprising of 1885, and the 1885 Resistance, have gone through three generations of interpretation within the Parks Canada system. First commemorated in the 1920s, they were originally seen as part of Canada's westward drive to become a transcontinental nation. This interpretation was hotly debated in the 1920s but remained substantially unchanged until the early 1950s, when it was replaced by an interpretation which gave some recognition to the Indigenous People who resisted this expansion. In the 1970s a third interpretational generation began to emerge which, while not abandoning the theme of Canadian expansion, placed considerable emphasis on the societies which this expansion displaced. Using Parks Canada public and internal documents, published history, and public commentary, this paper will trace the evolution in the interpretation of the 1885 sites from the 1920s to the present. It will set this evolution within the contexts of the Canadian government's Aboriginal policy and cultural policy, the growth of regionalism in Canada, the evolution of Canadian historiography, and evolving heritage policy within Parks Canada. Although the Board has commemorated at least 16 places, events, and persons related to the events of 1885,[4] it has lavished its attention on three key sites: Batoche, Cut Knife Hill and Fort Battleford (Figure 1). The three sites may be taken as representing three aspects (Métis, Native, and English-speaking Euro-Canadian) of the events of 1885.

Parks Canada's commemoration of the sites associated with the 1885 conflict has drawn the attention of historians before. C.J. Taylor's *Negotiating the Past: The Making of Canada's National Historic Parks and Sites* provides an analysis of the history and the interaction of the Historic Sites and Monuments Board and of the National Parks Branch (the predecessor of Parks Canada) in the years prior to 1965, while his "Some Early Problems of the Historic Sites and Monuments Board of Canada" includes a detailed study of the initial controversy which arose out of the commemoration of the 1885 sites. While admitting that the Board's structure, with regional representatives, provided for regional views on Canadian history, he argued that most of the original Board's members assumed the existence of a common national history. Their experience with the 1885 sites may not have destroyed this assumption, but it "demonstrated that the national perspective depended to

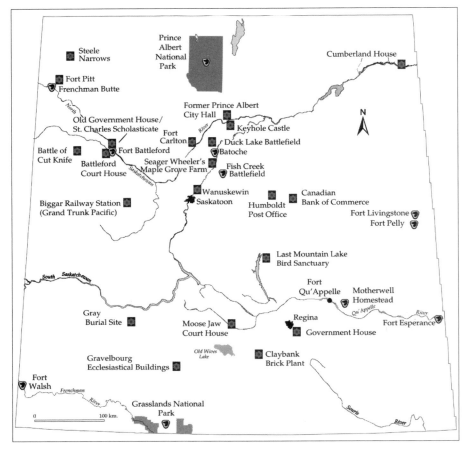

Figure 1. National Historic Sites and National Parks in Saskatchewan (Canadian Heritage, Parks Canada, *Canada's National Historic Sites and Parks Atlas*, March 1996).

a large degree on where one stood,"and that national significance was a "very elastic term."[5] Walter Hildebrandt has faulted both the Board and Parks Canada for imposing a central Canadian myth on the interpretation of Fort Battleford National Historic Park, and for ignoring both Native and settler history in the Battleford area.[6] More recently Frits Pannekoek has castigated the Board and Parks Canada for adhering to a nationalist storyline in interpreting its sites and for failing to embrace the post-modern concept of multiple narratives in its interpretation sites such as Batoche and Fort Battleford.[7] This article will not challenge the contention that the Board began with a strong central Canadian, or perhaps a traditional Canadian nationalist, interpretation of the events of 1885. It will suggest that both the

Board and Parks Canada began to adopt an interpretation which was much more sympathetic to regional perspectives in the 1950s, and that this sympathy has continued to evolve so that in one case, Batoche, the regional interpretation is now dominant. It will also argue that, in the case of Batoche, Parks Canada has attempted to implement, with limited success, the concept of multiple narratives. The paper will also consider, at least by inference, the role of a national heritage agency such as Parks Canada in framing a national history.

The Historic Sites and Monuments Board of Canada

The Historic Sites and Monuments Board of Canada was established in 1919 and given the responsibility of advising the Canadian government on the commemoration of sites of national historic significance. The creation of the Board came at the end of several decades of growing interest in Canadian history and in conservation both of natural and cultural resources. The two developments met in a movement to commemorate Canada's past through the preservation of historic landmarks. Although the move to commemoration and preservation was nationalist in inspiration, the nationalism took various regional forms—a celebration of the Loyalist/Imperialist tradition in Ontario and of the French-Canadian tradition in Québec, and a more diffuse celebration of the very early origins of European settlement in the Maritime provinces.[8] World War I intensified the movement towards conservation in Canada and, especially in English Canada, brought earlier diffuse national sentiment together. The Board members (E.A. Cruikshank, James Coyne, B. Sulte, W.C. Milner, and W.O. Raymond) who were appointed in 1919 all had some experience of the earlier preservation movement. They were historians, heritage activists and nationalists, and their early recommendations reflect the English-language "nation building" historiography of the time.

Although it was nominally an advisory body, in practice the Board operated as a semi-autonomous agency under the National Parks Branch (NPB) of the Department of the Interior. The Commissioner of National Parks, James Harkin, played an active role in the Board's decisions and the NPB implemented the Board's recommendations, but, until the 1950s, the Board's recommendations were seldom subject to political review.[9] Moreover, the Board had almost no support staff; generally speaking, members researched topics and drafted plaque texts themselves or enlisted the support of experts in the field. As a result the early commemorations, which set the tone of the commemoration program for half a century, were reflective of the members' interests and approach to history. From 1919 to 1939 Brigadier General E.A.

Cruikshank, an authority on the War of 1812, was the chairman of the Board. Under his influence early recommendations focussed on political and military history and on European exploration of Canada. Overall, the sites selected contributed to the "nation building" theme of Canadian history.

The rationale for establishing a system of national historic sites was not spelled out when the Board was created. It might be inferred from the context of the time that commemoration was intended both as a means of expressing and maintaining a Canadian nationalism. Certainly the chairman saw the Board's role as patriotic and didactic. The Board's principal form of commemoration was through bronze plaques mounted on stone monuments. Cruikshank favoured plaque texts which were brief and "factual"; they provided little overt interpretation or context and did not attempt to tell the whole story. Cruickshank hoped that the texts would inspire the reader's interest and curiosity; he did think it useful to include details, especially names, as a means of inspiring local interest.[10]

With the exception of Benjamin Sulte, a noted Québec historian, the original Board was Anglophone. Sulte died in 1923 and was succeeded by Victor Morin, a Montréal notary, active in the Québec heritage movement and president of the Montréal Antiquarian and Numismatic Society. He resigned after the Board refused to adopt his suggestion that all plaques, not just those in Québec, should be bilingual. Three successors resigned in turn, with the result that there was no effective voice on the Board for a French-speaking, Catholic interpretation of Canadian history during the 1920s when the 1885 sites were commemorated. As well, there were no members from the Prairie provinces until 1937. The British Columbia member, Judge F.W. Howay, who was appointed in 1923, generally spoke for western sites. A leading historian of British Columbia, he was not an expert on the Prairies and frequently consulted A.S. Morton, a fur trade historian at the University of Saskatchewan, on the 1885 sites. Howay also provided some balance to Cruikshank's enthusiasm for central Canadian military sites.[11]

Initial Commemoration and Interpretation

At its first meeting in 1919, the Board identified a provisional list of 171 Canadian sites which it hoped to commemorate; in eastern Canada the list was dominated by military sites, with a smaller group of exploration and settlement sites. Twenty-eight commemorations were proposed for western Canada with the emphasis on fur trade sites. Four battlefields from the 1885 Rebellion—Batoche, Cut Knife Hill, Duck Lake, and Fish Creek—were the most significant block of non-fur-trade sites. In 1920 the Board recommended that the 1885 sites be treated as a whole, and over the next few years other sites (Frog Lake, Frenchman Butte, Battleford) were added to the list. In 1923 Judge Howay drafted plaque texts for Batoche, Fish Creek, Frog Lake, Cut Knife Hill, and Battleford. Overall, the drafts and the final products focused, in each case, on the action and took the point of view of the Canadian forces. Howay had his texts reviewed by E.H. Oliver of Presbyterian College, Saskatoon,[12] by the other Board members and then, at the suggestion of Cruikshank, by Sir William Otter. Otter had commanded the Canadian forces at the Battle of Cut Knife Hill, where they were defeated by the Cree under the leadership of Poundmaker and Fine Day.

The Board members did not make any substantial changes to the drafts, although James Coyne of Ontario did make the revealing comment that he was not sure that the Board should advertise the "retreat of Col. Otter [from Cut Knife Hill] and the victory of Dumont [at Fish Creek]. In similar cases heretofore we have contented ourselves with honouring our own soldiers or citizens who fell."[13] However, Otter substantially rewrote the Cut Knife Hill text, with the result that it implied that the battle had been a victory for the Canadian forces under his command. At the time even Howay deferred to Otter's view.[14]

The monuments were erected in 1924 and unveiled in the summer of 1925. Almost immediately they were involved in a storm of controversy. Indeed, during the unveiling ceremony the Roman Catholic Vicar-General of Prince Albert denounced the Batoche plaque as a "gross insult to the men who fought under Riel," and a delegation from Québec boycotted the ceremony.[15] The Vicar-General's charge was widely reported in English language papers and was endorsed by many French-language papers. *Le Soleil* of Québec City wrote: "On a fait du monument un mémorial à la prussienne; c'est au milieu d'un peuple vaincu le souvenir de l'écrasement par les vainqueurs, sans le moindre égard pour le ressentiment des familles métisses."[16] "L'affaire Batoche" became a major embarrassment for the Board.

The Batoche text (Figure 2) was a straightforward presentation of an English and central Canadian view of 1885. It named General Middleton and the Canadian government units which participated in the battle, but did not deign to identify Louis Riel or Gabriel Dumont or to mention the Métis forces.

The monument was in front of the church at Batoche, on land which had been donated by the church. Harkin had written the Roman Catholic Bishop of Prince Albert in 1924, asking him to donate a plot for the monument and enclosing a photo of the plaque. The bishop responded that he would be pleased to transfer the land, provided that the monument respected the "sensibilities of the people" among whom it was to be erected and that it be in French as well as in English. Harkin thanked him for providing the site and remarked that although the plaque had already been cast in English, he was favourably disposed to having a separate plaque cast in French.[17] When Howay learned of the bishop's request for a bilingual plaque he wrote that he was "utterly opposed" to putting up a plaque in French; to do so in the West would, he predicted, lead to trouble.[18] The Board deferred preparing a French-language plaque, and only the English text was available at the time of the unveiling. This, together with the reference to the Métis as rebels, was taken as a double violation of the agreement with the bishop, who asked that a new plaque, with no reference to rebels or rebellion, be prepared. The bishop also objected to the

> NORTH WEST REBELLION
> BATOCHE
> HEADQUARTERS OF THE
> REBELS
>
> Its capture by General Middleton, after four days fighting, 9th, 10th, 11th and 12th May, 1885, ended the rebellion.
> The Midland Regiment, 10th Royal Grenadiers, 90th Regiment, Winnipeg Battery. "A" Battery Boulton's Mounted Infantry, and French's Scouts took part in the battle.

Figure 2. 1924 Batoche plaque text (LAC, RG84, Vol. 979, File BA2, Part 1, photograph, c. 1923–34).

plaque on the grounds that it implied that the clergy had supported the rising.[19] This last point serves as a useful reminder that the positions of the clergy and of the Métis were not identical, although the Board treated the clergy as intermediaries for the Métis.

At its 1926 meeting the Board declined to change the English text "in the interests of historical accuracy," while recommending that a French-language text be prepared.[20] There was little chance of a French-language text being accepted while the offending English-language text remained unchanged. By 1929 the plaque had been defaced with "certain words" chiselled off,[21] but it remained in place until 1939.

The controversy was extended to other sites by H.A. Kennedy. A prominent journalist, Kennedy had been present at the Battle of Cut Knife Hill as a war correspondent for the New York *Herald*. He had been on the speakers' platform at the unveiling of the plaques; it particularly irked the Board members that he had not criticized the plaques at the time of the unveiling but raised the issue later in newspaper columns under headlines such as "The Comedy of the Cairns" and "Blunders in Bronze." He echoed the bishop's criticism of the plaque at Batoche for being in English only and for using the words *rebellion* and *rebels* in a French-speaking, Roman Catholic, Métis community peopled by descendants of the Métis who had participated in the

NORTH WEST REBELLION
CUT KNIFE BATTLEFIELD

Site of fight, 2nd may 1885
between government troops
under Lieut. Col. W.D. Otter
and Indian rebels under Chief
Poundmaker whose junction with
another rebel, Chief Big Bear, it
was desirable to frustrate.
After an engagement of six
hours when this object had been
attained Lt. Col. Otter returned
to Battleford with a loss of eight
killed and fourteen wounded.

Figure 3. Text unveiled in 1924 at Cut Knife (LAC, RG84, HS 10-3-4, Part 1, Brass Rubbing, c. 1923–24).

1885 rising. At Cut Knife Hill he criticized the text (Figure 3) for being inaccurate—the battle had been a Canadian defeat, not a victory as the text implied—and for being in the wrong place. At Frog Lake, where the text (Figure 4) began "Here on 2 April 1885 rebel Indians under Big Bear massacred…," Kennedy argued that Big Bear had tried unsuccessfully to stop the massacre and that Wandering Spirit was the aggressive leader.

The Battleford plaque (Figure 5), which began, "Sacked by rebel Cree Indians under Poundmaker," showed, he wrote, "an astonishing looseness of language."[22] Poundmaker had no "autocratic powers": he had been overridden by his more "ignorant and excitable" followers, and "sack" was an inaccurate description for the looting which occurred. Kennedy accepted that the Métis and Indians had been rebels (he did not consider the term one of opprobrium, and referred to his own Scottish ancestors who had been rebels in '45) and that once it began, it was necessary to suppress the rebellion. However, he emphasized that the rebellion need never have happened if western development had not been so ineptly mismanaged by the federal government.

Kennedy's columns, which appeared in the Toronto *Globe*, in the *Mail and Empire*, and in the Calgary *Herald*, were picked up and commented upon in other papers. The Ottawa *Journal* remarked that the inaccuracy in the Cut Knife Hill plaque was "inexcusable."[23] Kennedy was active in

NORTH WEST REBELLION
FROG LAKE MASSACRE

Here on 2nd April, 1885, rebel
Indians under
Big Bear massacred Rev. Father Léon Adélard
Fafard, O.M.I, Father Félix Marchand,
O.M.I, Indian Agent Thomas Quinn, Farm
Instructor John Delaney, John Alexander Gowanlock,
William Campbell Gilchrist, George Dill
Charles Gouin, John Williscroft.

Figure 4. Text of 1924 Frog Lake Massacre plaque (Parks Canada, Ottawa, HSMBC Originals, Plaque Texts).

NORTH WEST REBELLION
BATTLEFORD

Sacked by the Rebel
Cree Indians under
Poundmaker. Here
on 26th May, 1885, after
the Battle of Batoche
and the capture of Riel
Poundmaker and his
band surrendered to
General Middleton.

Figure 5. Text of 1924 Battleford plaque (LAC, RG84, Vol. 1382, HS 10-3-6, Part 1, Brass Rubbing, c. 1923).

the Canadian Authors Association and he was probably responsible for the resolution passed at its Calgary meeting in 1929, which supported the Board's work but condemned inaccuracies in the texts, especially in Western plaques, and called for the appointment of members from the Prairies.[24]

In the case of the Cut Knife Battlefield plaque (Figure 3), erected on the Poundmaker Reserve, the population had not been consulted about the text, in spite of the fact that many veterans of the battle lived on the reserve. The population resented the text, but initially the Indian agent refused to support their protests out of deference to the HSMBC. When the accuracy of the texts became a public issue, the agent forwarded the Indians' protests to Ottawa. He wrote that the Indians claimed that "they were not rebels but were fighting for their rights and that Col. Otter retreated without attaining any object and in haste." They asked that the "Tablet should merely read that the monument was to commemorate the fight, stating names and date and omitting the objectionable features from the tablet."[25] The agent also noted that many old-timers in the district (by which he probably meant white settlers) also resented the text; this view was supported by an independent report which noted that the Cut Knife Hill plaque had been defaced with the words "All lies."[26]

A concern with historical accuracy, local pride, and the presence of many veterans of the battle on the Poundmaker reserve is sufficient to explain the protest launched by the band. However, it is worth noting that the Poundmaker reserve was a centre of Native political activity in the 1920s and 1930s. The Chief, Fine Day, was both a veteran of the battle and an active and resourceful defender of his followers' rights, especially their right to practice their traditional religion. John Tootoosis, a member of the band, was the principal organizer for the League of Indians in Saskatchewan during the 1930s; the League is generally considered to be the first political umbrella group representing Canadian First Nations.[27]

The Board was annoyed by the attacks and somewhat intimidated; for several years it viewed the 1885 sites as troublesome and to be avoided while there were less contentious topics to commemorate.[28] In 1930, when it

Poundmaker (courtesy of the Saskatchewan Archives Board/R-B8775).

was suggested that the site of Middleton's camp at Batoche should be protected, Howay wrote that the whole Batoche episode had been an unpleasant experience and that Batoche should be left to "fry in its own grease."[29] In the case of the Batoche, Battleford and Frog Lake plaques, the Board maintained that they were basically accurate and that Kennedy's criticisms were little more than nit-picking. The Cut Knife Hill plaque was more troubling. Howay accepted that it was in the wrong place and that it was inaccurate.[30] The error in locating the monument was explicable: it had been placed about a mile away from the actual site of the battle to make it more accessible by road. The error in the content of the text was more serious, and Howay pressed for a change; but the Ontario members, Cruikshank and Coyne, were reluctant to challenge the interpretation put forward by Sir William Otter. The Board debated the question at each of its annual meetings from 1927 to 1931. In an attempt to break the deadlock and to involve both more professional expertise and western opinion, it asked the heads of history departments in the three Prairie universities, A.L. Burt, A.S. Morton and Chester Martin, for drafts. It did not, so far as is known, consult with the First Nations. Finally in 1931 the Board agreed on a text which substituted the term "hostile Indians" for "Indian Rebels" and refrained from any suggestion that the Canadian force had accomplished its aims before it "retired to Battleford."[31]

This text was cast with the intention that it be erected in 1933, but the depression delayed action. In the meantime, George E. Lloyd, the Church of England bishop of Saskatchewan, took an interest in the plaque. He had been a chaplain to Canadian forces at the battle and he objected that the new text was "deliberately composed to spell 'defeat' without actually saying so."[32] In 1935 Bishop Lloyd attended a reunion of Veterans of the North West

Rebellion in Toronto which passed a resolution strongly condemning any change in the memorial at Cut Knife. The issue attracted some press coverage, and the powerful Toronto Conservative MP, Tommy Church, became involved. Speaking in the House of Commons, he supported the commemoration of the 1885 sites and spoke of the veterans of the North West Rebellion as men who went to the "northwest in 1885 to prevent this country from being dislocated and dismembered and to avenge the death of that great patriot, Thomas Scott."[33] Howay was asked to prepare a report in response to the veterans' resolution, and in 1936 the Board went to the unusual extent of reading into its minutes extensive extracts from standard histories to support its interpretation of the battle. In spite of this brave front, the revised plaque was never erected. This failure may have been a response to the opposition from the veterans, but it was probably also a result of the loss of energy and sense of direction which the Board experienced in the mid 1930s. The original version of the Cut Knife Hill text remained in place until 1952.

With the exception of the admitted inaccuracies in the Cut Knife Hill text, the Board's view was representative of the mainstream English-language historiography which had developed since 1885; essentially it ignored the possibility of the legitimacy of Métis and First Nations claims. This view was at odds with French-language historiography, which tended to identify the Métis cause with the cause of French-speaking, Roman Catholic Québec, and placed the 1885 Rebellion in a long line of confrontations including the Manitoba School Question, Bill 17 in Ontario, and conscription in World War I.

Shifting Personalities, Perspectives, and Interpretations

Kennedy's attack on the plaques revealed that there was a more nuanced interpretation of the rebellion current in English Canada and that the issue was more complex than the short, nationalist texts favoured by the Board were capable of dealing with. In a pamphlet, *The North-West Rebellion*, published by Ryerson Press in 1928, Kennedy mitigated Métis and Native responsibility in the rebellion. The federal government had "seemed deaf to all complaints"and in the early, non-violent stages, the protest had the support of some whites and of the Catholic clergy. At Frog Lake the most "savage" members of the band "set at naught their old chief Big Bear's" leadership, and Poundmaker was "practically a prisoner" in his camp. Above all, blame for the violent outcome was placed on Riel's shoulders. Kennedy's views were not simply an idiosyncratic interpretation; his pamphlet, which was aimed at school children, was recommended for use by the Ontario

Big Bear (courtesy LAC-c-1873).

provincial department of education and was endorsed by the Imperial Order Daughters of the Empire.[34]

His position has some points in common with those of George Stanley, whose *The Birth of Western Canada: A History of the Riel Rebellions* was published in 1936. Stanley saw the 1870 and 1885 rebellions as key events in the formation of a new region. This gave the risings legitimacy and shifted interpretation away from emphasis on the English/French conflict to a centre/ periphery issue. Stanley also emphasized the rebellions as struggles between old and new ways of life, between "primitive and civilized peoples."[35] Stanley's work was not widely disseminated in the 1930s, but it was reissued in 1960 and became, for a time, the most widely accepted interpretation of the rebellions in English-language historiography.

Changes in the Board's personnel and the active interest of local historians prepared the ground for a substantial shift in interpretation at the 1885 sites. In 1936 T.A. Crerar, a Manitoba MP, became the minister responsible for the Board. Crerar was first elected to Parliament in 1921 as a member of the Progressive Party, a regionally based party. Although he subsequently joined the Liberal Party, his western loyalties may have influenced his decision in 1937 to appoint Board members representing Manitoba and Saskatchewan. The Manitoba member, Father Antoine D'Eschambault, was a Roman Catholic priest, an active member of the Saint Boniface Historical Society, and a recognized historian. J.A. Gregory, a businessman and politician, was appointed to represent Saskatchewan. During Crerar's ministry, Gustave Lanctôt, a leading historian of French Canada, was appointed to the Board, ex officio, in his position as Dominion Archivist. He effectively replaced E.A. Cruikshank, who died in 1939. Howay, who had drafted the original texts, retired in 1944. This left only one member on

> Batoche
>
> Here, on the 15th May, 1885, after four days of fighting, the Métis under Louis Riel surrendered to General Middleton commanding the Canadian troops.
>
> Ici, le 15 mai 1885, après quatre jours de combat, les Métis sous Louis Riel se rendirent au Général Middleton, commandant des forces canadiennes.

Figure 6. 1947 plaque text (Parks Canada Ottawa Office, "Historic Sites and Monuments Board of Canada. Originals. Plaque Texts." Compiled c. 1973).

the Board, J.C. Webster of New Brunswick, who had been associated with the early controversies.

Gregory, the member of the Board for Saskatchewan, was a longtime mayor of North Battleford, a Liberal MLA (1934–40), and the MP (1940–45) for the Battlefords. As an MLA in 1938 he had spoken at length in the legislature on Métis' history and on their right to some consideration from the government; his speech was published in pamphlet form under the title "Metis Claims." The speech, unusual for its time, indicated a sympathy for the Métis which may have made him amenable to reconsidering the Board's interpretation of Batoche.[36]

In 1939 the plaque which had given such offense at Batoche was taken down. In another decision which suggests an increased responsiveness to other voices, the Board recommended in 1943 that the new plaque at Duck Lake should be in Cree syllabics as well as English. Given that only twenty years before the Board had resisted putting French on the Batoche plaque, this was a substantial concession. In 1943 Father D'Eschambault was asked to consult with clergy at Batoche on the text for a new plaque there. Father Allard at Batoche consulted with his parishioners, who agreed to a draft text, in French and English, which was subsequently approved by the Board. The new text avoided the use of the word *rebel* and in fact avoided any attempt to explain the significance of the battle. The plaque (Figure 6) was placed on the old monument in the summer of 1947. There was no ceremony; it was simply left with the parish priest who had it put in place. While this surrender to local sentiment, which had opposed the original plaque, may not have been gracious, it was an indication that the Board was willing to consider other views in preparing plaque texts.

Over the next five years there was a concerted campaign waged by local interests to expand NHS involvement at both Batoche and Battleford. In 1947 the Board agreed to consider the care of soldiers' graves at Batoche. In 1948 Walter Tucker, a Saskatchewan MLA and leader of the Saskatchewan Liberal Party, began to pepper the NPB with letters urging that something be done to preserve the trenches of Middleton's encampment which were on Alfred Caron's farm at Batoche. Gregory, the board member, visited Fish Creek and Batoche with Tucker and found that Caron was willing to sell the site. Gregory also remarked that there was a granite memorial in the Batoche cemetery with the names of the Métis and Indians who had died there, including Louis Riel. He suggested that perhaps enough time had passed that the government might undertake to care for the graves of "these misguided people."[37] In 1950 the Prince Albert Historical Society urged NHS to set aside the Batoche battlefield as a historic site; and in the debate on supply, two Saskatchewan Members of Parliament, J.H. Harrison and J.G. Diefenbaker, spoke in favour of preserving the 1885 sites. In 1950 the Board recommended that the trenches at Middleton's camp were of national significance and should be acquired. Negotiations to purchase the land began almost immediately. While they were going on, the priest at Batoche proposed that the government should buy the presbytery at Batoche for use as a museum, or, he suggested, NHS might buy the presbytery, the cemetery and the church and establish a substantial historic park. He remarked that the Métis resented the fact that the government was buying Middleton's campsite, which could be used to interpret the role of the government forces, and felt that their side of the story should be told as well.[38] Calculated or not, the remark played to the Board's willingness to give a more balanced interpretation to the Batoche site.

At the same meeting at which it recommended that Middleton's trenches should be acquired, the Board established a committee to review all of the 1885 sites. Father D'Eschambault and Campbell Innes, a local historian and heritage activist from Battleford who replaced Gregory on the Board in 1951, completed the review in May of 1952. They reported that the causes of the "events of 1885" were complex, and that it was "too simple to say it was a struggle between the ancient way of life, the border line and frontier existence and the incoming civilization." Responsibility "at least in greater part" was attributed to the "callous indifference and the later blundering of the Canadian authorities." They also reported that there was widespread support from the white community in the initial stages of the events. The report recommended the acquisition of the Batoche rectory, the Métis trenches at Batoche, and the Indian trenches at Frenchman Butte. The report also suggested a new interpretive framework, stating that "So far only the military operations have been given importance and consideration. Justice should be done to all participants in these tragic events which should be considered as a whole."[39]

While the report was in preparation, the prime minister, Louis St.

Laurent, intervened in the debate over the interpretation of the events of 1885. St. Laurent was a French-Canadian, a Roman Catholic, a Liberal, and an heir to the tradition of Sir Wilfrid Laurier who had taken up the defence of Riel and of the Métis in the aftermath of the rising. During a tour of Saskatchewan in August 1951, St. Laurent met Walter Tucker, the leader of the Saskatchewan Liberal Party, who told him of the "trouble" he had experienced with the Board over the wording of the plaque at Batoche. Subsequently, St. Laurent visited the museum at Fort Battleford, which had been transferred from a local historical society to the National Parks Branch in July of 1951. There, St. Laurent found "'rebels' and 'rebellion' splashed all over the place." Speaking with "intense feeling" he told J.D. Herbert, who was in charge of the museum:

> that the word "rebellion" was unfortunately chosen to describe the events of 1885 because the people involved on both sides of the affair were equally interested in the democratic process and in the interests of national unity which he and a great many others had been striving a long time to further, [and thus] he felt that the word rebellion should be dropped and should be properly referred to as simply an uprising.[40]

He went on to quote Sir Wilfrid Laurier as saying that the Métis "wanted to be treated like British subjects and not bartered away like common cattle," and that in 1885 they had been driven to crime by the government. St. Laurent declared that he would "take official steps to have the half-breed actions on the prairies in the last century referred to as an 'uprising' and not a 'rebellion'."[41]

St. Laurent's comments evoked a substantial press response. While some papers described his intervention as "rewriting history", others took the view that the rising was the result of government procrastination and that the Métis and Indians took up arms to "fight for some of the freedoms we Canadians have today." W.L. Morton, a historian of Manitoba and western Canada, agreed with St. Laurent in the broad political sense while pointing out that legally, the uprising was a rebellion.[42]

On his return to Ottawa, St. Laurent wrote to the minister responsible for the HSMBC, expanding on his remarks and suggesting that the Board might wish to consider his point of view. St. Laurent eloquently placed the events of 1885 in both a large and a small "L" liberal context:

> I have always looked upon as Toryism the application of condemnatory terms to those, who, after all, have been

largely responsible for the free institutions we now enjoy. I don't think of the Bishops and Barons at Runnymede [as rebels] nor do I think this of others who secured all the great charters, no not even William Lyon Mackenzie and Neilson and Papineau. As a matter of fact, you know, there are a great many Canadians of my race and religion who resent as cowardly the conduct of Sir John A. Macdonald and his government in allowing Riel to be hanged. I think we should be false to the attitudes so eloquently maintained in the House of Commons by Sir Wilfrid Laurier if we countenanced the continuation of inscriptions in a public museum that endorses the attitude then taken by the Macdonald government.[43]

The Prime Minister's intervention reinforced, and probably helped to shape, the recommendations in D'Eschambault and Innes' report on the 1885 sites, and in 1952 the Board agreed that the use of the term *rebellion* was "unwise."[44] The Board had already begun to move in the direction it was being pushed: in rewriting the Batoche plaque text in 1947 and the Cut Knife Battlefield text in 1951 it had avoided the use of the words *rebels* and *rebellion*. The exhibits at Fort Battleford, which had attracted St. Laurent's attention, were the responsibility of the National Parks Branch and the Board; but it seems likely that they had been developed by the local historical society, which had transferred the museum to the federal government only a month before St. Laurent's visit.

The report by D'Eschambault and Innes, the intervention by the prime minister, and the transfer of the museum at Fort Battleford to National Parks set the stage for the 1952 recommendation by the Board that the Batoche rectory was of national historic significance and should be acquired for use as a museum. The rectory was bought in 1955 and the church in 1970. By 1976 Parks Canada had acquired about 2,700 acres of land including the site of the village of Batoche, and was preparing to develop Batoche as a major historic site in western Canada.

In 1952 the Board replaced the original Cut Knife Hill plaque. As was the case at Batoche, the Board sought the prior approval of the local Aboriginal population in replacing the plaque. Unlike the case at Batoche, where the clergy acted as intermediaries for the Métis, the Aboriginal population at Cut Knife Hill was consulted directly. Thomas Favel, the chief at Poundmaker, gave permission for a monument to be erected on the battlefield and agreed to participate in the unveiling ceremony on the understanding that a new text would be prepared.[45]

CUT KNIFE BATTLEFIELD

Named after Chief Cut Knife of the Sarcee in an historic battle with the Cree. On 2nd May, 1885, Lt. Col. W.D. Otter led 325 troops composed of North West Mounted Police, "B" Battery, "C" Company, Foot Guards, Queen's Own and Battleford Rifles, against the Cree and Assiniboine under Poundmaker and Fine Day. After an engagement of six hours, the troops retreated to Battleford.

Figure 7. Text unveiled in 1952 (LAC, RG84, Vol.1381, HS 10-3-4, Part 3, Blue print c. 1951, T-14149).

The new text was approved in 1951 and unveiled in 1952 (Figure 7). The 1952 text followed fairly closely what the members of Poundmaker's reserve had suggested in 1926. It named the commanders on each side, identified the government units and tribal peoples involved, and concluded that after six hours the government troops retreated to Battleford. There was no mention of rebellious or hostile Indians nor of Poundmaker's surrender. Equally, the text avoided describing the battle as a Canadian defeat and avoided any discussion of the context of the battle, of the aims of the participants, or of the consequences of the battle. In its spareness the text is similar to the 1947 text at Batoche; apparently the only common ground which the descendants of the participants in the 1885 battles could agree on were the dates and the names of those involved.

When the Board had replaced the old plaque at Batoche it had done so almost by stealth. By contrast, the unveiling of the Cut Knife Hill plaque was done with full press coverage and in the presence of the Governor-General. The ceremony, on November 2, 1952, was hosted and organized by the chiefs of Poundmaker, Sweet Grass and Little Pine Reserves, who issued an invitation to the descendants of the Canadian militia and Indian warriors to attend. Prayers were offered by a Native catechist, Baptiste Pooyak, with a choir from the Little Pine Day School. The actual unveiling was done by Mrs. C. Parker, whose father, Paddy Bourke of the North-West Mounted Police, had been killed in the battle. The Governor-General, Vincent Massey, spoke at the ceremony and was quoted as saying there were "no truer Canadians anywhere" than "Her Majesty's Indian subjects."[46] Finally the names of those killed at the battle were read out by RCMP Inspector Hansen and by Chief Blackman. The front cover of the program bore an image of "Fine Day, General of the Indian Forces." The back cover had a cut of Major-General T.B. Strange, who had led a Canadian force in 1885 but who was not at Cut Knife Hill. Lieut.-Col. Otter, who had commanded the government forces in the battle, was not mentioned in the program. The shift in perspective which the new plaque and the ceremony

"Her Majesty's Indian Subjects" as prisoners of the North-West Mounted Police in Regina in 1885. The central figure with the mutton chop whiskers, seated fourth from left in the second row, is Lieutenant-Governor Edgar Dewdney. To his right is Superintendent Richard Burton Deane of the North-West Mounted Police, who has just placed his pillbox cap on the head of Chief Piapot, who is sitting in front of him (courtesy of the Saskatchewan Archives Board/R-B3819).

represented was picked up in the newspaper headlines reporting the ceremony: "Cut Knife Hill battle saw Indians give pasting to white soldiers," and "History revised. Referees do a double-take and Poundmaker cops a hill."[47]

The contrast between the profile given the replacement of the Batoche plaque in 1947 and the unveiling of the Cut Knife Hill plaque in 1952 can be seen both as an evidence of the evolution of the Board's views on the 1885 sites and the profile which St. Laurent's intervention and the acquisition of Fort Battleford as a national historic park had given historic sites in Saskatchewan. The prominence may also have been a recognition of the growing political sophistication of the Saskatchewan Native community and of the community on the Poundmaker reserve.

Unlike the sites at Batoche and Fort Battleford, Parks Canada has never owned any substantial property at Cut Knife and it has not developed a major interpretive program there. The site is on the Poundmaker Indian Reserve where the Poundmaker First Nation has established its own interpretation centre, the Chief Poundmaker Historical Centre and Teepee Village. There the events of 1885 are set in a broader history of the Cree people, including the story of how treaties were made and broken and how the Cree people preserved their traditions.[48]

THE BATTLE OF CUT KNIFE

On May 2 1885, after the relief of Battleford, Col. W. D. Otter and a flying column of 305 men advanced on Poundmaker's reserve at Cut Knife where the Cree and Assiniboine bands of Battleford Agency were gathered. The surprise attack failed and after six hours fighting Otter retreated to Battleford. On Poundmaker's orders the Indians declined pursuit but, convinced of white hostility, moved to join Riel at Batoche. When word came of the Métis defeat there, Poundmaker and his bands surrendered at Battleford on May 26.

Figure 8. Text approved 1971; installed in 1985 (HSMBC, Minutes, May 1971).

Although there appeared to have been a general acceptance of the Cut Knife text erected in 1952, a new text was drafted in 1971 and erected in 1985 (Figure 8). The new text (in Cree, English and French) is comparable in style to the 1954 text at Fort Battleford. It attempts to provide a narrative description of the event but it remains ambiguous as to causes, results and motives. Does, as I believe, its description of a "surprise" attack imply that Otter, representing the Canadian government, was the aggressor in the battle? Does the phrase "after the relief of Battleford" make, as Parks Canada historian Frieda Klippenstein suggests, a "very subtle explanation and legitimization of Otter's attack"?[49] Should the phrase "convinced of white hostility, [Poundmaker's band] moved to join Riel at Batoche" be taken as meaning that Otter's attack was another instance of government action driving loyal Indians into rebellion? On one point, that Otter was defeated, the current text seems clear where earlier texts were opaque or inaccurate.

At Battleford there was no pressure to change the interpretation presented by the 1924 plaque, which made reference to the "sack" of Battleford. Perhaps this was because the predominantly white community accepted the interpretation as an accurate account of the events of the rebellion. There was, however, pressure for the NPB to become more involved in interpreting the history of Battleford: the community had an active local history society, which published a series of memoirs of early pioneers with a particular emphasis on the 1885 experience. The society's moving spirit, Campbell Innes, replaced J.A. Gregory on the Board in 1951. Innes was largely responsible for persuading the provincial government to fund the restoration of several buildings at the old North-West Mounted Police post for use as a local museum. Work on the restoration began in 1945, and the "North West Mounted Police Memorial and Indian Museum" was formally opened in 1948. The museum was managed by the historical society; it occupied five

FORT BATTLEFORD

Here in July, 1876, Superintendent James Walker
established a post of the North West Mounted Police in the
heart of the Cree country. "The Fort" grew to a strength of 200.
during the uprising of 1885 it gave refuge to more than 400
people and was the base for operations at Cut Knife Hill and
Fort Pitt leading to the surrender of Chief Poundmaker and the
search for Big Bear. With the extension of settlement and
mechanization of the Force it ceased to be the barracks in 1924.

Figure 9. 1954 plaque text (HSMBC, Minutes, May 1953).

buildings and had exhibits on police history, Indian life, pioneer life, natural history, and agriculture.[50]

The historical society hoped to gain the support of the Indian Affairs Branch and of the Board for the project. In 1947 the Board appointed a committee headed by J.A. Gregory to consider a proposal that the Indian Affairs Branch become involved in the museum. The committee suggested that a series of regional museums devoted to Indian culture should be developed, and in 1948 the Board endorsed this concept.[51] Following a subsequent, and even more positive, report by the committee, the Board recommended the acquisition and operation of the museum by National Parks. As a result, the museum was transferred to the federal government in 1951.

In 1953 the Board approved a plaque text for Fort Battleford (Figure 9). The text was not a replacement for the original "sack" of Battleford text erected in 1924 (Figure 5), which remained in place until at least 1962.[52] The Fort Battleford text marked the acquisition of Fort Battleford as a national historic site. It focussed on the role of Fort Battleford as a police post, its place in the government's relations with the Cree Indians and in the events of 1885. The text represented a move to a new style which both commemorated and educated. It conveyed considerably more information than had the recent texts at Batoche or Cut Knife Hill. The expansiveness of the Fort Battleford text also reflects the fact that the plaque was being erected in a community which generally shared the Board's preconceptions. It is not known to what extent the Board consulted with the people of Battleford in preparing the text; however, Campbell Innes, the driving force behind the development of Fort Battleford, was also the Saskatchewan member of the HSMBC and, if usual Board practice was followed, would have drafted the text which was erected in 1954.

The rewriting of the Batoche, Cut Knife Hill and Fort Battleford plaque

The jury for Louis Riel's 1885 trial in Regina (courtesy of the Archives of Manitoba/ N12343).

texts marked a substantial shift in the Board's and the NPB's approach to the 1885 sites. This change was emphasized and confirmed in 1956, when the Board approved the commemoration of Louis Riel. The last lines of a plaque text to commemorate him (approved in 1964) indicate how far Riel had traveled since 1885—"After being found guilty of treason he was hanged at Regina, November 16, 1885. Riel is recognized as one of the founders of the Province of Manitoba."[53] In subsequent years the Board recommended the recognition of Poundmaker (1967) and Big Bear (1971), Cree leaders who had been imprisoned for their role in 1885, and Gabriel Dumont (1981), Riel's military commander in 1885. The rewriting of the texts and the recognition of Aboriginal leaders gave the Aboriginal interpretation of the 1885 uprising a legitimacy which had not been present in the early plaque texts.

Evolving Historiography—Growing Regional Identity— Changes at Parks Canada

Superficially, the shift in focus can be attributed to a change in personnel at the Board, and to the presence of active members from the Prairie provinces with a sympathy for a regional perspective on the events of 1885. At another level the change reflects evolving historiography, a growing regional identity, increased assertiveness on the part of Aboriginal people, and changes in the structure and approach of Parks Canada. Many of these changes were just becoming apparent in the 1950s, but they would become powerful trends during the 1960s and 1970s.

In the 1920s Howard Kennedy had suggested that there were legitimate grievances in western Canada which could explain but not excuse the Rebellion. George Stanley, writing in the 1930s, placed Riel and the Rebellions within a framework of regional protest and struggle between primitive and civilized peoples. Stanley's thesis was developed by Joseph K. Howard in *Strange Empire: Louis Riel and the Métis People*, published in 1952. Howard portrayed the Métis as romantic primitives struggling against a central government with Riel as their spokesman. Howard's work was less subtle than Stanley's, but it was more accessible and it fed into the growing counter-culture of the 1960s, which saw parallels in the anti-colonial struggle of the Métis in the 19th century and that of the Third World of the 20th.[54]

Stanley's view of Riel and the Métis as representatives of regional dissent was one which resonated with many historians and westerners. In 1948 H.C. Knox, in a letter to the editor of the Winnipeg *Tribune*, suggested that a statue should be erected to Riel as "the first man to fight for the recognition of the West and the rights of all Westerners."[55] Two years later when Charles Lightbody, a historian at the University of Saskatchewan, proposed that the government acquire Middleton's trenches at Batoche, he wrote: "This region is rapidly evolving a consciousness of a distinctive history and culture, within the framework of a developing national culture."[56] Western regionalism in historiography was exemplified in W.L. Morton's work. Morton was ultimately a Canadian nationalist, but he was also a leading regional historian and author of a study of the Progressive Party, a regional protest movement of the 1920s. He was able to sympathize with Riel and the Métis as regional voices while not accepting their specific goals or methods. The idea of regionalism as a framework of national history was legitimized by J.M.S. Careless. Writing in 1969, Careless was critical of the "nationbuilding" approach to Canadian history which, he suggested, "may tell us less about the Canada that now is than the Canada that should have been…"[57] As an alternative he suggested that Canadian history could be viewed as the articulation of limited identities based primarily on regions within one transcontinental state. Careless became a member of the HSMBC in 1972 and served as chairman from 1981 to 1985. His appointment in 1972 was symbolic of changing philosophy in Canadian historiography, and on the Board, for he succeeded Donald Creighton, who saw Canadian history as a story of nationbuilding centred in the St. Lawrence valley.

Riel's rehabilitation continued in the 1960s and 1970s when he was made to serve as a symbol for the French language in western Canada, at a time when bilingualism was being established as a national policy. In his role as a regional symbol he was acceptable to white and Aboriginal westerners,

Louis Riel (courtesy of the Saskatchewan Archives Board R-A2305).

French and English-speaking. In Manitoba he was acknowledged as the founder of the province with a heroic statue on the grounds of the legislature; another statue in Regina recognized his place in the history of Saskatchewan. In 1978 the Association of Métis and Non-Status Indians of Saskatchewan (AMNIS) asked that he be pardoned, as he had been driven to rebellion by the government; within a few years AMNIS withdrew this request, arguing that Riel, and the Métis, had done nothing wrong and therefore did not need a pardon. More recently Riel has been spoken of as a Father of Confederation—a member of the Canadian pantheon along with his nemesis, Sir John A. Macdonald. Riel has not been without his detractors, most notably Thomas Flanagan who focused on Riel's religious millenarian beliefs and mental instability. Flanagan places much of the blame for the rebellion on Riel's shoulders; moreover, he argues that the rebellion could not be justified in liberal democratic theory. In spite of his flaws, Riel became, in Douglas Owram's words, "one of Canada's special losers," comparable to Papineau and Mackenzie.[58]

The Métis cause was not identical with Riel, but it benefited from his rehabilitation. Beginning with Marcel Giraud's *Le Métis Canadien* in 1945, scholars began to look at the Métis not merely as participants in two failed risings but as a "new people" or nation. This approach blossomed in the 1970s and 1980s with a number of studies of Métis communities which were based in social rather than political history. One which was especially relevant to Batoche NHS was Diane Payment's *Batoche, 1870–1910* (St. Boniface: Éditions du Blé, 1983). Payment was a Parks Canada historian employed in the Prairie Regional Office, and the book was one of the products of her research towards the development of the Batoche NHS. Payment argued that the Métis were adapting relatively well to changed economic circumstances after 1870 and that the defeat at Batoche, although a setback, did not spell the end of the community or of the Métis people. Although she accepted that the Métis of Saskatchewan were a "people," she recognized that they were not monolithic and that not all Métis supported Riel.[59] Payment's work and that of others reinforced the view that the Métis were a "nation" comparable to the Cree or Blackfoot; this view received legal support in 1982 when the Canadian constitution recognized the Métis as Aboriginal people.

Riel and the Métis came to be viewed as representatives of the Aboriginal people and of their struggle to survive against the advance of Canadian society. This role linked 1885 to the growing Aboriginal rights debates of the 1970s and to the growing assertiveness of Native people. In 1945 the United States government had established an Indian Claims Commission to adjudicate native claims and, during the 1950s and 1960s, the Canadian government, in the face of an increasingly active Aboriginal population, considered establishing a similar commission. Then in 1969 the new Trudeau government launched its white paper on Indian Affairs which proposed a radical restructuring of Native/non-Native relations. The white paper proposed winding up the Department of Indian Affairs and essentially ending the special status which natives enjoyed or suffered under. This proposal was rejected by Native leaders and seems to have inspired them to a more determined pursuit of their interests. In 1973 the case of *Calder vs. Attorney General of British Columbia* forced the federal government to accept the possibility that some form of Aboriginal title might be recognized by the courts and that negotiation of such claims could no longer be avoided. In 1974 the Office of Native Claims was created to coordinate these claims.[60] As well as legitimizing the Native point of view, the office helped to fund extensive research on native history as it related to claims. Although this research was tailored towards the requirements of the legal system, it expanded the base for Aboriginal history in western Canada. Finally, the repatriated Canadian constitution of 1982 recognized and enshrined Aboriginal rights, without defining them.

During the 1950s both the structure and philosophy of NPB and of the Board began to change in ways which affected how national historic sites were identified, commemorated and interpreted. The Board's recommendation that the sites at Battleford and Batoche be acquired was unusual and indicative of the change. Through the 1920s, 1930s and 1940s the Board and National Historic Sites operated as a small, underfunded organization. Board members researched subjects and drafted plaque texts themselves.

The Board's focus was on commemoration rather than preservation; it generally resisted any attempt to involve it in a site beyond the level of a plaque. Preservation (as opposed to commemoration) was not part of its philosophy. The Parks Branch did operate some sites such as Fort Anne and Fort Chambly, which it had owned since before the creation of the Board. It also became involved in the partial restoration of sites such as Louisbourg and Fort Prince of Wales during the 1930s, and undertook the reconstruction of the Port Royal Habitation. Although individual Board members were sometimes involved in these projects, the Board itself was not committed to them.[61]

Not all of the Board members were satisfied with its focus during its first three decades. Howay, the British Columbia member, was uneasy with the emphasis on military sites which tended to favour central Canada. On two occasions he suggested that a halt be called to additional commemorations of sites associated with the War of 1812. In 1943 he submitted a review of the Board's achievements and recommendations for its future. He noted the geographic and thematic imbalance in commemorations: of 285 sites, 105 commemorated battles and war; 97 were in Ontario and 63 were in Québec. There were only 8 sites in Saskatchewan. He suggested that more attention be paid to economic, social and cultural growth, and that both distinctive and typical examples of Canadian buildings should be commemorated and preserved. The Board endorsed his report and although change was slow to come, it did come in the years following World War II.[62]

The booming post-war economy made more money available for heritage and for culture in general. In 1949 the government appointed the Royal Commission on National Development in the Arts, Letters and Sciences. Known as the Massey Commission, it was directed to investigate and encourage cultural "institutions which express national feeling, promote common understanding and add to the variety and richness of Canadian life…"[63] The Commission viewed the HSMBC as a key federal heritage institution, and supported an expansion of its role with an increase in its funding. It criticized the program for being uneven, with too few sites on the prairies, and recommended a more active role in consulting with local heritage groups. The Commission also suggested that in addition to commemoration, the Board should pay more attention to preservation, in particular to the preservation of architecturally significant buildings. The Commission repeated some of the concerns expressed in Howay's report of 1943 and supported the preservation initiatives which had been emerging within the Parks Program before World War II. However, the Commission operated at a much higher level than the Board and its recommendations received the full attention of a government which, in the post-war boom, was increasingly active.

During the 1950s the NHS program expanded rapidly. New sites were acquired; restoration and reconstruction became more common; and interpretation programs, including museums, became more elaborate. The expansive atmosphere was exemplified by the massive reconstruction of Louisbourg in the 1960s; C.J. Taylor, who wrote a history of the Board, referred to the 1960s as the "Era of the Big Project." The development and interpretation of large sites such as Louisbourg, Dawson City, and, ultimately, Batoche and Fort Battleford, demanded a more expansive interpretation than had been provided by the Board's plaques. It also opened the possibility of broader social and economic interpretations of historic events, as opposed to the political and military interpretations which had been current in the pre-war period.

The era of the big project also required a larger, more complex organization. Initially Parks Canada established regional offices in Calgary and Québec City. In 1973 it established additional regional offices in Halifax, Cornwall and Winnipeg. These offices were a response to specific requirements of managing a larger system, but they were also a part of a general government program of decentralization designed to defuse regionalism, spread employment benefits, and deflect criticism of a distant government. By the late 1970s most Parks Canada regional offices had a full planning and development capability including the capability to undertake a complex program of historical research and interpretation. Some had also developed a regional perspective and viewed "Headquarters" in Ottawa with ambivalence. Although Headquarters continued to exercise a policy and review role in site development, the regional offices were powerful new influences on the development of historic sites. Their identification with regional perspectives should not be underestimated as a factor affecting the development and interpretation of sites.

The growth of the Parks Canada program also influenced the Board's relationship to the program and to its political masters. By 1950 the Board was in practice semi-autonomous: while it relied on the staff of National Parks to implement its recommendations, the recommendations were approved neither by the bureaucrats nor by politicians. In the early 1950s the minister responsible for the Board became concerned about both the financial and political implications of the Board's activity. The incident, already described, in which Prime Minister St. Laurent took exception to the interpretation of the 1885 conflict at Fort Battleford, may have highlighted the political implications of historic sites. In 1952–53 the minister instituted administrative reforms and legislation which made it clear that the Board was only an advisory body. Its recommendations had to be approved by the minister before they came into effect and decisions as to how they were implemented were also in the minister's hands.[64]

The Board's relationship to the staff of National Historic Sites also changed as the program expanded. As National Historic Sites developed expertise in historical research, archaeology, material culture and other disciplines, and the scale of commemorations expanded, the Board had a less immediate relationship to the interpretation of sites. Whereas in 1924 Howay and the Board had drafted and approved the plaque text for Batoche, in the 1970s a range of planners, interpreters, historians, archaeologists and curators had input into the planning of Batoche National Historic Site and Fort Battleford NHS. While the development of Batoche remained grounded in the Board's 1923 recommendation that "Batoche is a site of national importance" and in a few subsequent amplifications, there was much room to manoeuvre in determining why the site was important and how this importance was to be communicated to the public. All of these changes had an effect on how commemoration and interpretation developed at the 1885 sites in the second half of the 20th century.

Fort Battleford

Both Batoche and Fort Battleford were to be developed as major historic sites with substantial investment in both preservation and interpretation. Fort Battleford had been developed as a museum by the local historical society, which in July of 1951 turned the site over to NHS. In making the transfer, the museum board requested that the name and focus of the museum be retained. In particular it asked that the relics of the pioneers keep a prominent place at the site and that the Indian museum continue to interpret the life and customs of the Native people.[65] The name of the park was changed to Fort Battleford National Historic Site, but other changes were slow to come. A report dated about 1968 stated that the exhibits had remained basically unchanged for 20 years.[66] The Superintendent's house at the fort was being restored to the period 1875–89; the Officer's Quarters housed exhibits on the early history of the district and the Territorial Council (which had sat at Battleford from 1876 to 1883); the Sick Horse Stable had exhibits explaining the importance of the horse to the police; the Guard Room had exhibits on the Uprising; and the Mess Hall housed a lecture hall and exhibits of Indian artefacts.[67]

New exhibits in the barracks and the refurbished commanding officer's residence were opened in 1969. Walter Hildebrandt, a historian of Fort Battleford who worked with the Prairie Regional Office in Winnipeg, argues that these exhibits, and the overall interpretation at Fort Battleford under Parks Canada's administration, present a "centralist" interpretation of Canadian history. In particular, he suggests, the role of the site as an "Indian Museum" suffered from an increased focus on the nation-building role of the North West Mounted Police.[68] Certainly, both local and Native history became relatively less significant but they were not eliminated. The increased focus on the police force and the events of 1885 was only part of what the founders of the museum had planned, but it was in keeping with the intent of the Board as it was expressed in the Fort Battleford plaque erected in 1954 (Figure 9).

The intent of the Board was, and remains, a key element in what is now referred to as commemorative integrity. According to Parks Canada's *Guiding Principles and Operational Policies*, "A historic place ... may be said to possess commemorative integrity when the resources that symbolize or represent its importance are not impaired or under threat, when the reasons for its significance are effectively communicated to the public and when the heritage value of the place is respected."[69] The reasons for a site's significance are established by the HSMBC in the light of its own collective understanding of Canadian history, on the advice offered by staff, and, increasingly, on the basis of consultation with individuals, groups and communities with an interest in the commemoration. While communities and individuals may be consulted, the Board is ultimately responsible and is required to make its recommendations in terms of "national historic significance." National significance is largely defined on the basis of the Board's tradition and its collective sense of the Canadian reality. The Board's tradition has evolved and is evolving; the concept of national significance is not static.

In spite of the dynamic nature of national historic significance and of consultation with local communities, tension among national, regional and local perspectives is common at historic sites. This is especially the case at older sites, such as those of 1885, which were commemorated when a nation-building view of history was popular and when there was no consultation with the local communities. Most national historic sites are recognized by the Board because of their relationship with a specific event, phenomenon or person which the Board judges to be of national significance. It is typical—indeed it is a requirement of commemorative integrity—for commemoration and interpretation at a site to focus on the elements which the Board has identified as having national significance. Equally typically, at a major site, there will be pressure to expand the focus either to include other events or persons which are considered significant or to provide context to the primary focus. Often the pressure for change comes from community groups which wish to tell the history of their community, but it may also come from regional or national groups which have a different perspective on the site than that identified by the Board. At Batoche NHS, the Board has modified its initial focus on the military events of 1885 substantially, in response to evolving historiography and to local and regional interests.

Fort Battleford NHS has evolved differently. It began as a community-based museum with the role of telling the entire story of the community. When it became a national historic site in 1951 its focus was narrowed, fitting it within what the Board had identified as being of national historic significance and within a larger system of national historic sites dedicated to telling the story of Canada. Although the focus has since widened to include more information on Native history, the process has not gone as far as it has at Batoche. One might speculate that this is because Fort Battleford is located in a predominately Euro-Canadian community (with a large Native minority) which is relatively comfortable with the story of Canadian expansion as represented by the North-West Mounted Police and Fort Battleford.

To the extent that a shift in focus towards the police theme represented a centralist focus, it had support from business interests in the local community. In 1957 the Battleford Board of Trade asked that the site be fully restored as a memorial to the police. The Board of Trade also suggested that the museum collection was of "secondary importance" and could be moved out of the Fort and housed in a rebuilt concert hall.[70] A decade later an editorial in the North Battleford *News-Optimist* declared that the site "should be operated less as a museum and more as a fort…" It should be restored as it was in 1885: "It is not enough to see the relics of an era… Fort Battleford needs some living Redcoats … some Indian Braves." This, the newspaper declared, was what the tourists expected to see.[71]

What "tourists expected to see" was becoming increasingly important. It would be misleading to suggest that before 1950 the Board was indifferent as to whether or not the public stopped to read the plaques it erected: as we have seen, in 1924 the Cut Knife Hill plaque was erected some distance from the site of the battle so as to make it more accessible to the public. However, the consequences of public indifference to a commemoration were more visible and more costly as the scale of commemoration increased. Visitation statistics became one measure of a site's success, and visitor reaction, real or anticipated, influenced how a site was developed and interpreted. Consideration of visitor reaction may have led to caution in approaching controversial or unpopular interpretations at sites. More positively, it meant that interpretations presented at sites had to be aware of a wide range of valid views on the history of sites such as Batoche, Fort Battleford, or Cut

Knife Hill. The expansion of the audience also affected the way in which sites were presented. Because both refurnished buildings, whether originals or reconstructions, and animated, as opposed to static, interpretation were popular with visitors, there was pressure to employ them. Finally, local communities (and quite possibly some heritage professionals) often favoured large-scale reconstructions and animated interpretation both as a tourist draw and as a source of employment. The "big project" complicated many of the decisions which had to be made in developing a historic site, at the same time as it gave many more people an input than had been the case in the early days of the Board.

In 1971–72 Parks Canada carried out a major review of its program, preparing formal management plans for all of the national historic sites which it operated. The 1972 management plan for Fort Battleford increased the emphasis on Fort Battleford as a police post, a centre of law enforcement and of territorial administration. Although the plan recognized the importance of the post's relations with Native people and settlers, and of the "siege" of 1885, it was clear that they were secondary themes. In particular, the plan stated that the involvement of the post with the events of 1885 should not be overemphasized.[72]

In the 1970s Parks Canada also began to plan for a substantial interpretation of the history of the police force at Fort Walsh in southwestern Saskatchewan. The duplication of effort at Forts Walsh and Battleford was a continuing cause of concern within Parks Canada. This concern, plus the increasing interest in Native history, led to the adoption of a new set of themes and objectives for Fort Battleford in 1986: "Native People, Territorial Administration, and Law Enforcement on the Northern Plains."[73] The new themes were an attempt to develop around the police post at Battleford a storyline which would tell of the interaction between the police and Native people from the arrival of the police at Battleford in 1876 until the aftermath of the Rebellion. Significantly, the graves of the nine Indians who were hung at Fort Battleford in 1885 were listed as one of the most important resources related to the theme.

Both the 1972 and the 1986 plans for Fort Battleford set new directions for the interpretation of Fort Battleford, but neither plan has been fully implemented and the interpretation presented at the site remains thematically divided. The principal static exhibit (in the Barracks) is essentially unchanged from the one prepared in the late 1960s.[74] Two videos shown at the site appear to be of more recent provenance. A 10-minute video presents both white and Native perspectives on 1885 while an 18-minute video "River People" presents a sympathetic history of the Cree peoples who inhabited and still inhabit the area. The Native perspective on the fort is reinforced by tour guides, some of whom are Native people. A recent evaluation of the site suggests that "Celebrating the police and their accomplishments remains at least as strong a focus at the site" as "presenting the Métis and Indian ... as victims caught in a trap."[75]

Batoche

At Batoche, Parks Canada acquired property and buildings but not existing museum exhibits. Exhibits were developed over a period of several years, and the museum was formally opened in 1961. The main exhibit had the general heading "Conflict of Cultures." It traced the history of the Métis, their exodus from Manitoba, the role of their "Blood Brothers" the Indians, and the "Advance of Foreign Culture." Slightly over one-third of the exhibit panels were devoted to the Rebellion of 1885. A secondary exhibit on the second floor of the rectory showed the history of the rectory as a priest's home, school and post office.[76] A brochure which was available at the time spoke of the Métis as "children of the fur trade," who "claimed an historic right to their share of the plains" although they had "no legal right to the land they occupied." "The government remained blandly indifferent to the troubles of the west."[77] The exhibit and brochure, while sympathetic to the Métis, retained something of George Stanley's view of the struggle as a conflict between primitive and civilized peoples. In the early 1960s, Stanley's interpretation was widely accepted; the explosion of research into both Métis and Indian culture was still a decade off. The brochure also echoed Stanley's and Morton's view of the rising as an expression of regional protest against a distant and insensitive government.

Prime Minister John Diefenbaker dedicated the museum on June 27, 1961. His speech echoed the tone of the Batoche brochure, describing the "uprising" as "the conflict of two ways of life, both with many admirable features."[78] He paid tribute to Gabriel Dumont and to the soldiers who had fought on both sides, but made no mention of Louis Riel or of Sir John A. Macdonald. The lesson he drew from the uprising was the importance of respecting minority rights and he linked the lesson to current issues with a reference to both the Canadian Bill of Rights, which his government had recently passed, and to the fact that it was only in 1959 that Canadian Indians had been granted the vote. One brief paragraph of his speech was delivered in French, a significant gesture on the part of the unilingual prime minister. The opening had a high profile, like the unveiling of the Cut Knife Hill plaque 10 years earlier, but it lacked the local involvement of the Cut Knife Hill ceremony. Although a nephew of Gabriel Dumont and the chiefs of the Beardy and One Arrow reserves were present on the platform, they played no active role in the event. The difference may well reflect the fact that at Cut Knife the ceremony was held on land owned and controlled by the Native people, while at Batoche the ceremony was on land administered by Parks Canada.

Diefenbaker's speech is a remarkable indicator of changing attitudes. Although he was a Conservative and an admirer of Sir John A. Macdonald, he was also a westerner and a spokesman for regional interests. Equally important, he was an advocate of human rights; his references to the importance of respecting minority rights would have been acceptable to his Liberal predecessor, Louis St. Laurent.

A year after the opening of the museum, a visit by a detachment of the Royal Regiment of Canada to Batoche reinforced the theme of understanding and rapprochement which both St. Laurent and Diefenbaker had voiced. The Royal Regiment was a successor to the Royal Grenadiers which had fought at Batoche in 1885, and it initiated the visit as part of its centenary celebrations. Saskatchewan government officials involved in planning the visit advised that the ceremony should give recognition to the Métis and Indians as well as to the Canadian military.[79] Two hundred members of the regiment attended a ceremony at Batoche which the Regina *Leader-Post* described as "a four hour exchange of compliments and expressions of 'Let's work together for the good of everyone.'" The guard of honour was inspected by Mrs. Monture, author, historian, and great-granddaughter of Joseph Brant. Mrs. Monture and Colonel Frost, who commanded the detachment, placed wreaths on the grave of Gabriel Dumont. Malcolm F. Norris, representing the Métis of Saskatchewan, paid "tribute and honor to all those who fell in the rebellion of 1885 … a struggle of brave men on both sides." He went on to say that the "Métis and Indians have a first right to more than has remained to them from the days when the whole land was theirs."[80] Norris' speech was an indication of the growing Aboriginal rights movement and a reminder that the interpretation at Batoche, and other 1885 sites, would continue to be contested.

The continuing shift in interpretive stance is evident in the management plan which Parks Canada developed for Batoche in 1972. The plan began with a statement of Batoche's historical significance, which lay in the proclamation of a "Provisional Government of Saskatchewan" under the leadership of Louis Riel and in the "decisive engagement" which effectively ended the "rebellion." The interpretive segment of the plan outlined the approach to be taken:

The main thrust of our interpretation at Batoche must be towards showing the visitor the life style of the Métis in the 1880s and what they were willing to fight to protect. Although Louis Riel played a crucial part in the story of the Rebellion, we believe the visitor must be made to realize the basic causes of the actions that were taken and fully understand the Métis and their point of view… . Every attempt will have to be made to have the visitor think of the story and the action from the Métis point of view.[81]

The plan went on to recommend the construction of a new Visitor Reception Centre with interpretive facilities, the period restoration of both the rectory and the church, and the interpretation of the village site as well as the battle site. The strong emphasis on having the "visitor think of the story and the action from the Métis point of view" was a reversal of the point of view displayed in the plaque which the Board had approved in 1923. Louis Riel, the military events of 1885 and the point of view of the Canadian government were not eclipsed, but they were to be observed from a new angle. The new focus recalled, and moved beyond, D'Eschambault and Innes's recommendation in 1952 that "So far only the military operations have been given importance and consideration. Justice should be done to all participants in these tragic events which should be considered as a whole."[82] Although the 1972 plan was eventually superseded, it guided research and development during the 1970s, and its point of view was incorporated into the subsequent plans.

During the later 1970s Parks Canada undertook archaeological and historical research in preparation for redeveloping the site. In keeping with the focus on the Métis point of view, the Parks Canada historian who was primarily responsible for Batoche, Diane Payment, carried out extensive oral history among the Métis population in the Batoche area. Her research contributed to the concept of the Métis as a people with an independent history which went beyond their involvement in two uprisings; it also built support and interest for the development of Batoche as a centre of Métis society. The plans to develop Batoche tapped into a growing activism and interest in preserving their heritage among the Métis: since at least 1971 Saskatchewan Métis had been organizing a "Back to Batoche" festival of Métis culture at Batoche. All of this activity culminated in the launching of a new round of management planning in the late 1970s, with the goal of using the centenary of the Battle of Batoche as a showcase for Parks Canada's 100th anniversary in 1985.[83]

Planning for the centennial began with the preparation of a new

The church and rectory at Batoche as viewed from the cemetery (courtesy of David McLennan, Canadian Plains Research Center).

statement of themes and objectives for the site. These were completed in 1979 and provided for two themes at Batoche: "The North West Rebellion of 1885" and "Métis Settlement in the Batoche District." The formal acceptance of two themes equal in importance was a significant innovation. The Board had never identified "Métis Settlement at Batoche" as a theme but, it was argued, the Board had "shown an increasing concern for the Métis perspective on the conflict"[84] and this concern required the Métis settlement to be interpreted on an equal basis with the political and military events of 1885. Whether or not Parks Canada was in advance of the Board on this issue became irrelevant in 1985 when the Board approved a new plaque text for Batoche (Figure 10) which effectively expanded the thematic framework to include both the North West Rebellion and Métis settlement.

The 1985 Batoche text gives almost equal play to the two themes commemorated at Batoche. It places the story of Batoche in a context which begins well before 1885, and it ends with an affirmation of the survival of the Métis community after the battle. It also provides a brief explanation of why the Métis engaged in resistance to the Canadian government. The word "resistance" is significant; it is used where St. Laurent had used "uprising" and the Board in 1924 had used "rebellion." The origin of the term resistance to describe the events of 1885 is unclear. In 1956 W.L. Morton described the

---

BATOCHE

In 1872 Xavier Letendre *dit* Batoche founded a village at this site where Métis freighters crossed the South Saskatchewan River. About 50 families had claimed the river lots in the area by 1884.
Widespread anxiety regarding land claims and a changing economy provoked a resistance against the Canadian Government. Here, 300 Métis and Indians led by Louis Riel and Gabriel Dumont fought a force of 800 men commanded by Major-General Middleton between May 9 and 12, 1885. The resistance failed but the battle did not mean the end of the community of Batoche.

Figure 10. 1985 plaque text (HSMBC, Minutes, June 1985).

events at Red River in 1869–70 as a "resistance" and by the 1970s some scholars were applying "resistance" to the events of 1885.[85] While it is possible that "resistance" was intended as a less emotive term than "rebellion," for many Canadians it was primarily associated with "the Resistance," the patriotic French underground which fought against the occupying German forces in World War II. For those familiar with feminist and Afro-American academic literature, "resistance" has the sense of a struggle against an oppressive hegemony of gender, race or class. Given these associations, resistance was no more neutral than was rebellion. Its use, however, is consistent with the 1972 management statement that "Every attempt will have to be made to have the visitor think of the story and the action from the Métis point of view.[86]

Public consultations on the future of Batoche NHS found that there was general support for the themes, for telling "both sides of the story," and for involving both the Métis and the Native people in the planning for the site.[87] The themes of Métis society and 1885 Rebellion were incorporated in the 1982 management plan which proposed the restoration of four of the surviving buildings on the site, the reconstruction of six buildings in the village of Batoche, and the construction of a modern Visitor Reception Centre to house interpretive programs. The work, with the exception of the reconstruction of buildings, was completed by 1985.

The new museum exhibit at Batoche presented a much a more detailed and sympathetic account of the Métis cause than had been available in earlier interpretations. It traced the history of the Metis from before the Red River Resistance in 1869–70 to the 20th century, and reduced the military events of 1885 to a very important event in that history. Given the two, co-equal themes at the site, and the changing historiography of 1885, this change was to be expected. Nevertheless the change in emphasis shifted the earlier focus of the site from a key episode in Canadian history to an important event in Canadian history which was also a pivotal episode in the history of one of the constituent peoples of Canadian society.

An elaborate and powerful audio-visual presentation was also developed for presentation at the site. The presentation, which is still in use, employs multiple perspectives on the history of Batoche using the voices of Métis inhabitants, Canadian soldiers, Gabriel Dumont, Louis Riel, General Middleton and Sir John A. Macdonald.[88] The approach is an adaptation of what has since come to be called a "Many Voices "technique. Frieda Klippenstein, a historian with Parks Canada, has explained the "many voices" concept:

> In a many voices context, visitors understand a site and its messages through a collage of vivid stories and images rather than one authoritative description and explanation of an event. It is reminiscent of some aspects of First Nations historical tradition. Though not uniform across all groups, one of the unique features of Native oral tradition is the idea that a person or group can tell only that part of the story that they have authority to tell, so each voice adds a component. The total picture of an event, then, requires a collage of these tellings.
>
> A many voices approach is … personal and multi-dimensional. It brings out the array of human impacts of a particular physical landscape, issue or event. Some key characteristics of a many voices approach are that it recognizes the validity of various perspectives on an historical event without having to synthesize them, or to judge which are most "true" in order to weed out contradictions. It concedes that historical accounts are constructions, posited by individuals, parties, or whole sectors of society for their own conscious or unconscious purposes. And it requires various individuals or groups to be involved in historical commemoration, to contribute authentic expressions of the multiple meanings of a person, place or event. … A key tenet of the many voices approach is to maintain the connection between story and storyteller.[89]

The goal is "to get across the overarching message that there is no one ultimately 'true' way to tell a story."[90] There are multiple meanings to a site such as Batoche, and the many voices approach is a means of reinforcing the multiplicity of potential messages.

At a theoretical level "many voices" may be a response to postmodern ambiguities in meaning and to the debate over the collapse of the concept of objective truth in history. If there is no authoritative version of an event, then the fairest and most objective way to describe it is through multiple, subjective perspectives or many voices. For a national heritage agency dealing with historical subjects on which there is no agreed interpretation, a balanced or "many voices" approach may be the wisest course. Avoidance of authoritative interpretations of historical events was raised to the level of policy in Parks Canada's Cultural Resource Management Policy statement of 1994:

> Parks Canada will present the past in a manner that accurately reflects the range and complexity of the human history commemorated at or represented in a national historic site, historic canal or national park.

> History will be presented with integrity. This will include the presentation of differing contemporary views, perspectives informed by traditional knowledge, and later interpretations. Parks Canada will not play the role of arbiter of Canada's human history.[91]

While this policy is well intended, it is disingenuous to suggest that Parks Canada, which implements the advice of the HSMBC, can avoid playing the role of arbiter of Canada's human history. The legislated role of the HSMBC is to provide advice on what is of national historic significance. The Board regularly makes recommendations to the minister on what is, and what is not, of national historic significance. Topics which the minister, on the advice of the Board, judges to be not of national significance are not given a voice at Parks Canada sites.

For example, in developing Batoche, Parks Canada carried out extensive consultations but these consultations were within the context of the existing themes for the site: "The North West Rebellion of 1885" and "Métis Settlement in the Batoche District." Suggestions from the public that post-1885 non-Métis settlement in the Batoche area be part of the interpretation were rejected on the grounds that it was not part of the themes established by the Board. Suggestions that First Nations involvement at Batoche receive greater prominence were rejected on the grounds that First Nations involvement in 1885 would be dealt with at other sites.[92]

In practical terms "many voices" is Parks Canada's approach to dealing with an important site where there is no consensus as to its meaning. The conscious decision to present multiple perspectives implies acceptance of a more complex historical reality than was present in early Board plaque texts. This complexity can only be conveyed to the visitor if credible accounts of the differing positions are presented. The success of the "many voices" approach depends largely on how well the "many voices" are selected and how sympathetically they are presented.

A visitor to Batoche in 1989 complained that the exhibit had not succeeded in presenting this complex historical reality. In a letter to his Member of Parliament, he described the audiovisual presentation as "elaborate and impressive", but complained that it did not "portray itself as just one perspective, but as the 'Real Story'." He noted that in the presentation an old Métis lamented that soon "there will be no one left to tell the real story," whereas, the visitor suggested, he should have said "our story." The visitor went on to give his interpretation of what he clearly regarded as the Second Riel Rebellion: "However pure Riel's motives were perceived, he still started an armed rebellion, he took innocent hostages and even had one executed. Issues such as these were not addressed in the presentation... Armed rebellions should not be taken lightly."[93]

The visitor was not alone. A 1990 report on the presentation of Aboriginal history at national historic sites stated:

> Staff at Batoche visitor centre report that the Métis who see the production are generally pleased with the way in which their (italics in original) history is presented in the a/v show. Any complaints voiced about the production come from individuals who feel that the show depicts Riel, Dumont and the Métis in an excessively favourable light, at the expense of the military force whom the Canadian government called upon to deal with the resistance. (In particular, General Middleton and Prime Minister Sir John A. Macdonald are thought to be caricatured.) It will likely be another generation or two before there is no controversy surrounding the historical place of Louis Riel and the movements of which he was part.[94]

The visitor's criticism might be dismissed as a misunderstanding of the audiovisual presentation. Moise, the "old Métis," was not intended to be an objective chronicler but a participant putting forward his view of the events. However, Moise is the principal narrator—he carries the story, with Riel, Dumont, Middleton, Macdonald and an unidentified Canadian soldier commenting at specific points. Moise, who may or may not be a historic figure, gives, through his voice and lines, a sympathetic portrayal of the Métis case. Sir John A. Macdonald, who would presumably have wished to articulate a case for Canada, is given lines which can be paraphrased as "we have no intention of stealing their miserable little plots" and "in a hundred years no one will remember Riel or the Metis but they will remember me."[95] He comes across as an overbearing, arrogant politician from outside of the region and culture, with no sympathy for the Métis or Riel. Whether or not the lines he is given are direct quotations from Macdonald's recorded speeches is not clear[96]; even if they are, it is improbable that this is the voice Macdonald would have chosen to tell his story. Presumably, if all the major participants in a historical event are to be given an opportunity to tell their version of it, they should be allowed to make the best case possible. If the "many voices" approach is intended to convey the message that "there is no one ultimately 'true' way to tell a story," then the different versions of the story which are told must be sufficiently credible that the public can appreciate the complexity of history.

A more balanced presentation would also help the visitor understand how earlier generations viewed historic events. Today, among both professional historians and Canadians generally there is substantial support for the Métis position and an equally broad condemnation of government mismanagement of the situation which led to the rising. The audiovisual presentation reflects present-day attitudes but gives little indication of how widespread support for the military suppression of the rebellion was in 1885. This was true even in French-speaking, Roman Catholic Québec; it was only when it became clear that the government intended to execute Riel that Québec came to view him as a martyr and the Métis as compatriots.[97] Although there was fervent opposition in Québec to Riel's execution, Macdonald's Conservative party, which supported his execution, nevertheless defeated the Liberals, who opposed the execution, in both Québec and the rest of Canada in the general election of 1887. This support is not made clear in the audiovisual presentation; a young Canadian soldier, who might be expected to provide the eastern Canadian public voice, delivers what is in effect a plaintive anti-war message. Although this message resonates with late-20th-century sensibilities, it does nothing to inform the viewer of the passions which explain the support for the war at the time.

Although Parks Canada may wish to avoid becoming the arbiter of Canadian history, it cannot avoid the responsibility of balancing different legitimate interpretations of events at sites which it interprets. The concept of 'many voices' provides a framework within which this balancing act can be carried out, but it requires all of the skills which are a part of traditional history. Moreover, to the extent that it is successful in conveying the message that "there is no one ultimately 'true' way to tell a story," it will remain con-

troversial. Unresolved stories are emotionally unsatisfying; more importantly, they do not supply validation which communities involved in Canadian
history seek.

The interpretation of the 1885 sites has never been static and it is not likely to become so. As this is being written, a new management plan, with
revised interpretive themes, for Fort Battleford is nearing completion. At the
same time Parks Canada and the HSMBC are engaged in a long-overdue
review of the interpretation of Native involvement in the 1885 rising. Both
of these revisions will be shaped by the same forces which have led to the
re-interpretation of Batoche.

Conclusion

The past is not a unitary state but an unstable federation of competing concepts, each with its supporters struggling for their place in the sun. In
Canada, as in many countries, different groups have supported different
views of the past as a means of defining their vision of their nation and of
strengthening their own identity within that nation. Each group has struggled to make its interpretation the accepted history, thereby legitimizing its
claim to power and strengthening its identity. Universal acceptance has
always eluded any one vision; competing visions survive to challenge, and
sometimes supplant, the dominant version.

Commemoration of historic events, people and places is an important
means of establishing and defining a common history, establishing consensus, and legitimating authority. Consequently, control of commemoration—
what is recognized and how it is presented—is a crucial aspect of defining
collective memories. In Canada there was a surge of commemorative activity in the late 19th and early 20th century; this activity was carried out by a
variety of individuals and groups with a diverse range of views and interpretations of Canadian history. The Historic Sites and Monuments Board of
Canada was established by the federal government in 1919 to undertake a
national program of commemoration. The Board received no explicit direction from the government as to the approach it should take to commemoration, but it was dominated by a small group of English-speaking professionals of about the same age and outlook. They developed a commemorative
program which can best be described as central Canadian, with a focus on
the survival and expansion of Canada in North America. Until 1937 none of
the members were from the Prairie provinces; French Canada was not
absent from the program but it was confined to Québec; ethnic minorities
and Aboriginal people were almost completely absent from the program.

In 1923 the Board recognized six sites associated with the 1885 North

West Rebellion—Batoche, Battleford, Duck Lake Battlefield, Fish Creek Battlefield, Cut Knife Battlefield, and Frog Lake Massacre—as sites of national historic significance. In the plaque texts which were erected at the sites, they were portrayed from a central Canadian viewpoint in the context of the expansion of Canada and western civilization across North America. This interpretation of Canada and the events of 1885 was contested, unsuccessfully, by some white Canadians and by many Native people and Métis. Many of the individuals on both sides of the debate could remember the events being commemorated, and some had been personally involved in them.

In the decade after 1945, the 1885 sites were reinterpreted. This reinterpretation was a response to continuing dissatisfaction with the original interpretation, growing pressure from local communities, developing regional consciousness, changing personnel on the Board and, not least important, changing historiography. In preparing new texts for Batoche, Cut Knife Hill and Fort Battleford, the Board consulted with some of the communities which had protested the original interpretation. The revised texts avoided an overtly triumphalist version of central Canadian history by focussing on the events of 1885, while avoiding any consideration of the causes or results of the events. In effect they avoided discussing the significance of the events and as a result were arid, uninformative and unsatisfying.

Within a few years of the second interpretation of the 1885 sites, a number of changes led to a third interpretation. A change in interpretive philosophy within Parks Canada, epitomized by the "big project," allowed a more complex interpretation of historic events than had been possible under the system of commemoration by plaques. The growth of a large bureaucracy, including heritage professionals, increased the number of individuals who had input into Parks Canada interpretations. The growth of regionalism, of the Aboriginal rights movement, and of a historiography sympathetic to both regional and Aboriginal rights required the development of interpretations which were more sympathetic both to regional and Aboriginal viewpoints. This led to much more extensive public consultations than had been done in the past. The reinterpretation has proceeded unevenly and is still in progress. Relatively little has been done at Cut Knife Hill or at sites such as Frog Lake; more has been done at Fort Battleford.

The third generation of interpretation is most fully developed at Batoche, which now carries two equal themes, the Battle of Batoche in 1885 and the history of the Métis settlement at Batoche. The interpretation is intended to present multiple perspectives on the events of 1885 without consciously attempting to reconcile them or to select one perspective as being the preferable one. However, the sympathetic portrayal of the Métis settlement at Batoche leaves the overall impression that the armed resistance of the Métis was both understandable and justifiable.

Between 1924 and 1985 the interpretive focus at the 1885 sites has shifted from "rebellion" to "resistance." The change in focus is a reflection of a general shift in the tone of most historical writing which now places much of the blame for the rebellion on the federal government. It is also a response to the growing self-confidence and influence of regions and of Aboriginal people who support a different version of Canada than General Cruikshank did 75 years ago. The new interpretation is not universally accepted; there are still those who believe that "armed rebellions should not be taken lightly" but they are among those protesting Parks Canada's current interpretation, much as the residents of Batoche and Poundmaker's Reserve were in the 1920s.

Appendix
Historic Sites and Monuments Board of Canada, Membership, 1919–60
(Taylor, *Negotiating the Past*, pp. 193–98)

Chairman		Ontario I	
1919–39	E.A. Cruikshank,	1919–39	E.A. Cruikshank
ON1939–42	Vacant	1939–54	Vacant
1943–44	F.W. Howay, B.C.	1955–59	Harry Walker
1945–50	J.C. Webster, N.B.	1959–61	A.R.M. Lower
1950–58	Fred Landon, Ont.		
1958–60	Mgr. A.	Ontario II	
	D'Eschambault, MB	1919–32	James Coyne
		1932–58	Fred Landon
Alberta		1958–72	D.G. Creighton
1944–55	M.H. Long		
1956	M.E. Lazerte	Prince Edward Island	
1957–59	Joel K. Smith	1950–58	Thane Campbell
1959–67	R.Y. Secord	1959–66	Earl Taylor
British Columbia		Québec I	
1923–44	F.W. Howay	1919–23	Benjamin Sulte
1945–59	W.N. Sage	1924–25	Victor Morin
1960–67	Margaret Ormsby	1925–26	Aegidius Fauteaux
		1927–29	P. Demers
Manitoba		1930–33	Maréchal Nantel
1937–59	Mgr. A.	1933–55	E.-F. Surveyer
	D'Eschambault	1955–60	Jules Bazin
1959–60	W. Smith		
		Québec II	
New Brunswick		1955–60	Édouard Fiset
1919–23	W.O. Raymond		
1923–50	J.C. Webster	Saskatchewan	
1950–61	A.G. Bailey	1937–50	J.A. Gregory
		1951–54	Campbell Innes
Newfoundland		1955–60	R. Mayson
1950–55	C.E.A. Jeffrey		
1959–60	Oliver Vardy	National Archives (ex officio)	
		1937–49	Gustave Lanctôt
Nova Scotia		1949–68	W. Kaye Lamb
1919–23	W.C. Milner		
1923–25	J.P. Edwards	National Museum of Canada	
1925–30	W. Crowe	(ex officio)	
1931–54	D.C. Harvey	1951–55	F. Alcock
1954	Thomas Raddall	1956–58	Vacant
1955–69	C. Bruce Fergusson	1959–61	Clifford Wilson

Notes

This article first appeared in *Prairie Forum* 27, no. 2 (2002): 161–98.

1. Robert Gildea, *The Past in French History* (New Haven: Yale University Press, 1994), 10, 1–12.

2. Ibid., 10. Gildea bases his discussion of collective memory on Maurice Halbwachs, *La Mémoire collective* (Paris: Presses Universitaires de France, 1950).

3. Ibid., 10.

4. Commemorations of places, people, and events related to 1885 include: Fort Battleford, Battle of Cut Knife Hill, Battle of Duck Lake, Battle of Fish Creek, Fort Carlton, Fort Pitt, Frenchman Butte, Steele Narrows, Frog Lake Massacre, Big Bear, Gabriel Dumont, Louis Riel, Poundmaker, Samuel Steele, Alberta Field Force, Battleford-Swift Current Trail.

5. C.J. Taylor, *Negotiating the Past: The Making of Canada's National Historic Parks and Sites* (Montreal and Kingston: McGill-Queen's University Press, 1990), xvi–xviii; C.J. Taylor, "Some Early Problems of the Historic Sites and Monuments Board of Canada," *Canadian Historical Review* 64, no. 1 (1983): 24.

6. Walter Hildebrandt, *View from Fort Battleford: Constructed Visions of an Anglo-Canadian West* (Regina: Great Plains Research Center, 1994), 103–9.

7. Frits Pannekoek, "Who Matters? Public History and the Invention of the Canadian Past," *Acadiensis* 29, no. 2 (Spring 2000): 206–10.

8. Taylor, *Negotiating the Past*, 3–31.

9. David McConnell, "Whether and how recommendations of the Historic Sites and Monuments Board of Canada were communicated to the Minister during the period covered by the archival records" (unpublished paper prepared for National Historic Sites Directorate, January 2000).

10. David McConnell, "E.A. Cruikshank: His Life and Work" (MA thesis, University of Toronto, 1965), 66, 68.

11. Taylor, *Negotiating the Past*, 85–88.

12. National Archives of Canada (hereafter NA), RG84, Vol. 1380, HS-10-3-2, Part 1, Howay to Harkin, September 18, 1925, T-14148.

13. Ibid., Coyne to Harkin, October 8, 1923, T-14148.

14. Ibid., Vol.1381, HS-10-3-4, Part 1, Howay to Harkin, November 20, 1923, T-14149.

15. Ibid., Vol. 979, BA2, Part 1, Clipping, Winnipeg *Free Press*, July 11, 1925.

16. Québec City, *Le Soleil*, quoted in C.J. Taylor, "Some Early Problems," 22.

17. The bishop's initial response is not on file and the wording of his conditions must be deduced from subsequent correspondence. NA, RG84, Vol. 979, File BA2, Part 1, Harkin to Prudhomme, July 5, 1924 and August 20, 1924, T-11020.

18. NA, RG84, Vol. 979, File BA2, Part 1, Howay to Harkin, September 8, 1924, T-11020.

19. Ibid., Prudhomme to Harkin, March 26, 1926, T-11020.

20. Ibid., Part 2, Board Minute, May 1926, T-11020.

21. Ibid., Murray to Macpherson, November 25, 1929, T-11020.

22. Ibid., Vol. 1379, HS-10-3, draft of "The Sack of Battleford," T-14147.

23. Ibid., Vol. 1381, HS-10-3-4, Part 1, Clipping, Ottawa *Journal*, August 29, 1925, T-14149.

24. Ibid., Kennedy to HSMBC, May 11, 1929, T-14149.

25. Ibid., Macdonald, Indian Agent, to Scott, July 26, 1926, T-14149.

26. Ibid., undated, unsigned memo, c. 1926, T-14149. The memo may have been written by A.S. Morton of the University of Saskatchewan.

27. Saskatchewan Indian, January/February 1989, p. 1, "John B. Tootoosis, 1899–1989," http://www.sicc.sk.ca/saskindian/a89jan01.htm

28. NA, RG84, Vol. 1380, File HS-10-3-1, Part 2, Howay to Harkin, May 4, 1927, T-14147.

29. Ibid., Vol. 979, File BA2, Part 2, Howay to Harkin, July 3, 1930, T-11020.

30. Ibid., Vol. 1381, HS10-3-4, Part 1, Howay to Harkin, September 16, 1925, T-14149.

31. Ibid., Part 2, Board Minute, May 29, 1931 and brass rubbing of text. The revised text read: NORTH WEST REBELLION/BATTLE OF CUT KNIFE HILL/At daybreak, 2nd May, 1885, Canadian forces under Lieutenant-Colonel William Dillon Otter, marching from Battleford to attack/ Poundmaker's camp, were discovered and fired upon by hostile Indians/concealed in the ravines on this slope. After some six hours'/fighting, the troops found their position untenable and retired to/Battleford.

32. Ibid., Saskatchewan to Harkin, January 3, 1930, T-14149.

33. Ibid., Forin to Howay, September 6, 1935; ibid., Draft "The Monument at Cut Knife" by Fred Williams; Canada, House of Commons, Debates, Vol. 1, p. 527, February 25, 1936.

34. Howard Angus Kennedy, The North-West Rebellion (Toronto: Ryerson Press, 1928).

35. Douglas Owram, "The Myth of Louis Riel," Canadian Historical Review 63, no. 3 (1982): 324–25. My interpretation of historiography on Riel, the Métis, and 1885 draws heavily on Owram and on J.R. Miller, "From Riel to the Métis," Canadian Historical Review 69, no. 1 (1988): 1–20.

36. NA, RG84, Vol. 979, File BA2, Part 3, Allard to D'Eschambault, March 1, 1944; ibid., D'Eschambault to Cromarty, March 6, 1944; ibid., Board minute, May 26, 1944, T-11020.

37. Ibid., Gregory to Cromarty, August 15, 1949, T-11020.

38. Ibid., Dubuc to Minister of Mines and Resources, September 11, 1951; ibid, Dubuc to Childs, October 14, 1951.

39. Ibid., Vol. 1379, HS-10-3, Part 2, "Committee to Report on the Events of 1885," c. May 1952, T-14147. The report, which was submitted after Prime Minister St. Laurent raised the issue of the appropriate terminology to describe the "events of 1885," avoided the use of the terms rebellion, uprising and resistance.

40. NA, MG26, L, Vol. 393, Clippings, Visits to Saskatchewan, North Battleford News, August 9, 1951, "Prime Minister Inspects N.W.M.P. Museum."

41. NA, RG84, Vol. 1379, HS-10-3, Part 2, clipping, Toronto Daily Star, August 9, 1951, T-14147; ibid., clipping, Prince Albert Herald, August 7, 1951, T-14157.

42. Ibid., Ottawa Journal, "Other Views: Rewriting History," August 21, 1951, T-14147; NA, MG26, L, Vol. 393, Clippings, Visits to Saskatchewan, North Battleford News, "The Prime Minister's Visit," August 16, 1951; Winnipeg Tribune, August 8, 1951, "P.M. Prefers Uprising to a 'Riel Rebellion'."

43. Ibid., Vol. 109, File HS-25-2-R, 1951–52, St. Laurent to Winters, August 1951.

44. NA, RG84, Vol. 1379, File HS-10-3, Part 2, Board Minutes, May 28–30, 1952, T-14147.

45. Ibid., Vol. 1381, HS10-3-4, Part 3, undated affidavit (c.1950) by Thomas Favel, T-14149.

46. Ibid., Clipping, unnamed North Battleford paper, "No truer Canadians Gov. Gen. tells Indians," T-14149.

47. Saskatoon StarPhoenix, October 24, 1952; Regina Leader-Post, November 4, 1952.

48. Brochure issued by "Chief Poundmaker Historical Centre and Teepee Village. Poundmaker Cree Nation, Canada."

49. Frieda Klippenstein, "First Nations Involvement in the 1885 North West Rebellion/Resistance," HSMBC Agenda Paper, 1999-12A, p. 488.

50. NA, RG84, Vol. 1057, File BA2, Part 1,"Memorial and Museum Plans," T-11975.

51. Ibid., "Report of the Committee on the Proposed Indian Museum at Battleford," T-11974; ibid., Board Minute, May 17–19, 1947.

52. Ibid., Vol. 1379, HS-10-3, Part 3, Herbert to Tatro, [February] 20, 1962, T-14147.

53. The full text of the Riel plaque read: LOUIS RIEL/1844–1885/Born at St. Boniface, October 27, 1844. When the Hudson's Bay Company/ceded Ruperts Land to the Canadian Government in 1869–70 he led the Métis/of Red River and established a "Provisional Government." Following the/execution of Thomas Scott, he fled to the United States. He returned to/Canada in 1884 and the next year led the Metis uprising. Following/military defeat at Batoche he surrendered and after being found guilty of/treason he was hanged at Regina, November 16, 1885. Riel is recognized as/one of the founders of the Province of Manitoba.

54. John Coulter, *The Crime of Louis Riel* (Toronto: Playwrights Coop, 1976), Forward [*sic*], makes this link to the Third World explicit.

55. Winnipeg *Tribune* files, Roll 99, Northwest Rebellion, H.C. Knox to the Editor, December 24, 1948.

56. NA, RG84, Vol. 1379, File HS-10-3, Part 2, Lightbody to Secretary, HSMBC, June 9, 1950, T-14147.

57. J.M.S. Careless, "Limited Identities in Canada," in Carl Berger (ed.), *Contemporary Approaches to Canadian History* (Toronto: Copp Clark Pitman Ltd., 1987), 6.

58. Miller, "From Riel to the Métis," 7–8; Owram, "The Myth of Louis Riel," 333.

59. Miller "From Riel to the Métis," 9.

60. Richard C. Daniel, "A History of Native Claims Processes in Canada, 1867–1979" (unpublished report prepared for Research Branch, Department of Indian and Northern Affairs, February 1980, Chapters 10 and 12).

61. Taylor, *Negotiating the Past*, 103, 107–8, 126.

62. Ibid., 87, 130–31; HSMBC Minutes, May 19, 1943, p. 4.

63. Quoted in Taylor, *Negotiating the Past*, 131.

64. McConnell, "Whether and how recommendations…," 3–4.

65. NA, RG84, Vol. 1057, File FBA2, Part 1, Stewart to Smart, July 7, 1951, T-11975.

66. Ibid., Vol. 1060, File FBA318, Part 3, undated report, c. 1968, T-11977.

67. Ibid., Vol.1059, File FBA109, Part 5, Clipping *News-Optimist*, June 28, 1968, T-11976.

68. Walter Hildebrandt, "Where Myth Meets History," *Newest Review* (April/May 1989): 27.

69. Parks Canada, *Guiding Principles and Operational Policies* (Canada: Minister of Supply and Services 1994), 119.

70. NA, RG84, Vol. 1059, File FBA155, Part 1, Battleford Board of Trade to Minister of Northern Affairs and Natural Resources, June 24, 1957, T-11976.

71. Ibid., File FBA109, Part 4, undated clipping North Battleford *News-Optimist*, "A Challenging Future."

72. Parks Canada, File 8400/F4, Battleford Management Plan, January 20, 1972.

73. Parks Canada, "Themes and Objectives. Fort Battleford National Historic Park" (1986), 3–5.

74. Photos of the exhibit taken c. 1970, show substantially the same panels and artefacts as were present in May 2000. Parks Canada, Winnipeg Office, Tatro Photos, Battleford, nos. 59 to 150. The panel on the events of 1885 has the title "The Uprising 1885/La

Rebellion de 1885" with a more recent addition to the panel giving the title "The North-West Resistance of 1885."

75. Klippenstein, "First Nations Involvement," 488, 505.

76. NA, RG84, Vol. 981, File BA318, Part 2, Tatro to Herbert, November 24, 1960, T-11114; ibid., Herbert to Wilson, September 14, 1961, T-11114.

77. Department of Northern Affairs and Natural Resources, National Historic Sites Division, *Batoche National Historic Site* (Ottawa: Queen's Printer, 1960).

78. NA, Diefenbaker Papers, MG26, M, Vol.176, File313.25, Saskatchewan, pp. 145610–689, Reel M-7867, Notes for an address by the Rt. Hon. J.G. Diefenbaker, "The Official Opening of Batoche National Historic Site."

79. Ibid., Vol. 578, File 918-Batoche, pp. 440326–28, Reel M-8926, Hill to Frost, September 28, 1961.

80. Regina *Leader-Post*, "Soldiers meet Indians Metis again at Batoche," July 5, 1962, p. 36.

81. Department of Canadian Heritage, Parks Canada File 8400/B3, Batoche Management Plan, March 2, 1972.

82. NA, RG84, Vol. 1379, HS-10-3, Part 2, "Committee to Report on the Events of 1885," c. 1952, T-14147.

83. "Batoche Management Guidelines," approved October 26, 1979, p. 1.

84. "Batoche National Historic Park, Themes and Objectives," Approved September 14, 1979.

85. Morton wrote: "The term Resistance is used deliberately. Not only was it frequently employed at the time, it also possesses the merit of describing precisely the spirit and intent of the actions of the *métis* in 1869–70, without resorting to the legally accurate but nevertheless misleading term 'rebellion.' The opinion advanced is that Riel and his followers did commit acts of rebellion, but did so in the belief that they were both morally and legally justified." W.L. Morton, *Alexander Begg's Red River Journal and Other Papers Relative to the Red River Resistance of 1869–1870* (Toronto: The Champlain Society, 1956), 1, fn. 2. David T. McNab used the term resistance in his article on the Colonial Office and the Prairies in *Prairie Forum* in 1978.

86. Department of Canadian Heritage, Parks Canada File 8400/B3, Batoche Management Plan, March 2, 1972.

87. Parks Canada, *Batoche Alternatives* (February 1981), 3.

88. The audiovisual presentation prepared in 1985 was revised in the late 1990s. This discussion is based on a viewing in May 2000.

89. Frieda Esau Klippenstein, "On a New Approach to Heritage Presentation at National Historic Sites," *Research Links* (Summer/Autumn 1999): 3–4.

90. Personal communication, F. Klippenstein to A. McCullough, February 28, 2000.

91. Canadian Heritage, Parks Canada, *Guiding Principles and Operational Policies* (Ottawa: Minister of Supply and Services, 1994), 105–6.

92. Heritage Canada, Parks Canada, 8400/B3, Vol. 1, Batoche NHS. "Public Comments on Themes and Objectives" August 1980.

93. Parks Canada, 8400/B3, vol. 1, Campbell to Hawkes, July 17, 1989. The reference to a hostage being executed suggests that Mr. Campbell conflated the Resistance of 1869–70 in Manitoba with the 1885 Rebellion in the North West Territories. The error does not invalidate his point; indeed the vehemence of Ontario's demand for Riel's execution in 1885 owed much to its memory of the execution/murder of Thomas Scott in 1870.

94. A.J.B. Johnston, *Toward a New Past: Report on the Current Presentation of Aboriginal History by Parks Canada* (Ottawa: Canadian Heritage, Parks Canada, 1995), 234.

95. These are paraphrases, taken during a viewing of the audiovisual show in May 2000. Parks Canada was unable to provide me with a copy of the script.

96. Diane Payment, the primary Parks Canada historian of Batoche, wrote "The Batoche video is more like a docu-drama than a historical documentary. The script writer was Jake MacDonald who had access to historical studies that Walter Hildebrandt, myself and others had done on Batoche. The lines that you quote from Macdonald were either direct quotes, paraphrases and I suspect some literary licence based on Macdonald's words." Diane Payment to Alan McCullough, June 28, 2000. Some of Macdonald's lines—for example, "Riel shall hang though every dog in Quebec barks"—are recognizable quotations. The ones cited in the text are not familiar to me. Parks Canada does not have a policy which deals with the attribution of lines to historic characters in audiovisual presentations. Given that these documentaries are seen by far more people than Parks Canada's meticulously documented research reports, this is a significant gap.

97. A.I. Silver, *The French-Canadian Idea of Confederation, 1864–1900* (Toronto: University of Toronto Press, 1997), 153 and ch. 7.

Index

The Prairie Provinces

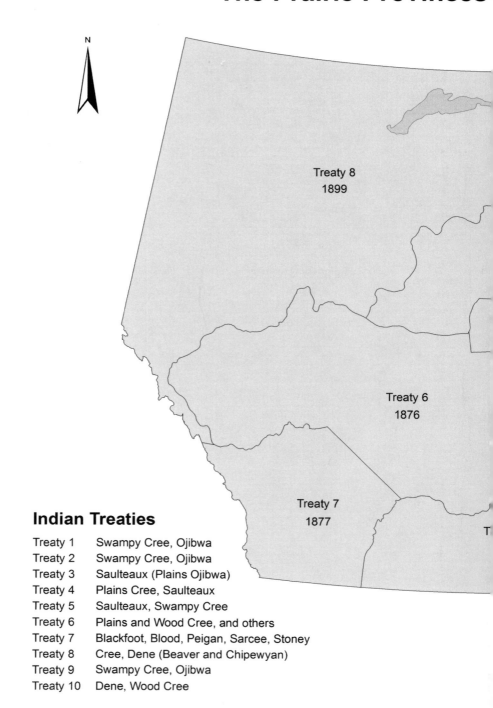

N

Treaty 8
1899

Treaty 6
1876

Treaty 7
1877

Indian Treaties

Treaty 1	Swampy Cree, Ojibwa
Treaty 2	Swampy Cree, Ojibwa
Treaty 3	Saulteaux (Plains Ojibwa)
Treaty 4	Plains Cree, Saulteaux
Treaty 5	Saulteaux, Swampy Cree
Treaty 6	Plains and Wood Cree, and others
Treaty 7	Blackfoot, Blood, Peigan, Sarcee, Stoney
Treaty 8	Cree, Dene (Beaver and Chipewyan)
Treaty 9	Swampy Cree, Ojibwa
Treaty 10	Dene, Wood Cree